Dictionary

of Chinese

Biography

BERKSHIRE

Dictionary
of Chinese
Biography

宝库山中华传记字典

Kerry Brown

Lau China Institute at King's College, London

Editor in Chief

VOLUME 4

BERKSHIRE PUBLISHING GROUP
Great Barrington, Massachusetts

© 2016 Berkshire Publishing Group LLC

Berkshire Publishing Group
122 Castle Street
Great Barrington, Massachusetts 01230-1506 USA
Email: info@berkshirepublishing.com
Tel: +1 413 528 0206
Fax: +1 413 541 0076

Permissions may also be obtained via Copyright Clearance Center, 222 Rosewood Drive, Danvers, MA 01923, USA, telephone +1 978 750 8400, fax +1 978 646 8600, info@copyright.com.

Digital editions. All volumes of the *Berkshire Dictionary of Chinese Biography* are available online through Oxford Reference Library, Oxford University Press, at www.oxfordreference.com.

Library of Congress Cataloging-in-Publication Data

Berkshire dictionary of Chinese biography / editor in chief: Kerry Brown, King's College, London.
     pages cm
  Includes bibliographical references and index.
   ISBN 978-1-933782-66-9 (3-volume set : hardcover : alk. paper)—
ISBN 978-1-61472-975-4 (4-volume set : hardcover : alk. paper)—
ISBN 978-1-61472-900-6 (volume 4 : hardcover : alk. paper) 1. China—
Biography—Dictionaries. I. Brown, Kerry, 1967-
  DS734.B47 2014
  951.003—dc23
                          2013042493

Praise for the
Berkshire Dictionary of Chinese Biography, Volumes 1–3

"All students of China and indeed of East Asia and world history will be greatly aided in their studies by this comprehensive reference work, a true milestone in collaborative historical research."

—**Wm. Theodore de Bary, Columbia University**

"We have long needed a new, comprehensive dictionary of Chinese biography that satisfies both China specialists and teachers/students interested in famous Chinese across the ages. . . . No comprehensive biographical dictionary of China has successfully replaced Herbert Giles's [1898] work until the new *DCB*. It's about time!"

—**Benjamin A. Elman, Princeton University & Fudan University**

"Chinese history is enriched by the lives of distinguished men and women, and finally their lives are made accessible in a concise and accurate way in these volumes. This magnificent work will surely be a must-have for serious libraries around the world."

—**Rana Mitter, University of Oxford**

"The *Berkshire Dictionary of Chinese Biography* will be an invaluable resource for students, teachers, and anyone who wants to supplement what they hear and see from our media coverage of China today."

—**Stephen A. Orlins, President of the National Committee on U.S.-China Relations**

Table of Contents

List of Biographies A–Z

Introduction to the *Berkshire Dictionary of Chinese Biography*

The guiding principle behind the first three volumes of the *Berkshire Dictionary of Chinese Biography,* issued in 2014, was simply to attempt to populate and make more knowable and appreciated, at least to a non-specialist and English-speaking audience, the vast sweep of Chinese history from the earliest dynasties up to the modern era. Rather than simply producing a long series of emperors and officials, we tried give some sense of the diversity of important players and their contributions over this four-millennia-long period.

This fourth volume covers figures, most of whom are still alive, who influenced events from 1979 onwards. The challenge here has been the reverse of previous volumes. Far from being dominated by one particular type of figure or one guiding narrative that has become the consensus view and has had time to become accepted and embedded in our understanding, modern Chinese history almost splinters, into dozens of different paths along which we can wander endlessly. Not only figures within the People's Republic of China, Hong Kong, and Taiwan (an area we can capture with the term Greater China) but those from the global Chinese diaspora start to become more important, as do cultural figures, film stars, singers, activists, writers, and business people. Details about their lives are abundant rather than restricted. The key task becomes not one of detection and assemblage of whatever facts we can find, but rather of exclusion and selectivity. And unlike with historic figures in the more remote past, whose careers and contributions we have had time to reflect on in order to reach some kind of common appreciation, our judgments of these recent lives are more conditional, provisional, and for that reason sometimes contentious.

The break at 1979 between the first three volumes and this one is very deliberate. The bridge between the end of the Maoist period from 1976 and the start of the Deng Xiaoping reforms in 1978–1979 gave birth not only to economic changes in the People's Republic, but to a new form of hybrid Chinese modernity which, over time, started to transcend the boundaries of the country and reach into the rest of the world. We are still living in this era, labeled as "Reform and Opening Up" in China, but by many other terms in the rest of the world. One scholar I spoke to a few years ago used the simple term, "The Great Transformation." Others have simply called it the start of Global China. The British writer Martin Jacques has even labeled this date the start of the twenty-first century. The only consensus inside and outside China seems to be that the country is a different place after this watershed, as is the very quality of what it is to be Chinese. The biographies in this final volume map that difference, and give it a human face.

The first illusion that might be shed when reading through this series of biographies is that there is no easy, unified sense of what China is, what its most recent history has meant, and what its core current values are. There are figures here profoundly supportive of the mission from Beijing to create a strong country guided by largely Chinese Communist ideology and institutions, and others deeply antagonistic and opposed to this who assert a different vision, some of them from communities in the rest of Greater China or the world

beyond. Some have expressed their views in political polemic, some in more symbolic form; some took direct action, through law or other means. Others have retreated into a more symbolic mode of opposition or expression of difference.

The only safe conclusion one can draw when stepping back and looking at recent history through some of these key life stories is that there was no easy entity called "China" nor a neat set of values and ideas that could be labeled distinctly Chinese. Instead, ideas flowed in and out of China and impacted intellectual, cultural, and political life, sometimes producing startling new forms. Unsurprisingly, this collection also pays tribute to the figures who have shaped life in Hong Kong, before and after its reversion from British to Chinese sovereignty in 1997, and in Taiwan, which has continued to develop its own highly distinctive pathway as part of the Chinese cultural world, while becoming increasingly politically and economically separate, despite Beijing's strong antipathy to this.

The fragmentariness of modern China comes across in the very different styles in which our contributors have rendered particular figures. With Chinese mainland political leaders, the tone is one appropriate in accounting for the sober procession through various formal positions up the hierarchy to senior leadership and influence. Sometimes glory awaited them—witness the tale of current President Xi Jinping. But others fell by the wayside; Bo Xilai is the cause célèbre here. Some have exercised influence in more subtle ways, like Qiao Shi, a low-key politician in the Jiang Zemin era. Others gained, even in their lifetimes, a sort of infamy. Li Peng, linked to the Tiananmen Square Incident in 1989 is the most prominent example of this.

And then there are the cultural figures, who have sometimes flourished, at least if they were based in the mainland, and sometimes been victimized. A figure like Jet Li, feted in Hollywood and now a global star, typifies the new face of global China, a person bought up in Beijing in the 1960s, a product of the state film industry who took his chance in the 1980s and sought fame and fortune in Hong Kong and then in the United States. Straddling the language worlds of Chinese and English, he captures some of the ambiguity and torn nature of modern China: belonging to two places, located mostly in one but often nostalgic and deeply loyal to his roots.

But of course, there are the more marginal voices, the most prominent of them figures like Nobel Prize Laureate Liu Xiaobo, imprisoned since 2009 despite international criticism, and a person whose forensic critiques of the Communist Party's moral behavior in the modern era have so riled figures of authority in Beijing. Alongside Liu were previous forces of criticism and opposition, figures like Liu Binyan, one of the finest modern journalists whose

work in the 1950s exposing early Communist corruption and misbehavior earned him over two decades in jail or detention. Liu was to end his days as a émigré in America—a common fate for many of the most outspoken critics, but as his entry in this collection makes clear, he is linked to a lineage of honest, upright, and fearless intellectual figures who have been a characteristic of Chinese history.

The one similarity that this final volume shares with the previous three, which covered years pre-1979, is questions about how to define whom to include and whom to leave out. In a period of such rapid change and increased diversification, who can be called truly representative in their field? Some figures have already secured a place in history, among them the late scientist and father of China's atom bomb Qian Xuesen, because of the unique and momentous nature of their achievements. But others, like pianist Lang Lang, are probably significant because they are the first in their fields to have become globally known Chinese practitioners. In that sense, beyond their intrinsic talents and technical mastery in any particular field, the fact that they were Chinese path-breakers gives them added importance.

Unlike the figures in the first three volumes, many of those covered in this collection are still in the midst of their careers, and much of their work remains to be done. Xi Jinping has been leader of China only since 2012. Those like Lang Lang are still relatively young. The authors of their entries may speculate about their future endeavors, but of course, one thing we can take for granted in the course of events is how unexpected outcomes often are and how hard they can be to predict even for individuals working in very defined areas.

In a period when many make firm claims about the importance of Chinese culture and a unified sense of Chinese identity, contemplating the diversity of lives there and their different tones and trajectories helps to guard against oversimplification. The China that comes through in this volume is one that is dispersed, rich in different ideas and identities, often contradictory, sometimes fractious, but full of creative human complexity. The lives rendered here represent this; some were heroic, some tragic, and many inspirational. Some are given trenchant criticism, and some are celebrated with a sense of wonder and awe. It would be interesting to speculate on how this collection might look in fifty years, or after a century. Would someone dusting it off from a library bookshelf, intrigued by the title, wonder who on earth these largely forgotten figures were? Or would they be fascinated by the early assessments of people who had gone on to become truly historic figures, their reputations lasting beyond their lifetimes. Of course, as editor I hope that

the majority will fall into the latter category. But at the very least, this is one of the first, perhaps the first attempt, to address the issue of whose contribution in whichever field they were prominent in will have historical longevity. This volume, therefore, differs in that many of the figures portrayed occupy a pioneering role with little of the scholarship and reflection concerning their legacy that was utilized in earlier volumes.

We hope that by placing the three volumes covering historic China with this more modern volume, readers might get a sense both of history already made alongside that of history being made, and what this means in a China that often seems alienated from its past while trying to recover and reconnect with it. Every figure covered in this final work has made a contribution to this endeavor, through what they did or what they tried to achieve. That in the end is the connection, or link, between the Chinas of now and the Chinas that came before—an attempt to create a national or cultural narrative that is full of heroic peaks and some devastating troughs, but which is fated to always be a mission in process, rather than something that can ever be proclaimed complete.

Kerry Brown

Kerry Brown, Editor in Chief

Kerry Brown is Professor of Chinese studies and director of the Lau China Institute, King's College in London. Until November 2015, he was director of the China Studies Centre at the University of Sydney. Before moving to Australia, he was head of the Asia Programme at Chatham House, an independent policy institute based in London, and led the Europe China Research and Advice Network (ECRAN) funded by the European Commission. Educated at the University of Cambridge, University of London, and University of Leeds, he worked in Japan and the Inner Mongolian region of China before joining the Foreign and Commonwealth Office. He worked in the China Section and served as First Secretary in Beijing from 2000 to 2003, and was head of the Indonesia East Timor Section from 2003 to 2005.

He is the author of *What's Wrong with Diplomacy: The Case of the UK and China* (2015), *China and the EU in Context* (2014), *The New Emperors: Power and the Princelings in China* (2014), *Carnival China: China in the Era of Hu Jintao and Xi Jinping* (2014), *Hu Jintao, China's Silent Leader* (2012), *Ballot Box China* (2011) and the edited collection *China 2020* (2011), *Friends and Enemies: The Past, Present and Future of the Communist Party of China* (2009), *The Rise of the Dragon—Chinese Investment Flows in the Reform Period* (2008), *Struggling Giant: China in the 21st Century* (2007), and *The Cultural Revolution in Inner Mongolia* (2006). He was a coeditor of the *Berkshire Encyclopedia of China* (2009) and editor in chief of the *Berkshire Dictionary of Chinese Biography, vol. 1–3* (2014). His study *Xi Jinping: China's CEO* will be published in early 2016.

Reader's Guide

The entries in the *Berkshire Dictionary of Chinese Biography, volume 4* are written in such a way that they can be read as stand-alone articles. They are organized alphabetically, as reflected in the list of biographies (see p. ix). Within each article, individuals with their own full entry are marked with an asterisk * in front of their name, and they are bolded in the index and the biographical directory (Appendix 2).

Structure of the Articles

All articles are structured in a similar way, and contain certain standard elements. Below the title is a bio-line, with life dates and a short description. If applicable, alternate names are added below the bio-line. Each article opens with a short summary (in bold) that gives the reader a quick glance of the figures' life and article's content. A section of recommended further readings is included at the end of each article, and a general bibliography is available in Appendix 7.

A portrait image is included in nearly every article, and sources and copyright information for these images are credited in the back matter (p. 573).

Use of Chinese Characters

In this fourth volume, we have included *either* simplified or traditional characters in the articles, depending on the main linguistic environment of the individual discussed; for mainland Chinese figures simplified characters are used, while individuals from Hong Kong and Taiwan have traditional characters. In the appendices, both simplified and traditional Chinese characters are included whenever applicable.

In general, we use the pinyin transliteration system to transcribe Chinese names. For several figures, however, we chose the most commonly used transcription, which isn't always in line with pinyin. Alternate names are mentioned at the top of each article, and in the index and appendix, a cross-reference to the main title is included (e.g., Chang, Eileen. *See* Zhang Ailing). A pinyin–Wade-Giles (pinyin's predecessor) conversion table is included in Appendix 1.

☌ Bā Jīn 巴金

1904–2005—One of the most popular writers of the 20th century

Alternate names: b. Lǐ Yáotáng 李尧棠/李堯棠; style name: Lǐ Fèigān 李芾甘

Summary

Ba Jin is among the best known of twentieth-century Chinese writers. A prolific writer of fiction from the 1920s through the 1940s, he was extremely popular in China and later became known to many non-Chinese readers through his novel *Family*. After enduring dreadful political persecution from the 1950s through the late 1970s, he lived to be one hundred years old.

Ba Jin is counted among the most popular Chinese writers of the twentieth century. He published twenty novels and more than seventy short stories from the late 1920s through the 1940s. Ba Jin's fiction, with its combination of realistic social criticism and captivating, emotionally saturated plots, held strong appeal for readers of the time. Ba Jin's literary fame largely comes from his most famous novel, *Family* (*Jiā* 家), published in 1933, although Ba Jin's last work of fiction prior to 1949, *Cold Nights* (*Hányè* 寒夜, 1947), is considered by many to be his best novel. In *Family* and many of his other works, Ba Jin's characters, themes, and settings reflect the author's passionate commitment to social change, which he advanced through his promotion of anarchism.

After the Chinese Civil War and the Communist victory in 1949, Ba Jin complied with the political demands placed upon writers by the Chinese Communist Party (CCP). The oppressive political climate, however, seemed to have largely put an end to his creative writing. He ceased writing novels and published only a few collections of short stories between the 1950s and 1961. He was targeted during several political campaigns, especially the Cultural Revolution (1966–1976). In the late 1970s he returned to writing, publishing more than a dozen collections of essays in the form of personal reflections, letters, and remembrances. Despite Ba Jin's popularity with readers, literary scholars have been fairly critical of his stories and novels.

Early Life

Ba Jin was born Li Yaotang on 25 November 1904 into a wealthy and influential landowning family in Chengdu, the capital of Sichuan Province. Ba Jin's mother was the most influential person in the first decade of his life. A practicing Buddhist who taught her son compassion for all living things, she also helped instill in Ba Jin a love for literature, reciting favorite poems to him and his brothers.

In early 1911, amid violent demonstrations against the policies of the Qīng 清 dynasty (1644–1911/12), Ba Jin's father resigned from his government post and moved the family from Guanyuan in northern Sichuan to Chengdu. The Li family tried to keep Ba Jin and his young siblings and cousins insulated, within their luxurious compound, from the chaos of the Xinhai revolution raging outside. By the end of 1911, the Qing dynasty—the last of China's centuries-old dynastic system—had crumbled.

Several months before Ba Jin's tenth birthday, his mother died, followed four months later by his eldest sister's death. His father and grandfather died in 1917 and 1919, respectively.

From Anarchist to Author

As early as 1918, Ba Jin began to read Western works of fiction in translation, and in 1919 news of the May Fourth Movement 五四运动 (during which Confucian values were denounced and Western-inspired worldviews were promoted as part of a project to rejuvenate Chinese culture) reached the Li family compound, largely in the form of journals and pamphlets. Through their reading of such May Fourth–era journals as *New Youth* (*Xīn qīngnián* 新青年), Ba Jin, his brothers, and cousins absorbed radical ideas about world affairs, Chinese nationalism, culture, and society. The direction of his intellectual, political, and literary development was heavily influenced by the Western ideas and literary styles promoted in these journals.

Anarchism had by far the greatest impact on Ba Jin's beliefs and attitudes. By his own account, anarchism helped to give form and structure to feelings of sympathy for the poor and downtrodden that he had felt from an early age. So influential was this philosophy that he may have created his pen name Ba Jin (adopted around 1928, although he used at least thirty-seven different pen names in his career) from the Chinese transliterations of the surnames of the anarchist thinkers he most admired— taking the "Ba" from Bakunin and the "Jin" ("kin") from Kropotkin. Ba Jin later denied this well-known origin of his pen name, but his denial may have been made while under duress. Whatever the origins of his pen name, by the winter of 1920, Ba Jin was referring to himself as an "anarchist." Ba Jin's life as writer commences with essays related to his anarchist activities, namely the 1921 publication (under the name Feigan) of his first essay, "How to Establish a Truly Equal and Free Society." Ba Jin also emulated the style and content of Russian, German, and French writers such as Turgenev, Leopold Kampf, Zola, Maupassant, and Romain Rolland. This is perhaps most notable in his emotional, realistic, and sympathetic portrayals of the poor and dispossessed.

An important rite of passage for iconoclastic young Chinese intellectuals at the time was to study abroad. In January 1927, Ba Jin left for France and spent most of the next two years in Paris and Château-Thierry, a small town outside Paris, returning to China in early 1929. His years in France were disappointing, marked by boredom, loneliness, depression, and news of his family's bankruptcy. Ba Jin made his first attempt at novel writing while in France, marking the start of a productive period of literary creativity.

Literary Career

Ba Jin is most known for the many works of fiction (especially novels) he wrote during the 1930s and 1940s. His first novel, *Destruction* (*Mièwáng* 灭亡, 1929) was inspired by contemporary events in China, the 1927 execution of the Italian-born anarchists Nicola Sacco and Bartolomeo Vanzetti in the United States, and his "intensive preoccupation with Russian literature and with the history of the Russian revolutionary movement" (Lang 1967). *Destruction* tells the story of a sensitive young intellectual, Du Daxin, who is single-minded in his hatred of oppression and inequality; the suffering of the masses pains him. He knows he is dying of tuberculosis and comes to realize the sacrifice he must make for his ideals. The novel, enthusiastically received by readers at the time, is written in a straightforward style and is easy to read, though rather predictable.

Ba Jin's next novel, *The Dead Sun*, deals with bourgeois intellectuals; it attacks imperialism and idealizes the working classes. The book resonated with the sentiments of many readers in the early 1930s but has not been highly regarded by critics, and even Ba Jin himself called the book a "failure" (Lang 1967).

The Big Breakthrough: *Family*

Ba Jin began to publish the novel *Torrent* (or *Turbulent Stream*, *Jīliú* 激流) in serial form in the newspaper *The Times* (*Shíbào* 时报) in April 1931. It created a sensation as *Family*, the title under which it appeared in book form in 1933, and remains Ba Jin's most famous work. The great success of *Family* eventually inspired Ba Jin to write a sequel, *Spring* (*Chūn* 春, 1938), and a third novel, *Autumn* (*Qiū* 秋), forming a trilogy collectively entitled Torrent. The trilogy received critical acclaim, but only *Family* has since been canonized as one of the great masterpieces of modern Chinese literature.

Family chronicles the breakdown of the Gao family, a large and wealthy multigenerational family of the traditional scholar-gentry class, living within the walls of their vast compound. The novel's main characters are three brothers, grandsons of the contemptible patriarch, Master Gao: Gao Juexin, followed by Gao Juemin and Gao Juehui. The three struggle against their family to gain control over their own lives and develop a sense of individuality. Family, as Ba Jin portrays it, is, ironically, a hotbed of cruelty, corruption, greed, hypocrisy, misogyny, and infighting. The dissension between the generations generates the dramatic events of the novel and, allegorically, represents the conflicts between traditional and modern world views then raging in China.

In the following extract from Ba Jin's famous novel Family, Juexin, the oldest brother and a brilliant student, graduates from middle school, only to find his dreams of studying in China or abroad crushed by his father's announcement of an arranged marriage.

Handsome and intelligent, he [Juexin] was his father's favourite. His private tutor also spoke highly of him. People predicted that he would do big things, and his parents considered themselves fortunate to be blessed with such a son. [. . .]

But then, one day, his dreams were shattered, cruelly and bitterly shattered. The evening he returned home carrying his diploma, the plaudits of his teachers and friends still ringing in his ears, his father called him into his room and said:

"Now that you've graduated, I want to arrange your marriage. [. . .] I've already arranged a match with the Li family. The thirteenth of next month is a good day. We'll announce the engagement then. You can be married within the year. . . ."

The blow was too sudden. Although he understood everything his father said, somehow the meaning didn't fully register. Juexin only nodded his head. He didn't dare look his father in the eye, although the old man was gazing at him kindly.

Juexin did not utter a word of protest, nor did such a thought ever occur to him. He merely nodded to indicate his compliance with his father's wishes. But after he returned to his own room, and shut the door, he threw himself down on his bed, covered his head with the quilt and wept. He wept for his broken dreams.

Source: *Family* by Ba Jin. Translated by Sidney Shapiro. Beijing: Foreign language university Press, 1989 (pp. 36).

The story takes place between 1919 and 1923, as tumultuous historical events transpire outside the walls of the Gao family compound, including the student-led May Fourth Movement. The relationship between literature, enlightenment, and the transformation of Chinese society is reflected both in the content of the story as well as in the novel's popular reception. Just as the youthful characters in the story are inspired by journal articles coming out of social and intellectual movements of the early 1920s, so were 1930s and 1940s readers of *Family* moved by its indictment of the traditional family system.

Among Ba Jin's most preferred techniques in *Family* is the didactic description of a character's responses to a decisive, potentially transformative event. This is likely intended to inspire readers to contemplate and act accordingly when confronting similar situations. For example, when Juehui magnanimously gives some money to a poor beggar on a cold night, he is haunted by a voice that criticizes the stopgap nature of individual acts of charity. The voice implies that only when collective, large-scale change is undertaken will Chinese society be reformed and China's people truly saved:

A voice seemed to shout at him in the silence: "Do you think deeds like that are going to change the world? Do you think you've saved that beggar child from cold and hunger for the rest of his life? You—you hypocritical 'humanitarian' what a fool you are!" (Ba Jin 1989, 104).

A Prolific Author

Until the late 1930s, Ba Jin published several novellas, novels, and another trilogy. Although never as popular with readers as *Family* or the Torrent Trilogy, Love: A Trilogy (*Àiqíng de sān bù qǔ* 爱情的三部曲) was nonetheless a favorite of the author's, with many characters modeled after Ba Jin's friends. The conflict between romantic love and commitment to social change is central to all three novels.

In between publishing translations, working on Love: A Trilogy, writing essays on recent travels in southern China, and cofounding a literary magazine (*Harvest*), Ba Jin found time to pursue his interest in the short-story form, publishing several collections of short stories. *Revenge* (*Fùchóu* 复仇, 1931) was based on his life in France, and his second collection, *Light*, also known as *Brightness* (*Guāngmíng* 光明, 1932), focuses on both Westerners and Chinese.

In most of Ba Jin's works before July 1937, the author's political agenda supersedes artistic and entertainment concerns. Ba Jin never disguised his emphasis on the didactic and political or his disdain for pure literary artistry. In an essay collected in *Confessions of a Life* (*Shēng zhī chànhuǐ* 生之忏悔, 1936), as quoted by the literary critic C. T. Hsia, Ba Jin writes, "Many, many people are taking hold of my pen to express their sorrow....Do you think I can still pay attention to form, plot, perspective, and other such trivial matters?" (Hsia 1971, 238). It is safe to say that didactic, undisguised political content and unambiguous, emotionally charged characterization are both the hallmarks of Ba Jin's fiction and the sources of his popularity.

During the early war years (1937–1945), Ba Jin published several volumes of essays and translations and, in 1940, the novel *Autumn*, the final installment in the Torrent Trilogy. In late 1940 and early 1941, Ba Jin published the first and second installments of the yet another trilogy, Fire (Huǒ 火). Before 1949, he published two more collections of short stories and two more full-length novels, but his most critically acclaimed novel came out in 1947.

Cold Nights, Ba Jin's last work of fiction prior to 1949, is considered by many to be his best novel. The story takes place in 1944, during the bleak final phase of the war, and conveys a sense of the times through a dual focus on the siege atmosphere and constant threat of bombing raids on the one hand and the economic deprivation and gloom of city life in the Chinese interior (Chongqing) on the other. While *Cold Nights* links the characters' suffering to the Japanese and the corrupt Nationalist government, the novel nonetheless demonstrates how the unrelenting problems of the public and private worlds overlap and influence one another, making the characters' personal experiences complex and ambiguous, rather than the mere result of or reaction to the Japanese or the Nationalists.

Career after 1949

After the founding of the People's Republic of China (PRC) in 1949, the quality and quantity of Ba Jin's work declined. Though he complied with the political demands imposed on writers by the Chinese Communist Party (CCP), he did not receive favorable treatment from them. Beginning in the 1950s, he was the target of political persecution, which became especially vicious during the decade of the Cultural Revolution. He was targeted for numerous reasons, including his pre-1949 anarchist political activities and his literary works. In his "Random Thoughts" ("Suíxiǎng lù" 随想录) essays of the 1980s, Ba Jin recounted many of his difficult experiences after 1949, which included physical, mental, and material assaults, such as being forced to kneel on broken glass while being harangued at a rally in People's Stadium in Shanghai. He was tormented at other "struggle sessions" (*pīdòuhuì* 批斗会), his wife died (having been denied medical treatment), and his art collection and library were destroyed, the latter of which contained a large archive of anarchist literature.

Ba Jin was officially rehabilitated by the CCP in 1977. Decades later, he continued to draw accolades and in 2002 was referred to as "the only survivor of the 'six contemporary literature giants of China'" in the *China Daily* (3 July 2002; the other five are Lu Xun, Guo Moruo, Mao Dun, Lao She, and Cao Yu). A lifelong heavy smoker, Ba Jin suffered from chronic bronchitis and Parkinson's disease, and was reportedly confined in the Shanghai Huadong Hospital starting in 1999. The title of the *China Daily* article quoted the then ninety-seven-year-old writer as saying that "longevity is a punishment for me." He eventually died in Shanghai, age one hundred, on 17 October 2005.

Nicholas A. KALDIS
Binghamton University (SUNY)

Further Reading

Ba Jin. (1929). *Miewang* 灭亡 [Destruction]. Shanghai: Kaiming shudian chubanshe.

Ba Jin. (1933). *Mengya* 萌芽 [Sprouts]. Shanghai: Xiandai shuju.

Ba Jin. (1934). *Ba Jin zizhuan* 巴金自传 [Ba Jin's Autobiography]. Shanghai: Diyi chubanshe.

Ba Jin. (1936a). *Aiqing de sanbu qu* 爱情的三部曲 [Love: A trilogy]. Shanghai: Liangyou tushu yinshua gongsi.

Ba Jin. (1936b). *Xue* 雪 [Snow]. Shanghai: Wenhua shenghuo chubanshe.

Ba Jin. (1938). *Chun* 春 [Spring]. Shanghai: Kaiming shudian chubanshe.

Ba Jin. (1940). *Qiu* 秋 [Autumn]. Shanghai: Kaiming shudian chubanshe.

Ba Jin. (1978). *Cold nights: A novel by Pa Chin* (Nathan K. Mao and Liu Ts'un-yan, Trans.). Hong Kong: The Chinese University Press, 1978. (Original work published 1947)

Ba Jin. (1981). *Autumn in spring and other stories* (Wang Mingjie, Trans.). Beijing: Panda Books.

Ba Jin. (1989). *Family* (Sidney Shapiro, Trans.). Beijing: Foreign Languages Press. (Original work published 1931)

Ba Jin. (1997). *Ba Jin yiwen quanji* 巴金译文全集 [Ba Jin's complete translations] (10 vols.). Beijing: Renmin wenxue chubanshe.

Hsia, C. T. (1971). Chapter 10: Pa Chin (1904–). In *A history of modern Chinese fiction* (pp. 237–256). New Haven, CT: Yale University Press.

Jia Zhifang, Tang Jinhai, Zhang Xiaoyun, & Chen Sihe (Eds.). (1985). *Ba Jin zuopin pinglun ji* 巴金作品评论集 [Annotated collection of Ba Jin's work]. Beijing: Zhongguo wenlian chubanshe gongsi.

Kaldis, Nicholas A. (2007). Ba Jin. In Thomas Moran (Ed.), *Dictionary of literary biography—Chinese fiction writers, 1900–1949* (pp. 310–325). New York: Thomson Gale.

Kaldis, Nicholas A. (2003). Ba Jin. In David Levinson (Ed.), *Encyclopedia of modern Asia* (vol. 1, pp. 209a–209b). New York: Scribner's.

• Ba Jin •

Kaldis, Nicholas A. (2003). Ba Jin's *Jia*. In Joshua Mostow (Ed.), *The Columbia companion to modern East Asian literature* (pp. 411–417). New York: Columbia University Press.

Lang, Olga. (1967). *Ba Chin and his writings: Chinese youth between the two revolutions*. Cambridge, MA: Harvard University Press.

Larson, Wendy. (1991). Shen Congwen and Ba Jin: Literary authority against the "world." In *Literary authority and the modern Chinese writer: Ambivalence and autobiography* (pp. 61–85). Durham, NC: Duke University Press.

Lau, Joseph S. M. (1981). Pa Chin (1904–). In Leo Ou-fan Lee & C. T. Hsia (Eds.), *Modern Chinese stories and novellas, 1919–1949* (pp. 292). New York: Columbia University Press.

Li Cun'guang. (1994). *Ba Jin zhuan* [Ba Jin biography]. Beijing: Beijing shiyue wenyi chubanshe.

Mao, Nathan. (1978). *Pa Chin*. Boston: Twayne.

Rey Chow. (1989). Ba Jin's *Jia* (The family) (1930). In *Woman and Chinese modernity: The politics of reading between West and East* (pp. 96–102). Minneapolis: University of Minnesota Press.

Shapiro, Sidney, & Wang Mingjie (Trans.). (1988). *Selected works of Ba Jin*. Beijing: Foreign Languages Press.

Tang Xiaobing. (2000). The last tubercular in modern Chinese literature: On Ba Jin's *Cold nights*. In *Chinese modern: The heroic and the quotidian* (pp. 131–160). Durham, NC: Duke University Press.

Yang Yi. (1981). An interview with Ba Jin. In *Autumn in Spring and other stories* (pp. 133–147). Beijing: Panda Books.

♂ Bào Tóng 鲍彤

b. 1932—Government official, dissident, activist, and writer, imprisoned after the Tiananmen protests

Alternate name: trad. 鮑彤

Summary

Bao Tong is one of China's best-known political dissidents, imprisoned as a result of the crackdown on the 1989 democracy movement. In the 1980s, he served as political secretary to Premier Zhao Ziyang and played a key role in formulating many major reform policies. Just before the violent suppression of the 1989 Tiananmen protests, Bao was detained and eventually charged with revealing state secrets and making counterrevolutionary propaganda. He served seven years in prison but has continued to promote democratic reform in China.

Bao Tong is the highest-ranking official to have been tried and imprisoned in connection with the Tiananmen Incident of 1989, in which thousands of protesters occupied Tiananmen Square in the call for political reform and liberalization. Bao had been the closest aide to former premier *Zhào Zǐyáng 赵紫阳 (1919–2005) and, like Zhao, sympathized with the protesters and thought that they should be dealt with in accordance with legal proceedings. Bao was eventually tried for counterrevolutionary agitation and imprisoned for seven years. Since his release, he has actively criticized the government and worked to further the causes of human rights and reform.

Early Life

Born in Haining, Zhejiang Province, in 1932, Bao Tong grew up and received his primary and secondary education in Shanghai. The most influential person in Bao's formative years was his maternal uncle Wú Shìchāng 吴世昌, a well-known political commentator in the 1930s and 1940s, and, in his later life, an expert on the great Qīng 清 dynasty (1644–1911/12) classical novel *Dream of the Red Chamber*. Wu was a major

*People marked with an asterisk have entries in this dictionary.

contributor to *The Observer* (*Guānchá* 观察), a key journal of Chinese liberal intellectuals in the 1940s. It was mainly through the influence of this liberal uncle that Bao turned to political liberalism and left-wing ideology (New Democracy, promoted by the Chinese Communist Party [CCP] in particular), when he was still a high school student. He joined the CCP at Shanghai Nanyang High School in 1949, prior to the establishment of the People's Republic of China (PRC).

Contribution to Reform

Bao Tong worked at the Organization Department (in effect, the CCP's personnel department in charge of appointments) for over two decades, first in Shanghai until 1954, and at the CCP Central Committee after 1954. He was deputy director of the Research Office of the CCP Central Organization Department and secretary for Ān Zìwén 安子文, director of the CCP Central Organization Department, prior to the Cultural Revolution (1966–1976). When An was felled during the Cultural Revolution, Bao refused to denounce him and was persecuted as a capitalist roader as a result of this connection.

Bao was rehabilitated in 1977 and introduced by An Ziwen to *Dèng Xiǎopíng 邓小平 (1940–1997), joining the team that drafted Deng's well-known science and technology conference speech that recognized "intellectuals as part of the proletarian class." Bao was also a participant in the Theoretical Conference of the CCP Central Committee in 1979.

Bao became the most important aide to Zhao Ziyang in 1980 when Zhao was appointed premier. He served as political secretary for Premier Zhao for seven years and continued to serve as Zhao's political secretary for another three years when Zhao was the general secretary of the party. During this period, Bao was also put in charge of the State Commission for Economic System Reform, the Office of Political Reform of the CCP Central Committee, and then the Drafting Small Group for the Thirteenth Congress of the CCP. At the same time, Bao was elected as a member of the CCP Central Committee at the Thirteenth Congress in 1987. While serving in these key positions, Bao worked with many noted reformers and facilitated the formation of many key reform theories and proposals, such as "the theory of the initial stage of socialism," "separation of the government from enterprises," and "separation of the party from the government."

Political Dissident

The inaugural president of the Beijing Association of Young Economists in 1984, Bao Tong had already established extensive connections with the emerging civil society when working as a party official of ministerial rank. Bao's official career, however, was disrupted during the 1989 pro-democracy movement. Like Zhao Ziyang, Bao sympathized with the movement, attempted to find common ground with the demonstrators, and insisted on "settling the issue in accordance with democratic and legal procedures." After Zhao refused to follow Deng Xiaoping's order to crush the movement by force and lost his position as general secretary of the party and his freedom, Bao was arrested in Beijing on 28 May 1989, just before the 4 June Tiananmen Incident. While Zhao was held under house arrest for the rest of his life, Bao was detained for two years and then subjected to a brief show trial in 1992. He was expelled from the party and sentenced to seven years' imprisonment for the "crime of revealing state secrets" 泄露国家秘密罪 and the "crime of counterrevolutionary propaganda and agitation" 反革命宣传煽动罪. He served the full term of his imprisonment in solitary confinement at Qincheng prison, and then was held at a government compound on the outskirts of Beijing for an additional year without any legal proceedings. Since his release in 1997, he has been under around-the-clock surveillance, with his visitors being screened or blocked. His phone has been tapped or cut off entirely, and he has been followed by plain-clothes police and occasionally prevented from leaving his apartment during "sensitive" events, such as the anniversary of the Tiananmen Square massacre, the party congresses, or Zhao Ziyang's funeral in 2005.

Bao Tong has never regretted his association with Zhao Ziyang nor his confrontations with the hard-liners of the party, and has continued to be an important voice for human rights and democracy in China. He appealed for the restoration of Zhao Ziyang's civil and political rights from 1998 until Zhao's death. He was instrumental in the May 2009 publication of Zhao Ziyang's memoir, *Journey of Reform* (*Gǎigé lìchéng* 改革历程), based on audiotapes that Zhao made secretly while under house arrest, which were discovered after his death in 2005. Bao has published regularly on the Internet and in overseas journals, analyzing Chinese current affairs, criticizing government policies and measures he deems harmful to society, and promoting human rights and democracy. In 1998, he was named Chinese Outstanding Democracy Activist by Chinese Democracy Education Foundation, and he was a signatory of Charter 08, released in December 2008, calling for China's transformation to constitutional democracy.

Chongyi FENG
University of Technology, Sydney

Further Reading

Bao Tong 鲍彤. (2000). *Zhongguo de yousi* 中国的忧思 [Worries about China]. Hong Kong: The Pacific Century Press.

Bao Tong 鲍彤. (2012). *Bao Tong wenji* 鲍彤文集 [A collection of essays by Bao Tong]. Hong Kong: New Century Press.

Johnson, Ian. (2012, June 14). 'In the current system, I'd be corrupt too': An interview with Bao Tong. *The New York Review Blog*. Retrieved June 12, 2015, from http://www.nybooks.com/blogs/nyrblog/2012/jun/14/china-corruption-bao-tong-interview/

Leavenworth, Stuart. (2015, February 2). Torn apart by Tiananment, father, son still fight for free speech in China. *McClatchy DC*. Retrieved June 12, 2015, from http://www.mcclatchydc.com/2015/02/02/255207/torn-apart-by-tiananmen-father.html

Lim, Louise. (2014). *The People's republic of amnesia: Tiananmen revisited*. Oxford, UK: Oxford University Press.

Song, Yuwu. (2013). Bao Tong. In Yuwu Song (Ed.), *Biographical dictionary of the People's Republic of China* (pp. 16–17). Jefferson, NC: McFarland.

Sullivan, Lawrence R. (2012). Bao Tong. In *Historical dictionary of the Chinese Communist Party* (pp. 22–23). Plymouth, UK: Scarecrow Press, Inc.

Tatlow, Didi Kirsten. (2014, October 5). Bao Tong, recalling Tiananmen, calls on Hong Kong protesters to 'take a break'. *The New York Times: Sinosphere*. Retrieved June 12, 2015, from http://sinosphere.blogs.nytimes.com/2014/10/05/bao-tong-recalling-tiananmen-calls-on-hong-kong-protesters-to-take-a-break/?_r=1

The Asia Watch Committee. (1990). Bao, Tong. In *Repression in China since June 4, 1989* (pp. 80). US: Human Rights Watch.

Wu Guoguang 吴国光. (1997). *Zhao Ziyang yu zhengzhi gaige* [Political reform under Zhao Ziyang]. Taipei, Taiwan: Yuanjing chuban shiye gongsi.

Wu Wei 吴伟. (2013). *Zhongge bashi niannai zhengzhi gaige de taiqian muhou* 中国80年代政治改革的台前幕后 [Political reform in China in the 1980s]. Hong Kong: New Century Press.

鲍彤

♂ Běi Dǎo 北岛

b. 1949—Contemporary Chinese poet, a key figure of the Misty Poets movement, living in exile since 1989

Alternate names: b. Zhào Zhènkāi 赵振开; trad. 北岛

Summary

No figure looms larger than Bei Dao in Chinese poetry of the last forty years. He is synonymous with Misty Poetry, which originated in the 1970s and fundamentally changed the landscape of contemporary Chinese poetry. Renowned for his complex images and opacity, Bei Dao is frequently the subject of controversy, whether because of his innovative poetics or his entanglement in China's politics.

Widely recognized as the most eminent living Chinese-language poet, Bei Dao writes poetry that is an exercise in survival, a battle of voices, and a strategy of mapping out the vanishing self against all antagonistic forces—real or imagined—in contemporary societies. He lives and writes in two worlds. In China he is a legend of the 1980s whose groundbreaking poetry influenced a generation and sparked the democracy movement that helped accelerate the country's reform and openness. In the West he is a reminder of China's political intolerance, a poetic enigma whose elliptical syntax and cryptic imagery represent a complex interior response to a hostile exterior world. Such different reactions toward Bei Dao underscore the transformation of the poet himself—from an uncompromising young rebel in pre-1989 China to a mellowing and meditative poetic voice in exile in the West.

Now that Bei Dao has found a home in Hong Kong and is allowed to visit mainland China, he is able to reconnect Chinese readers with a body of poetry that has evolved from his legacy of Misty Poetry (so named because it has been officially denounced as "hazy" and "obscure") and yet is distinct from it. Bei Dao's poetry is unabashedly individualistic but also deeply synchronistic with traditional Chinese and postmodernist aesthetics, and it characteristically challenges the conventions of meaning and interpretative certitude. What emerges in these works is the familiar Bei Dao, whose ingrained skepticism is present in every word-image, a skepticism that originated from his frustrating experiences with the force-fed Maoist ideology during his formative years and that now expands to produce a suspicion about all discourses of power that oppress and corrupt.

Misty Poetry and the Making of a Rebel

Bei Dao is the pen name of Zhao Zhenkai, who was born in 1949 in Beijing. His father was a middle-level government official and his mother a doctor. The year of Bei Dao's birth coincided with the founding of the People's Republic of China, an auspicious beginning for this "baby of New China." He attended No. 4 High School, a famous public school for children of Beijing's privileged class. The accidental drowning of his beloved younger sister and the start of the Cultural Revolution (1966–1976) interrupted normal school activities for Zhao Zhenkai and had a profound impact on his writing years later.

Young Zhao Zhenkai joined the Red Guard, but only briefly. He then went to the countryside to be "reeducated" as ordered by Chairman Máo Zédōng 毛泽东 (1893–1976); unlike millions of other young people who scattered across China to remote rural villages, however, Zhao Zhenkai ended up in a western Beijing suburb working in construction. This eleven-year ordeal ended in 1980 when Bei Dao was allowed to return to

Beijing on account of work-related health problems.

Poetry, as Bei Dao recalls, is an accident that happened to him. He would not have become a poet if not for his experience with bricks and cement. Young and restless, yet stuck in a back-breaking job that taxed his body and soul, Bei Dao found writing down lines of words a convenient way to dispel the feelings of boredom and despair. The lines of words accumulated to become poems, soon to be shared with a few poetry-loving friends from his high school days. The circle of friends grew and formed a sort of "underground poetry club" that included aspiring young poets such as Mang Ke, Jiang He, and Duo Duo. In 1978 a thin, stencil-printed poetry journal called *Today* (*Jīntiān* 今天) was published without official government permission, a standard practice for all print publications in China. The journal reached its readers through direct sales on Beijing's street corners and university campuses and through limited mail orders for the rest of China. In less than two years the journal was shut down by the authorities, but a new kind of poetry was born in China.

Conditions were ripe for this new poetry, which deliberately differentiated itself from the official poetry of the time in terms of language, style, and theme. By the end of the 1970s, China had just awakened from the nightmare of its Cultural Revolution, and the oppressive

Maoist ideology had lost much of its credibility. After years of being overfed the formulaic propaganda of socialist literature, the public, especially young readers, was ready for an alternative. Thus, Bei Dao's personal pulse became that of a generation. Although his writings paralleled the official poetry in the style of grandiosity and sloganism, they could not be more different in their messages. The significance of a simple statement, such as "I—do—not—believe!" (Bei Dao 1983), can only be grasped by those who must believe nothing else but the personal cult of Mao.

The central concern of Bei Dao's poetry in this period was a plea for the restoration of personal space and life's ordinariness against the previous decade's general deprivation of humanity in China. "I am no hero," he writes, "In an age without heroes / I just want to be a man" (Bei Dao 1988, "Declaration"). Being a man, Bei Dao repeatedly clarifies, means living a life of dignity and fulfillment without political consequences. Such apolitical ideas were given a political reading by both the student protesters of the late 1980s and the Chinese government.

When Bei Dao's influence spread, the literary establishment launched a campaign against him and other young poets associated with *Today* and denigrated their works as "Misty Poetry," a label that, interestingly, Bei Dao took as a badge of honor and gleefully embraced. The official hostility made Bei Dao famous, but it ultimately led to his forced exile in 1989 following the Tiananmen student protests.

Exile in the West: The Self in Crisis

"The exile of the word has begun," Bei Dao announced upon his arrival in Europe. He immediately became the symbol of China's abortive democracy movement. He revived his journal *Today* and made it an important forum for the community of exiled Chinese writers. As difficult as exile has been for his family life—moving between half a dozen countries in a span of eighteen years without a permanent home in any one place—Bei Dao has relished the unexpected freedom of travel and the opportunity to work "the word" to attain the realm of pure poetry, a poetry of linguistic exactitude and aesthetic bliss.

In terms of style and technique, he has become an even bolder experimentalist than before with truncated word combinations and disjointed images. He has also reinvigorated his efforts to draw on classical Chinese poetry as well as his favorite Western poets, such as Paul Celan and César Vallejo. Removed from familiar sensations and relationships, Bei Dao seizes the singularity of his life in exile and contextualizes his heightened sense of subjectivity in everything that is happening—be it an accidental mosquito bite, a Bach concert, or a phone call home. In this mundaneness of life, however, an opponent always lurks, invisible and in some cases unnamable, working to undermine life's promise and fragment the self.

That the exile of the poet is foremost the exile of the word is Bei Dao's unique take on his experience away from China. His poem "A Local Accent" poignantly captures Bei Dao's reconfigured relationship with China through language:

> I speak Chinese to the mirror
> a park has its own winter
> I put on music
> winter is free of flies
> I make coffee unhurriedly
> flies don't understand what's meant
>   by a native land
> I add a little sugar
> a native land is a kind of local accent
> I hear my fright
> on the other end of a phone line

> 我对着镜子说中文
> 一个公园有自己的冬天
> 我放上音乐
> 冬天没有苍蝇
> 我悠闲地煮着咖啡
> 苍蝇不懂得什么是祖国
> 我加了点儿糖
> 祖国是一种乡音
> 我在电话线的另一端
> 听见了我的恐惧

(Bei Dao 1991)

The poem rests beautifully on a dual narrative structure in which the two sides close out each other. A subjective world fragmented by mechanical acts runs parallel to an incomprehensible and incommunicable objective world. The local accent as a false emblem of that native land no longer bears the marks of identification, yet it is arduously preserved between "I" and its mirrored self, for there is nowhere to go beyond that "last line of defense" constructed by the Chinese language.

It is almost a hackneyed notion that exile brings about freedom, but it is a notion that still retains much force for exiled writers such as Bei Dao. Still, new opportunities come with new perils. In exchange for the distance from the center of power and more freedom, the poet in exile is thrown into an unfamiliar territory of irrelevance, in which writing has become less meaningful to the world even as it is acquiring increasing significance to the poet himself. Poetry then has the potential of becoming "pure," of becoming the poet's very being. This may explain why Bei Dao's poetry in exile has become far more obtuse and abstract, hidden behind a labyrinth of imaginative images accessible only to the most sensitive readers. Even though "obscurity" has been Bei Dao's trademark, thanks to China's literary bureaucracy, life as an exile forced the poet to negotiate anew in the "unreality" of the West once the threat of a repressive ideology was removed. In this way, it can be argued that exile is only an occasion for Bei Dao's profound sense of alienation and pessimism and that he is reiterating a truth about modern life in general, a truth that is more powerful and long-lasting than a single political ideology.

Return to China: Finding No Home

On 24 November 1994, five years after he left China, Bei Dao arrived at the Beijing International Airport. The agents of the National Security Bureau were waiting for him. After an interrogation lasting more than twelve hours, Bei Dao was expelled and sent back to the United States on the same airplane. In the years that followed, Bei Dao would keep trying to go home, but to no avail. Finally, in December 2001 the Chinese authorities granted him a visit to his ailing father and aging mother. This trip was followed by more visits to his home country, particularly after Bei Dao's move to Hong Kong in 2007, when he became a professor of humanities at the Chinese University of Hong Kong. The exile has seemingly ended, but the nature of his homecoming is shrouded in Chinese-style ambiguity. Officially, Bei Dao is no longer an "unwelcome person" in China, but he is by no means considered a "hero" in the press. Bei Dao has achieved a measure of peace with his new and restricted life in China, for living under surveillance is a familiar experience, a reminder of the life Bei Dao left behind.

The return to a China that is strangely familiar has provided a new round of poetic inspirations for Bei Dao. His beloved city of Beijing and almost everywhere else in China have changed vastly, so the native son relies on his memory to navigate a geophysical landscape that impresses but does not respond. The city has all the markings of a place once lived but gives no directions as to where things are, a feeling that Bei Dao poignantly captures in the paradoxical image of a "black map," in a poem of the same name:

> In the end, cold crows piece together
> the night: a black map
> I've come home—the way back
> longer than the wrong road
> long as life
>
> ....
> Beijing, let me
> toast your lamplights
> let my white hair lead
> the way through the black map
> as though a storm were taking you to fly
>
> I wait in line until the small window
> shuts: O the bright moon
> I've come home—reunions
> are less than good-byes
> only one less

寒鸦终于拼凑成
夜：黑色地图
我回来了——归程
总是比迷途长
长于一生

……

北京，让我
跟你所有灯光干杯
让我的白发领路
穿过黑色地图
如风暴领你起飞

我排队排到那小窗
关上：哦明月
我回来了——重逢
总是比告别少
只少一次

(from "Black Map," Bei Dao 2011b;
translation by the author)

The metaphor of the night once again becomes the means for articulating a poetic event. It is a centralizing thought that unifies the speaker's seemingly chaotic and painful experience of return—it is compared to "spring water and horse pills," a rainbow above the black market, and flying in a storm. Life returns in its vanishing traces, such as the absence of the former lover. That memories assault and invoke both sweet nostalgia and bitter disappointment is vividly represented in this line: "I wait in line until the small window shuts." It recalls the old times of Beijing, the days of economic shortage, when people waited in line daily to live their rationed lives. Whatever the speaker waited for, he did not get it, for "the small window shuts" before his turn comes up.

Emptied of the past's substance and particularity, Bei Dao makes his memory work in a purely formalist fashion, focusing on the act of remembering rather than on what is to be remembered. But memory emits its most power when retained as a formal expression of emotions, not as a tool of reconstructing the past. Using a colon to dissolve the line into the symbol of the moon (a clear allusion to Li Bai's well-known poem about homesickness), Bei Dao links his personal experience to the collective longing for return in Chinese culture that has made the sorrow of homesickness an aesthetic bliss over the centuries. Bei Dao quickly reins in, however, this very aesthetic bliss, this nostalgia derived from the context of Li Bai's poem, by privileging farewell over reunion. "Reunions / are less than good-byes / only one less," he writes, indicating the choice of a life of constant farewells. In other words, the return is not going home at all, but a visit, the beginning of another round of good-byes. In such an eloquent expression of the tormented feeling of rootlessness brought about by China's rush to modernization, Bei Dao once again proves to be the poet of our times.

Dian LI
Sichuan University, Chengdu

Further Reading

Bei Dao. (1983). *Notes from the city of sun: Poems by Bei Dao* (Bonnie S. McDougall, Ed. & Trans.). Ithaca, NY: Cornell University East Asia Papers.

Bei Dao. (1988). *The August sleepwalker* (Bonnie S. McDougall, Trans.). London: Anvil Press.

Bei Dao. (1991). *Old snow* (Bonnie S. McDougall and Chen Maiping, Trans.). New York: New Directions.

Bei Dao. (1994). *Forms of distance* (David Hinton, Trans.). New York: New Directions.

Bei Dao. (1996). *Landscape over zero* (David Hinton with Yanbing Chen, Trans.). New York: New Directions.

Bei Dao. (1999). *Nightwatch* (David Hinton, Trans.). Hopewell, NJ: Pied Oxen Printers.

Bei Dao. (2000). *Unlock* (Eliot Weinberger and Iona Man-Cheong, Trans.). New York: New Directions.

Bei Dao. (2001). *At the sky's edge* (David Hinton, Trans.). New York: New Directions.

Bei Dao. (2010). *The rose of time: New and selected poems* (Eliot Weinberger, Trans.). New York: New Directions.

Bei Dao. (2011a). *Endure* (Clayton Eshleman and Lucas Klein, Trans.). Boston: Commonwealth Books, Black.

Bei Dao. (2011b). *Beidao zuo pin jing xuan* 北岛作品精选 [Selected works of Be Dao]. Wuhan, China: Changjiang wenyi chubanshe.

Janssen, Ronald R. (2002). What history cannot write: Bei Dao and recent Chinese poetry. *Critical Asian Studies*, 34(2), 259–277.

Li, Dian. (2006). *The Chinese poetry of Bei Dao, 1978–2000: Exile and resistance.* New York: The Edwin Mellen Press.

McDougall, Bonnie S. (1985). Bei Dao's poetry: Revelation and communication. *Modern Chinese Literature*, 1(2), 225–252.

Owen, Stephen. (1990). What is world poetry? *The New Republic*, 19, 28–32.

Tan, C. L. (2014). Engagement and integration: The post-exile poetics of Bei Dao. *Quarterly Journal of Chinese Studies*, 2(4), 1–14.

Van Crevel, Maghiel. (2008). Exile: Yang Lian, Wang Jiaxin and Bei Dao. In Maghiel van Crevel, *Chinese poetry in times of mind, mayhem and money* (pp. 137–186). Leiden, The Netherlands: Brill.

Yang Xiaobin 杨小滨. (1995). Jintian de "Jintian pai" shige: lun Bei Dao, Duoduo, Yan Li, Yang Lian de haiwai shizuo 今天的"今天派"诗歌：论北岛, 多多, 严力, 杨炼的海外诗作 [Poetry of the Today school today: On Bei Dao, Duoduo, Yan Li and Yang Lian's overseas works]. *Jintian*, 4, 244–261.

Běi Dǎo •

☿ Bó Xīlái 薄熙来

b. 1949—Politician, Chongqing party secretary (2007–2012), convicted of corruption in 2013

Alternate name: trad. 薄熙來

Summary

In 2013, Bo Xilai was the first senior member of the Chinese "princelings" to be convicted of corruption offences since 1985. While party secretary of Chongqing in the early 2000s, he had electrified Chinese politics and become a favorite of the "New Left" and those who yearned for socialist equality and a more dynamic China. He was also criticized by liberal intellectuals who saw recurrences of the lawless brutality of China's Maoist past. These divisions became apparent after Chongqing's police chief fled the city and told officials that Bo had attempted to cover up his wife's murder of an English family friend.

Bo Xilai was an ambitious Communist Party aristocrat who tore up the monochrome façade of post-Deng politics. As party secretary of Chongqing (2007–2012), Bo made waves by boldly acknowledging a growing national crisis of inequality, corruption, and bureaucratization, in contrast with the Party's generally triumphal official line. "Corruption is the party's mortal wound, and degeneration of its working style is its chronic disease," Bo said on television in December 2009, using bodily metaphors favored by both Mao and Stalin. "Without help the disease will become fatal."

Bo's efforts to rejuvenate the Communist Party catalyzed what was arguably the closest thing to an open political contest that China had witnessed since 1989. He was hugely popular among China's resurgent leftists as well as many fellow-descendants of founding revolutionaries. Some powerful peers and superiors, however, believed Bo and the surgery that he proposed were more dangerous than the underlying disease. His career was ultimately destroyed by the political struggle he started, in a bruising process which exposed weaknesses in China's one-party structure. Bo is best known for a movie-like conspiracy of corruption, murder, and betrayal which led to his ejection from power in the lead-up to the Eighteenth Party Congress of November 2012.

Early Life

Bo was born in July 1949, just months before the communist "liberation" of China, and he grew up within the cloistered walls of Zhongnanhai, the walled compound in Beijing where highest-level officials live and work. His childhood was defined by the extensive privileges and acute traumas associated with the status of his father, *Bó Yībō 薄一波 (1908–2007), a founding revolutionary who rose to be vice premier in the early years of the People's Republic. Bo Xilai attended China's most exclusive school, No. 4 Middle School, where classmates remember him as being reserved and studious. Powerful myths have evolved about Bo's behavior during the Cultural Revolution that purportedly foreshadowed the person he became. Prominent commentators have endorsed stories told by rivals that Bo was a Red Guard who helped to beat two people to death and physically assaulted his own father to the point of breaking his ribs (Sina 2012). But there are no plausible accounts of when or where these events might have occurred. "It couldn't have happened," the student leader of Bo Xilai's class, Fu Yang, told the author. "He

didn't have any opportunity to see his father, so how could he have beaten him?" Fu added that the murder allegations "must be fabricated" (Garnaut 2012, interview with Fu Yang).

There is no doubt, however, that Bo's cloistered world was up-ended by the Cultural Revolution. His father was taken by Red Guards in December 1968, when he was recuperating from illness with his wife, Hu Ming, in the southern city of Guangzhou. The following month he was dragged to Beijing's Workers' Stadium with his head shackled in an iron rack. Bo Xilai and two brothers were banished to the 789 "thought-reform" camp in Beijing's western suburbs. They later discovered that their mother had been harassed into suicide midway on the train journey from Guangzhou to Beijing.

Early Career

In 1979, more than two years after Mao's death, Bo Yibo was released from jail and reinstated as vice premier, responsible for economics. He returned to Zhongnanhai with his seven children and never remarried. Bo Xilai studied world history at Peking University and shifted to the Chinese Academy of Social Sciences to complete a master's degree in international journalism. In 1982, Bo received career-building appointments in the central party secretariat and general office. In 1984, he was assigned as deputy party secretary in Jinzhou and proceeded up the ranks of the local and provincial

---

*People marked with an asterisk have entries in this dictionary.

government in Liaoning, on the Bohai Sea. He left his high-born wife and married another, Gu Kailai, in 1986.

Bo Xilai strengthened friendships and alliances with key families from his father's "white area" factional base who supported the rise to power of President *Jiāng Zémín 江泽民 (b. 1926) after the "turmoil" of 1989, according to acquaintances. He also sharpened divisions with families that had been rivals of his father, particularly those close to the purged liberal leader *Hú Yàobāng 胡耀邦 (1915–1989). In the 1990s, while still in Liaoning Province, Bo had a reputation for being a charismatic, modernizing leader who could charm foreign dignitaries and cultivate crony businessmen. He also gained a reputation for ruthlessly persecuting critics.

Bo's Chongqing Model

Bo's career spanned the era of Reform and Opening Up (gǎigé kāifàng 改革开放), a period of mostly economic reforms begun by *Dèng Xiǎopíng 邓小平 (1904–1997) in 1978. Bo spent most of that time in the northeast rustbelt province of Liaoning, which became the epicenter of a redundancy program which saw nearly fifty million Chinese workers laid off from state-related enterprises in the decade leading up to 2003 (Naughton 2007, 186; cf. official figure of 28.2 million). The mass privatization and restructuring of "iron rice bowl" enterprises triggered a backlash against China's perceived "neo-liberal" turn, particularly within the intellectual New Left and conservative segments of the Party. In 2004, Bo was promoted as the minister of commerce. After Bo was promoted to the Politburo at the Seventeenth Party Congress of November 2007, and was sent to run the province-level municipality of Chongqing, he rode this wave of discontent.

In Chongqing, Bo conspicuously projected his personality to the public and across the municipal bureaucracy with a series of campaign-style programs to build affordable housing, attract foreign investment, and plant millions of trees across the city. He gained national prominence with a "strike black" and "sing red" law-enforcement and propaganda campaigns. His state-centric policies, nostalgic Mao-era imagery, and charismatic manipulation of popular opinion made him the hero of leftists who were pushing back against the liberal-minded lawyers, journalists, and scholars who dominated China's nascent, Internet-enabled civil society. Supporters hailed Bo's "Chongqing Model" as a new solution to the old contradictions of political dictatorship and market-oriented economics. A civil society backlash gathered strength from late in 2009, when Bo arrested (and later re-arrested) a well-regarded and connected Beijing lawyer, Li Zhuang, who had robustly defended an entrepreneur who said he had been pressured to falsely confess to triad links. The Li Zhuang case galvanized old family rivals within the elite against him.

Catalyzing China's Political Divide

Several top leaders went out of the way to endorse Bo's program, particularly those who owed their promotions to former president Jiang. The most striking statement of support came from the then vice president, *Xí Jìnpíng 习近平 (b. 1953), in December 2010, shortly after he received a crucial military promotion. Interviews with the author reveal, however, that Xi also showed strong support for Bo's opponents who were warning that Bo's Chongqing Model threatened to revive the most lawless and despotic episodes in the Party's history. "In recent years, for whatever reason, there seems to be a 'revival' of something like advocating the Cultural Revolution," said Hu Deping, eldest son of the purged 1980s party secretary Hu Yaobang, speaking at a gathering of liberal-minded "princelings" and intellectuals in August 2011 (Garnaut 2012a). Hu Yaobang, a crucial supporter of Xi's father, had been toppled in a purge led by Bo's father.

At the same time, associates of Bo's flamboyant police chief, Wang Lijun, came under pressure from central investigators in 2011. Evidence suggests that these investigations contributed to a chain reaction of sordid and extraordinary events. On 14 November 2011, Wang assisted Bo's wife, Gu Kailai, in the murder of an English family friend, Neil Heywood, by getting him drunk and pouring a cyanide cocktail down his throat (court accounts show that Gu imagined that Heywood was plotting to harm Gu and Bo's son, Bo Guagua). Wang assisted Gu in covering up the murder, before falling out with her (their relationship had been so close that Bo expressed frustration about having to put away Wang's shoes in his own home). In late January 2012, Bo demonstrated his displeasure with Wang by punching him in the face (which Bo described in court as a "slap," although it drew blood). On 6 February, Wang fled for his life and sought asylum at the US consulate in the city of Chengdu, in what quickly became China's most dramatic and closely watched political event since 1989. On 7 February, after tense negotiations between Washington and Beijing, Wang was escorted by a vice minister of State Security, Qiu Jin, out of the US embassy to catch an Air China flight and surrender himself to central authorities in Beijing.

Bo Xilai's fate appeared to be hanging in the balance in March 2012 when he gave a rousing defense of his conduct in a press conference during the National People's Congress. "I was mentally prepared for the fact that attacking organized crime and expunging evil would affect some people's interests," he said, dismissing lurid claims that had been circulating about him. "There are many people who have poured filth on Chongqing, including pouring filth on me and my family" (Garnaut 2012b).

Days later, on 14 March, Premier *Wēn Jiābǎo 温家宝 (b. 1942) foreshadowed

Bo's imminent demise by echoing the language of Hu Deping and linking Bo with the worst excesses under Mao. "After the implementation of reform and opening up, the mistakes of the Cultural Revolution and feudalism have not been completely eliminated," said Wen, who had publicly advocated democratic and legal restraints on state power. "Without the success of political reform, economic reforms cannot be carried out. The results that we have achieved may be lost. A historical tragedy like the Cultural Revolution may occur again" (Xinhua 2012)

Bo was removed from the Politburo the following day, on 15 March. On 10 April, he was stripped of his Chongqing post. In August, Bo's wife received a suspended death sentence for murder. In September, Wang Lijun, the police chief, received a fifteen-year jail sentence for defection, bribe-taking, and abuse of power. On 28 September, ahead of the Eighteenth Party Congress and following months of messy political struggle, the Politburo finally sealed Bo's fate by expelling him from the Party and accusing him of a broad range of crimes. Bo faced trial in September 2013 in the Jinan Intermediate People's Court. He was sentenced to life in jail for bribery, embezzlement, and abuse of power.

Bo Xilai's Legacy

Bo's downfall exposed deep flaws in China's one-party structure, with even officials publicly conceding that he damaged the image of the Party. His outspoken and combative style was seen as a threat to other leaders who had stuck to the Party's strict requirements of public conformity. His performance in Chongqing also heralded the rise of a cohort of "princeling" leaders who were more forceful, charismatic, and willing to take risks than the consensus-focused leaders who had ruled since the Party's founding revolutionaries had faded from the political stage. Beyond this, however, assessments of Bo's legacy remain highly contested.

Supporters, including those within the "princeling" elite, maintain that Bo was a potential Communist Party savior who was politically persecuted for the sins of others. They point out that the financial misdemeanors involving Bo's cronies and family members were less serious than those of other Politburo colleagues who have not been prosecuted (such as Premier Wen, whose family had accumulated US$2.7 billion in assets, according to the *New York Times*.) Opponents argue that Bo operated like an imperial-era lord, or Mao-like despot, who threatened to derail China's reforms and its progress towards modernity.

Prior to the Eighteenth Party Congress, some commentators had argued that Xi Jinping was factionally aligned but ideologically opposed to Bo. But subsequent developments do not support this view. Bo's life sentence, which was handed down after Xi had taken power, was considerably harsher than most observers expected. The early years of the Xi era have been characterized by a ferocious anti-corruption campaign which has targeted prominent protégés of former president Jiang Zemin and mostly spared senior leaders associated with 1980s leader Hu Yaobang and former president *Hú Jǐntāo 胡锦涛 (b. 1942).

In the wake of Bo's demise, Xi appears to have borrowed from Bo's playbook to concentrate power in his own hands like no other leader in the post-Mao era. He has led a revival of Mao-era theories (like the "mass line") and techniques (like criticism, self-criticism, and the public humiliation of political opponents). In retrospect, the Bo trial can be seen to have announced the beginning of Xi's political ascendancy. At the time of writing, those who had hoped or argued that removing Bo would catalyze political reform in China have been disappointed.

John GARNAUT
The Sydney Morning Herald

Further Reading

Bo Zhiyue. (2007). *China's elite politics: Political transition and power balancing*. East Asian Institute, National University of Singapore, Singapore.

Nathan, Andrew J., & Gilley, Bruce. (2003). *China's new rulers: The secret files* (127–130). New York: New York Review of Books.

Garnaut, John. (2012a). *The rise and fall of the House of Bo: Penguin Specials*. London: Penguin UK.

Garnaut, John. (2012b, March 27). Death on the Yangtze—a mystery that's gripping China. *The Sydney Morning Herald*, p.7.

Ho Pin, & Xin Gao. (1993). *Princes and princesses of Red China*. Union City, CA: Pan Asian Pubns

Ho Pin, & Huang Wenguang. (2013). *A death in the Lucky Holiday Hotel: Murder, money, and an epic power struggle in China*. New York: Public Affairs.

Li, Cheng. (2001). *China's leaders: The new generation*. Lanham MD: Rowman & Littlefield.

Naughton, Barry. (2007). *The Chinese economy*. Cambridge, MA: MIT Press.

Sina Blog. (2012). 薄一波文革冤为叛徒, 遭亲儿子薄熙来的"敌对" [Bo Yibo during the Cultural Revolution wrongfully turned into a traitor, running into the "enemy" of his own son Bo Xilai]. Retrieved December 23, 2014, from http://blog.sina.com.cn/s/blog_4c0141c10102e0fo.html

Song, Yuwu. (2013). Bo Xilai. In Song Yuwu (Ed.), *Biographical dictionary of the People's Republic of China* (pp. 20–21). Jefferson, NC: McFarland.

Liu, Jen-Kai. (2009). Bo Xilai. In Zhang Wenxian & Ilan Alon (Eds.), *Biographical dictionary of new Chinese entrepreneurs and business leaders* (pp. 3–5). Northampton, MA: Edward Elgar Publishing.

Xinhua. (2012, 14 March). Wen says China needs political reform, warns of another Cultural Revolution if without. Retrieved July 7, 2015, from http://news.xinhuanet.com/english/china/2012-03/14/c_131466552.htm

♂ Bó Yībō 薄一波

1908–2007—Party elder, political and military leader

Summary

One of the seminal leaders of the Chinese Communist Party, Bo Yibo enjoyed a career that ranged from the foundational era of revolutionary activism in the 1920s and 1930s, through the establishment of the People's Republic of China, and deep into the latter part of the twentieth century. He was persecuted during the Cultural Revolution and yet went on to be reinstated as vice premier under Deng Xiaoping. Considered one of the Eight Immortals of the Party, Bo remained an influential figure up until his death at the age of ninety-eight.

One of the Chinese Communist Party's original leaders, Bo Yibo is known as the great survivor of Chinese modern politics and father of the Bo clan. He was unique in being a revolutionary activist in the 1920s and 1930s; an active supporter of clampdowns on rightists in the 1950s; a victim in the Cultural Revolution (1966–1976); and then, one of the hard-liners, after his rehabilitation in the Reform Era after 1978, of the clampdown on the Tiananmen Square student protests of 1989. One of the few elite leaders to have produced extensive memoirs of his lengthy time in office, he died at almost a hundred years old in the twenty-first century, the last surviving member of his generation of founding leaders and of the so-called Eight Immortals (an illustrious group of officials wielding the most power during the 1980s and 1990s).

Childhood

Bo Yibo was born in Taiyuan, Shanxi Province, in 1908 at the twilight of the Qīng 清 dynasty (1644–1911/12). He was from a poor background; his father was employed in a paper workshop. One story tells that a newborn was drowned at birth because the family did not have the means to support another child. Despite his disadvantaged background, as an adolescent he studied at Beijing University, although he never formally graduated, migrating instead to activism for the Chinese Communist Party (CCP), which he joined in 1925, four years after its foundation.

Career

Bo was an activist both in Beijing and then back in his native Shanxi through the late 1920s. During the breakdown of the First United Front (1922–1927), the period during which the Communists and the competing Nationalists (Guómíndǎng 国民党, or GMD) worked with each other for national unification, a major purge of over five thousand Communist movement leaders took place in April 1927. Bo went underground, primarily working in the city of Tianjin. This did not prevent him from being arrested by the Nationalists several times; during the final one, from 1931 to 1936, he was held in jail until he signed an anti-communist confession, with implicit Party approval, to secure his release. With the start of the Second Sino-Japanese war (1937–1945), a new era of concord between the Nationalists and the Communists was ushered in, and Bo, newly released, was able to participate in the war as part of a patriotic mass organization called the Sacrifice League, set up by warlord Yán Xíshān 阎锡山, also from Shanxi.

Bo eventually joined the Communist Eighth Route Army, and from 1943 he trained at the Central Party School at the revolutionary base of Yan'an in northern Shanxi, where the Communist Party was based, under the increasing ascendancy of Máo Zédōng 毛泽东 (1893–1976). While the victory of the United Front over the Japanese in 1945 liberated China from external aggression, it plunged the nation into internal conflict, with a civil war between the Nationalists and Communists raging from 1946 to 1949. Bo worked underground during this period, as a political commissar in the People's Liberation Army, in charge of ideological indoctrination.

With the victory of the Communists in the Chinese Civil War in 1949 and the foundation of the People's Republic of China (PRC), Bo became one of the key leaders. He served as minister of finance until 1953 and chairman of the State Planning Commission, in charge of directing the "command style" economy (in which the government rather than the market determines goods produced and at what prices) being set up by the government; in 1953, he launched the first Five-Year Plan, to promote heavy industry and technology over agriculture. In this era of relative harmony amongst the elite leadership, Bo was initially close to Mao Zedong. But his support for policies regarded as too liberal caused him to fall under a political cloud from the launch of the Great Leap Forward of 1958 (a disastrous period of industrialization and collectivization that eventually led to widespread famine). Despite this, he was a supporter of the Anti-rightist purges over this period, and remained a member of the Politburo, the leading decision-making Party body.

Cultural Revolution

During his early career, Bo had been close to Liú Shàoqí 刘少奇 (1898–1969); although Liu went on to become president of China, his falling out with Mao in the early 1960s led to his persecution and removal from office during the Cultural Revolution. Bo himself became one of the most prominent targets during this time, victimized in particular because of the confession he signed in 1936 to gain release from imprisonment by the Nationalists. A particular target of Mao's sinister head of internal security, Kāng Shēng 康生 (1898–1975), Bo was caught by rebellious groups (more popularly known as Red Guards) late in 1966 and subjected to torture, incarceration, and public humiliation. Bo, however, was to prove no pushover. Despite the possible murder of his wife (though there remains confusion over whether she was killed or committed suicide) and his inability to see his three young sons, Bo refused to issue any admission of guilt. In his public struggle sessions, he also loudly proclaimed his fidelity to Communism. His years as an underground worker and then a soldier had given him a toughness and resilience that meant he survived, making it through to his rehabilitation when the Cultural Revolution formally ended after Mao's death in 1976.

Post-Mao

Bo, a key ally of *Dèng Xiǎopíng 邓小平 (1904–1997) after the Reform and Opening Up era (*gǎigé kāifàng* 改革开放) commenced in late 1978, was restored to membership in the Politburo as vice premier. A visit to the United States, during a period when the Party was looking closely at foreign models of development, reinforced his earlier instincts to pursue more pro-growth liberal economic policies. But as with Deng, this did not translate to pursuing more radical ideas in the political sphere. Bo was instrumental in the removal of the party secretary *Hú Yàobāng 胡耀邦 (1915–1989) from his position in 1987, and he supported the military crackdown of the student demonstrations in June 1989, even though he was no longer occupying any formal position of power. Throughout the 1990s, Bo remained supportive of the continuing efforts to reform China's economic model, even as he supported crackdowns on any form of political opposition. His main political influence increasingly came through one of his sons, *Bó Xīlái 薄熙来 (b. 1949), who had pursued a political career of his own and was to go on to be minister of trade and then Politburo member himself before being felled in 2012 for corruption.

Influence and Legacy

Uniquely among leaders of his generation, Bo produced his own memoirs in 1991, and while they gave a highly edited

---

*People marked with an asterisk have entries in this dictionary.

version of his career (claiming, for instance, that he had been a participant of the Long March, despite the fact that he was incarcerated then), they offer the most complete inside view of a political figure's career in the CCP in the twentieth century. In these memoirs, Bo reveals himself first and foremost as a faithful servant of the Party, despite the suffering he had endured at its hands. The person who had been so viciously attacked in the 1960s, reportedly even by members of his own family, and who was able to shout back to Red Guards, demanding his capitulation, that they were acting against true communism evidently had a profound faith in the mission of the Party. It stayed with him till the end, and upon his death on 15 January 2007, his grieving family was able to celebrate his label as "an outstanding Party Member and revolutionary" (Xinhua 2007).

Kerry BROWN
Lau China Institute, King's College

Further Reading

Biography of Bo Yibo. (2007). *China Daily*. Retrieved December 18, 2014, from http://www. chinadaily.com.cn/cndy/2007-01/17/content_785104.htm

Bo Yibo 薄一波. (1991/2008). *Ruogan zhongda juece yu shijian de huigu* 若干重大决策与事件的回顾 [Reflections on certain major policy decisions and events]. Beijing: Zhonggong dangshi chubanshi.

Garnaut, John. (2012). *The rise and fall of the house of Bo: How a murder exposed the cracks in China's leaderships*. London: Penguin UK.

Gittings, John. (2007). Bo Yibo: Veteran Chinese leader and "immortal" whose loyalty to the party survived its purges. *The Guardian*. Retrieved October 29, 2014, from http://www.theguardian.com/news/2007/jan/24/guardianobituaries.obituaries1

Kahn, Joseph. (2007). Bo Yibo, leader who helped reshape Chinese economy, dies at 98. *New York Times*. Retrieved October 29, 2014, from http://www.nytimes.com/2007/01/17/world/asia/17bo.html?_r=0

Montgomery, Laszlo. (2012, April 12). *China history podcast: CHP-080-Bo Yibo*. Retrieved June 10, 2015, from http://chinahistorypodcast.com/chp-080-bo-yibo

Wortzel, Larry M., & Higham, Robin D. S. (Eds.). (1999). *Dictionary of contemporary Chinese military history* (pp. 32–33). Palo Alto, CA: ABC-CLIO.

Song, Yuwu. (2013). Bo Xilai. In Song Yuwu (Ed.), *Biographical dictionary of the People's Republic of China* (pp. 20–21). Jefferson, NC: McFarland.

Sullivan, Lawrence R. (2007). Bo Yibo. In *Historical dictionary of the People's Republic of China* (p. 80). Lanham, MD: Scarecrow Press.

Teiwes, Frederick C. (2003). Bo Yibo. In Colin Mackerras, Donald H. McMillen & Andrew Watson (Eds.), *Dictionary of the politics of the People's Republic of China* (pp. 57–58). London: Routledge.

Xinhua. (2007). Remains of Bo Yibo cremated in Beijing. Retrieved April 13, 2015, from http://english.cri.cn/2946/2007/01/21/53@187249.htm

Bó Yibō

♂ Cha, Louis

Zhā Liángyōng 查良鏞

b. 1924—Novelist and co-founder of the Hong Kong-based Ming Pao media franchise

Alternate names: Cha Leung-yung; pen names: Jīn Yōng 金庸, Yáo Fùlán 姚馥蘭, Lín Huān 林歡; simpl. 查良镛

Summary

Louis Cha is best known as Jin Yong, the twentieth century's preeminent author of martial arts chivalry fiction. As founder of Hong Kong-based Ming Pao Holdings, he also ranks among the most influential journalists and media tycoons of the Cold War era. In the 1980s, Cha helped negotiate Hong Kong's 1997 handover to People's Republic of China sovereignty.

Louis Cha is a martial arts novelist who emerged in the twentieth century under his pen name Jin Yong. His novels' blend of classical Chinese themes with deft narrative has earned him hundreds of millions of fans and spawned numerous adaptations. Cha also founded Ming Pao Holdings, a Hong Kong print conglomerate that published both authoritative coverage of Communist China and fiction serials. In his later years, Cha was appointed to a committee to negotiate Hong Kong's return to People's Republic of China sovereignty, and he developed contacts and collaborations with several mainland institutions. To many, Cha remains an exemplar of *wénrén bànbào* 文人辦報—a literatus newsman.

Early Years

Cha was born to a scholarly lineage near Hangzhou on 6 February 1924. His father's family had taken the imperial civil service exams for generations, frequently attaining the *jìnshì* 進士 degree (presented scholar) and serving the imperial court. His mother was a relative of the Shanghai poet Xú Zhìmó 徐志摩.

Brought up on Chinese classics and fiction, a teenaged Cha pursued a more modern education at a nearby boarding school. The 1937 Japanese invasion sent Cha, with his teachers and classmates, fleeing to the interior. Cha's teachers saw a creative and prodigious writer with a gift for foreign languages; his conflicts with administrators, however, led to multiple expulsions. He enrolled in the Central Politics University in the wartime capital of Chongqing in 1943, but did not graduate.

In 1947 Cha moved to Shanghai to work as an international news translator for *Ta Kung Pao* 大公報, a major national paper. With the help of a prominent relative in Shanghai, he was able to study international law part-time at the city's branch of Soochow University, but again did not graduate. With the rest of *Ta Kung Pao*'s staff, Cha moved to British Hong Kong in 1948 to escape the worsening Communist-Nationalist Civil War.

In 1950, after Máo Zédōng 毛泽东 (1893–1976) and the Chinese Communist Party (CCP) came into power, Cha traveled to Beijing to apply for work at the new regime's Ministry of Foreign Affairs. He was rejected due to bad class background and returned to Hong Kong. Then, in 1951, during a Communist land reform campaign, Cha's father was shot and the family estate expropriated.

As *Ta Kung Pao* became a more established leftist voice in Hong Kong—that is, one that supported the Mao regime—Cha found his politics diverging from that of the newspaper. He took freelancing opportunities presented by the fluid media market under laissez-faire British administration. He worked as a screenwriter and film critic, gaining an appreciation of cinematic narrative.

Fictional Beginnings

In 1954, a martial arts charity competition in the neighboring Portuguese colony of Macau rekindled public appetites for martial arts novels (*wŭxiá xiǎoshuō* 武侠小說). In 1955 Cha began publishing installments of his first martial arts novel, *The Book and the Sword* 書劍恩仇錄, in *The New Evening Post* 新晚報 under the name Jin Yong. With a growing readership, Cha emerged along with several other famous *wuxia xiaoshuo* writers of the mid-twentieth century, including Liáng Yǔshēng 梁羽生, Ní Kuāng 倪匡, and Gǔ Lóng 古龍. In a broad genre, Cha found his niche by blending China's literary tradition—poems, classics, histories, epic novels—with Western narrative styles influenced by Alexandre Dumas and Victor Hugo.

Early *Ming Pao*

In 1957, amid growing political disagreement with his *Ta Kung Pao* colleagues, Cha quit the paper and in 1959 started his own, *Ming Pao Daily News*. *Ming Pao Daily* was one of many new papers at the time, relying on a small staff of classically trained journalists under a loose management structure. *Ming Pao Daily* gained notice in the early 1960s for its double-barreled editorials criticizing both Mao's Great Leap Forward—which sent famine refugees over the border to Hong Kong—and the British authorities' poor treatment of new arrivals.

Cha's prominence as an editorialist grew amid his polemical fights ("pen wars," or *bǐzhàn* 筆戰) with former *Ta Kung Pao* colleagues. In 1964 his editorial criticizing Marshal Chén Yì's 陈毅 prioritizing China's nuclear weapons program over citizens' welfare caught the marshal's attention. Chen himself is reputed to have ordered *Ta Kung Pao*'s "editorial ceasefire" with Cha.

In 1966 and 1967, unrest in Hong Kong inspired by the Cultural Revolution (1966–1976) claimed the life of local radio host Lam Bun 林彬, whose assassination by the colony's leftist underground put anti-Communist journalists on notice. Leftist activists named Cha as next on the hit list, and he briefly fled to Singapore for safety.

Also in 1966, Cha founded *Ming Pao Monthly*. The highbrow periodical joined several other titles under the Ming Pao aegis. It sought to assert traditional Chinese cultural values against the Cultural Revolution's destruction. *Ming Pao Monthly* remains a respected outlet to this day, publishing literary articles from Chinese academics and writers from around the globe. Its stature approximates the *New York Review of Books* or *Times Literary Supplement* in the Anglophone world.

The Cha Canon

Through the late 1950s to the founding of Ming Pao Holdings and several years into the Cultural Revolution, Cha continued to publish martial arts fiction serials. Some ran in *Ming Pao Daily* alongside other fiction serials; others in specialty *wuxia* magazines. Cha's film connections eased adaptation for movies, radio, and later television. The exposure has multiplied the cultural impact of Cha's novels and raised their author to icon status.

Cha's characters and plots have entered the cultural vernacular of Greater China. His most popular works include *The Book and the Sword*; the Condor Heroes Trilogy (including *Legend of the Condor Heroes* 射鵰英雄傳, *Return of the Condor Heroes* 神鵰俠侶, and *Heaven Sword and Dragon Saber* 倚天屠龍記); *Demi-Gods and Semi-Devils* 天龍八部; *The Smiling, Proud Wanderer* 笑傲江湖; and *The Deer and the Cauldron* 鹿鼎記. Cha declared his canon complete (*fēngbǐ* 封筆) in 1971 and set about revising his fiction serials for a bound, published release by Ming Pao's publishing arm. The first of *Jin Yong's Complete Works* 金庸作品 were released in 1975.

In some cases, revisions were substantial. Distraught by divorce from his second wife and his eldest son's suicide, both in 1976, Cha altered some books' emotional tenor. In other instances, serials were amended for plot cohesion or to reassert authorship; Cha excluded sections of *Demi-Gods and Semi-Devils* written by Ni Kuang.

Ming Pao Publishing's first editions of Cha's complete works continued into the 1980s. Eventually, Nationalist authorities in Taiwan and the CCP in mainland China would permit sales as well.

Return to China and Political Role

During his 1950 trip to Beijing's Foreign Ministry, Cha had expressed a patriotic interest in public service. In 1981, after three decades outside mainland China, he became the highest-profile Hong Kong resident invited for an early meeting with *Dèng Xiǎopíng 邓小平 (1904–1997), Mao's successor, in Beijing. Deng professed himself a fan of Cha's novels and arranged for the eventual easing of a Mao-era ban on martial arts fiction. This cleared the way for sales of Cha books in the mainland, the primary reason Cha is today the best-selling living author in the Chinese language.

Deng and Cha discussed his father's conviction and execution, arranging for a posthumous rehabilitation of his reputation and expunging of his "class enemy" status. In addition, Cha agreed to help begin exploring possibilities for returning Hong Kong to People's Republic of China sovereignty in 1997, the expiry date for Britain's ninety-nine-year lease. After the 1984 Sino-British Joint Declaration established a framework for "One Country, Two Systems," Cha was appointed to the Basic Law Drafting Committee. The committee considered various plans to balance Hong Kong autonomy with Chinese sovereignty. Cha's incremental proposals

on a timetable for democratic representation drew criticism from liberal Hong Kong residents. Many saw Cha as too accommodating of Beijing's authoritarianism; students burned *Ming Pao Daily* outside its headquarters.

Amid the declaration of martial law and crackdown during the 1989 Tiananmen Incident, in which the military and student protestors clashed and many people were killed, Cha resigned from the Basic Law committee and gave a tearful television interview. In spring of 1993 he returned to Beijing and was photographed alongside *Jiāng Zémín 江泽民 (b. 1926), general secretary of the CCP, during a party meeting. In the ensuing years, Cha developed a variety of official and unofficial contacts with mainland institutions, including Zhejiang University, where he accepted a vice-chancellorship.

After Ming Pao

Cha sold Ming Pao Holdings in 1993 to Yu Pun Hoi 于品海, a media entrepreneur whose management inexperience and criminal record nearly destroyed the company. Industry observers considered the succession choice to be Cha's greatest failing as a businessman. A controlling interest in the company was eventually purchased by Malaysian-Chinese tycoon Tiong Hiew King 張曉卿, who retains ownership today. Despite a ban in mainland China, Ming Pao remains among the strongest brands in the global

---

*People marked with an asterisk have entries in this dictionary.

Chinese-language media industry. Besides several prestigious titles published out of Hong Kong, *Ming Pao Daily* has several overseas editions. Hong Kong's *Ming Pao Daily* remains respected for its serious editorial voice in a shrill media market. The Ming Pao brand remains indelibly associated with Louis Cha's name and legacy.

During the 1990s Cha lived part-time in a Hangzhou villa near the West Lake, financed and attended conferences about his fiction, and sought English-language translators to achieve wider recognition for his novels. In 1997 a stroke weakened his health.

Regretful that he never finished his education, Cha earned a Chinese history doctorate in 2008 from Cambridge University, where he has endowed a scholarship. He was awarded another graduate degree at Peking University in 2013; his acceptance of the achievement was one of his final public appearances. Currently, his health is precarious. He lives in Hong Kong with his third wife. His children are occasionally profiled in local media.

Literary Legacy

Cha's literary status remains controversial in China. *Wuxia xiaoshuo* emerged as a genre in the twentieth century, combining the martial *wu* and chivalrous errantry *xia* with chapter-style (*zhānghuí xiǎoshuō* 章回小說) late imperial Chinese vernacular fiction. While some scholars classify *wuxia* novels—and Cha—as

modern fiction meriting scholarly analysis, others find his work too sentimental, or shoddily structured. Many young Chinese readers, however, credit their knowledge of Chinese culture to the richness of Cha's novels in historical setting and literary allusion. *Wuxia* remains a popular genre in many media, including video games and Internet fan fiction. Regardless of the literary establishment's verdict, the enormous popularity of Cha's books ensures that Jin Yong's name will long outlive him.

Nicholas FRISCH
Yale University

Further Reading

Cha, Louis. (1997). *The deer and the cauldron: The first book.* (John Minford, Trans.). Oxford, UK: Oxford University Press.

Cha, Louis. (2000). *The deer and the cauldron: The second book.* (John Minford, Trans.). Oxford, UK: Oxford University Press.

Cha, Louis. (2003). *The deer and the cauldron: The third book.* (John Minford, Trans.). Oxford, UK: Oxford University Press.

Cha, Louis. (2005). *The book and the sword.* (G. Earnshaw, Trans.; R. May & J. Minford, Eds.). Oxford, UK: Oxford University Press.

Chen Pingyuan 陈平原. (1998). *Chaoyue "yasu"—Jin Yong de chenggong ji wuxia xiaoshuo de chulu* 超越"雅俗"——金庸的成功及武侠小说的出路 [Beyond "highbrow/lowbrow"–Jin Yong's success and the future direction of martial arts chivalry fiction]. *Dangdai Zuojia Pinglun* 当代作家评论, 5.

Cheung Kwai Yeung 張圭陽. (2000). *Jin Yong yu baoye* 金庸與報業 [Jin Yong and the news industry]. Hong Kong: Ming Pao Publishing.

Fu Guoyong 傅国涌. (2013). *Jin Yong zhuan (Xiudingban)* 金庸传(修订版) [The Jin Yong story (rev. ed.)]. Hangzhou: Zhejiang renmin chubanshe.

Hamm, John Christopher. (2005). *Paper swordsmen: Jin Yong and the modern Chinese martial arts novel*. Honolulu: University of Hawai'i Press.

Huss, Ann, & Liu Jianmei. (2007). *The Jin Yong phenomenon: Chinese martial arts fiction and modern Chinese literary history*. Amherst, NY: Cambria Press.

Jin Yong. (2004). *Jinyong zuopin ji* 金庸作品集 [The collected Jin Yong] (New rev. ed., 12 vols.).

Ng, Margaret 吳靄儀. (1998a). *Jin Yong xiaoshuo de nüzi* 金庸小說的女子 [Women in Jin Yong's fiction]. Taipei: Yuan-Liou Publishing Co.

Ng, Margaret 吳靄儀. (1998b). *Jin Yong xiaoshuo de qing* 金庸小說的情 [Emotion in Jin Yong's fiction]. Taipei: Yuan-Liou Publishing Co.

Ng, Margaret 吳靄儀. (1998c). *Jin Yong xiaoshuo de nanzi* 金庸小說的男子 [Men in Jin Yong's fiction]. Taipei: Yuan-Liou Publishing Co.

Ng, Margaret 吳靄儀. (1998d). *Jin Yong xiaoshuo kan rensheng* 金庸小說看人生 [Views on life in Jin Yong's fiction]. Taipei: Yuan-Liou Publishing Co.

Ni Kuang 倪匡. (1997). *Wo kan Jin Yong xiaoshuo* 我看金庸小說 [My views on Jin Yong's fiction]. Hong Kong: Ming Pao Publishing.

Yan Jiayan 严家炎. (2007). *Jin Yong xiaoshuo lungao* 金庸小说论稿 [A study of Jin Yong's fiction]. Beijing: Beijing daxue chubanshe.

• Cha, Louis •

♀ Chan, Anson

Chén Fāng Ānshēng 陳方安生

b. 1940—Hong Kong's chief secretary under the British colonial government (1993–1997) and the Special Administrative Region government (1997–2001)

Alternate names: Anson Maria Elizabeth Chan Fang On-sang; simpl. 陈方安生

Summary

The first woman and the first ethnic Chinese to serve as chief secretary, Anson Chan was a prominent head of the Hong Kong government before and after the handover from Britain to the People's Republic of China. After her resignation in 2001, she was elected to the Legislative Council (Hong Kong's de facto parliament) in 2007. She remains politically active and is the founder of the Hong Kong 2020 democracy advocacy group.

Anson Chan, whose full name is Anson Maria Elizabeth Chan Fang On-sang (with Fang being her surname and Chan her husband's surname) was the last chief secretary of British colonial Hong Kong and the first chief secretary of the Hong Kong Special Administrative Region (SAR). In 1999, she agreed to delay her retirement until June 2002, but then resigned in January 2001 and stepped down in April of that year. During her tenure she was called the Iron Lady of Hong Kong, and, later, the epitome of "Hong Kong's Conscience."

Early Career

Chan was born in Shanghai on 17 January 1940 and followed her father, Fang Shin Hau, to Hong Kong in 1948 during the Chinese Civil War. Her father died two years later, leaving her mother, Fang Zhaoling, to raise eight children. After Chan's mother took two of her sons to study in England, Chan and five of her siblings were taken in by their grandmother and an uncle in Hong Kong. Under her grandmother's discipline and expectations, Chan was expected to be honest and hard-working.

Chan graduated from Sacred Heart Canossian College in 1957 and went on to St. Paul's College. She then entered the University of Hong Kong, where she studied English language and literature, and met her future husband, Archibald Chan Tai Wing. She worked as a private tutor and initially made the decision to become a social worker. She eventually joined the civil service, however, as an administrative officer in 1962 and served in the economics section of the financial branch, followed by positions in the Department of Agriculture and Fisheries and the Department of Commerce and Industry. She was promoted to assistant financial secretary in 1970 and then assistant territories secretary in 1972.

From 1975 to 1987, Chan served as the principal assistant secretary of social affairs, rising to vice director and then to director of the Department of Social Welfare, the first female civil service director in Hong Kong. In 1986, she was criticized for her handling of a child custody case, popularly known as the "Daughter of Kwok-A Incident," in which a six-year-old child was supposedly illegally detained by her mother. The public questioned the necessity of breaking into the house and separating the family by force, and criticized the department for flagrant abuse of power. Despite being cleared of wrongdoing, the case tainted her career for some time and she was criticized for being inconsiderate and authoritarian. As she herself said:

> For the first ten years or so, you would always question whether the decisions were right or wrong, but you have to learn to put things behind you once a decision is made. You can't be wishy-washy about it. (Chan 2001a)

Tenure as Chief Secretary

Anson Chan served as secretary for economic services from 1987 to 1993, before finally being appointed in 1993 as chief secretary, the head of the civil service. The first ethnic Chinese to hold the highest administrative position in the Hong Kong government, she came to be known as "Iron Lady." She would eventually serve as chief secretary for more than seven years, the longest of any chief secretary since World War II.

Hong Kong Handover

On 1 July 1997, after more than 150 years of colonial rule, the sovereignty of Hong Kong was handed from the United Kingdom to China, and Hong Kong became a Special Administrative Region of the People' Republic of China (PRC), enjoying a high degree of autonomy. At first, China's policy of "One Country, Two Systems" worked well in Hong Kong, and China permitted Hong Kong to run its own affairs without much interference.

The great majority of British Hong Kong's officials were transferred to the new Special Administrative Region's government. Some emerging internal challenges, however, placed the new government under considerable stress. The first chief executive, businessman *Tung Chee-hwa 董建華 (b. 1937), could

• Chan, Anson •

---

*People marked with an asterisk have entries in this dictionary.

be described as conservative and interventionist. His chain of proposed reforms, such as providing eighty-five thousand housing flats annually and granting the Cyber Port Project (a large campus-like area aimed to strengthen the local information technology and service sector) without an open tender, provoked stern opposition and resistance from almost all affected stakeholders. As head of the Development Steering Committee since 1994, Chan herself was involved in the chaos caused during the move from the old Kai Tak Airport and the opening of the new Chek Lap Kok Airport in 1998, with the public blaming her for the lack of supervision of this project. On the other hand, when the Radio Television Hong Kong (RTHK) was attacked for being a platform for discussions about Taiwan-mainland relations in 1999, Chief Executive Tung did not respond, but Chan rushed to its defense, stressing the importance of press freedom and publication. She stated publicly that Beijing was not in the position to debate RTHK's role.

Continuing Participation in Government

In 1999, shortly before Chan would reach retirement age, she accepted an invitation to stay on as chief secretary until June 2002. In April 2001, eighteen months before her term was due to end,

however, Chan stepped down. In a speech from January 2001, Chan herself stated that:

> Our economy has staged a strong recovery. Public confidence and consumer sentiment have both improved. Most of the reforms to the Civil Service are in place. The Chief Executive has also delivered his Policy Address, outlining Government's major initiatives in the next few years. I feel that it is time for me to step down and make way for new blood. (Chan 2001c)

The real reasons for her stepping down remain unclear. Two important issues that have led to her continuing participation in Hong Kong's affairs, however, were the legislation of an anti-subversion law and the lack of institutional reforms towards full democracy after 2004. Protests against the anti-subversion bill resulted in the mass demonstration in Hong Kong on 1 July 2003, causing the bill to be shelved indefinitely. The implementation of democratic changes was stopped in 2004 by the Standing Committee of the National People's Congress in Beijing, ruling against the introduction of universal suffrage in Hong Kong before 2012.

After her retirement, Chan took a prominent role in the campaign for democratization in Hong Kong. She was active in promoting the implementation of universal suffrage and formed the

陳方安生

Core Group to develop proposals in September 2006. The group aimed to develop a constitutional reform proposal acceptable to the Hong Kong and central governments before the Commission on Strategic Development produced a road map to universal suffrage. Chan said the pro-democracy blocs had to address concerns that a democratic government might be anti-business and endanger the prosperity and stability through excessive social welfare, and opponents of democratization needed to change their mind-set and position. In March 2007, "The Road to Democracy" recommended the phasing in of universal suffrage for election of the chief executive and all members of the Legislative Council no later than 2016. The decision of the Standing Committee of the National People's Congress of the PRC was that election of the chief executive by universal suffrage would be introduced in 2017 and for all members of Legislative Council in 2020.

Chan stood as a candidate in the December 2007 by-election for a seat on the Legislative Council and was successfully elected. She dissolved the Core Group and set up the Citizens' Commission for Constitution Development in April 2008. This steering group lent active support to initiatives that promoted achievement of universal suffrage. She was criticized, however, for being so active in the political arena following her retirement from the civil service, and the Civil Commission was said to be a mirror organ of the official one.

Chan then launched the group Hong Kong 2020 to monitor, give recommendations, and work towards consensus on constitutional changes in Hong Kong in order to achieve the universal suffrage promised by Beijing. This universal suffrage was seen as a means of ensuring the legitimacy of the chief executive, securing good governance, maintaining the lifestyle of citizens, and preserving the rule of law, rights, and freedom in Hong Kong.

During her professional career as a civil servant and then as chief secretary, Anson Chan showed deep support for democracy and freedom. Even after her retirement from official positions, she participated actively in politics, and marched for universal suffrage. The announcement in 2014, however, that instead of universal suffrage a selection committee would put forward two to three people for election as chief executive beginning in 2017, showed that Chan's attempts to secure greater suffrage have so far failed. The large protests that followed the decision do show, however, that Chan's ideals of democracy for Hong Kong are still very much alive.

HUNG Chung Fun Steven
The Hong Kong Institute of Education

Further Reading

Chan, Anson. (2013). Press conference to launch "Hong Kong 2020" opening statement, on 24 April 2013.

Chan, Anson. (2001a). Speech commenting on her handling the controversial 1986 child custody case. Retrieved June 17, 2015, from http://knowledgerush.com/encyclopedia/Anson_Chan/

Chan, Anson. (2001b). In retrospect and anticipation. Speech by the honorable Mrs. Anson Chan, GBM, JP, Chief Secretary for Administration, Hong Kong SAR Government. Retrieved January 28, 2015, from http://asiasociety.org/retrospect-and-anticipation

Chan, Anson. (2001c). Statement by Chief Secretary for Administration at a media session at the Central Government Offices this (January 12) afternoon. Retrieved January 28, 2015, from http://www.info.gov.hk/gia/general/200101/12/0112226.htm

Cheng, Joseph Yu Shek. (Ed.). (2014). *New trends of political participation in Hong Kong*. Hong Kong: City University Press.

Ching, Frank. (2001). The handling of sensitive political and legal issues by the Hong Kong Government of the HKSAR. In Joseph Y. S. Cheng (Ed.), *Political development in the SAR* (pp. 119–138). Hong Kong: City University of Hong Kong.

Lo, Sony ShiuHing. (2008). *The dynamics of Beijing-Hong Kong relations: A model for Taiwan?* Hong Kong: Hong Kong University Press.

• 陳方安生 •

☿ Chan, Jackie

Chén Gǎngshēng 陳港生

b. 1954—Hong Kong-born actor, stuntman, and director, internationally known for his comic roles in kung fu action movies

Alternate names: b. Chan Kong-sang; simpl. 陈港生

Summary

Jackie Chan has developed his own unique style of filmmaking over half a century. He has appeared in more than 150 films and has continuously reinvented himself by integrating martial arts, stunt performance, acting, situational comedy, singing, writing, directing, and producing into his impressive body of work. Thanks to repeated and consistent efforts throughout his career, he has reached global popularity for his achievements in both acting and directing, and continues to expand his influence in the world of film by mentoring the next generation.

Jackie Chan is one of the few Chinese male actors to have reached a global popular status, alongside *Bruce Lee 李小龍 (1940–1973) and *Jet Li 李连杰 (b. 1963), and has stars on both the Hong Kong Avenue of Stars and the Hollywood Walk of Fame. But under the mask of the international superstar hides a multitalented and multifaceted character.

Aside from his lauded skills as an actor, stuntman, and martial artist, Jackie Chan is also a trained singer in Chinese opera who has sung in both Cantonese and Mandarin. He has integrated that talent with his art and his passion for filmmaking by singing on some of the soundtracks for his films. His acting style has developed over a long-standing career, from the *wǔxiá* 武侠 (literally "martial hero," or more commonly called "sword films") and kung fu films from the 1970s, to the urban themes of the 1980s, to his break into Hollywood at the end of the 1990s, and his more recent use of dramatization in the 2000s. Over the years, Jackie Chan has also evolved to become equally active and successful both in front of and behind the camera.

---

*People marked with an asterisk have entries in this dictionary.

Early Years

Jackie Chan was born in Hong Kong on 7 April 1954 and grew up in the years following World War II. Hong Kong had received many refugees from the Chinese Civil War (1946–1949), and these included Chan's parents, Charles Chan (Chén Zhìpíng 陳志平, 1914–2008) and Lee-Lee Chan 陳莉莉 (born Chén Yuèróng 陳月榮, 1916–2002). In his early years, Jackie Chan, who was nicknamed "Pao Pao" (cannonball) due to his liveliness and his energetic character, was raised in very difficult financial conditions. His parents reportedly planned to sell him to an English doctor to cover the cost of his birth before they ultimately found a way to raise the money to keep him.

Chan was soon sent to the Peking Opera School in Beijing to study under Yu Jim-yuen (Yú Zhānyuán 于占元, 1905–1997), a martial arts and drama master. There he learned Chinese operatic singing, martial arts, and stage acting for the following ten years under a draconian discipline in which corporal punishment was very frequent. This very difficult upbringing seems to have given Chan the technical skills that launched him into his career in film, his discipline, and his will to surpass himself, as well as his generosity and modesty.

During these formative years, Jackie Chan was selected by the school to be included in a special performance group called the "Seven Little Fortunes" along with Sammo Hung and Yuen Biao, with whom he later partnered on a number of performances and film projects as the Three Brothers or Three Dragons. Jackie Chan's first appearance in a film was at age seven in *Big and Little Wong Tin Bar* 大小黃天霸 (1962) as part of this group.

Due to the Japanese occupation followed by the Chinese Civil War, Chinese film studios had been relocated from Shanghai to Hong Kong (Curtin 2007; Fu and Desser 2002; Fu 2003; Szeto 2011). As a consequence of this shift, the Hong Kong film industry became very prolific from the 1930s onward and later offered Jackie Chan a set of unparalleled opportunities to break into the world of cinema.

In this context, Jackie Chan decided to move away from the rigid lifestyle at the academy and started his independent career as an extra on the masterpiece *A Touch of Zen* 俠女 (1971).

A Multifaceted Artist

After Jackie Chan left the martial arts school in Beijing, he worked primarily as an extra before he reached the next level, that of stunt performer, working for Bruce Lee in *Fist of Fury* 精武門 (1972) and *Enter The Dragon* 龍爭虎鬥 (1973). Up to that point, the Shaw Brothers Studio was the only sizable and vertically integrated production house (i.e., a single entity that controls all aspects of film production including development, finance, production, and distribution) in

Selected Filmography of Jackie Chan				
Year	English Title	Chinese Title	Director	Notes
1962	*Big and Little Wong Tin Bar*	大小黄天霸 *Dàxiǎo huáng tiān bà*	Lung To	First appearance
1962	*7 Little Fortunes*			
1971	*A Touch of Zen*	俠女 *Xiá nǚ*	King Hu	
1972	*Fist of Fury*	精武門 *Jīng wǔmén*	Lo Wei	Stuntman for Bruce Lee
1973	*Enter the Dragon*	龍爭虎鬥 *Lóng zhēng hǔ dòu*	Robert Clouse & Bruce Lee	Stuntman for Bruce Lee
1978	*Snake in the Eagle's Shadow*	蛇形刁手 *Shé xíng diāo shǒu*	Yuen Woo-ping	Role: Chien Fu
1978	*Drunken Master*	醉拳 *Zuì quán*	Yuen Woo-ping	Role: Wong Fei Hung
1979	*The Fearless Hyena*	笑拳怪招 *Xiào quán guài zhāo*	Jackie Chan	Role: Shing Lung
1980	*Battle Creek Brawl*	殺手壕 *Shāshǒu háo*	Robert Clouse	Role: Jerry Kwan
1981	*The Cannonball Run*		Hal Needham	Role: Subaru Driver #1
1983	*Project A*	A 計劃 *A jìhuà*	Jackie Chan	Role: Sergant Dragon Ma Yue Lung
1985	*Police Story*	警察故事 *Jǐngchá gùshì*	Jackie Chan	Role: Chan Ka Kui
1985	*The Protector*		James Glickenhaus	Role: Billy Wong
1986	*Armour of God*	龍兄虎弟 *Lóng xiōng hǔ dì*	Jackie Chan & Eric Tsang	Role: Asian Hawk
1995	*Rumble in the Bronx*		Stanley Tong	Role: Keung
1998	*Rush Hour*		Brett Ratner	Role: Lee
1998	*Jackie Chan: My Story*		Media Asia, JC Group	Documentary
1999	*Jackie Chan: My Stunts*		Media Asia, JC Group	Documentary
2000	*Shanghai Noon*		Tom Dey	Role: Chon Wang
2003	*Shanghai Knights*		David Dobkin	Role: Chon Wang
2008	*The Disciple*	龍的傳人 *Lóng de chuánrén*	Jackie Chan	TV Show
2009	*Shinjuku Incident*	新宿事件 *Xīnsù shìjiàn*	Derek Tung-Shing Yee	Role: Steelhead

Hong Kong, with a monopoly in the film industry, particularly after the demise of the Cathay Studio (Curtin 2007). The studio catered to television and cinema audiences, and promoted a stardom system similar to Hollywood's by contractually locking in actors and directors. But a new studio emerged—Golden Harvest—founded by the entrepreneurs Raymond Chow and Leonard Ho, and it became successful thanks to the popularity and international success of Bruce Lee. Golden Harvest gave artists more freedom to express their creativity as compared to the traditional structure of Shaw Brothers. This suited Jackie Chan's aspirations, but after Bruce Lee's premature death, he had to wait until late 1978 to combine his stunt and comedy skills in films such as *Snake in the Eagle's Shadow* 蛇形刁手 (1978) and *Drunken Master* 醉拳 (1978) and truly reveal his talent both as a stunt professional and as an actor.

Jackie Chan has achieved mastery in many of the facets of filmmaking, but he has been most successful as a stunt performer, comedian, and director. While performing these roles, he has also expanded his creative freedom.

The Stuntman

During the late 1970s, most of the films produced in Hong Kong were either kung fu or *wuxia* films, which used wide angles for action scenes, and this meant that Chan had to take more risks to convey his sense of action to his audience.

As a result, Jackie Chan has suffered multiple injuries throughout his career. He damaged his lower spine when he fell from a clock tower in *Project A* A計劃 (1983), in a scene played as a tribute to Harold Lloyd in *Safety Last!* (dir. Fred C. Newmeyer and Sam Taylor, 1923). Although he was able to recover from this and other accidents, today Jackie Chan still bears the painful consequences of these episodes, and no insurance company is willing to cover him. In spite of this, Jackie Chan has an obsession with not "cheating" his audience (Chan 1998). This shows genuine integrity and respect for his peers and his public, at the risk of pain and bodily damage. Thanks to his stunt work, however, Jackie Chan has been able to reach audiences and connect with local artists worldwide through the universal theme of action.

The Actor

In the 1970s, the Hong Kong film industry was blossoming largely because of the volume of production of commercial, popular films and the use of its own distribution networks (Szeto 2011). Hong Kong used its diaspora to create a large distribution network throughout Asia and within the Chinese communities around the world, notably in the United States (Bordwell 2000). This network helped to launch Bruce Lee in the United States and internationally, and later supported Jackie Chan's career abroad.

陳港生

The Hong Kong film industry continued to increase significantly in the 1980s and the 1990s, reaching a climax when it ranked third in the world in terms of volume of film production, just behind Hollywood and Bollywood (the Hindu language film industry, centered around Mumbai, India), and the second largest film exporter in the world. This buoyant period helped to raise Chan's popularity across borders. At the same time, Chan started integrating his stunts skills and experience with comedy. His friend and manager, Willie Chi-Keung Chan (b. 1941), supported him regarding the development of his career as a comedian and advised him to make use of his martial arts skills in addition to his visual creative ideas.

In his films, Jackie Chan regularly used aspects of the environment where the action sequences take place to increase their comedic nature: for instance, Chan and his team often use everyday objects in their fight scenes, such as a bicycle in the famous battle scene that takes place in a narrow street in *Project A*. Jackie Chan generally presents action as a creative strategy, not just a trick, a stunt, or an expression of violence. He has often expressed his dilemma regarding violence and prefers to use the word *action* (Chan 1998). He has set his own code of conduct to diminish the violence used in his films. He refers to it as "good violence" (Chan 1998), and it is mostly depicted in a comedic fashion, which aims to entertain the audience (Gallagher

2006). As a result, he appeals to children as well as adults, crossing age and national boundaries, making him a truly universal and popular artist.

While continuing his career in Hong Kong with such popular films as *Police Story* 警察故事 (1985) or *Amour of God* 龍兄虎弟 (1986), and after a few unsuccessful attempts in the United States, including *Battle Creek Brawl* (1980) and *Cannonball Run* (1981), it was *The Protector* (1985) that truly opened the doors in Hollywood for Jackie Chan. Ten years later, *Rumble in the Bronx* (1995) brought him further exposure. The release of *Police Story III: Supercop*'s American version in the 1990s, his appearance on American TV, and his documentaries *Jackie Chan: My Story* (1998) and *Jackie Chan: My Stunts* (1999) strengthened his transnational signature and reinforced his popularity with American audiences.

In 1997, the year of the retrocession of Hong Kong to the People's Republic of China, Jackie Chan saw one of his dreams come true: he left his first imprints on Hollywood's Walk of Fame. With *Rush Hour* (1998), Jackie Chan temporarily managed to avoid the Hong Kong and mainland China nexus and was propelled to international star status.

Chan's acting has evolved over his long career from the slapstick comedy of his early films, which he refers to as unnatural comedy, to situational comedy, as in *Shanghai Noon* (2000) or *Shanghai Knights* (2003), to dramatic acting, as in *Shinjuku Incident* 新宿事件 (2009).

The Director

From 1979, with *The Fearless Hyena*, Jackie Chan has integrated his roles of stuntman and actor with that of director. Without going to film school, Jackie Chan has developed his own filmmaking style just as he has developed his stunt work and acting talent: through experience and hard work. Jackie Chan had already gained valuable experience as a fight director in Hong Kong, which gave him the necessary knowledge and skills to move on to direct his own films.

As a director, Jackie Chan chose to sign on early with Golden Harvest rather than the giant Shaw Brothers, because the relatively small size of Golden Harvest allowed him to have more creative freedom (Szeto 2011). Due to the creative control that he has been able to nurture over the years, Jackie Chan has pioneered some editing techniques himself, such as the double cut that takes the same scene from two different angles successively in rapid succession. His methods have been very influential, as other action filmmakers around the world have adopted these techniques.

Jackie Chan's influences include the cartoons of Warner Bros. and Tex Avery, which inspired him to avoid direct violence. He also worked as a fight director on *The Protector*, an American production that received popular acclaim both in the United States and Hong Kong. To appeal to these very different audiences, the fight sequences were adapted for the different markets. This seems to have reinforced Jackie Chan's understanding of universal themes in his films.

The Man behind the Mask

Reflecting both his modesty and universality, Jackie Chan has been a popular humanist who has used his name to improve the lives of others. He has worked with such international organizations as the Salvation Army, UNICEF, and UNAIDS to help people without distinctions of age, race, or gender. He has also been associated with causes connected to endangered animal species, notably the pandas of China, and pollution.

Jackie Chan's next dream seems to focus on the education of the next generation of martial artists and filmmakers. In 2008, he initiated and produced the TV series *The Disciple* 龍的傳人 (lit. "disciple of the dragon") in which he tries to find successors to his work.

Chan was called upon to be the ambassador for the 2008 Beijing Olympics and to host the first Beijing International Film Festival in 2011, which confirms his role in China as a conduit between East and West, and a vehicle to promote Chinese soft power abroad.

Patrice POUJOL
Independent Researcher

Further Reading

Blunt, Emily. (2003). *Bluntly Shanghai'd: An Emily Blunt interview*. Retrieved October 10, 2014, from http://www.jackiechankids.com/files/Emily_Blunt_Interview.htm

Bordwell, David. (2000). *Planet Hong Kong: Popular cinema and the art of entertainment*. Cambridge, MA: Harvard University Press.

Chan, Jackie (Director). (1998). *Jackie Chan: My story* [Motion Picture]. Hong Kong: Media Asia, JC Group.

Chan, Jackie (Director). (1999). *Jackie Chan: My stunts* [Motion Picture]. Hong Kong: Media Asia, JC Group.

Chan, Jackie, & Yang J. (1998). *I am Jackie Chan: My life in action*. New York: Ballantine Books.

Cheuk, Pak Tong. (2008). *Hong Kong New Wave cinema (1978–2000)*. Bristol, UK: Intellect.

Cooper, Richard, & Leeder, Mike. (2002). *100 per cent Jackie Chan: The essential companion*. London: Titan Books.

Curtin, Michael. (2003). The future of Chinese cinema: Some lessons from Hong Kong and Taiwan. In Chin-Chuan Lee (Ed.), *Chinese media, global contexts* (pp. 237–255). New York: Routledge.

Curtin, Michael. (2007). *Playing to the world's biggest audience: The globalization of Chinese film and TV*. Berkeley: University of California Press.

Fu, Poshek, & Desser, David. (2002). *The cinema of Hong Kong: History, arts, identity*. Cambridge, UK: Cambridge University Press.

Fu, Poshek. (2003). *Between Shanghai and Hong Kong: The politics of Chinese cinemas*. Stanford, CA: Stanford University Press.

Gallagher, Mark. (2006). *Action figures: Men, action films, and contemporary adventure narratives*. New York: Palgrave Macmillan.

Gentry, Clyde, III. (1997). *Jackie Chan: Inside the dragon*. Dallas, TX: Taylor Publishing Company.

Knox, Andrea. (2014). *Jackie Chan 76 success facts: Everything you need to know about Jackie Chan*. Toronto: Emereo Publishing.

Lee, Bruce. (1971, December 9). *The Pierre Berton Show: Interview*. Canada: CTV.

Lee, Ip. (2012). *Jackie Chan biography: Kung fu master, actor, writer, director, philanthropist* [Kindle edition]. Retrieved from Amazon.com.

Logan, Bey. (1995). *Hong Kong action cinema*. Woodstock, NY: The Overlook Press.

Rovin, Jeff. (1997). *The essential Jackie Chan source book: A fan's unauthorized guide to the star*. New York: Pocket Books.

Szeto, Kin-Yan. (2011). *The martial arts cinema of the Chinese diaspora: Ang Lee, John Woo, and Jackie Chan in Hollywood*. Carbondale: Southern Illinois University Press.

Tarantino, Quentin, & Ratner, Brett. (2007). *Rush Hour: Lights, camera, action! The blockbuster companion to the Jackie Chan–Chris Tucker trilogy*. New York: HarperCollins Publishers.

Teo, Stephen. (1997). *Hong Kong cinema: The extra dimensions*. London: British Film Institute.

Tucker, Chris. (2013, June 6). *Chris Tucker at Jackie Chan's hand & footprint immortalization ceremony*. Retrieved June 19, 2015, from http://www.toponlinemart.com/watch/e8WkEoJZSTw

Yang, Jeff. (2003). *Once upon a time in China: A guide to Hong Kong, Taiwanese, and mainland Chinese cinema*. New York: Atria.

☿ Chén Guāngchéng
陈光诚

b. 1971—Blind civil rights activist best known for his activities as a "barefoot lawyer"

Alternate name: trad. 陳光誠

Summary

A self-taught legal advocate, Chen Guangcheng has worked on behalf of the rural poor and for women forced to have abortions or coerced into sterilization due to China's family-planning practices. In 2012, the blind activist gained fame with a daring escape from detention, taking refuge in the American embassy in Beijing, which led to a negotiated exile to the United States.

Chen Guangcheng first came to public attention in 2002 when *Newsweek International* featured the thirty-year-old Chen in its cover story about a new Chinese phenomenon—"barefoot lawyers." The story focused on how, in some parts of rural China, people with no formal legal education were beginning to play roles traditionally associated with lawyers, negotiating with government agencies and even representing people in court. Chen, *Newsweek* noted, was especially striking because not only was he learning and applying law on behalf of largely impoverished and uneducated clients, but he was managing to do this despite the fact that he has been blind since infancy.

Early Life and Education

Chen was born in 1971 in Dongshigu, a remote village in Yinan County, Shandong Province. He was the youngest of five brothers, and when he was about six months old he suffered a severe fever that destroyed his optical nerves, causing him to go blind. It wasn't until 1989 that a school for the blind was opened in his region, and Chen at last started school at age eighteen. From 1994 to 1998 he attended high school, and in 1998 he enrolled in the Nanjing University of Traditional Chinese Medicine, where, at that time, acupuncture and massage were the only specializations accessible to the blind. After graduating in 2001, Chen, who had encountered many

Chen Guangcheng and his family in their hometown, Dongshigu village. From left to right: Eldest brother, father, Chen Guangcheng, mother, wife (Weijing) and their daughter (Chen Kerui), eldest brother's wife. Photo by Joan Lebold Cohen.

instances of official discrimination against himself and others, decided that a career representing people as a social activist would be more satisfying for him than one as a masseur.

Because Chen's many unhappy experiences as a disabled person had made him familiar with the national legislation promulgated to protect the disabled, he was increasingly attracted to the prospect of using the law as an instrument to correct abuse. Despite his lack of formal legal education, Chen began his informal activities as a "barefoot lawyer" in Dongshigu, the dirt-poor village where he had grown up. His local "clients" were underprivileged, often disabled, farmers who needed help in dealing with problems such as unfair taxation, arbitrary denial of a business license, and mistreatment by local police. In order to help them, Chen used legal texts that were read to him by his wife and eldest brother. Chen not only helped in legal matters but had also persuaded the British embassy in Beijing to arrange financing for an electric water well system for the village.

Chen often discussed with foreign guests how to train the two hundred colleagues he estimated would be required to meet the demands of the poor for legal services that Yinan County's few licensed lawyers had ignored for financial and political reasons. At the time, Chen, an optimist, thought that the rural government would not interfere with the training of a large number of "barefoot lawyers," even though they would surely complicate the work and lives of local officials.

Connecting with the World

The *Newsweek* story of 2002 led American diplomats based in China to offer Chen an opportunity to join the United States government's International Visitor Leadership Program, which invites foreign nationals identified as possible future leaders of their countries to tour the United States for several weeks in order to become acquainted with American life and to meet professional counterparts. In the summer of 2003, the State Department contacted my (Jerome A. Cohen, the author of this essay) law school office at New York University (NYU) in an effort to set up an appointment for Chen and his wife, Yuan Weijing, to meet me. Despite my initial reluctance to meet him because of his lack of any formal legal training, once I learned more about him I agreed to do so and was impressed by his story.

Although he had grown up in a very poor, isolated village of only five hundred people and started his education at a late age, Chen proved to be a charismatic personality and highly intelligent. He spoke Mandarin clearly and well. Moreover, he radiated confidence and conviction from behind the dark glasses that seemed to enhance rather than diminish his good looks. Here was an authentic son of the Chinese soil who had known and overcome extraordinary hardships, unlike so many officially sponsored Chinese visitors who hailed from intellectual, bureaucratic, or even bourgeois families. And he was evidently eager to reveal the many injustices of the Chinese countryside and to seek help in curing them.

Two months after his visit to the United States, while I was teaching at Tsinghua University Law School in Beijing, I invited Chen and his wife for a visit and introduced them to two senior Tsinghua University scholars as well as to a prominent Chinese lawyer. Chen spoke eloquently, urging them to support the selection and training of many more "barefoot lawyers." Except for the law school's dean, however, he received a surprisingly frosty reception, apparently because of the hostility that many Chinese lawyers and scholars have for their less well-educated, unlicensed countryside counterparts, who, they fear, will damage the Chinese legal profession's efforts to improve its traditionally poor reputation.

陈光诚

The Barefoot Lawyer in Trouble

Before a program to train more "barefoot lawyers" could be instituted, however, Chen ran afoul of the local authorities on unforeseen ground—their lawless detention and abuse of the families of thousands of women who had gone into hiding to avoid compulsory abortion or sterilization. Chen, who in the early days of his untutored lawyering had achieved some success with the county courts, was totally unsuccessful in obtaining judicial relief for the persecuted families, since the local Communist Party and government officials dominated the courts and were determined to meet the strict birth control quotas imposed on them by higher levels of government. Frustrated by his inability to help the many victims, Chen decided to resort to less conventional means to expose the situation and obtain help. He pursued two tracks—domestic and international—in the hope of attracting the concern of the central government.

The domestic track involved enlisting the help of Beijing law professor Teng Biao, and other human rights activists, who made a video about the lawless detentions taking place in Yinan County and managed to post it briefly on the Internet. The international track involved enlisting the attention of the foreign press, an even more dangerous course. In August 2005, the *Washington Post* published a front-page story revealing the dire situation in Yinan County. Soon after, Shandong Province police kidnapped Chen off the streets of Beijing and forced him and his family into illegal captivity in their own farmhouse, cutting off all contact with the world. There they were kept prisoner for almost six months until the Linyi municipal authorities responded to domestic and foreign protests against the Chens' confinement, not by releasing them but instead by prosecuting and convicting Chen on fabricated charges. He was sentenced to four years and three months in prison after a farcically unfair trial. Nor did Chen's nightmare cease when he completed his sentence in mid-2010, since the authorities then imposed on the entire family an even stricter house arrest than before the prosecution. This time they deployed up to two hundred men to maintain the Chens' around-the-clock detention and total isolation from the world.

Escaping China

That remained the situation until late April 2012, when Chen stunned the world by miraculously escaping from his captivity and, although injured in a fall, making his way to Beijing with the help of courageous activists. After three days evading detection in the nation's capital, he obtained refuge in the American embassy, thereby precipitating a major dispute between Washington and Beijing just as Secretary of State Hillary Clinton was en route to Beijing for the annual

Chen Guangcheng (middle) counseling disabled villagers. Photo by Joan Lebold Cohen.

陈光诚

Sino-American Strategic and Economic Dialogue. There followed five days of intense Sino-American negotiation that finally produced an intergovernmental agreement in which the People's Republic of China (PRC), while refusing to permit Chen to leave the country, promised that he would be spared further confinement and allowed to study law in China "with the same degree of freedom as any Chinese student." Chen, under great pressure from American officials eager to end what had become a diplomatic crisis, with great trepidation finally accepted this imaginative but risky compromise.

Chen left the embassy for the hospital where he was to reunite with his family and recover from his ordeal before pursuing his planned course of study. That night, however, he changed his mind. After the American diplomats who had accompanied him to the hospital left him to get some sleep, Chen spoke with Teng Biao and other Chinese friends he had been unable to contact for years and came to regret his risky agreement to stay in China. He then told the foreign media that he insisted on leaving the country.

Now, the American diplomats and their Chinese counterparts were confronted with a more acute crisis than ever. It was only resolved twenty-four intense hours later, just as the bilateral Strategic and Economic Dialogue was getting under way, when, amid the heat of world publicity, the Chinese leadership reluctantly agreed to allow Chen to apply to go abroad to study law at NYU. Two tense weeks later, on 19 May 2012, Chen, his wife, and two children arrived in New York.

Building a Life in the United States

Hosted by NYU, with no expense spared to improve the chances for him and his family to make a safe and beneficial adjustment to American life and learning, Chen enjoyed an extremely stimulating and challenging first year. He was in enormous demand as a speaker in the United States and many other countries, and not only on academic campuses and at human rights programs but also in political and foreign policy circles. His first six months in the United States coincided with the heated finale of the 2012 American presidential election, and both Republicans and Democrats sought to exploit his extraordinary story. Republicans would have been delighted if he had vindicated their accusations that the Obama administration had botched the negotiations with the PRC over his fate, and the Democrats were eager to have him support their portrayal of this complex incident as a demonstration of the diplomatic skills of Secretary Clinton and her staff. Chen, who generally heeded advice to sidestep the campaign's temptations, was careful not to offer either side fuel for its fire. Nor did

he succumb to efforts by anti-abortion activists to transform his courageous opposition to China's forced abortions and sterilization into broader opposition to women's rights.

A misunderstanding between Chen and NYU over the duration of his fellowship, which was clearly indicated to be limited to one year, marred the last weeks of Chen's stay at NYU. In order to ease his forthcoming transition, as early as January 2013, six months before the scheduled end of his NYU tenure, university officials, together with his host, NYU's US-Asia Law Institute, began a painstaking process of exploring and negotiating what might be his most favorable next steps. A few months later, however, Chen claimed that the university was forcing him to leave its premises prematurely because the university was allegedly under pressure from the PRC to terminate its support for him. Chen's claims, which to this day remain unsubstantiated, led to the termination of final negotiations about a three-year appointment to the staff of the Committee to Support Chinese Lawyers based at Fordham University Law School's Leitner Center for Law and Justice. Happily, Chen soon found another source of support in the Witherspoon Institute, a conservative organization devoted to the dissemination of democratic principles that reportedly agreed to sponsor his affiliation with Catholic University and the Lantos Foundation for Human Rights & Justice in Washington, D.C. After a second, transitional year in

• Chén Guāngchéng •

New York, Chen and his family moved to the Washington suburbs.

Although no evidence has yet come to light of the PRC expressing dissatisfaction with NYU's offer to host Chen, the PRC did show signs of dissatisfaction with Chen's decision to visit Taiwan at the end of his NYU year in June 2013. Although the Nationalist Party-led Taiwan government grudgingly granted Chen a visa, President *Ma Ying-jeou 马英九 (b. 1950) and various legal officials and judges declined to receive him. Nevertheless, Chen's spirited academic and human rights lectures and exchanges were highly appreciated by Taiwan law schools, bar associations, non-governmental organizations, and opposition politicians.

Moving Forward

After leaving NYU in mid-2013, Chen completed work on an autobiography, *The Barefoot Lawyer*, subtitled *A Blind Man's Fight for Justice and Freedom in China*. In it he recounts the many exciting chapters in his life until his widely heralded arrival in New York. His later experience will presumably be the topic of a second volume that will help us understand to what extent he is managing to avoid the fate of many previously exiled Chinese human rights activists, who have tended to lose their influence both in China and the West after a brief flurry of publicity in their new homeland.

Jerome A. COHEN
New York University School of Law

Further Reading

Clinton, Hillary Rodham. (2014). *Hard choices.* New York: Simon & Schuster.

Chen Guangcheng. (2015). *The barefoot lawyer: A blind man's fight for justice and freedom in China.* New York: Henry Holt and Co.

Cohen, Jerome A. (2014, July 28). Chen Guangcheng goes to Washington. *The Diplomat.*

Kaufman, Joyce P. (2013). Chen Guangcheng: The case of the blind dissident and US-China relations. In Ralph G. Carter (Ed.), *Contemporary cases in U.S. foreign policy: From terrorism to trade* (pp. 249–271). Thousand Oaks, CA: CQ Press.

Johnson, Ian. (2012, June 26). 'Pressure for change is at the grassroots': An interview with Chen Guangcheng. Retrieved January 6, 2015, from http://www.nybooks.com/blogs/nyrblog/2012/jun/26/chen-guangcheng-interview

*People marked with an asterisk have entries in this dictionary.

♂ Chén Kǎigē 陈凯歌

b. 1952—Contemporary film director, key figure of the so-called Fifth Generation directors

Alternate name: trad. 陳凱歌

Summary

Chen Kaige, part of the group of filmmakers known as the Fifth Generation, has made his imprint on both Chinese and world cinema. His early films helped mark the beginning of a "Chinese New Wave" that brought Chinese cinema to international prominence. His later films, reflecting the new commercial environment of the 1990s, tended to balance art and entertainment.

Chen Kaige, who has made over a dozen films, is one of the first contemporary Chinese film directors to have made a name for himself internationally. He is part of the group of filmmakers known as the Fifth Generation, which introduced a new type of Chinese cinema to the world in the 1980s. Not long after China ended its chaotic Cultural Revolution (1966–1976), Chen began to establish himself as one of the most innovative filmmakers of his time. His successful yet sometimes controversial career both represents and symptomatizes the Chinese new cinema over the past decades. Chen's early films in the 1980s, for example, characterized by their crude realism, bold symbolism, powerful imagery, and ideological ambiguities, moved sharply away from the prevailing socialist-realist cinematic establishment of the time and immediately attracted international attention. In the 1990s, however, when China began a steady transformation into an increasingly commercialized society, Chen's productions began to shift more toward entertainment values, while still trying to preserve their arthouse aesthetics. In addition, as Chen was becoming more influential in the international film arena, his productions began exhibiting increasingly transnational features. Controversies began to arise about the loss of critical and innovative edge in these later commercial films. But throughout his career, Chen has consistently shown, in his own words, "a fundamental suspicion and questioning of our environment, society, and culture" in his filmmaking, "an attitude of questioning and criticizing" (Berry 2005, 104).

Early Life

Chen Kaige was born into a prominent film family in Beijing on 12 August 1952. His father, Chén Huái'ǎi 陈怀皑 (1920–1994), was a well-known film director in his own right, whose representative works include the influential film *The Song of Youth* 青春之歌 (1959). Chen Kaige's mother, Liú Yànchí 刘燕驰, worked as a script editor and consultant at the Ministry of Culture's Film Bureau and the Beijing Film Studio. Chen attended a relatively privileged primary school and junior middle school, and some of his schoolmates were children of his parents' colleagues. One of Chen's childhood friends was Tián Zhuàngzhuàng 田壮壮 (b. 1952), who later became his classmate at the Beijing Film Academy and a fellow Fifth Generation director. Despite his exposure to filmmaking influences in childhood, however, Chen was not particularly interested in the activity at the time, though the elite intellectual environment he experienced as a boy ultimately had a profound impact on his career.

When the Cultural Revolution started in 1966, Chen was obliged to end his formal education, but he devoted himself to reading historical writings and classical novels. He soon joined the

Red Guards, groups of young people who made it their cause to become Mao Zedong's loyal followers. Like many other young members of the Red Guards, Chen was led to denounce his father. The son later regretted this, and he made efforts to redeem himself through films such as *Farewell My Concubine* 霸王别姬 (1993) and *Together* 和你在一起 (2002).

In 1968, following the Chinese Communist Party's call for youths to go to the countryside, Chen volunteered to go to the southwest Yunnan Province; this experience as a "sent-down youth" (*zhīshi qīngnián* 知识青年)—that is, an educated young person who left the urban districts in China to live and work in rural areas—was later critically reflected in his film *King of the Children* 孩子王 (1987). He returned to Beijing after demobilization from the army in 1975 and was assigned to work in a laboratory in the Beijing Film Processing Factory. For the following three years he spent time with people who had had similar experiences in the Cultural Revolution, such as the writer Zhōng Āchéng 钟阿城 (better known as Āh Chéng 阿城, b. 1949) and the poet *Běi Dǎo 北岛 (b. 1949), and who shared his view that dramatic changes in the intellectual field were imminent.

Early Films

Chen was admitted to the Beijing Film Academy in 1978 and became a member of the very first class of the academy to graduate after the Cultural Revolution.

---

*People marked with an asterisk have entries in this dictionary.

It was during his studies at the academy that he was first exposed to a large number of Western films, the viewing of which previously had been denied to a common audience on ideological grounds. This training and exposure to another kind of film reshaped his perspective toward filmmaking.

After Chen graduated in 1982, he was assigned to the Beijing Film Studio, where he worked as an assistant to other directors. Dissatisfied with the lack of opportunity to direct his own films, Chen joined his former classmate, cinematographer and director *Zhāng Yìmóu 张艺谋 (b. 1951), upon the latter's invitation, at the Guangxi Film Studio in Nanning to make his first film, *Yellow Earth* 黄土地 (1984). The remote location of Guangxi, as well as the "smallness and newness of the studio," played a crucial role in paving the way for the Fifth Generation (Clark 2005, 77). Unlike large and established studios in Beijing and Shanghai, where young directors had to wait years for the chance to make their own films, the studio in Guangxi provided Chen with an immediate opportunity and greater liberty in making his debut film. This resulted in a highly innovative film that deviated sharply from the existing cinematic conventions. With its brutally realistic depiction of peasant life in the poverty-stricken northwest, the film called into question the socialist-realist narrative that had held this region as a sacred place of the country's revolutionary tradition, as well as the cradle of

Chinese civilization. Zhang Yimou's stylized cinematography produced a meditative ambience that urged the audience to contemplate the relationship between human beings, on the one side, and nature and culture, be it traditional or socialist, on the other. The movie created a filmic aesthetic that was entirely new to an audience accustomed to the socialist-realism that had dominated Chinese film aesthetics for decades.

After directing a TV drama, *Forced Takeoff*, Chen moved on to direct his second film, *The Big Parade* 大阅兵 (1986). Presenting the story of a military division in training for eight months to participate in the 1984 big parade in Tiananmen Square, this film charted individual aspirations against collective services, complicating propagandist views of commitment and loyalty. This central tension, which was heightened by Zhang Yimou's experimental use of the camera, served, as Paul Clark observes, "as a metaphor for the fifth-generation's attitudes to China and their place in the nation" (Clark 2005, 150).

Chen's third film, *King of the Children*, adapted from his friend Ah Cheng's novella, was semiautobiographical and recalled his time in southwest Yunnan Province as part of the Red Guards. Telling the story of a sent-down youth bringing new ideas in teaching to the children in a closed community in Yunnan, the film reflected the simultaneously liberating and confining nature of Chinese culture—a theme of the "roots-seeking" movement that the film was part of. His fourth film, *Life on a String* 边走边唱 (1991), tells the story of two blind musicians attempting to find, through belief, perseverance, love, and disillusionment, the meanings of their lives. Made two years after the 1989 Tiananmen Square Incident, in which civilian protestors were killed by the military after several weeks of protests for more democratization, the film presented, in accordance with the gloomy atmosphere then shrouding China, the loneliness and desolation of human beings trapped in a spiritual void.

This early stage in Chen's filmmaking, characterized by bare stories, stylized audio and aural presentation, philosophic ideas, and the challenge to the establishment, came to a conclusion in the early 1990s. These films, paradoxically, were direct products of the social system of which they were so critical; the not-yet-commercialized system working by way of state assignment provided the filmmakers with a rare opportunity for cinematic experiment without having to consider the box office. As this system was gradually replaced by a market-oriented one in the 1990s, the Fifth Generation as a wave, which Chen was such a significant part of, was over.

Transnational Filmmaking

The social transformation in China in the 1990s, in addition to Chen's growing international influence, rendered his filmmaking more transnational, catering simultaneously to both international art-house circles and the mainstream public in China. In fact, Chen's transnational filmmaking started with the making of *Life on a String*, which was co-sponsored by China, the United Kingdom, Germany, and Japan. But it was his epic film *Farewell My Concubine* 霸王别姬 (1993) that marked the peak of this phase of his career. Adapted from Hong Kong writer Lilian Lee's (Lǐ Bìhuá 李碧华, b. 1959) novel, this film tells the story of the ups and downs of two Peking Opera actors in tumultuous twentieth-century China. Incorporating elements of homoeroticism, politicized historicity, and oriental exoticism, this film masterfully delineated the intricacy of human feelings under political turmoil. It won the Palme d'Or at the 1993 Cannes Film Festival.

Because of the sweeping success of *Farewell My Concubine*, Chen again teamed up with its stars, Leslie Cheung (Zhāng Guóróng 张国荣, 1956–2003) and *Gǒng Lì 巩俐 (b. 1965), for his next production, *Temptress Moon* 风月 (1996). This film, however, was a box-office failure, mainly due to Chen's heightened narrative and cinematographic aesthetics, as well as his unfamiliarity with the culture in Republican Shanghai, where the story was set. Chen's 2008 semi-biopic, *Forever Enthralled* 梅兰芳, brought his focus back to Beijing and Peking Opera. Depicting the life of the Peking Opera master Méi Lánfāng 梅兰芳 (1894–1961), the film highlighted Mei's individual

Selected Filmography of Chen Kaige			
Year	English Title	Chinese Title	Notes
1984	*Yellow Earth*	黃土地 *Huáng tǔdì*	Director, writer
1986	*The Big Parade*	大閱兵 *Dà yuèbīng*	Director
1987	*The King of Children*	孩子王 *Háizǐ wáng*	Director
1987	*The Last Emperor*	末代皇帝 *Mòdài huángdì*	Actor: Captain of the Imperial Guard
1991	*Life on a String*	邊走邊唱 *Biān zǒu biān chàng*	Director, writer
1993	*Farewell My Concubine*	霸王別姬 *Bàwáng bié jī*	Director
1996	*Temptress Moon*	風月 *Fēng yuè*	Director, writer
1999	*The Emperor and the Assassin*	荆轲刺秦王 *Jīng Kē cì Qín Wáng*	Director, writer, actor (role: Lü Buwei)
2002	*Killing Me Softly*		Director
2002	*100 Flowers Hidden Deep*		Director; Segment in the anthology film *Ten Minutes Older: The Trumpet*
2002	*Together*	和你在一起 *Hé nǐ zài yīqǐ*	Director, producer, writer, actor (role: Yu Shifeng)
2005	*The Promise*	無極 *Wú jí*	Director, writer
2007	*Zhanxiou Village*		Director; Vignette in the anthology film *To Each His Cinema*
2008	*Forever Enthralled*	梅兰芳 *Méi Lánfāng*	Director
2009	*The Founding of a Republic*	建国大业 *Jiàngúo dàyè*	Actor
2010	*Sacrifice*	趙氏孤兒 *Zhào shì gūér*	Director
2012	*Caught in the Web*	搜索 *Sōusuǒ*	Director
2015	*The Monk*	道士下山 *Dàoshì xià shān*	Director

integrity along with his artistic pursuit and national dignity.

Chen's fascination with history resulted in the making of *The Emperor and the Assassin* 荆轲刺秦王 (1999) and *Sacrifice* 赵氏孤儿 (2010). The former retold the well-known historical incident of Jing Ke's failed assassination of Qin Shihuang (260–221 BCE), the First Emperor of China; the latter was adapted from the Yuán 元 dynasty (1279–1368) opera *The Orphan of Zhao* (attributed to Jì Jūnxiáng 纪君祥, and the earliest Chinese play to be known in Europe), which was loosely based on the historical story of Zhao Wu seeking revenge for his clan in the Jin State of the Spring and Autumn period (770–476 BCE). Retelling history from a modern perspective, both films demonstrated Chen's critical reflections on traditional values—such as the imperial view of "all under heaven" and the Confucian view of sacrifice for loyalty—and his consistent concern for humanity.

In the early 2000s Chinese martial arts films experienced a resurgence in the global market, and in 2005 Chen joined in with a martial arts fantasy, *The Promise* 无极. Though it had an enviable pan-Asian lineup of stars and was financed with the priciest investment in Chinese cinema to that point (US$41.9 million), the film was received only lukewarmly by both critics and the public. An amateur director, Hú Gē 胡戈 spoofed the film with his video *A Bloody Case Caused by a* Bun (*Yige mántou yǐnfā de xuè'àn* 一个馒头引发的血案, 2005), which

immediately went viral on the Internet. This incident arguably triggered a widespread spoof (*ègǎo* 恶搞) phenomenon in mainland China. Chen's 2012 film, *Caught in the Web* 搜索, can be regarded as his belated response to the spoof. Adapted from an Internet novel that tells the story of the death of a girl caused by the "human flesh search engine" (*rénròu sōusuǒ* 人肉搜索)—a phenomenon where netizens use the Internet to locate and expose personal information about (perceived) wrongdoers as a form of social punishment—the film questions the ethics of the overall contemporary media in China and that of the Internet in particular.

Other Activities and Legacy

Chen served as a visiting scholar at the New York University Film School on a fellowship from the Asian Cultural Council in 1987, and he spent the following three years in the United States. In 1989, he filmed a music video for the song "Do You Believe in Shame" by Duran Duran. In 2002, he directed his first—and to date only—English-language film, *Killing Me Softly*, an erotic thriller that proved disappointing for the director, critics, and the audience. But these experiences helped Chen broaden his vision and offered him an opportunity to reflect on filmmaking and Chinese culture.

Chen has also displayed a talent for acting. He played roles not only in his own films *The Emperor and the Assassin* and *Together*, but also in Bernardo Bertolucci's *The Last Emperor* (1987) and Huang Jianxin's star-studded historical film, *The Founding of the Republic* 建国大业 (2009).

But Chen is known mostly for the role he played in Chinese cinema's increasing involvement in the global film market beginning in the 1980s and for his transnational films of the 1990s and afterward. His later films, which balanced art and the market and which exemplified his diverse social and cultural concerns, consistently maintained an intellectualism that some held dear but others deemed anachronistic as Chinese society was becoming increasingly diversified.

Haomin GONG
Case Western Reserve University

Further Reading

Berry, Michael. (2005). *Speaking in images: Interviews with contemporary Chinese filmmakers*. New York: Columbia University Press.

Chen Kaige 陈凯歌. (2009). *Wo de qingchun huiyilu: Chen Kaige zizhuan (diyibu)* 我的青春回忆录：陈凯歌自传（第一部）[Remembrance of my youth: Chen Kaige's autobiography I]. Beijing: Zhongguo renmin daxue chubanshe.

Chen Kaige; Wan Zhi; & Rayns, Tony. (1989). King of the Children *and the new Chinese cinema*. London: Faber and Faber.

Clark, Paul. (2005). *Reinventing China: A generation and its films*. Hong Kong: The Chinese University Press.

Gong, Haomin, & Yang Xin. (2010). Digitized parody: The politics of *egao* in contemporary China. *China Information*, 24(1), 3–26.

Kun Qian. (2009). Love or hate: The First Emperor on screen—Three movies on the attempted assassination of the First Emperor Qin Shihuang. *Asian Cinema, 20*(2), 39–67.

Lu Tonglin. (2002). *Confronting modernity in the cinemas of Taiwan and mainland China*. Cambridge, UK: Cambridge University Press.

McDougall, Bonnie S. (1991). The Yellow Earth: *A film by Chen Kaige, with a complete translation of the filmscript*. Hong Kong: Chinese University Press.

Ni Zhen. (2002). *Memoirs from the Beijing Film Academy: The genesis of China's Fifth Generation* (Chris Berry, Trans.). Durham, NC: Duke University Press.

Wang Yiyan. (2007). *The Emperor and the Assassin*: China's national hero and myth of state origin. *Media Asia*, 34(1), 3–13.

♂ Chén Shuǐ-biǎn
陳水扁

b. 1950—Mayor of Taipei, chairman of the DPP, and president of the Republic of China (2000–2008)

Alternate names: A-Bian; simpl. 陈水扁

Summary

Born into an impoverished family in southwest Taiwan, Chen Shui-bian rose to become a prominent lawyer, the mayor of Taipei, and the president of the Republic of China for two terms, from 2000 to 2008. He served with an agenda of a flourishing national identity for Taiwan, which meant distant and often frosty relations with mainland China. Corruption scandals plagued him and his family during his second term, and he was eventually tried and found guilty of graft and corruption.

Chen Shui-bian was born on 12 October 1950 to a family of poor and illiterate farmers in Hsi-chuang, a village in the southwest of the Republic of China (ROC; also known as Taiwan). When he came into the world he was so weak that his parents thought he would not survive and did not register him at the local temple until seven months later. Against all odds, he became a strong child and an exemplary law student at the famous National Taiwan University 國立台灣大學. As a lawyer, he gained a national reputation by defending dissidents jailed by the martial law government during the so-called Kaohsiung Incident (Gāoxióng shìjiàn 高雄事件) in 1979. Then he was pushed toward politics as an active member of the Tangwai (Dǎngwài 黨外) movement, expressing harsh criticism against the hegemonic power of the Nationalist Party (Kuomintang 國民黨, KMT). In 1989, after the end of martial law which had lasted for more than thirty-eight years (the longest imposed in the world), Chen was elected as a member of the Legislative Yuan (Lìfǎ Yuàn 立法院), Taiwan's de facto parliament, as an Independent, and in 1994 was elected as mayor of Taipei. In 2000, he was voted president of Taiwan as a member of the Democratic Progressive Party (DPP, Mínjìndǎng 民進黨), putting an end to fifty-five years of Nationalist government. In 2004, Chen was reelected but by a much smaller margin after he had survived an apparent assassination attempt. Both his terms (2000–2004 and 2004–2008) were marked by his pro-independence policies challenging the cross-Strait status quo. In 2008, at the end of his second term and after losing elections, he left office under suspicion of corruption. Shortly afterward, he was detained and, in September 2009, sentenced to life imprisonment.

Early Life: Frail to Famous

Although Chen Shui-bian's (informally known as A-Bian) official biographies state he was born on 18 February 1951 in the village of Hsi-chuang (modern-day Guantian Township, Tainan County), in fact he was born seven months before that. The reason is that after his birth, he was so frail that his parents had doubts he would survive and only issued his birth certificate some months later. His parents were poor and uneducated tenant farmers contracted out as sugarcane factory workers and day laborers. They borrowed money to send him to school, where he achieved a remarkable first rank from primary school up to university. In 1969, he passed the joint national College and University Entrance Examination with the highest score. He entered the well-known National Taiwan University in 1969, and after shifting from business administration to law the following year, he graduated with a bachelor of laws (LL.B.) degree with the

Outstanding Performance Award in 1974. While at university, he met Wu Shu-shen 吳淑珍, the daughter of wealthy doctors, who would become his wife in 1975. The following year, he was hired by the Formosan International Marine and Commercial Law Office as an attorney specializing in maritime law, where he served as a senior partner until 1989. In 1979, Chen gained national standing after legally representing dissidents detained by the martial law government during the Kaohsiung Incident. Martial law was imposed on Taiwan in 1949 to suppress communist and independent activities in Taiwan that would undermine the political control of the island. The emergency decree prevented the formation of political parties and gave strict powers to the secret military police to arrest anyone voicing disapproval of the government. On 10 December 1979, Tangwai movement members (Tangwai literally means "outside the party," i.e., the Nationalist Party), headed by veteran opposition politicians in the Legislative Yuan held the island's first major human rights demonstration in an effort to support and claim democracy in Taiwan. In the streets of Kaohsiung, a coastal city in southern Taiwan, marchers hurled provocative statements at police officers, who brought out tear gas, and violence soon escalated. The editors of *Formosa* magazine (*Měilìdǎo zázhì* 美麗島雜誌) and other publications were charged with incitement to rebellion by the government. Their offices were raided and shut down by the government; however, the race to democracy had already begun. The legal protection afforded by Chen, who saved them from the death penalty, was extensively publicized at the time. This marked a turning point in Chen's life and career, projecting him to a new political dimension.

A Politician on the Rise

After the Kaohsiung Incident, Chen Shui-bian also became a member of the Tangwai movement, mostly an intellectual movement that used journals to express their political opinions and criticism of the monopolistic political position of the KMT. At that time, opposition parties were still not allowed in Taiwan, and Tangwai members formed various united fronts that aimed at supporting "individual" candidates and candidacies to political offices.

In 1981, Chen Shui-bian entered the Taipei City Council as the youngest elected councilor to serve the city. In 1985, he ran for county head in Tainan, at tremendous political and personal costs. Not only did he lose the contest but the following day, his wife was hit by a truck in an accident that paralyzed her from the chest down. Chen's supporters believed the "accident" may have been politically motivated, although there was no proof that this was the case. In 1986, after a piece of writing criticizing the pro-KMT philosopher Elmer Hu-hsiang Fung (Féng Hùxiáng 馮滬祥)

was published in *Formosa* magazine, Chen was processed for defamation due to his chairmanship. He was forced to resign from the city council and soon after was held in Tucheng Penitentiary for eight months. After the incident, a magazine called *Neo-Formosa* was published, claiming to be an alternative to the *Formosa* magazine. (After this new version was also banned, the magazine re-appeared in electronic form in 2009.) Meanwhile, Chen's wife had entered the Legislative Yuan, taking political advantage of the protests over his detention. In the same year and benefiting from the end of martial law, the Tangwai movement formed the Democratic Progressive Party (DPP), which was only completely legalized in 1991. The DPP became the first major opposition party, and Chen served as a member of its Central Standing Committee. In 1989, he was elected as a member of the Legislative Yuan, serving as co-convener of the National Defense Committee and Rules Committee. His oratorical skills were very much appreciated, as well as his determination. In 1994, he was elected mayor of Taipei, implementing an ambitious political program based on the city's new transport mobility system, eradicating corruption, fighting crime, and clamping down on Taipei's sex industry. *Time* magazine put him on its "Global 100" list of forthcoming young leaders for the new millennium, and *Asiaweek* considered Taipei one of best cities in Asia. His popularity was huge among Taipei residents, with approval ratings reaching about 70 percent. In 1998, his political opponents were able to put him out of office in the following election; however, this only paved the way for a new presidency race.

In 1996, Taiwan had held its first presidential election under direct democracy, which *Lee Teng-hui 李登辉 (b. 1923) from the KMT won with 54 percent of the votes. Mainland China tried to disrupt the elections by launching missiles near the island, but the move proved counterproductive. In spite of some pro-Chinese voices that accused him of instigating insecurity in the Taiwan Strait, the truth is that Lee actually increased his reputation among the Taiwanese voters, including many DPP supporters. The result of the election was that Taiwan paved the way to democracy, and opened a period of even greater division from mainland China.

Presidential Years

On 18 March 2000, Chen Shui-bian ran in Taiwan's second direct presidential elections and won. He was elected with 39.3 percent of the votes, benefiting from a division within the KMT, with James Soong (Sòng Chǔyú 宋楚瑜) running as an Independent with 36.84 percent of the votes and leaving *Lien Chan 連戰 (b. 1936), the Nationalist candidate, with

---

*People marked with an asterisk have entries in this dictionary.

just 22.1 percent. The KMT had held power on the island for an uninterrupted period of fifty-five years, some of them under a strict authoritarian regime. The election was a historical landmark and represented the end of the KMT party-state authoritarian rule imposed for decades and a political project idealized in mainland China.

Many believed that Chen would start a new project of "de-Sinification," but that would not be realized. Although he started with a very high approval rate (77 percent), unemployment, bad economic performance, and tensions with China reduced this number. Lien Chen and James Soong planned a new alliance in order to defeat Chen Sui-bian in the following elections, but to no avail. Chen was elected again, in March 2004, defeating the KMT candidate some days after surviving an apparent assassination attempt (also known as the 3-19 [March 19] shooting). His opponents suspected the incident was planned, but after an enquiry, the case was officially terminated due to insufficient evidence.

Both of Chen's terms were marked by his strong charisma in delivering populist speeches, but for the most part, DPP's policies were barred by the coalition within the KMT and other minor parties (also known as the Pan-Blue Coalition, associated to the traditional color of the KMT) that controlled the Legislative Yuan. Controversial policies included the expansion of nuclear power, the removal of pictures of historical figures from public buildings, and a pro-independence stance that provoked Beijing security concerns. Chen abolished the National Unification Plan in 2006, introduced amendments to the ROC's constitution, and tried to push a referendum on Taiwan access to the United Nations. At the same time, he introduced a new approach to Taiwan's national identity that included policies of promoting the island as different from China, and he tried to conceal the historical legacy of the KMT. Symbolically, he changed the name of the postal service from China Post to Taiwan Post and the name of the Chiang Kai-shek Memorial Hall to the Taiwan Democracy Memorial Hall. Many consider the strengthening of the national identity as one of Chen's most important political contributions as president. Chen's assertive national identity policy strained relations not only with mainland China but also with the United States; both believed he was moving toward an independency strategy. While Beijing repeated that there is "only one China" and Taiwan can never be independent, Chen said that in addition to the "one China reality," the future of Taiwan should be decided by Taiwanese people. In 2005, in response to Chen's attempts, mainland China approved the Anti-Secession Law (Fǎn fēnliè guójiā fǎ 反分裂國家法) sanctioning "non-peaceful means" to protect territorial integrity by the mainland. The KMT put forward a new strategy of conciliation with China that would bring

positive results in the 2008 presidential elections. At the same time, Chen was dragged into a scandal of mishandling government money. In spite of internal divisions in Taiwan and cross-Strait tensions, Chen's eight years of government in Taiwan brought important domestic reforms, including gender equality legislation, anticorruption measures, constitutional reform of the electoral system, expansion of social welfare, and progress of labor rights.

The Specter of Corruption

Chen Shui-bian's political career was affected by suspicions of corruption, in particular the misuse of a secret presidential fund earmarked for international diplomatic missions. Taiwan's opposition immediately called for the president's resignation, but Chen refused and protected himself with presidential immunity. On 20 May 2008, when *Ma Ying-jeou 馬英九 (b. 1950) took office as the newly elected president of the ROC, Chen lost his immunity and was put under surveillance by Taiwanese prosecutors in order to prevent him from leaving the island. The allegations of corruption also involved presidential aides, his wife, and numerous relatives. On 11 September 2009, Chen Shui-bian received a life sentence for embezzlement, bribery, and money laundering. According to his prosecutors, he accepted bribes related to a land deal, laundered money through Swiss bank accounts, and forged documents. Many DPP supporters claimed that the verdict was motivated by politics, particularly for Chen's anti-Beijing ideas. Meanwhile, the process was complicated by legal proceedings that threw out initial convictions and added new ones on other cases. Chen has spent his days writing a lengthy prison diary, in which he calls himself "the son of Taiwan," while his health condition slowly deteriorates. In 2010, the high court reduced his life sentence to a total prison time of twenty years.

Jorge TAVARES DA SILVA
Institute of Information and Administration Science (ISCIA), University of Minho

Further Reading

Choy, Peter C.Y. (2012). *National identity and economic interest: Taiwan's competing options and their implication for regional stability.* London: Palgrave Macmillan.

Davison, Gary Marvin. (2003). *A short story of Taiwan: The case for independence.* Westport, CT: Praegar.

East, Roger, & Thomas, Richard. (2003). *Profiles of people in power: The world's government leaders.* London: Europa Publications Limited.

Fell, Dafydd. (2012). *Government and politics in Taiwan.* London: Routledge.

Government Information Office. (2002). *The Republic of China yearbook 2002.*

Guo, Baogang, & Teng, Chung-Chian. (Eds.). (2012). *Taiwan and the rise of China.* Lanham, MD: Lexington Books.

Keating, J. F. (2008). *Taiwan: The search for identity.* Taipei, Taiwan: SMC Publishing Inc.

McCarthy, Terry. (2000, March 27). Profile of a president. *Time Asia, 155*(12). Retrieved April 24, 2015, from http://content.time.com/time/world/article/0,8599,2053775,00.html

• Chén Shuǐ-biǎn •

☿ Chén Xītóng 陈希同

1930–2013—Member of the Politburo of the Chinese Communist Party, mayor of Beijing (1983–1993), and party secretary of Beijing (1992–1995)

Alternate name: trad. 陳希同

Summary

A prominent member of the conservative wing of the Chinese Communist Party, Chen Xitong is best known for his role as Beijing's mayor during the Tiananmen Square Incident of 1989. Chen was considered a leading advocate of the government crackdown on student protests, which resulted in widespread casualties. In 1995 he was charged and eventually found guilty in one of the highest-level corruption cases in the history of modern China. Before his death in 2013, Chen said that the Tiananmen Square crackdown was "a regrettable tragedy that could have been avoided."

C hen Xitong was the mayor of Beijing from 1983 until 1993, and the party secretary of Beijing from 1992 until he was charged with corruption in 1995 and sentenced to sixteen years in jail in 1998. As mayor of Beijing during the Tiananmen Square protests in the spring of 1989, Chen was concerned with restoring order in the capital. He provided

*Dèng Xiǎopíng 邓小平 (1904–1997) with information (possibly exaggerated) about the protests, which reportedly influenced Deng's harsh crackdown against the student protesters that resulted in widespread casualties. In the years that followed 1989, Chen was promoted within the Chinese Communist Party (CCP).

Early Life

Chen was born in Anyue County, Sichuan Province, on 10 June 1930, and was raised by his widowed mother. From 1948 to 1949, he received a scholarship to study Chinese literature at Beijing University. Chen eventually married his professor's daughter, Ye Zi, and had two sons, Chen Xiaotong and Chen Xiaoxi. In the 1940s and 1950s, Chen became interested in politics and took positions within the Beijing Party Committee and the Beijing government. From 1966 to 1971, during the Cultural Revolution (1966–1976), Chen was sent down to the

---

*People marked with an asterisk have entries in this dictionary.

countryside along with hundreds of thousands of other young people to do manual labor.

Positions in Government

Chen abandoned his interest in Chinese literature and pursued a political career. He joined the CCP in 1949 and rose through the party ranks. From 1973 to 1979 he was the secretary of the CCP for Changping District, Beijing. In 1979, he was appointed the deputy mayor of Beijing, and in 1981 he became the party secretary of Beijing. In 1983, Chen was appointed the mayor of Beijing. He was a member of the Twelfth Central Committee of the CCP (1982–1987) and of the Thirteenth Central Committee (1987–1992), and he served on the Fourteenth Central Committee from 1992 to 1997. He was appointed a member of the Politburo in 1992 and served until he was removed on corruption charges in 1995. Chen had a reputation for being a powerful and controlling politician.

In the early 1990s, Chen led Beijing's effort to win the 2000 Summer Olympic bid (Sydney, Australia, was the winner). During this time, as an effort to promote Beijing's image in light of the Olympic bid, Chen introduced a type of architecture that would preserve the "Chineseness" and traditional aesthetic of the city while at the same time promote the city's modern image abroad. The style, which became known as the "Xitong hats" (Xītóng dǐng 希同顶), consisted of small pagodas with traditional-looking pavilions featuring upturned corners and tiled roofs that sat on top of large and modern buildings.

Context and Events

Chen was a member of the Beijing leadership at a pivotal point in Chinese history. The student protests in Tiananmen Square from April to June of 1989 revealed the fragility of the legitimacy of the CCP as well as its internal fragmentation. The charges levied against him in 1995 culminated in one of the highest-level corruption cases in China's recent history.

Student Protests in Tiananmen Square

In the spring of 1989, a student-led popular protest calling for political reform and an end to corruption and abuse of power converged on Tiananmen Square in Beijing. The protests were in part sparked by the death, on 15 April 1989, of former secretary general of the CCP *Hú Yàobāng 胡耀邦 (1915–1989). As a member of the post-Mao ruling elite, Hu promoted economic and political reform, eventually losing his position in 1986 due to party elders' unhappiness about his liberal views. Hu was viewed as a potential ally to the pro-democracy movement. A week after his death, over 100,000 protesters gathered in Tiananmen Square to demand political reforms such as freedom of the press, transparency and accountability among political leaders, an end to corruption, and a more democratic political system in China. The movement intensified throughout April and May of 1989, culminating in the student occupation of Tiananmen Square and more specific calls for political and economic reform. On 27 May, students from the Central Academy of Fine Arts erected a 10-meter-tall Goddess of Democracy statue made of foam and papier-mâché and modeled after the Statue of Liberty. Some students participated in a hunger strike. By mid-May, the protests spread to over four hundred cities throughout China, threatening to create a political stalemate and openly fragment the party leadership.

Adding another layer to the Tiananmen protests, on 16 May 1989, Soviet president Mikhail Gorbachev made a historic visit to Beijing to reestablish diplomatic relations after twenty-nine years. The international press corps was gathered in Beijing to cover the Deng-Gorbachev summit. This meant that the world's focus was on Beijing while the protests unfolded.

The initial government response, guided by the conservative wing, was to issue threatening statements in an attempt to intimidate and disband the students, but these only provoked the movement's leaders and accelerated the demonstration. General Secretary *Zhào Zǐyáng 赵 紫阳 (1919–2005) disagreed with a crackdown, thus creating a split among the ruling elites. Zhao succeeded Hu Yaobang in 1986 as general secretary and was also a liberal reformer who was more sympathetic to the demands of the Tiananmen protesters.

When the Politburo Standing Committee voted on the crackdown, Zhao Ziyang and Hu Qili voted against it, while Premier *Lǐ Péng 李鹏 (1909–1992) and Vice Premier Yáo Yīlín 姚依林 voted for it. Chen Xitong, as the city's top leader, did not have the same power as the Standing Committee members. His concern was to restore order in Beijing, and to those ends he sided with the hard-liners. It is not clear if his support for the crackdown was ideologically driven or simply a response to avoid chaos and disorder in the city of Beijing. While Zhao was on a planned state visit to North Korea in late April, the hard-liners consolidated power. On 20 May 1989, Li Peng, Chen's political ally, declared martial law on parts of Beijing that began the violent suppression of the student protesters. On 4 June, the government ordered 300,000 troops into Tiananmen Square to stop the protesters.

According to Nicholas Kristof, Beijing bureau chief of the *New York Times* in 1989, Chen Xitong and CCP boss Lǐ Xīmíng 李锡铭 were a focus of the student protesters' anger and were increasingly portrayed as "villains." In *Conversations with Chen Xitong*, published in Hong Kong by the scholar Yao Jianfu and based on interviews during Chen's medical parole from prison in 2011 and 2012, Chen gave his own version of his role in the Tiananmen Square protests. In response to Li Peng's assertion in his book (*Dairies of Li Peng*) to the effect that Chen was the commander-in-chief of the forces upholding martial law during the Tiananmen protests, Chen asked where was the official document of such appointment, which agency issued it, and who appointed him. He also denied playing a key part in Deng's eventual decision to crack down on the protests, saying Deng had other sources of information. Calling his corruption conviction the biggest miscarriage of justice since the Cultural Revolution, he claimed that he was made a scapegoat by those who essentially staged a coup to oust Zhao (i.e., party elders and Li Peng).

Chen was quoted as saying, he was "sorry" and that he was only following orders. He told the book's author that the event was "a regrettable tragedy that could have been avoided" (Chow 2012).

Anti-corruption Campaign

Chen maintained a powerful role within the Party in the years following the crackdown in Tiananmen Square. In 1993, however, a new president, *Jiāng Zémín 江泽民 (b. 1926), took power and launched an anti-corruption campaign led by Jiang's Shanghai clique—an informal group of powerful party officials. Chen was charged with accepting US$86,000 in bribes and using public money to build luxury homes in 1995, and sentenced to sixteen years in prison. Chen was already famous for keeping mistresses, accepting gifts, having a private secretary who would accept bribes to see the boss, and owning multiple luxury villas at which he would throw lavish parties (Sun 2004). Chen's two sons, Chen Xiaoxi and Chen Xiaotong,

embezzled money and were known for lavish vacations to Hawaii and fancy dinners during which pornographic videos were shown to guests (Gilley 1998).

Chen's corruption charges came during what some viewed as a power struggle between Chen and President Jiang Zemin. According to the journalist and editor Bruce Gilley,

Jiang and Chen never got along well. On at least three occasions since Jiang had become party general secretary, Chen has openly challenged his authority. In 1992, for example, Chen had made a glaring attempt to paint Jiang unfairly as a conservative by allowing the daily *Beijing ribao* to report on Deng's southern tour the day before Jiang overcame propaganda conservatives in the central party to have a national report issued. He then personally arranged for Deng's tour in May of that year of the Capital Iron and Steel plant, styling himself as the mouthpiece for Deng's reforms. Most enraging, however, was Chen's unwillingness to submit to Jiang's unquestioned political authority, even after it had been put in writing by the September 1994 plenum. (Gilley 1998, 242)

Chen's son Chen Xiaotong was also charged and sentenced, as was Chen's protégé, Beijing's vice mayor, Wang Baosen. Wang committed suicide in 1994.

• Chén Xītóng •

Public Reaction and Recognition

In the last years of Chen's life, two books were released that provided new information on Chen's political career. The first was Zhao Ziyang's memoir, *Prisoner of the State: The Secret Journal of Premier Zhao Ziyang*, published by Simon & Schuster in May 2010, but with segments available in China as early as the previous year. In it, Zhao makes comments that suggest Chen played a key role in the government's interpretation of the events of April–June 1989. Zhao suggests that instead of reporting that the protests were dying down, which was widely believed, Chen reported to Deng Xiaoping that they were escalating and required more serious action. According to Zhao's telling, it was because of Chen's alarmist portrayal of the demonstrations that Deng decided to respond harshly.

The second book, *Conversations with Chen Xitong*, published after Zhao's memoir, presents a very different story. Some believed this book was a response to Zhao's book and an attempt to clear Chen's name. The book implies that Chen was a pawn in a system controlled by forces greater than himself. "I hoped we would solve the case peacefully," Chen is quoted (Ewing 2012).

Reputation and Influence after Death

Chen died of colon cancer at the age of eighty-two on 2 June 2013 in Beijing. In 2006, Chen was released from jail on medical parole. His death came just three months before his jail sentence would have ended. A father of one victim of the Tiananmen Square crackdown was quoted as saying that Chen's death was punishment for his sins (Cheung and Chan 2013). But according to Yao Jianfu in an interview with the *New York Times*, "He was a tragic figure; he was a puppet used by more powerful people." Speaking of Chen's possible regrets, Yao goes on, "He started as a Chinese literature student at Peking University and could have become a poet or writer. But he joined the revolution and became a politician, and he'll always be known for his role in the June 4 tragedy" (Buckley 2013).

After the 2013 ousting of *Bó Xīlái 薄熙来 (b. 1949), party secretary of Chongqing, for corruption and abuse of power, the Chinese public and media have become more sympathetic to Chen's fate, linking together Chen and other accused officials such as Chen Liangyu, party secretary of Shanghai, and Bo as victims of power struggles in the upper echelons. As victims, they are viewed more sympathetically. Some scholars believe it is unfair that Deng, who was the ultimate decision maker during the crackdown, remains a lauded figure both in China and overseas, while Chen takes much of the blame.

Lucia GREEN-WEISKEL
Queens College, City University of New York

陈希同

Further Reading

Baum, Richard. (1991). *Reform and reaction in post-Mao China: The road to Tiananmen*. New York: Routledge.

Branigan, Tania. (2012, May 29). Tiananmen crackdown was a tragedy, says former Beijing mayor. *The Guardian*. Retrieved June 22, 2015, from http://www.theguardian.com/world/2012/may/29/tiananmen-square-deaths-beijing-mayor

Buckley, Chris. (2013, June 5). Chen Xitong, Beijing mayor during Tiananmen protests, dies at 82. *The New York Times*. Retrieved June 22, 2015, from http://www.nytimes.com/2013/06/06/world/asia/chen-xitong-mayor-during-tiananmen-protests-dies.html

Cheung, Gary, & Chan, Minnie. (2013, June 5). Death of Chen Xitong is retribution for his sins, says father of Tiananmen student victim. *The South China Morning Post*. Retrieved June 22, 2015, from http://www.scmp.com/news/china/article/1253688/death-chen-xitong-retribution-his-sins-says-father-tiananmen-student

Childs, Martin. (2013, June 7). Obituary: Chen Xitong: Disgraced former mayor of Beijing. *The Independent*. Retrieved June 22, 2015, from http://www.independent.co.uk/news/obituaries/chen-xitong-disgraced-former-mayor-of-beijing-8650180.html

Chow Chung-yan. (2012). June 4 "could have been avoided". *South China Morning Post*. Retrieved February 25, 2015, from http://www.scmp.com/article/1002311/june-4-could-have-been-avoided

The death of Chen Xitong. (2013, June 8). *The Economist*. Retrieved June 22, 2015, from http://www.economist.com/news/china/21579045-death-chen-xitong

Ewing, Kent. (2012, June 6). Tiananmen villain seeks to clear his name. *Asia Times Online*. Retrieved June 22, 2015, from http://www.atimes.com/atimes/China/NF06Ad02.html

Gilley, Bruce. (1998). *Tiger on the brink: Jiang Zemin and China's new elite*. Oakland: University of California Press.

Kristof, Nicholas. (1989, November 12). China update: How the hardliners won. *The New York Times*. Retrieved June 22, 2015, from http://www.nytimes.com/1989/11/12/magazine/china-update-how-the-hardlinerswon.html

Liu, Melinda. (2012, June 7). Senior Chinese leaders flouted rules to call out troops in Tiananmen Square, New Book Says. *The Daily Beast*. Retrieved June 22, 2015, from http://www.thedailybeast.com/articles/2012/06/07/senior-chinese-leaders-flouted-rules-to-call-out-troops-intiananmen-square-new-book-says.html

Sapio, Flora. (2007). L'altra faccia della lotta alla corruzione: Luci ed ombre del caso Chen Xitong [Tales of corruption control: The "Chen Xitong saga and its shadows". In Annamaria Palerrno (Ed.), *La Cina e l'Altro* (pp. 631–650). Napoli, Italy: Il Torcoliere.

Yan Sun. (2004). *Corruption and market in contemporary China*. Ithaca, NY: Cornell University Press.

Yao Jianfu (Ed). (2012). *Chen Xitong qinmu: Zhong kou shuo jin nan shuo zhen* 陳希同親述 ： 衆口鑠金難鑠真 [Conversations with Chen Xitong]. Hong Kong: Xin shi ji chu ban ji chuan mei you xian gongsi.

Zhao Ziyang. (2010). *Prisoner of the state: The secret journal of Premier Zhao Ziyang*. New York: Simon & Schuster.

☿ Chén Yún 陈云

1905–1995—Old-guard political leader and economic thinker, one of the so-called Eight Immortals

Alternate names: b. Liào Chényún 廖程雲; trad. 陳雲

Summary

A long-lived revolutionary and government official, Chen Yun is best known as a key party economic thinker and ideological theorist from the 1950s to the 1980s. He developed the bird cage theory of limited economic freedom after the Cultural Revolution and promoted slow, steady development in opposition to Deng Xiaoping's quest for rapid modernization. The apparent success of Deng's reforms sidelined Chen, and he died in 1995 as one of the last of the old guard.

Noteworthy for his continuous place in the inner group of Chinese leaders and his long service on the Central Committee and Politburo of the Chinese Communist Party (CCP), Chen Yun was never a contender for top leader from the 1930s until the 1980s, and only a potential leader until his death in 1995. Born in Qingpu near Shanghai on 13 June 1905, he worked as a typesetter in Shanghai before joining the CCP in 1924.

He later served as a union organizer, guerrilla soldier, and secret agent. Promoted to the Central Committee in 1931, he participated in the Long March (1934–1935) and went to Moscow for training in ideology and organization. Several other key communists, most notably "third generation" leaders *Lǐ Péng 李鹏 (b. 1928) and *Jiāng Zémín 江泽民 (b. 1926), also studied in the Soviet Union. Though he received only an elementary school education, Chen emerged as a key economic thinker and ideological theorist, especially during the 1942 Rectification Campaign when he wrote key papers on ideology, party organization, and training of cadres.

Rise Towards the Top

In 1949, Chen became the head economic planner, responsible for stabilization and reconstruction after World War II. In charge of financial and

---

*People marked with an asterisk have entries in this dictionary.

economic affairs, he crafted the first Five-Year Plan, based on Soviet central planning and industrialization models. Emphasis would now be placed on high growth, by privileging heavy industrial development over agriculture. Soviet planners assisted Chinese bureaucrats in drafting the plan, while Soviet engineers and technicians helped with a large number of industrial and infrastructure projects. By 1957, all private industry had been transferred to state or joint ownership, and farmers were encouraged to form large agricultural cooperatives.

Close to premier Zhōu Ēnlái 周恩来 (1898–1976) and vice premier *Dèng Xiǎopíng 邓小平 (1904–1997) in outlook, Chen agreed with Zhou on the need for incentives to spur agricultural production. From 1956 to 1957, however, he clashed with CCP chairman Máo Zédōng 毛泽东 (1893–1976) over the direction of economic development. Mao called for quick economic advance, based on mobilization of Chinese masses, while Chen wanted a slower, steadier development involving a balance of local markets and national economic planning. This became the core of his "bird cage" theory, where limited economic freedom would be allowed (the bird), but within centralized planning (the cage). The Great Leap Forward launched in 1958 was Mao's attempt to use the Chinese masses to quickly achieve high-speed growth. Relying on assumed high agricultural productivity, peasants were

diverted to infrastructure and small-scale steel smelting projects. With not enough peasants in the fields and a severe drought, agricultural productivity collapsed and a mass famine hit various rural areas.

At the critical Lushan Conference in 1959 to review the dismal results of the Great Leap Forward, Chen remained silent and did not criticize Mao. Defense minister Péng Déhuái 彭德怀 (1898–1974) and other leaders, on the other hand, did criticize Mao for the disastrous results of the program. Mao reacted strongly to this criticism, replacing Peng with Lín Biāo 林彪 (1907–1971). During the conference, Mao was eventually asked to stay out of economic policymaking, and agreed to step down as party chairman, and the Great Leap Forward was curtailed. To mollify Mao, the Party launched an Anti-Rightist campaign against his opponents.

Following the Great Leap Forward, Chen toured the countryside to assess the program's failures, voicing his criticism to other leaders. His ideas became central to the moderate policies of Deng and president Liú Shàoqí 刘少奇 (1898–1969) beginning in 1962, and he provided a theoretical justification for their economic reforms with his "bird cage" concept (i.e., some economic freedom, but within centralized limits). Chen's efforts to reduce the costs of grain shipments to urban areas, however, also laid the groundwork for the later internal deportation of youth during the Cultural Revolution (1966–1976). Mao opposed

• Chén Yún •

these policies, but kept a low profile until 1965.

A Moderate During the Cultural Revolution

The Cultural Revolution began as a cultural campaign by which Mao hoped to regain control over the CCP. By 1966, it had expanded into a major effort by Mao and radical leftists to dismantle the party leadership, using the Red Guards (bands of young pro-Maoist zealots). Liu Shaoqi was sacked as president in 1968, and Deng Xiaoping was purged from his positions. By 1967, alarm at excesses by the Red Guards led the army to restore control throughout the country and to send millions of urban young people to the countryside to "learn from the peasants." "Set aside" from all of his positions except membership on the Central Committee though not punished for his moderation during the Cultural Revolution, Chen began to formulate many ideas that later formed the core of the Deng-era reforms. He disagreed with Deng only over timing of the early reforms, and worked closely with the paramount leader for a time, but from 1984 criticized the reform process for going too far. Initially, their policies were intended to stimulate agriculture, which had collapsed during the Great Leap Forward. They allowed peasants to retain private plots, and allowed some local markets for the selling of produce.

A Conservative During Economic Reforms

Chen supported Deng's second return to power in 1977, and was rewarded with chairmanship of the newly created Central Disciplinary Inspection Committee in 1978. Though not formally set forth in the party constitution, the committee nonetheless has several important functions, including maintaining party discipline and morale, controlling party organizations, and investigating violations of party order. In the Reform and Opening Up era (gǎigé kāifàng 改革开放), these investigations most often have concerned corruption. In the 1980s, Chen criticized Deng's reforms for abandoning his bird cage concept, for downplaying the importance of grain distribution, for unbalanced growth of regions, and for contributing to budget deficits. Chen held no other high positions during the 1980s, except for his membership on the Central Committee; due to his prestige and influence, however, he was considered fifth in the hierarchy and one of the Eight Immortals (the most powerful of China's elderly leaders in the 1980s and 1990s), and retained much behind-the-scenes influence. Besides Chen, the Eight Immortals included Deng Xiaoping, *Péng Zhēn 彭真 (National People's Congress chairman, 1902–1997), *Yáng Shàngkūn 杨尚昆 (president, 1907–1998), *Lǐ Xiānniàn 李先念 (president, 1909–1992), *Bó Yībō 薄一波 (Central Advisory Committee vice chairman, 1908–2007), and *Wáng Zhèn 王震 (Central Advisory Committee vice chairman, 1908–1993). Accounts differed on the identity of the eighth "immortal." In China, they are also referred to as the "Eight Eminent Officials" or "Eight Elders."

Rumors of Deng's death sparked fears that Chen would replace him, and led the Hong Kong stock market to drop several times. Though he resigned from the Central Committee in 1987, Chen was a crucial supporter of Deng's hard line during the Tiananmen Incident of 1989. He nevertheless aided efforts to sideline Deng after 1989, and fought Deng's last reform campaign in 1992. The perceived success of the reforms by the mid-1990s discredited most of his moderate socialist notions. His death on 10 April 1995 was marked as a significant passing of the old guard.

Joel R. CAMPBELL
Troy University

Further Reading

Becker, Jasper. (2002). *The Chinese.* New York: Oxford University Press.

Chen Yun. (n.d.). Retrieved March 5, 2015, from http://www.answers.com/topic/chen-yun

Chinaposters. (2014). Chen Yun. Retrieved March 5, 2015, from http://chineseposters.net/themes/chenyun.php

Dreyer, June Teufel. (2010). *China's political system: Modernization and tradition* (7th ed.). New York: Longman.

Evans, Richard. (1995). *Deng Xiaoping and the making of Modern China.* London: Penguin.

Fairbank, John King. (1987). *The great Chinese revolution, 1800–1985.* New York: Harper Perennial.

Morton, W. Scott, & Lewis, Charlton M. (2004). *China: Its history and culture* (4th ed.). Englewood Cliffs, NJ: McGraw-Hill.

Roberts, J. A. G. (2006). *A concise history of China* (2nd ed.). London: Palgrave Macmillan.

Salisbury, Harrison. (1993). *The new emperors: China in the era of Mao and Deng.* New York: Harper Perennial.

Spence, Jonathan. (1999). *The search for modern China.* New York: W. W. Norton & Co.

Wang, James C.F. (2001). *Contemporary Chinese politics.* New York: Prentice-Hall Publishers.

• Chén Yún •

♀ Chen, Joan

Chén Chōng 陈冲

b. 1961—Shanghai film actress, director, and producer

Alternate name: trad. 陳沖

Summary

One of contemporary China's most globally recognized actresses, Joan Chen has appeared in films by five generations of mainland China's directors, Hong Kong New Wave directors, directors from the Asian diaspora, and high-profile international filmmakers. She was the youngest-ever recipient of China's Hundred Flowers Award. Beloved in China for her contributions to Chinese cinema following the Cultural Revolution, Chen's personal and career decisions have also made her a controversial figure.

Joan Chen (or Chen Chong), one of contemporary China's most globally recognized film actresses, was born on 26 April 1961 into a family of doctors in Shanghai. Her paternal grandfather, Chén Wénjìng 陈文镜 (1903–1987), studied at Shanghai's St. John's Medical School and later became a surgeon at the Shanghai No. 9 People's Hospital. Her maternal grandfather, Zhāng Chāngshào 张昌绍 (1906–1967), had a doctoral degree in pharmacology from London University and also trained at Harvard Medical School. He was known for laying the groundwork to establish pharmacology in the People's Republic of China. Chen's father, Chén Xīngróng 陈星荣 (b. 1931), is a renowned radiologist at Shanghai's Huashan Hospital.

Revolutionary Roles

Chen grew up during the Cultural Revolution (1966–1976), when schools were closed, teachers persecuted, and youth "sent down" to the countryside. In 1967, Zhang Changshao committed suicide after being politically persecuted, traumatizing his six-year-old granddaughter. The family persevered to continue her education despite the circumstances. Joan Chen learned to play piano and accordion at a young age and participated in stage performances as a teen. Her given name, Chōng 冲 ("charging forward"), is representative of the family's high expectations for her.

Chen's acting career started at the age of fifteen, the year the Cultural Revolution ended. Shanghai Film Studio's veteran director Xiè Jìn 谢晋 (1923–2008) invited her to play the lead role in *Youth* 青春 (1976), a revolutionary melodrama about a young girl who overcomes her muteness and even manages to work as an army switchboard operator. In 1978, Chen began studying English at the reopened Shanghai Institute of Foreign Languages. Her early film roles were often musical and emotionally charged, providing her audiences emotional outlets as the devastating Cultural Revolution came to an end. During college she played a young singer in *Hearts for the Motherland* 海外赤子 (1979), a People's Liberation Army soldier's little sister in *Little Flower* 小花 (1979), and a pianist in *Awakening* 苏醒 (1981).

Chen's role as Xiaohua in *Little Flower* made her a household name. In May 1979 she was featured in *Popular Cinema*, the most important film magazine in the People's Republic of China (PRC), and a year later she became the youngest-ever recipient of the magazine's Hundred Flowers Award. Fans identified with Chen's screen persona so much that they fondly called her Xiaohua (Little Flower). Critics praised her straightforward acting style and hardworking spirit.

The vacuum of acting talent in the late 1970s helped propel Chen's quick rise to teen stardom. Since the early 1950s China's film industry had been nationalized. Máo Zédōng's 毛泽东 (1893–1976) political campaigns had dictated the development of filmmaking. During the Cultural Revolution, film directors, actors, script writers, and critics went through even tougher political scrutiny and persecution than others, and Chinese universities and film schools were shut down. This legacy left a shortage of trained professionals, and inexperienced teen talent, including Joan Chen, consequently found unprecedented opportunities.

Acting Career in America

In 1981, Chen decided to go to America and study medicine, as her protective family urged her to evade the public attention associated with her unanticipated teen stardom. She never finished her medical training; instead, she became the PRC's first actress to pursue a career in Hollywood. She performed in stage dramas and on television shows before she ran into producer Rafaella De Laurentiis in a parking lot and landed her first big film role in America, as a Scottish businessman's mistress named May-May in *Tai-pan* (1986). *Tai-pan* was a flop, but it led to the opportunity to play Empress Wǎnróng 婉容 in *The Last Emperor* (1987), winner of nine Academy Awards.

Chinese audiences vehemently criticized Chen's personal and career decisions. Her departure to America, a country often seen as ideologically and

Chen, Joan

Selected Filmography of Joan Chen				
Year	**English Title**	**Chinese Title**	**Director**	**Notes**
1976	*Youth*	青春 *Qīngchūn*	Xie Jin	Role: Shen Yamei
1979	*Hearts for the Motherland*	海外赤子 *Hǎiwài chìzǐ*	Xing Jitian	
1979	*Little Flower*	小花 *Xiǎohuā*	Zhang Zheng	Role: Zhao Xiaohua
1981	*Awakening*	苏醒 *Sūxǐng*	Teng Wenji	Role: Su Xiaomei
1985	*Miami Vice*			Role: May Ying
1986	*Tai-pan*		Daryl Duke	Role: May-May
1987	*The Last Emperor*		Bernardo Bertolucci	Role: Empress Wanrong
1988	*Heartbeat*		Harry Winer	Role: Cathryn
1989	*The Blood of Heroes*		David Webb Peoples	Role: Kidda
1990-91	*Twin Peaks*		Creators: Mark Frost & David Lynch	Role: Jocelyn Packard
1992	*Shadow of a Stranger*		Richard Friedman	Role: Vanessa
1993	*Heaven and Earth*		Oliver Stone	
1993	*Tales from the Crypt*		Rodman Flender	
1993	*Temptation of a Monk*	诱僧 *Yòu sēng*	Clara Law	Role: Princess Hong-e, Qing-shao
1994	*Red Rose White Rose*	红玫瑰白玫瑰 *Hóng méiguī bái méiguī*	Stanley Kwan	Role: Wang Jiao-rui
1995	*Judge Dredd*		Danny Cannon	Role: Dr. Isla Hayden
1997	*Homicide: Life on the Street*		Tim McCann	Role: Elizabeth Wu
1997	*Happily Ever After: Fairy Tales for Every Child*		Edward Bell	Role: Princess Jade
1998	*The Outer Limits*		Helen Shaver	Role: Major Dara Tarif
1998	*In a Class of His Own*		Robert Munic	Role: Linda Ching

Year	English Title	Chinese Title	Director	Notes
1998	*Xiu Xiu: The Sent-Down Girl*	天浴 *Tiānyù*	Joan Chen	Director, producer, writer
1998	*Green Card Clan*	绿卡族 *Lǜ Kǎzú*		TV Show
2000	*What's Cooking*		Gurinder Chadha	Role: Trinh Nguyen
2000	*Autumn in New York*		Joan Chen	
2004	*Avatar (Cyber Wars)*		James Cameron	Film, actress
2004	*Jasmine Flower*	茉莉花开 *Mòlìhuā kāi*	Hou Yong	Role: Elder Mo
2004	*Saving Face*		Alice Wu	Role: Hwei-Lan Gao
2005	*Sunflower*	向日葵 *Xiàng rì kuí*	Zhang Yang	Role: Zhang Xiuqing
2006	*Americanese*		Eric Byler	Role: Betty Nguyen
2007	*The Sun Also Rises*	太阳照样升起 *Tàiyǎng zhàoyàng shēngqǐ*	Jiang Wen	
2007	*Lust, Caution*	色戒 *Sè jié*	Ang Lee	Role: Madam Yee Tai Tai
2008	*Seventeen*	十七 *Shí qī*	Ji Cheng	Role: Mother
2008	*24 City*	二十四城 *Èrshísì chéng*	Jia Zhangke	Role: Gu Minhua
2010	*Color Me Love*	爱出色 *Ài chūsè*	Chen Yili	Role: Zoe
2010	*Journey to the West*	西游记 *Xīyóujì*		TV Show
2010	*Love in Disguise*	恋爱通告 *Liàn ài tōng gào*	Wang Leehom	Role: Joan
2011	*1911*	辛亥革命 *Xīnhài gémìng*	Zhang Li & Jackie Chan	Role: Empress Longyu
2012	*Let It Be*	稍安勿躁 *Shāo ān wù zào*	Song Jinxiao	Role Niu Jie
2012	*Sui Tang Heroes*	隋唐英雄 *Suí Táng yīngxióng*		Role: Empress Dugu
2014	*Marco Polo*		Joachim Rønning, et al.	Role: Empress Chabi
2015	*Lady of the Dynasty (Yang Guifei)*	王朝的女人: 杨贵妃 *Wángcháo de nǚrén: Yáng Guìfēi*	Shi Qing (with Zhang Yimou & Tian Zhuangzhuang)	Role: Consort Wu

politically opposed to China since the establishment of the PRC, was seen by many as an act of betrayal, made even more hurtful because Chen's most memorable roles in China had been patriotic, encouraging identification with the PRC and its ideologies despite the Cultural Revolution. In 1985 Chen returned to China for the first time and briefly appeared at China Central Television's New Year's Gala, only to find herself criticized afterward for having called her motherland "China." *Reference News*, a publication circulated to senior decision-makers in China, stated that her sensual role in *Tai-pan* was politically humiliating. A critic even blamed her for starting the trend for award-winning Chinese actresses to leave their motherland for morally questionable Western countries. Joan Chen's politically conscious grandmother authored a series of articles defending her granddaughter.

Chen's Hollywood career was marked by success—she became a member of the American Film Institute, was featured on magazine covers, and served as a judge at film festivals. Racial typecasting, however, constrained her acting career. Her brilliant performance in *The Last Emperor* was limited by the film's general lack of interest in developing Empress Wanrong into a complex character. In films such as *The Blood of Heroes* (1989), *Judge Dredd* (1995), and *Avatar* (also known as *Cyber Wars*, 2004), Chen's Asian appearance was used to enhance the "otherness" nature of the time and place. She also played many pan-Asian roles, including a Vietnamese mother in both *Heaven and Earth* (1993) and *What's Cooking* (2000).

Chen has acted in some American television series throughout her career as well. Her work before 2000 includes *Miami Vice* (1985), *Heartbeat* (1988), *Twin Peaks* (1990–1991), *Shadow of a Stranger* (1992), *Tales from the Crypt* (1993), *Homicide: Life on the Street* (1997), *Happily Ever After: Fairy Tales for Every Child* (1997), *The Outer Limits* (1998), and the television movie *In a Class of His Own* (1998).

Directing Career

Chen planned for a directorial career as early as 1993. In 1998 she produced, wrote, and directed *Xiu Xiu: The Sent-Down Girl* 天浴, a film that was secretly shot in a remote plateau area in China and banned in the country. It depicts a fifteen-year-old girl's descent from an enthusiastic and innocent student longing for revolution to a disillusioned and homesick young woman hopelessly using her body for the slightest chance of returning home. Her death in the end of the film challenges the mainstream discourse's oblivion of the pain inflicted upon Chinese people by Maoist campaigns. Chen established herself as a critically acclaimed director through this film, which received seven Golden Horse Awards in Taiwan.

In 2000 Joan Chen directed her second film, *Autumn in New York,* a romantic drama featuring Richard Gere and

Winona Ryder. Gere played a forty-eight-year-old restaurant owner and womanizer falling in love with a nineteen-year-old girl who has only weeks to live due to a tumor. Despite it being a modest box-office success, Chen was not satisfied with the film, citing her unfamiliarity with Western film production. Reviewers and audiences responded lukewarmly, unimpressed by the clichéd plot and the unattractive pairing of Gere and Ryder.

Return to the Chinese-Language Cinema

In the early 1990s, Joan Chen returned to Chinese-language cinema through two Hong Kong New Wave films. In *Temptation of a Monk* (1993), a drama adapted from a Lilian Lee 李碧华 (b. 1959) novel set in seventh-century China, Chen doubles as a tragic princess, whom the protagonist falls for, and a sensual mistress, whose seduction quenches the protagonist's last worldly desire. In *Red Rose White Rose* 红玫瑰白玫瑰 (1994), a romantic drama based on a *Zhāng Àilíng 张爱玲 (1920–1995) novella, Chen plays a strong-willed woman falling for her husband's friend. Chen received a Golden Horse Award for this role.

The television series *Green Card Clan* 绿卡族 (1998) ushered in Chen's return to the big screen in mainland China. In films set in modern China, she has personified two types of middle-aged women. The first type is the mother figure, as seen in *Jasmine Flower* 茉莉花开 (2004), *Sunflower* 向日葵 (2005), and *Seventeen* 十七 (2008), where she was either widowed or alienated from her husband and child. The second type is the socially powerful, sexually unsatisfied, and mentally fragile woman. Portrayals of this type of woman include the doctor sexually involved with her patient in *The Sun Also Rises* 太阳照样升起 (2007), the fashion business superwoman caught in a strained relationship with her husband in *Color Me Love* 爱出色 (2010, the Chinese version of *The Devil Wears Prada*), and the village head's wife secretly longing for romantic love in *Let It Be* 稍安勿躁 (2012).

The memorable roles of Chen's early career have been evoked in roles of her later career for various purposes. Her role as Empress Lōngyù 隆裕 the palace matriarch in 1911 辛亥革命 (2011), resembles her role in *The Last Emperor*. In the docudrama *24 City* 二十四城 (2008), by director *Jiǎ Zhāngkē 贾樟柯 (b. 1970), Chen plays a factory worker who used to be so beautiful that people nicknamed her Xiaohua. The factory worker mentions Joan Chen, who played and is playing Xiaohua, in the third person. This reference allows the director to simultaneously pay his tribute to and distance himself from Chinese national cinema.

As mainland China's film industry became more market-driven in the 1990s,

---

*People marked with an asterisk have entries in this dictionary.

Chen's international recognition began to be considered a favorable credential. Her long acting career—working with Xie Jin (from China's so-called Third Generation of filmmakers) and Teng Wenji (Fourth Generation) in the 1970s and early 1980s; Sixth Generation directors Jiāng Wén 姜文, and Zhāng Yáng 张扬, and Jia Zhangke in the 2000s; directors born after the 1980s, such as Jī Chéng 姬诚; and finally Fifth Generation directors, such as Tián Zhuàngzhuàng 田壮壮 in *Lady of the Dynasty* 杨贵妃 (2015)—reflects the development of Chinese cinema for more than three decades.

Joan Chen remains active in films by the Asian diaspora. In *Ang Lee's 李安 *Lust Caution* 色戒 (2007), she played Madam Yee, who was able to hide her hurt feelings after she discovered her husband's affair. Other films in this category include *Saving Face* (2004), *Americanese* (2006), and *Love in Disguise* (2010). She also continues to act in television series, including *Journey to the West* 西游记 (2010) and *Sui Tang Heroes* 隋唐英雄 (2012).

Family Life and Continuous Controversy

Joan Chen was married to Jim Lau, a personal trainer, from 1985 to 1990. She has been married to cardiologist Peter Hui since 1992, and they have two daughters. But like her decision to pursue a career in Hollywood, a personal decision related to her family caused a scandal in the eyes of the Chinese public. In 1998, the couple attempted to adopt twin girls from China. After Chen became pregnant with her own child, however, she "transferred" custodianship of the twins to friends in New York. Around 2010, the Chinese public discovered this and began furiously questioning the couple's integrity.

Today the Chinese public remains divided about Chen and her work. While some appreciate her beauty, talent, perseverance, and international visibility, others question these attributes and find her earlier sensual roles and her recent custodianship scandal distasteful.

Jie ZHANG
Trinity University

Further Reading

Chen Chong. (2007). Interview with Yang Lan. Retrieved February 18, 2015, from http://video.sina.com.cn/v/b/5852579-1188622761.hmtl

Chow, Rey. (2006). Seeing modern China: Toward a theory of ethnic spectatorship. In D. Eleftheriotis & G. Needham (Eds.), *Asian cinemas: A reader and guide* (pp. 168–199). Honolulu: University of Hawai'i Press.

Cui, Shuqin. (2003). *Women through the lens: Gender and nation in a century of Chinese cinema*. Honolulu: University of Hawai'i Press.

Shih, Alice. (2007). Interview: Joan Chen: Actor, screenwriter, director, Chinese American, woman, mother: Who is Joan Chen? *Cineaction*, 46–52.

陈冲

Stringer, Julian. (2003). Scrambling Hollywood: Asian stars / Asian American star culture. In Thomas Austin & Martin Barker (Eds.), *Contemporary Hollywood stardom* (pp. 229–242). London: Arnold.

Xiao Zhiwei, & Zhang Yingjin. (2002). Chen, Joan. In Yingjin Zhang (Ed.), *Encyclopedia of Chinese film* (pp. 113). New York: Routledge.

Yan Geling. (1994). Chen Chong zhuan 陈冲传 [Biography on Chen Chong]. Shanghai: Shanghai yuandong chubanshe.

Zhang, Jie. (2014). Joan Chen: National, international, and transnational stardom. In Leung Wing-Fai & Andy Willis (Eds.), *East Asian film stars* (pp. 96–112). London: Palgrave Macmillan.

• Chen, Joan •

♀ Cheung, Maggie

Zhāng Mànyù 張曼玉

b. 1964—Transnational Hong Kong actress

Alternate names: Man-yuk Cheung; simpl. 张曼玉

Summary

Maggie Cheung's acting career spanned an important and productive period in Hong Kong cinema. Beginning with roles in comedies and action films in the 1980s, Cheung established herself as a dramatic actress in the mid-1990s with a series of high-profile box-office hits. Later, her casting in a number of international art house and crossover films emphasizing her multilingual ability further extended the reach of her transnational stardom.

Actress Maggie (Man-yuk) Cheung was born in Hong Kong on 20 September 1964 but grew up in England after her family migrated there in the early 1970s. She returned to Hong Kong for a holiday at the age of eighteen and stayed in the territory after being talent-spotted as a model. In 1983, her second-place finish in the Miss Hong Kong beauty pageant led to her casting as the affable but vapid girlfriend of action star

*Jackie Chan's 陳港生 (b. 1954) "super-cop" headline character in the popular *Police Story* series. More dramatic, and critically acclaimed, performances in the 1990s in films by well-known Hong Kong filmmakers saw her star profile evolve, and by the early 2000s she had transitioned into the international art house market and had won a number of acting awards at international film festivals.

Over this period, Hong Kong's cultural politics, cinema included, were responding to the return of the former British colony to the political jurisdiction of the People's Republic of China (PRC), a move that brought to the fore questions of personal, political, cultural, and historical identities and identifications within the territory. From the mid-1980s through 1997, many films across different genres—from comedy to action to horror—took on the abstract notion of

---

*People marked with an asterisk have entries in this dictionary.

"Hong Kong" as their core subject; in this way they were able to explore the fractiousness of what it meant to be "Chinese" and what it meant to be "from Hong Kong" (as opposed to from Britain or China), as well as fears and anxieties for the future (Teo 1997).

Maggie Cheung's work with some of the key filmmakers of this period, including Mabel Cheung 張婉婷, Ann Hui 許鞍華, Clara Law 羅卓瑤, Stanley Kwan 關錦鵬, *Wong Kar-Wai 王家衛 (b. 1958), and Tsui Hark 徐克, along with other stars of the same cohort, to some extent made her one of the more recognizable faces of Hong Kong cinema of the period.

Early Beginnings

In the *Police Story* series, which starred and was directed by Jackie Chan, who was already a superstar within the Hong Kong film industry, Cheung was cast as May, the slightly helpless and equally hapless girlfriend whose accidental stumblings onto the crime scenes provided convenient plot devices and much of the films' screwball humor. Cheung reprised this role twice after the first film, *Police Story* 警察故事 (1985), appearing in *Police Story 2* 警察故事續集 (1988) and *Police Story 3: Supercop* 警察故事 3: 超級警察 (1992). The last film in particular saw her role relegated even further to an inept comedy sidekick, as second billing in the film was given to female action star Michelle Yeoh 楊紫瓊,

who in the fight sequences seemed to match Jackie Chan blow for blow.

By 1992, however, Cheung already had a number of lead dramatic roles under her belt. She was cast in Hong Kong auteur Wong Kar-wai's first feature, *As Tears Go By* 旺角卡門 (1988), as well as his second, *Days of Being Wild* 阿飛正傳 (1990), alongside other Hong Kong stars Andy Lau 劉德華 and Leslie Cheung 張國榮. In 1990 she also appeared in three other key films: Stanley Kwan's *Full Moon in New York* 人在紐約 (1990), about three Chinese women working in America; Ann Hui's *Song of the Exile* 客途秋恨 (1990), about a young Chinese woman who learns about her Japanese mother's past; and Clara Law's *Farewell, China* 愛在別鄉的季節 (1990), about a couple from China struggling with the trauma of migration to America. The rapid rate of production was the norm for Hong Kong cinema of the period (Bordwell 2000). Additionally, it was not unusual for stars to be involved in a number of projects concurrently. What is significant about Cheung's contributions is that among the plethora of films made, many of which have been forgotten, these films are today considered some of the more central works in the canon of Hong Kong cinema during this period.

Career Peaks

The 1990s saw Maggie Cheung's stardom expand internationally, particularly

Selected Filmography of Maggie Cheung				
Year	English Title	Chinese Title	Director	Notes
1985	*Police Story*	警察故事 *Jǐngchá gùshì*	Jackie Chan	Role: May
1988	*Police Story 2*	警察故事續集 *Jǐngchá gùshì xùjí*	Jackie Chan	Role: May
1988	*As Tears Go By*	旺角卡門 *Wàngjiǎo kǎmén*	Wong Kar-wai	Role: Ngor
1990	*Days of Being Wild*	阿飛正傳 *Āfēi zhèngzhuàn*	Wong Kar-wai	Role: Su Li-zhen
1990	*Full Moon in New York*	人在紐約 *Rén zài Niǔyuē*	Stanley Kwan	Role: Lee Fung-Jiau
1990	*Song of the Exile*	客途秋恨 *Kètú qiū hèn*	Ann Hui	Role: Cheung Hueyin
1990	*Farewell, China*	愛在別鄉的季節 *Ài zài biéxiāng de jìjié*	Clara Law	Role: Li Hung
1992	*Police Story 3: Supercop*	警察故事 3: 超級警察 *Jǐngchá gùshì 3: Chāojí jǐngchá*	Stanley Tong	Role: May
1992	*Center Stage/ Actress*	阮玲玉 *Ruǎn Língyù*	Stanley Kwan	Roles: Ruan Ling-yu and herself
1992	*New Dragon Gate Inn*	新龍門客棧 *Xīn lóngmén kèzhàn*	Tsui Hark, Ching Siu-tung, Raymond Lee	Role: Gam Sun-Yeuk
1993	*Green Snake*	青蛇 *Qīng shé*	Tsui Hark	Role: Siu Ching

張曼玉

Year	English Title	Chinese Title	Director	Notes
1994	*Ashes of Time*	東邪西毒 *Dōng xié xī dú*	Wong Kar-wai	Role: The Woman
1996	*Comrades, Almost a Love Story*	甜蜜蜜 *Tián mìmì*	Peter Chan	Role: Qiao Li
1996	*Irma Vep*		Olivier Assayas	Role: Maggie
1997	*The Soong Sisters*	宋家皇朝 *Sòngjiā huángcháo*	Mabel Cheung	Role: Soong Ching Ling
1997	*Chinese Box*		Wayne Wang	Role: Jean
1999	*Augustin, Roi du Kung Fu*		Anne Fontaine	Role: Ling
2000	*In the Mood for Love*	花樣年華 *Huā yàng nián huà*	Wong Kar-wai	Role: Su Li-zhen
2002	*Hero*	英雄 *Yīngxióng*	Zhang Yimou	Role: Flying Snow
2004	*Clean*		Olivier Assayas	Role: Emily Wang
2004	*2046*	*2046*	Wong Kar-wai	Role: Su Li-Zhen

with her portrayal of the silent film star Ruǎn Língyù 阮玲玉 (1910–1935) in Stanley Kwan's *Center Stage / Actress* 阮玲玉 (1992). Shot as a film within a film and rather than presenting Ruan's life as a conventional biopic, *Center Stage* intersperses footage from her classic and most well-known films, *The Goddess* (*Shénnǚ* 神女, 1934) and *New Women* (*Xīn Nǚxìng* 新女性, 1935), with reconstructed scenes from her films with Cheung acting as Ruan within them. These sequences are then further intercut with meta-filmic scenes of the present, where members of the production—Stanley Kwan, Cheung, and co-star Carina Lau 劉嘉玲—appear as themselves. *Center Stage* won a string of Hong Kong Film Awards, including Best Actress for Cheung. It was her Silver Bear for Best Actress at the Berlin International Film Festival, however, that brought the actress international attention. She also won a Best Actress award at the Chicago

International Film Festival. *Center Stage* is perhaps the first film where Cheung literally holds center stage, and it is her performance—one that slides fluently between Cantonese, Mandarin, and Shanghainese—that holds together what is essentially a film with a modernist structure and multiple realities.

No longer confined to supportive girlfriend/daughter roles, Cheung followed up *Center Stage* with a series of varied performances, including as the vivacious innkeeper in Tsui Hark's *New Dragon Gate Inn* 新龍門客棧 (1992) and as the seductive snake spirit in *Green Snake* 青蛇 (1993), also by Tsui Hark. She also appeared in Wong Kar-wai's *Ashes of Time* 東邪西毒 (1994) alongside many of the biggest stars in Hong Kong. This film was not widely seen in Hong Kong at the time (Chan 2012). It certainly made the art house and festival circuits, however, and foreshadowed Cheung's later, more memorable appearance in Wong's biggest international hit, *In the Mood for Love* 花樣午華 (2000).

Although *Center Stage* was a critical success, the decade's best commercial triumph went to Peter Chan's sentimental *Comrades, Almost a Love Story* 甜蜜蜜 (1996), in which Cheung played one-half of a couple who had to endure separation across time (ten years) and space (from Hong Kong to America) before eventually reuniting. The film swept nearly all of the major prizes at the Hong Kong Film Awards. Cheung was by this time a household name in Hong Kong

and also in countries within East and Southeast Asia where Hong Kong films are popular.

By 1997, handover anxiety and anticipation came to a head in Hong Kong, and Hong Kong cinema produced, among other films, the lavish *The Soong Sisters* 宋家皇朝 (1997) by Mabel Cheung. This historical epic covered the tumultuous events leading to the Civil War (1946–1949) and the eventual founding of modern China and Taiwan. Maggie Cheung once again won Best Actress at the Hong Kong Film Awards, this time for her role as Soong Ching Ling, the historical figure who married Sun Yat-sen, the first president and founding father of the Republic of China.

Transnational Stardom

By the late 1990s, Cheung was not taking on as many projects as she had in earlier years. Handover anxiety notwithstanding, the Hong Kong film industry was experiencing a period of crisis and production fell drastically. A number of reasons have been offered for this development, including the Asian currency crisis, changing audience demographics, video piracy, and increased competition from Hollywood. During this period Cheung began to take on projects outside of Hong Kong, which extended her range and showcased her fluency in English and French.

Cheung's closest brush with Hollywood came in the form of a film set around the time of the handover called

Chinese Box (1997), which also starred Jeremy Irons and *Gǒng Lì 巩俐 (b. 1965) and was directed by Asian American filmmaker Wayne Wang, who was born and raised in Hong Kong. In the film, Cheung plays Jean, a "typical" Hong Kong woman who seems to simply live for the moment and for her own self-interest.

More intriguing roles emerged from projects in France, beginning with one in which French director Olivier Assayas (who was married to Cheung from 1998 to 2001) made the unusual decision to cast Cheung in the titular role of *Irma Vep* (1996), a remake of a classic silent serial, *Les Vampires* (1915–1916). The unusual pairing of a Hong Kong actress in a French role generated much critical attention in film scholarship in English. In contrast, Cheung's role in the French comedy *Augustin, Roi du Kung Fu* (1999) by Anne Fontaine, in which Cheung plays the local acupuncturist whom the protagonist falls for, is a little-known addition to her oeuvre.

Cheung's final feature before semi-retiring from films was *Clean* (2004), which was directed by her then ex-husband, Olivier Assayas. She plays a musician and a junkie who struggles with her addictions in order to be with her young son. In the film, which is set in Paris, France, and Vancouver, Canada, Cheung switches between speaking English and French (and a smattering of Cantonese) with ease in a naturalistic role that won her the Best Actress award at the Cannes Film Festival, making her the first Asian actress to receive this honor. By the end of *Clean*, Cheung's character embarks on a renewed career as a rock musician, a move that the actress herself, a screen veteran of over eighty films, appears to be mirroring: She held her debut concert at the Strawberry Music Festival in Beijing in May 2014.

Felicia CHAN
The University of Manchester

Further Reading

An, Grace. (2000). Par-Asian screen women and film identities: The vampiric in Olivier Assayas's *Irma Vep. Sites: The Journal of Twentieth-Century/Contemporary French Studies revue d'études français*, 4(2), 399–416.

Bordwell, David. (2000). *Planet Hong Kong: Popular cinema and the art of entertainment.* Cambridge, MA: Harvard University Press.

Chan, Felicia. (2012). From world cinema to world cinema: Wong Kar-wai's *Ashes of Time* and *Ashes of Time Redux*. In Rajinder Dudrah, Lucia Nagib, & Chris Perriam (Eds.), *Theorizing world cinema* (pp. 93–110) London, UK: IB Tauris.

Chan, Felicia. (2014). Maggie Cheung, "une Chinoise": Acting and agency in the realm of transnational stardom. In Leung Wing-Fai & Andy Willis (Eds.), *East Asian film stars* (pp. 83–95). Basingstoke, UK: Palgrave Macmillan.

Conley, Tom. (2000). Revamping Irma: Immodest reflection on French cinema and globalization. *Sites: The Journal of Twentieth-Century/Contemporary French Studies revue d'études français*, 4(2), 417–433.

Cui, Shuqin. (2000). Stanley Kwan's *Center Stage*: The (im)possible engagement between feminism and postmodernism. *Cinema Journal, 39*(4), 60–80.

Hudson, Dale. (2006). Just play yourself, Maggie Cheung: *Irma Vep*, rethinking transnational stardom and unthinking national cinemas. *Screen, 47*(2), 213–232.

Khoo, Olivia. (1999). "Anagrammatical translations": Latex performance and Asian femininity unbounded in Olivier Assayas's *Irma Vep. Continuum: Journal of Media & Cultural Studies, 13*(3), 383–393.

Pak Tong Cheuk. (2008). *Hong Kong New Wave Cinema (1978–2000)*. Bristol, UK: Intellect.

Stringer, Julian. (1997). *Centre Stage*: Reconstructing the Bio-Pic. *CineAction, 42*.

Teo, Stephen. (1997). *Hong Kong cinema: The extra dimensions*. London: British Film Institute.

Wang, Yiman. (2007). Screening Asia: Passing, performative translation, and reconfiguration. *Positions: East Asia Cultures Critique, 15*(2), 319–343.

Williams, Tony. (2003). Transnational stardom: The case of Maggie Cheung Man-yuk. *Asian Cinema, 14*(2), 180–196.

Yue, Audrey. (2010). *Ann Hui's* Song of the Exile. Hong Kong: Hong Kong University Press.

• 張曼玉 •

♂ Chow Yun-fat

Zhōu Rùnfā 周潤發

b. 1955—Hong Kong TV and film actor

Alternate name: simpl. 周润发

Summary

Chow Yun-fat, a TV and film actor, is one of Hong Kong's most successful stars. After a short stint in Hollywood, in which he struggled to overcome typecasting but nonetheless earned a leading romantic role in the block-buster *Anna and the King*, Chow returned to Chinese-language cinema in the mid-2000s.

Since landing his first acting role in the 1970s, Chow Yun-fat has become one of Hong Kong's most successful stars. For over three decades he has developed an acting career across various cultural industries, geographical borders, and media platforms. Many of his screen works have been both commercial and critical successes.

In 1995, Chow moved to Hollywood. His Hollywood career was not very successful, however, due to language, racial, and cultural barriers. Since 1995 Chow has starred in only a small number of Hollywood-produced films, many of which are B movies. Nevertheless, Chow's experiences of working in different film industries, particularly in Hollywood, are highly valued by the increasingly transnational Chinese-language cinema, which is seeking ways to enter the global commercial film market, including casting stars with international fame.

Beginning in the mid-2000s, Chow gradually moved his career back to China. While early in his career he mostly played rebellious Hong Kong youths, in recent years Chow has been cast more often in the role of a patriarch who reconciles and defends the authority power. To a large extent, the trajectory of Chow's screen roles illustrates the shift of Hong Kong screen culture since the 1970s, as well as the complex relationship between Hong Kong, the previous colonial city, and mainland China before and after the city's return to the People's Republic of China (PRC) in 1997.

Early TV Career

Born on 18 May 1955 in Hong Kong, Chow is the youngest son of a working-class family. To help out his family financially, a teenage Chow quit school to work a number of odd jobs, including shop assistant, hotel bellboy, and postman. In 1973 he applied to study acting in a drama class organized by Television Broadcasts Limited (TVB), the first commercial television station in Hong Kong. One year later he became a TVB-contracted actor. During the first few years of his TV acting career, Chow was assigned many undemanding minor roles, such as Jiang Yuhan in *Dream of the Red Chamber* 紅樓夢 (1975) and some nameless characters in *Chinese Folklore* 民間傳奇 (1974–1975).

In 1976 Chow got his first leading role as Shao Huashan in *Hotel* 狂潮 (created by Wong Tin Lam and Selina Chow), TVB's first long-running drama miniseries set in modern times (Zhong 2004, 253). Through this role, Chow began to attract public attention. Tall, handsome, and lean, Chow

Selected Filmography of Chow Yun-fat				
Year	English Title	Chinese Title	Director	Notes
1975	*Dream of the Red Chamber*	红楼梦 *Hónglóu mèng*		Role: Jian Yuhan
1976	*Hotel*	狂潮 *Kuáng cháo*	Wong Tin Lam, Selina Chow (creators)	TV Show
1979	*Man in the Net*	网中人 *Wǎngzhōng rén*	Ng Yun Chen, et al.	TV Show
1980	*The Bund*	上海滩 *Shànghǎi Tān*	Chiu Chun-keung, et al.	TV Show
1980	*Family Feeling*	亲情 *Qīnqíng*	Li Tiansheng	TV Show
1981	*The Fate*	火凤凰 *Huǒ fènghuáng*	Li Tiansheng	TV Show; Role: Ngai Chun
1981	*Good Old Times*	鳄鱼潭 *Èyú tán*	Ma Yuhui	TV Show; Role: Ouyang
1981	*The Story of Woo Veit*	胡越的故事 *Húyuè de gùshì*	Ann Hui	
1982	*The Lone Ranger* (*The Mavericks*)	孤城客 *Gū chéng kè*	Yu Kairong	TV Show
1984	*The Smiling Proud Wanderer*	笑傲江湖 *Xiào ào jiāng hú*	Producer: Lee Ding-lun	TV Show

Year	English Title	Chinese Title	Director	Notes
1984	*Hong Kong 1941*	等待黎明 *Dèngdài límíng*	Po-Chih Leong	Role: Yip Kim Fay
1986	*A Better Tomorrow*	英雄本色 *Yīngxióng běn sè*	John Woo	Role: Mark
1987	*An Autumn's Tale*	秋天的童话 *Qiū tiān dí tóng huà*	Mabel Cheung	Role: Samuel Tang
1987	*All About Ah Long*	阿郎的故事 *Āláng de gùshì*	Johnnie To	Role: Ah Long
1987	*City on Fire*	龙虎风云 *Lóng hǔ fēng yún*	Ringo Lam	Role: Ko Chow
1988	*The Eighth Happiness*	八星报喜 *Bā xíng bào xǐ*	Johnnie To	Role: "Handsome" Long
1988	*The Greatest Lover*	公子多情 *Gōngzǐ duō qíng*	Clarence Yiu-leung Fok	Role: Qian Jin
1989	*God of Gamblers*	赌神 *Dǔshén*	Wong Jing	Role: Ko Chun
1989	*The Killer*	喋血双雄 *Diéxuè shuāngxióng*	John Woo	Role: Ah Long
1991	*Once a Thief*	纵横四海 *Zòng héng sì hài*	John Woo	Role: Red Bean Pudding (Joe)
1998	*The Replacement Killers*		Antoine Fuqua	Role: John Lee
1999	*The Corruptor*		James Foley	Role: Nick Chen
1999	*Anna and the King*		Andy Tennant	Role: King Mongkut
2000	*Crouching Tiger, Hidden Dragon*	卧虎藏龙 *Wòhǔ cánglóng*	Ang Lee	
2006	*Curse of the Golden Flower*	满城尽带黄金甲 *Mǎnchéng jìndài huángjīnjiǎ*	Zhang Yimou	Role: Emperor Ping
2010	*Confucius*	孔子 *Kǒngzǐ*	Hu Mei	Role: Confucius
2012	*The Assassins*	銅雀臺 *Tóng què tái*	Zhao Linshan	Role: Cao Cao
2014	*The Monkey King*	大闹天宫 *Dà nào tiāngōng*	Cheang Pou-soi	Role: Jade Emperor

showed the TV studio his star quality as a leading man and became a household name in Hong Kong with his performance in *Man in the Net* 網中人 (also known as *The Good, the Bad, and the Ugly*) in 1979. His performance in 1980's drama *The Bund* 上海灘 was well-received even beyond Hong Kong's borders, which not only solidified Chow's TV stardom in the city, but also made him one of the best-known Hong Kong stars in mainland China.

Chow's star image was rather distinctive on Hong Kong's TV screen during the late 1970s and early 1980s. Unlike many other leading stars of the time, such as Adam Cheng 鄭少秋, Damian Lau 劉松仁, and Lawrence Ng 伍衛國, Chow rarely starred in a TV drama set in ancient China, except for *The Lone Ranger* 孤城客 (1982) and *The Smiling Proud Wanderer* 笑傲江湖 (1984). Many local audiences and critics regarded Chow's image as too modern to play a premodern character (Feng 2010, 198). The Hong Kong public's rejection of Chow's star image as an ancient Chinese man was at least partially because of the city's awakening sense of self-identification. During the early period of TV in Hong Kong, historical dramas and martial arts serials were the two dominant genres. Rapid economic growth in Hong Kong, however, caused local audiences to call for a new icon who could represent their modern urban identity.

Chow quickly built up a star image as a modern urban young man. Soon after the releases of *Hotel* and *Man in the Net*, TVB cast Chow in a number of serials set against a similar backdrop of contemporary Hong Kong, including *Family Feeling* 親情 (1980) and *The Fate* 火鳳凰 (1981). Even in dramas set in the 1930s and 1940s, Chow's characters, such as his Hui Man Keung in *The Bund* and Ouyang Han in *Good Old Times* 鱷魚潭 (1981), were more Westernized and adapted to city life than many other characters. Often set in contemporary spaces with which Hong Kong audiences would have been familiar, these TVB dramas not only injected an urban and Westernized image into Chow's star personae, but they also highlighted Chow's star image as a modern Hong Kong citizen.

Hong Kong Film Career

Meanwhile, Hong Kong cinema was experiencing a period of modernization. A new generation of filmmakers, such as Hark Tsui 徐克, Ann Hui 許鞍華, and Patrick Tam 谭嘉明, had come of age in the late 1970s and were sensitive to the local community and social changes that occurred while the city transitioned from a regional manufacturing city to a global financial center (Sek 1999). The regeneration of Hong Kong cinema saw the industry boom in the 1980s. It was around this time that Chow started to develop his career in the film industry.

His early attempts, however, did not meet with much success. Chow failed to find any significant cinematic stardom, despite the fact that his performances in

The Story of Woo Viet 胡越的故事 (1981) and *Hong Kong 1941* 等待黎明 (1984) were critically well-received, with the latter winning Chow his first film acting award at the Asia-Pacific Film Festival. It was not until 1986 that his performance of Mark Gor in *John Woo's 吳宇森 *A Better Tomorrow* 英雄本色 became an overnight sensation in Hong Kong, both commercially and critically. During this period of his Hong Kong career, Chow starred in more than seventy films across a wide range of genres, including melodramas, action films, comedies, thrillers, and westerns, and created many iconic screen characters, such as Boat-head in *An Autumn's Tale* 秋天的童話 (1987), Ah Long in *All About Ah Long* 阿郎的故事 (1987), and Ko Chun in *God of Gamblers* 賭神 (1989).

As was the case with his TV career, many of Chow's well-received film roles were as Hong Kong local citizens who demonstrated a strong emotional attachment to the city and local society. For instance, in many of Chow's best-known action films, such as *A Better Tomorrow*, *City on Fire* 龍虎風雲 (1987), and *The Killer* 喋血雙雄 (1989), his action heroes often embody a man's sense of *yì* 義, or righteousness, justice, altruism, and horizontal loyalty between brothers and friends. Unlike many other action stars' films, such as those of *Jackie Chan 陳港生 (b. 1954) and *Jet Li 李連杰 (b. 1963), in

which good and evil are clearly defined and order is always reestablished at the end, Chow's action films frequently positioned the star's character between culturally defined moral standards and statutory obligations in urban Hong Kong. As such, many of Chow's action films point to the hybrid nature of Hong Kong's urban culture and the instability of Hong Kong citizens' position within modern society, demonstrating Hong Kong cinema's imagination of the local anxiety to the social crisis associated with the city's return to the PRC in 1997. Compared to macho action heroes around the world during of the same time, such as Sylvester Stallone, Arnold Schwarzenegger, and Jean-Claude Van Damme, Chow inserted a touch of sentiment into his star image as a suffering action hero. Successfully delivering multiple layers of emotions, Chow demonstrated his acting ability by incorporating seemingly contradictory characteristics into a complex masculinity.

To many Hong Kong local citizens, however, Chow's popularity extends far beyond action cinema. Chow's comedies, such as *The Eighth Happiness* 八星報喜 (1988), *The Greatest Lover* 公子多情 (1988), and *Once a Thief* 縱橫四海 (1991), also mirror the social mentality during the late 1980s and early 1990s. In these comedies, Chow's characters are frequently shown traveling around the world, accessing or owning items that are symbolically related to foreign culture. Although the Chinese associations

---

*People marked with an asterisk have entries in this dictionary.

have never been completely removed from Chow's star image, the media focus on the construction of Chow's star image centered around the influences of global contact and modernization, which again conveyed Hong Kong cinema's intention of distinguishing the city from the traditional Chinese agricultural culture. Chow's portrayal of man's dilemma in modern society was well-received not only in Hong Kong but it also caught Hollywood's attention.

Career beyond Hong Kong

In the 1980s Hong Kong became one of the most important cities for film production in Asia. After more than a decade of prosperity, however, Hong Kong cinema went into a long period of recession. Mo Jianwei (n.d.) notes that the local film industry's annual production dropped by nearly 40 percent, from 242 films in 1993 to 150 in 2000. The decline of the Hong Kong cinema saw a number of local stars and filmmakers migrating overseas. Following his friends and long-time collaborators John Woo, Ringo Lam 林嶺東, and Terence Cheung 張家振, who moved to America in the early 1990s, Chow announced his decision to continue his career in Hollywood in 1995. As was the case with many other Chinese stars who developed their careers in Hollywood during the same period, Chow was introduced as an action star by Hollywood studios to the global commercial film market. Chow's

first two Hollywood roles, however—John Lee in *Replacement Killers* (1998) and Nick Chen in *The Corruptor* (1999)—are criticized by many film scholars, such as Gina Marchetti (2001, 37) and Kwai-Cheung Lo (2004, 69), as a confirmation of Hollywood's perceived stereotypes of Asians. Chow's capacity as a refined dramatic actor was severely restricted because of the Hollywood studios' type-casting and his English-language barrier (Fore 2004, 97). Although Chow's third American film, *Anna and the King* (1999), made him the first male Chinese actor to play the leading role in a major Hollywood romantic epic, it remains to this day the only Hollywood-produced blockbuster to cast a male East Asian actor as a romantic lead.

In the meantime, the number of films being produced in Hong Kong continued to decline (Zhong 2004, 2). At the same time, the commercial cinema in mainland China was expanding at an unprecedented rate. The fast growth of the Chinese film market and the development of transnational Chinese cinema demanded a large number of film talents. Subsequently, many Hong Kong stars and filmmakers, whether they remained in or left Hong Kong in the 1990s, started to work in mainland China beginning in the early 2000s. It is under this context that Chow returned to Chinese-language cinema. In contrast to the construction of Chow's early star image, in which the influences of global contact, Western culture, and modernization on

Hong Kong citizens' social mentality and lifestyle are emphasized, the media focus on Chow's star image is gradually shifting to that of Chineseness and traditional values of Chinese culture.

Since 2000 Chow increasingly has been cast in films set in historical China, including *Crouching Tiger, Hidden Dragon* 臥虎藏龍 (2000), *Curse of the Golden Flower* 滿城盡帶黃金甲 (2006), *Confucius* 孔子 (2010), *The Assassins* 銅雀臺 (2012), and *The Monkey King* 大鬧天宮 (2014). In these films Chow often plays a father figure who upholds the Confucian code *xiào* 孝, which promotes filial piety, respect, subordination, and vertical loyalty from youngsters to their parents, ancestors, and other senior members. Highly valued in the Confucian doctrine, the notion of *xiao* not only endows senior members with prestige and power but also plays a significant role in maintaining the stability and the continuity of the father's authority in a Chinese patriarchal society.

The refocused cinematic construction of Chow's star image to some degree shows China's intention of promoting the country as a peaceful, rising global superpower. As the political scientist Zheng Yongnian points out, one of the primary concerns of the Chinese central government today is to preserve unity and stability in China and to reinforce the one-party policy as the country experiences fast economic growth (Zheng 2010, 43). Confucianism served the ruling society well for thousands of years in Chinese history, and the Chinese government has started to reimbibe and repromote Confucianism in recent years. Defending authority and institutional power, Chow's recent roles on the Chinese big screen seem to have a particular and timely conformance with Chinese commercial cinema's embracing of the government's promotion of the ideas of social stability, unity, harmony, and loyalty to the ruling party.

Lin FENG
University of Hull

Further Reading

Feng, Lin. (2010). Chow Yun-fat: Hong Kong's modern TV *Xiaosheng*. In Mary Farquhar & Yingjin Zhang (Eds.), *Chinese film stars* (pp. 196–206). London: Routledge.

Feng, Lin. (2014). Translocal imagination of Hong Kong connections: The shifting of Chow Yun-fat's star image since 1997. In Leung Wing-fai & Andy Willis (Eds.), *East Asian film stars* (pp. 113–127). London: Palgrave MacMillan.

Fore, Steve. (2004). Home, migration, identity: Hong Kong film workers join the Chinese diaspora. In Esther M. K. Cheung & Chu Yiu-wai (Eds.), *Between home and world: A reader in Hong Kong cinema*. Oxford, UK: Oxford University Press.

Lo, Kwai-Cheung. (2004). Double negations: Hong Kong cultural identity in Hollywood's transnational representations. In Esther M. K. Cheung & Yiu-wai Chu (Eds.), *Between home and world: A reader in Hong Kong cinema*. Oxford, UK: Oxford University Press.

Marchetti, Gina. (2001). Hollywood's construction, deconstruction, and reconstruction of the "Orient." In Roger Garcia (Ed.), *Out of the shadows: Asians in American cinema*. Milan: Edizioni Olivares.

Mo Jianwei. (n.d.). *Xianggang dianying gongye yu dianying zhengce* 香港电影工业与电影政策 [Hong Kong film industry and film policy]. *Media Digest*. Retrieved October 24, 2014, from http://www.rthk.org.hk/mediadigest/20021216_76_55191.html

Sek, Kei. (1999). Achievement and crisis: Hong Kong cinema in the '80s. In Hong Kong Urban Council (Eds.), *The 15th Hong Kong International Film Festival: Hong Kong cinema in the eighties: A comparative study with Western cinema* (Rev. ed., pp. 54–55). Hong Kong: Hong Kong Urban Council Publication.

Stringer, Julian. (2003). Scrambling Hollywood: Asian stars/Asian American star cultures. In Tomas Austin & Martin Barker (Eds.), *Contemporary Hollywood stardom* (pp. 229–242). London: Hodder Arnold.

Zheng Yongnian. (2010). *The Chinese Communist Party as organizational emperor: Culture, reproduction and transformation*. London: Routledge.

Zhong Baoxian. (2004). *Xianggang dianshiye bai nian* 香港影视业百年 [Hundred years of Hong Kong film and television industry]. Hong Kong: Joint Publishing Co. Ltd.

• 周潤發 •

☿ Cuī Jiàn 崔健

b. 1961—One of China's first and most famous rock musicians

Summary

Cui Jian is China's most famous and influential rock musician. He rose to fame after releasing the country's first rock album in 1989 and was China's first rock musician to perform abroad. His music and lyrics had a strong impact on youths of his generation, but over the course of his career he met with occasional censorship of his material. Cui remains committed to rock music but also has successfully pursued other artistic endeavors, including film.

Cui Jian's career as a rock musician began in Beijing's underground during the reform period of the 1980s. By the end of the decade, he had achieved nationwide fame with his album *Rock 'n' Roll on the New Long March*, which combined previously unknown sounds and rhythms in China with a new message of individualism and authenticity. Beginning in the early 1990s, he was joined by an increasing number of rock bands. He also began to see the availability of alternative music styles, changing audience preferences, a new commercial pop culture, and exclusion from the state-owned media. Cui, however, was open to experimenting with new musical trends and continued his "Long March" to establish rock music as a serious and meaningful form of music culture in China. Around 2000, Cui also began to engage in other musical and cultural activities. Today he is a respected artist in and outside of China, although he is less popular among the younger generation than he once was, and he continues to raise his critical voice in a highly commercialized and censored cultural sphere.

Laying the Foundation for Rock Music

Cui was born into an ethnically Korean and musically supportive family: his father was a trumpet player and his mother worked at the Central Song and Dance Troupe. He grew up in Beijing and at age fourteen, close to the end of the Cultural

Revolution (1966–1976), began learning to play the trumpet. Later he was employed by the prestigious Beijing Symphony Orchestra (1981–1987), while at the same time being introduced to new foreign sounds and music forms that had entered China from the beginning of the reform period in 1978. In 1984, Cui formed the band Seven-Ply Board 七合板 with six other classical musicians and began performing in hotels and small restaurants in Beijing. The band released a (tape) recording of Western songs (*Qīge bǎn yǎnchàng zhuānjí* 七合板演唱专辑) in 1985, the same year the American pop duo Wham! shook an audience of fifteen thousand at Beijing's Workers' Stadium.

Meanwhile, Cui had already recorded an album of Chinese pop ballads, *Vagabond's Return* 浪子归 (1984), which reflected the growing influence of popular music from Hong Kong and Taiwan. Cui did not write the lyrics for this album. His first original composition was the song "It's Not That I Don't Understand" 不是我不明白 (1985), in which he reflects upon the rapid changes of Chinese society in a synthesis of rock and funk, inspired by music from the Beatles, the Rolling Stones, the Talking Heads, and the Police. Cui rose to fame with his song "Nothing to My Name" 一无所有, which debuted on 9 May 1986 when he performed it at a state-organized and nationally broadcasted concert in Workers' Stadium commemorating the Year of World Peace.

By 1987, pirated copies of his song were circulating in China, and Cui became a victim of the "Campaign against Bourgeois Liberalization," due to the official critique of some of his lyrics and unconventional stage manners. He left the Beijing Song and Dance Ensemble and began working with the young Sino-foreign band ADO. In 1988, Cui and ADO were invited to play a concert in Seoul and together recorded China's first rock album, *Rock 'n' Roll on the New Long March* 新长征路上的摇滚. The album, finally released in February 1989, reflected Western rock influences, elements of funk, and a significant proportion of Chinese sounds such as the zither (*gǔzhēng* 古筝) and the Chinese oboe (*suǒnà* 唢呐); its official release concert was held in March 1989. Audiences were struck not only by the new sounds, but also by Cui's rough voice, individualistic performance style, and sincere lyrics, which expressed the sentiments, emotions, and experience of his generation. In March and April, Cui participated in London's first Asian Popular Music Awards and joined a music festival in Paris. Meanwhile, the album appeared with the title *Nothing to My Name* on the overseas markets in Hong Kong and Taiwan. Soon thereafter, the song "Nothing to My Name" became one of the unofficial anthems of the Tiananmen demonstrations.

In 1990, in support of the Asian Games to be held in Beijing, Cui was permitted to go on a nationwide tour.

The tour, however, was cancelled after the fourth concert because official sponsors were concerned that audiences were getting worked up by what the music represented: individualism, freedom, and desire for alternatives to the party line, for example. Meanwhile, Cui released his second album, *Solution* 解决 (EMI Hong Kong, 1990). Musically it was more powerful, reflecting influences of The Clash, and contained songs with ambiguous lyrics, such as those in "Like a Knife" 象一把刀子, "The Last Shot" 最后一枪, "A Piece of Red Cloth" 一块红布, "Let Me Run Wild on the Snow" 快让我在雪地上撒点儿野, and a reinterpretation of the revolutionary classic "Nanniwan" 南泥湾 (1943), a song Cui had been performing since the late 1980s that had gotten him in trouble early in his rock career. In 1993, Cui and his band were also featured in one of China's first independent films, *Beijing Bastards* 北京杂种. The film was directed by Zhāng Yuán 张元, who had also directed the award-winning music video for "Let Me Run Wild on the Snow" (1992). Cui was deeply involved in the film as producer, funder, star, and film-score writer.

For Cui and the "first generation" of rock musicians in China, rock music was a new means of self-expression they had to fight for; this was emphasized by invoking the revolutionary spirit of the historic and heroic Long March (1934–1935) of the Chinese Communist Party. The often-discussed "rock spirit" (*yáogǔn jīngshén* 摇滚精神) combined seriousness, individualism, creativity, and authenticity with a certain attitude and lifestyle, and it clearly challenged the state-controlled sphere of popular culture. In the words of Cui, "Western rock is like a wave, and Chinese rock is like a knife." Consequently, Chinese rock does not immediately overwhelm large numbers of people; rather, it is felt more like a deep stitch or sting that can't be removed and that increases its impact over time.

The 1990s saw the rise of China's rock community, with Beijing as the center. Enthusiastic about the fame of Cui and Beijing's growing underground scene, record companies from Hong Kong and Taiwan tried to capitalize on the new genre. Cui, seen as representing this musical genre in China, was also invited to several concert tours and festivals abroad in Japan (1992, 1994, 1995), Germany (1993), Switzerland (1993), the United States (1994, 1995, 1999), Denmark (1996), and Malaysia (1998).

Changing Styles

In China, however, the overall spirit among youths had changed. They had become disillusioned with politics and were more consumer- and career-oriented. New forms of popular music were en vogue, and rock music remained largely an underground phenomenon, even though early rock bands like Black Panther, Tang Dynasty, Cobra, and others were playing shows at filled stadiums. Caught in an atmosphere between new

• Cuī Jiàn •

market reforms and a Patriotic Education Campaign, Cui had trouble booking concerts but was able to release his third album, *Balls Under the Red Flag* 红旗下的蛋 (EMI Hong Kong, 1994). With its synthesis of rock, funk, jazz, and Chinese musical sounds, the album was more complex than his previous two, while the lyrics continued to reflect on China's society and its changes.

Inspired by his first visit to the United States and bands such as Public Enemy, Cui began to experiment more with hip hop and rap sounds as well as electronic music. The results were presented in the single "Get over That Day" 超越那一天 (1997) and on his fourth album, *The Power of the Powerless* 无能的力量 (1998), which was marketed by the musician's own Beijing East-West Manufacturing Corporation. When Cui went on his second tour to the United States in 1999, he celebrated the tenth anniversary of his first rock album and (an unusual) second release in China.

Beyond Rock Music: Free Style

In 2000, probably due to China's ongoing negotiations regarding the World Trade Organization (WTO), things began to change for Cui. Hunan-TV broadcasted a special performance of his—the first in ten years. Cui also appeared live on television and on a large stage in Beijing for the first time in seven years when he performed one song at the Anti-Piracy Concert in the famous Workers' Stadium. The Netherlands honored him with the Prince Claus Award for his outstanding contribution to culture and society. In 2000, Cui played twenty-eight shows in China and began to pursue various other artistic endeavors.

He wrote the music for *Devils at the Doorstep* 鬼子来了 (2000), director Jiang Wen's satire on the Second Sino-Japanese War, and collaborated with the Hong Kong Modern Dance Company to produce the experimental dance musical *Show You Colours* 给你一点颜色, which premiered in February 2001. Cui also acted as a village music teacher in the movie *Roots and Branches* 我的兄弟姐妹 (dir. Yú Zhōng 俞钟, 2001) and published a book titled *Free Style* 自由风格, in which he discusses his experience and philosophy of rock music in a dialogue with Zhōu Guópíng 周国平, an essayist and philosopher from the Chinese Academy of Social Sciences.

In 2002, Cui was the main organizer behind one of China's first open-air rock music festivals. China's "highest" (about three thousand meters) and largest open-air festival, The Snow Mountain Music Festival 丽江雪山音乐节, took place in Lijiang, Yunnan Province, with a total of eighteen Chinese bands playing for an audience of about ten thousand. The festival was called "Chinese Woodstock" and was reportedly a success that cleared the way for a new concert culture in China. It also gave Cui the opportunity to launch a movement against playback

崔健

"lip-synched" singing, which was a common practice in China's mass media and TV-festival culture. The Real Sing Movement 真唱运动 was carried out at universities and other venues throughout China.

Political Rehabilitation and New Activism

In 2005, Cui released his fifth album, *Show You Colours* 给你一点颜色. That same year saw the beginnings of Cui's political rehabilitation. The state-owned TV channel CCTV 10 featured him in the program *People* 人物 in a respectful one-and-a-half-hour documentary entitled *Rock 'n' Roll on the New Long March*, (produced by Zhào Shūjìng 赵淑静, 2005), and on 24 September he played a full concert at the Beijing Capital Stadium, his first in Beijing in twelve years. In the following years Cui received several awards and performed regularly in and outside of China, including in then unusual and unlikely places such as Lhasa (2005), Taipei (2007, 2009), and Stanford University, California (2008).

Cui, who had already acted as an opener for Deep Purple (2004), performed with the Rolling Stones in Shanghai in 2006. His portrait also appeared on the front page of the first issue of China's *Rolling Stone* magazine. Two years later he initiated a benefit concert with other rock bands for the victims of the Sichuan earthquake. The natural disaster also served as the backdrop for Cui's first

engagement as a film director, for 2009's *Chengdu, I Love You* 成都我爱你. Also in 2009 Cui celebrated the twentieth anniversary of his first rock album on a China tour called "Rock 'n' Roll on the New Long March," and in 2010 he performed two concerts at the Workers' Stadium in Beijing as part of the "New Year's Concerts of Rock Symphony." Cui and his band shared the stage with the prestigious Beijing Symphony Orchestra, his former work unit, performing a selection of his "revolutionary" repertoire. The concerts provided the material for a 3D concert film and documentary on Cui Jian entitled *Transcendence 3D* 超越那一天 (prod. Bai Qiang, 2012).

In 2014, Cui Jian was honored with a wax replica of himself at Madame Tussaud's Wax Museum in Beijing. He also released his feature film *Blue Sky Bones* 蓝色骨头, a story about history, music, and politics covering the years from the Cultural Revolution to the present; this oeuvre developed over twenty-five years.

Today he still adheres to a rock spirit that seeks to be noncommercial, sincere, and authentic—a spirit that also inspires his films, which are always concerned with music. Critics claim that this spirit belongs to the past, which may explain why he has more freedom to perform than before. It may also explain why he is less popular among China's younger generation, which either does not know him or denotes him as the "Godfather of Chinese Rock and Roll." Cui, however, usually plays sold-out concerts and has a

• Cuī Jiàn •

large fan base, even though he hasn't released an album since 2005.

In addition, he has learned to successfully navigate his interests and projects through a jungle of commercial and political obstacles, and still demonstrates his limits when cooperating with the authorities. In 2014, he was asked to participate in the annually celebrated, nationally broadcasted popular New Year's Spring Festival Gala. After much rumor and long negotiations, he rejected the offer because he was denied permission to perform the song "Nothing to My Name." This decision earned him widespread respect, especially from within China's rock community, and underscores the symbolic value of his songs and the ongoing tensions in China's cultural sphere.

Andreas STEEN
Aarhus University, Denmark

Further Reading

Campbell, Jonathan. (2011). *Red Rock. The long, strange march of Chinese rock & roll.* Hong Kong: Earnshaw Books.

Cui Jian 崔健, & Zhou Guowei 周国平. (2001). *Ziyou fengge* 白由风格 [Free Style]. Guilin, Guangxi: Pedagogical University Publishing House.

Cui Jian. Homepage. Retrieved February 11, 2015, from www.cuijian.com.

De Kloet, Jeroen. (2010). *China with a cut—Globalisation, urban youth and popular music.* Amsterdam: Amsterdam University Press.

Guo Facai 郭发财. (2007). *Jiasuo yu benpa—1980–2005 Zhongguo yaogunyue duli wenhua shengtai guancha* 枷锁与奔跑—1980-2005 中国摇滚乐独立文化生态观察 [Chained and running – Detailed inspection of China's independent culture of rock 'n' roll, 1980–2005]. Wuhan: Hebei People's Publishing House.

Jones, Andrew F. (1992). *Like a knife—Ideology and genre in contemporary Chinese popular music.* New York/Ithaca: Cornell University.

Jones, Andrew F. (1994). The politics of popular music in Post-Tiananmen China. In Jeffrey N. Wasserstrom & Elizabeth J. Perry (Eds.), *Popular protest and political culture in modern China* (2nd ed.) (pp. 148–165). Boulder, Co: Westview Press.

Lu Lingtao 陆凌涛, & Li Yang 李洋. (Eds.). *Nahan weile Zhongguo cengjing de yaogun* 呐喊为了中国曾经的摇滚 [SCREAM for China's rock 'n' roll yesterday]. Guilin, Guangxi: Pedagogical University Publishing House.

Steen, Andreas. (1996). *Der Lange Marsch des Rock 'n' Roll. Pop- und Rockmusik in der Volksrepublik China.* Hamburg, Germany: Lit-Verlag.

Steen, Andreas. (2011). Long live the revolution? The changing spirit of Chinese rock. In Ian Peddie (Ed.), *Popular music and human rights, Volume II: World music* (pp.131–146). Aldershot: Ashgate.

Ying Xiao. (2013). Chinese rock 'n' roll film and Cui Jian on screen. In John Richardson, Claudia Gorbman, & Carol Vernallis (Eds.), *The Oxford handbook of new audiovisual aesthetics* (pp. 266–283). New York: Oxford University Press.

Zhao Jianwei 赵健伟. (1992). *Cui Jian: Zai yiwu suoyou zhong nahan: Zhongguo yaogun beiwanglu* 崔健：在一无所有中呐喊 – 中国摇滚备忘录 [Cui Jian: Shouting while having nothing—Memorandum of Chinese rock]. Beijing: Beijing Normal University Publishing House.

♀ Dài Qíng 戴晴

b. 1941—Environmental journalist, writer, and human rights activist

Alternate names: b. Fù Xiǎoqìng 傅小慶; Fù Níng 傅凝

Summary

Dai Qing, who began her career as a missile engineer and intelligence agent for the Communist Party, is a journalist world-renowned for her activism on behalf of environmental issues in China, especially in regards to the Three Gorges Dam project. Her criticism of government policies has led to imprisonment, surveillance, and censorship of her writings. Garnered with awards and fellowships from overseas, Dai continues to live and work in Beijing on behalf of environmental and human rights issues.

One of the most prominent environmental journalists in contemporary China, Dai Qing is world-renowned for her activism against the Three Gorges Dam project. In 1989, she published *Yangtze! Yangtze!* in China, a collection of essays and documents critical of the dam construction, followed by *The River Dragon has Come!* which was published abroad in 1998. Although she is censored in China and faces harassment and surveillance by the authorities, she continues to live and work in Beijing, where she writes about environmental issues and government accountability.

Early Career

Born on 24 August 1941 in the southwestern city of Chongqing in Sichuan Province, Dai Qing was originally known as Fu Ning but changed her name in 1979 after becoming a short story writer and active journalist. Her parents, father Fù Dàqìng 傅大庆 and her mother Yáng Jié 杨洁, worked in the underground organization of the Chinese Communist Party (CCP) during the War of Resistance against Japan when they were captured in 1944, tortured, and ultimately executed. Adopted by three separate stepfathers including, most prominently, General *Yè Jiànyīng 叶剑英 (1897–1986),

---

*People marked with an asterisk have entries in this dictionary.

a friend of her father and later one of the ten highest-ranking marshals in the People's Liberation Army (PLA), with whose family she lived for years, Dai Qing attended the PLA's Harbin Institute of Military Engineering in the department of guided missile engineering from 1960–1966.

Following her graduation, Dai was assigned to two research institutes under the headquarters of the PLA General Staff, one where she worked on surveillance equipment and another where she helped design gyroscopes for ballistic missiles. Considering herself a loyal Communist after joining the CCP in 1965 and declaring her total "loyalty" (zhōng 忠) to Chairman Mao Zedong and his "thought," she enthusiastically joined a Red Guard organization at the beginning of the Cultural Revolution (1966–1976). Along with her husband, Wáng Déjiā 王德嘉, she was later "sent down" to the countryside in Guangdong and Hunan provinces to perform land reclamation labor.

In 1972, Dai and her husband fled back to Beijing to reunite with their young daughter, Wáng Xiǎojiā 王小嘉, whom they had not seen since the age of one. Still a member of the Army, from 1978 to 1981 she continued to work at the headquarters of the PLA General Staff, where she studied English at its Foreign Language Institute. Her long-held desire was to translate English language children's books, as virtually none were available in Chinese for youngsters like

her daughter (a topic of one of her first short stories, which won her broad national acclaim.) Despite having begun to question her political loyalties to the Communist regime during her exile in the countryside, where she witnessed the brutality of PLA units toward the local population, from 1980–1982 she also worked for the Foreign Affairs Liaison Office of the Chinese Writers' Association and as an agent for the intelligence section of the PLA General Staff, both of which were charged with keeping track of "foreign enemies," especially from the Soviet Union and its Eastern European allies both in China and abroad. With her proficiency in English, Dai was also assigned to spy on visiting American writers and intellectuals, including the famous writer Louis "Studs" Terkel (1912–2008), with whom she later struck up a strong personal relationship.

Making of a Journalist and Activist

After leaving the Army in 1982, Dai joined the *Enlightenment Daily*, China's premier newspaper for intellectuals, and during the next several years of "ideological emancipation" inaugurated by China's then paramount leader *Dèng Xiǎopíng 邓小平 (1904–1997), she wrote a column "Interview with Intellectuals" in which she reported on the opinions and views of some of China's most distinguished and often liberal intellectuals and scientists, including the prominent and often outspoken astrophysicist *Fāng Lìzhī* 方励之 (1936–2010). It was also during this period at *Enlightenment Daily* that Dai became increasingly aware of the growing debate within China over environmental policies, especially those involving the controversial Three Gorges Dam.

Assigned to cover one of the many conferences convened to study construction of the dam, which had been initially proposed in the 1910s by the first president of the Republic of China, Dr. Sun Yat-sen, Dai was ordered not to report on the ongoing reassessment of the project and yet still managed to collect numerous documents, articles, and interviews especially by its major opponents among Chinese hydrologists and engineers. This led, in 1989, to the publication of *Yangtze! Yangtze!* by the Guizhou [Province] People's Publishing House, in which many of these documents were made publicly available for the first time and presented to delegates attending meetings of the Chinese People's Political Consultative Conference and the National People's Congress in March–April 1989. Dai also traveled to Japan to convince officials not to extend loans to finance the project, which the United States Bureau of Reclamation also ultimately refused to support.

After the outbreak of the student demonstrations in April and the subsequent hardline military crackdown in

Environmental Disaster or Engineering Miracle?

Constructions on the Three Gorges Dam, the world's largest engineering feat aiming to provide almost 10 percent of China's electricity requirements, began in 1994. Despite some favorable outcomes, like being the world's biggest source of clean, renewable energy, social and environmental challenges have wreaked havoc on the surrounding area. For example, 1.3 million people living near the Yangzi (Chang) River, where the dam was constructed, were forced to relocate, some sinking into extreme poverty.

The rising waters submerged more than homes. Around 1,600 industrial enterprises in the area retained tons of unmitigated hazardous waste—all of which continued to flow unrestricted into the reservoir. Algal blooms flourish as a result, causing widespread calamities, such as the pollution of domestic water impacting the fifty thousand citizens of Fengdu County in 2008.

Trapped silt behind the static reservoir waters also presents issues. Silt deposits reduce hydropower capacity of tributary dam

• Dài Qǐng •

projects and, though the dam reduces catastrophic downstream flooding, it blocks much of that silt from enriching the lowland soils, as it had done for centuries—pressuring farmers to find new lands to cultivate.

Rising water is not the only change in the landscape: frequent landslides and bank collapses plague the area, killing citizens and forcing survivors to move. On 25 June, 2015, there was a landslide that sent large waves crashing against fishing boats, and sent residents around the Daning River fleeing from their homes.

As a result of the Three Gorges Dam, citizens worldwide are left wondering where the balance is between innovation and destruction, and whether the benefits of the former are worth the repercussions of the latter.

—Eliza J. MITCHELL, *Berkshire Publishing Group*

Sources: Cunha, Stephen F. (2009). Three gorges dam. In Linsun Cheng & Kerry Brown (Eds.), *Berkshire encyclopedia of China* (pp. 2256–2259). Great Barrington, MA: Berkshire Publishing Group.

Kuo, Lily. (2015, June 25). The world's biggest hydropower project may be causing giant landslides in China. *Quartz*. Retrieved June 29, 2015, from http://qz.com/436880/the-worlds-biggest-hydropower-project-may-be-causing-giant-landslides-in-china/

Tiananmen Square on 4 June 1989, Dai Qing, who in protest to the crackdown resigned from the CCP, was soon arrested and imprisoned while her book was banned for having supposedly "contributed to the turmoil" (Dai 2005). Despite attempts by Dai during the demonstrations to convince the protesting students to leave the square and return to their campuses, she was imprisoned for ten months in Beijing's Qincheng Prison and was at one point even threatened with execution.

Greater Recognition and Persecution

Following her release into a prisoner halfway house, Dai returned to her home in Beijing but was prohibited from taking up her former job at *Enlightenment Daily*. Virtually all of her published works were banned, while her residence was placed under constant police surveillance. In 1993, during a visit to China by then United States Secretary of State James Baker, Dai was

A view of the Three Gorges Dam, the world's largest feat of engineering, which will supply China with much-needed hydroelectric power when fully operational in 2009. Photo by Berkshire Publishing Group.

forcibly prevented from meeting him as she was whisked off to temporary detention outside Beijing.

Throughout this period, Dai was granted several fellowships in the United States and Australia, including Harvard University, the Woodrow Wilson International Center for Scholars in Washington D.C., and the Australian National University. For her work on environmental and other issues in China, Dai received several prizes and awards including recognition from PEN International (1962), and the Goldman Environmental Prize and Condé Nast Environmental Award (both in 1993). A prolific writer, several of her books have been translated and published in English including *Yangtze! Yangtze!*, *The River Dragon Has Come! The Three Gorges Dam and the Fate of China's Yangtze River and Its People*, and *Tiananmen Follies: Prison Memoirs and Other Writings*. Other published works covering Dai's long-time interest in the persecution of liberal Chinese intellectuals within the CCP include *Wang Shi Wei and "Wild Lilies": Rectification and Purges in the Chinese Communist Party, 1942–1944*, *Piquant Essays I, II*, and, in Chinese, *In the Palm of Buddha's Hand: Zhang Dongsun and His Era*.

Still a resident in Beijing who stoutly rejects the label of "Chinese dissident," Dai Qing has worked closely with other prominent Chinese environmental journalists such as *Mǎ Jūn 马军 (b. 1968) in

• Dài Qīng •

opposing the giant South-to-North Water Transfer Project along with international NGOs like International Rivers Network and Canada's Probe International. While her publications remain officially banned in China, interested readers are reportedly able to access them via the Internet. In October 2005, in her first public appearance since 1989, Dai gave a talk without government interference on the ongoing issue of the Three Gorges Dam at the Sanwei Bookstore in Beijing. But in 2009, upon the insistence of the Chinese government, she was barred from official participation in the Frankfurt Book Fair in Germany, which in that year was devoted to Chinese books and publications. In 2010, she began an oral history project on the reactions and opinions of Beijing residents to the problems of the city's increasing water scarcity and pollution. Still under police surveillance, her friends were reportedly prevented from holding a surprise seventieth birthday in her honor in 2011. Describing herself as a "pessimistic activist," Dai continues work on her oral history and other projects concerned with China's increasingly deteriorating environment (Probe International 2005).

Lawrence R. SULLIVAN
Adelphi University

Further Reading

Barme, Geremie. (1993). Using the past to save the present: Dai Qing's historiographical dissent. *East Asian History*, 1, 141–181.

Dai Qing. (1993). *Wang Shiwei and "wild lilies": Rectification and purges in the Chinese Communist Party, 1942–1944* (Nancy Liu & Lawrence R. Sullivan, Trans.). Armonk, NY: M.E. Sharpe.

Dai Qing. (1994). *Yangtze! Yangtze!* (Patricia Adams & John Thibodeau, Eds.; Nancy Liu; Wu Mei; Sun Yougeng; & Zhang Xiaogang, Trans.). London & Toronto: Earthscan.

Dai Qing. (1998). *The river dragon has come!: The Three Gorges Dam and the fate of China's Yangtze River and its people* (John Thibodeau & Philip B. Williams, Eds.; Ming Yi, Trans.). Armonk, NY: M.E. Sharpe.

Dai Qing. (2005). *Tiananmen follies: Prison memoirs and other writings*. Norwalk, CT: EastBridge.

Garschagen, Oscar. (2009). The Uninvited: A visit with shunned Chinese writer Dai Qing. *Spiegel Online International*. Retrieved March 13, 2015, from http://www.spiegel.de/international/world/the-uninvited-a-visit-with-shunned-chinese-writer-dai-qing-a-655297.html

Probe International. (2005). Dai Qing: "I have been trying to make a public speech for the past 16 years." Retrieved March 13, 2015, from http://journal.probeinternational.org/2005/11/23/dai-qing-i-have-been-trying-to-make-a-public-speech-for-the-past-16-years

Sullivan, Lawrence R. (2011). Dai Qing. In Lawrence R. Sullivan, *Historical dictionary of the Chinese Communist Party* (p. 73). Plymouth, UK: Scarecrow Press.

Zheng Wang. (1988). Three interviews: Wang Anyi, Zhu Lin, Dai Qing. *Modern Chinese Literature*, 4(1/2), 99–148.

Zhu Tianbao. (2003). Dai Qing. In Lily Xiao Hong Lee & A. D. Stefanowska (Eds.), *Biographical dictionary of Chinese women. The twentieth century, 1912–2000* (Vol. 2) (pp. 125–128). Armonk, NY: M.E. Sharpe.

戴晴

♂ Dèng Xiǎopíng 邓小平

1904–1997—Military leader; general secretary of the CCP; deputy premier and deputy chairman of China

Alternate names: b. Dèng Xiānshèng 邓先圣; trad. 鄧小平

Summary

Deng Xiaoping was China's preeminent leader from 1978 to 1992, a man who guided the transformation of China from a poor, divided, and chaotic country and achieved the dream of Chinese leaders since the Opium War of setting China on a path of enriching the people and becoming a global power. He joined the Communist movement in France in 1923, and became a revolutionary leader and a soldier. From 1952 to 1966 he held key positions implementing Mao Zedong's policies. He fell from office three times, but as top leader from the late 1970s, he maintained order, developed good relations with major foreign powers, transformed the Communist Party from a revolutionary party to a ruling party, opened markets, and sent tens of thousands abroad to bring in modern technology and management. Several hundred million people were raised above the poverty line under Deng's leadership.

Deng Xiaoping was the paramount figure who led the transformation of China to a modern nation. A revolutionary leader from the mid-1920s and a high-level political commissar in the military from the late-1930s through the 1940s, Deng led the establishment of Communist power in China's southwest from 1949 to 1952. After being brought to Beijing by Máo Zédōng 毛泽东 (1893–1976) in 1952, Deng served as vice president and general secretary of the Communist Party for over a decade. He was three times removed from office and subjected to criticism, but since he joined the Communist movement in 1923, he was never thrown out of the Party. From 1978 to 1992 he was China's preeminent leader, guiding the bold Reforms and Opening Up (*gǎigé kāifàng* 改革开放) that set the country on a new path and brought rapid modernization, and enabling China to play a major role in world affairs.

Childhood and Early Education

Deng was born in Paifang village (also known as Yaoping), Sichuan Province, in 1904. His father, Deng Wenming, was a landlord who had several farm hands. Deng initially received a classical Confucian education, but switched to a local public elementary school in 1915 that taught modern subjects, such as history, mathematics, and science.

In 1919, in the wake of World War I, Deng Xiaoping, not yet fifteen, joined in the patriotic demonstrations taking place around the country against negotiations about handing over Chinese territory from Germany to Japan. From that time on he was deeply concerned with strengthening China so it could resist being dominated by foreign countries.

France, and the Start of a Political Career

That same year, Deng was sent to a school that prepared him for going abroad to study, and upon graduation the next year, he and eighty-three other boys boarded a ship for France, where they would receive education in modern subjects and then return home to play a role in the modernization of China.

After arriving in France, however, the political and economic situation made it increasingly difficult to find a job, and Deng, like the vast majority of the other young Chinese intellectuals in France, did not have enough money to attend high school or university. The "worker-students" became only workers, and those who had read Marx and Engels, and those familiar with the Russian Revolution that took place in 1917, found the explanations that fit their own experience.

Party Politics in France

The student politics in France reflected the politics of the time in China, where the Communists and Nationalists worked together in the First United Front (1923–1927). Deng, called "Mr. Mimeograph," became an assistant to Zhōu Ēnlái 周恩来 (1898–1976), the leader of the Communist students in France, and as an editor, writer, and mimeographer he helped put out a news sheet distributed to Chinese in France, promoting the leftist cause within the Nationalist Party (Guómíndǎng 国民党, or GMD). In 1923, Deng became a member of the Communist Party, and at the end of 1925, after taking part in demonstrations against the French government, he had to escape through Germany and Poland to Moscow.

Soon after Deng arrived in Moscow in January 1926, he was assigned to be a member of the first class of the newly established Sun Yat-sen University (Zhongshan University), set up by Moscow leaders to train Communist Party members for China and elsewhere in Asia.

Return to China

Deng was in Moscow a year when, even before graduation, he was assigned to return to China. After the split between the Nationalists and the Communists in 1927, he was assigned to the Communist underground. In 1929, at age twenty-five, he was sent to cooperate with some small warlords in Guanxi Province to lead urban insurrections in Baise and Longzhou. After a battle in which they suffered heavy losses, Deng was separated from his troops, and chose to return to Party headquarters in Shanghai.

After some months of waiting in Shanghai, Deng was allowed to join Mao's forces in Jiangxi where they aimed to set up a rural base that would gain the strength necessary to take on the Nationalists. Like Mao, Deng disagreed with the Party leaders in Shanghai, and was soon dismissed from his posts, but was soon brought back on to head provincial propaganda work. During the Long March—a 9,600-kilometer (6,000-mile) series of military retreats undertaken by the CCP's Red Army—Deng was responsible for putting out a newssheet to buoy up the troops on the March. After the Long Marchers arrived in Yan'an in 1937, Japan invaded China, and the Communists and Nationalists forged a second period of United Front. Deng was assigned to be a political commissar, responsible for the military's political education, organization, and loyalty to the government.

After the end of World War II in 1945, and as the Civil War broke out between the Nationalists and the Communists, Deng continued to fight against the Nationalist Army. After the Communist victory over the Nationalists, culminating in the founding of the People's Republic of China in 1949, Deng, together with his former Army comrade Liu Bocheng, was placed in charge of the southwest region (headquartered in Sichuan, Deng's home province). In 1952, Deng and many other leaders transferred to Beijing. Deng first became deputy premier in the government, and served as finance minister for a year from 1953. Along with Mao, Deng participated in campaigns against counter-revolutionaries, landlords, profiteering officials, and business people. Indeed, Deng played a major role in implementing the Anti-Rightist Campaign. Although Liu Shaoqi was officially Mao's successor, it was clear to many that Mao considered Deng a leading candidate to be his successor.

The Great Leap and the Cultural Revolution

In mid-1958, the Great Leap Forward was launched and in the autumn Deng traveled to various provinces supporting the efforts to establish rural communes and to speed up industrialization. He began to comment on problems, and warned that the Communist Party still needed to "seek the correct path from facts" (*shíshì qiúshì* 实事求是) (i.e., look at the real situation and not be guided by ideology alone). Although Deng did not criticize Mao's policies in public, by reporting to Mao less often, he obtained a measure of freedom to do what he regarded as necessary to adapt to the problems.

Tens of millions are estimated to have died from unnatural causes due to the failures of the Great Leap Forward. Despite these devastating results, Mao tried to keep alive the leap to a higher stage of socialism combined with class struggle and continuing revolution, resulting in 1966 in the mass mobilization of the Cultural Revolution, attacking not only old customs but "officials in authority" who had constrained his efforts in the early 1960s.

Beginning in October 1966 Liu Shaoqi and Deng Xiaoping were openly criticized by Red Guards—groups of students who made it their cause to become Mao Zedong's loyal followers—as the leading persons pursuing the capitalist road, and by the end of 1966 they no longer appeared in public.

In October 1969, Deng was sent to the outskirts of Nanchang, Jiangxi Province, where he received an hour per day of political training on "Mao Zedong Thought"—the collective name for the ideology of the Chinese party-state—and worked in a county-level tractor repair factory where he and his wife worked at lathes. Mao only allowed Deng to return to Beijing in February 1973.

Return to Mao's Good Graces

By December 1973, Mao judged Deng to have proved his loyalty. Deng, while tutored by Premier Zhou Enlai, was gradually given more responsibility for foreign affairs, and in the course of 1974 to 1975 hosted many foreign leaders. In 1974, Mao named Deng deputy premier. By mid-1974, Mao had decided that more order and economic progress was required to avoid the risk of the country falling apart, and he allowed Deng in 1975 to begin to bring back order. To give a quick boost to the economy and to set an example for the rectification required to bring order and economic progress, Deng focused on Xuzhou, in Jiangsu Province in eastern China, where badly needed coal and other supplies piled up because rebels blocked the smooth flow of freight. In short order, Deng had troops occupy the place, clean out the obstacles, and rally the rebelling workers to criticize the old leadership who had led them astray and to undertake more efficient operations. It was a quick success that instantly increased industrial production in the surrounding regions and served as an example for rectification elsewhere, which Deng began to undertake.

After Mao

By the end of 1975, however, as Deng began to criticize officials at Tsinghua University who had supported Mao in the Cultural Revolution, Mao began to have doubts about whether Deng as successor would support the people and the policies Mao favored. After Zhou Enlai died in January 1976, Mao appointed Huá Guófēng 华国锋 (1921–2008) to be responsible for the premier's work and a few months later officially removed Deng from his position (his third fall). When Mao died in September 1976, Hua became the preeminent leader. Mao's widow Jiang Qing and her associates (known as the "Gang of Four") continued to take radical positions and began trying to gain power. In October 1976, a few weeks after Mao's death, Hua cooperated with a small number of others to arrest the Gang of Four. With that, the radical pressures of the Cultural Revolution were over.

In July 1977, Deng was allowed to return and he volunteered to work on education, science, and technology, which he and many others believed

Deng Xiaoping applauds as President Jimmy Carter stands behind a podium at the White House, Washington, D.C., on 29 January 1979. US news & World Report Magazine Photograph Collection. Library of Congress.

to be crucial to prepare for the "four modernizations" 四个现代化 (science and technology, industry, agriculture, and national defense). Immediately after returning to work, Deng announced that there would be an immediate reopening of universities, most of which had been closed since the beginning of the Cultural Revolution. Deng also announced that entrance to universities would be determined entirely by examinations and that political considerations for admission, which Mao had always insisted on, would be abolished.

In mid-November 1978, key senior party leaders decided that Hua Guofeng lacked experience in foreign relations and the military, was following Mao too closely, and so Deng was called deputy premier and deputy chairman, while *Chén Yún 陈云 (1905–1995), the one other person with seniority qualifications comparable to Deng, was also to approve important decisions.

Reform and Opening Up

Deng was not the only one who had given thought to reforms and opening up (even Hua Guofeng wanted some opening and reforms), and he had the same goal as generations of Chinese leaders: to enrich the people and strengthen the country. But while

___
*People marked with an asterisk have entries in this dictionary.

Chinese leaders had failed to find the path to success for over a century, Deng found that path.

Deng was a brilliant political manager and he worked with many able officials. He was more pragmatic than ideological, and his formulations such as "Chinese-style socialism" gave him the flexibility to adapt and to allow "seeking the correct path from facts." Under his leadership, the Communist Party was transformed to a ruling party that promoted stability, high educational standards, meritocracy, scientific development, and economic growth. He said that if starvation was a serious problem in certain areas, farmers should be allowed to find their own ways to survive. Some of them chose to engage in household farming, and to ensure that there was enough food to feed those in the cities, Deng was willing to have the government set quotas and make contracts with the households so that they produced what was needed for the country. They were then given the freedom to sell excess produce in markets. He did not immediately allow private companies to form, but he allowed enterprises in towns and villages to have their own companies, which allowed far more flexibility to respond to market conditions than the large state enterprises could. Rather than create massive unemployment in state enterprises, he first allowed these town and village enterprises to grow and provide large-scale employment before he began to put pressure on the state enterprises.

Deng found a way to depart from Mao but also put Mao on a pedestal so that he did not lose the support of those who worshipped Mao: Mao, he made clear, made enormous contributions; everyone is human and makes mistakes and Mao made some in his later days. He did not criticize Mao for being too ideological; he simply said, "It doesn't matter if the cat is black or white as long as it catches the mice."

On the World Stage

Deng wanted to have good relations with other countries, especially major countries, so China could concentrate on domestic development. On the eve of his Reforms and Opening Up, Deng visited Japan where, for the first time in history, a Chinese leader met the emperor. He made friends with Japanese leaders, brought Japanese movies and television series to China to improve relations between the countries, and visited Japanese factories, enabling him to get help from Japan in finance, technology, and management that would play a major part in Chinese growth in the 1980s. He completed the normalization process with the United States, allowing China to send massive numbers of students to the United States.

Deng had criticized the Soviet Union for making too many enemies and exhausting its resources to build up its military. In the 1980s he was ready to improve relations with the Soviet Union if the Soviets would withdraw troops from China's northern border, pull out of Afghanistan, and get Vietnam to reduce its military control over Cambodia. When by 1989 the Soviet Union had completed these conditions, he welcomed Mikhail Gorbachev (b. 1931, General Secretary of the Communist Party of the Soviet Union 1985–1991), to Beijing.

Many Britons and Hong Kong residents feared that when the leases on the New Territories of Hong Kong came due in 1997 that China's insistence on resuming sovereignty could lead to a quarrel or to a mess; Deng negotiated that China would take over sovereignty in 1997 but allowed Hong Kong to keep its own systems for at least fifty years, thus resolving that issue.

Although historically China had been an Asian power rather than a global power, Deng welcomed China's participation in the United Nations, the World Bank, the International Monetary Fund, and other organizations. Deng was generally well-liked by foreign leaders who met him. They praised Deng for being direct, smart, attentive, humorous—an honest broker who represented his nation's interests but adjusted to realities and sought to solve problems.

Tiananmen Square and Deng's Legacy

Early in his administration, Deng chose *Hú Yàobāng 胡耀邦 (1915–1989) as his Party general secretary and *Zhào

Dèng Xiǎopíng

Zǐyáng 赵紫阳 (1919–2005) as his premier. Hu Yaobang, completely dedicated to encouraging people to liberate their thinking and to responding flexibly to needs, traveled the country supporting local people. He was very popular with young people in particular. In January 1987, Deng allowed Hu to be removed because he feared that he was too soft in dealing with student and intellectual protests. Zhao Ziyang made great contributions throughout the 1980s in guiding the difficult process of gradually opening up the economy. In 1988, Zhao supported a high level of inflation to support growth and Deng decided to decontrol prices, but this created enormous worry among salaried people that their livelihoods were in danger.

In 1989, when Gorbachev came to Beijing and the world press corps came in large numbers, students in Beijing, who had first taken to the streets to mourn the death of Hu Yaobang a month earlier, continued their protests, demanding more democracy and criticizing official corruption. On 20 May 1989, Deng approved the sending in of troops unarmed to restore order, but they were stopped by demonstrating students and by citizens who worried about inflation and who objected to troops moving in to control the people. On the night of 3 June, with Deng's approval, troops were told to do what was necessary to restore order, and citizens were told to stay off the streets.

Massive numbers of people blocked the troops and when they could not get through, they used their weapons to restore order and, by daylight on 4 June, to clear out the demonstrators from Tiananmen Square.

Although there are no precise numbers of how many were killed, the most careful estimates are that over seven hundred, including soldiers and civilians, were killed. Deng was denounced at home and abroad for killing students and other demonstrators and for not handling the situation better. Chinese intellectuals as well as foreigners criticized Deng for not doing more to establish democracy and the rule of law. Those who supported Deng explained that China was on the verge of chaos and that as tragic as the situation was, Deng had no other choice but to restore order, and that China did not yet have the circumstances that would allow more freedom. In their view, China was not able to make sustained progress in the chaotic conditions from the Opium War until 1949 and during the Cultural Revolution, and that millions died in the turmoil because the country was too chaotic; public order was essential for national progress. Zhao Ziyang, who had been made general secretary after Hu Yaobang was eliminated, refused to join in sending the troops in the spring of 1989, and was subsequently removed and replaced by someone who had not been part of the clampdown in Beijing: *Jiāng Zémín

江泽民 (b. 1926), who was brought from Shanghai to replace Zhao Ziyang.

After the Tiananmen tragedy, other nations imposed sanctions. Deng urged the Chinese people to remain calm and said that China should not only remain open but should open wider. He believed that foreign countries had short memories and that within several years, foreign businessmen who wanted access to the China market would convince their country's leaders that they should not isolate China. After 1989, Deng was very upset that conservatives had gained control over economic policy and that growth had slowed down from 1989 to 1992. Although he no longer had formal power, in the spring of 1992 he took a "Southern Tour" to rally the local people for further openness and faster growth. He succeeded, and at the Fourteenth Party Congress in October 1992, at age eighty-eight, he made it clear that he supported Jiang Zemin and Jiang's successful efforts to speed up growth and further opening. At that point, Deng waved good-bye to the political stage. He died in 1997. While Mao's body remained on display in Tiananmen Square, Deng's body was cremated and his ashes dispersed into the sea.

Under Deng's leadership, China for the first time in its long history had become an active participant in world affairs and world organizations. Once his administration was well underway, economic growth reached a level unprecedented by any country in world history: roughly 10 percent a year for three decades. Several hundred million people were raised above the poverty line. China, which for millennia was an overwhelmingly rural society, was well on its way to becoming a predominantly urban society. The basic system and policies Deng established have continued after his death, and he ensured China was on its way to becoming an important country in world affairs. Having brought several hundred million people out of poverty and set a weak country on the path to become one of the two major global powers, Deng had a greater long-term impact on world history than any other twentieth-century world leader.

Ezra F. VOGEL
Harvard University

Further Reading

Chen Yun 陳云. (2000). *Chen Yun nianpu* 陳云年譜 [Chen Yun chronicles] (3 vols.). Shanghai: Zhongyang wenxue chubanshe.

Deng Xiaoping. (2005). *Deng Xiaoping nianpu* 邓小平年譜 1975–1997 [Deng Xiaoping chronicles]. (2 vols.). Shanghai: Zhongyang wenxue chubanshe.

Deng Xiaoping. (2009). *Deng Xiaoping nianpu* 邓小平年譜 1904–1974 [Deng Xiaoping chronicles]. (3 vols.). Shanghai: Zhongyang wenxue chubanshe.

Deng Xiaoping. (1994). *Selected works of Deng Xiaoping* (3 vols.). Beijing: Foreign Language Press.

Deng Maomao. (1995). *My father: Deng Xiaoping*. New York: Basic Books.

Deng Rong. (2002). *Deng Xiaoping and the Cultural Revolution: A daughter recalls the critical years*. Beijing: Foreign Languages Press.

Cheng Zhongyuan 程中原, & Xia Xiangzhen 夏杏珍. (2003). *Lishi zhuanzhe de qianzou: Deng Xiaoping zai 1975* 历史转折的前奏：邓小平在 1975 [The prelude to the historical turning point: Deng Xiaoping in 1975]. Beijing: Zhongguo qingnian chubanshe.

Deng Xiaoping. (2004). *Deng Xiaoping junshi wenji* 邓小平军事文集 (3 vols.) [Collection of Deng Xiaoping's military writings]. Beijing: Junshi kexue chubanshe and Zhongyang wenxian chubanshe.

Qian Qichen. (2005). *Ten episodes in China's diplomacy*. New York: HarperCollins.

Ruan Ming. (1994). *Deng Xiaoping: Chronicle of an empire*. Boulder, CO: Westview.

Shambaugh, David L. (Ed.). (1995). *Deng Xiaoping: Portrait of a Chinese statesman*. New York: Oxford University Press.

Teiwes, Frederick, & Sun, Warren. (2007). *The end of the Maoist era: Chinese politics during the twilight of the Cultural Revolution, 1972–1976*. Armonk, NY: M. E. Sharpe.

Tyler, Patrick. (1999). *A great wall: Six presidents and China: An investigative history*. New York: Public Affairs.

Vogel, Ezra F. (2013). *Deng Xiaoping and the transformation of China*. Cambridge, MA: The Belknap Press of Harvard University Press.

Yang Tianshi 杨天石 (Ed.). (2005). *Deng Xiaoping xiezhen* 邓小平写真 [A portrait of Deng Xiaoping]. Shanghai: Shanghai cishu chubanshe.

Yu Guangyuan. (2004). Deng Xiaoping shakes the world: An eyewitness account of China's Party Work Conference and the Third Plenum (November–December 1978). Edited by Ezra F. Vogel and Steven I. Levine. Norwalk, CT: EastBridge.

Zhongyang wenxuan publishers (Ed.). (2004). *Bainian Xiaoping* 百年小平 [One hundred years Deng Xiaoping]. Shanghai: Zhongyang wenxuan chubanshe.

邓小平

☿ Fāng Lìzhī 方励之

1936–2012—Physicist and cosmologist, lived in exile since 1990

Alternate names: pen name: Wang Yunran; trad. 方勵之

Summary

Fang Lizhi was a cosmologist, physicist, and vice president of the University of Science and Technology of China. His call for liberal democratic reforms and support for the student movement that resulted in the Tiananmen Square protests of 1989 led to his ouster from the Chinese Communist Party and exile to the United Kingdom and the United States.

Fang Lizhi occupied a unique position in contemporary China. A world-class cosmologist and physicist, working in one of the most technical and abstruse of areas, he was also one of the country's most prominent and outspoken intellectual opponents of the Chinese Communist Party (CCP). Expelled from the party not once but twice and, because of links to the 1989 Tiananmen Square protests, forced into exile first to the United Kingdom and then the United States, Fang's career exemplifies the initial strong support and then deep disenchantment with party rule first under Máo Zédōng 毛泽东 (1893–1976) and then *Dèng Xiǎopíng 邓小平 (1904–1997) among intellectuals.

Early Career During Troubled Times

Fang Lizhi was born in Beijing on 12 February 1936, the son of a Hangzhou postal clerk. Such modest beginnings may have inspired his initial enthusiasm for the Communist Party, which was a victimized underdog during his early adolescence, when in 1946 he reportedly joined a sympathetic underground group during the Chinese Civil War. After the foundation of the People's Republic of China (PRC) in 1949, Fang was able to enroll at prestigious Peking University at the age of sixteen. His specialism in physics meant he belonged among those

---

*People marked with an asterisk have entries in this dictionary.

whose knowledge and skills were of most practical use in the task of reconstructing and defending the country during the early years of the party's rule. After graduation, in the late 1950s, he worked on the first phases of China's atomic bomb, a project Mao closely linked to the mission of making China strong and able to defend itself.

During this time, Fang met his wife, Lǐ Shūxián 李淑娴, who was also from a technical background. She would later take the main role in the first set of events that would turn Fang against the political movement he had so strongly supported till then. In the 1956 Hundred Flowers Campaign, Mao Zedong requested open criticism of how the government and party were performing, however the quantity and intensity of negative feedback caused the campaign to end after only a few weeks. Li, then based in the physics department of Peking University, together with Fang, who was working at the newly established Institute of Modern Physics, had written a stinging letter of criticism of some aspects of the Party's practices. While hardly a declaration of opposition, it showed precisely the sort of thinking authorities regarded as antagonistic and disloyal. She was expelled from the Party, and Fang sent to Hebei Province near Beijing for a year to do hard labor. On his return, he was similarly expelled from the Party, but because of his evident skills as a science researcher

he was given a job at the University of Science and Technology.

Allowed to live a relatively normal life again in the early 1960s, Fang even managed to produce research papers, though first under a penname, Wang Yunran. His field of interest moved towards particle physics and laser physics. Productive throughout the decade in terms of research, though never able to openly declare his authorship because of his disgraced status and lack of party membership, he was almost exiled from Beijing again on the eve of the Cultural Revolution (1966–1976), though he was saved through top-level patronage.

Cultural Revolution, Tiananmen Square Protests, and Exile

Increasing tensions with the Soviet Union, in part precipitated by the party's debunking of Stalin's rule in the late 1950s and through the virulent language used against the former communist ally as the Cultural Revolution heated up, resulted in the Third Front policy, whereby China's key strategic industrial and technical entities were moved away from the capital and the main coastal regions and towards the western hinterland. The University of Science and Technology ended up in Hefei, Anhui Province. This necessitated Fang being separated from his wife once more and

方励之

going to live at the new campus in 1969. At the same time, he became a target of the Cultural Revolution, then raging in China, because of his "unreliable" background during the Hundred Flowers Campaign in the 1950s, when he had criticized the Party. He was forced to undertake hard labor once he was in Anhui, some of which reportedly involved building the brick walls of the institution where he had been sent to do research.

The one benefit of this difficult period was that he had time to study physics books, one of which introduced him to the theory of relativity. This resulted, in 1972, with Fang and some colleagues publishing a paper called "A Solution of the Cosmological Equations in Scalertensor Theory, with Mass and Blackbody Radiation." Remarkably, such an arcane title still managed to attract attacks from some of the noisiest radicals, with one in particular, Yáo Wényuán 姚文元, later playing a leading role in the group subsequently known as the Gang of Four. Yao was to issue a rebuke to Fang's paper, stating that the big bang theory he had supported there contradicted Engel's notion that the universe in time and space was infinite. Brickbats continued until 1976, when Mao's death ended the radical era and the party adopted more pragmatic politics.

In the new Reform and Opening Up era, with its emphasis on the critical importance of science, Fang's party membership was restored and he was inducted into the Chinese Academy of Science. He was even elevated to the position of vice president of the University of Science and Technology in 1984, after which he brought in leading Western experts for the first time, including a young Stephen Hawking. Able to travel around the world, Fang looked like he had finally been embraced as a trusted member of the elite. But this period was to prove short-lived. With student unrest beginning in 1986 over rising prices, inflation, and corruption, Fang's public comments in support of faster political reforms were seen as exacerbating the situation rather than helping to stabilize it. In 1987, Fang and a group of other distinguished veteran intellectuals, among them the renowned journalist *Liú Bīnyàn 刘宾雁 (1925–2005), sent an open letter to the paramount leader Deng Xiaoping asking him to implement what the jailed dissident and activist from the Democracy Wall Movement of 1979 *Wèi Jīngshēng 魏京生 (b. 1950) had called "the Fifth Modernization"—democracy.

Deng reacted furiously, demanding to know how people writing such things could call themselves communists. With the fall of the Party's general secretary, *Hú Yàobāng 胡耀邦 (1915–1989), in April 1987, partially because of his refusal to condemn Fang, the physicist (who had been sent from Hefei to Beijing to work at the National Astronomy Observatory) was, for the second time,

• Fāng Lìzhī •

expelled from the Party. His speeches to students in support of greater democratic freedoms and human rights continued throughout 1988 and into 1989, as the events leading up to the 4 June Tiananmen Square Incident intensified. Trying to reach the Great Wall Hotel for a reception attended by US President George H. W. Bush in early 1989, Fang was prevented and forced to return home. His blatant criticisms of Communist Party policy and rule were blamed after 4 June as being a significant precipitating factor mobilizing students and causing them to take part in the protests. Fang and his wife sought refuge in the US embassy, living there for a year before being released under a special deal between China and the United States on 25 June 1990. He was taken immediately to the United Kingdom, where he spent some time in Cambridge, and then moved on to Princeton in the United States before settling for the rest of his life in Tucson, Arizona, as a professor of physics at the university there.

Influence and Legacy

Fang's writings on political matters belonged to the classical tradition of Western liberal democratic and human rights ideals, and for that reason he proved to be very popular in the West. The Chinese government's campaign of vilification once he left the country was replaced, beginning in the mid-1990s, by attempts to simply erase him from domestic history. In this, they were to prove largely successful. Better known in the West than in his homeland after his exile, his death in 2012 created barely a stir in China. His post-1989 fate typifies the tragedy of many of those who stood so courageously for their beliefs while in China, but then were forcibly evicted and sent to places where they had neither the language community nor the environment to continue to be truly effective. In a kinder time, Fang would almost certainly have enjoyed a long career in China as a lauded expert, a model public intellectual willing to speak out not just on technical but also wider social and political issues, his contributions winning him domestic fame and public admiration. As it was, he was to spend nearly the last three decades of his life in exile. His career is representative of how almost every area of life in China since 1949 has been politicized, and how even people who peer into the beginnings of the universe and its outermost limits are still perfectly capable of irritating, and being punished, by the ruling party.

Kerry BROWN
Lau China Institute, King's College

Further Reading

Fang Lizhi. (1989). *Fang Lizhi zi xuan ji* 方勵之自選集 [Selected speeches and writings] (vols. 1–3). Singapore: World Scientific.

Fang Lizhi, & Williams, James H. (1991). *Bringing down the Great Wall: Writings on science, culture and democracy in China*. New York: Knopf.

Schell, Orville. (1988). China's Andrei Sakharov. *The Atlantic Monthly*. Retrieved March 31, 2015, from http://www.theatlantic.com/past/docs/unbound/flashbks/china/fang.htm

The Economist. (2012, 14 April). Fang Lizhi, obituary. Retrieved March 31, 2015, from http://www.economist.com/node/21552551

Williams, James H. (1990). Fang Lizhi's expanding universe. *China Quarterly*, *123*, 459–484.

Wines, Michael. (2012, 7 April). Fang Lizhi, Chinese physicist and seminal dissident dies at 76. *The New York Times*. Retrieved March 31, 2015, from http://www.nytimes.com/2012/04/08/world/asia/fang-lizhi-chinese-physicist-and-dissident-dies-at-76.html

• Fāng Lìzhī •

☿ Fèi Xiàotōng 费孝通

1910–2005—Professor of sociology and anthropology, father of sociology in China

Alternate names: Hsiao-Tung Fei; trad. 費孝通

Summary

Known as the father of Chinese sociology, Fei Xiaotong was most noted for his research of village life and ethnic groups in China. Author of the classic text, *From the Soil*, Fei delineated the underlying organizational principles of Chinese society in comparison to the West. Scholars and anthropologists have utilized his concepts and theories to describe Chinese society up to the present day.

Fei Xiaotong was a professor in sociology and anthropology at Peking University who played two major public roles throughout his life. As a scholar, he was no doubt one of China's finest sociologists and anthropologists, and was instrumental in laying a solid foundation for the development of sociological and anthropological studies in China, and introducing them to the world. As a practitioner and politician, he was vice chairman of the Standing Committee of the National People's Congress, as well as holding many other official posts. His work helped to influence China's social and economic development and raised cultural awareness in Chinese and global societies.

The Course of Fei's Career

Fei Xiaotong was born in Wujiang County, Jiangsu Province, on 2 November 1910. His father, Fèi Pǔ'ān 费朴安, was educated in the Chinese classics, earned a *shēngyuán* 生员 civil service degree, studied in Japan, and founded a middle school. He was also elected as Head of the Wujiang County Council and participated in democratic activities. Fei's mother, Yáng Rènlán 杨纫兰, the Christian daughter of a government official, graduated from Shanghai Wuben Girls' School and went on to establish her own nursery school. She also wrote articles for magazines to promote ideas of freedom. Fei Xiaotong was the youngest of five children, and in primary school, was always teased for being a "little wasted person" because he was always ill and his surname had the same pronunciation as the word for waste (*fèi* 废). Fei's family moved to Suzhou in 1920, when his father was working as education supervisor of Jiangsu Province. Fei was sent to Zhenhua Girls' School, partly to protect him from being teased again by boys, and partly to gain a better education, because the headmistress was a friend of Fei's mother and was considered highly qualified, having graduated from the University of Illinois. Fei's reading at this time included much local history, materials and notes brought home from his father's business visits to nearby places, as well as reports that his father wrote. Fei went on to Soochow University Affiliated High School, where he flourished, publishing his first essay at the age of fourteen and many others afterwards, which demonstrated the way he had begun thinking about the nature of society.

In 1928, Fei Xiaotong went to the medical school of Soochow University, but as a student leader, he was involved in a student protest and had to leave the university. After visiting various heads of departments at Yenching University in Beijing, Fei registered as a student in the department of sociology in 1930, where he was heavily influenced by Professor Wú Wénzǎo 吴文藻 and Robert E. Park, the University of Chicago sociologist on a semester visit in China. From 1933 to 1935, Fei completed his

master's in sociology and anthropology at Tsinghua University, where he studied with the Russian anthropologist S. M. Shirokogoroff, and gained a strict theoretical and methodological training in anthropology.

During fieldwork on Yao Mountain in Guangxi Province, Fei's leg was crushed by a tiger trap, and his new wife, Wáng Tónghuì 王同惠, a fellow anthropologist, fell to her death while seeking help. In memory of her, Fei wrote a book, *Social Organization in Yao Society*, in hospital while recovering from his injury, and published it under their joint names (Fei and Wang 1936). Fei then spent two months doing fieldwork in Kaixiangong village, a placement arranged by his sister Fèi Dáshēng 费达生, one of the pioneers of rural industry in China in the 1930s. Based on this fieldwork material, Fei Xiaotong obtained his PhD at the London School of Economics and Political Science in 1938, and published his thesis as *Peasant Life in China* (1939).

In November 1938, Fei Xiaotong returned to a war-torn China and in 1939 married Mèng Yín 孟吟, with whom he had a daughter, Fèi Zōnghuì 费宗惠. He chaired a research station in Kunming that was jointly founded by Yenching University and Yunnan University. Fei and his colleagues and students studied three villages and Fei published more than a dozen journal articles and some books in Chinese based on these studies. From 1943–1944, with support from Professor John K. Fairbank at Harvard

University, Fei visited the United States, where he published a book on rural industry, *Earthbound China* (Fei and Chang 1945), also based on his Yunnan village studies. In 1945, Fei became a professor at Tsinghua University, in its wartime Yunnan exile. He also joined the China Democratic League and participated actively in the democratic movement. However, when the democratic intellectuals Lǐ Gōngpǔ 李公朴 and Wén Yīduō 闻一多 were assassinated by the Nationalists, Fei took refuge in the US consulate in Kunming, together with some left-wing professors. He was then invited to visit the United Kingdom for a few months. In 1947, Tsinghua University moved back to Beijing, after which Fei Xiaotong taught there and published extensively.

After the liberation in 1949, Fei continued to work at Tsinghua University until 1952, when he was appointed as a vice president at the Central University for Nationalities (CUN). He was also appointed as vice minister in 1956 of the State Ethnic Affairs Commission (SEAC) of the Government of the PRC. Although sociology was treated as a "bourgeois pseudo-science" and was eliminated as a field in 1952, Fei conducted intensive field survey in areas of minority nationalities and worked on the construction of ethnology. During the Hundred Flowers Campaign of 1956–1957, when citizens were encouraged to voice their opinions of communist leaders and policies, Fei spoke out for the restoration of sociology and called for utilizing the talents of intellectuals. For this he was accused of being a "rightist" during the ensuing Anti-Rightist Movement in 1957, and all his positions in the CUN and the state were revoked. From 1958 to 1966, Fei was allowed to do some writing and translation at home, but he was not able to escape attack during the Cultural Revolution (1966–1976). He was sent to the Cadres School of CUN from 1969 to 1972 for political reeducation. Fairbank visited China and was able to meet with Fei Xiaotong after US President Richard Nixon's visit in 1972. The change in the China-US relationship enabled Fei to return to the CUN, where he worked with fellow anthropologist and sociologist Wu Wenzao and others on translating a world history and other documents until the end of Cultural Revolution.

In 1978, Fei was appointed as vice director of the Institute of Ethnology, Chinese Academy of Social Sciences (CASS). After the field of sociology was re-established, Fei was elected president of the Chinese Sociological Association (CSA) in 1979, and then appointed director of the Institute of Sociology, where he served from 1980 to 1984. He worked for the establishment of sociology departments in universities, and also travelled widely in China and overseas. In 1985, Fei established the Institute of Sociology and Anthropology in Peking University and worked there for the last twenty years of his life. During this period, Fei wrote prolifically, including field visit notes, research reports, as well as reflective essays on theoretical and methodological thinking.

Academic Contributions

Of the twenty volumes of *Fei Xiaotong's Completed Works* (Fei 2010), only two books are well known in the West. One is his PhD thesis, *Peasant Life in China*, published in English in 1939 and translated into Chinese as *Jiāngcūn jīngjì* 江村经济 by Dài Kèjǐng 戴克景 in 1986. In his preface to the book, the anthropologist Bronislaw Malinowski wrote that he regarded it as "a landmark in the development of anthropological fieldwork and theory" (1939, xix). Malinowski believed that the future course of social anthropology lay in studying societies, such as China's, that had long and complex histories of civilization (Freedman 1963). As the first instance of social anthropology of this kind, and also a case of fieldwork conducted by a native in his own society, *Peasant Life in China* was a significant contribution to the development of classic ethnography.

The second major book was entitled *Xiāngtǔ Zhōngguó* 乡土中国 (1947), translated into English as *From the Soil* (1992) by Gary Hamilton and Zheng Wang. This book demonstrated Fei's major theoretical and methodological contributions to the understanding of Chinese people and society. Gary Hamilton found that in *From the Soil*, Fei's twin concepts of *chāxùgéjú* 差序格局 (differential mode of association) and *tuántǐgéjú* 团体格局 (organizational mode of association) offer a guide to thinking about how Chinese and Western societies are differently organized. He suggests that

institutions of domination in the West have a "jurisdictional quality," meaning that legitimate authority can only be exercised within prescribed organizational boundaries. This is *tuantigeju*. In China, the institutions work according to the logic of relationships, which are controlled at a basic level through Confucius's "*li*", which I would define as a studied obedience to social roles, both conformity to one's own roles and monitoring the conformity of others to theirs. This is *chaxugeju*. Each "principle of domination" generates its own distinctive institutions. (Hamilton and Chang 2014, 108)

This is why, after discussions between Hamilton and Fei himself, the subtitle *The Foundations of Chinese Society* was added to the English version (Hamilton and Chang 2011). For Hamilton, these two concepts were "profound and go to the core meaning patterns of the two societies, to what German sociologists call *Weltanschauungen*, or what we call in English 'a world view'" (Hamilton 2014, 52).

Anthropologists in the West and in China have translated and interpreted these terms in different ways. Stephan Feuchtwang, emeritus professor at the London School of Economics, translated *chaxugeju* and *tuantigeju* as "social egoism" and "corporatism" (Feuchtwang 2014). According to Feuchtwang's understanding of Fei's work, Chinese society is formed as circles of social relatedness spreading out from each person, the immediate circle being a family or small lineage, which is an efficient, flexible and expandable, multi-functional organization, but has no fixed boundaries. Yúnxiáng Yán 严云翔, a native of Beijing and professor of anthropology at University of California, Los Angeles, holds that Fei's concept of *chaxugeju* is an ideal type of social structure in China. For Yan, *chaxugeju* contains *xu*, a vertical dimension of moral hierarchy and order, and *cha*, a horizontal dimension of relational distance and differentiation. This hierarchal dimension thus has a certain influence on the cultural construction of the Chinese (Yan forthcoming 2015).

Although Fei never revealed how he arrived at the concept of *chaxugeju*, it in fact covers all the dimensions mentioned by others about a half century later: individual, family, neighborhood, party, country, and *tiānxià* 天下 (world and heaven). Fei Xiaotong made it clear, moreover, that *chaxugeju* was maintained by a set of morals and ethics as an assurance mechanism of a *li*-, or ritual-, based society (*lǐ zhì shèhuì* 礼治社会) (Fei 1985, 29–35). Furthermore, to contrast the conventional view of Western society as having "a rule of law" (*fǎzhì* 法治) and Chinese society as "a rule of man" (*rénzhì* 人治), Fei invented another term, "rule of ritual" (*lǐzhì* 礼治), to further describe Chinese society (1985, 48–53).

In Fei's later years, he paid more attention to globalization, which can be seen as an implication of *chaxugeju* at the *tianxia* level. Fei treated the world as one global society (or "world society" in his words of the 1940s). His ideas about the importance of building patterns of multicultural and international "pluralistic unity" within "one world" can be understood as part of his broader conceptualization of global governance. Fei always believed that social-scientific contributions drawing on Chinese society should be studies of how Chinese people make and maintain relationships in order to live peacefully and harmoniously. In his last paper, he emphasized that Chinese civilization is founded on Confucian *li*-centered culture. Here *"li"* means ceremony, gift, ritual, courtesy, propriety, rite, or manners. Fei believed this philosophy of individual self-discipline promoted a harmonious social order (Fei 2005). It thus accords with his early ideas in *From the Soil*.

Fei wrote prolifically in the last fifteen years of his life, mainly in Chinese, but only a small portion of his work has been translated and most studies cover

费孝通

only a minor part of his completed works, which consists of over seven million Chinese characters (Hamilton and Chang 2014, 106). To fully understand and appreciate Fei's contribution to the field of anthropology in China and beyond, it is important to take all his works into consideration.

CHANG Xiangqun
University College London

Further Reading

Arkush, R. David. (1981). *Fei Xiaotong and sociology in revolutionary China*. Cambridge, MA: Harvard University Press.

Fei Xiaotong. (1939). *Peasant life in China*. London: Routledge; New York: Dutton.

Fei Xiaotong. (1946). *Neidi de nongcun* 内地的农村 [Villages of the interior]. Shanghai: Shenghuo.

Fei Xiaotong. (1947). *Shengyu zhidu* 生育制度 [The Institutions for Reproduction]. Shanghai: Shangwu.

Fei Xiaotong. (1948). *Xiangtu chongjian* 乡土重建 [Rural recovery]. Shanghai: Guancha.

Fei Xiaotong. (1953). *China's gentry*. Chicago: University of Chicago Press.

Fei Xiaotong. (1989). *Zhonghua minzu duoyuan yiti geju* 中华民族多元一体格局 [The pattern of Chinese nationalities' pluralistic unity]. Beijing: Central University for Nationalities Publishing House.

Fei Xiaotong. (1992). *From the soil: The foundations of Chinese society*. (Gary Hamilton & Zhang Weng, Trans.). Berkeley: University of California Press. (Original work published 1948/85)

Fei Xiaotong. (2005). Meimei yu gong he renlei wenming 美美与共和人类文明 [Common Beauty and Human Civilization]. *Quanyan 1*, 17–20; *2*, 13–16.

Fei Xiaotong. (2010). *Fei Xiaotong: Quanji* 费孝通：全集 [Fei Xiaotong: Complete works] (20 vols). Hohhot: Neimenggu People's Publishing House.

Fei Xiaotong, & Wang Tonghui. (1936). *Hualan yao shehui zuzhi* 花篮瑶社会组织 [Hualan Yao social organization]. Shanghai: Shangwu Yin Shu Guan.

Fei Xiaotong, & Chang Chih-yi. (1945). *Earthbound China*. Chicago: University of Chicago Press.

Feuchtwang, Stephan. (2009). Shehui ziwo zhuyi yu geren zhuyi 社会自我主义与个人主义 [Social egoism and individualism]. (Gong Haoqun & Yang Qingqing, Trans.). *Kaifang Shidai, 3*, 67–82.

Feuchtwang, Stephan. (2014). Social egoism and individualism: surprises and questions that arise from reading Fei Xiaotong's idea of "the opposition between East and West. *Journal of China in Comparative Perspective, 1*(2), 75–95.

Freedman, Maurice. (1963). A Chinese phase in social anthropology. *British Journal of Sociology, 14*(1), 1–19.

Hamilton, Gary. (2010). World images, authority, and institutions: a comparison of China and the West. *European Journal of Social Theory, 13*(1), 31–48.

Hamilton, Gary. (2014). What Western social scientists can learn from the writings of Fei Xiaotong. *Journal of China in Comparative Perspective, 1*(2), 49–73.

Hamilton, Gary, & Chang Xiangqun. (2011). *China and world anthropology: A conversation on the legacy of Fei Xiaotong* (1910–2005). *Anthropology Today, 6*, 20–23.

Hamilton, Gary, & Chang Xiangqun. (2014). Fei Xiaotong's contribution to sociology and anthropology: A dialogue between a Western scholar and a Chinese scholar. *Journal of China in Comparative Perspective*, 1(2), 91–116.

Malinowski, Bronislaw. (1939). Preface. In: Fei Xiaotong, *Peasant life in China*. London: G. Routledge and New York: Dutton.

Xu Ping. (2009). *Fei Xiaotong Ping Zhuan* [A critical biography of Fei Xiaotong]. Beijing: Minzu Cubanshe

Yan Yunxiang. (forthcoming 2015). Moral hierarchy and social egoism in a networked society: The Chaxugeju thesis revisited. In Stephan Feuchtwang; Chang Xiangqun; & Zhou (Eds.), *Globalization of Chinese social sciences — Commemorating the 105th anniversary of professor Fei Xiaotong's birth*. London: Global China Press.

Zhang Guansheng. (1996). *Xiangtu zuyin – Fei Xiaotong zuji, biji, xinji* 乡土足音——费孝通足迹笔迹心迹 [Footsteps from the soil: Fei Xiaotong's footprints, handwritings and heart's pursuit]. Beijing: Qun Yan Publishing House.

费孝通

♂ Féng Xiǎogāng 冯小刚

b. 1958—Film director, well-known for his New Year films

Alternate name: trad. 馮小剛

Summary

Feng Xiaogang is one of the most active and prolific filmmakers in China. He is unique among modern Chinese filmmakers for his combination of productivity and popularity, and his career was deeply impacted by both commercialization and censorship in Chinese cinema. Feng's first films were lighthearted romantic comedies, but he later made films about more serious subjects. His recent films alternate between these two genres.

Entering the filmmaking industry with little professional training, Feng Xiaogang started his career as an assistant to an art director in the early 1990s. Within several years Feng had become one of the most influential film directors in contemporary China. His New Year comedy films, or *hèsuìpiàn* 贺岁片, made after 1996, earned substantial profits in the domestic film market and were even more successful at the box office than some Hollywood blockbusters. From 2000 to 2014, Feng made eleven films—almost one film a year—surpassing the productivity of most other Chinese filmmakers, including winners of international film awards such as *Zhāng Yìmóu 张艺谋 (b. 1951) and *Chén Kǎigē 陈凯歌 (b. 1950). Additionally, Feng has demonstrated an ability to handle multiple genres, including comedy, epic, war, and history.

Success did not come immediately for Feng, however. His four earliest productions made between 1994 and 1995, including one film and three television dramas, were either censored or failed to attract much attention from critics and audiences. These failures led to the bankruptcy of his first production company. It was not until 1997 that his films began to attract audience attention and became popular at the box office. Throughout his career Feng has utilized various modes of

*People marked with an asterisk have entries in this dictionary.

film production, from independent production to foreign investment, and has been forced to deal creatively with challenges ranging from censorship, a lack of stable financial resources, and competition from Hollywood blockbusters.

Early Life

Feng was born in Beijing in 1958. After his parents divorced, he lived with his mother and sister in a "grand courtyard" (*dàyuàn* 大院), a compound containing offices, apartments, and public facilities such as restaurants, stores, and medical offices. In this environment, Feng became familiar with the living conditions of the so-called "little characters"—that is, the insignificant people situated at the bottom of the power hierarchy—who later became the protagonists in his films.

Feng's childhood coincided with the Cultural Revolution (1966–1976). Too young to join the Red Guards, he stayed in Beijing throughout this period and remembers it as a time of peace and quiet. All schools were closed, and older children were sent to the countryside for reeducation. During this time Feng developed an interest in art and began to learn painting (Feng 2003, 35–40). When the Cultural Revolution was redefined as a "ten year disaster" (*shínián hàojié* 十年浩劫) at the end of the 1970s, Feng experienced neither the iconoclasm nor the disillusionment that many in China felt. In fact, unlike in other films and works of art of this period, the Maoist era is portrayed in Feng's films with a great sense of nostalgia and sentiment rather than criticism and disillusionment.

In 1978, when Chinese universities and colleges reopened, Feng passed the entry examination of the Department of Art Direction at the Beijing Film Academy. Because his mother could not afford the cost of art supplies, however, he had no choice but to give up this opportunity. Instead of entering the academy, he joined the army, where he worked as a set designer in a Military Art Ensemble based in Beijing.

Film Career

In 1985, Feng began to work as a staff member of the Beijing City Construction Workers Union 北京城建开发总公司工会 and then joined the Beijing TV Drama Production Center 北京电视剧制作中心 and worked as an assistant to the set designer and art director for several television shows, including *Returning in Triumph at Midnight* 凯旋在子夜 and *Plainclothes Police Officer* 便衣警察. In the early 1990s, he started to write scripts for television dramas and films (Feng 2003, 25–35).

Feng's filmmaking career can be divided into three periods: the formative stage, the New Year film period, and the post-New Year film period.

Formative Stage (1991–1996)

In 1991, Feng wrote his first screenplay for the film *Unexpected Passion* 遭遇激情 (1991), directed by Zhèng Xiǎolóng

郑晓龙. The film, a tragic love story about a young unemployed urban dweller and a mysterious girl he meets in a bar, received four Golden Rooster nominations, the most prestigious film award in China, including one for Best Screen Script. In 1993, Feng wrote another film script, *After Separation* 大撒把 (1993) based on Zheng Xiaolong's personal experience of his life after his wife went to live abroad, which also received a Golden Rooster nomination for Best Screen Script.

In 1993, Feng and the popular author *Wáng Shuò 王朔 (b. 1958) co-founded a television and film production company, Good Dream TV and Film Production & Consulting 好梦影视策划公司. Feng worked first as a scriptwriter, then as a director. Good Dream was not only where Feng got his first training as a businessman, it was also where he began to experiment with different subjects and styles of cinema.

Wang Shuo later left for another production company, and Feng became the central figure at Good Dream. The company's six productions are all associated with Feng, and he worked in multiple capacities as director, scriptwriter, and actor. During its four years in existence, the company produced three television dramas, all directed by Feng, and two films, including *Chicken Feather* 一地鸡毛 (1995), *Elegy for Love* 情殇 (1995), *Dark Side of the Moon* 月亮背面 (1996), *Gone Forever with My Love* 永失我爱 (1994), and *I Am Your Dad* 我是你爸爸 (dir. Wang Shuo, 1995).

As a result of Feng and Wang Shuo's collaboration, the cynicism and "black humor" of Wang Shuo's writing also became characteristic of Feng's work. Feng's directorial debut, *Gone Forever with My Love* is an adaptation based on two short stories by Wang, "Flight Attendant" ("Kōngzhōng xiǎojiě" 空中小姐) and "Died after Enjoyment" ("Guò bǎ yǐn jiù sǐ" 过把瘾就死), which is a sentimental nostalgic love story along with a strong sense of disillusionment toward love and idealism, all hallmarks of Wang's early writing style. While working at Good Dream, Feng also began to express more-insightful and direct critiques of social and cultural issues in contemporary China. During the four years of its existence, the company produced three television dramas and three films with subjects such as social issues, the depravity of human beings, and injustice between classes, reflecting Feng and Wang's social conscience and their desire to produce meaningful commentary on problems in contemporary Chinese society. This caused several unpleasant encounters with censorship.

In 1996, Good Dream did not register with Beijing Industry and Commerce Administration BICA, and it was closed in 1997. The closing of Good Dream was the most devastating event in Feng's career, but it was also a turning point. Learning from the failures of his productions at Good Dream, Feng explored the new genre of New Year films, which brought him to the center of national attention.

• Féng Xiǎogāng •

Selected Filmography of Feng Xiaogang			
Year	English Title	Chinese Title	Notes
1986	*Returning in Triumph at Midnight*	凯旋在子夜 *Kǎixuán zài zǐyè*	Set-designer
1987	*Plainclothes Police Officer*	便衣警察 *Biànyī jǐngchá*	Set-designer
1991	*Unexpected Passion*	遭遇激情 *Zāoyù jīqíng*	Script-writer
1993	*After Separation*	大撒把 *Dà sǎ bǎ*	Script-writer
1994	*Beijinger in New York*	北京人在纽约 *Běijīng rén zài Niǔyuē*	Co-director
1994	*Gone Forever With My Love*	永失我爱 *Yǒng shī wǒ ài*	Director
1995	*Elegy for Love*	情殇 *Qíng shāng*	TV drama
1995	*Chicken Feather*	一地鸡毛 *Yīdì jīmáo*	TV drama
1996	*Dark Side of the Moon*	月亮背面 *Yuèliang bèi miàn*	TV drama
1996	*Living a Miserable Life*	过着狼狈不堪的生活	Project aborted
1997	*Party A, Party B*	甲方乙方 *Yǎfāng yǐfāng*	Director
1998	*Be There or Be Square*	不见不散 *Bújiàn búsàn*	Director

New Year Films (1997–1999)

Starting in 1997, in order to avoid direct conflict with the censorship board, Feng changed his style from "social conscience" to a safer alternative, comedy, and found other ways to draw attention to the issues he wanted to expose. In 1996, inspired by a suggestion from Hán Sānpíng 韩三平, the director of the Beijing Film Studio, Feng decided to adapt

Year	English Title	Chinese Title	Notes
1999	*Sorry, Baby!*	没完没了 *Méiwán méiliǎo*	Director
2000	*Sigh*	一声叹息 *Yī shāng tànxi*	Director
2001	*Big Shot's Funeral*	大腕 *Dàwàn*	Director
2003	*Cellphone*	手机 *Shǒujī*	Director
2004	*A World Without Thieves*	天下无贼 *Tiānxià wú zéi*	Director
2006	*The Banquet*	夜宴 *Yè yàn*	Director
2006	*Assembly*	集结号 *Jí jié hào*	Director
2009	*If You Are the One*	非诚勿扰 *Fēichéng Wùrǎo*	Director
2010	*Aftershock*	唐山大地震 *Tángshān Dà Dìzhèn*	Director
2010	*If You Are the One II*	非诚勿扰2 *Fēichéng Wùrǎo 2*	Director
2011	*Remembering 1942*	温故 1942 *Wēngù 1942*	Director
2013	*Personal Tailor*	私人订制 *Sīrén dìngzhì*	Director

the popular Hong Kong New Year film genre for a mainland audience. New Year films were so named because they were released in theaters specifically during the New Year holidays.

Feng wrote and directed his first New Year film, *Party A, Party B* (1997), based on Wang Shuo's short story "You Are Not a Common Person" ("Nǐ búshì ge sú rén" 你不是个俗人). The film achieved box-office earnings as high as 15 million yuan (around US$2 million) in Beijing, the highest earnings of any film that year. Feng's other New Year films included *Be There or Be Square* 不见不散 (1998), *Sorry Baby!* 没完没了 (1999), and

From Hollywood to *Hesuipian*

The emergence of New Year films in 1996 was the result of a series of transformations in the Chinese film industry brought about by industry reforms and Hollywood imports.

In the early 1990s, a new round of industry reforms focused more fundamentally on pushing the state-owned studios to the forefront of commercialization. With limited state sponsorship, and an enormous burden from overstaffing, many studios had to rely for their earnings on the sale of licenses to private productions companies or the collection of "management fees" from co-productions with foreign studios. Therefore, in the mid-1990s, even though the ownership of film production studios was still in the hands of the state, films produced by private or semi-private production companies demonstrated a great potential for success in the film market.

An important external force also began to show its influence in 1995. In 1994, the Chinese Film Import and Export Corporation signed a contract with major Hollywood studios to import ten Hollywood films each year with a promise to raise the quota gradually until China's entry into the World Trade Organization (WTO), after which Hollywood would be allowed to export films to China without any restrictions or quotas. In 1995, ten Hollywood blockbusters, including *True Lies* and *The Fugitive*, entered Chinese movie theaters, attracting Chinese audiences back to movie theaters, and thus functioned as a driving force in the rejuvenation of a weak film market. It was against this background that in 1996 Feng Xiaogang changed his style from "social conscience" to New Year comedy, a genre that was not only more easily accepted by the censors, but also more attractive to audiences and thus more profitable.

Rui ZHANG

Big Shot's Funeral 大腕 (2001). All these films are light comedies focusing on the lives of ordinary people in various odd situations and circumstances. By infusing stories of ordinary people with deliberate satire and cynicism, his films both appealed to the general public and supported mainstream official ideology. Starting in this period, Feng's films began to demonstrate the "doubleness" of popular culture, in which he expressed his concerns for social problems in implicit or explicit ways but also endorsed the current social order by providing solutions for the problems from within the system. For example, in *Sorry Baby*, the male protagonist, a tour-bus driver named Han Dong (played by the well-known actor Gě Yōu 葛优), kidnaps his boss's girlfriend, because the boss refuses to pay his salary. This reflects a permeating social problem for many unpaid employees. At the end of the film, however, while the stingy boss still refuses to pay his girlfriend's ransom, the girlfriend herself pays Han the money. As Han decides to surrender to the police, she also testifies that he didn't kidnap her, and he is subsequently set free. Furthermore, the girlfriend eventually breaks up with the boss and falls in love with Han. Thus, not only are all problems solved, the protagonist is also rewarded with love.

Post-New Year Films (2000–Present)

In 2000, Feng shifted his focus again from comedy to more-serious subjects, which brought about the arrival of the third stage of his career. In this stage, while his films still had traces of witty and humorous dialogue, there was a definite turn toward dark and cynical themes.

The movie *Sigh* 一声叹息 (2000) can be seen as Feng's first attempt to test the waters of censorship. The film tells the story of a successful writer who, despite being happily married, finds himself falling for his young and attractive assistant. For several years, he lives a double life and is torn between breaking up with his lover and divorcing his wife (played by Xú Fān 徐帆, Feng's second wife who appeared in many of his films). Originally the movie ended with a scene in which the husband sneaks out to see his lover, many years after their breakup. Film censors advised that this scene be changed, however, because the affair "ought" to have ended after the husband returned home. The final version of the film thus ends with the husband and his family on vacation. As he answers a call on his cell phone, he turns around and looks directly at the camera with a fearful gaze (Short 2010). Although the ending of the film was changed according to the censor's requirement, the fact that the film passed at all signals a loosening of the ideological restrictions circumscribing the Chinese film industry. The relaxed restrictions enabled a shift in emphases in Feng's films from light-hearted comedies with hidden criticism to serious examinations of the darker side of humanity.

Starting in 1998 Feng began to collaborate with Huayi Bothers Media Group 华谊兄弟传媒集团. His recent films, including *Cellphone* 手机 (2003), *The Banquet* 夜宴 (2006), *Assembly* 集结号 (2006), *If You Are the One* 非诚勿扰 (Part one 2009, Part two 2010), *Aftershock* 唐山大地震 (2010), *Remembering 1942* 温故 1942 (2011), and *Personal Tailor* 私人定制 (2013), were all made under Huayi's sponsorship.

Feng's films feature many recurring themes, such as the portrayal of "little characters," satirical mockery of the privileged stratums, and implicit and explicit social commentary. Different cultural and political forces, including ideological control, film industry reform, and the importation of Hollywood films, have influenced Feng's films. The interactions between the filmmaker and the film authorities represented by the former's resistance, negotiation, and compromise with the authorities and the latter's attempt to control this medium through both governmental legislation and arbitrary film censorship also had an effect on Feng's career. Another aspect that cannot be ignored in a general portrayal of Chinese cinema at the turn of the twenty-first century—or, by extension, during Feng's filmmaking career—is the impact of commercialization of the Chinese film industry and Hollywood cinema.

Although his early career suffered from film censorship, Feng greatly benefited when the Chinese film industry entered the corporate era, but he also fell victim to the drive for profits. In the 2000s, although the pressure from film officials regarding film ideology was reduced, the demand to maximize profits forced Feng to insert as many tie-ins (i.e., references to other products or media properties) as possible to satisfy his investors, while still attempting to maintain the integrity of the narrative. Simultaneously, Feng became a billionaire because of his stock options in Huayi, after the company went public in 2009.

Rui ZHANG
Tsinghua University

Further Reading

Feng Xiaogang 冯小刚. (2003). *Wo ba qingchun xian gei ni* 我把青春献给你 [I dedicated my youth to you]. Beijing: Changjiang wenyi.

McGrath, Jason. (2008). *Postsocialist modernity: Chinese cinema, literature, and criticism in the market age.* Stanford, CA: Stanford University Press.

Short, Stephen. (2001). Interview with director Feng Xiaogang, *Time Asia*.

Zhu Ying. (2003). *Chinese Cinema during the reform era: The ingenuity of the system.* Westport, CT: Praeger.

Zhang Rui. (2008). *The cinema of Feng Xiaogang: Censorship and commercialisation of Chinese cinema after 1989.* Hong Kong: Hong Kong University Press.

冯小刚

♂ Fok, Henry

Huò Yīngdōng 霍英東

1923–2006—Hong Kong business leader, politician, and sportsman

Alternate names: b. Fok Koon Tai 霍官泰; Henry Ying-Tung Fok; simpl. 霍英东

Summary

Dr. Henry Fok was China's window to the world before the country's opening-up in the late 1970s. While his childhood was a struggle for survival, he won fame and fortune when he started shipping strategic supplies to China during the Korean War, against a United Nations embargo. Gaining China's trust later paved the way for his subsequent rise in business and politics.

D r. Henry (Ying-Tung) Fok was a trailblazer in business, politics, and sports. What he did in these three areas changed the course of history of Hong Kong and China. In 1993 he became the first Hong Kong-born Chinese to become vice chairman of the Chinese National People's Political Consultative Committee (CNPPCC), which offers advice to the Central Committee of the Chinese Communist Party and has significant influence and status.

Early Life and Career

Born to a sampan fishing-boat family on 10 May 1923, Fok lost his two elder brothers at the age of seven when a rogue wave hit them. After his cancer-stricken father died soon afterwards, his mother moved into a slum area in Wan Chai, where as a preteen Fok worked in various manual trades before making his way to study at Queen's College, one of the top government-run secondary schools. In 1941, when he was eighteen, his course of study was cut short by the Japanese occupation of Hong Kong. He married at age twenty and started a small hawker business. Through a combination of hard work and business acumen, his hawker business flourished and he started bidding in post-war government auctions of materials and supplies.

Ferrying Supplies to China

A major turning point in Fok's fortune came in 1950 with the outbreak of the Korean War. Gathering equipment purchased from public auctions of residual war-related supplies, he outfitted a small fleet of fishing boats and started shuttling these much-needed supplies to China, circumventing a United Nations (UN) shipment embargo that was strictly enforced by the British colonial administration. Years later, Fok would deny rumors of weapon smuggling to China, admitting only to shipping such resources as iron plates, iron sheets, pipes, gasoline, hardware, and medical supplies. What was undisputed was that the three years of clandestine shipments to China earned him his first fortune and the trust of Chinese Communist Party (CCP), laying the foundation for his subsequent rise within the Chinese unofficial pecking order. At the same time, it also earned him blacklisting by the British colonial rulers in Hong Kong.

It is hard to tell to what extent the outcome of the Korean War would have been different without Fok's supplies, which sustained China's campaign. But amidst some lingering rumors that Fok profiteered on China's "national calamity" during the war, Fok's effort was officially recognized in the early 1980s when Liao Chengzhi, then director of the Overseas Chinese Affairs Office of the Chinese State Council, declared: "I want to vindicate Mr. Fok for his contribution. What he 'smuggled' during the Korean War was our much needed strategic supplies. He contributed to our effort against the US in support of Korea" (Li Wenshen 2011, 170). On 25 October 2000 at an official memorial function in Beijing to mark the fiftieth anniversary of the Korean campaign, Fok was the only overseas guest invited to attend.

Business Ventures: From Hong Kong to China

Fok's business ventures during Hong Kong's post-war reconstruction boom suffered many British-inflicted setbacks. He was the only bidder in 1965 for a naval-barracks site that subsequently became Admiralty and Pacific Place, between Hong Kong's central business district and Wan Chai. It was the first time the colonial government invited international tenders for a piece of land in Hong Kong, but with Fok as the only bidder, the government refused to release the site.

Two years later, during the 1967 riots in Hong Kong by those sympathetic to the Cultural Revolution being waged across the border, Fok's Star House in Tsimshatsui—a prime commercial property in Kowloon—became the target of commercial hostility by British-American interests who severed the supply of water, electricity, and telephone lines, rendering the property unsustainable. Fok was forced to sell it on the cheap to the British firm Hong Kong Land.

While the British frustrated Fok, China facilitated his business. As real estate development boomed in post-war Hong Kong, Fok moved to the property market and pioneered the sale of uncompleted residential flats, which remains the standard modus operandi for property developers in Hong Kong. In 1961, he joined hands with *Stanley Ho (b. 1921) to start a casino business in Macao, although Fok himself was anti-gambling and never involved himself in the management of the gaming industry. He subsequently donated to charity his entire 27.7 percent holdings in the gaming empire. In 1973, he started doing petroleum business with China, and in 1983 developed the White Swan Hotel in Guangzhou, which became the icon of China's opening up. Among its guests was *Dèng Xiǎopíng 邓小平 (1904–1997), who checked into the hotel three times, including one time in which he met with Fok to discuss the issue of Hong Kong's 1997 return to China. Fok was the first to get a one-on-one with the Chinese paramount leader when Beijing started contemplating the "One Country, Two Systems" concept for the management of governance post-1997 in Hong Kong.

Fok's last investment was in Nansha in Guangdong, where he injected US$800 million to develop a science and technology park in collaboration with the Hong Kong University of Science and Technology.

Second Career: Sports

Fok contributed to China's sports diplomacy, but first he re-made himself as a sportsman. Back when Hong Kongers loved soccer and tennis as much as their colonial masters, Fok at the age of forty-three trained to become a League A soccer player, Hong Kong's equivalent of the British Premier League soccer player. From 1972 to 1977, he was Hong Kong's champion in tennis doubles for six years in a row. He was then already in his fifties. After quitting premier league soccer, he went on to become the chairman of the Hong Kong Football Association for twenty years and then a member of the FIFA committee. He has donated billions of Hong Kong dollars for sports scholarships to support China's and Hong Kong's Olympians. Locals regarded him as a sports legend both on and off the field.

Through his connections in regional and global sports circles, he lobbied hard to restore China's membership in international sporting associations at a time when Taiwan was the official China representative. He had to win the support of international bodies and also to convince Beijing's hardliners who advocated the "China won't come if Taiwan doesn't get out" position. In 1974, the Asian Football Confederation restored China's membership while preserving Taiwan's membership as part of the China membership. Other international bodies including FIFA and the International Olympics Committee followed suit. This political solution to China's membership in international bodies was in the same spirit as the "One Country, Two Systems" concept conceived by Deng Xiaoping to resolve Hong Kong's return to China.

---

*People marked with an asterisk have entries in this dictionary.

Political Status and Legacy

In 1989, Fok openly wept for the death of students in the Tiananmen Incident and joined nineteen leading Hong Kong and Macau community figures in denouncing the use of force against the protesters. But no friendship was lost with Beijing. In 1993, he was made a vice chairman of the CPPCC National Committee.

Fok died of cancer on 28 October 2006 and received a state burial of the highest order. China's official obituary called him "a close friend of the Chinese Communist Party," an accolade reserved for very few trusted CCP allies.

Chee Kong YEUNG
Chinese University of Hong Kong

Further Reading

Li Wenshen 李敏生. (2011). *Huo Yingdong yu kangmei yuan chao zhanzheng* 霍英東與抗美援朝戰爭 [Henry Fok and the Korea War]. Beijing: Jiefangjun Chubanshe.

Li Wenshen 李敏生 (Ed.). (1997). *Huo Yingdong yu tijiao* 霍英東與體育 [Henry Fok and Sports]. Beijing: Beijing Social Science Chronicle.

Leng Xia 冷夏. (2005). *Huo Yingdong quanzhuan* 霍英東全傳 [Henry Fok—A complete biography]. Beijing: Zhonghua Huaju.

Leng Xia 冷夏. (2010). *Shiji huimou: Huo Yingdong hui yilu* 世紀回眸：霍英東回憶錄 [Henry Fok tells his story]. Hong Kong: Mingliu Chubanshe.

CPPCC National Committee Office (Eds.). (2007). *Huo Yingdong Fengfan changchun* 霍英東風範長存 [Tribute to Henry Fok]. Beijing: Zhonghua wenshi.

☿ Gāo Xíngjiàn 高行健

b. 1940—Writer, artist, director, and filmmaker who won the 2000 Nobel Prize for Literature

Summary

Gao Xingjian became a celebrity in Chinese literary circles through his book *Preliminary Explorations into the Art of Modern Fiction* and with the staging of several of his plays. His play "The Other Shore" was banned at rehearsal, and he was subjected to various forms of harassment. Relocating to Paris in 1987, he excelled as an artist, novelist, playwright, director, and filmmaker. By interrogating Chinese and European aesthetics and practices he produced unique creations that have led to prestigious awards including the Nobel Prize for Literature in 2000.

Born into a middle-class family in Nationalist China, Gao Xingjian was exposed to the cosmopolitan cultural influences of those times from an early age. As a child he took violin lessons and listened to European classical music on a gramophone, and also spent much time browsing through the family library, which included numerous volumes on European literature and art. Fascinated by the European masters, he saved pocket money to buy tubes of paint and by his teenage years was taking lessons in oil painting to prepare for further study in an art college. By the time he finished his high school education, the politics of establishing a new socialist society prevailed, and a career in art meant painting propaganda posters. Gao enrolled instead in a five-year degree course in French at the Foreign Languages Institute in Beijing.

Education and Career in China

While in the outside world Chinese books were being trashed or stored in basements by the censors, Gao read through the Institute's library holdings of French literature and French translations of writings in other languages. His reading fuelled his desire to actualize in word and image his inchoate thoughts and feelings. He was assigned work as a translator and editor at the Foreign Languages Press in 1962. Meanwhile he began to write in secret because he knew what he wrote failed to conform to the stipulated guidelines for socialist cultural production. He also painted with Chinese ink, which could be completed with a few calligraphic strokes and would dry instantly. When Red Guards began ransacking homes to find evidence of counterrevolutionary activities at the outbreak of the Cultural Revolution (1966–1976), he had no choice but to hastily burn his suitcase of unpublished manuscripts. During this chaotic time he spent five years working as a peasant and then as a village teacher; only as the Cultural Revolution drew to an end in 1975 was he able to resume work in Beijing.

China gradually began opening to the world after decades of isolation, and the draconian censorship on cultural activities relaxed. In 1979 and 1980, Gao Xingjian made two short trips to Europe, first travelling as the interpreter for a delegation of writers to France led by veteran writer *Bā Jīn 巴金 (1904–2005), and then as a member of a delegation of writers to France and Italy. In the grand museums of Europe, he saw the originals of artworks he had long admired and knew that it was futile to think he could ever produce comparable oil

paintings. Returning from the second trip, he turned fully to exploring the potential of Chinese ink to give expression to his artistic impulses. His early studies of the nude female body dating back to the early 1960s already indicate a radical departure from the conventions of traditional Chinese ink painting, and from 1980 he rapidly developed his own distinctive style of Chinese expressive painting.

Preliminary Explorations and Popular Plays

In 1980, Gao was reassigned to work as a playwright for the People's Art Theatre in Beijing, and his prolific output of short stories, novellas, plays, writings on French literature, and theoretical works on fiction and drama began appearing regularly in literary publications. In 1981, his book *Preliminary Explorations into the Art of Modern Fiction* 现代小说技巧初探 was published and immediately sold out. The work audaciously challenged the official socialist guidelines for cultural production with its claim that the masterpieces of Chinese and Western literature all had characters with human impulses, emotions, motivations and sensitivities that made them credible and authentic depictions of real human beings; the book further proposed that literature should not be used to preach. When the book was reprinted in 1982, Gao came under the surveillance of the custodians of cultural production who

---

*People marked with an asterisk have entries in this dictionary.

directed the Writers Association and the Department of Propaganda.

Preliminary Explorations into the Art of Modern Fiction was one of the most widely read books at the time, and Gao's celebrity credentials as a writer were consolidated by the staging of his plays "Absolute Signal" 绝对信号 in 1982 and "Bus Stop" 车站 in 1983 to wildly ecstatic audiences. Like the short stories and novellas he was writing at the time, both plays confirmed the effectiveness of his proposal for character portrayal. His characters were neither the revolutionary-hero nor counterrevolutionary-villain stereotypes that were obligatory in revolutionary plays, but instead bore a likeness to real people. His primary interest was the psychology of his characters, and the staging of these first two plays demonstrates his emerging theater aesthetics in which theatricality and humor were essential elements.

Official Opposition in China

In early 1983, Gao Xingjian was summoned to appear at three separate mass meetings held in different locations to hear condemnations that his book *Preliminary Explorations into the Art of Modern Fiction* was allegedly leading young writers astray. All three meetings failed to achieve the desired outcome for the organizers because veteran writers came forward to speak in defense of both the book and the author. Exhilarated by this outcome, Gao proceeded to rehearse and stage "Bus Stop" without obtaining the required authorization. The play was banned after the tenth performance with the launch of a new political campaign to combat "spiritual pollution."

On learning that he would be sent to a prison farm in Qinghai Province for re-education, Gao immediately fled for parts unknown in the mountain forests of southwest China. When the political campaign lost momentum towards the end of the year, he returned to Beijing. Publishers were required to shelve his manuscripts for several months, but a number of his short stories as well as essays on literary aesthetics were published that year, and in 1984 and 1985 a continuous stream of his publications appeared in literary magazines. In 1985, his third play "Wild Man" 野人 was staged in the main auditorium of the People's Art Theatre, where he also held a solo exhibition of his Chinese ink paintings in the theater foyer. He then traveled on a German Academic Exchange Service (DAAD) fellowship to Germany, and spent months traveling around Europe, presenting lectures, and exhibiting his paintings.

While his plays found their way onto European stages and radio stations, and French translations of his short stories began to appear, in China his new play, "The Other Shore," was banned after a few rehearsals in 1986, and he became the target of a vendetta that used insidious tactics to block his creative endeavors.

Selected Bibliography of Gao Xingjian			
Year	English Title	Chinese Title	Notes
1981	*Preliminary Explorations into the Art of Modern Fiction*	现代小说技巧初探/ 现代小說技巧初探 *Xiàndài xiǎoshuō jìqiǎo chūtàn*	Literary Criticism
1982	Absolute Signal	绝对信号/絕對信號 Juéduì xìnhào	Play
1983	Bus Stop	车站/車站 Chēzhàn	Play
1985	Wild Man	野人 Yěrén	Play
1985	Collected Plays by Gao Xingjian	高行健戏剧集/高行健戲劇集 Gāo Xíngjiàn xìjù jí	Collected plays
1986	The Other Shore		Play (banned after a few rehearsals)
1988	*Buying a Fishing Rod for My Grandfather*	给我老爷买渔竿/給我老爺買魚竿 *Gěi wǒ lǎoyè mǎi yúgān*	Short story collection (translated in 2004)
1988	*In Search of a Modern Form of Theatre*	对一种现代戏剧的追求/對一種现代戲劇的追求 *Duì yīzhǒng xiàndài xìjù de zhuīqiú*	Literary criticism
1990	*Soul Mountain*	灵山/靈山 *Língshān*	Autobiographical novel (translated in 2000)
1993	*Six Plays by Gao Xingjian*	高行健戏剧六种/高行健戲劇六種 *Gāo Xíngjiàn xìjù liùzhǒng*	Collected plays
1995	Weekend Quartet (Quatre quatuors *pour un week-end*)	周末四重奏 /週末四重奏 Zhōumò sìchóngzòu	Play (translated in 1999)
1996	*Without Isms*	没有主义 /没有主義 *Méiyǒu zhǔyì*	Literary criticism

Year	English Title	Chinese Title	Notes
1999	*One Man's Bible*	一个人的圣经 /一個人的聖經 *Yīge rén de shèngjīng*	Autobiographical novel (translated 2002)
2000	Snow in August	八月雪 *Bāyuè xuě*	Opera (translated in 2003)
2004	The Man Who Questions Death (Le quêteur de la mort)	叩问死亡/叩問死亡 Kòuwèn sǐwáng	Play (translated in 2007)
2007	*Silhouette / Shadow (La silhouette si non l'ombre)*	侧影或影子/ 側影或影子 *Cèyǐng huò yǐngzi*	Art film
2008	*After the Flood (Après le déluge)*	洪荒之后 /洪荒之後 *Hónghuāng zhī hòu*	Art film
2008	*Aesthetics and Creation*	论创作 / 論創作 *Lún chuàngzuò*	Essay collection (translated 2012)
2012	*Wandering Spirit and Metaphysical Thoughts*	游神与玄思/ 游神與玄思 *Yóushén yú xuánsī*	Essay collection
2013	*Requiem for Beauty (Le Deuil de la beauté)*	美的葬礼/ 美的葬禮 *Měi de zànglǐ*	Art film

Relocation to France

Gao travelled to Germany in late 1987 and by the end of the year had settled in Paris, where he immediately began recouping the decades of his creative life that had been squandered by Chinese politics. He was able to support himself abroad by selling his paintings. Informed by his interest in both oil painting and black-and-white photography, his art-works are distinguished by their rich textures and sense of distance that are absent in traditional Chinese expressive painting.

Nobel Prize for Literature 2000

When Gao Xingjian was crowned Nobel Laureate for Literature in 2000, it was the first time in its nearly one-hundred-year history that the award had been given for a body of work originally created in the Chinese language. Most of his plays had been collected in *Collected Plays by Gao Xingjian* 高行健戏剧集 (1985) and in *Six Plays by Gao Xingjian* 高行健戏剧六种 (1993). His opera *Snow in August* 八月雪 (2000) was released as a single volume. Several of his plays had been staged in various languages on five continents and testified to their ability to transcend cultural barriers. His major works of fiction included the short stories in *Buying a Fishing Rod for My Grandfather* 给我老爷买渔竿 (1988) as well as two lengthy autobiographical novels, *Soul Mountain* 灵山 (1990) and *One Man's Bible* 一个人的圣经 (1999). He had also published three volumes of critical writings on fiction and drama: besides the acclaimed *Preliminary Explorations into the Art of Modern Fiction* (1981), these include *In Search of a Modern Form of Theatre* 对一种现代戏剧的追求 (1988), and *Without Isms* 没有主义 (1996).

Translations and Research

Only one of the Nobel adjudicators read Chinese, so translations and writings in major European languages were imperative for the judging process. By 1990, English translations of individual plays had appeared in magazines or anthologies: "Absolute Signal" (1996), "The Bus Stop" (1996, 1998) and "Wild Man" (1990). At different times during the 1990s, a number of academics from different parts of the world sought Gao Xingjian's permission to translate and arrange publication of his major works. The Nobel adjudicators therefore had access to reading selections of Gao Xingjian's plays and short stories, as well as his two novels in the Swedish translations of Göran Malmqvist and the French translations of the husband and wife team Noël and Liliane Dutrait. They also had access to two volumes of his works

in English: *The Other Shore: Plays by Gao Xingjian* (1999) translated by Gilbert C. F. Fong (Chinese University of Hong Kong), and his novel *Soul Mountain* translated by Mabel Lee (University of Sydney).

From the early 1980s, English-language studies of Gao Xingjian's work began appearing in academic journals, and the Nobel adjudicators would have read copies of these essays that Kwok-kan Tam later collected and published in 2001 with the title *Soul of Chaos: Critical Perspectives on Gao Xingjian*. Perhaps of critical importance was the publication in 2000 of the English-language monograph *Towards a Modern Zen Theatre: Gao Xingjian and Chinese Theatre Experimentalism* by Henry Y. H. Zhao.

Post-Nobel Career

The Chinese authorities were critical of the decision to award Gao the Nobel Prize, and both his art and his writings are in effect banned in China. He has nonetheless maintained a substantial international audience. His plays continue to be staged in many languages all over the world, and his literary works are studied in the original or in translation in high schools and universities. In 2002, he directed his grand opera, *Snow in August*, at the National Theater in Taipei, and in early 2003 he directed the Comédie Français premiere of his play "Weekend Quartet" 周末四重奏 (1995). Later that year he co-directed his play

高行健

"The Man Who Questions Death" as part of the cultural events held by the city of Marseille to celebrate "Gao Xingjian Year."

His major recent works also include three art films *Silhouette / Shadow* 侧影或影子 (2007), *After the Flood* 洪荒之后 (2008) and *Requiem for Beauty* 美的葬礼 (2013). He has most recently produced a collection of essays, *Aesthetics and Creation* 论创作 (2008), and his first collection of poetry, *Wandering Spirit and Metaphysical Thoughts* 游神与玄思 (2012). In 2013, his black-and-white photography reproduced on silk was exhibited for the first time at iPreciation Gallery in Singapore and then at the University of Maryland in the United States.

Self-censorship has largely stifled serious Gao Xingjian research publications in China, and even attempts to exhibit his paintings continue to be stymied. He has been virtually airbrushed from existence by the Chinese authorities since his Nobel lecture in which he argues for the right to freedom of artistic expression and condemns authoritarian states for denying people this right. Both first published in Taiwan before 2000, his autobiographical novels *Soul Mountain* and *One Man's Bible* are highly artistic portrayals of his life in China. The former documents his solitary journey on the fringes of society after escaping the authorities at the beginning of the "anti-spiritual-pollution" campaign in 1983, and feature his reflections on history, society, literature, language and art, and

his own psychology. Importantly, *Soul Mountain* introduces his unique use of pronouns instead of characters with names, a writing technique that he would also later use in some of his plays. Pronouns are also used in *One Man's Bible*, which confronts his own psychology and behavior during the Cultural Revolution. The "he" of those abnormal times is indicted as cowardly, stupid, and easily manipulated by politics. By extension the suggestion is that, just like "he," the entire population had succumbed to the same form of intimidating manipulation, and therefore effectively controlled by its political masters. Although China's modern political history is critically examined in a few works, Gao clearly perceives political dynamics in social relationships as dating from the beginning of time, as seen in his play "Of Mountains and Seas."

Recent Gao Xingjian research publications in English are substantial, and include monographs such as Sy Ren Quah's *Gao Xingjian and Transcultural Chinese Theater* (2004), Izabella Łabędzka's *Gao Xingjian's Idea of Theatre: From the Word to the Image* (2008), and Jessica Yeung's *Gao Xingjian's Writing as Cultural Translation* (2008), and also essays such as those collected in *Polyphony Embodied: Freedom and Fate in Gao Xingjian's Writings* (2014), edited by Michael Lackner and Nikola Chardonnens, as well as large numbers of other uncollected essays. Gao's writings are linguistically and culturally porous, lending themselves easily to translation into various languages and to theater performances all over the world. Like his paintings and films, his novels and plays have as their primary aim the exploration of what it is to be human, and this accounts for their universal appeal.

Mabel LEE
The University of Sydney

Further Reading

Bergez, Daniel. (2013). *Gao Xingjian: Painter of the soul.* London: Asia Ink.

Gao Xingjian. (1999). *The other shore: Plays by Gao Xingjian* (Gilbert C. F. Fong, Trans.). Hong Kong: The Chinese University Press.

Gao Xingjian. (2000). *Soul mountain* (Mabel Lee, Trans.). Sydney, New York & London: Harper-Collins. (Original work published 1990)

Gao Xingjian. (2002). *One man's bible* (Mabel Lee, Trans.). Sydney, New York & London: Harper-Collins. (Original work published 1999)

Gao Xingjian. (2003). *Snow in august* (Gilbert C. F. Fong, Trans.). Hong Kong: The Chinese University Press. (Original work published 2000)

Gao Xingjian. (2004). *Buying a fishing rod for my grandfather* (Mabel Lee, Trans.). Sydney, New York & London. (Original work published 1988)

Gao Xingjian. (2007). *Escape & The man who questions death* (Gilbert C. F. Fong, Trans.). Hong Kong: Chinese University Press. (Original work published 2004)

Gao Xingjian. (2007). *La fin du monde* (Beate Reifenscheid, Ed.). Bielefeld, Germany: Kerber Verlag.

Gao Xingjian. (2007). *Silhouette/shadow: The cinematic art of Gao Xingjian.* (Fiona Sze-Lorrain, Ed.). Paris: Contours.

Gao Xingjian. (2007). *The case for literature* (Mabel Lee, Trans.). New Haven and London: Yale University Press.

Gao Xingjian. (2008). *Of mountains and seas: A tragicomedy of the gods in three acts* (Gilbert C. F. Fong, Trans.). Hong Kong: Chinese University Press.

Gao Xingjian. (2012). *Aesthetics and creation* (Mabel Lee, Trans.). Amherst, NY: Cambria. (Original work published 2008)

Gao Xingjian 高行健. (2012). *You shen yu xuansi* 游神与玄思 [Wandering spirit and metaphysical thoughts). Taipei: Lianjing.

Gao Xingjian. (2015). *City of the dead and Song of the night.* (Gilbert C. F. Fong & Mabel Lee, Trans.) Hong Kong: Chinese University Press.

Kuo, Jason C. (2013). On Gao Xingjian's films, paintings, and photographs. In Gao Xingjian, *After the flood* (pp. 10–18). Singapore: iPreciation.

Łabędzka, Izabella. (2008). *Gao Xingjian's idea of theatre: From the word to the image.* Leiden and Boston: Brill.

Lackner, Michael & Chardonnens, Nikola. (Eds.). (2014). *Polyphony embodied: Freedom and fate in Gao Xingjian's writings.* Berlin and Boston: De Gruyter.

Lee, Mabel. (2007). Aesthetic dimensions of Gao Xingjian's painting. In Gao Xingjian, *Between figurative and abstract: Paintings by Gao Xingjian* (pp. 127–145). Notre Dame, Indiana: Snite Museum of Art.

Lee, Mabel. (2012). The writer as translator: On the creative aesthetics of Gao Xingjian. In

Kwok-kan Tam & Kelly Kar-yue Chan (Eds.), *Culture in translation: Reception of Chinese literature in comparative perspective* (pp. 1–18). Hong Kong: Open University of Hong Kong Press.

Liu, Jianmei 刘剑梅. (2012). Lingshan: Xiandai Zhuangzi de kaixuan 灵山：现代庄子的凯旋 [*Soul mountain*: The triumph of modern Zhuangzi]. In Liu Jianmei (Ed.), *Zhuangzi de xiandai mingyun* 庄子的现代命运 [The modern fate of Zhuangzi] (296–320). Beijing: Shangwu yinshuguan.

Liu Zaifu. (2011). *Gao Xingjian yinlun* 高行健引论 [Introductory essays on Gao Xingjian]. Hong Kong: Dashan wenhua.

Quah, Sy Ren. (2004). *Gao Xingjian and transcultural Chinese theater*. Honolulu: University of Hawai'i Press.

Tam, Kwok-kan. (Ed.). (2001). *Soul of chaos: Critical perspectives on Gao Xingjian*. Hong Kong: The Chinese University Press.

Yeung, Jessica. (2008). *Ink dances in limbo: Gao Xingjian's writing as cultural translation*. Hong Kong: Hong Kong University Press.

Zhao, Henry Y. H. (2000). *Towards a modern Zen theatre: Gao Xingjian and Chinese theatre experimentalism*. London: SOAS Publications.

• Gāo Xíngjiàn •

♀ Gǒng Lì 巩俐

b. 1965—Actress associated with films from China's Fifth Generation directors

Alternate name: trad. 鞏俐

Summary

Gong Li is a popular actress who was first introduced to Chinese and Western audiences in the 1980s. At the beginning of her career, she worked regularly with the film director Zhang Yimou, a key figure among China's so-called Fifth Generation directors. She later worked with other directors and attempted to make a career in Hollywood, though she eventually returned to China.

Gong Li is one of the most well-known Chinese actresses of the twentieth and twenty-first century. Her work has gained attention from Western critics, such as scholar John Berra, who selected her—along with leading actresses Ruǎn Língyù 阮玲玉 (1910–1935), Lí Lìlì 黎莉莉 (1915–2005), Zhōu Xùn 周迅 (b. 1974), and Zhào Tāo 赵涛 (b. 1977)—as one of the five most iconic Chinese actresses of all time (Berra 2014). While many contemporary Chinese actresses, such as Fàn Bīngbīng 范冰冰, Lǐ Bīngbīng 李冰冰, and Gāo Yuányuán 高圆圆, aim to establish and manage their images through magazine covers and highly stylized photo shoots, Gong Li remains, in terms of the recognition of Chinese female actresses in Western reviews and academia, slightly conventional in comparison. Her beauty and mannerisms reveal a natural and realistic charisma reminiscent of the 1980s.

Born on 31 December 1965 in Liaoning, Shenyang Province, Gong Li moved to Jinan with her parents at a very young age. Early on she showed interest in both singing and dancing. She appeared on stage during her school years and eventually ended up at the Central Academy of Drama, an institution known for training successful actors and actresses. The person who really introduced her to Chinese and international audiences, however, was the director *Zhāng Yìmóu

---

*People marked with an asterisk have entries in this dictionary.

张艺谋 (b. 1951), who was considered part of China's so-called Fifth Generation of filmmakers.

The Zhang Yimou Period

Zhang Yimou first brought Gong Li to the silver screen with his film *Red Sorghum* 红高粱 (1987), which is based on the novel *The Family Saga of Red Sorghum* by *Mò Yán 莫言 (b. 1955). Gong Li plays the main role of Jiu'er, whose father marries her off for money to an old man who owns a distillery. Jiu'er, however, bravely challenges traditional morals by exploring and accepting her own feelings and sexuality. As the narrative progresses, the Japanese army attacks and commits crimes in the village where Jiu'er lives. Seeking revenge, she again stands up to authority and supports her lover and friends, only to be killed by the Japanese soldiers.

Red Sorghum won the Golden Bear Award at the 38th Berlin International Film Festival, in addition to seventeen other international awards. All of a sudden, Gong Li's and Zhang Yimou's names appeared regularly in film critics' conversations and reviews. Gong Li's portrayal of Jiu'er, a countrywoman who has been repressed by traditions and values but who is at the same time daring and brave, opened the eyes of international cinema visitors. Western audiences found it exciting to experience the journey of a Chinese woman fighting for a fulfilling existence amid feudalism and

war. Gong Li, her appearance, and her image became representative of a female hero.

After the success of *Red Sorghum*, Zhang Yimou continued to make films that followed a similar theme, focusing on a repressed countrywoman and how she challenges traditions and explores her own feelings. Zhang's films, *Codename Cougar* 代号美洲豹 (1989), *Ju Dou* 菊豆 (1990), *Raise the Red Lantern* 大红灯笼高高挂 (1991), *The Story of Qiu Ju* 秋菊打官司 (1992), and *To Live* 活著 (1994) all starred Gong Li as the lead actress.

Gong Li's greatest achievements while working with Zhang Yimou came when she was named Best Actress at the Golden Rooster Awards and the Golden Phoenix Awards and received the Volpi Cup for her role in *The Story of Qiu Ju*, and when she was named Best Actress at the Hundred Flowers Awards for her role in *Raise the Red Lantern*. These awards, however, came at a price: For a long time, Gong Li's image as an actress was associated almost exclusively with the role of a repressed and exploited countrywoman. Because of this, she was associated with a narrow range of roles and mostly linked to Zhang Yimou in her early career, which made her seem more limited than she was.

Post-Zhang Yimou Period

Apart from appearing regularly in Zhang's films, Gong Li also appeared in works by other directors, such as *The*

Selected Filmography of Gong Li				
Year	English Title	Chinese Title	Director	Notes
1987	*Red Sorghum*	红高粱 *Hóng gāo liáng*	Zhang Yimou	Role: Jiu'er
1989	*Codename Cougar*	代号美洲豹 *Dài háo měi zhōu bào*	Zhang Yimou, Yang Fengliang	Role: Ah Li
1989	*The Empress Dowager*	一代妖后 *Yī dài yāo hòu*	Li Han-hsiang	Role: Guilian
1990	*A Terracotta Warrior*	古今大战秦俑情 *Gǔ jīn dà zhàn qín* *yǒng qín*	Ching Siu-tung	Role: Winter/ Lili Chu
1990	*Ju Dou*	菊豆 *Jú Dòu*	Zhang Yimou, Yang Fengliang	Role: Ju Dou
1991	*Raise the Red Lantern*	大红灯笼高高挂 *Dà hóng dēng lóng* *gāo gāo guà*	Zhang Yimou	Role: Songlian
1991	*God of Gamblers III:* *Back to Shanghai*	赌侠2之上海滩赌圣 *Dǔ xiá zhī* *Shànghǎitān dǔshèng*	Wong Jing	Role: Yu San/ Yu Mong
1991	*The Banquet*	豪门夜宴 *Háo mén yè yàn*	Alfred Cheung, Joe Cheung, Tsui Hark, Clifton Ko	Role: waitress
1992	*The Story of Qiu Ju*	秋菊打官司 *Qiū Jú dǎ guān sī*	Zhang Yimou	Role: Qiu Ju
1992	*Mary from Beijing* (AKA: *Awakening*)	梦醒时分 *Mèng xǐng shí fèn*	Sylvia Chang	Role: Ma Lei/ Mary
1993	*Farewell my* *Concubine*	霸王别姬 *Bàwáng Bié Jī*	Chen Kaige	Role: Juxian
1993	*Flirting Scholar*	唐伯虎点秋香 *Táng Bóhǔ diǎn* *Qiū xiāng*	Stephen Chow, Lee Lik-chi	Role: Chen Heung
1994	*To Live*	活着 *Huó zhe*	Zhang Yimou	Role: Xu Jiazhen

Year	English Title	Chinese Title	Director	Notes
1994	*Dragon Chronicles: The Maidens* (AKA: *The Maidens of Heavenly Mountains, Semi-Gods and Semi-Devils*)	天龙八部之天山童姥 *Tiān lóng bā bù zhī tiān shān tóng lǎo*	Andy Wingk-Keung Chin	Role: Mou Hang-wen (Tin-san Tung-lo)
1994	*A Soul Haunted by Painting*	画魂 *Huà hún*	Huang Shuqin	Role: Pan Yuliang
1996	*Temptress Moon*	风月 *Fēng yuè*	Chen Kaige	Role: Pang Ruyi
1997	*Chinese Box*	中国匣 *Zhōngguó xiá*	Wayne Wang	Role: Vivian
1998	*The Emperor and the Assassin*	荆轲刺秦王 *Jīng Kē cì Qín Wáng*	Chen Kaige	Role: Lady Zhao
2004	*2046*		Wong Kar-wai	Role: Su Li-zhen
2004	*Eros*	爱神 *Àishén*	Wong Kar-wai, Michelangelo Antonioni, Steven Soderbergh	Role: Miss Hua (in "The Hand")
2005	*Memoirs of a Geisha*		Rob Marshall	Role: Hatsumomo
2006	*Curse of the Golden Flower*	满城尽带黄金甲 *Mǎn chéng jìn dài huáng jīn jiǎ*	Zhang Yimou	Role: Empress Phoenix
2006	*Miami Vice*		Michael Mann	Role: Isabella
2007	*Hannibal Rising*		Peter Webber	Role: Lady Murasaki
2010	*Shanghai*		Mikael Håfström	Role: Anna Lan-Ting
2011	*What Women Want*	我知女人心 *Wǒ zhī nǚrén xīn*	Chen Daming	Role: Li Yilong
2014	*Coming Home*	歸來 *Guīlái*	Zhang Yimou	Role: Feng Wanuy
2016	*Monkey King 2*	西游记之三打白骨精 *Xī yóu jì zhī sān dǎ bái gǒ jīng*	Cheang Pou-soi	Role: Baigujing

• Gŏng Lì •

Empress Dowager 一代妖后 (1989), *A Terracotta Warrior* 古今大战秦俑 (1990), *God of Gamblers III: Back to Shanghai* 赌侠2之上海滩赌圣 (1991), *The Banquet* 豪门夜宴 (1991), *Mary from Beijing* 梦醒时分 (1992), *Dragon Chronicles: The Maidens of Heavenly* 天龙八部之天山童姥 (1994), and *A Soul Haunted by Painting* 画魂 (1994). In addition to her partnership with Zhang Yimou, she frequently worked with another Fifth Generation director, *Chén Kǎigē 陈凯歌 (b. 1950), by appearing in *Farewell My Concubine* 霸王别姬 (1993), *Temptress Moon* 风月 (1996), and *The Emperor and the Assassin* 荆轲刺秦王 (1998). She also had an opportunity to work with Stephen Chow 周星驰 in the film *Flirting Scholar* 唐伯虎点秋香 (1993), one of the few Hong Kong productions she participated in.

By the end of the 1990s, Gong Li had become one of the most experienced film actresses in China of her generation. It was inevitable that she began to take on more challenging roles. Before she worked with Zhang Yimou again in 2006 for *Curse of the Golden Flower* 满城尽带黄金甲, Gong Li attempted several times to shed the image of a repressed but brave countrywoman. For example, she attempted to work with directors from abroad in an effort to break into Hollywood. Gong Li worked on a movie in English for the first time in 1997; *Chinese Box* was directed by Hong Kong diaspora director Wayne Wang, and it was Gong Li's first experience acting with English dialogue. Later, following *Memoirs*

of a Geisha (2005), *Miami Vice* (2006), *Hannibal Rising* (2007), *Shanghai* (2010), Gong Li and her agent seemed focused on getting deals from Hollywood and establishing the actress internationally. Apart from *Memoirs of a Geisha*, however, which gained a little attention from the popular blockbuster film audience, the rest of the films were not well-received enough to help Gong Li achieve a second big breakthrough. Furthermore, although *Memoirs of a Geisha* gained some attention, many thought the actresses in the film were less important than the exotic fantasy that the film offered. In other words, the actresses could have been anyone, as long as they looked Asian. Gong Li appeared in additional films where the main requirement seemed to be simply to look and act like the stereotypical Western view of an Asian woman rather than to demonstrate any real acting ability. Gong Li also worked with Hong Kong director *Wong Kar-wai 王家卫 (b. 1958) in two of his films in 2004, *2046* and *Eros* 爱神. Both works demonstrated that she had rich acting skills and a powerful screen presence. These were her most challenging roles, where she had the opportunities to explore two emotionally complex characters. Both films gained attention from international critics, which helped her to complicate the conventional country woman image so familiar among Western audiences.

In 2011, Gong returned to the Chinese market and audience, playing a role in *What Women Want* 我知女人心, a

China-Hong Kong production that also starred Andy Lau 劉德華. In 2014 she returned to the director who first introduced her to audiences, Zhang Yimou, starring in his most recent work, *Coming Home*. It seemed, however, that the chemistry that had once existed in the partnership between the two had vanished. According to most critics, *Coming Home* lacks the sparks that were present in the pair's films from the 1980s and 1990s. In 2016, Gong Li will be playing a role in a Chinese blockbuster sequel, *The Monkey King 2*.

In 2008, two years before her divorce from spouse Ooi Hoe Seong, Gong obtained Singaporean citizenship, something she was criticized for and which led to her expulsion from the China Film Association (CFA). Such a well-known and beloved actress will have no trouble getting roles in the Chinese or international market, but audiences that truly appreciate her talent and beauty will wish to see her in more challenging roles, where she is able to really shine.

Hiu M. CHAN
Cardiff University

Further Reading

Berra, John. (2014). Five iconic Chinese actresses. Retrieved January 11, 2015, from http://www.bfi.org.uk/news-opinion/news-bfi/lists/five-iconic-chinese-actresses

Berry, Chris & Farquhar, Mary Ann. (2013). *China on screen: Cinema and nation.* New York: Columbia University Press.

Chow, Rey. (1995). *Primitive passions.* New York: Columbia University Press.

Lu, Hsaio-peng & Lu, Sheldon. (1997). *Transnational Chinese cinemas: Identity, nationhood, gender.* Honolulu: University of Hawai'i Press.

Sukhmani, Khorana. (Ed.). (2013). *Crossover cinema: Cross-cultural film from production to reception.* New York: Routledge.

Zhang, Zhen. (2007). *Urban generation: Chinese cinema and society at the turn of the twenty-first century.* Durham, NC: Duke University Press.

• Gǒng Lì •

♂ Gou, Terry

Guō Táimíng 郭台銘

b. 1950—Founder and chairman of Foxconn

Alternate name: Terry Tai-ming Gou; simpl. 郭台铭

Summary

As the founder and chairman of Foxconn Group, one of largest manufacturing companies in the world, Terry Gou has been helping to shape the electronic industry in Taiwan since the 1990s. Implementing his own business model of production, Gou has seen his company expand worldwide, manufacturing electronics for such brands as Apple and Nokia, and seen his factories come under scrutiny for the working conditions of its labor force.

The business tycoon Terry (Tai-ming) Gou has been a prominent figure in the business development of Taiwan in the 1970s and 1980s, when he started to expand his company's operations based on the practice of contract manufacturing. His personal fortune amounts to US$5.5 billion dollars, which ranks him 136th on Forbes's list of billionaires (Parry and Jones 2010).

Early Life

Very few details are known about Gou's early life and education. He was born in Banqiao on 8 October 1950 to a rather poor family who had fled China in 1949. He worked in factories in his area to put himself through college, and after his graduation from the Taipei College of Maritime Technology in 1971, he worked as a clerk in a large shipping company. Only three years later, Gou took his first steps towards becoming Taiwan's most wealthy entrepreneur.

Establishment and Development of Foxconn

In 1974, Gou founded Foxconn 富士康 (also known as the Hon Hai Precision Industry 鴻海精密工業股份有限公司) with an initial capital of 300,000 New Taiwanese Dollars (around US$9000) (Asamoto 2013a). Initially a small firm producing components for televisions, Foxconn developed rapidly. Beginning in 1980, the company became involved in the production of connectors and imported high-end technological equipment from America and Japan (Asamoto 2013a). The company also expanded its industrial base into different areas in Taiwan. In 1988, Foxconn established a new factory in Shenzhen in order to capitalize on the abundant supply of land and labor on the mainland (Asamoto 2013a).

Beginning in the 1990s, Foxconn started to develop its international portfolio and it is now the supplier of electronic components and products to multinational companies such as Apple, Dell, Hewlett-Packard, and Microsoft. Foxconn itself has also become an exemplar for the globalized economies of scale (new globalized model) in manufacturing and raw materials procurement. The company has been involved in the production of a wide range of products, including notebooks, desktops, mobile phones, and digital cameras, and began to develop its research and development capacity (Asamoto 2013a). Gou migrated most of Foxconn's operation to Shenzhen, which became an industrial hub for the company. Since 2000, the company put substantial effort into the development of communication technology, and its collaboration with multinational enterprises became more apparent. By 2002, Foxconn became the largest exporting enterprise in China and the third-largest foreign investor in the country (Asamoto 2013a).

Gou's Business Empire and the New Global Economy

Over the last twenty years, Gou introduced a new business model of supply chains that gradually transformed the global system of production in the electronic industry sector. He emphasized client-orientation in business operations and the importance of adapting to the growing diversity of business challenges (e.g., the rapid changes of information technology). More importantly, he has developed a stylized approach to contract manufacturing known as the eCMMS model, which evolved from an early idea of CMM (components, modules, moves) (Lin 2013; Asamoto 2013b). To date, the idea of eCMMS (e-enabled components, modules, moves, and services) has become a guiding principle in the everyday operation of Foxconn. A vertically integrated "one-stop shopping business model," eCMMS integrates "mechanical, electrical, and optical capabilities." It covers a huge range of solutions "from moulding, tooling, mechanical parts, components, modules, system assembly, design, manufacturing, [and] maintenance" (Foxconn n.d.). It also emphasizes the importance of service in the whole cycle in production. Foxconn offers two kinds of services, namely Joint DeVelopment Manufacturing (JDVM) and Joint DeSign Manufacturing (JDSM), which enable the company to both meet the needs of clients and to develop its own

Gou, Terry

research-and-development capacity (Lin 2013; Asamoto 2013b).

While adhering to the spirit of Fordism—a mode of manufacturing based on industrialized and standardized production—in structuring its business operations, Foxconn has been able to transform itself with reference to the changing characteristics of the global production network. The transnationalization of supply chain has been seen by Gou as a key opportunity to rethink ways to realize his corporate vision globally. To date, Foxconn has established its global production chain across Asia, Europe, Russia, and South America (Lin 2013). In China alone, Gou has established large factories and become the greatest private employer in China. Foxconn has also capitalized on the emergence of an intellectual property rights regime to protect its business interests. With the help of its dedicated legal team, the company has filed 127,500 patent applications in 2013 globally, with 63,300 applications being endorsed (Foxcon 2009). The use of property right law for safeguarding business interests has become one of the key operational features of Foxconn in the advent of the knowledge economy.

Company Scandals

Inside Foxconn, Gou is known for his military-style, highly individualized management philosophy. Gou has emphasized the importance of talent over speed, cost, and quality in accounting for the success of his business empire. While all recruitments and promotions are performance-based, absolute loyalty is considered to be important in ensuring the success of the enterprise, which in turn justifies the idea of "righteous dictatorship" advocated by Gou. Gou also encourages whistle-blowing as a means to ensure the integrity of the company (Parry and Jones 2010). Foxconn is also known by the public for its attractive system of remuneration. Outstanding employees can receive company shares. Yet, while Gou is seen to have demonstrated strong business leadership and to have articulated his commitment to social responsibility (Alden 2010), his business practices have not gone without criticism.

News stories about difficult working conditions and labor malpractice has drawn international and scholarly attention. From 2011 to 2013, reports emerged of Chinese workers committing suicide under tremendous pressure while working at Foxconn factories. Many of these cases were put down to the soulless environment in which workers found themselves, with high levels of regimentation despite perks like gyms, social clubs, and other amenities. The Foxconn factory in Shenzhen in particular is known for its size (half a million workers) and the number of suicides recorded there. In response to pressures from his contractors, the senior management of Foxconn, including Gao himself, made a number of visits to the factories concerned and promised to investigate the matter.

Within Foxconn, there is growing concern about the increase in minimum wage for Chinese labor, and how this will affect business dealings on the mainland. In the political context, Gou has been known as a supporter of the Kuomintang in Taiwan, which endorses the "three noes" policy of no unification, no independence, and no use of force between the countries, and has urged employees stationed in China to cast their votes in the latest presidential election. For Gou, the economic ties between the mainland and Taiwan are something too important to be neglected (Kuomintang 2014).

Dennis Lai Hang HUI
The Hong Kong Institute of Education

Further Reading

Alden, William. (2010). Billionaire Terry Gou, Foxconn CEO: I have no idea how much money I have, I'm working for society. Retrieved February 24, 2015, from http://www.huffingtonpost.com/2010/09/10/terry-gou-foxconn-ceo_n_711859.html

Asamoto, Teruo. (2013a). Kōnomi (Hon Hai) ni okeru hatten no nazo o saguru 鴻海（ホンハイ）における発展の謎を探る [Exploring the development of Hon Hai]. *Koryo, 865*, 1–11.

Asamoto, Teruo. (2013b). Kironitatsu Kōnomi (hon hai) no "shōri no hōteishiki" ― sekai dai 1-i no emusu kigyō no sentaku 岐路に立つ鴻海（ホンハイ）の"勝利の方程式" ―世界第 1 位の EMS 企業の選択 [Hon Hai to stand at the crossroads of (Hon Hai) "winning formula." The world's top EMS companies in the corporate world]. *Koryo, 866*, 8–15.

Foxconn. (n.d.). Competitive advantages. Retrieved December 10, 2014, from http://www.foxconn.com/GroupProfile_En/CompetitiveAdvantages_sub.html

Foxconn. (2009). Zhihui chanquan 智慧产权 [International property rights]. Retrieved May 6, 2015, from http://www.foxconn.com.cn/wisdomproperty.html

Kuomintang. (2014). Democracy vs. economics: Terry Gou and Ko Wen-Je speak different languages. Retrieved February 23, 2015, from http://www.kmt.org.tw/english/page.aspx?type=article&mnum=113&anum=15425

Lin Jiaheng 林家亨. (2013). *ODM da pojie: Guoji dai gong sheji zhizao maimai heyue zhongdian jiexi* ODM 大破解：國際代工設計製造買賣合約重點解析. Taipei: Showwe Information.

Parry, Simon, & Jones, Richard. (2010). He spent £21m on a penthouse—but turns lights off to save money: Inside the amazing world of secret billionaire Terry Gou. Retrieved February 24, 2015, from http://www.dailymail.co.uk/news/article-1289811/Terry-Gou-billionaire-manufacture-Apple-Dell-products-spent-21m-penthouse--turns-lights-save-money.html

• Gou, Terry •

☿ Hán Hán 韩寒

b. 1982—Novelist, online commentator, and motor sports star; best known for his popular blog

Summary

Han Han is best known for his popular satirical blog posts about Chinese culture and society. He regularly pushes the envelope and sometimes attracts censorship. Han Han is also a best-selling novelist, magazine editor, and racecar driver.

Han Han is a novelist, online commentator, and motor sports star who is based in Shanghai but enjoys nationwide celebrity status in China. He became famous by winning the "New Concept" literary prize competition in 1999. This competition, sponsored by the country's top universities, aimed at discovering writing talent among secondary school pupils. As soon as Han won the prize, he dropped out of school the same year and refused an offer to attend literature classes at the elite Fudan University. The next year, when Han Han was still only eighteen, he published his first bestseller, a cynical dissection of the Chinese education system titled *Triple Gate* (*Sān zhòng mén* 三重门).

Han Han started blogging in 2005, when the popular Sina blog site was launched. By that time he was already famous throughout China for his printed novels, and he accumulated half a million followers for his blog in no time. From then on he gained increasing acclaim (and attracted occasional censorship) for the satirical essays, mainly commenting on current affairs, that he published on his blog. His novels continued to appear only in print. He never published any creative writing on the Internet and used his blog only for social and cultural critiques. He has also been active as a magazine editor and a film director, and as a professional rally driver.

Themes in Han's Work and Opinions

A key theme in Han Han's writing is skepticism toward state institutions and a strong endorsement of the private sector. In addition to his critique of the state school system with its excessive emphasis on rote learning and lack of incentive for creative individual development, he vehemently criticized the state-sponsored Writers Association, famously comparing writers joining the association to kept mistresses. In a protracted online debate with the critic Bai Ye in early 2006, which he later removed from his blog site, Han Han repeatedly argued that the only good literature is that written by professional writers whose livelihoods depend on being able to attract real readers rather than on pleasing the authorities in exchange for writing stipends. Similarly, after the 2008 Wenchuan earthquake, Han Han publicly stated his refusal to donate money through official channels and lauded the efforts by private individuals and privately owned corporations in providing disaster relief.

In 2010 Han Han launched the glossy magazine *Chorus of Solos* (*Dúchàngtuán* 独唱团), promising to pay contributors publication fees up to ten times as high as those offered by state-supported cultural journals. When the magazine was banned after the first issue for failing to obtain the correct type of state-issued "book number," he moved the whole operation online, setting up a mobile application called One (*Yīge* 一个) through which users of handheld devices can access new content daily that is similar to the type of content he had in mind for his printed magazine.

Han Han was also a key figure in the establishment of the Writers Legal Protection Union, which took Internet giant Baidu to court for violation of copyrights through its Baidu Library. Users were freely uploading and sharing illegal copies of printed books through this library, thereby depriving professional writers of their livelihoods.

Social Critiques

As a blogger Han Han became especially well-known for his biting social critiques, which were often aimed directly or indirectly at official corruption and popular nationalism. In 2008, for example, Chinese nationalists took to the streets to boycott French goods because of controversy over the treatment of a disabled Chinese athlete during the Olympic torch relay in Paris that year, and Han Han praised them for making it difficult for corrupt cadres to purchase luxury items. When those same nationalists got angry about Japanese claims on the Diaoyu Islands, Han Han memorably retorted that he saw no reason to get upset about whether or not China owned a piece of rock in the ocean, considering Chinese citizens were not even allowed to own the land on which their houses were built (because all land is still owned by the state).

As with most critical online discourse in China, Han Han's writing relies heavily on the use of satire and irony—that is, stating the opposite of

• Hán Hàn •

what he really thinks in such a way that his readers realize what he is criticizing and consider themselves in on the joke. Some of the titles of his blog posts, such as "Han Feng is a Fine Cadre" (about a corrupt official) and "Three Gorges is a Fine Dam" (about the dam's damaging ecological effects) inevitably provoke laughter and skepticism, while not breaking any obvious rules that might attract intervention by censors.

Nevertheless, Han Han's blog posts are occasionally the target of censorship. In most cases he himself agrees to censors' requests to remove certain posts. Even in deleting his own writings,

however, Han often employs a form of satire by leaving the title of the offending piece and replacing the text under it with a single full stop. When his online followers see the full stop appearing under a title, they often respond by the thousands, leaving encouraging comments about a post that has no content.

Han Han is unusual among online celebrities in that he does not use the Internet to interact with his readers and he never responds to their online comments. Perhaps for similar reasons, he has not taken as enthusiastically as others to social media, where constant interaction is crucial. Although he does have

Han Han, who is not only a well-known writer but also a successful racecar driver, competing at WRC Rally Australia (2009). Photo by Livewireshock.

a Sina Weibo account (akin to a Twitter account) linked to his Sina blog page, he uses it mainly to upload links to his writings that are published elsewhere.

As with his blog posts, irony and wordplay play an important role in Han's offline literary productions. In 2010 he published a novel with the title *1988*, which became an instant bestseller (and later served as the basis of the script for his 2014 movie, *The Continent* [*Hòu huì wúqī* 后会无期]). There was no obvious reason why the novel should have that particular title, but presumably Han was playing a joke on the censors, who would have had to ban the work if its title had been *1989*—a possible reference to the June Fourth Incident of that year in Tiananmen Square. Similarly, his magazine *Chorus of Solos* actually carried on the cover the English title *Party*, which subtly suggested that Han Han had done something that no one else in China is allowed to do: found his own "party."

Han Han's image took somewhat of a hit in 2012 when he was unable to convincingly refute accusations that some of his works, including the early novels that brought him his fame, were ghost-written by his father, Hán Rénjūn 韩仁均. In 2013 and 2014 Han Han published a combined total of only seven blog posts, the last one being a censored post consisting of a single full stop—followed by fifty-seven pages of supportive readers' comments. Despite this lack of new material, Han Han's blog remains one of the top ten most-visited weblogs on the

Sina site, having been visited by a total of more than 600 million unique users.

Michel HOCKX
SOAS, University of London

Further Readings

Fumian, Marco. (2009). The temple and the market: Controversial positions in the literary field with Chinese characteristics. *Modern Chinese Literature and Culture, 21*(2), 126–166.

Han Han. (2012). *This generation: Dispatches from China's most popular blogger* (Allan H. Barr, Ed. & Trans.). London: Simon and Shuster.

Han Han. Blog Homepage. Retrieved March 2, 2015, from http://blog.sina.com.cn/twocold

Hockx, Michel. (2015). *Internet literature in China.* New York: Columbia University Press.

Martinsen, Joel. (2012). Han Han the novelist versus Fang Zhouzi the fraud-buster. Retrieved February 17, 2015, from http://www.danwei.com/blog-fight-of-the-month-han-han-the-novelist-versus-fang-zhouzi-the-fraud-buster

Wasserstrom, Jeffrey. (2012). Make way for Han Han. Retrieved February 1, 2015, from http://wordswithoutborders.org/dispatches/article/make-way-for-han-han

Yang, Guobin. (2010). Chinese Internet literature and the changing field of print culture. In Cynthia Brokaw & Christopher A. Reed (Eds.), *From woodblocks to the Internet: Chinese publishing and print culture in transition, circa 1800 to 2008* (pp. 333–352). Leiden, The Netherlands: E. J. Brill.

Yang, Guobin. (2009). *The power of the Internet in China: Citizen activism online.* New York: Columbia University Press.

• Hán Hán •

♂ Ho, Stanley

Hé Hóngshēn 何鴻燊

b. 1921—Entrepreneur and founder of the gaming industry in Macao

Alternate names: Hung San; simpl. 何鸿燊

Summary

As an entrepreneur and casino tycoon, Stanley Ho has been a prominent figure in the socio-economic development in Macao and Hong Kong. He has played an important role in transforming Macao from an underdeveloped colonial backwater to a modern city renowned for its gaming industry. His investments also include transportation, real estate, entertainment, and he has been involved in developing casinos abroad.

Over the course of his long career, Stanley Ho has contributed to the economic and political development of Macao, amassing a considerable fortune along the way, to such an extent that his name has become nearly synonymous with the city.

Early Life

Stanley Ho Hung San was born on 25 November 1921 to a wealthy Hong Kong family. He was the grand-nephew of Sir Robert Hotung, an influential Eurasian businessman who was knighted twice by the British crown. After completing secondary school, Ho earned a scholarship to the University of Hong Kong, but his course of study was cut short when the Japanese invaded the island during World War II. Ho fled with his family to Macao as a refugee (ATV 2010), and soon after arriving began his career at one of the local trading companies. With a one-million dividend issued by this trading company, Ho established a kerosene company in Macao in 1943. After the war ended, he returned to Hong Kong while maintaining his business interests in Macao. He then started to invest in real estate in Hong Kong, further amassing his personal fortune.

A Career on the Fast Track

In the 1960s, Ho became interested in the development of the gambling industry in Macao. In 1962, he formed the Sociedade de Turismo e Diversões de Macau

(STDM) with a consortium of businessmen, namely *Henry Fok 霍英東 (1923–2006), Teddy Yip, and Yip Hong. The company was able to win the monopoly from the Portuguese colonial government, although Ho has expressed that the bidding process was an uphill battle. On the one hand, he had to personally fly to Portugal six times to negotiate with the government there and make promises of commitment to ensure the growth and development of Macao (ATV 2010). On the other hand, he faced hostile resistance from local factions that had extensive vested interests in the gambling sector of Macao. Notwithstanding repeated threats from these local factions, STDM was able to begin casino operations at the Estoril Hotel in 1963. Meanwhile, to further the expansion of his casino empire and to fulfill the requirements imposed by the colonial government, Ho started to build a team of ferries operating between Hong Kong and Macao. In 1964, STDM bought the first jetfoil, which shortened the trip between Hong Kong and Macao substantially (Zhu and Xin 2005, 109). Later, the ferry service between Hong Kong and Macao became regularized by Ho's Shun Tak Enterprises, which was incorporated in 1973 (*South China Morning Post* 1973).

Ho established the Casino Lisboa in 1970, which became a prototype casino-cum-hotel complex. The 1970s and 1980s witnessed a period of rapid expansion of Ho's Empire, with the number of casinos expanding to five by the end of 1985. In 1989, Ho consolidated his influence in the gaming sector of Macao by acquiring a 51 percent stake in the Macao Jockey Club, rescuing it from a worrying financial position (Zhu and Xin 2005). Ho also engaged in a wide range of management reforms by professionalizing the casino industry. He introduced training programs to equip casino employees with sector-specific knowledge and adopted the junket system, which provides a substantial source of revenue for his casinos by bringing gamblers over from China and even lending them money for betting (Zhu and Xin 2005).

In contrast, Ho's track-record in expanding his empire abroad has been a mixed one. His plan to develop a racecourse in Tehran in the late 1970s was shattered by the Islamic Revolution in 1979, while his casino business in the Philippines was disrupted by the changing political factionalism in the government there (Zhu and Xin 2005). Even in Macao, his business empire encountered challenges beginning in the 2000s when the gaming sector became infiltrated by triad societies (Lo 2005). Intensification of clashes between triad societies and junket operators have resulted in a new scale of violence. Scholars thus argue that casino development in Macao can no longer be considered purely an economic issue; rather, it is a baffling

---

*People marked with an asterisk have entries in this dictionary.

Stanley Ho built the Macau Tower Convention and Entertainment Center (also known as the Macau Tower) after seeing the Sky Tower in New Zealand. Photo by Toby Oxborrow.

question involving the state, the casino operators, and the criminals (Lo 2005). Meanwhile, the Macao Special Administrative Region (SAR) government started to conceive of a proposal to liberalize the casino sector. Ho conceded that the proposal would inevitably impact the revenue of his casinos, and since this liberalization the market share of STDM has fallen from 89 percent in 2004 to 27 percent in 2009 (McCartney 2010). Yet, Ho believed that by opening up the casino industry, Macao's economy could acquire new momentum (Zhu and Xin 2005).

To date, STDM is operating eighteen casinos in Macao and has been able to benefit from the increase in Chinese travelers to Macao over the past decade. Meanwhile, the entry of new competitors in this sector has compelled STDM to adopt a more innovative way of expanding its empire. The increasing crackdown on conspicuous consumption by the Beijing authorities since 2013, however, has meant that STDM and its competitors are facing a new uncertainty.

Given his extensive connection with different sectors of Macao, it isn't surprising that Ho has been a powerful influence on the political economy of the colony. While he did not participate directly in the colonial affairs of Macao, he sought to extend his political leverage by attempting to install his aides in different decision-making bodies, although with mixed success (Zhu and Xin 2005). Since the retrocession of sovereignty to China, Ho became more vocal in the political affairs of Hong Kong and Macao. In particular, he reiterated the importance of upholding the "One Country, Two Systems" principle and the need to continue the capitalist economic system in the two SARs (McCartney 2010). Ho has also been increasingly visible in the political scene of China. He has been a member of the Chinese People's Political Consultative Conference. He is also the member of the Consultative Committee for the Basic Law of the Hong Kong SAR (McCartney 2010, 178).

Family Affairs

Ho has seventeen children born to four women (*The Telegraph* 2011), and his family has received a lot of attention from the local media. On the business level, family members such as Pansy Ho and Angela Leung have been active in the casino-related aspect of Ho's empire. For example, Pansy Ho is now the managing director of Shun Tak Holding. His family made the headlines of local newspapers in 2011 when they were drawn into a feud involving a dispute over Ho's assets (*South China Morning Post* 2011). His health condition has also been receiving attention from the media since the late 2000s.

Dennis Lai Hang HUI
Hong Kong Institute of Education

Further Reading

ATV. (2011). He Hongshen 何鴻燊 [Stanley Ho]. Hong Kong: Asia Television Limited.

Lo, Shiu Hing. (2005). Casino politics, organized crime and the post-colonial state in Macau. *Journal of Contemporary China*, 14(43), 17–34.

McCartney, Glenn. (2010). Stanley Ho Hungsun: the "King of Gambling." In Richard W. Butler & Roslyn A. Russell (Eds.), *Giants of tourism* (pp. 170–181). Wallingford, Oxfordshire, UK: CABI.

South China Morning Post. (1973, January 19). Shun Tak shares oversubscribed 154 times, p. 33.

South China Morning Post. (2011, March 11). Stanley Ho calls truce in family feud over fortune: Casino magnate drops second lawsuit, p. 1.

The Telegraph (2011). Stanley Ho: the Macao gambling king who defied the odds. Retrieved March 6, 2015, from http://www.telegraph.co.uk/news/worldnews/asia/macau/8282097/Stanley-Ho-the-Macao-gambling-king-who-defied-the-odds.html

Zhu, Chunting 祝春亭, & Xin Lei 辛磊. (2005). *Aomen Duwang Hehongshen Quan Chuan* 澳门赌王何鸿燊全 [A biography of Stanley Ho, the casino tycoon]. Wuhan, China: Hubei renmin chuban she.

☌ Hou Hsiao-hsien

Hóu Xiàoxián 侯孝賢

b. 1947—Taiwanese film director, screenwriter, and producer

Alternate name: simpl. *侯孝贤*

Summary

Hou Hsiao-hsien is one of Taiwan's most influential filmmakers of the past forty years. His work is closely associated with the New Taiwan Cinema movement, and he has gained widespread recognition as an important voice in international art house cinema thanks to his innovative cinematic techniques, such as empty shots, the long take, non-linear narrative, use of dialects, and employment of non-professional actors. Many of Hou's films are regarded as classics of world cinema.

Hou Hsiao-hsien is an award-winning filmmaker associated with the New Taiwan Cinema (Táiwān xīn diànyǐng 台灣新電影) movement, which combined social realism with experimental innovations to portray and explore Taiwan's modern history.

Career in Filmmaking

Born in Mei County, Guangdong Province, on 8 April 1947, Hou immigrated to Taiwan while still an infant after his father accepted a post as a civil servant. After a somewhat rebellious adolescence, Hou enrolled in an arts school and worked as a calculator salesman before beginning his apprenticeship in the Taiwan film industry in 1973. Hou gained experience working under veteran directors such as Lee Hsing 李行 on several dozen mainstream films as a screenwriter and assistant director. In 1980 Hou struck out on his own with a string of romantic comedies that proved very successful at the Taiwan box office. These early films were produced in concert with Hou's creative partner, cinematographer Chen Kun-hou 陳坤厚, with whom Hou collaborated on numerous films including 1980's *Cute Girl* 就是溜溜的她 and 1983's *Green, Green Grass of Home* 在那河畔青草青.

Although Hou got his start in the commercial film industry making mainstream romantic comedies, he began to eschew his commercial roots in favor of a new film style that would go on to redefine world art cinema, beginning in 1983 with *The Sandwich Man* 兒子的大玩偶. Hou's use of nonprofessional actors and his groundbreaking employment of long shots and the long take, coupled with his courageous exploration of personal memories and national trauma, helped forge a bold new cinematic voice. Hou's technique for expressing his "aesthetics of violence" (*bàolì de měixué* 暴力的美學)—in which violence often plays out off-screen, is alluded to, is portrayed through extreme long shots, or is juxtaposed with empty shots of nature—is another key aspect of his unique approach.

New Taiwan Cinema Movement

During the 1980s Hou was closely associated with the New Taiwan Cinema movement, alternatively referred to as the Taiwan New Wave (Táiwān xīn làngcháo 台灣新浪潮), which emerged when local talent like Hou joined forces with another group of young Taiwanese filmmakers who had studied abroad and introduced concepts drawn from Western film theory and art cinema. The creative marriage of filmmakers who had extensive hands-on training in the local industry with filmmakers who had studied in the United States and Europe, like Edward Yang 楊德昌, resulted in a powerful dynamic that challenged Taiwan's mainstream genre cinema, which had been dominated by romantic comedies, war films, gangster films, and martial arts films. The New Taiwan Cinema movement's fresh approach created a new aesthetic rooted

in realism and Taiwan's modern history with an experimental spirit. Hou's films such as *The Sandwich Man* (1983) and *The Boys from Fengkuei* 風櫃來的人 (1983) were some of the most important early artistic statements to emerge from the movement.

Hou's career can be divided into several phases, each of which marked a shift in his style and the themes his films explored. Following his commercial romantic-comedy period of 1980–1983, Hou directed a quartet of classic bildungsroman films from 1983–1986. *The Boys from Fengkuei, Summer at Grandpa's* 鼕鼕的假期 (1984), *A Time to Live, A Time to Die* 童年往事 (1985), and *Dust in the Wind* 戀戀風塵 (1986) were all coming-of-age films drawn from Hou's and his collaborators' own autobiographical stories.

Hou followed this remarkable string of films with his acclaimed Taiwan Trilogy (Táiwān Sānbùqǔ 台湾三部曲), which explored some of the darker corners of Taiwan's history under martial law such as the February 28th Incident of 1947, when thousands of protesters were killed, and the ensuing White Terror, during which thousands more were imprisoned. The trilogy, which was produced between 1989 and 1995 and included *City of Sadness* 悲情城市 (1989), *The Puppetmaster* 戲夢人生 (1993), and *Good Men, Good Women* 好男好女 (1995), pushed Hou's explorations of nonlinear narratives, multiple storylines, and cinematic form in new directions and won him wide critical acclaim. These

Selected Filmography of Hou Hsiao-hsien			
Year	English Title	Chinese Title	Notes
1980	*Cute Girl* (AKA *Loveable You*)	就是溜溜的她 *Jiùshì liūliū de tā*	Director
1981	*Cheerful Wind*	風兒踢踏踩 *Fēng' ér tī tācāi*	Director
1983	*The Green, Green Grass of Home*	在那河畔青草青 *Zài nà hépàn qīngcǎoqīng*	Director
1983	*The Sandwich Man*	兒子的大玩偶 *Érzǐ de dà wán'ǒu*	Co-director
1983	*The Boys From Fengkuei* (AKA: *All the Youthful Days*)	風櫃來的人 *Fēngguì lái de rén*	Director, actor
1984	*A Summer at Grandpa's*	冬冬的假期 *Dōng dōng de jiàqī*	Director
1985	*A Time to Live, A Time to Die*	童年往事 *Tóngnián wǎngshì*	Director
1985	*Taipei Story*	青梅竹馬 *Qīng méi zhú mǎ*	Actor. Role: Lung
1986	*Dust in the Wind*	戀戀風塵 *Liàn liàn fēng chén*	Director
1987	*Daughter of the Nile*	尼羅河的女兒 *Níluóhé de nǚ'ér*	Director
1989	*A City of Sadness*	悲情城市 *Bēiqíng chéngshì*	Director
1991	*Raise the Red Lantern*	大紅燈籠高高掛 *Dà hóng dēnglóng gāogāo guà*	Producer
1992	*Dust of Angels*	少年吔, 安啦 *Shàonián yē, ānla*	Producer
1993	*The Puppetmaster*	戲夢人生 *Xì mèng rénshēng*	Director

Year	English Title	Chinese Title	Notes
1994	*A Borrowed Life*	多桑 *Duō sāng*	Producer
1995	*Good Men, Good Women*	好男好女 *Hǎonán hǎonǚ*	Director
1995	*Heartbreak Island*	去年冬天 *Qù nián dōng tiān*	Producer
1996	*Goodbye South, Goodbye*	南國再見, 南國 *Nánguó zàijiàn, Nánguó*	Director
1998	*Flowers of Shanghai*	海上花 *Hǎi shàng huā*	Director
2001	*Millennium Mambo*	千禧曼波 *Qiānxī mànbō*	Director
2003	*Café Lumière*	咖啡時光 *Kāfēi shíguāng* (jap. *Kōhī Jikō*)	Director
2005	*Three Times*	最好的時光 *Zuìhǎo de shíguāng*	Director
2005	*Reflections*	愛麗絲的鏡子 *Ài lì sì de jìngzi*	Producer
2008	*Flight of the Red Balloon*	紅氣球的旅行 *Hóng qìqiú zhī lǚ*	Director
2010	*One Day*	有一天 *Yǒu yī tiān*	Producer
2010	*Taipei Exchanges*	第 36 個故事 *Dì 36 ge gùshì*	Producer
2011	*Hometown Boy*	金城小子 *Jīnchéng xiǎozǐ*	Producer
2013	*Beyond Beauty: Taiwan from Above*	看見台灣 *Kànjiàn Táiwān*	Producer
2013	*Young Style*	青春派 *Qīngchūn pài*	Actor
2015	*The Assassin*	聶隱娘 *Nièyǐnniáng*	Director

highly controversial films were also crucial in opening up new public forums for discussing and rethinking modern Taiwan's history and how that history could be represented in film. The trilogy had begun to appear in the immediate wake of Taiwan's martial law period, which lasted from 1947 until 1987 and during which many personal freedoms, including free speech, were restricted and discussion of topics like the brutal 28 February Incident and the White Terror were political taboos. Hou's trilogy was crucial in boldly exploring these sensitive topics so soon after the lifting of martial law.

Many of Hou's films from 1998 to the present have taken on a distinctly global sensibility in terms of funding, distribution, and even setting. Since the 1990s Hou has increasingly relied on Japanese and French financing for his films, and several films were shot partially or entirely on location outside Taiwan: *Millennium Mambo* 千禧曼波 (2001) and *Café Lumiere* 咖啡時光 (2003) were shot in Japan, for example, and *Flight of the Red Balloon* 紅氣球之旅 (2008) in France.

Another important facet of Hou's work is his team of key collaborators, which includes screenwriter Chu Tien-wen 朱天文; cinematographer Mark Lee Ping-bing 李屏賓; editor/producer Liao Ching-sung 廖慶鬆; sound designer Tu Tu-chi 杜篤之; composer Lim Giong 林強; and actors Shū Qí 舒淇, Jack Kao 高捷, Chang Chen 張震, Lee Tien-lu 李天祿, and others.

Activism, Awards, and Influence

Besides his work as a screenwriter and director, Hou has also been active in a number of other related film activities. He is the artistic director of iSpot (Táiběi guāngdiān 台北光點), an art house cinema/cultural hub in Taipei; he served as director of the Golden Horse Film Festival (Jīnmǎ diànyǐng jié 金馬電影節); and he has fostered the development of many younger filmmakers such as Hou Ji-ran 侯季然 and Yao Hung-I 姚宏易 through his work as a producer. Hou has also taken on a high-profile role as a social activist when it comes to democracy, labor rights, and other issues. He has been honored for his work in film with the Golden Lion award at the 1989 Venice International Film Festival and the Jury Prize at the 1993 Cannes Film Festival, and he has been hailed by film critics as one of the most important living film directors. While many have compared Hou to Yasujiro Ozu and other international art house filmmakers, Hou has instead emphasized the profound impact of Chinese writers like Shěn Cóngwén 沈从文, whose "detached coldness" in terms of narrative style impacted many of his classic films. As his style developed, however, Hou clearly began to embrace cinematic influences with full-length feature films dedicated to Ozu (*Café Lumiere*) and Albert Lamorisse's *The Red Balloon* (*Flight of the Red Balloon*). The impact of

侯孝賢

Hou can be seen in the work of film-makers around the globe, from the French director Olivier Assayas to the Japanese director and producer Hirokazu Koreeda.

Michael BERRY
University of California, Santa Barbara

Further Reading

Chen, Kuan-Hsing; Willemen, Paul; & Ti Wei. (Eds.). (2008). Hou Hsiao-hsien special issue. *Inter-Asia Cultural Studies 9*(2).

Frodon, Jean-Michel. (Ed.). (1999). *Hou Hsiao-hsien*. Lonrai, France: Editions Cahiers du cinema.

Lu Tonglin. (2002). *Confronting modernity in the cinemas of Taiwan and mainland China*. Cambridge, UK: Cambridge University Press.

Lupke, Christopher. (2004). The muted interstices of testimony: *A City of Sadness* and the predicament of multiculturalism in Taiwan. *Asian Cinema, 1*(15), 5–36.

Ma, Jean. (2010). *Melancholy drift: Marking time in Chinese cinema*. Hong Kong: Hong Kong University Press.

Reynaud, Berenice. (2002). *A city of sadness*. London: British Film Institute.

Suchenski, Richard I. (Ed.). (2014). *Hou Hsiao-hsien*. Vienna, Austria: Filmmuseum Synema Publikationen.

Udden, James. (2009). *No man an island: The cinema of Hou Hsiao-hsien*. Hong Kong: Hong Kong University Press.

Yeh, Emilie Yueh-yu, & Darrell William Davis. (2005). *Taiwan film directors: A treasure island*. New York: Columbia University Press.

Yip, June. (2004). *Envisioning Taiwan: Fiction, cinema, and the nation in the cultural imaginary*. Durham, NC: Duke University Press.

• Hou Hsiao-hsien •

♂ Hú Jiā 胡佳

b. 1973—Environmental and human rights activist

Alternate name: b. Hú Jiā 胡嘉

Summary

Hu Jia is one of China's best-known political activists. He participated in the 1989 Tiananmen Square protests and has worked for environmental and public health nongovernmental organizations. His work as an AIDS activist, his support of fellow activists who criticized government policies, and his lobbying on behalf of human rights issues has led to his house arrest, and imprisonment from 2008 to 2011. Hu currently lives in Beijing under close supervision by the authorities.

Hu Jia is one of the most prominent of a new generation of human rights activists in the People's Republic of China. In his career he has migrated from environmental issues, considered relatively safe territory, to the highly contentious issue of HIV-contaminated blood and the associated AIDS crisis, on to equal rights for same-sex couples, and the legacy of the 1989 Tiananmen Square movement. For this, despite international support, he has paid a high price in China, being placed under house arrest and imprisoned. His career illustrates the harsh trajectory of those who work in arenas that attract the antipathy of the authorities.

Background

Hu Jia was born in Beijing on 23 July 1973, towards the end of the Cultural Revolution (1966–1976) and into a home already disadvantaged by being associated with a "bad" class background. His mother and father were both students at elite universities—his father at Tsinghua University in Beijing and his mother at Nankai University in Tianjin—when they were each accused of being rightists during the Anti-Rightist Campaign of 1957–1958. They met at the start of the Cultural Revolution, and did not manage to settle down for a number of years because of the

胡佳

uncertainty and social turbulence of that era.

Career as an Activist

Hu was brought up in Beijing, and in interviews has referred to the relatively open environment he experienced as an adolescent during the early years of Reform and Opening Up in the 1980s. All of this changed, however, with the removal in 1987 of *Hú Yàobāng 胡耀邦 (1915–1989) from his position as party

―――――――

*People marked with an asterisk have entries in this dictionary.

secretary and an increasingly acrimonious battle among the political elite, between economic conservatives and liberals. By the time of the student demonstrations in the spring of 1989, Hu already showed a strong interest in supporting this cause, despite being only fifteen, and was present in Beijing's Tiananmen Square up until the night of 3 June, when the bloody military clampdown occurred. Hu has subsequently said that he was not present in the final stage of the protests because his father, fearing for his safety, prevented him from attending. "We didn't have any experience but we had a sense of responsibility," Hu stated in an

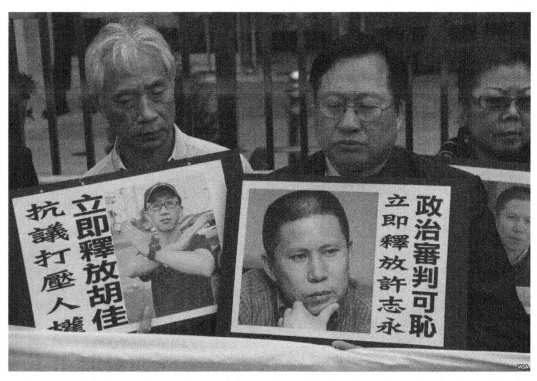

Protesters in Hong Kong gather in support of the activists and dissidents Hu Jia and Xu Zhiyong (2014). Photo by Voice of America (Chinese).

interview about this period in 2014. "We wanted democracy, we wanted an end of corruption. We wanted dialogue" (Johnson 2014).

After studying information engineering at the Beijing School of Economics, in the late 1990s Hu started becoming involved first in environmental projects, and then in the much more controversial problem of HIV-contaminated blood. Environmentalism had been growing in China over the previous two decades, once the extent to which China's natural resources and environment were being decimated due to intense industrialization became clear. The journalist and activist *Dài Qíng 戴晴 (b. 1941) and others had already written about this issue, and had set up a number of non-governmental organizations (NGOs), and while they were operating in novel legal territory (NGOs simply did not exist in the era of the all-powerful central state under Mao), they were largely tolerated.

The issue of HIV-contaminated blood, however, was much less straightforward for activists. Throughout the 1990s, at a time when the government was largely promoting the line that AIDS was a foreign disease that only existed in China inasmuch as it had been brought in and spread by non-Chinese, blood donor scams were operating in a number of provinces, the most extreme being in highly populated central Henan. Unscrupulous blood traders were paying farmers and others small amounts of cash to become donors, using recycled and dirty syringe needles to extract the blood, and then storing the collected plasma in vats where it was mixed together. Unsurprisingly, HIV started to spread and by the end of the decade reports surfaced of whole villages blighted with AIDS. The government's initial response was a news clampdown and blanket denial. But the work of activists like Hu Jia made this reaction untenable, and finally the government had to openly admit the problem, although it blamed the crisis on "evil" business people rather than government agents, and offered minimal compensation.

Hu's role in Aizhixing, an NGO established by fellow AIDS activist Wán Yánhǎi 万延海, his public support for the blogger Liú Dí 刘荻 (writing under the name Stainless Steel Mouse 不锈钢老鼠) who was imprisoned in 2003 for posting articles critical of the Party and government, and his lobbying of the European Parliament and other external bodies about human rights issues in China all contributed to his detention, under house arrest, beginning in 2006. This period coincided with a marked deterioration in the human rights situation in China, with a number of other like-minded rights lawyers and advocates being harassed, perhaps the most prominent being Nobel Prize laureate *Liú Xiǎobō 刘晓波 (b. 1955). By early 2008, Hu was formally sentenced to three to five years in jail, his stated crime being the very broad "inciting subversion of state power."

The specific cause was an open letter to the government he had co-authored with the highly regarded human rights lawyer Téng Biāo 滕彪 in 2007, entitled "The Real China and the Olympics." The government's nervousness over the Olympics, due to be held in Beijing in August 2008, was only intensified by the uprising in April of that year in Tibet, and the subsequent unrest in Xinjiang in 2009, and Inner Mongolia in 2011. All of this exacerbated the harsh treatment of activists and people labeled as dissidents.

While Hu was freed in 2011, he has remained under close official supervision, and his wife, the documentary filmmaker and activist Zēng Jīnyàn 曾金燕, has been forced to relocate to Hong Kong with their daughter because of persistent harassment by police and other state agents. These conditions come close to those of his house arrest several years before. Hu has maintained an active web presence, and was one of the main proponents in June 2014 of an attempt to mark the twenty-fifth anniversary of the Tiananmen Square Incident, which was aborted due to official pressure and obstruction. In recent years, he has suffered ill health, namely hepatitis, due to his time spent in prison.

Hu Jia's career and treatment are symptomatic of one of the less positive aspects of modern China—intolerance of political dissent, and brutal recriminations for those who dare question the legitimacy of the party. As such, he is symbolic of a small, though highly vocal, minority who hold views that differ from those of the authorities but who, in more free societies, would be allowed to at least speak their opinions peacefully and engage in legal advocacy. Instead, Hu has been imprisoned and bullied, and had silence sporadically enforced upon him.

Kerry BROWN
Lau China Institute, King's College

Further Reading

Johnson, Ian. (2014). You won't get near Tiananmen!: Hu Jia on the continuing crackdown. *The New York Review of Books*. Retrieved December 19, 2014, from http://www.nybooks.com/blogs/nyrblog/2014/jun/02/you-wont-get-near-tiananmen-square-talk-hu-jia

Hu Jia. (2003). A tale of two crises: SARS vs. AIDS. (Stacy Mosher, Trans). *China Rights Forum*, 3, 56–63. Retrieved December 19, 2014, from http://iso.hrichina.org/sites/default/files/PDFs/CRF.3.2003/Hu_Jia.pdf

Hu Jia, & Zeng Jinyan. (2006–2007). *Prisoners in freedom city*. Retrieved December 19, 2014, from https://www.youtube.com/playlist?list=PL7562A31EDB814BE2

Teng Biao, & Hu Jia. (2007). The real China and the Olympics. Retrieved December 19, 2014, from: http://www.hrw.org/sites/default/files/related_material/teng_biao080220.pdf

• Hú Jiā •

♂ Hú Jǐntāo 胡锦涛

b. 1942—Former president of China (2003–2013) and general secretary of the CCP (2002–2012)

Alternate name: trad. 胡錦濤

Summary

As China's paramount leader, Hu Jintao was known during his tenure as a devotee to the Chinese Communist Party, a hard-boiled autocrat who rose up from the western provinces with a reputation for cracking down on dissent and unrest. Governing during a time of increasing economic disparity, Hu also oversaw a period in which China became the world's third-largest economy, the second-largest exporter, and the host of the 2008 Summer Olympics.

By the end of the first decade of the twenty-first century, Hu Jintao was the most powerful man in the People's Republic of China (PRC). He was concurrently the president of China (a largely symbolic post), chair of the Central Military Commission (CMC, with final say on China's military forces) and, most significantly of all, general secretary of the Chinese Communist Party (CCP). With this brace of positions, he held his hand on all the main positions of power.

Early Years

Little is known about Hu's early life and he has barely ever mentioned his early years, or his family background. He was born of Anhui parents, perhaps in Anhui, or Jiangsu, or even Shanghai, in 1942. By 1959, he had been sent to the water conservancy department at elite Tsinghua University in Beijing. He joined the CCP in 1964, and remained at Tsinghua after completing his first degree to do political work and be a postgraduate.

When the Cultural Revolution started in 1966, Tsinghua was one of the first, and most active, centers of revolution. Like any future leader from this generation, Hu has been dogged by questions of what he got up to during this anarchic time, when students were encouraged to attack teachers and other figures of authority. All Hu's official biographical data records was that he "participated in research and development," but some have claimed that he was a Red Guards group leader. There is another gap in his biography during the years 1968 to 1974. Whether he was still engaged at Tsinghua or had been sent to other parts of the country to engage in revolutionary work is unclear. By 1975, however, Hu was recorded as a low-level party official in the construction sector in the remote western province of Gansu. His political journey had now started.

The Road to Power

Hu was based in the arid and impoverished Gansu region for the next eight years. It was subsequently claimed, when he became a national leader, that this experience framed his outlook and informed his political worldview. He was not of the elite, Beijing-based group but had come up from the grassroots. His time in Gansu introduced him to another key organization in his career, the China Youth League. In the early 1980s, he worked briefly as the head of this organization at a local level in Gansu, before being sent to Beijing to be chairman of the national Youth League. This was to be a great networking and training ground for his future positions.

Return to the Provinces

In addition to his position in the Youth League, Hu had been voted into the Central Committee of the Party (at the time, a four-hundred-strong decision-making elite) in 1982. The famously "anti-ideological" nature of Chinese politics in the mid-1980s is typified by *Dèng Xiǎopíng's 邓小平 (1904–1997) endlessly quoted line, "It doesn't matter if a cat is white or black, as long as it catches mice," and the frequent interdictions by then party secretary, *Hú Yàobāng 胡耀邦 (1915–1989), and his deputy, *Zhào Zǐyáng 赵紫阳 (1919–2005), that politics needed to be given a back seat while China's economy and society entered into the twentieth century. This, however, did not occur without opposition.

In 1984, 1986, and finally in 1987, there were national clampdowns against "spiritual pollution." Entrepreneurs who had gone too far in terms of setting up private companies were viewed as practicing blatant capitalism rather than working within the Party rubric to create a strong, socialist country. They were slapped down, and some even temporarily imprisoned. The other targets were the intellectuals who were most unrestrained in questioning the legitimacy of the Party and its right to have a monopoly on political power. They too were reined in. In the middle of the decade, Hu was appointed Party leader of a remote, poorer region, in order to gather more leadership experience. He was to remain in the west for another seven years.

---

*People marked with an asterisk have entries in this dictionary.

Guizhou and Tibet

To many, Hu's "reward" by being made party boss of the impoverished Guizhou Province would have seemed like rough justice. Even so, custodianship of an area like this was a chance to prove that Hu could administer and lead. He did well enough to finally be rewarded with the even more sensitive "prize" of Tibet, the massive but sparsely populated autonomous region covering most of the extreme west of the PRC. From 1988 to 1992, he was the party secretary there.

As party secretary of the area, Hu was both the highest-ranking leader, with responsibility for the security and stability of the area, and also the guardian of the Party's control over unity in the area. Beginning in 1987, disturbances occurred in the region, with Lhasa exploding in full scale riots in April 1989. Against the backdrop of social unrest across the country in Tibet, there were the specific issues of rights for minority communities, dissatisfaction with the treatment of specific religious figures, anger over the continuing exile of the Dalai Lama, and fury over the unequal benefits available in the region, with Han settlers accused of getting far better conditions than native locals. It was at this critical juncture that Hu authorized the deployment of over fifteen thousand security personnel into the region to restore order.

The brutality of Hu's crackdown was to lead to shocked compliance among most of the populace in Tibet. It is still not clear to this day how many were killed, but the decisiveness of his actions won him at least one major fan in Beijing: the eighty-seven-year-old paramount leader Deng Xiaoping. When the then party secretary, Zhao Ziyang, was put under house arrest for failing to deal with the issues of Tiananmen Square in 1989, Deng cleared a route for Hu's return to the political center. By 1992, Hu was given new appointments, the most important of which was membership in the Standing Committee of the Politburo, the most powerful decision-making body in China, and at that time consisting of only seven members. He was also made head of the Party School in Beijing, the main generator of new ideas and initiatives.

A National Leader

As one of the chief deputies and allies of the new party secretary and country president, *Jiāng Zémín 江泽民 (b. 1926), Hu was part of a period that saw both massive opportunities and huge potential risks. While the era of Deng was finally drawing to a close (Deng passed away in 1997), and Jiang and the new generation (the third, as it came to be called) still had other elder party leaders to contend with, the path had become a little clearer for them to be their own men.

When Hu Jintao was elevated to the position of vice president in 1998, talk began of his likely future leadership of the Party. He visited the United States and undertook other foreign tours, getting some badly needed experience in foreign affairs. Despite all the prophesies of potential fall-out around the leadership transition, in the end it happened seamlessly. In late 2002, Hu Jintao stood as the paramount leader of the most populous nation on the planet. He was also elected president. After his predecessor, Jiang Zemin, relinquished his role as chair of the Central Military Commission in 2004, Hu Jintao was in charge of all key institutional levers of power in China.

Domestic Challenges

The country he led was one of stark contrasts. It became, under his leadership, the world's largest holder of US debt, its third-largest economy after the United States and Japan, its second-largest exporter, and its largest holder of foreign currency reserves. But it was also a country which still had huge numbers of impoverished people, and which was alone among the world's top-ten economies in remaining a state where there were no free national elections.

Hu, with his premier, *Wēn Jiābāo 温家宝 (b. 1942), having succeeded in the first smooth and peaceful transition of power from one generation of leadership to another, now needed to face the key issues of their term in power. The foremost of these were domestic: how to deal with the inequalities that had occurred in Chinese society as a result of the

economic reforms of the last two decades. Another issue was how to maintain good gross domestic product (GDP) growth, continuing to lift people out of poverty. These were both seen as critical to maintain the Communist Party's hold on power. In international affairs, they hoped to reassure the world that, despite its continuing rise and prominence, China was a force for good, and that its different political model should not be interpreted negatively. These goals were to present massive challenges, and Hu and Wen's successes were only partial.

Inequality in particular had been the bugbear of the economic reforms. For all its success in creating GDP growth (almost 10 percent a year since 1979) China had gone from being one of the most equal societies in the world in 1984, measured by the Gini coefficient, which measures income distribution, to being as unequal as Brazil in 2007. While coastal areas boomed, the western provinces where Hu had spent much of his career remained dominated by state-owned industry, or agriculture, with large swathes of poverty, lack of development, and farmers who felt that the economic edifice was biased against them. Hu and Wen knew that discontent in the countryside led to massive uprisings in the past and from 2004, in particular, Hu talked more in his key speeches about a harmonious society (*héxié shèhuì* 和谐社会) and the need to embrace the poorest in society, to create a more level, balanced society. The brute fact remained, however, that while China created many thousands of millionaires, poverty remained entrenched in many parts of the country; and that, in 2005, China had 20 million more illiterate people than fifteen years earlier, a damning indictment of its educational provision outside of cities.

Maintaining continuing economic growth was the other great challenge. The path of reform and opening up had to continue, and that meant more radical economic change. Chinese enterprises were allowed to become active abroad. From its entry into the World Trade Organization (WTO) in 2001, foreign investment continued to flow into China. The whole country became like a Special Economic Zone (SEZ, Jīngjì tèqū 经济特区), with almost every province and sector open to foreign investment. By 2008, the domestic market had also

become important, with one particular landmark in 2009 when China overtook the United States as the world's biggest market for cars.

These domestic issues lay at the heart of the party's need to demonstrate legitimacy. Corruption of officials and party members was rampant, but from time to time Hu, like his predecessor Jiang, was able to strike with surprising effectiveness against potential opponents, usually using the anti-corruption banner.

International Exposure

China's economic rise had created more opposition than had been expected, and the need to communicate a calm, peaceful, and benign intent to the world had been recognized from 2005. In making the so-called Confucius Institutes one of the key elements of China's face abroad, the

Hu Jintao (right) shaking hands with Korean President Lee Myung-bak. Photo by the Republic of Korea.

leadership under Hu turned their back on Maoist visceral hatred of Confucius's place in Chinese intellectual and spiritual tradition. China's articulation of its global position became particularly important, but as the problems in the lead-up to the Beijing Olympics showed, there were plenty of people who had been unsettled by the country's fast and vast growth, and distrusted its intentions. Hu, as the face and voice of new China, was not exactly either approachable or comprehensible. His stiff public manner, lack of ability in speaking foreign languages, and inscrutable demeanor all boded ill.

The Party Man

But for his domestic challenges, which were, after all, the key ones, Hu had one major challenge and one alone. That was to ensure that the Party continued to enjoy a monopoly on power and that it survived, despite the sea of threats around it. Neither the economy nor the international situation could push the Party from its preeminent position. So those who had hoped to see a reformer in Hu in his rise to power in the 1990s were in for a rude shock. There were no major legal reforms under his rule, no easing up on dissidents, who were treated as harshly as those under previous leaders. Property rights were slightly revised, but the Party maintained its grip in the key areas of social and political life. Hu's one concession was to talk more of internal party democracy, bringing in a little more

transparency to administrative and legal decision-making. The need for the Party to at least open up a bit and sort out its own house was an important admission.

But it was on this issue that Hu also showed his greatest limitations. If there was one defining characteristic of him as a person, and of his leadership, it was the utter preeminence of the Party and its legitimacy, rule, and continuation over all else. Hu was a creature of the Party. He owed everything to it and was created in its mold. Perhaps this alone was why Deng had seen so much in him. More than anyone else in modern China, he exemplified the interests of the Party and its style of rule. He had no evident personal likes and dislikes beyond the Party, and made decisions solely with the interests of the Party at their heart.

For those issues of the day that needed vision, courage, or imagination, Hu was evidently not the man. His reaction to most threats was to authorize repression or co-option. On the haunting issue of political reform, he stuck resolutely to gradualism, allowing people in the Party School to talk of potential fundamental reform in the next fifty years, rather than by 2020. No mercy was show to anyone who attempted to set up organized political opposition. The issue of Xinjiang, in particular, and of Tibet, was dealt with by flooding the area with security personnel, and then unleashing extensive crackdowns. Hu's administration shied away from talk of a possible global G2 partnership with the United States, perhaps

• Hú Jǐntāo •

wisely saying that China was both unready and unwilling to take up this position. But even in places like North Korea and Africa, where China had strong interests and influence, it wished to continue to keep a low profile. At a time when communication was necessary, therefore, Hu failed to show that he could speak for China in a way that the world understood. This may well be seen as his greatest limitation.

Hu the Man

Those who met Hu personally could be divided into those who remarked on how he resembled a benign, diffident academic, and those who felt he was almost mechanical, resembling an automaton. His remarkable memory for names was often commented on, along with his administrative ability. When he showed the Queen around a British Museum exhibition in London during his state visit in 2005, he briefly came alive, explaining some of the exhibits to her and displaying a good knowledge of ancient China. But his technocratic background meant that he displayed next to no interest in art or culture, never expressed any opinion about books or films, and seemed devoid of interest in any issues beyond politics.

He married Liú Yǒngqīng 刘永清 after studying with her at Tsinghua University, and they had two children: one son, Hu Haifeng, who is a businessman, and one daughter, Hu Haiqing, who lives in the United States. Both keep very low profiles.

His period in office ended in 2012, with the transition to a new generation of leadership. The fact that the transition went in a largely orderly fashion (despite some turbulence around the time of the fall of Chongqing party secretary *Bó Xīlái 薄熙来 [b. 1949]) was a testament to Hu's fidelity to the interests of the Party, and his largely low key, impersonal style of leadership. He largely disappeared from public view after 2012, unlike his own predecessor, Jiang Zemin, who had been very much present even after leaving office. Hu's period in power can be best characterized as one in which China grew richer than it had ever been before, but also in which its internal governance grew increasingly complex. These were the challenges that Hu left to his successors.

Kerry BROWN
Lau China Institute, King's College

Further Reading

Brown, Kerry. (2009). *Friends and enemies: The past, present and future of the Communist Party of China.* New York: Anthem Press.

Lam, Willy Wo-Lap. (2006). *Chinese politics in the Hu Jintao era: New leaders, new challenges.* Armonk, NY: M.E. Sharpe.

Li, Cheng. (2001). *China's Leaders: The new generation.* Lanham, MD: Rowman & Littlefield Publishers.

Shambaugh, David. (2008). *The Communist Party of China: Atrophy or adaptation.* Berkeley: University of California Press.

⚲ Hú Yàobāng 胡耀邦

1915–1989—General secretary of the CCP (1980–1987), supporter of economic and political reforms

Summary

Hu Yaobang was a Chinese Communist Party leader noted for his reform-mindedness and support of intellectuals. A long-term political ally of Deng Xiaoping, he was ousted from power in 1987 after party elders criticized his handling of student protests. Hu's untimely death in 1989 caused wide-spread public mourning which escalated into the 4 June Tiananmen Square Incident.

Hu Yaobang was the most prominent reformist political leader among the People's Republic of China's (PRC) "second generation" leadership, alongside *Zhào Zǐyáng 赵紫阳 (1919–2005). Hu's major contributions to the 1978 reforms included the rehabilitation of unjustly purged victims of Mao-era persecution, and his lobbying for a "liberation of thinking" from Maoist doctrine. Throughout his political career,

Hu actively built networks of reform-minded intellectuals and provided political patronage for a number of critical thinkers within the Chinese Communist Party (CCP).

Groomed as the successor to *Dèng Xiǎopíng 邓小平 (1904–1997) since 1980, Hu was forced to resign as CCP general secretary in early 1987 when veteran leaders criticized his handling of student protests. Hu's death in April 1989 triggered massive outpourings of public mourning, which culminated in the 1989 Tiananmen Square demonstrations. As a result of the 4 June military crackdown, Hu's life and memory, while not strictly taboo, have been part of PRC public discourse only sparingly.

Early Life and Activism

Hu Yaobang was born into a peasant family on 20 November 1915 in Nanxiang, Liuyang County, Hunan Province. A gifted pupil, he received a comparatively good primary school education,

---

*People marked with an asterisk have entries in this dictionary.

and attended Zhonghe village school and Liwen Elementary School in Wenjia town, where he was recruited into the Communist Youth League by a teacher. After passing the entrance examination of Liuyang County Middle School in 1928, Hu studied there until its closing due to political instability a year later. He joined the Communist revolution at age fourteen, and in the spring of 1931 left his home and joined the Jiangxi Central Soviet base, one of three major Communist strongholds formed in 1930 in central China.

Wartime Activities and Functions (1931–1949)

During his time at the Jiangxi Central Soviet, Hu first worked as a communications officer and head of the Youth Office of the Soviet District Anti-Imperialist Alliance, becoming secretary general of the Central Bureau of the Chinese Communist Youth League in 1933. Later that year, Hu was admitted into the Communist Party, and in early 1934 took over as secretary general of the Central Committee of the Chinese Communist Youth League, until they had to retreat from advancing Nationalist forces in October 1934.

During the Long March, when Chinese Communists marched from Jiangxi Province in southeast China to Shaanxi Province in northwest China in retreat from the Nationalists, Hu was in charge of ideological work among the Youth League members of his military unit. On 15 February 1935, he fought in the battle for the Loushan Pass, reportedly showing exemplary heroism. After having been seriously wounded, Hu continued the retreat and later worked as head of the Welfare Brigade of the Third Red Army Corps. Hu's unit reached Wuqi in the Shaanxi-Gansu Soviet District in late October 1935. At age nineteen, Hu was one of only about seven thousand Long March survivors.

After the Long March, Hu became captain of the Shilou County Work Brigade, carrying out the communist land reform program and spreading anti-Japanese propaganda. In late 1935, Máo Zédōng 毛泽东 (1893–1976) himself promoted Hu to membership of the Central Office of the Chinese Communist Youth League, where Hu became involved in the league's reorganization, aiming at recruiting youths for anti-Japanese resistance work.

In the spring of 1937, Hu was selected for training at the newly established Resistance University (Kàngdà 抗大) in Yan'an, which was modeled after the Nationalist's Whampoa (Huángpǔ 黄埔) military academy. In Yan'an, Hu studied Mao's early works with Mao himself. These essays formed the backbone of Hu's critical understanding of "Mao Zedong Thought" during the 1978 "Truth Criterion" debate launched for the liberation of thinking from pseudo-Maoist doctrine. In 1938/1939, Hu became active in United Front work to expand CCP influence in the Yan'an region. At age

Hu Yaobang in Yan'an, between 1937 and 1940.

twenty-three, he was appointed director of the Organization Department of the Military Commission's General Political Bureau, and thus put in charge of military cadre policy. During the Chinese Civil War (1946–1949), Hu commanded troops in numerous guerilla attacks and mobile warfare campaigns.

On 1 October 1949, Hu attended the founding ceremony of the People's Republic of China in Beijing. During November and December, Hu again commanded troops against remaining Nationalist forces in Sichuan.

Marriage and Children

In 1942, at age twenty-seven, Hu married twenty-one-year-old Lǐ Zhāo 李昭, a student at the Chinese Women's College in Yan'an. They had four children: a son, Hú Dépíng 胡德平 (b. 1942), later a vice

chairman of the All-China General Chamber of Industry & Commerce and Standing Committee member of the Chinese People's Political Consultative Conference (CPPCC); a son named Liú Hú 刘湖 (b. 1945), who was initially given to the care of foster parents due to political turmoil and therefore received the surname Liu, and who later worked in the leadership of the Hong Kong-based state-owned enterprise China Resources; a third son named Hú Déhuā 胡德华 (b. 1949), a scientist and officer at the Chinese Academy of Sciences; and a daughter named Lǐ Héng 李恒 (b. 1952), an officer for the Chinese Medical Association, who received her mother's surname as a sign of equality between the sexes.

Political Career During the Mao Era (1949–1976)

In 1950, Hu was put in charge of north Sichuan's economic and finance work. Working under Deng Xiaoping's direct supervision for nearly three years, he developed a close rapport with him.

In August 1952, Mao transferred both Deng and Hu to Beijing. Hu was put in charge of the New Democratic Youth League (in 1957 renamed the Chinese Communist Youth League). During Hu's tenure, membership grew from about two million members to about twenty million in 1956. In September 1956, Hu was elected to the CCP's Central Committee. He actively promoted the 1957 Hundred

Flowers Campaign in the Youth League and argued for leniency with the dissenting voices who had been encouraged to speak out. However, during the 1958 Anti-Rightist Campaign backlash, he adhered to Mao's hard line and initially also supported the Great Leap Forward propaganda effort, which aimed to advance China's agricultural and industrial development through agricultural collectivization and other ill-advised schemes, in the Youth League's publications.

After local inspection tours conducted by Hu in 1961 to Tang County, Hebei Province and in 1962 to Anhui Province revealed the disastrous consequences of the Great Leap Forward, Hu was prompted to promote local measures to quickly enhance food production through individual farming. In 1963, Hu obtained permission to move to southern Hunan as local committee secretary to study agricultural affairs with the aim of developing sound economic development policies.

In March 1966, he was recalled to Beijing to take personal charge of Youth League leadership amidst early signs of the impending Cultural Revolution. In December 1966, a violent Red Guard attack overturned his fourteen-year tenure as the Youth League's leader. From January 1967, Hu was "struggled against," publicly paraded and humiliated, and locked up in a shed for two and a half years. His family was divided and all members suffered persecution as "reactionary elements." From late 1968,

Hu was sent to the countryside for "re-education" through manual labor until he fell ill and received permission to get treatment in Beijing in early 1971, where he remained in forced retirement.

In 1972, Hu wrote a letter to the central leadership asking to return to work, which he was allowed to do in 1973. In July 1975, he was appointed as vice president of the Chinese Academy of Sciences (CAS) in charge of party organization work, where he tried to constrain ideological dominance over research in accord with Deng's ideas. In early 1976, this policy led to a Maoist backlash, and Hu was ousted from power until after Mao's death in September 1976.

Post-Mao Leadership Functions (1976–1987)

When Deng returned to the central government in May 1977, Hu was appointed vice president of the Central Party School in Beijing. In August 1977, he was elected into the CCP's Eleventh Central Committee and in December 1977 became director of the CCP's Central Organization Department.

Contribution to Reform and Opening Up (1976–1980)

The Central Party School post allowed Hu to build a network of young cadres destined for higher positions in various state and party organs, including the major newspapers. Hu quickly moved to organize writing teams to promote reformist ideas, arguing for the rehabilitation of unjustly purged cadres, and criticizing blind adherence to Maoist policies. Starting from Deng Xiaoping's May 1977 criticism of Party Chairman Huá Guófèng's 华国锋 "Two Whatevers" doctrine of unswerving loyalty to Mao—"Let us resolutely defend *whatever* policy decisions Chairman Mao made, and steadfastly abide by *whatever* instructions Chairman Mao gave"— Hu in the spring of 1978 orchestrated the collaborative drafting and strategic publication of the article "Practice is the Sole Criterion for Testing Truth" which challenged the notion that Mao's words had to be taken as unfailing truth, and argued for a comprehensive review of Mao's writings in the context of Marxist philosophy and actual experience. The essay was reprinted in all leading party newspapers in May 1978, and kickstarted the so-called "Great Truth Criterion Debate" which continued for months. The aim of this was to undermine the Hua leadership's claim to power and to support Deng's reform agenda.

As director of the Central Organization Department, Hu simultaneously started a massive initiative to redress unjust purges of cadres labeled "rightists" since the 1957 Anti-Rightist Campaign. Expressing regret at his earlier failure to stand up for those attacked, Hu organized the reexamination of hundreds of thousands of cases nationwide, starting with former minister of defense Péng Déhuái 彭德怀, who had been one of the highest-profile victims of the Cultural Revolution. Until 1980, about 540,000 "unjust verdicts" (the so-called *yuān jiǎ cuò àn* 冤假错案) were overturned, earning Hu widespread sympathy among those affected. This measure enlarged the support base for Deng's reform course among party cadres.

Hu's hugely successful strategy prepared the ground for the political turn towards Reform and Opening Up at the Third Plenum of the Eleventh Central Committee in December 1978. At that Plenum, Hu became a Politburo member and a secretary of the CCP's Central Discipline Inspection Committee.

Top Party Leader and Reformer (1980–1987)

In February 1980, Hu was appointed secretary general of the re-established CCP Central Committee's Secretariat, and in June 1981, became CCP chairman following Hua Guofeng's resignation, and was also appointed director of the Central Committee's Propaganda Department. In September 1982, the position of party chairman was abolished and Hu instead became general secretary of the Central Committee, a post he held until his forced resignation in 1987.

During his tenure as party chief, Hu worked for the consolidation of the reform course against its numerous critics who feared "spiritual pollution" from "bourgeois liberalization" (i.e., Western political values and Western popular culture), and actively promoted reforms in the CCP's cadre system with an aim to recruiting younger, better qualified people into leadership positions. He also argued for establishing a routine modus for leadership succession. His initiative to set a fixed retirement age for leaders was however construed as an attack on Deng Xiaoping's and other veteran leaders' special status by his political opponents. Hu likewise alienated fellow reformist leader, State Council Premier *Zhào Zǐyáng 赵紫阳 (1919–2005), with his outspoken stance on economic issues and political reform, prompting Zhao to frequently complain about Hu's interventions into his own portfolio. Other controversial activities which undermined Hu's support base among party elders were his attempts to combat corruption among the children of high-ranking cadres, including those of Hú Qiáomù 胡乔木, *Wáng Zhèn 王震 (1908–1993), and *Bó Yībō 薄一波 (1908–2007).

Ousting From Power and Death (1987–1989)

When high inflation rates and student protests in December 1986 made social tensions palpable, Hu's critics blamed his leadership. Deng Xiaoping withdrew his support and on 16 January 1987 forced him to resign as CCP general secretary amidst a purge against pro-reform intellectuals such as *Liú Bīnyàn 刘宾雁

(1925–2005), *Fāng Lìzhī 方励之, and Wáng Ruòwàng 王若望, who had all been supported by Hu.

Zhao Ziyang, after harshly criticizing Hu, succeeded him as CCP general secretary. Although permitted to remain on the Politburo's Standing Committee and thus not technically purged, the severity of the verbal attacks launched on him by party elders and fellow reformers such as Zhao reportedly shocked Hu deeply.

For the remainder of his life, Hu continued to attend Politburo meetings and other official functions. During a Politburo meeting on 8 April 1989, Hu suffered a heart attack and collapsed. Despite immediate treatment, he passed away on 15 April. This unexpected death only two years after his shameful ousting from power came as a shock to a sympathetic public, and quickly gave rise to mourning activities on Tiananmen Square resembling those commemorating Zhōu Ēnlái 周恩来 during the earlier 1976 Tiananmen Incident. These resulted in unprecedented public protest demonstrations criticizing the CCP leadership, which were ultimately suppressed violently during the 4 June 1989 Incident.

Public Reaction, Legacy, and Recognition

According to his biographer, Yáng Zhōngměi 杨中美, the major contribution of Hu Yaobang and his collaborators consisted in an obvious rejection of Mao

Contemporary artist rendition of Hu Yaobang on a wall in France (2008). Photo by thierry ehrmann.

(Hu 2011). On 15 April 2010, then State Council premier *Wēn Jiābǎo 温家宝 (b. 1942) for the first time officially commemorated Hu in a *People's Daily* (*Rénmín rìbào* 人民日报) article. Numerous other commemorative writings have been published in Hong Kong, including a collection of popular poems dedicated to his memory entitled "Words from the Heart of the People" (Gao 2008).

Sarah Katharina KIRCHBERGER
University of Hamburg

Zedong's style of socialism and a determined effort to push for a more intelligent reform path (Yang 1988). The various reform initiatives of the late 1970s orchestrated by Hu and his associates have been commemorated in numerous monographs and articles. Many of these emphasize the positive leadership, creative working style, tolerance for dissent, and fidelity to humanist ideals shown by Hu throughout his entire career (Ruan 1994, Shen 1997, Wang 1997, Dai 1998, He 1999, Hu 2011, and Xu 2013).

In recent years, erstwhile political associates and relatives of Hu have lobbied for his full rehabilitation. The outspoken Beijing-based history magazine *China Through the Ages* (*Yánhuáng chūnqiū* 炎黄春秋*)*, which was founded in 1991 by former associates of Hu Yaobang and Zhao Ziyang, has printed numerous related materials, and since late 2014 has been led by Hu's eldest son, Hu Deping, who has also published a book on his father's reform course in Hong Kong

Further Reading

Baum, Richard. (1994). *Burying Mao: Chinese politics in the age of Deng Xiaoping*. Princeton, NJ: Princeton University Press.

Dai Huang 戴煌. (1998). *Hu Yaobang yu pingfan yuan, jia, cuo an* 胡耀邦与平反冤假错案. [Hu Yaobang and the redressing of unjust, false and erroneous cases]. Beijing: Xinhua chubanshe.

Gao Yongqi 高勇氣. (Ed.). (2008). *Renmin de xinsheng: jinian Hu Yaobang shiciji* 人民的心聲：紀念胡耀邦詩詞集 [Words from the heart of the people: A collection of commemorative poems for Hu Yaobang]. Hong Kong: Shidai guojihua.

Goldman, Merle. (1991). Hu Yaobang's intellectual network and the theory conference of 1979. *The China Quarterly, 126*, 219–242.

He Zai. (1999). *Yuan, jia, cuo an shi zheyang pingfan de* 冤假错案是这样平反的. [This is how the unjust, false and erroneous cases were redressed]. Beijing: Zhonggong zhongyang dangxiao chubanshe.

Hu Deping 胡德平. (2011). *Zhongguo weishenmo yao gaige : huiyi fuqin Hu Yaobang* 中國為什麼要改革: 回憶父親胡耀邦 [Why China needs reforms-remembering my father Hu Yaobang]. Hong Kong: Zhonghe publishing.

Kirchberger, Sarah. (2011). Dogma oder Praxis? Der Wahrheitskriterium-Text von 1978 als Beispiel für 'Politik durch Dokumente'. [Dogma or praxis? The Truth Criterion Article of 1978 as an example of 'documentary politics']. *Oriens Extremus, 50,* 249–281.

Ruan, Ming. (1994). *Deng Xiaoping: Chronicle of an empire.* (Nancy Liu et al., Trans.). Boulder, CO: Westview Press.

Schoenhals, Michael. (1991). The 1978 Truth Criterion Controversy. *The China Quarterly, 126,* 243–268.

Shen Baoxiang 沈宝祥. (1997). *Zhenli biaozhun wenti taolun shimo* 真理标准问题讨论始末 [The history of the Truth Criterion Debate]. Beijing: Zhongguo qingnian chubanshe.

Vogel, Ezra F. (2011). *Deng Xiaoping and the transformation of China.* Cambridge, MA, & London: The Belknap Press.

Wang Ruoshui 王若水. (1997). *Hu Yaobang xiatai de beijing : rendaozhuyi zai Zhongguo de mingyun* 胡耀邦下臺的背景 ： 人道主義在中國的命運 [Behind Hu Yaobang's step down : the fate of humanism in China]. Hong Kong: Mingjing chubanshe.

Wen Jiabao 温家宝. (2010, April 14). Zai hui xingyi yi Yaobang 再回兴义忆耀邦 [Upon returning to Xingyi I miss Yaobang]. *Renmin Ribao*, p. 2. Retrieved February 17, 2015, from http://paper.people.com.cn/rmrb/html/2010-04/15/nw.D110000renmrb_20100415_1-02.htm

Xu, Baojia 許保家. (2013). *Gaige xianqu Hu Yaobang* 改革先驅胡耀邦 [Vanguard of the reform: Hu Yaobang], Hong Kong: Tiandi tushu.

Yanhuang Chunqiu 炎黄春秋. (2015). History monthly homepage. Retrieved May 8, 2015, from http://www.yhcqw.com

Yang Jisheng 楊繼繩. (2010). *Zhongguo gaige niandai de zhengzhi douzheng* 中國改革年代的政治鬥爭. [Political conflict during the Chinese Reform Years]. Hong Kong: Tiandi/Cosmos Books.

Yang Zhongmei. (1988). *Hu Yaobang; A Chinese biography*. London: M.E. Sharpe.

胡耀邦

☿ Huáng Guāngyù
黄光裕

b. 1969—Founder of Gome Electrical Appliances, convicted for bribery and insider trading

Alternate names: former name Huáng Jùnliè 黃俊烈; Wong Kwong Yu; trad. 黃光裕

Summary

Until 2008, Huang Guangyu's story was a classic "rags to riches" tale. Founder of Gome, the nation's largest electrical appliances retailer, Huang was a billionaire by the age of thirty-seven. In 2008, however, he was arrested and eventually sentenced to fourteen years in prison for bribery and insider trading in 2010. Despite this setback, Huang is still in effective control of the company through his large shareholding and continues to influence management from behind bars.

Hugely successful as the founder of Gome Electrical Appliances (Guóměi Diànqì 国美电器), Huang Guangyu demonstrates through his career the enormous opportunities that have opened up in China during the reform period, especially for people with entrepreneurial talent. His eventual downfall also illustrates the difficult balancing act that private entrepreneurs must engage in to maintain profitability in China's cutthroat market while staying on the right side of the ever-evolving law.

Childhood and Early Education

Huang Guangyu was born in Shantou, Shandong Province on 24 June 1969. Little is known about his childhood, except that he was raised in a poor farming family and has at least an older brother (Huang Junqin) and a sister (Huang Yanhong). He dropped out of school at the age of sixteen, and went into the electronics business with his brother (some sources indicate he and his brother first tried to sell clothing, without success). Around 1986, he opened roadside stalls in the north selling electronics from the south. At this time, China's distribution system was not well developed, and many products from the more advanced Guangdong coastal region were not available in other parts of China, including Beijing, except at a very high premium. It was very common to see individual entrepreneurs (*gètǐhù* 个体户) like the Huangs riding trains from Guangdong to Beijing and other northern cities loaded down with as many electronic goods as they could carry, then selling them for a small profit before starting the process again (Branigan 2010; Bristow 2010).

Rise of a Tycoon, Fall of a Cheat

Huang Guangyu's career is closely tied to the rapid development of Gome. By early 1987, the Huangs had sufficiently developed their own distribution channels to open their first electrical appliances retail store in Beijing. By 1993, they had several stores operating and they adopted the brand name Gome for the first time. In July 1999, Gome opened its first store outside the Beijing region, in the city of Tianjin, signifying the start of its national expansion strategy (Gome 2014a).

In the early 2000s, Gome continued to expand rapidly both by opening new stores and through the acquisition of struggling competitors. The company was doubtless assisted by the huge growth in demand for consumer electronics among China's population in this period of rapid economic expansion. In addition, the constant advancement of television, mobile phone, and computer technologies quickly made earlier models obsolete and put pressure on consumers to continuously upgrade their appliances. Gome also gained a strong reputation for providing competitive prices with excellent service, and its retail model became the subject of numerous public seminars and business school case studies (Gome 2014a; Branigan 2010). Several other electrical appliance retailers such as Dazhong, Suning, and Yongle were competing fiercely with Gome, but apparently were unable to match its profitability and price structure. By 2007, Gome had listed its shares on the Hong Kong Stock Exchange (in 2004) and was the largest electrical appliance retailer in China, having absorbed Yongle and Dazhong through acquisition. In 2006 and 2007, Huang Guangyu's net worth, based largely on his shareholdings in Gome and affiliated companies, placed him at the top of China's richest person list, as estimated by Hurun (Yu et al 2008; *China Daily* 2010; Gome 2014a).

How did Gome achieve success in such a fiercely competitive business environment? Much of the firm's competitive edge appears to have come from Huang Guangyu's unorthodox and occasionally illegal financing techniques, which were revealed in Chinese media reports leading up to his trial in 2010. Initially, Huang took advantage of the trading convention that allowed retailers like Gome ninety days to pay their suppliers for goods that in most cases sold immediately in Gome's stores. Instead of paying suppliers immediately, Huang would offer short-term loans to cash-starved businesses and consumers at high interest rates, making more profit from this money-lending venture than he did from selling the low-margin electrical goods in the first place. This was illegal, though, as Huang was not a licensed financial services provider.

Huang also greatly boosted Gome's cash flow by cultivating a relationship with Niú Zhōngguāng 牛忠光, president of the Beijing branch of the Bank of China, who helped to disguise unauthorized and unsecured loans from the bank to Gome as fake mortgages and car loans. Gome allegedly borrowed up to 1.3 billion yuan in this way, and the money was apparently used by Gome to acquire land and other competing businesses, and possibly also to lend at higher interest rates.

Lastly, Huang used Gome's huge cash flow to engage in manipulation of the stock prices of various affiliated companies on the Chinese stock markets. For example, he secretly caused his associates to buy up shares in the publicly traded Zhongguancun Science and Technology Group (in which Huang and Gome had previously purchased a large stake at 0.78 yuan per share), despite the fact that he knew Zhongguancun was weighed down by huge debts. The effect of his associates' share purchases was to lift Zhongguancun's share price and thereby attract outside investors to jump on the bandwagon and buy more shares. The ultimate plan was to offload the company to unsuspecting investors at a much higher share price and give Huang, Gome, and his associates a huge profit (Yu et al 2008). Huang allegedly also engaged in insider trading of the shares of another company that he controlled, Beijing Centergate, making a trading profit of 309 million yuan (*China Daily* 2010).

When the police, anti-corruption investigators, and tax authorities began to crack down on Huang, Gome, and affiliated companies in 2006, Huang bribed them to drop the charges. Initially, he was successful, but a broader anti-corruption campaign in 2008 ensnared his official protectors too, and the charges against Huang were re-introduced. In 2010, Huang was convicted of illegal business dealings, insider trading, and corporate bribery and sentenced to fourteen years in prison and fined 600 million yuan, along with the confiscation of 200 million yuan worth of property. His wife, Du Juan, who was closely involved in managing Huang's companies, was sentenced to three and a half years for insider trading and fined 200 million yuan. Several government officials who had been bribed by Huang received lengthy jail terms, including an assistant minister of public security, three officials from the Beijing economic crimes investigation unit, and a senior official from the State Administration of Taxation (*China Daily* 2010).

Despite his conviction, Huang was still the largest shareholder of Gome, and was able to continue influencing the company's management from jail. For example, he ousted Chen Xiao, former CEO of Yongle, who had replaced him as chairman at Gome, in favor of his own candidate, Zhang Dazhong (Wei 2011). In addition, the fines exacted against him and his wife apparently made only a small dent in his fortune, as his stake in Gome was already worth around 18 billion yuan in 2008 (Yu et al, 2008). His legal difficulties, however, have continued up to the present, with the Hong Kong Securities and Futures Commission in 2014 ordering Huang and his wife to pay a total of HK\$420 million (US\$54 million) back to Gome due to a breach of directors' duties back in 2008. Huang and Du had caused Gome to purchase millions of dollars' worth of shares from Huang to help him pay off a personal loan without considering whether the purchase was in the company's best interests (Hong Kong Securities & Futures Commission 2014).

Influence and Legacy

Though Huang built up Gome very rapidly and was briefly ranked as the richest person in China, he is better known today as a typical "get rich quick entrepreneur" (*bàofāhù* 暴发户): someone who is prepared to use any means possible, including extensive corruption, to make a fortune and then keep the authorities at bay. It is unlikely that Gome would have survived and prospered as a private business in the complex Chinese environment without Huang engaging in some illegal activities. His disguised loans from the Bank of China, for example, were essential to fund Gome's growth, and could not have been obtained legitimately due to discrimination by Chinese state-owned banks against private-enterprise borrowers in the 1980s and 1990s. Likewise, Huang's habit of lending out Gome's cash flow to short-term borrowers at high interest rates was probably the only way that Gome could make enough profit in the low-margin consumer electrical appliance business to gain an edge over rivals. Huang's mistake was that he continued taking bigger legal risks in the 2000s, such as engaging in obvious insider trading and market manipulation, and failed to regularize his business practices after being investigated. Instead he relied on the high risk and ultimately unsuccessful strategy of bribing numerous officials to let him off the hook (Hogg 2010).

Ironically, Huang's example also shows that the Chinese government's attitude towards private entrepreneurs has changed significantly and for the better since the 1980s. Despite the huge amount of illicit gains made by Huang and his wife, he did not face the death penalty, and his major shareholding in Gome was not confiscated. Certainly he

黄光裕

will need to serve his time in prison, but when he eventually gets out, he will still be a very wealthy man.

Colin HAWES
University of Technology, Sydney

Further Reading

Branigan, Tania. (2010). Chinese electronics tycoon becomes country's richest prisoner. *The Guardian.* May 18. Retrieved August 27, 2014, from http://www.theguardian.com/world/2010/may/18/huang-guangyu-gome-jailed

Bristow, Michael. (2010). Profile: Huang Guangyu. *BBC News.* May 18. Retrieved August 27, 2014, from http://news.bbc.co.uk/2/hi/asia-pacific/8634862.stm

China Daily. (2010). Chinese tycoon Huang gets 14 years in prison. *China Daily online.* May 19. Retrieved December 7, 2014, from http://www.chinadaily.com.cn/china/2010-05/19/content_9866895.htm

Gome. (2014). Milestones. Retrieved December 7, 2014, from http://www.gome.com.hk/html/about_milestones.php

Hogg, Chris. (2010). What brought down China's Huang Guangyu? *BBC News.* 18 May. Retrieved August 27, 2014, from http://news.bbc.co.uk/2/hi/asia-pacific/8688638.stm

Hong Kong Securities & Futures Commission. (2014). SFC obtains court orders for GOME to receive HK$420 million compensation from founder and wife over breaches in share repurchase. Retrieved December 7, 2014, from http://www.sfc.hk/edistributionWeb/gateway/EN/news-and-announcements/news/enforcement-news/doc?refNo=14PR52

Lattemann, Christoph. (2009). Huang Guangyu. In Zhang Wenxian, & Ilan Alon, (Eds.). *Biographical dictionary of new Chinese entrepreneurs and business leaders* (pp. 58–59). Cheltenham, UK & Northampton, MA: Edward Elgar Publishing.

Poza, Ernesto. (2013). *Family business.* Mason, OH: Cengage Learning.

Wei, Michael. (2011). Gome Electrical's chairman Chen quits after boardroom battle with founder. *Bloomberg News.* March 9. Retrieved December 8, 2014, from http://www.bloomberg.com/news/2011-03-09/gome-electrical-says-chairman-chen-xiao-resigns-replaced-by-zhang-dazhong.html

Yu Ning, Li Qing, & Luo Changping. (2008). Dead end for a tycoon's creative financing. *Caijing Magazine.* December 12. Retrieved December 8, 2014, from http://english.caijing.com.cn/2008-12-11/110037416.html

♂ Jiǎ Zhāngkē 贾樟柯

b. 1970—Film director, screenwriter, and producer; leading member of the Sixth Generation

Alternate name: trad. 賈樟柯

Summary

The most influential film director of the Sixth Generation, Jia Zhangke has directed shorts, feature-length films, and documentaries. Jia's work is distinctive for his critical engagement with social issues concerning contemporary China, his intentional blurring of documentary and fiction film, and his attention to a realist aesthetic. Jia's films have consistently topped film critics' polls and been awarded many major international film prizes.

Jia Zhangke is regarded as the most influential film director of the Sixth Generation (Dì liùdài 第六代), a group of independent filmmakers who came to prominence in the 1990s.

Jia was born in Fenyang, a midsize town in Shanxi Province, in 1970. He attended the Beijing Film Academy (BFA), where he studied "film literature," a major that emphasizes film theory. During his BFA years Jia directed three student short films, *Du Du* 嘟嘟, *One Day in Beijing* 有一天, 在北京, and *Xiaoshan Going Home* 小山回家. After screening the last title at an independent film festival, he began to form a strong creative relationship with a trio of Hong Kong filmmakers trained overseas: cinematographer Yu Lik-wai 余力为, producer Lee Kit-ming 李杰明, and producer/editor Chow Keung 周强. With the help of this team and their production company, Hu Tong Productions, Jia made a series of films that rewrote the rules for Chinese independent cinema.

The Hometown Trilogy

Jia's first major cinematic statement was a series of films that would come to be referred to as the Hometown Trilogy (Gùxiāng sānbùqǔ 故乡三部曲). *Xiao Wu* 小武 (1997), *Platform* 站台 (2000), and *Unknown Pleasures* 任逍遥 (2002) make up a remarkable group of films that broke new ground in terms of their sophisticated use of film language, documentary-film aesthetics, realist tone, employment of nonprofessional actors, and complex, layered storylines. Each film was shot in a different format (16 mm, 32 mm, and digital, respectively) and spanned a different time period (1996, the 1980s, and 2002, respectively), yet collectively they created one of the most consistent and powerful cinematic statements to come out of the contemporary Chinese film scene. All the films eschewed portrayals of both the "backward" countryside and the "modern" big city usually seen in Chinese cinema in favor of "small town," everyday China. The trilogy also eschewed emphasis on traditional "heroes," instead focusing on average, marginalized protagonists—dancers, pickpockets, and delinquents—in an attempt to reveal the texture of Chinese reality.

Highlighting a few days in the life of a small-time pickpocket in Fenyang, *Xiao Wu* reveals the breakdown of interpersonal relationships in Xiao Wu's world. The film utilized a documentary-like approach, yet woven into the handheld camera work and gritty style was a carefully designed structure that traced the tragic destruction of Xiao Wu's relationships with his former best friend, a would-be girlfriend, and ultimately his parents. Playing out against Xiao Wu's story is the larger story of mass-scale demolition and forced relocation carried out in his (and the director's) hometown of Fenyang. More ambitious, *Platform* spans the entire decade of the 1980s, from the early days of the Reform and Opening Up era in the late 1970s up until the time of the Tiananmen Incident in 1989. Unfolding against this canvas of massive social change is a more quotidian story of a group of young dreamers who are members of a song and dance troupe attempting to navigate the changing world around them. *Unknown Pleasures* provided an updated take on China's transformation to 2002, portraying two lost teenagers whose coming-of-age story is plagued by a series of misfortunes and missteps. Shot entirely in digital, the film was also instrumental to early digital filmmaking in China.

Neorealism

While the Hometown Trilogy established Jia internationally, in China his films were limited to small screenings in film clubs, universities, independent film festivals, and underground DVDs. It was not until his 2004 film, *The World* 世界, that Jia's films began being commercially screened in China. *The World* also marked a turning point in Jia's film aesthetic. The film, which portrays a group of migrant workers employed at a large theme park in Beijing, still employed the director's trademark techniques and themes, but this time Jia surprised viewers with a thumping electronic music soundtrack, dreamlike Flash animation vignettes, and touches of what could almost be described as magic realism.

In 2006's *Still Life* 三峡好人, winner of the Golden Lion award at the Venice

Selected Filmography of Jia Zhangke			
Year	English Title	Chinese Title	Notes
1994	*One Day in Beijing*	有一天，在北京 *Yǒu yī tiān, zài Běijīng*	Director
1995	*Xiao Shan Going Home*	小山回家 *Xiǎoshān huí jiā*	Director
1996	*Du Du*	嘟嘟 *Dūdū*	Director
1997	*Xiao Wu (aka The Pickpocket)*	小武 *Xiǎo wǔ*	Director
2000	*Platform*	站台 *Zhàntái*	Director
2001	*In Public*	公共场所 *Gōng gōng cháng sǔo*	Director
2002	*Unknown Pleasures*	任逍遥 *Rèn xiāo yáo*	Director & actor
2004	*The World*	世界 *Shìjiè*	Director
2006	*Still Life*	三峡好人 *Sānxiá hǎorén*	Director
2006	*Dong*	东 *Dōng*	Director
2007	*Useless*	无用 *Wúyòng*	Director
2007	*Our Ten Years*	我们的十年 *Wǒmén de shí nián*	Director
2008	*24 City*	二十四城记 *Èrshísì chéngjì*	Director
2008	*Cry Me a River*	河上的爱情 *Héshàng de àiqīng*	Director
2008	*Plastic City*	荡寇 *Dàngkòu*	Producer
2010	*I Wish I Knew*	海上传奇 *Shànghǎi chuánqí*	Director
2012	*Fidaï*		Producer
2013	*A Touch of Sin*	天註定 *Tiān zhù dìng*	Director
2015	*Mountains May Depart*	山河故人 *Shānhé gùrén*	Director

International Film Festival, Jia again tested the boundaries between fiction film and documentary, while simultaneously pushing his magic-realist tendency even further with painted Peking Opera actors, tightrope walkers, and spaceships all intermittently appearing among the ruins of a soon-to-be submerged city. The film seemed to take Jia's themes of demolition and destruction, first introduced in *Xiao Wu*, to their ultimate destination, with an entire city slated to be "relocated" in anticipation of the rising level of the Yangzi (Chang) River due the Three Gorges Dam project. The film was produced in concert with a companion documentary film, *Dong* 东 (lit. East), which focused on painter Liú Xiǎodōng's 刘小东 portraits of workers and residents in the same city. Jia's neorealist style is deeply engaged with documentary film strategies, on-the-spot realism, and deep concern for social issues in contemporary China; however, his films also employ an array of techniques from science fiction, traditional arts, magic realism, and the fantastic in order to fully convey the contradictions, complexities and absurdities of Chinese society.

Documentaries

Continuing to alternate between feature films and documentaries, Jia made two more feature-length documentary films, *Useless* 无用 (2007) and *I Wish I Knew* 海上传奇 (2010), the latter of which was produced in cooperation with the 2010 Shanghai Expo. His 2008 film, *24 City* 二十四城记 (2008), again played with the line between documentary and fictional filmmaking, casting professional actors like *Joan Chen 陈冲 and Zhào Tāo 赵涛 alongside real-life interview subjects. The film was a nostalgic look back at the factory system of socialist China and the fate of the workers whose lives were once entirely bound by the structure of the factory work unit. In 2013 Jia released what was perhaps his most controversial film, testing his sometimes tenuous relationship with China's film censors. Inspired by a series of authentic news reports, *A Touch of Sin* 天注定 (2013) documented a group of loosely intertwined stories about individuals frustrated, abused, exploited, or otherwise disenfranchised by society. In each of the stories, individuals pushed to their limits explode—or implode—triggering a series of violent acts that capture the disenchantment and frustrations lurking just beneath the surface of economic prosperity.

Other Activities

Beyond his important contributions as a film director, Jia has been consistently active in a variety of other film activities. He has published more than half a dozen

*People marked with an asterisk have entries in this dictionary.

books, including a highly influential collection of essays on cinema. He is a major spokesperson and advocate for Chinese independent filmmaking, and he has fostered the development of younger talent by producing films by up-and-coming directors such as Hán Jié 韩杰 and Diāo Yìnán 刁亦男. Jia makes Hitchcock-esque cameos in nearly all of his feature films and also has appeared in cameo roles in films by popular blogger, race-car driver, and director *Hán Hán 韩寒 and other directors. While his own works represent very different trends than those seen in mainstream commercial cinema in China today, Jia has managed to consistently evolve while remaining true to the probing, independent spirit of his early work. His films reveal the underbelly of contemporary China's economic miracle while also capturing the social and ethical quandaries of a China in transition.

Michael BERRY
University of California, Santa Barbara

Further Reading

Berry, Michael. (2009). *Jia Zhangke's "Hometown Trilogy": Xiao Wu, Platform, Unknown Pleasures.* New York: Palgrave Macmillan.

Byrnes, Corey. (2012). Specters of realism and the painter's gaze in Jia Zhangke's *Still Life. Modern Chinese Literature and Culture, 24*(2), 52–93.

Cui, Shuqin. (2010). Boundary shifting: New generation filmmaking and Jia Zhangke's films. In Ying Zhu & Stanley Rosen (Eds.), *Art, politics, and commerce in Chinese cinema* (pp. 175–194). Hong Kong: Hong Kong University Press.

Jia Zhangke. (2014). *Jia Zhangke speaks out: The Chinese director's texts on films* (Claire Huot, Tony Rayns, Alice Shih & Sebastian Veg, Trans.). Piscataway, NJ: Transactions Publishers.

Lin Xiaoping. (2005). Jia Zhangke's cinematic trilogy: A journey across the ruins of post-Mao China. In Sheldon Lu & Yueh-Yu Yeh (Eds.), *Chinese-language film: Historiography, poetics, politics* (pp. 186–209). Honolulu: University of Hawai'i Press.

Lu Tonglin. (2003). Music and noise: Independent film and globalization. *The China Review, 3*(1), 57–76.

McGrath, Jason. (2008). *Postsocialist modernity: Chinese cinema, literature, and criticism in the market age* (pp. 129–164). Stanford, CA: Stanford University Press.

Pernin, Judith, & Veg, Sebastien. (Eds.). (2010). Special Feature: Independent Chinese Cinema; Filming in the 'Space of the People'. *China Perspectives*, 1.

Silbergeld, Jerome. (2009). Facades: The new Beijing and the unsettled ecology of Jia Zhangke's *The World.* In Sheldon Lu & Jiayan Mi (Eds.), *Chinese ecocinema: In the age of environmental challenge* (pp. 113–128). Hong Kong: Hong Kong University Press.

Wang Yanjie. (2011). Displaced in the simulacrum: Migrant workers and urban space in *The World. Asian Cinema, 22*(1), 152–169.

☿ Jiāng Zémín 江泽民

b. 1926—President of China (1993–2003) and general secretary of the Chinese Communist Party (1989–2002)

Alternate name: trad. 江澤民

Summary

Jiang Zemin became China's top leader after the Tiananmen Square Incident in 1989, and went on to oversee a period of rapid socioeconomic development and openness and pragmatism in foreign affairs. As the core of China's "third generation" leadership, he is best known for his theory of the Three Represents, which redefined the Communist Party's guiding ideology. Jiang will also be remembered for the economic disparities and rampant corruption that arose during his tenure.

Jiang Zemin arrived, suddenly and unexpectedly, at the pinnacle of the Chinese leadership in the wake of the Tiananmen crackdown of 1989. Initially considered a mere transitional figure, Jiang would go on to rule over China for the next thirteen years, a crucial period in China's regeneration and modernization.

Early Life

Jiang Zemin was born in Yangzhou, Jiangsu Province on 17 August 1926, the third of five children in a well-off family. He grew up in a time of great upheaval in China. As he started elementary school in 1931, Japan began its invasion of China's northeast and by the time he was at university in Shanghai, China was gripped by a civil war between the Nationalist (Guómíndǎng 国民党, or GMD) and Communist forces. Official accounts claims that at age thirteen, Jiang became the adopted son of his uncle Jiāng Shàngqīng 江上清, who was a Communist martyr. Unofficial history has raised questions about this claim, but there is no doubt that Jiang's post-1949 career benefited from this linkage to his martyr uncle.

Graduating from university with a major in engineering in 1947, Jiang's first job was as an engineer in the power-supply department of a food-making factory in Shanghai. In the first few years of the People's Republic of China (PRC), Jiang, with his university training which was in short supply, emerged as a competent engineer highly useful for the new state's economic recovery.

In these years Jiang made his first contact with party cadre Wāng Dàohán 汪道涵, a revolutionary colleague of Jiang's adopted father during the 1930s. Wang took it upon himself to look after the younger Jiang and would later play a crucial role in several junctures of Jiang's elevation through party ranks.

During the 1950s and early 1960s, Jiang held positions at China's First Automobile Plant in Changchun, then at Shanghai- and Wuhan-based research institutes of the First Machine Building Ministry. In 1970, after having been suspended from his position and attacked during the political campaigns of the Cultural Revolution (1966–1976), he was reinstated at the Ministry and served as the deputy director of the Ministry's foreign affairs bureau, which began his career as a bureaucrat and politician. By 1982 he was moved into a role as vice-minister of the Ministry of Electronics Industry. At this point, Jiang also became a member of the Central Committee of the CCP at the Twelfth Party Congress, held later in that year, indicating he had been selected into the top echelon of party cadres.

Rise to Power

In 1985, Jiang was appointed to the mayoralty of Shanghai. As China's biggest city, Shanghai was home to the country's largest and most advanced industrial capacity in those years. Jiang's mentor, Wang Daohan, was pivotal again in his elevation, having been the incumbent mayor and wielding influence over the choice of his successor. Jiang would spend four years in Shanghai, two as mayor and then two as party chief. The Shanghai mayoralty, however, would prove a daunting challenge to Jiang. Through the 1980s, the city had been in decline as it was still under tight central government control, while many other coastal cities prospered amidst China's Reform and Opening Up policies.

Wang Daohan, before 1949. Wang was one of Jiang Zemin's main supporters and mentors throughout his career.

During this time, Jiang succeeded in cultivating relationships with a number of key senior leaders, including *Chén Yún 陈云 (1905–1995) and *Lǐ Xiānniàn 李先念 (1909–1992), both of whom often spent winters in Shanghai with their wives. Chen and Li would eventually be two of Jiang's key backers in his eventual rise to the top of the Party. Yet it was in early 1989 that a critical incident helped Jiang establish himself as a tough defender of the Party, and win the trust of *Dèng Xiǎopíng 邓小平 (1904–1997) and other elder leaders. After the Tiananmen Square crackdown, the CCP was left without a general secretary when *Zhào Zǐyáng 赵紫阳 (1919–2005) was blamed for the disturbances and removed from power. Designating a replacement was a delicate process for Deng Xiaoping and the senior leaders around him. The new general secretary needed to be younger than the remaining "second generation" leaders and yet still acceptable to them. Given the events surrounding Tiananmen, the replacement had to be demonstrably unyielding on political dissent, but still a committed economic reformer in order for China to continue on the path of Reform and Opening Up. It was also important that the successor not be tainted with any direct involvement in the indecision and infighting which plagued the leadership leading up to the Tiananmen Incident.

———
*People marked with an asterisk have entries in this dictionary.

Jiang became the eventual choice, and he was formally elected as the new general secretary of the CCP and installed as the "core" of the "third generation" of leaders at an enlarged Politburo meeting in June 1989. In theory, general secretary is the highest formal position in the Chinese party-state machinery, but Jiang's command on power was far from indisputable. It was an extremely uncertain time both for Jiang and for China.

Consolidation of Power

In November 1989, Deng relinquished his role as chairman of the Central Military Commission (CMC) to Jiang, who now theoretically controlled all the formal power as the top leader of China. In practical terms, however, Jiang's hold on power was far from secure. The Tiananmen Incident, and the exit of many party elders during its aftermath, had greatly altered the power distribution within the Party's top leadership, and Jiang was left to find his own way through this power minefield. The necessity for political stability worked in Jiang's favor, as Deng put his support behind him by endorsing him as the "core" of the "third generation" leadership.

Following a brief period of indecision and cautiousness, Jiang eventually committed himself wholeheartedly to the reformist line, after Deng had shown his dissatisfaction with the stalling of reforms during his Southern Tour in 1992.

• Jiāng Zémín •

Eventually Deng retained his support of Jiang, who was re-elected as party secretary at the Twelfth Party Congress. In March 1993, Jiang took the presidency from *Yáng Shàngkūn 杨尚昆 (1907–1998), after convincing Deng Xiaoping that the greatest threat to stability in the Chinese leadership came from Yang and his half-brother Yáng Báibīng 杨白冰, who was secretary-general of the Central Military Commission. This completed for Jiang the trio of top positions in the Chinese political system: general secretary of the CCP, state president, and chair of the CMC.

Jiang's next four years were spent consolidating his power base. This was done by promoting his own allies into powerful positions within the Party, but also by manufacturing the downfall of some rivals, including Beijing party chief *Chén Xītóng 陈希同 (1905–1995).

Domestic Politics

From his position at the top, Jiang oversaw a key phase in China's continued development. With substantial involvement from *Zhū Róngjī 朱镕基 (b. 1928), a past colleague in Shanghai and then first vice-premier, Jiang's leadership made fundamental changes to the governance system in China. Jiang and Zhu's fiscal reforms implemented in 1993 brought greater fiscal power to the central government, giving it better control over the provinces and much needed resources for many big national development programs.

As Jiang consolidated his power, Taiwan remained a policy area where his predecessor Deng had not achieved satisfactory results, and an issue that carried grave implications for the legitimacy of the Party as well as his own political legacy. In January 1995, he issued his Eight-Point Proposal for the development of relations between the mainland and Taiwan. The tone of the proposal was mild and it was duly snubbed by Taiwanese President *Lee Teng-hui 李登辉 (b. 1923). Jiang soon came under pressure to retort from hardliners in the party, especially from within the military.

In 1995, when President Lee visited the United States, despite assurances from the White House to Beijing that he would not be granted a visa, Jiang ordered a show of military strength in the Taiwan Strait. Such a move satisfied hardliners in the Party and military, and gave Jiang his first opportunity to be seen as a leader at war. It did not, however, lead to any major breakthroughs in cross-Strait relations, in fact creating even more difficult relations for Jiang and his successors.

Foreign Affairs

Due to the negative impacts of the Tiananmen crackdown, when Jiang became China's top leader in 1989, China's relations with major Western powers were at their lowest since China's opening up in the late 1970s. Jiang and his colleagues tried to break the blockage by taking a detour to a number of important third-world

江泽民

countries. Formal relationships were quickly established with South Korea, Saudi Arabia, Israel, and resumed with Indonesia, significantly expanding China's international space. In 1997, Jiang Zemin made a landmark visit to the United States, which was returned by a visit by President Clinton the following year, signifying a period of cordial relationships between the two powers.

After an extended period of negotiations that dragged on for over a decade, China's WTO accession would eventually take place under Jiang's leadership in December 2001. Jiang was also at the helm when Beijing succeeded in its bid to host the 2008 Olympic Games in July 2001. This was a great boost to the public morale in China, as it regained its standing in the international community as a modern and prosperous nation.

Economic Development under Jiang

China's economic reform and development took new strides following the 1992 Party Congress, when the leadership fully embraced marketization. Jiang did not specialize in economic issues, and economic reform and management were largely within the purview of Zhu Rongji, first vice premier (1993–1998) and then premier (1998–2003). Throughout Jiang's tenure, however, and until 2002, the economy continued to develop apace, in spite of some heady challenges. Even in the face of the Asian Financial Crisis in 1997–1998, China's economy continued to confound critics who had predicted its downfall.

Supreme Leader and the Three Represents

The Fifteenth Party Congress in 1997 was Jiang Zemin's unofficial coronation as supreme leader. Deng Xiaoping had passed away earlier in the year. Shortly thereafter, Jiang had played a significant role in the handover of Hong Kong from Britain to China.

This was also the time during which the Chinese top leadership took up several monumental tasks of economic reform, most notably the shaking up of state-owned-enterprises (SOEs). Capably executed by the then premier, Zhu Rongji, many of the SOEs were privatized and millions of workers were laid off.

It was in the area of party-building that Jiang would make a contribution for which he would be remembered: what he called the Three Represents 三个代表. First enunciated in early 2000, during a study trip to Guangdong Province, China's reform forefront, the Three Represents stipulates that the CCP should represent the advanced social productive forces, advanced culture, and the interests of the overwhelming majority. This is a major departure from the Marxist-Leninist orthodoxy which maintains that the Party should represent the proletariat (workers and peasants in the Chinese context). The Three Represents theory hence cleared the way for admitting capitalists and private business owners into the party. It signified a profound ideological shift for the CCP and institutionalized the gradual changes the party had been going through as it governed an increasingly complex, pluralist, and dynamic country. It was highly criticized, however, by party conservatives as the party's ideological degeneration. In the end, the Three Represents was enshrined in the Chinese constitution at the Sixteenth Party Congress of 2002 and therefore became one of the guiding ideologies of the CCP.

Exiting the Stage

Jiang stepped down as general secretary of the CCP at the Sixteenth Party Congress and handed over the reins to *Hú Jǐntāo 胡锦涛 (b.1942). He then handed over the presidency to Hu the following year. Although this would be the first peaceful handover of power in the PRC's history, Jiang held onto the post of chairman of the Central Military Commission when it had been expected that he would stand down and he succeeded in stacking the Politburo and Standing Committee with his own allies, creating barriers for the new leader to consolidate his power. With these arrangements he continued to exert political influences despite not having any formal position in the Party.

Family

Jiang and his high-school sweetheart, Wáng Yěpíng 王冶坪, were wed in December 1949. They had two sons, Mianheng and Miankang, who studied engineering abroad and returned home to China in the early 1990s. With partial assistance from Jiang, Mianheng once held the position of vice chief commander of China's spacecraft program, the Shenzhou or Divine Vessel Program. Jiang's step-sister (a daughter of his adopted father), Zehui, is a professor of forestry science, and served as the president of the Chinese Academy of Forestry.

Public Reaction and Recognition

Jiang's greatest achievement as leader was to have navigated China through a difficult period in its reform and development process. Having just emerged from the Tiananmen crackdown, the Chinese government faced a legitimacy crisis and was boycotted by most Western powers. Domestically, economic reforms slowed following the policy failures of the late 1980s that had in part led to the 1989 political crisis.

Although he started with a weak base, Jiang managed to slowly consolidate his own power, and increasingly saw through an era of profound economic reform, achieving impressive economic growth in the process. By 2002, China was firmly on the road to becoming one of the world's largest economies and top exporters, as well as a big power in regional and global affairs.

江泽民 •

But Jiang's reign also had many disappointments. The growth model of Jiang's era overwhelmingly favored the wealthier urban groups, at the expense of the poorer rural and inland areas. The environmental costs of those years of development were also high, and corruption in government became endemic. These negative effects became major sources of social unrest in China, and addressing it has been one of the cornerstones of Jiang's successors' policies.

Despite making some progress in institutionalizing politics at the elite level, at times Jiang ensured that his own cronies, above all allies from his time in Shanghai, were promoted to prominent positions. While the Three Represents theory he advocated may have moved the Party onto a renewed ideological foundation, it was also seen by some as merely serving Jiang's obsession of leaving behind a personal legacy on a par with those of Mao and Deng.

Although the peaceful returns of Hong Kong and Macau to Chinese sovereignty took place under his watch, Jiang made little progress on the Taiwan issue. In foreign affairs he was known for giving too much emphasis to the big powers such as the United States and Russia, while generally overlooking relations with developing countries such as those in Southeast Asia and Africa.

Jiang's personality endeared him to foreign leaders. He loved to be the center of attention, and he was a competent linguist, having passable capabilities in Russian, Romanian, and English. When meeting with foreign leaders he enjoyed making allusions to famous speeches in their languages. He was also wont to exhibit his musical and literary skills, never shy to grab center stage by conducting, singing, playing a musical instrument, or reciting poems at public events. His demeanor was considered the most "Western" of any Chinese leader, but within China he was seen as too frivolous and overtly obsessed with his image.

Zhengxu WANG
University of Nottingham

Marcel AUSTIN-MARTIN
China Europe International Business School

Further Reading

Baum, Richard. (1998). The fifteenth national party congress: Jiang takes command? *The China Quarterly, 153*, 141–156.

Gilley, Bruce. (1998). *Tiger on the brink: Jiang Zemin and China's new elite*. Berkeley: University of California Press.

Huang Yasheng. (2008). Chapter 3: A great reversal. In *Capitalism with Chinese characteristics: Entrepreneurship and the state*. New York: Cambridge University Press.

Mulvenon, James. (2003). The PLA and the 16th party congress: Jiang controls the gun? *China Leadership Monitor, 5*, 20–29.

Mulvenon, James. (2002). The PLA and the "Three Represents": Jiang's bodyguards or party-army? *China Leadership Monitor, 4*.

Nathan, Andrew J., & Gilley, Bruce. (2002). *China's new rulers: the secret files*. New York: New York Review of Books.

People's Daily Online. (n.d.) The daily routine of Jiang Zemin: Biography. Retrieved April 20, 2015, from http://en.people.cn/leaders/jzm/biography.htm

Suettinger, Robert L. (2004) *Beyond Tiananmen: The politics of U.S.-China relations, 1989–2000*. Washington D.C.: Brookings Institution Press.

Tien, Hung-Mao, & Chu, Yun-Han. (Eds.). (2000). *China under Jiang Zemin*. Boulder, Co: Lynne Rienner Publishers.

Wang Zhengxu. (2006). Hu Jintao's power consolidation: groups, institutions, and power balance in China's elite politics. *Issues and Studies, 42*(4), 97–136.

Xinhua. (2004). *Jiang Zemin shenghuo baodao zhuanji* 江泽民生活报道专集 [Collection of coverage on Jiang Zemin's life, 1998–2003]. Retrieved April 20, 2015, from http://www.xinhuanet.com/newscenter/ldrbdzj/jzm2003.htm

• 江泽民 •

♀ Kadeer, Rebiya

Rèbǐyǎ Kǎdé'ěr 热比娅・卡德尔

b. 1946—Businesswoman and political activist, president of the World Uyghur Congress (2006–present)

Alternate names: Uygur: قادر رابيـي; trad. 熱比婭・卡德爾

Summary

Rebiya Kadeer, whom the Chinese authorities once hailed as a successful Uygur businesswoman and philanthropist, is now an exiled overt critic of Chinese policies in Xinjiang and leads the World Uyghur Congress to promote the rights of Uygurs in China. Although she is often described by Western media as a human rights champion, the Chinese government depicts her as a separatist and believes that she orchestrated the July 2009 riots in Xinjiang from abroad—an accusation she has continually denied.

Rebiya Kadeer is an ethnic Uygur activist from the Xinjiang Uygur Autonomous Region (XUAR), also known as East Turkestan. Before she began publicly criticizing the Chinese government in 1997, the authorities widely hailed her as a successful Uygur businesswoman and philanthropist. Her relationship with the authorities, however, deteriorated

and she was jailed in 1999 for passing state secrets. In 2005, she was released on medical parole to the United States, where she became the leader of the Uygur overseas movement and held leadership positions in various Uygur diasporic organizations, such as the Uyghur American Association (UAA) and the International Uyghur Human Rights and Democracy Foundation (IUHRDF) in Washington D.C. (The Dui Hua Foundation 2005). Since 2006, Kadeer has also been the president of the German-based World Uyghur Congress (WUC), an international umbrella organization advancing Uygur human rights.

Early Life and Career

Rebiya Kadeer rose to prominence during the 1990s, running a multimillion-dollar trading company and a department store in Urumchi, the capital of XUAR. Using space in her department store, she operated free classes to educate children from poor families.

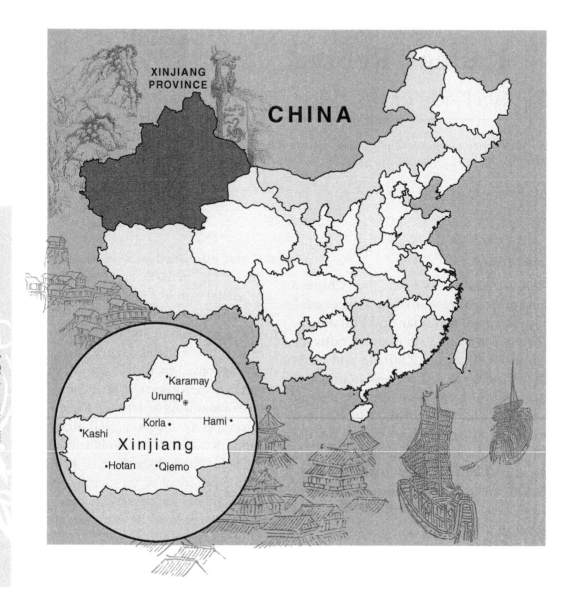

Initially, the Chinese government praised her philanthropic work. She was appointed to the Chinese People's Political Consultative Conference, an elite advisory group consisting of party and non-party members, and in 1995 she was a member of China's delegation to the United Nations Fourth World Conference on Women held in Beijing.

After publicly criticizing China for violation of human rights and mistreatment of her people in 1997, however, Kadeer was barred from traveling abroad, and in 1998 she lost her government post when she refused to denounce her husband, Sidik Rouzi—who worked in the United States and was accused by the Chinese government of inciting separatism in China. On her way to meet a US congressional delegation on 11 August 1999, she was arrested and sentenced to eight years in prison for releasing state secrets and intelligence to foreigners, on the grounds that she had sent local newspaper clippings to her husband.

International human rights organizations, such as Amnesty International and Human Rights Watch, publicized Kadeer's case and actively campaigned for her release, focusing on her as a political victim. On 17 March 2005, just three days before newly appointed US Secretary of State Condoleezza Rice was to make her first visit to Beijing, Kadeer was released on medical parole and fled

to the United States, where she now lives in exile. After her release, the United States immediately announced that, unlike the previous year, it would not pursue a resolution condemning China's human rights violations at the (former) UN Commission on Human Rights's annual meeting in Geneva (Halpin and Hogrefe 2006). A report by congressional staff indicated that although both the Chinese and US governments denied a quid pro quo, "the timing of the event leaves the impression that a deal for Ms. Kadeer's release had been struck" (Halpin and Hogrefe 2006).

Later Career

When Kadeer moved to the United States, the Chinese government warned her not to engage in political activism. She soon

Ellen Sauerbrey, former head of the United States Department of State's Bureau of Population, Refugees, and Migration, meets with Rebiya Kadeer to discuss human rights of the Uygur minority living in Xinjiang Province (2006). Photo by U.S. Department of State.

did so, however, by using her reputation in the Uygur community. For instance, with other activists such as Omer Kanat, she collected donations to finance her political activities. She was the president of the UAA, and she is the current president of the WUC based in Munich, Germany. She frequently travels between the United States and Europe to engage in her political activism. In 2000, Human Rights Watch honored her as a global rights defender. In 2004, the Norwegian Rafto Foundation for Human Rights awarded her the Rafto Prize for human rights. She was also nominated for the Nobel Peace Prize on multiple occasions.

The 10 Conditions of Love

In 2009, writer and director Jeff Daniels filmed a documentary about Kadeer called *The 10 Conditions of Love*. The premiere was scheduled for an international film festival in Melbourne, Australia. However, the festival organizer's decision to show the documentary faced severe obstruction from Chinese diplomatic representatives and China supporters in Australia. China supporters even hacked the festival's website, which led to a police investigation. Various news providers covered the incident, resulting in a strong public backlash in Australia.

Chinese Treatment of Kadeer

Whereas the WUC and Western media depict Kadeer as a human rights activist, Chinese writers' depiction of her has changed over the years. The story of how Kadeer obtained her wealth was originally noted as a point of inspiration and pride for Xinjiang and the Uygur people. She was described as "diligent," "tenacious," "with a brilliant business mind," and possessing "eyes of wisdom" that epitomize Uygur women (Chen 1994, 45–46). Glowing accounts were offered of how she excelled in business and provided jobs to local women and youth (Chen 1994, 45–46). But after her conflict with the Chinese government, she was labeled a traitor and terrorist, and questions were raised about how she obtained and managed her wealth. Suddenly, her wealth was attributed to tax evasion, financial fraud, and other illegal activities (Wang 2009, 6–7). Chinese writers comment that Kadeer's fear of being discovered may have pushed her into joining the separatist movement.

Chinese writers tend to downplay Kadeer's significance to the diasporic movement. According to Wu (2009, 24), Kadeer is not well educated and is not proficient in any foreign language. According to this account, her lack of credentials disqualifies her for the role of WUC president. Despite this, she was elected WUC president because of her legendary background—as a successful Muslim businesswoman, politician, convicted political prisoner, political exile, and human rights award winner—and is seen as the spiritual mother of the Uygurs.

Chinese writers acknowledge that the aforementioned conditions have boosted

Xinjiang Uygur Autonomous Region

Xinjiang Uygur Autonomous Region, located in northwestern China, is bordered by Russia to the north, Mongolia to the northeast, the Chinese provinces of Gansu and Qinghai to the east, Tibet (Xizang) Autonomous Region to the southeast, Afghanistan and India to the south and southwest, and Kyrgyzstan, Kazakhstan, and Tajikistan to the west. Xinjiang Uygur Autonomous Region is the largest political unit in China, covering 1.6 million square kilometers: slightly smaller than Iran. However, despite its size, Xinjiang is one of the least-populated regions of China.

Xinjiang has long been China's gateway to central Asia. As far back as the Han (206 BCE–220 CE) and Tang (618–907 CE) dynasties, the oasis towns scattered throughout Xinjiang were the backbone of the great Silk Roads, a highway over which merchants carried luxury goods from the Chinese empire to the Arab empires of the Middle East and the kingdoms of central Asia. Despite its strategic location, Xinjiang retained considerable independence during much of its history. The region's current name, which in Chinese means "new frontier," can be traced to the conquest of the region by the Manchu armies of the Qing dynasty (1644–1912) during the mid-eighteenth century. Even after 250 years of Chinese control, however, Xinjiang retains much of its traditional culture. The region's largest ethnic group continues to be the Muslim Uygurs, although several other minority nationalities, including Uzbeks, Kazakhs, and Tajiks, also have sizable populations. The "minority" population of Xinjiang in 1997 was 10.58 million (61.6 percent of the region's total population). This population figure is all the more noteworthy because, since 1949 when the Chinese Communist Party took over the governance of Xinjiang, central authorities have had a policy of settling Han (ethnic Chinese) in the region in an attempt to solidify their rule.

Xinjiang Uygur Autonomous Region is a central element of China's Developing the West program, which was announced by Premier Jiang Zemin in 2000.

Source: Perrins, Robert John (2009). Xinjiang Uygur Autonomous Region. In Linsun Cheng, et al. (Eds.), *Berkshire encyclopedia of China* (pp. 2519–2522). Great Barrington, MA: Berkshire Publishing.

• Kadeer, Rebiya •

Kadeer's popularity among Western countries and have placed her at the forefront of separatist groups. They also assert that such groups made her their pawn, for they are scattered around the world and need to project a positive image in the West. Sympathetic Western countries consider Kadeer's persona worthy of cultivation, encouraging her image as the face of WUC solidarity and a figure comparable to the Dalai Lama (Wang 2009, 6–7).

Chinese writers also discuss Kadeer's autobiography, *Dragon Fighter: One Woman's Epic Struggle for Peace with China*, which shows that she genuinely sees herself as a warrior and that the enemy is the "dragon" (Chen 2009, 33). Thus, Chinese writers see her autobiography as an attempt to strengthen her position within the Uygur movement (Wu 2009, 51) and as part of the strategy of the overseas movement to portray her as a bold fighter, regardless of whether there is any truth to the claim.

Some Chinese writers point out that Kadeer is not without critics, even within her own diasporic group. Such writers suggest that she has acquired an unfavorable reputation among her colleagues because of her "whimsical character, greed, and nepotism" (Wang 2009, 6–7; Wu 2009, 51).

Lastly, according to China-based writers (Wu 2009, 23), Kadeer, the WUC, other East Turkestan separatist groups, and terrorist groups, are all said to be the invisible hands behind the July 2009 riots in Xinjiang—an accusation Kadeer and the WUC have continually denied.

Future of Kadeer and Her Movement

China's depiction of Kadeer's life story seeks to raise questions about her credentials and motivations for assuming a leadership role within the Uygur diasporic community. In the Chinese government's version of events, the leader whom the WUC works so assiduously to legitimize is a traitor and a criminal. Despite this, she continues to receive sympathy from communities outside China, and has lobbied bodies such as the European Parliament, the US Congress and others, raising the profile of the Xinjiang issue which still remains highly contentious. The Uygur community, however, continues to suffer from having a leader of similar statue to the Dalai Lama with the Tibetans.

Julie Yu-Wen CHEN
Palacky University

Further Reading

Amnesty International. (2007). *People's Republic of China: Rebiya Kadeer's personal account of Gulja after the massacre on 5 February 1997*. London: Amnesty International.

Chen Wuguo 陈伍国. (1994). Rangshijie zhenjingdi Zhongguo nudaheng 让世界震惊的中国女大亨 [The female tycoon who shocked the world]. *Jizhe guancha* 记者观察, 10, 45–46.

Chen Yunqiu 陈韵秋. (2009). Rebiya zhi bian 热比娅之变 [The changing of Rebiya]. *Baokanhuicui* 报刊荟萃, *11*, 33–34.

Chen Yu-Wen. (2014). *The Uygur lobby: Global networks, coalitions and strategies of the World Uyghur Congress.* London: Routledge.

Culpepper, Rucker. (2012). Nationalist competition on the Internet: Uyghur diaspora versus the Chinese state media. *Asian Ethnicity*, *13*(2), 187–203.

Halpin, Dennis, & Hogrefe, Hans. (2006). Findings of staff delegation visit to Urumqi, PRC, May 30–June 2, 2006, *Momorandum to Chairman Henry Hyde and Ranking Member Tom Lantos.* Pennsylvania: Institute for Corean-American Studies. Retrieved November 19, 2014, from http://www.icasinc.org/2006/2006l/2006ld2h.html

Kadeer, Rebiya, & Cavelius, Alexandra. (2009). *Dragon fighter: One woman's struggle for peace with China.* Carlsbad, CA: Kales Press.

Millward, James. (2004). *Violent separatism in Xinjiang: A critical assessment.* Washington D.C.: East-West Center.

Millward, James. (2007). *Eurasian crossroads: A history of Xinjiang.* London: Hurst & Company.

Naoko Mizutani 水谷尚子 (2007). Chugoku O Owareta Uigurujin: Bomeisha Ga Kataru Seiji Dan'atsu 中国を追われたウイグル人——亡命者が語る政治弾圧 [Uygurs expelled from China]. Tokyo: Bungeishunju.

O'Brien, David. (2011). The Mountains are high and the emperor is far away: An Examination of ethnic violence in Xinjiang. *International Journal of China Studies*, *2*(3), 389–406.

Shichor, Yitzhak. (2006). Changing the guard at the World Uyghur Congress. *China Brief*, *6*(25), 12–14.

Shichor, Yitzhak. (2009). *Ethno-Diplomacy: The Uyghur Hitch in Sino-Turkish Relations.* Honolulu: East-West Center.

The Dui Hua Foundation. (2005). Statement on the release of Rebiya Kadeer. Retrieved 27 November 2014, from http://duihua.org/wp/?page_id=1739

Wu Xiaofan 吴晓芳. (2009). Jiangdu hetadi toutoumen 疆独和他的头头们 [Uygur independence and its leaders]. *Shijie zhishi* 世界知识, *15*, 23–25.

Wang Yan 王燕. (2009). Sikai Rebiyadi choulou zuilian 撕开热比娅的丑陋嘴脸 [Tearing off the ugly mask of Rebiya]. *Xinwen Tiandi* 新闻天地, *8*, 6–7.

• Kadeer, Rebiya •

♂ Lài Chāngxīng 赖昌星

b. 1958—Founder and chairman of Yuanhua Group, kingpin of one of China's largest smuggling rings

Alternate name: trad. 賴昌星

Summary

A peasant-turned-entrepreneur, Lai Changxing made his fortune through legal and illegal means, including running a multibillion-dollar smuggling empire in China aided by his bribery of government officials. After hiding in Canada for over a decade, he was repatriated to China in 2011 and convicted of smuggling, tax evasion, and bribery in what is allegedly the biggest case since the founding of the People's Republic of China in 1949.

Born into a poor family in Shaocuo village, in Jinjiang City, Fujian Province, at the beginning of the Great Leap Forward in 1958, Lai Changxing came from humble beginnings. He worked his way up to become a powerful entrepreneur running a multibillion-dollar smuggling ring out of Xiamen, Fujian Province, in the 1990s. But his life took a dramatic turn when the racket he was running was exposed and he became China's most wanted fugitive. As a result, he fled China to Canada and hid there for a decade. Lai was finally deported to China in 2011 after lengthy extradition negotiations between China and Canada, and he was convicted of smuggling and bribery, with a sentence of life in prison.

Initial Success

The seventh of eight children, Lai grew up the son of a poor farmer during the upheavals caused by the Cultural Revolution (1966–1976). He barely finished his formal primary education because of the poverty and chaotic situations during that time. In his teenage years, he went back to the village farm to work in the fields with his brothers.

When he was older, Lai joined one of his brothers in digging wells for the army and later digging air-raid shelters in Quanzhou, a town in Fujian, before moving back to his hometown. He then worked for a local village agricultural machinery plant marketing its products and getting paid on commission. In 1976, towards the end of the Cultural Revolution, a campaign was launched to "strike new bourgeois elements," during which time some emerging successful business leaders were accused of and condemned as being capitalists. Nevertheless, Lai was undeterred from pursuing his interests in the business world.

He and his fellow villagers pooled together a few hundred yuan (about US$180) each and opened an auto-parts plant in their village in 1979. It was an exciting time, right at the beginning of *Dèng Xiǎopíng's 邓小平 (1904–1997) Reform and Opening Up (gǎigé kāifàng 改革开放) era. The auto-parts plant was Lai's first investment. Later he invested in a textile machinery plant. While the first business opportunity was a joint investment, the second was his sole investment. He bought a building across from his own house and remodeled it into a plant. It was during this time that he met his future wife and business partner, Zéng Míngnà 曾明娜.

In the early 1980s more and more enterprises, mostly village and township enterprises in coastal regions in Zhejiang, Fujian, and Guangdong provinces, engaged in the processing of customer-provided materials to manufacture items such as garments and toys. Textile machineries were in high demand. Lai seized the opportunity and shifted away from making textile machinery accessories in favor of machine tools, which was much more profitable. With tenacity and hard work, he traveled around the country expanding his businesses and earning his initial fortune. Over the next few years, Lai's businesses kept growing. He launched a new enterprise that produced umbrellas and paperboard cartons as well as provided printing services. He reinvested the profits earned from his businesses into new ventures, including an electronics store, a shipping enterprise, a general investment company, and a cigarette plant.

Illegal Dealings

In the early 1980s smuggling became rampant in the southern coastal region. Many people smuggled goods into China in order to get rich quick. This was in line with the official slogan of the time, which said that "getting rich is glorious." The whole country became obsessed with making money and building wealth. Lai was no exception, and this ultimately led to his downfall. As the author and journalist James McGregor argues, "Lai Changxing fell into this terrible predicament because he had jumped aboard the roller coaster of Chinese economic reform at the very beginning and had taken it for the full ride, right into the dark heart of the Chinese political and economic system" (McGregor 2007, 95).

In 1989, Lai met a business partner in Shishi, a smuggling-infested small coastal

---

*People marked with an asterisk have entries in this dictionary.

city not far from Jinjiang. Together they opened a garment factory there. Around this time Lai found a new way of making easy money quickly—by smuggling goods into China.

Lai moved to Hong Kong in 1991 on allegedly fake documents. He invested in the city's real estate and was quite successful, since Hong Kong was experiencing a recession at that time. Later he launched an import-export firm doing business between Hong Kong and the mainland, delivering goods from Hong Kong to Xiamen. In early 1994 Lai went back to Xiamen as a successful Hong Kong businessman and investor, establishing a company called Xiamen Yuanhua Electronics Co., Ltd., with a registered capital of more than US$1 million. Later it became Xiamen Yuanhua Group Ltd.

According to Chinese government investigations, Yuanhua Electronics Co., Ltd. never set up any production facilities or hired factory workers. Rather, Lai was busy setting up a completely different operation. He spent his time and money hosting banquets and giving gifts and so-called *hóngbāo* 红包, or red envelopes with money in them, to establish connections with customs officials, members of the harbor patrol and commodities inspection office, and officials at different levels. In this way, he recruited them to be his accomplices in his large-scale smuggling operation. Between 1991 and 1999 Lai bribed sixty-four government officials—including Li Jizhou, the deputy minister of public security in Beijing, and Lan Pu,

the vice mayor of Xiamen municipal government—with cash, assets, and cars worth more than 39 million yuan (US$6.2 million). Yuanhua Ltd. lacked the necessary permits to import goods, but corrupt local officials helped the company import dutiable goods free of duty. Tax officials provided fake value-added tax (VAT) receipts so that the smuggled goods could be sold on the Chinese market.

In 1996, Lai built a seven-story Yuanhua headquarters in Xiamen, which became known as the "Red Mansion," a pleasure palace that featured luxury apartments, a banquet hall, a cinema, a sauna, a swimming pool, a massage parlor, and several karaoke rooms. Lai entertained his "guests" there by providing special services and bribes. According to state media, Lai's Red Mansion was a warren of decadence, dripping with US$20 million worth of decoration.

Lai reached the pinnacle of his so-called success in early 1999 when he built an eighty-eight-story skyscraper and a thirty-story luxury hotel, bought an A-league soccer team for Xiamen, and built a replica of the Heavenly Gate from Beijing (complete with a portrait of Chairman Mao Zedong) outside of Xiamen. Lai's Yuanhua empire, however, was about to crash to the ground. On 20 April 1999 the government launched an investigation into his smuggling operation after receiving a seventy-four-page tip-off letter containing details of the operation and evidence such as bills of sale. Chinese authorities

赖昌星

conducted an investigation called the "4-20 Investigation" (named after the date the investigation started) and discovered a massive smuggling operation allegedly masterminded by Lai, his wife, and the Yuanhua Group founded by him.

One day in August 1999, Lai took an urgent phone call from an old friend, Zhuang Rushun, head of public security in the nearby provincial capital city of Fuzhou, who had heard that the police in Xiamen were planning to arrest Lai the next day. Lai caught a speedboat out of Xiamen, landing in Hong Kong on 11 August. From there, he and his family fled to Vancouver, Canada, three days later on a tourist visa. He was later arrested on a *gambling* spree at a Niagara Falls *casino* in 2000. He and his wife divorced in 2005.

Canada and Extradition

For more than a decade Lai fought in Canadian courts to secure refugee status, appealing for asylum, and trying to avoid being sent back to China on the grounds that he might face torture and execution and that he would be unable to receive a fair trial if he returned. After a lengthy extradition battle and diplomatic negotiations between Canada and China, during which Canada received "extraordinary assurances" that Lai would not be tortured or executed, the Canadian high court upheld Lai's deportation order, and he was repatriated to China on 23 July 2011. He was arrested upon his arrival in Beijing at the airport.

In China Lai faced criminal charges and was sentenced to life in prison for smuggling and bribery on 18 May 2012 by the Intermediate People's Court in Xiamen, Fujian. He was also deprived of political rights for life and saw all of his personal property confiscated. According to the court, Lai had formed a smuggling ring by establishing firms and bases in Hong Kong and Xiamen since 1991. From December 1995 to May 1999, Lai's Yuanhua Group smuggled cigarettes, cars, refined oil, vegetable oil, chemical materials, textile materials, and other commodities worth more than 27 billion yuan (US$4.3 billion) and evaded duties of 14 billion yuan (US$2.2 billion).

This case is still one of the most talked about corruption cases in China and typifies an era in which excess grew out of control. To this day, Lai remains synonymous with corruption.

Weidong ZHANG
Winona State University

Further Reading

August, Oliver. (2007). *Inside the Red Mansion: On the trail of China's most wanted man*. London: John Murray.

Beech, Hannah. (2002). Smuggler's blues. Retrieved October 1, 2014, from http://content.time.com/time/world/article/0,8599,2056114,00.html

Lee, Khoon Choy. (2005). *Pioneers of modern China: Understanding the inscrutable Chinese*. Hackensack, NJ: World Scientific.

• Lài Chāngxīng •

McGregor, James. (2007). *One billion customers: Lessons from the front lines of doing business in China.* New York: Free Press.

Ramzy, Austin. (2011). End of the road for Lai Changxing, one of China's most wanted fugitives. Retrieved October 1, 2014, from http://world.time.com/2011/07/22/end-of-the-road-for-lai-changxing-one-of-chinas-most-wanted-fugitives

Song Yuwu. (2013). Lai Changxing. In Song Yuwu (Ed.), *Biographical dictionary of the People's Republic of China* (pp. 163). Jefferson, NC: McFarland.

Xu Wei, & Zhang Yan. (2012). Smuggling kingpin Lai gets life in jail. Retrieved October 1, 2014, from http://usa.chinadaily.com.cn/china/2012-05/19/content_15335661.htm

Zhang Lu 张鹭. (2011). Lai Changxing Qianzhuan 赖昌星前传 [Biography of Lai Changxing, the first half]. *China Newsweek.*

Zhang Weidong. (2009). Lai Changxing. In Zhang Weidong, & Ilan Alon (Eds.), *Biographical dictionary of new Chinese entrepreneurs and business leaders* (pp. 70–71). Northhampton, MA: Edward Elgar Publishing.

♂ Lai, Jimmy

Lí Zhìyīng 黎智英

b. 1948—Entrepreneur and founder of Next Media Group in Hong Kong

Alternate names: Lai Chee-ying; nickname: Fatman Lai

Summary

A legendary business leader who has transformed the news media in Hong Kong and Taiwan, Jimmy Lai exemplifies a classic story of rags to riches. He transformed himself from a poor immigrant to a successful fashion merchant to a media tycoon. A staunch supporter of freedom and democracy, he plays an important role in the pro-democratic camp in Hong Kong as a media owner and financial supporter.

Jimmy Lai is an interesting and important figure in Hong Kong. His reputation as a successful business leader is unquestioned, and his way of doing business has been admired and studied. The success stories of his businesses Giordano, *Apple Daily*, *Next Magazine*, and Apple Action News are well known, as are the failed attempts of others, such as adMart and Apple TV. Lai commands huge influence through his media empire both in Hong Kong and Taiwan, and has shaped the development of these two societies significantly.

Lai is also a controversial figure, particularly in the political arena. His involvement in Hong Kong politics is a topic of interest for the general public and different political camps. A prolific writer, he has contributed a weekly column to his *Next Magazine* for many years, and many of his ideas and experiences can be found in the twenty books he has published since 1998. He and his wife are both Catholic, and he has close ties with Cardinal *Joseph Zen 陳日君 (b. 1932) and founding chairman of the Democratic Party in Hong Kong, *Martin Lee 李柱銘 (b. 1938).

Early Years and Giordano Success

Born on 8 December 1948, in a village in Guangzhou Province, Jimmy Lai had a

---

*People marked with an asterisk have entries in this dictionary.

difficult childhood and from the age of eight had to earn a living to support his family. Entering Hong Kong via Macau as an illegal immigrant when he was just twelve, he worked in a garment factory for a few years and became a manager before the age of twenty.

Despite having only a primary education, he continuously tried to improve himself by reading books voraciously. After making some money in the stock market, he decided to take control of the failing garment factory where he had once worked. In 1981, Lai launched Giordano, which was a chain store selling fashion both locally and overseas.

Business Strategies

The success story of Giordano exemplifies the unique ways Lai does business. He is not afraid to try new things or to be innovative. He made mistakes in the beginning, but learned from them, gaining valuable experience. He borrows good ideas from others and also comes up with new ways of thinking on his own. These methods increased efficiency and effectiveness, ultimately yielding enormous profits.

Lai also seeks business opportunities by understanding and fulfilling customer wants and needs, responding to the market situation quickly to offer fresh and innovative products and services. He emphasizes solving problems, adding value, and above all simplifying things.

Political Fashion

During the 1989 protests, when citizens in Beijing poured into the streets in support of democratic reforms, Lai's Giordano company donated 200,000 T-shirts to the protesters. This move, and the clear involvement of Lai behind it, came with the consequence that Giordano began to face difficulties in its business dealings in China. In July 1994, after Lai moved on to establish his first media publication, he published an open letter in *Next Magazine* criticizing then Chinese Premier *Lǐ Péng 李鹏 (b. 1928). Although Lai had already removed himself from Giordano by that time, the business was blocked from opening stores in China.

Transformation into Media Tycoon

After the 1989 student movement, Lai became interested in the media business, and in 1990 launched *Next Magazine* in Hong Kong after selling all his shares of Giordano. He made a huge investment in this weekly news magazine, and the quick success of *Next Magazine* prompted him to try an even bigger media project. In 1995, the newspaper *Apple Daily* was launched and it also became a major success, with daily circulation rising to half a million copies. It was estimated that his wealth ballooned to more than 500 million US dollars during this time. Next Media group also publishes other weekly magazines, including *Sudden*

Weekly, *Easy Finder*, *Eat & Travel Weekly*, *Trading Express/Auto Express*, etc.

Lai continues with his unique brand of business strategies in the media industry. Some people see his ways as unconventional, even bordering on illogical. When starting *Apple Daily* in Hong Kong, he reduced the retail price of a newspaper from five dollars to two. He invested several hundred million Hong Kong dollars for the launch, and paid top salaries while raiding journalists working from other newspapers. Modeled after *USA Today*, *Apple Daily* was colorful, user-friendly, and rich in content, so that readers from different social strata could find something of interest to read. Yet, its sensational style and use of checkbook journalism as well as paparazzi led to controversy among journalists and the public. The boundary between entertainment news and hard news in *Apple Daily* was blurred, but Lai insisted that journalism should feel the market's pulse and the readers' feelings. Criticism of the government and the powers that be, including Lai's good friends, was the rule and was without exceptions.

Business Failures

In June 1999, Lai started an online retail business called adMart. He invested about 700 million Hong Kong dollars but in less than two years the expensive experiment had failed, and Lai lost more than a billion Hong Kong dollars as a result. There were various reasons leading to the failure, one of which were the fiercely defensive actions taken by two giant supermarket chains that were direct competitors. The management of the logistics of adMart as well as the quality of services and goods delivered were also questionable. Another factor was that Internet shopping in Hong Kong was not yet popular, given the convenience of offline shopping in this compact city. Lai then attempted to build a large web portal in 2000 for his various businesses, but the move proved to be unwise. Hundreds of employees were subsequently laid off.

Move to Taiwan

After the bitter experiences of adMart and his web portal, Lai shifted his attention to Taiwan as another playing field. Taiwan represented a larger market for Lai, and is known to be more traditional. While he wished to carry over his successful Hong Kong publication experience to start a modernized media empire there, he also proclaimed Taiwan a good place for doing business and expanding democracy in the Chinese context.

Lai launched the Taiwan edition of *Next Magazine* in 2001 and *Apple Daily* in 2003. The sensational style and the use of paparazzi by these two publications created shock waves in the media industry in Taiwan. In terms of politics, many local Taiwanese publications either sided with the Nationalist Party (Kuomintang) or the Democratic Progressive Party. Jimmy Lai's publications did neither and opted to take a critical stance toward both parties. The Taiwanese editions of the magazine and newspaper were very popular and quickly carved a significant niche among top-selling publications.

More Media

The free newspaper initiative started in Europe in the 1990s and soon began to catch up in Asia. In 2002, *Metro Daily* made its foothold in Hong Kong and quickly became profitable, with two more free newspapers following suit in 2007. Jimmy Lai was a bit late in this area, opting to launch his own free newspaper, *Sharp Daily*, in Taiwan in 2006 and in Hong Kong in 2011. The Hong Kong edition, however, was criticized by the public for its sensational style and pornographic content, and folded in less than two years.

Lai then launched the Next TV project at the end of 2010. It also proved to be a difficult investment and he soon had to sell it. But his Apple Action News, launched in 2009, has been a major hit in both Taiwan and Hong Kong and has helped *Apple Daily* to consolidate its lead in the media market. The presentation of news through computer-generated graphics is ground-breaking but controversial, with public outcry over sensationalism and the trivialization of news.

Political Stance and Participation

Jimmy Lai is a great admirer of economist and philosopher Friedrich Hayek, who defended classical liberalism; the economist Milton Friedman, who advocated free markets; and former financial secretary of Hong Kong, John James Cowperthwaite, whose free market policies helped turn Hong Kong into a financial powerhouse. Lai's belief in freedom is also closely linked to his support for the democracy movement in Hong Kong. He was an advocate of the protest march on 1 July 2003, when half a million Hong Kong people took to the streets to protest against the then chief executive, Tung Chee-hua, and his attempts to usher in Hong Kong Basic Law Article 23, a anti-succession and anti-subversion law. *Apple Daily* distributed a lot of posters to the protesters on that day.

In October 2011, it was reported that Lai had donated tens of millions of dollars to some pan-democrats and religious leaders between 2006 and 2010. His publications took a clear stand of supporting the pro-democracy camp in the various elections, and have been critical of both the Hong Kong SAR government and the central government in Beijing. Lai also participated in the Occupy movement in 2014 by staging many sit-ins himself. His publications ran stories in support of the protesters, which led some pro-establishment groups to fight back by blocking the entrance of *Apple Daily* after midnight, so that the trucks loaded with newspapers could not leave the premises. Lai was subsequently arrested on 11 December 2014 and three days later announced that he would no longer be the chairman of Next Media.

Emails written by Lai's top aide, Mark Simon, were hacked and documents were leaked to the press in 2014. There were cyberattacks on Next Media's network in 2014, and Lai was placed under investigation by the Independent Commission Against Corruption. Firebombs were hurled at Lai's home and office in 2015. The pro-China news media alleged that Lai was closely linked with the US embassy in Hong Kong and had been a close friend of the former US deputy secretary of defense, Paul Wolfowitz. Lai was also accused of financially supporting the Occupy Central movement in Hong Kong.

Reputation and Controversies

Jimmy Lai is viewed by many as a legend in Hong Kong. His poverty-stricken origins in mainland China and phenomenal success in Hong Kong represent the struggle and dream of his generation. His acute business sense and innovative strategies made him a billionaire, and his impact on the news media scene is unparalleled. He is seen by some as a staunch freedom fighter, and by others as the man who disrupts Hong Kong. Many are curious about how Lai amassed such a financial fortune and whether he has any hidden agendas. His huge influence in both the mass media and the political arena is welcomed by friends

and loathed by foes. The controversies he has been involved in are subject to different interpretations and will remain a fascinating social phenomenon worthy of continued attention.

Clement Y. K. SO
Chinese University of Hong Kong

Further Reading

Lai, Chee-ying 黎智英. (2001). *Shishi yu pianjian* 事實與偏見 [Facts and biases]. Hong Kong: Yi Chuban.

Lai, Chee-ying 黎智英. (2003). *Wo shige chiguo kutou di fuqin: Shizhi yu pianjian 7* 我是個吃過苦頭的父親——事實與偏見 7 [I am a father who has suffered: Facts and biases 7]. Taipei: Shangzhou Chuban.

Lai, Chee-ying 黎智英. (2007). *Woshi Li Zhiying: Cong yiyuan gangbi dao wuyi meiyuan di chuangye chuanqi* 我是黎智英——從一元港幣到五億美金的創業傳奇 [I am Lai Chee-ying: A legend of entrepreneurship from one Hong Kong dollar to 500 million U.S. dollars]. Taipei: Shangzhou Chuban.

Lai, Chee-ying 黎智英. (2007). Shengyi: Li Zhiying ruhe dazao dazhong shangpin 生意：黎智英如何打造大眾商品 [Business: How does Lai Chee-ying make mass commercial products]. Taipei: Shangzhou Chuban.

Lai, Chee-ying 黎智英. (2012). *Jingyan chu zhihui: Shishi yu pianjian 18* 經驗出智慧——事實與偏見 18 [From experience to wisdom: Facts and biases 18]. Hong Kong: Yi Chuban.

Lai, Chee-ying 黎智英. (2013). *Goule! Tuixiu!: Shishi yu pianjian19* 夠了！退休！——事實與偏見 19

[Enough! Retire!: Facts and biases 19]. Hong Kong: Yi Chuban.

Leung, Grace L. K. 梁麗娟. (2006). *Pingguo diao xialai* 蘋果掉下來 [Apple falling down]. Hong Kong: Sub-Culture Publishing Co.

Lui, Ka-ming 呂家明. (1997). *Li Zhiying chuanshuo* 黎智英傳說 [Legendary stories of Lai Chee-ying]. Hong Kong: Mingbao Chubanshe.

So, Clement Y. K. 蘇鑰機. (1997). Wanquan shichang daoxiang xinwen xue: Pingguo ribao gean yanjiu 完全市場導向新聞學：《蘋果日報》 個案研究 [Complete market-driven journalism: The case of Apple Daily]. In Joseph M. Chan 陳韜文, Leonard L. Chu 朱立, & Zhongdang Pan 潘忠黨 (Eds.), *Dazhong quanbo yu shichang jingji* 大眾傳播與市場經濟 [Mass communication and market economy] (pp. 215–233). Hong Kong: Lu Feng Society.

Zeng, Mengzhuo 曾孟卓. (2009). *Pinguo di ziwei: Yiyao shangyin di xingxiao guanli chuangyi xue* 蘋果 滋味：一咬上癮的行銷管理創意學 [The taste of apple: One bite addictive creative sales management]. Taipei: Shangzhou Chuban.

♂ Láng Lǎng 郎朗

b. 1982—China's most distinguished contemporary pianist

Summary

The most famous of Chinese virtuoso pianists, Lang Lang was a child prodigy who drew acclaim for his performances by the age of five and went on to study in Philadelphia with Gary Graffman. Residing in the United States, Lang Lang has become a global citizen, performing throughout the world and reaching an ever greater audience through his appointment as UN Messenger of Peace, with a special focus on education.

Undoubtedly the most famous pianist that modern China has produced, Lang Lang is known as a charismatic and expressive performer. As a Chinese citizen who has settled in the United States and constantly travels the world, he also exemplifies the significant impact people from China are having now on the international Western classical music scene.

Early Years

Lang Lang's first years coincided with the early stages of economic reforms led by *Dèng Xiǎopíng 邓小平 (1904–1997). Through this process, Deng Xiaoping opened up not just China's economy but, to some extent, its culture and society to Western and other influences. In June 1981, the Chinese Communist Party (CCP) formally criticized the Cultural Revolution (1966–1976), which had imposed an extremely narrow and tight framework on China's cultural life.

Lang Lang was born on 14 June 1982 in Shenyang, the capital of Liaoning Province in northeast China. His parents were both passionately interested in music, his father being a good player of the traditional two-stringed bowed fiddle (*èrhú* 二胡), but they were unable to pursue their dreams fully due to the

---

*People marked with an asterisk have entries in this dictionary.

constraints of the Cultural Revolution. Both were from social classes condemned by Máo Zédōng 毛泽东 (1893–1976) and his followers at that time, in particular Lang's father, Láng Guórèn 郎国任, who came from a distinguished Manchu family with aristocratic connections.

Lang Lang was a child prodigy and showed great interest in classical piano music at the age of two. His father, who had a very strong personality, encouraged his passion, found him a good teacher, and mercilessly drove him to practice and develop his skills and to reach the top. Lang Lang says in his autobiography that, for his father, "no result could be anything less than Number One" (Lang 2009, 39).

Insistence on being "Number One" carried with it a conviction on Lang Guoren's part that his son must win piano competitions. At age five, Lang entered and won his first official competition, the Shenyang Piano Competition, a contest for all piano students under the age of ten. Shortly thereafter, he gave his first public recital.

Lang moved to Beijing with his father, where he studied at the Central Chinese Conservatory. In 1994, he won first prize at the Fourth International Competition for Young Pianists, held in Ettlingen, Germany. In addition, he was awarded a "special prize for the most outstanding artistic performance" in the history of the competition (Lang 2009, 155). In 1995, he won first place at the even more significant International Tchaikovsky Competition for Young Musicians held in Japan. The next year he played in front of President *Jiāng Zémín 江泽民 (b. 1926) at the inaugural concert of the China National Symphony Orchestra.

In March 1997, Lang Lang won a scholarship to study under Gary Graffman, a concert pianist who was president of the famous Curtis Institute of Music in Philadelphia. Highly appreciative of Chinese culture and able to speak Chinese, Graffman persuaded Lang Lang to give up his obsession with winning contests, arguing that these "direct your energy away from the process to the prize" (Lang 2009, 203), an attitude he thought deleterious to true musical artistry. As an admirer of the United States, Lang Lang settled there and made it his base.

Lang Lang continued to travel and perform internationally, and to play with the world's top orchestras and conductors. In particular, he was the first Chinese pianist to be engaged by the New York, Vienna, and Berlin Philharmonic Orchestras. Among his most noteworthy successes was his 2001 BBC Proms debut at the Royal Albert Hall in London.

Repertoire and Recordings

Lang Lang has a wide repertoire, although there are a few composers for whom he has developed a particular affinity and whose works he has recorded, most notably Liszt, Tchaikovsky, Rachmaninov, Beethoven, Chopin, and Mozart.

In 2011, to commemorate the bicentenary of the birth of Franz Liszt (1811–1886), Lang Lang released a CD/DVD entitled *Liszt: My Piano Hero* under the Sony Classical label. As a child, Lang Lang had watched a Tom and Jerry cartoon featuring Liszt's Hungarian Rhapsody no. 2, and it was this that ignited his interest in piano playing. This childhood incident in some way explains Lang Lang's lifelong dedication to and love of Liszt's piano music.

Lang Lang has recorded many of the great piano concertos of Tchaikovsky, Rachmaninov, Chopin, Beethoven, and Mozart, as well as individual pieces by many of the greatest piano masters, including Liszt, Chopin, Beethoven, Haydn, Mozart, and Brahms; he has also acknowledged some Chinese composers, such as *Tán Dùn 谭盾 (b. 1957). He has taken part in other kinds of piano recording exercises, which include playing the music of film soundtracks, such as *The Painted Veil* (2007), as well as contributing to recordings by other artists, such as the blind Italian tenor Andrea Bocelli.

A Chinese and International Performer

Lang Lang has traveled to numerous countries, and has mentors, contacts, and a career worldwide, which have

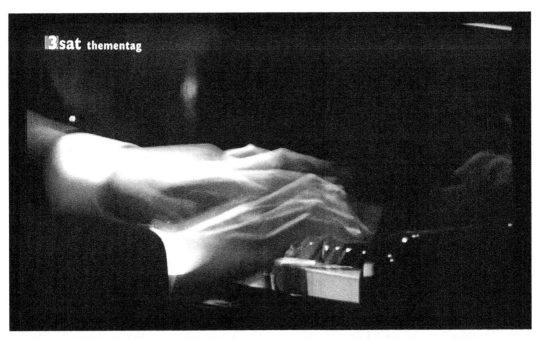

Lang Lang is known (and at times criticized) for his excessive showmanship and emphasis on technique over emotions. Here, he is playing at the Summer Night Concert, Schönbrunn, Germany (2014). Photo by digital cat.

shaped him into an international citizen. His autobiography, however, states that he tries "to stay involved in issues regarding my beloved China" (Lang 2009, 281). The fact that he was selected to play at the Beijing Olympics' opening ceremony and promoted there as a symbol of the youth and future of China suggests that he is held in very high regard in his native country.

He has played in front of numerous important dignitaries, including Barack Obama, Jiang Zemin, *Hú Jǐntāo 胡锦涛, Vladimir Putin, Nicholas Sarkozy, Queen Elizabeth II, and Kofi Annan. He has also played at many significant occasions, among them the opening ceremony of the Beijing Olympic Games in August 2008 and, along with tenor Plácido Domingo, the Rio de Janeiro FIFA World Cup concert in July 2014.

Relations with His Father

Lang Lang's relationship with his father has been unstable. At first his father was enormously domineering, with extreme demands that Lang Lang practice continually, and he always insisted on accompanying him wherever he went. After Lang Lang moved to the United States, his father came with him, but his lack of English reduced his power over his son, changing the balance in Lang Lang's favor. Until going to the United States, Lang Lang endured a very reluctant but nevertheless very

real dependence on his father, although he has finally been willing to recognize the enormous help his father's intervention had for his career. In November 2003, as an encore for his debut performance in New York's Carnegie Hall, Lang Lang accompanied his father's playing of a virtuoso piece on the *erhu*. Lang described this as "a moment of great triumph and reconciliation" (Lang 2009, 274).

Social Involvement

In October 2013, United Nations Secretary-General Ban Ki-Moon chose Lang Lang as a UN Messenger of Peace, with a special focus on education, the first such to be born in China. Ban called Lang "a true global citizen," adding that he influences people "not only through his music but through his passion to build a better world through education" (Barris 2013).

Evaluation and Significance

In 2009, *Time* magazine included Lang Lang among "The 100 Most Influential People." The rationale for this choice was that Lang Lang was a mixture of high and low, Chinese and American culture; moreover, he had a remarkable capacity to group different techniques and cultures into classical piano playing. The US jazz pianist Herbie Hancock noted that Lang Lang had started the Lang Lang International Music Foundation, which was "dedicated to supporting young pianists around the world" (Hancock 2009).

As is the case for many Chinese artists, Lang Lang has sometimes suffered criticism for emphasizing technique over emotion and for excessive showmanship. Although he resented the kind of criticism that claimed "Lang Lang's Mozart sounds more Lang Lang than Mozart," he was prepared to learn from it. In his autobiography, he says he came to see that "the criticism was helping. It made me controversial, and, funnily enough, controversy sells" (Lang 2009, 261). Yet the charge of showmanship has to some extent persisted, with many finding his stage playing mannerisms distracting and excessively flamboyant.

As he has matured, his playing has deepened, increasing in sensitivity and humaneness. In his discussion of Lang Lang in *Time* magazine, Herbie Hancock comments, "You hear him play, and he never ceases to touch your heart" (Hancock 2009). He regularly receives passionately enthusiastic reviews and a comment made in the *New York Times* (Wakin 2007) that he may well be "the hottest artist on the classical music planet" is frequently cited. Despite the criticism on Lang Lang's performance style, he remains one of the best-known classical musicians from China and stands at the forefront of China's contributions to the international music community.

Colin MACKERRAS
Griffith University

Further Reading

Barris, Michael. (2013, October 29). Lang Lang a "messenger of peace." *China Daily USA*. Retrieved October 12, 2014, from http://usa.chinadaily.com.cn/epaper/2013-10/29/content_17065877.htm

Hancock, Herbie. (2009, April 30). The 2009 *Time* 100: Artists and Entertainers; Lang Lang. *Time*. Retrieved October 11, 2014, from http://content.time.com/time/specials/packages/article/0,28804,1894410_1893836_1894420,00.html

Lang Lang, & French, Michael (with Andrew Pang). (2008). *Lang Lang: Playing with flying keys.* New York: Delacorte Press.

Lang Lang (with David Ritz). (2009). *Journey of a thousand miles: My story.* New York: Spiegel & Grau.

Lang Lang Piano Academy. (2014). *Mastering the piano* (5 levels). London: Faber Music.

Wakin, Daniel J. (2007, April 4). Increasingly in the West, the players are from the East. *The New York Times*. Retrieved October 18, 2014, from http://www.nytimes.com/2007/04/04/arts/music/04clas.html?pagewanted=all&_r=0.

Wu, Grace. (2010). *Chinese biographies: Lang Lang* 郎朗. Boston: Cheng & Tsui.

• Láng Lǎng •

♂ Lee Teng-hui

Lǐ Dēnghuī 李登輝

b. 1923—Taiwanese politician and first democratically elected president of the Republic of China (1988–2000)

Alternate name: simpl. 李登辉

Summary

Lee Teng-hui served twelve years as president of the Republic of China (Taiwan) from the death of President Chiang Ching-kuo in 1988 until 2000. Working with the opposition and liberal elements within his own party, Lee instigated and consolidated Taiwan's democratization and won a landslide victory in the first popular election of a Taiwan president, held in 1996. Lee has been fairly judged as Taiwan's Mr. Democracy.

Lee Teng-hui was born on 15 January 1923 near Tamshui, northwest of Taipei, midway through the Japanese colonial period in Taiwan (1895–1945). The son of a policeman who came from a wealthy family, Lee received his education through secondary school in Taiwan and read widely, including philosophical texts and literary classics (Lee 1999a, 21–28). In October 1943, following his graduation from Taipei High School in August, Lee went to Japan and became a student of agricultural economics at Kyoto Imperial University. In December 1944, he became a "student soldier" in the Japanese Army.

When Lee returned to a tumultuous Taiwan after World War II, he participated in reading groups and later stated, "I did attend several meetings convened by the Taipei Settlement Committee [a part of the 28 February 1947 anti-government uprising known as the 228 Incident], but I definitely did not participate in the discussions because I felt it was very dangerous" (Kamisaka 2001, 63). In the end, thousands were massacred by the Nationalist government, which soon began what is known as the White Terror period in Taiwan, during which thousands more were imprisoned or killed. (See Sidebar below on the 228 Incident.)

Lee continued his studies of agricultural economics at National Taiwan University, graduating on 1 August 1949 and becoming a tutor at the university. A few months earlier, at the age of twenty-six, he married Tseng Wen-hui (Zēng

Wénhuì 曾文惠), a marriage that united the "wealthy Tseng family with the learned Lee family" (Kamisaka 2001, 46).

Lee then obtained a Sino-American scholarship and went to Iowa State University, where he obtained an MA in agricultural economics in 1953. He returned to Taiwan where, in addition to teaching at National Taiwan University, he worked as an economist at the Taiwan Cooperative Bank, the Department of Agriculture and Forestry of the Taiwan provincial government, and the Joint [Taiwan and the United States] Commission on Rural Reconstruction (JCRR). In September 1965, Lee went to Cornell University in

upstate New York, where he received his PhD in 1968 with an award-winning dissertation about Taiwan economic development (published as Lee 1971).

In June 1969, within a year of his return to Taiwan from Cornell, Lee had a frightening experience when the Taiwan Garrison Command, then one of Taiwan's leading security agencies, called him in for questioning that lasted a week. Afterwards, a Taiwan Garrison Command officer told Lee, "No one but Chiang Ching-kuo would dare use someone like you" (Lee 1999a, 51). Later, Lee was promoted to chief of the Rural Economic Division of the JCRR and joined the Nationalist Party (Kuomintang 國民黨, KMT) in October 1971 "in order to solve Taiwan's agricultural problems" (Zhang et al. 2004, 44).

The Chiang Ching-kuo School of Politics (1972–1988)

The first important step in Lee Teng-hui's political career came in 1972, when newly appointed Premier Chiang Ching-kuo (son of the Nationalist leader Chiang Kai-shek 蔣介石) appointed him a minister without portfolio, undertaking special tasks in the areas of agriculture and agricultural development, the petrochemical industry, and vocational training. In 1976, after having been a cabinet minister for more than four years, Lee became a member of the KMT's Central Committee. Lee served in the cabinet for six years.

Lee Teng-hui as a young boy wearing a traditional Japanese Kendo uniform.

• Lee Teng-hui •

Lee's six years in the cabinet began his training in what he calls "Chiang Ching-kuo's 'school of politics'" (Lee 1999a, 197). When Chiang was elected president in 1978, he appointed Lee mayor of Taipei. During Lee's first three months as mayor, President Chiang would come three or four times a week after work to the municipal guest house and question Lee on the problems he faced and his solutions to these problems. After three months of intensive instruction, President Chiang said he felt confident with Lee's administration of the city and would no longer make these visits. While mayor, Lee became a member of the KMT's Central Standing Committee on 14 December 1979.

The 228 Incident

The February 28 Incident, known in Taiwan as "2-2-8" (*èr èr bā* in Chinese), began in the evening of 27 February 1947 when an angry crowd gathered in front of Taipei's Police Bureau on Taiping Street. The crowd was upset with the manner in which police and Nationalist Party officials treated an elderly woman, who reportedly had been roughed up for selling black-market cigarettes. The ill-trained and panicked police fired what was supposed to be a warning shot at the crowd but ended up killing a bystander.

On 28 February the crowds gathered around governor general Chen Yi's office, demanding redress and punishment for the police involved in the previous day's violence. Chen Yi, however, called out the military, who fired indiscriminately into the crowds. Although the violent crackdown on the protesters did end the immediate problem, it led to an even greater one—an all-out attempt at insurrection to overthrow Chen Yi and the Kuomintang government on Taiwan.

In the weeks after the February 28 Incident rebels took control of many parts of the island. But by early March, Chen Yi declared martial law and his superior armed forces managed to breach the rebel strongholds, and most of the rebel groups were jailed or killed. The subsequent crackdown became known as the start of the period of "White Terror" on Taiwan as the government hunted down suspected rebel "sympathizers." Some of the people arrested might indeed have had ties to the rebels, but others were merely local elites, people who happened to be at the wrong place at the wrong time.

李登輝

Eventually, Chen Yi was executed in 1950 for mishandling the February 28 Incident, during which an estimated eighteen thousand to twenty-eight thousand people were killed. The incident was a forbidden subject for decades under the authoritarian rule of Chiang Kai-shek and his son Chiang Ching-kuo. In 1995, President Lee Teng-hui finally officially acknowledge the incident and apologize on behalf of the government. February 28 was made a national memorial day in 1997, and each year a bell is rung in Taipei in honor of the dead.

Source: Chai, Winberg. (2009). February 28th Incident. In Linsun Cheng, et al. (Eds.), *Berkshire Encyclopedia of China*, pp. 801–802. Great Barrington, MA: Berkshire Publishing.

In November 1981, President Chiang appointed Lee governor of Taiwan Province. In July 1983 Lee gave a report to the Central Standing Committee on "methods the provincial government uses to send down roots" (*shěngzhèng xiàng xià zhāgēn de zuòfǎ* 省政向下紮根的做法), which Chiang Ching-kuo praised. Lee's reputation in Taiwan's political circles continued to rise. President Chiang's choice of Lee to be his vice-presidential running mate gave Lee his most important political opportunity. Lee was not the first native Taiwanese chosen to be vice president as his predecessor, Hsieh Tung-min (Xiè Dōngmǐn 謝東閔), was elected in 1978. But Hsieh was a "half-mainlander" (*bànshān rén* 半山人) who had worked on the mainland with the Nationalists during the Japanese colonial period (Jacobs 1990). Lee had not served on the mainland and thus was a "pure" Taiwanese. President Chiang did not tell Lee that he was to be his running mate until just before the public announcement in February 1984.

Lee's three years and eight months as vice president clearly helped him prepare to become president upon Chiang's death on 13 January 1988. Chiang had given Lee a variety of tasks and responsibilities, including aspects of foreign relations and dealing with political prisoners. Chiang clearly trusted Lee, but their relationship remained fairly formal and Lee did not belong to Chiang's inner circle of supporters, all of whom were mainlanders. Some people today argue that it was Chiang Ching-kuo who established democracy in Taiwan. Chiang did liberalize twice, once in the early 1970s in order to gain support for his new role as premier and once in the late 1980s towards the end of his life. But Chiang did not establish democracy. During Chiang's presidency, the president was still chosen by a rump electoral college, the National Assembly, and not by the people. Taiwan's citizens could only vote for less than half of the legislators. Politics, including the military and security agencies, remained in the hands of a small group of mainlanders who had come from China with Chiang Kai-shek after 1945 and who accounted for less than 15 percent of the population. People continued to be imprisoned for such political crimes as peacefully advocating a democratic or independent Taiwan.

Lee's Presidency and Taiwan's Democratization

When President Chiang Chiang-kuo died, many members of the mainlander elite were prepared to allow Lee to become president in accord with the constitution, but they also intended to sideline him politically. Debate raged for two weeks before the Central Standing Committee agreed on 27 January 1988 to make Lee the *acting* chairman of the KMT. Lee only became the formal chairman at the Thirteenth Congress in July 1988, almost six months after Chiang's death. President Lee then moved quickly to increase the numbers of native Taiwanese politicians in key positions. Although native Taiwanese accounted for over 85 percent of Taiwan's population, they had never held a majority of positions in the cabinet or in the Central Standing Committee until after Lee Teng-hui became president

and KMT chairman (Jacobs and Liu 2007, 379–380).

Lee also began the process of democratization in Taiwan, and in early 1988 the KMT invited the newly formed opposition Democratic Progressive Party (DPP) to discuss political questions. Lee also released several long-term political prisoners.

Internal Strife and Student Protests

By early 1990, the KMT had splintered into two main factions: Lee's Mainstream Faction (Zhǔliú pài 主流派) and the old mainlander elite's Anti-Mainstream Faction or Non-Mainstream Faction (Fēi zhǔliú pài 非主流派). The first open contest between these two factions occurred over the 1990 presidential election, the last to be conducted by the National Assembly. The KMT nominated Lee Teng-hui, but the Anti-Mainstream ran their own candidates, who only withdrew at the last minute. During this election, students also conducted "Wild Lily" (Yěbǎihé 野百合) demonstrations demanding substantial political reform. The day after his election as president, Lee met with student representatives and engaged in a dialogue.

Lee accepted one key demand of the students: the convening of a National Affairs Conference (Guóshì huìyì 國是會議). This June–July 1990 conference, which brought together members of the KMT, the DPP opposition, and recently

李登輝

released political prisoners, debated a wide variety of issues and opened the way for consensus on Taiwan's future. Just before the National Affairs Conference, Taiwan's Council of Grand Justices delivered Constitutional Interpretation No. 261 on 21 June, which stated that all central parliamentarians (members of the Legislature, the Control Branch, and the National Assembly) who had been elected in China during 1947 and 1948 had to retire by 31 December 1991. This order removed the 76 percent of central parliamentarians with lifetime positions in one step. Elections for the entirely new National Assembly were held in December 1991 and for the entirely new Legislature in December 1992 (Jacobs 2012, 70–79).

Further Democratization

Under President Lee, Taiwan implemented six sets of constitutional amendments. The first set ended martial law, which had been in place since the retreat of the Nationalists from the mainland in 1949, on 31 July 1992. The second set, passed by the newly elected National Assembly in May 1992, declared that the provincial governor and the mayors of Taipei and Kaohsiung would be elected by popular vote instead of being appointed by the central government, and also established "universal health insurance coverage." The Legislature amended Article 100 of the criminal code so that people could no longer be charged with the crime of insurrection and imprisoned simply for advocating an idea such as Taiwan independence or for non-violent action, and it also abolished the Taiwan Garrison Command, a key military-security agency (Jacobs 2012, 80–84).

In 1990, a key dispute arose over whether the president should be elected directly or indirectly. When the National Assembly passed the third set of constitutional amendments on 28 July 1994, however, this dispute no longer existed and the amendments provided for the direct election of the president and vice president.

Taiwan's voters went to the polls to elect their president directly for the first time on 23 March 1996. Altogether there were four candidates: President Lee from the KMT, a DPP candidate, a New Party (formed from the Anti-Mainstream) candidate, and one Independent. Despite— or because of—interference from China, President Lee won an absolute majority of 54 percent of the vote (Jacobs 2012, 106–126).

Cross-Strait Relations

From 1988 Lee proclaimed that Taiwan was a part of China. These statements, however, did not receive a positive response from China, which used military threats and missile launches during the legislative and presidential campaigns of 1995 and 1996 to threaten Taiwan. Subsequent talks between China and Taiwan did not progress smoothly. Finally, in 1999, Lee said that relations between

China and Taiwan are "a state-to-state relationship or at least a special state-to-state relationship, rather than an internal relationship between a legitimate government and a renegade group, or between a central government and a local government" (Lee 1999b). Lee received considerable criticism from conservative groups within Taiwan as well as from China for this so-called "two states theory" (*liǎngguó lùn* 兩國論). The idea of Taiwan as a sovereign state, however, has by now become widely held among the vast majority of Taiwan's citizens (Jacobs and Liu 2007, 388–390; Jacobs 2012, 135–138).

Lee was also honest in stating that the Nationalist regime of Chiang Kai-shek and Chiang Ching-kuo was a "regime that came [to Taiwan] from the outside" (*wàilái zhèngquán* 外來政權) (Jacobs and Liu 2007, 383). This too upset many conservatives, but for the vast majority of native Taiwanese, Lee's statement was correct.

Retirement as President

President Lee retired in 2000 after twelve years in Taiwan's highest office. The KMT nominated former premier and vice-president *Lien Chan 連戰 (b. 1936) as its presidential candidate and Lee fully supported Lien during the campaign. James Soong (Sòng Chǔyú 宋楚瑜), a politically powerful mainlander, was

angered not to receive the presidential nomination, however, and ran a splinter campaign. In the end, the DPP candidate, *Chen Shui-bian 陳水扁 (b. 1951), won the 2000 election over the divided Nationalists and, for the first time in its fifty-five years of rule, it lost the presidency.

Lee resigned the chairmanship of the party in March of the same year. Over a year later, Lee became "spiritual leader" of a new, small splinter party, the Taiwan Solidarity Union (Táiwān tuánjié liánméng 台灣團結聯盟) or TSU, which advocates a strong Taiwan identity. In this role, he has acted as an elder statesman occasionally commenting on political circumstances in Taiwan.

Evaluating Lee Teng-hui

Lee Teng-hui has proved to be a controversial figure in Taiwan politics. Many from the former mainlander elite have condemned him for being dictatorial and for betraying the party. A more generous view credits Lee with greatly contributing to Taiwan's democratization and ending the mainlander dictatorship of Chiang Kai-shek and Chiang Ching-kuo (Jacobs 2012, 171–172).

A survey conducted in early May 2000, just at the end of his presidency, affirms that Taiwan's citizens have given Lee overwhelmingly passing marks in "promotion of democratic reform," "maintaining Taiwan's sovereignty," and "handling cross-strait relations." In "promoting democracy," Lee received

---

*People marked with an asterisk have entries in this dictionary.

overwhelming passes from members of all parties, from all ethnic groups (whether identified as "Chinese," "Taiwanese," or both), and from all sectors of the economy. Clearly, all elements of Taiwan's society have affirmed Lee's presidency and its contribution to Taiwan's development (Lin and Tedards 2003, 46–48; Jacobs 2012, 171–172).

Since his retirement as president, Lee Teng-hui has continued to speak up on issues that concern Taiwan's democratization and its development as a nation.

J. Bruce JACOBS
Monash University

Further Reading

Jacobs, J. Bruce. (1990). Taiwanese and the Chinese Nationalists, 1937–1945: The origins of Taiwan's "half-mountain people" (Banshan ren). *Modern China, 16*(1), 84–118.

Jacobs, J. Bruce. (2012). *Democratizing Taiwan.* Leiden, The Netherlands: E.J. Brill.

Jacobs, J. Bruce, & Liu, I-hao Ben. (2007). Lee Teng-hui and the idea of "Taiwan." *China Quarterly, 190*, 375–393.

Kamisaka Huyuko 上坂冬子. (2001). *Hukou de zongtong: Li Denghui yu Zeng Wenhui* 虎口的總統: 李登輝與曾文惠 [President in the tiger's lair: Lee Teng-hui and Tseng Wen-hui]. (Luo Wensen 駱文森 and Yang Mingzhu 楊明珠, Trans.). Taipei: Xianjue.

Lee Teng-hui. (1971). *Intersectoral capital flows in the economic development of Taiwan, 1896–1960.* Ithaca and London: Cornell University Press.

Lee Teng-hui. (1999a). *The road to democracy: Taiwan's pursuit of identity.* Tokyo and Kyoto: PHP Institute, Inc.

Lee Teng-hui. (1999b). Interview of Taiwan President Lee Teng-hui with *Deutsche Welle* radio. Retrieved April 27, 2015, from http://www.taiwandc.org/nws-9926.htm

Lin, Chia-lung & Tedards, Bo. (2003). Lee Teng-hui: Transformational leadership in Taiwan's transition. In Wei-chin Lee & T.Y. Wang (Eds.), *Sayonara to the Lee Teng-hui era: Politics in Taiwan, 1988–2000* (pp. 25–62). Lanham, MD: University Press of America.

Tsai, Henry Shih-shan. (2005). *Lee Teng-Hui and Taiwan's quest for identity.* London/New York: Palgrave Macmillan.

Zhang Yanxian 張炎憲 et al. (2004). *Li Denghui xiansheng yu Taiwan minzhuhua* 李登輝先生與台灣民主化 [Mr Lee Teng-hui and Taiwan's democratization]. Taipei: Yushanshe.

• Lee Teng-hui •

♂ Lee, Ang

Lǐ Ān 李安

b. 1954—Taiwanese American film director who gained both local and international success

Summary

Ang Lee is an internationally renowned Taiwanese American director who has broken cultural and linguistic barriers between filmmaking in the East and West, with films in Mandarin Chinese, Taiwanese, and English. Best known for the commercial success of *Sense and Sensibility; Brokeback Mountain; Lust, Caution;* and *The Life of Pi,* Lee was the first person of Asian descent to win an Oscar, Golden Globe, and BAFTA for Best Director.

Ang Lee first came to the attention of the film world in 1993 with his second feature, *The Wedding Banquet* 喜宴, a Mandarin Chinese film shot on a shoestring budget. Ang Lee continually reinvents himself for each film, from low-budget productions to A-list Hollywood movies; in many ways he is experimenting with various genres and venturing into unique artistic territory.

The Long Road to Filmmaking

Born on 23 October 1954, in Pingdong—the southernmost tip of Taiwan—Ang Lee spent his childhood moving across the island to Taidong, Hualian, and Tainan. Lee did not begin his career as a professional filmmaker until he was thirty-seven years old. His father, Lee Sheng, was a high school principal and a traditional Confucian who valued filial piety and higher education. When Lee failed the national university entrance exams twice, this brought great shame to his father. Lee finally enrolled in the theater and film program at the Taiwan Academy of Arts (now the National Taiwan University of Arts) which in 1973 was a vocational school rather then a prestigious university, and thus a step down in the eyes of his father. As a film major, Lee embarrassed his father even further because film was not considered a respectable profession in the conservative environment of 1970s Taiwan. Lee was delighted with his experience as a film major, in any case, which he described as: "My spirit was liberated for the first time" (Zhang 2002, 34).

In 1978, at the age of twenty-three, Lee moved to the United States and enrolled as a theater major at the University of Illinois at Urbana-Champaign. There he met his future wife, Jane Lee, and graduated with a BFA (Bachelor of Fine Arts) in 1980. He then went on to New York University (NYU), to complete a master's degree in film production. At NYU, Lee had the chance to work with classmate Spike Lee, and his thesis film project, *Fine Line* (1984), won the prestigious Wasserman Award at the university. In the same year (1984), Lee's eldest son, Hann, was born. Lee has described the ensuing six years between 1984 and 1990 as "development hell" (Zhang 2002, 52). He spent these years as a house-husband of sorts, cooking and also looking for filmmaking opportunities. He wrote screenplays, and his agent occasionally found him work as a production assistant on other films. Lee has often praised his wife and family publicly for not giving up on him during this period. Lee submitted his screenplay "Pushing Hands" to the screenwriting contest held by the Taiwan government in 1990, and, almost as an afterthought, included in his submission another old screenplay "The Wedding Banquet."

The breakthrough for Lee finally occurred in late 1990, when these two screenplays won the two top prizes in the contest. Lee received US$16,000 in prize money to make the winning script, "Pushing Hands," into a film. Lee's first two films, *Pushing Hands* 推手 (1992) and *The Wedding Banquet* (1993), both filmed in the United States, were based on stories of Taiwanese Americans, focusing on themes of cultural and generational differences. *Pushing Hands* tells the story of a martial arts teacher who emigrates from Taiwan to live with his son in New York, but then moves out due to different ideas about family and life. *The Wedding Banquet* is a comedic family melodrama about a gay Taiwanese immigrant to the United States who plans to hide his true identity from his parents by marrying a woman.

A Career Taking Flight

The low budget *The Wedding Banquet* was a big hit, bringing in a worldwide profit of US$32 million. The film was nominated for both an Academy Award and Golden Globe Award for Best Foreign Language Film, won the Golden Bear at the Berlin Film Festival, and swept the Golden Horse Awards in Taiwan with six prizes. Ang Lee's third feature, *Eat Drink Man Woman* 飲食男女, his first film shot entirely in Taiwan, was released in 1994. This film, about a Chinese chef with three unmarried and unconventional daughters who challenge traditional notions of Chinese culture, earned Lee his second Oscar nomination, and was one of the most

Selected Filmography of Ang Lee			
Year	English Title	Chinese Title	Notes
1992	*Pushing Hands*	推手 *Tuī shǒu*	Director, writer, editor
1993	*The Wedding Banquet*	喜宴 *Xǐyàn*	Director, writer, actor
1994	*Eat Drink Man Woman*	飲食男女 *Yǐn shí nán nǚ*	Director, writer, editor
1995	*Sense and Sensibility*		Director
1995	*Siao Yu*	少女小漁 *Shàonǚ xiǎoyú*	Producer, writer
1997	*The Ice Storm*		Director, producer
1999	*Ride with the Devil*		Director
2000	*Crouching Tiger, Hidden Dragon*	臥虎藏龍 *Wòhǔ cánglóng*	Director, producer
2002	*The Hire*		Director
2003	*The Hulk*		Director
2005	*Brokeback Mountain*		Director
2007	*Lust, Caution*	色，戒 *Sè jiè*	Director, producer
2007	*Hollywood Chinese*		Actor
2009	*Taking Woodstock*		Director, producer
2012	*The Life of Pi*		Director, producer
TBA	*Billy Lynn's Long Halftime Walk*		Director

李安

successful foreign-language films in the United States. Featuring the Taiwanese actor Sihung Lung (Láng Xíong 郎雄), who plays the role of the father and also appeared in *Pushing Hands* and the *Wedding Banquet*, this film concludes the series known as the Father Knows Best trilogy.

The success of the trilogy attracted the attention of Hollywood studios. Lee's next three films were in English, made with access to international funding and audiences. Producer and director Sydney Pollack of the Mirage Enterprises production company was seeking a director to bring the classic Jane Austen novel *Sense and Sensibility*, a comedy of manners about the courtship of two sisters, to the screen, and he and his colleague Geoff Stier soon turned their attention to Lee. Lee was very surprised to be asked to work on this British classic, but he agreed to take on the challenge. This film brought Lee great success in 1995, with seven Academy Award nominations and a prize for Emma Thompson (Best Adapted Screenplay). From the marginalized foreign-language film director category, Lee had moved to join the leading forces in Hollywood.

In 2000, Lee directed *Crouching Tiger, Hidden Dragon* 臥虎藏龍, about a warrior in search of a stolen sword and based on the martial arts-romance series Crane-Iron Pentalogy (Hè tiě xìliè 鶴鐵系列) set during the Qīng 清 dynasty (1644–1911/12), by novelist Wáng Dùlú 王度廬. The film merged the Chinese martial arts genre with a Western-style romance, became the highest-grossing foreign film in many countries, and won an Academy Award for Best Foreign Language Film. Lee had re-introduced martial arts movies to the West and set a new standard for this genre that was followed by other Chinese directors such as *Zhāng Yìmóu 张艺谋 (b. 1951).

Lee's success was followed in 2003 by *Hulk*, which didn't achieve its full artistic potential and was badly received by critics and at the box office. The failure of *Hulk*, based on a Marvel Comics character who, after a lab accident, has the ability to turn into a muscled green-tinged monster, sent Lee into a depression, during which he considered quitting his career as a filmmaker. His father persuaded him to make another movie, and Lee turned his attention to *Brokeback Mountain*, which was adapted from the short story of the same title by the writer Annie Proulx. This controversial film, which blends the traditional western genre with a gay theme, was released to widespread critical acclaim in 2005, and reinvented and challenged the traditional American film genre of the western as a compassionate tale about the homosexual relationship between two Wyoming cowboys. *Brokeback Mountain* won seventy-one awards and an additional fifty-two nominations. It won the Golden Lion Award at the

*People marked with an asterisk have entries in this dictionary.

• Lee, Ang •

Venice International Film Festival and was named 2005's best film by Los Angeles, New York, Boston, and London film critics. Lee also earned his first Oscar for Best Director.

Lee then directed the sexually charged spy drama, *Lust, Caution* 色戒 in 2007, based on a short story by famed Chinese author *Zhāng Àilíng 張愛玲 (Eileen Chang, 1920–1995), set in Shanghai in the 1940s during World War II. Although scenes considered overly erotic or political were edited out, the Chinese government permitted the theatrical release of the film, and it was a huge success in China. The uncut version circulated as pirated DVDs and was readily downloadable on the Internet in China. Some mainland Chinese even traveled to Hong Kong to view the uncut version, since, as a Special Administrative Region of China, the city has more freedom in terms of film censorship. Lee's next film, *Taking Woodstock* (2009), about the famed music festival in 1969, was less successful. In 2012, Lee made *The Life of Pi*, adapted from the novel written by Yann Martel about an Indian boy from Pondicherry who survives a shipwreck but is stranded on a lifeboat in the Pacific Ocean with a Bengal tiger. Filled with 3-D special effects in post-production, 20th Century Fox invested US$120 million in the film. Unlike with most other sci-fi movies, Lee explores the artistic horizon of 3-D effects and pushes the boundary of how this technology can serve the movie's artistic

vision. Again, *The Life of Pi* challenged Hollywood genre film traditions by subverting the 3-D film convention of majestic scenes. *The Life of Pi* earned eleven Academy Award nominations in 2013 and won four awards, including Best Picture and Best Director.

East Meets West

Ang Lee is a product of both Chinese and American culture. He draws his artistic and philosophical traditions from both backgrounds, and this multicultural approach has made him an inspired and distinguished director. The Chinese philosophical themes of Confucianism, Daoism, and Buddhism, while more prevalent in his Chinese-language films, have been detected by some scholars in some of Lee's English-language works like *Brokeback Mountain* and *Sense and Sensibility*. The exploration of individual freedom and cultural constraints can be seen as one of the most significant unifying philosophical themes in Lee's works. His protagonists are typically caught in a struggle to define themselves. This thematic focus on personal freedom is a part of Lee's effort to scrutinize cross-cultural significance. While Lee's first trilogy is a clear example of the effects of globalization on culture and identity, his later films, such as *The Ice Storm*, deal with hybridized identity, or loss of identity, in the dimension of postmodern global society.

Lee also deals with sexual identity in many of his films. *The Wedding Banquet*, *Brokeback Mountain*, and *Taking Woodstock* deal with the social conflicts stirred by homosexual men confronting and expressing their sexual identity. Other films like Lee's earliest trilogy; *Crouching Tiger, Hidden Dragon*; *Sense and Sensibility*; and *Lust, Caution* deal with the sexual and social identity of women. The women in these films define themselves against the patriarchal authority that is prevalent in both Western and Eastern culture.

Ang Lee has said in interviews that he feels he in some ways embodies the deepening relationship between American and Asian cinema. "It used to be a one way street from West to East: we were receiving and the West was producing. I think we're getting closer and closer. The gap between the cultures is getting erased every day…The world's getting smaller" (Halbfinger 2005, 4). Ang Lee appeals to a more globalized audience and his career demonstrates that an ethnic Chinese can break into Hollywood, leaving his mark on the industry by becoming one of the most celebrated directors in the world. His deep understanding of both the Chinese way of life and Western traditions lends a unique aspect to his filmmaking. Lee's works are neither purely Asian American, nor purely Chinese, but they are the hybrid forms of art that serve to connect the two cinema worlds. Ang Lee is renowned as an all-round and fearless filmmaker whose films resonate with viewers not only because of his skill, but because they investigate issues that are universally important to human beings.

Grace Yan-yan MAK
Hong Kong Baptist University

Further Reading

Arp, Robert; Barkman, Adam; & McRae, James. (Eds.). (2013). *The philosophy of Ang Lee*. Kentucky: University of Kentucky Press.

Berry, Michael. (2005). *Speaking in images: Interviews with contemporary Chinese filmmakers*. New York: Columbia University Press.

Chen Bao-Xu 陳寶旭. (1994). *Yin shi nan nu: Dianying juben yu paishe guocheng* 飲食男女：電影劇本與拍攝過程 [Eat, Drink, Man, Woman: The screenplay and the shooting process]. Taipei: Yuan-Lui Publications.

Chang, Eileen; Wang Hui Ling; & Schamus, James. (2007). *Lust, Caution: The story, the screenplay, and the making of the film*. New York: Pantheon Books.

Cheshire, Ellen. (2001). *Ang Lee*. Chicago: Trafalger Square Publishing.

Dariotis, W. M., & Fung, E. (1997). Breaking the soy sauce jar: Diaspora and displacement in the film of Ang Lee. In Sheldon H. Lu (Ed.), *Transnational Chinese cinemas: Identity, nationhood, gender* (pp. 187–220). Honolulu: University of Hawai'i Press.

Dilley, Withney Crothers. (2007). *The cinema of Ang Lee: The other side of the screen*. London: Wallflower Press.

Halbfinger, David M. (2005, November 6). The delicate job of transforming a Geisha. *The New York Times*, 4.

Ma Shen-mei. (1996). Ang Lee's domestic tragicomedy: Immigrant nostalgia, exotic/ethnic tour, global market. *Journal of Popular Culture, 30*(1), 191–120.

Marchetti, Gina. (2004). Hollywood/Taiwan: Connection, countercurrent, and Ang Lee's HKLK. *Film International: Journal of World Cinema, 12*, 42–51.

Marchetti, Gina. (2012). Eileen Chang and Ang Lee at the movies: The cinematic politics of *Lust, Caution*. In Kam Louie (Ed.), *Eileen Chang: Romancing languages, cultures and genres*. Hong Kong: Hong Kong University Press.

Wu Huaiting, & Chan, Joseph Man. (2003). Globalizing Chinese martial arts cinema: The global-local alliance and the production of *Crouching Tiger, Hidden Dragon*. Paper presented at the International Communication Association Annual Convention, May 23–27, 2003, San Diego, CA.

Zhang Jinpei 张靓蓓. (Ed.). (2002). *Shinian yijiao dianying meng* 十年一觉电影梦 [A Ten-Year Dream of Cinema]. Taipei: Times Culture.

Zhang Ziyi. (2006, April 30). Ang Lee. *Time*. Retrieved on December 12, 2008, from http://www.time.com/time/magazine/article/0,9171,1187225,00.html

李安

♂ Lee, Bruce

Lǐ Xiǎolóng 李小龍

1940–1973—Kung fu movie star and martial arts cult idol

Alternate names: b. Lee Jun-fan 李振藩; simpl. 李小龙

Summary

Bruce Lee found worldwide fame as a kung fu movie star in the 1970s. A succession of popular Hong Kong films at the start of the decade (including *Fist of Fury*) launched his reputation and led to the Hollywood-produced *Enter the Dragon*, which showcased his talents for a Western audience. His mysterious death in 1973, aged thirty-two, turned him into a cult figure, and his influence continues to permeate popular culture around the globe.

Since his premature death in 1973, Bruce Lee has exerted a profound influence on global popular culture. His international stardom derived from a string of highly profitable kung fu movies produced in Hong Kong during the 1970s: *The Big Boss* 唐山大兄 (1971), *Fist of Fury* 精武門 (1972), *The Way of the Dragon* 猛龍過江 (1972), *Enter the Dragon* 龍爭虎鬥 (1973), and *Game of Death* 死亡遊戲 (1978). With the success of these films, Lee effectively globalized the martial arts genre. A worldwide wave of "kung fu fever" attended the international release of *Enter the Dragon* (a Hong Kong-US coproduction), and martial arts spectacle has since become central to Hollywood action cinema. One aspect of Lee's global importance is the change he precipitated in Hollywood's racial depictions. His prominence prompted Hollywood to reflect upon its ignominious history of Orientalist stereotyping and racial discrimination. Lee also pioneered an influential martial arts system (Jeet Kune Do 截拳道, or "The Way of the Intercepting Fist"). His star image, moreover, has informed more cultural texts (films, songs, television shows, comic books) than is possible to canvass.

By the time Lee achieved global renown, his screen persona had already crystallized. His physique was breathtaking and remains an object of fascination, a prime source of his films' spectacle. His sculpted, angular face was highly expressive, and he soon developed a repertoire of trademark facial gestures: a skeptically cocked eyebrow, a chastened pout, a twitch of the nostrils meant to convey indignation or contempt. In his scenes of physical combat—all of which Lee choreographed—he combines whip-crack speed and explosive force with an animalistic caterwaul, his muscular, sinewy body taut with emotion. At times he punctuates a flurry of high kicks with a staccato shuffle, displaying the limber gait of a boxer. The fights themselves harbor emotional complexity. For Lee's protagonists, to kill is to become wrought with rage and remorse: when he eliminates an enemy in *Fist of Fury*, he clutches his own trembling fist as if to quell the elemental rage within. Characteristically, the Bruce Lee protagonist is

Selected Filmography of Bruce Lee				
Year	English Title	Chinese Title	Director	Notes
1941	*Golden Gate Girl*		Esther Eng	
1950	*The Kid/My Son A-Chang*	細路祥 *Xì lù xiáng*	Fung Fung	Role: Ah-Cheung
1960	*The Orphan*	人海孤鴻 *Rén hǎi gū hóng*	Sun-Fung Lee	Role: Ah Sam
1966–67	*The Green Hornet*		George W. Trendle (Creator)	TV Show Role: Kato
1969	*Marlowe*		Paul Bogart	Role: Winslow Wong
1971	*The Big Boss*	唐山大兄 *Táng shān dà xiōng*	Wei Lo	Role: Cheng Chao-an
1972	*Fist of Fury*	精武門 *Jīng wǔ mén*	Wei Lo	Role: Chen Zhen
1972	*The Way of the Dragon*	猛龍過江 *Měng lóng guò jiāng*	Bruce Lee	Role: Tang Lung
1973	*Enter the Dragon*	龍爭虎鬥 *Lóng zhēng hǔ dòu*	Robert Clouse	Role: Lee
1978	*Game of Death*	死亡遊戲 *Sǐwáng yóuxì*	Bruce Lee, Sammo Hung, Robert Clouse	Role: Billy Lo

unremittingly virtuous, typically chaste, and an outsider even among his own comrades.

The Road to Global Stardom

The son of a successful Cantonese opera actor, Lee was born in San Francisco on 27 November 1940. He made his film debut as an infant in the US production *Golden Gate Girl* (1941), before the Lee family relocated to Hong Kong in 1941. More film roles followed during his childhood, and he soon became a favorite of the Cantonese cinema. He won local fame in *The Kid*, also known as *My Son A-Chang* 細路祥 (1950), in which he revealed himself an eccentric and endearing performer. The film puts on display what would later become Lee trademarks: the affectation of bravado and hubris; the penchant for buffoonery and mimicry; the marginalized, poorly educated, destitute figure vulnerable to deception. Above all, the fledgling actor delivers a highly physical performance, fitting for a star later to espouse "the art of expressing the human body." A series of Cantonese melodramas during the 1950s culminated in *The Orphan* 人海孤鴻 (1960), a social-problem drama featuring Lee as an *ah fei* (juvenile delinquent). This film can be seen as an update of *The Kid*, and here again Lee animates his role physically. He deftly implies that the delinquent's posture of cool indifference is too studied to be sincere, hinting at frailty beneath a youthful machismo.

In 1959, Lee returned to America, seeking stardom. Instead he encountered institutional racism and Yellow Peril paranoia (i.e., Western fear of Asian invasion and supremacy). On screen, Hollywood's Orientalist stereotypes held sway. Asians were routinely depicted as grotesques (Dr. Fu Manchu) or quasi-mystics (Charlie Chan); moreover, these roles were invariably portrayed by Caucasian actors in "yellow face" (Oriental-style make-up). In this context, few Asian actors found work. Lee filled his time opening martial arts schools on the west coast, recruiting several Hollywood celebrities. Gradually his profile increased, and he won a major role in ABC's *The Green Hornet* series

Bruce Lee (right) in his role as Kato, together with actor Van Williams, in the ABC television series *The Green Hornet* (1966).

(1966–1967). Lee's character (Kato) was both progressive and problematic, on the one hand a depiction of Asian heroism, on the other hand a racist recycling of the indentured man-servant topos. Moreover, though the series rejected the convention of yellow face, it still relied on cross-ethnic casting (Kato is putatively Japanese). Stymied by Hollywood prejudice, Lee returned to Hong Kong in 1970, accepting a two-picture deal at the newly formed Golden Harvest studio.

Bruce Lee's Chinese Nationalism

By 1970, the martial arts genre dominated Hong Kong's film industry. The swordplay films (*wŭxiá piān* 武侠片) produced by the Shaw Brothers studio established a tradition of highly stylized Mandarin-language action cinema. Formulaic plots depicted flying swordsmen capable of evincing "palm power," their hands emitting potent energy rays. Febrile zoom shots, accelerated motion, saturated color, and wirework conspired to create a fictional world far removed from reality. An emergent strain of kung fu cinema retained these aesthetic features, even as it substituted fists and feet for bladed weaponry. What these martial arts films lacked in realism they compensated for through sheer visual brio.

Into this milieu came Bruce Lee, whose kung fu films not only developed out of this *wuxia* tradition but departed from it as well. Lee sought to revolutionize the martial arts film, but he did not radically break with local norms of action cinema. On the one hand, he innovated a realist mode of kung fu filmmaking, seeking verisimilitude at all levels of narration. He dispensed almost entirely with the hoists, pulleys, and trampolines responsible for the remarkable feats of Shaw Brothers heroes, favoring instead an action style grounded in plausibility. He jettisoned palm power, flying, and other outlandish conventions. He also promoted the use of actual locations, rejecting the local custom of filming outdoor scenes in the studio. Under Lee's aegis, director Lo Wei subdued the *wuxia pian*'s feverishness. Both *The Big Boss* and *Fist of Fury* demote and decelerate the genre's ubiquitous zoom shot, and substitute a naturalistic color palette for a brightly embroidered set design. If the *wuxia* directors sacrificed realism for impact, Lee created impact through realism. Pledged to authenticity, he downgraded the *wuxia*'s outré elements in pursuit of stronger affect.

Lee preserved the nationalistic tenor of the *wuxia* film, and even intensified it. Revenge—a mainstay of the *wuxia* plot—is in Lee's films predicated on national and racial conflict, the retribution meted by Lee's hero a reaction to racial slurs against the Chinese. He often demonstrates national superiority by pitting his abilities against foreign opponents. In *Fist of Fury*, Lee and his compatriots suffer harsh indignities under Japanese occupation: at a Shanghai Bund park, a

李小龍

sign declares "No dogs and Chinese allowed," while another character disparages the Chinese as "the sick men of Asia." That Lee defeats his Japanese oppressors using a pair of Japanese nunchakus—a two-sectioned staff, the star's customary weapon—is significant, the hero asserting Chinese superiority by routing the Japanese with their own weaponry. Lee more generally pushed Chinese cultural nationalism into the fiber of his persona. Like the *wuxia* warriors, Lee's protagonists embrace an ethical creed rooted in Chinese philosophy (Buddhism, Daoism). Their physical prowess, moreover, springs from a specifically Chinese form of physical training and combat: kung fu. In body and mind, Lee came to personify China, exemplifying "Chineseness" for a local audience receptive to positive depictions of Chinese identity. (This persona differed sharply from Hollywood's Orientalist stereotypes and it is inconceivable that Lee could have cultivated it *in* Hollywood during this period.)

Lee's Chineseness, however, is far from simple or univocal. Though ethnically Chinese, he was born and partly educated in America, and he claimed US citizenship. His screen roles could be strange cultural hybrids: Kato in *The Green Hornet* is an English-speaking Asian superhero who dresses in a Mao jacket and bears a Japanese name. Lee's trademark nunchakus and battle cry (the *kiai*, derived from Japanese karate) tether his fighting technique at least partly to Japanese culture. Moreover, his Mandarin-language films tend to conflate Hong Kong and mainland China, making his cultural heritage ambiguous. From one angle, Lee's eclectic persona undermines his claim to authentic, archetypal Chineseness. Yet it is precisely Lee's cultural heterogeneity that ensures his enduring and far-reaching influence. His cultural ambiguity admits multiple points of identification. Diasporic audiences find an affinity through Lee's wayfaring protagonists, always adrift and struggling to assimilate to an alien culture (e.g., Thailand in *The Big Boss*, Italy in *The Way of the Dragon*). Other immigrant and ethnic groups, including African Americans and Hispanics, have appropriated Lee as a locus of inter-ethnic identification. For these groups, Lee signifies not so much *Chinese* superiority as racial empowerment, the triumph of the ethnic minority over foreign (white) persecutors. At the same time that this act of appropriation deracinates Lee and displaces his nationalism, it guarantees his widespread popular appeal—an ethnic rather than Chinese subject, a victor over oppressors, a figure of identification for disenfranchised peoples everywhere.

His unexplained death on 20 July 1973 in Hong Kong triggered genuine disbelief, not least because at age thirty-two he epitomized youthful vitality and physical excellence, but this only added to his fame. Lee's cultural identity was repurposed even further after his death, in movies such as Quentin Tarantino's

Kill Bill (2003), in which the vigilante heroine dresses in a yellow tracksuit famous from Lee's *Game of Death*. Here again the Lee icon serves as shorthand not for Chineseness but for emancipation and agency (in this case, of women navigating a brutally masculinist milieu). A posthumous exploitation industry coalesced in the mid-1970s, comprised partly of low-grade movies—labeled by critics as Bruceploitation cinema—that tapped Lee's global popularity. Representative titles include *Bruce Lee Fights Back from the Grave* (1976) and *The Dragon Lives Again* (1977), and starred so-called clones bearing names such as Bruce Li, Bruce Le, or Bruce Thai. As one critic puts it, "With his death, Lee became an object, even a fetish" (Teo 1997, 120). The point here is not only that Lee's nationalism becomes lost in the welter, but that the "Bruce Lee persona" now extends far beyond the films that Lee himself made. From the start his image was highly polysemous, but the significations it has accrued in the decades since his death are impossible to enumerate.

His cultural cachet shows no signs of waning. A statue in his image on Kowloon's waterfront attracts a regular flow of visitors. New audiences continue to discover his films. His popularity straddles several fields—cinema, sports, philosophy. Even the Bruceploitation juggernaut rumbles on, albeit elevated to a more prestigious form. Remakes, biopics, and spin-offs, including *Fist of Legend* (1994), *Dragon: The Bruce Lee Story* (1993), *The Green Hornet* (2011), and

Portrait of Bruce Lee's real-life kungfu master Ip Man. Photo by Dever.

Legend of the Fist: The Return of Chen Zhen (2010), pay respectful homage to Lee's oeuvre and present putative heirs to his legacy (*Jet Li 李连杰, Jason Scott Lee, Jay Chou, Donnie Yen). A cluster of Hong Kong films centered on Ip Man 葉問, Lee's real-life *shīfu* 師傅 (martial-arts teacher) have also leveraged Lee's cult status. *Ip Man* (2008), *Ip Man 2* (2010), and *Ip Man: The Final Fight* (2013) have furnished Hong Kong cinema with a new mythic hero, one cast in the Bruce

*People marked with an asterisk have entries in this dictionary.

Lee mold: devoutly patriotic, repelling imperial enemies, and exemplifying the virtues of the classic knights-errant. The canonization of Ip Man continued in *Wong Kar-wai's 王家衛 (b. 1958) meditative biopic *The Grandmaster* (*Yī dài zōng shī* 一代宗師, 2013), which incorporates a crowd-pleasing albeit oblique allusion to the pre-adolescent Lee. As film scholar Paul Bowman notes, "Lee has a kind of spectral and structural presence in [these] films, even if they are not literally about him" (Bowman 2014, 29). More than forty years after his death, Bruce Lee remains the spiritual father of Chinese martial arts cinema.

Gary BETTINSON
Lancaster University

Further Reading

Bettinson, Gary. (Ed.). (2012). *Directory of world cinema: China*. Bristol and Chicago: Intellect Press.

Bowman, Paul. (2014). Fists of Bruce Lee: Shanghai's martial arts film legacy. In John Berra & Wei Ju (Eds.), *World film locations: Shanghai* (pp. 28–29). Bristol & Chicago: Intellect Press.

Bowman, Paul. (2010). *Theorizing Bruce Lee: Film-fantasy-fighting-philosophy*. Amsterdam & New York: Rodopi.

Bordwell, David. (2000). *Planet Hong Kong: Popular cinema and the art of entertainment*. Cambridge, MA: Harvard University Press.

Glaessner, Verina. (1974). *Kung Fu: Cinema of vengeance*. Norfolk, CT: Bounty Books.

Hunt, Leon. (2014). Bruce Lee. In Gary Bettinson (Ed.), *Directory of world cinema: China 2* (pp. 53–56). Bristol & Chicago: Intellect Press.

Hunt, Leon. (2003). *Kung fu cult masters: From Bruce Lee to* Crouching Tiger. London: Wallflower Press.

Li Cheuk-to, & Keith Chan. (Eds.). (2010). *Bruce Lee lives*. Hong Kong: Hong Kong International Film Festival Society.

Li Cheuk-to (Ed.). (1984). *A study of Hong Kong cinema in the seventies (1970–1979)*. Hong Kong: HKIFF/Urban Council.

Little, John. (1998). *Bruce Lee: The art of expressing the human body*. Boston & Vermont & Tokyo: Tuttle Publishing.

Little, John. (2000). *Bruce Lee: The celebrated life of the golden dragon*. Boston: Tuttle Publishing.

Miller, Davis. (2000). *The Tao of Bruce Lee*. London: Vintage.

Teo, Stephen. (1997). *Hong Kong: The extra dimensions*. London: BFI.

Thomas, Bruce. (1997). *Bruce Lee: Fighting spirit*. London: Pan Books.

☿ Lee, Martin

Lǐ Zhùmíng 李柱銘

b. 1938—Hong Kong lawyer, legislator, and political activist

Alternate names: Lee Chu-ming; simpl. 李柱铭

Summary

To his admirers, Martin Lee is the "Father of Democracy" in Hong Kong or, at least, of the pro-democracy movement. To the Chinese government and its representatives in Hong Kong, his words and actions have bordered on the treasonous. The successful lawyer and founding chairman of the Democratic Party has worked in the years before and after the handover as a legislator and activist to promote democratic elections in the Hong Kong Special Administrative Region.

Martin Lee, the elder statesman of Hong Kong's democracy movement, was born in Hong Kong on 8 June 1938, the son of a former Nationalist (Guómíndǎng 國民黨, GMD) general, Li Yin-wo 李彥和, and raised in Guangzhou, Guangdong Province, where his father was based. Lee attended secondary school at the Jesuit-run Wah Yan College in Kowloon, where his father taught Chinese after the Civil War (1946–1949) between the Nationalists and the Communists ended. More than half a century later, a priest, Father Joseph Mallin, recalled in an interview to mark his hundredth birthday that "Martin Lee was very sharp" (McHugh 2013, 70).

Lee was baptized at the age of fourteen and acquired the Christian name Martin. He became a devout Catholic and his religion played a part even during his political life as he worked closely with the anti-communist bishop (later cardinal) *Joseph Zen 陳日君 (b. 1932), and *Jimmy Lai 黎智英 (b. 1948), another convert to Catholicism and founder of the *Apple Daily* and other publications.

There is little indication that Lee was especially interested in politics in his early years. After graduation from Wah Yan College, he went on to the University of Hong Kong, where he received a degree in philosophy and then worked as a

*People marked with an asterisk have entries in this dictionary.

teacher before going on to study law at Lincoln's Inn in London. He was called to the bar in 1966 and was appointed to the Queen's Counsel in 1979. The next year, Lee became chairman of the Hong Kong Bar Association and served for three years. This period coincided with the holding of Sino-British negotiations on the future of Hong Kong, preparing it for the planned 1997 handover of the then British colony to mainland China, and marked the beginning of Lee's political life.

One Country, Two Systems

In November 1984, after the Sino-British Joint Declaration was unveiled, the Hong Kong government announced that, in 1985, the Legislative Council would for the first time include elected members, and one seat was reserved for lawyers. At that time, Lee had already been appointed to serve on the Basic Law Drafting Committee to draft Hong Kong's post-1997 mini-constitution, which would implement the new policy of "One Country, Two Systems" under which Hong Kong's economic and political systems would remain unchanged despite officially belonging to socialist mainland China. Lee was one of fifty-nine members of the committee, of whom twenty-three were from Hong Kong and thirty-six from the mainland. On the committee, he and Szeto Wah 司徒華, head of the Hong Kong Professional Teachers Union, were known as backers of democracy.

Lee ran for the legislative council seat and won handily, and by 1985 he was deeply immersed in politics, serving as both a legislator and a Basic Law drafter. Those were heady days that ended abruptly on 4 June 1989 when tanks rolled into Tiananmen Square in Beijing to crush the student-led pro-democracy movement. Lee and Szeto founded an organization called the Hong Kong Alliance in Support of Patriotic Democratic Movements in China 香港市民支援愛國民主運動聯合會 (or 支聯會 for short), which called for the overthrow of the rule of *Dèng Xiǎopíng 邓小平 (1904–1997), Premier *Lǐ Péng 李鹏 (1909–1992) and President *Yáng Shàngkūn 杨尚昆 (1907–1998). As a result, both Lee and Szeto were ousted from the drafting committee.

Lee was also no longer allowed to travel to mainland China. "It's obviously painful," Lee said to *Time* magazine. "As a Chinese citizen, I'm not allowed back to my own country even though I'm welcome in every other country in the world" (*Time* 2008).

First Direct Elections

In 1991, the first direct elections were held in Hong Kong. Before that, the colony had no political parties. But in 1990, the first party, United Democrats of Hong Kong (UDHK), was formed with Lee as its chairman. It was quickly followed by the first pro-Beijing party, the Democratic Alliance for the Betterment of Hong Kong

(DAB). In 1995, UDHK—by then renamed the Democratic Party—won twelve of the twenty directly elected seats, while its allies won five, giving democrats seventeen of the twenty directly elected seats.

Lee, honed by years of courtroom argumentation, was good at producing "sound bites" for the media. Thus, after the formation of the DAB, he quipped that the letters stood for "Democracy According to Beijing." Another time, when talking about China and press freedom, he said China loved to "press freedom," going through the motion of pressing down with his hand.

Lee and others knew that they would have to leave office on 30 June 1997 (the day before the handover to mainland China) to make way for an unelected Provisional Legislative Council put in place by Beijing for one year. Lee's flair for the dramatic was well known. Shortly after the lowering of the British flag at midnight, he appeared on the balcony of the Legislative Council to make a farewell address, with the tacit approval of the incoming leader, *Tung Chee-hwa 董建华 (b. 1937).

Lee was in his element, announcing:

This is a glorious day for all Chinese people everywhere. For we are leaving behind the legacy of more than 150 years of British colonial rule and begin a new era for Hong Kong as part of China …

As we stand here this early morning in democratic solidarity, we declare that Hong Kong people want democracy. They have seen it work. The flame of democracy has been ignited and is burning in the hearts of our people. It will not be extinguished. Nay, it will only grow stronger. We say to those of you gathered here and to Hong Kong's friends around the world: we shall return! (Lee 1997)

And return they did. In the first elections after the handover, in 1998, of the twenty directly elected seats, democrats won fifteen, while the pro-Beijing government DAB won just five. But the election showed that pro-Beijing candidates, too, could win seats. This first elected Legislative Council replaced the appointed Provisional Legislative Council. In 2000, the Democratic Party still won nine directly elected seats, but by 2004 the number dropped to seven, despite the increase in directly elected seats to thirty. This to some extent reflected the emergence of another pro-democracy grouping, the Article 45 Concern Group, which later became the Civic Party.

Angering China

Lee often adopted a provocative, confrontational style. Indeed, despite his expression that China was his homeland, his distrust of China frequently found voice in his speeches. While Lee's acerbic criticisms of pro-Beijing politicians and politics in Hong Kong often irked Chinese officials, what angered them more were his ventures overseas to seek support from foreign governments. In April 1997, just weeks before the handover, he flew to Washington and saw President Bill Clinton, who warned Chinese leaders to "live up to their agreement" with Britain.

What angered China most was when Lee appeared before a US Senate subcommittee in 2004 and, in his capacity as a member of the Hong Kong Legislative Council, testified on the then current situation in Hong Kong. At the time, there was a strong demand for universal suffrage during the elections for the chief executive to be held in 2007 and for the whole legislature in 2008. Lee explained before leaving for Washington that his aim was merely to describe the situation in Hong Kong and not to urge the United States to take any action. He appeared before the East Asian and Pacific Affairs Subcommittee of the Senate Foreign Relations Committee on 4 March 2004 (Article 23 2004).

Lee's appearance before a foreign legislature was strongly criticized by Chinese officials. State Councilor Tang Jiaxuan said, "There is no need at all to run overseas and pay a visit to a temple, inviting foreign Buddhas to say this and that." Ān Mín 安民, vice minister of commerce, called Lee a traitor (*Taipei Times* 2004).

Retirement from Electoral Politics

The following month, China's National People's Congress Standing Committee (NPCSC) issued a decision in which it said that universal suffrage elections should not be used in elections in 2007 and 2008. After Hong Kong's democrats then focused on 2012 as the year for universal suffrage, Beijing ruled out that year too. But then, in December 2007, the NPCSC gave the green light to universal suffrage elections for chief executive in 2017.

In March 2008, months before his seventieth birthday, Lee announced that he would not run in the next elections. Six years earlier, he had relinquished the chairmanship of his party and was succeeded by Yeung Sum 楊森, former chairman of Meeting Point and a lecturer in the department of social work at the University of Hong Kong.

Lee's retirement from electoral politics did not signal an end to his political activities but he was no longer involved in running the party. In fact, in April 2013, he put forward a plan for nominating candidates for chief executive that was immediately repudiated not only by other pro-democracy parties, but also by Emily Lau 劉慧卿, chair of the Democratic Party. Lau said Lee had not consulted the party and was merely giving his own view. Lee withdrew his proposal and apologized.

Dispute over Universal Suffrage

The following year Lee, together with *Anson Chan 陳方安生 (b. 1940), who had served as chief secretary before 1997 under Patten and after 1997 under Tung, traveled to the United States and Britain—again raising China's ire for allegedly inviting foreign interference—as feelings ran high in Hong Kong over how the chief executive elections by universal suffrage would be held in 2017.

In Washington in April, the two met Vice President Joe Biden, triggering a charge from Beijing that Washington was "meddling" in Hong Kong's internal affairs. Upon their return to Hong Kong, Lee announced that the United States had decided to revive its annual reports to Congress on Hong Kong under the US-Hong Kong Policy Act of 1992, which required such reports for ten years only (Siu 2014). *Xinhua*, the official Chinese news agency, called Lee and Chan "mischief-makers" (Xinhua 2014a).

In July, Lee and Chan were on the move again, this time to the United Kingdom. There, they secured a meeting with Deputy Prime Minister Nick Clegg. This triggered a formal Chinese protest (Xinhuanet 2014b). The Chan-Lee visit evidently spurred the Foreign Affairs Committee of the House of Commons to announce that it would hold hearings on Hong Kong. Various Chinese agents, including China's ambassador to London, Liú Xiǎomíng 劉曉明, called for the cancellation of such hearings (Wong 2014).

Despite the efforts of Lee and Chan, and threats by the Occupy Central movement to paralyze the business district, China took an unyielding stance and the NPCSC announced on 31 August 2014

that the Nominating Committee would in effect be a copy of the 2012 Election Committee, and only two or three candidates would be nominated.

The efforts of Martin Lee and others are unlikely, in the foreseeable future, to bring about a democratic system in Hong Kong, one that will result in anti-Beijing candidates being nominated in the chief executive elections. Though not one of the three official organizers of the 2014 Occupy Central Movement, Lee was very much involved, speaking to the media, providing pro bono legal services and addressing the protesters, recalling his decades of championing the democratic cause in Hong Kong.

In 2015, Lee is Hong Kong's most senior barrister. Although his tenure on the Basic Law Drafting Committee was abbreviated because of his support for pro-democracy students during the Tiananmen protests of 1989, he was able to make significant contributions to the drafting of Hong Kong's mini-constitution. For instance, he claims credit for the incorporation in Article 159 of the words: "No amendment to this Law shall contravene the established basic policies of the People's Republic of China regarding Hong Kong."

Despite China's vehement objections to Lee's overseas activities, Lee did play a part in ensuring the continuation of the most-favored nation (MFN) status for China in the 1990s, in the aftermath of the Tiananmen Square Incident. His credentials as a pro-democracy activist plus his status as a Hong Kong legislator lent credence to his appeal to the US Congress that ending MFN would have a devastating effect on the Hong Kong economy.

Frank CHING
Independent Scholar

Further Reading

Article 23. (2004). Four local democrats attend US Senate hearing. Retrieved February 27, 2015, from http://www.article23.org.hk/english/newsupdate/mar04/0303e1.htm

Ching, Frank. (1985). *Hong Kong and China: For better or for worse*. China Council of The Asia Society and the Foreign Policy Association.

Hong Kong Government. (1984, July). *Green paper: The further development of representative government in Hong Kong*. Retrieved May 1, 2015, from https://archive.org/stream/greenpaperfurthe00hong/greenpaperfurthe00hong_djvu.txt

Hong Kong Government. (1984, November). *White paper: The further development of representative government in Hong Kong*. Retrieved May 1, 2015, from http://archive.org/stream/whitepaperfurthe00hong/whitepaperfurthe00hong_djvu.txt

Ip, Kelly, & Luk, Eddie. (2013, June 21). March of time. *The Standard*. Retrieved October 7, 2014, from http://www.thestandard.com.hk/news_detail.asp?art_id=134794&con_type=3

Joint declaration of the government of the United Kingdom of Great Britain and Northern Ireland and the government of the People's Republic of China on the question of Hong Kong. (1984). Retrieved May 1, 2015, from http://www.legislation.gov.hk/blis_ind.nsf/CurEngOrd/034B10AF5D3058DB482575EE000EDB9F?OpenDocument

Lee, Martin. (1997). Speech from the legislative council balcony by Democratic Party chairman Martin Lee Chu-ming. Retrieved May 1, 2015, from http://www.martinlee.org.hk/July1Declaration.html

McHugh, Fionnuala. (2013, September 14). My life: Father Joseph Mallin. *Post Magazine*. Retrieved October 7, 2014, from http://www.scmp.com/magazines/post-magazine/article/1308371/my-life-father-joseph-mallin

Siu, Phila. (2014, April 14). US to revive annual report to Congress on Hong Kong politics. *South China Morning Post*.

The Basic Law of the Hong Kong Special Administrative Region of the People's Republic of China. (1990). Retrieved May 1, 2015, from http://www.basiclaw.gov.hk/en/basiclawtext/images/basiclaw_full_text_en.pdf

War of words over Martin Lee's trip to US intensifying. (2004, March 9). *Taipei Times*. Retrieved October 7, 2014, from http://www.taipeitimes.com/News/world/archives/2004/03/09/2003101761

Wong, Alan. (2014, September 5). British response to election limits upsets activists in Hong Kong. *International New York Times*.

Xinhua. (2014a, April 19). China voice: Don't talk democracy while selling sovereignty. Retrieved October 7, 2014, from http://news.xinhuanet.com/english/china/2014-04/19/c_133274054.htm

Xinhua. (2014b, July 17). China lodges protest with Britain over Hong Kong affairs. Retrieved July 4, 2015, from http://news.xinhuanet.com/english/china/2014-07/16/c_133489121.htm

• Lee, Martin •

☿ Lee, Yuan Tseh

Lǐ Yuǎnzhé 李遠哲

b. 1936—Scientist and Nobel Prize laureate in Chemistry (1986)

Alternate name: simpl. 李远哲

Summary

Taiwan-born Lee Yuan Tseh has had two careers. As a scientist in the United States, he made discoveries about the mechanism and dynamics of chemical reactions, and in 1986, was co-recipient of the Nobel Prize in Chemistry. In 1994, he returned to Taiwan and served as the president of Academia Sinica, transforming the level of scientific research and education in his home country. Lately, his attention has turned to solving global problems, and he has served as the president of the International Council for Science.

A s a premier scientist and educator, Lee Yuan Tseh's life and oeuvre exemplify how far talent, hard work, and dedication can go. He has served scientific progress with his experiments and discoveries; he has also helped his homeland, Taiwan, by lifting its level of science and education. Toward the end of his career, he has also been concerned with solving global problems of sustainability.

Family Background and Youth

Lee Yuan Tseh was born on 19 November 1936 in Hsinchu, Taiwan, into a scholarly middle-class family. Both his parents were schoolteachers, but his father eventually became a well-recognized artist of watercolor painting; his career lifted the family from near poverty to reasonable wealth. Lee's mother collected the work of authors worldwide. Yuan was the "generation name" of all the boys in the family, but Tseh (*zhé* 哲), meaning "philosophy," was uniquely Lee's own, and his mother chose it because she expected him to become a scholar. Lee's affinity for mechanics manifested itself early on, when he repaired her sewing machine to reduce its noise.

During the bombings of World War II, the family had to leave their home and move to a safer mountainous area of

Taiwan. The bombings brought another lesson for the young Lee: if the planes released bombs directly above them, they knew the bombs would not hurt them, because momentum would move them away. After the war, Lee resumed his education. Both in elementary school and high school, Lee combined academic interest with extracurricular activities. He liked tennis, was on the school's baseball and table tennis teams, and played trombone in the school's marching band. Above all, he was a voracious reader, and his interest in books covered both social science and natural science. When he read Madame Curie's biography, he knew he would become a scientist.

Lee excelled in high school and, in 1955, entered National Taiwan University without an entrance examination.

Book about Lee Yuan Tseh's boyhood. Image courtesy of Lee Yuan Tseh.

By the end of his first year, he decided to become a research chemist. He understood that to become an innovative researcher in chemistry, he should learn how to blow glass and how to design and build mechanical and electronic equipment, and he mastered these skills. This proved a foresight for his future career. For his bachelor of science thesis, he solved a problem in analytical chemistry involving a recent technique for the separation of two metals from each other.

In 1959, Lee enrolled at National Tsinghua University for his graduate studies. His thesis work under Professor H. Hamaguchi was about the determination of the naturally occurring radioisotopes in a mineral of hot spring sediment. When he earned his master of science degree in 1961, he stayed on to learn another important technique, X-ray diffraction analysis, under Professor C. H. Wong.

Berkeley–Harvard–Chicago

In order to continue his education, Lee moved to the United States in 1962 and became a doctoral student of the University of California at Berkeley. Lee did his research under the supervision of Professor Bruce H. Mahan (1930–1982). Lee studied the behavior of simple molecules under some drastic experimental conditions to enhance the understanding of the nature of the bonding in these molecules, and already he showed originality in the design of his experiments. Some of his observations went against conventional expectations, but his results proved sound and reliable.

The main thrust in his graduate work, as well as in his later research career, focused on one of the most fundamental questions in chemistry. Chemistry is about how materials transform and how to produce new materials with desired properties. In this, the time element is important—that is, how fast the transformations occur. The chemical reactions usually consist of many elementary steps, and it is impossible to understand the mechanism of a chemical reaction without comprehending these steps. This kind of research needs a deep understanding of theory and skills in building and operating complex equipment. Lee prepared himself eminently for solving such problems.

In 1965, he earned his PhD degree and stayed at Berkeley as Mahan's postdoctoral fellow. He continued the investigation of the mechanism of elementary reactions. His results brought him reknown among the top scientists of his field. In 1967, he moved to Harvard University, as a postdoctoral fellow in Professor Dudley Herschbach's group. Lee was already thirty-one years old, but he was not in a hurry to become independent, and his patience paid off. In Herschbach's group, he further developed his experiments and built new equipment. In some of Herschbach and Lee's experiments, they used a technique in which two beams of molecules crossed each other. This approach brought them additional valuable information about the dynamics of the reactions they studied.

Lee spent only a year and a half with Herschbach, but this was an exceptionally fruitful period for his research. Now he was ready to become fully independent and to build his own laboratory. The opportunity came when in 1968, the University of Chicago invited him to became an assistant professor in its chemistry department. He moved up the academic ladder quickly and received a promotion to full professorship in 1973. He continued his research, but soon his Chicago period was over, and in 1974 he made his final move in American academia, back to the University of California at Berkeley. That the same year, he became an American citizen.

At the Top of His Field

The move to Berkeley brought Lee back to the venue of his doctoral studies, but this time he had a double faculty appointment: he was a professor of chemistry in the chemistry department and a principal investigator at the Lawrence Berkeley National Laboratory, adjacent to the university campus. He continued and expanded his research of the mechanism of elementary reactions and built more sophisticated apparatuses for studying them. He also investigated marine, atmospheric, and even astrophysical chemistry. His fame and creativity attracted students to his laboratory from many places in the world.

At the summit of his scientific career, Lee, jointly with Herschbach and the Canadian John C. Polanyi, received the Nobel Prize in Chemistry in 1986. The award was for their contributions to the studies of the dynamics of elementary chemical reactions. Lee titled his Nobel lecture "Molecular Beam Studies of Elementary Chemical Processes" and delivered it in Stockholm on 8 December 1986 (Lee 1992).

Lee has received numerous forms of recognition, including membership in the US National Academy of Sciences in 1979; the Academia Sinica, Taiwan in 1980; the Pontifical Academy of Sciences in 2007; honorary membership in the Japan Academy in 2007; and numerous other learned societies. He has received the US National Medal of Science (1986, from President Ronald Reagan), the Ernest O. Lawrence Award of the US Department of Energy (1981), and the Faraday Medal of the Royal Society of Chemistry (London, 1992), among many other awards. He has received honorary doctorates from forty universities: twelve from Taiwanese and eight from American schools, and the rest from twelve other countries.

After the Nobel Prize, Lee continued his high-level research at Berkeley for eight more years. However, like many Nobel laureates, he started thinking about whether he should consider other goals beyond his research in physical chemistry. He had returned to Taiwan for visits, and in 1972, he spent his sabbatical leave there. His impression was that the country was not yet ready for an increased role of science and educational reform, so over the years, he contributed to Taiwanese science, and his help gradually intensified as he acquired fame internationally. The situation in Taiwan appeared to be changing rapidly by the early 1990s, and Lee felt himself ready for a major career move.

Statesman of Science in Taiwan and Globally

In 1994, Lee returned to Taiwan and was appointed president of Academia Sinica, previously a lifetime appointment. This academy has an important place in Taiwan; it has about 230 members, of whom about one-third live in Taiwan and the rest reside abroad, most in the United States. Lee did not think that lifetime appointments were a healthy way of governing this institution, so he went to the Congress of Taiwan, which changed the law to limit the academy presidency to a maximum of two five-year terms. When the law was adopted, Lee had already completed seven years as president and could have stayed on for ten more years, but he limited his stay in office to a total of twelve years and stepped down in 2006.

As Academia Sinica president, Lee had two principal goals. One was bringing scientific research in Taiwan to the front of international science; the other was educational reform. For a country of about eighteen million people and limited resources, it was impossible to compete in all areas of science. The priorities of science in Taiwan, the so-called national project, revolved around "info-nano-bio." Lee thought this choice of priorities was consistent with Chinese traditional interests since ancient times, namely the creation of the universe, the origin of life, and the structure of and the forces operating in matter. Taiwan created new research institutes during Lee's tenure, and the percentage of the gross national product for research and development rose from 1.8 percent to 2.8 percent. Lee has used his possibilities for building bridges between the scientific establishments of China and Taiwan.

Lee did not retire after the presidency, because the demands for his participation in various projects, domestic and international, only intensified. Between 2008 and 2011, he was president-elect of the International Council of Science (ICSU), and he served as president between 2011 and 2014. ICSU is a nongovernmental organization representing scientific bodies of 141 countries and 31 international scientific unions. Lee spoke out on global issues, such as our sustainable future and global science. He has taken account of the challenges of modern society and has made recommendations on how to face them.

Human Aspects

Lee and his wife, Bernice Wu, first met at elementary school. She was ambitious and studied foreign languages and literature. At one point, however, the couple decided that only one of them should pursue an academic career. They have three children, all of whom were born and live now in the United States: Ted (b. 1963), Sidney (b. 1966), and Charlotte (b. 1969).

Lee was an exceptional mentor, and fifteen of his former associates are serving as professors in major universities. His personal and professional interests have blended. He often uses chemical analogies to describe human relations and human characteristics—especially borrowed from sports—to explain scientific concepts. In his Nobel lecture, for example, he presented a simple cartoon to explain the conversion of kinetic

Illustration of the conversion of kinetic energy into potential energy. As Lee explained in his Nobel lecture in 1986: "An acrobat bounced off the plank converts his kinetic energy into potential energy on his way to forming a delicate three-man formation." Image from Lee's 1986 Nobel Lecture, in Frängsmyr & Malström (1992), p. 337.

energy (energy from motion) into potential energy (energy from position).

At one of Lee's birthday receptions, he gave a cup to all his guests, which bore an inscription in Chinese characters: "Learning is a lifelong endeavor" (Herschbach 1997, 6344). This summarizes his leitmotif. According to Lee, "Dedication to education is a cultural heritage in Confucian teaching" (Hargittai and Hargittai 2006, 447).

Lee Yuan Tseh's career has had a double significance. He had an extraordinary impact on science in the United States in his younger years. His impact in later life was social in nature for the Taiwanese people. These activities have formed a unified whole, and this has made him a role model for many in Asia and worldwide.

Balazs HARGITTAI
Saint Francis University, Loretto, PA

Istvan HARGITTAI
Budapest University of Technology and Economics

Further Reading

Hargittai, Istvan, & Hargittai, Magdolna. (2006). Yuan Tseh Lee. In Istvan Hargittai & Magdolna Hargittai, *Candid science vi: More conversations with famous scientists* (pp. 438–457). London: Imperial College Press.

Herschbach, Dudley. (1997). The odyssey of Yuan Tseh Lee: "Should be all right." *Journal of Physical Chemistry A, 101,* 6341–6344.

Kemsley, Jyllian. (2010). Yuan T. Lee. *Chemical & Engineering News, 88*(21), 38.

Lee Yuan Tseh. (1992). Molecular beam studies of elementary chemical processes. In Tore Frängsmyr & Bo G. Malmström (Eds.), *Chemistry 1981–1990: Nobel lectures* (pp. 320–354). Singapore: World Scientific.

Lee Yuan Tseh & Yang Wei-Chih. (2011). Chemistry, science, and our sustainable future. *Angewandte Chemie International Edition, 50,* 10260–10261.

♂ Leung Chun-ying

Liáng Zhènyīng 梁振英

b. 1954—Politician, third chief executive of Hong Kong (2012–)

Alternate name: C. Y. Leung

Summary

Leung Chun-ying served as the third chief executive of the Hong Kong Special Administrative Region, beginning in 2012. During his tenure, the government was beset with constitutional challenges and social unrest, and Leung with accusations that his loyalties lay too much with Beijing.

Leung Chun-ying, also known as C.Y. Leung, was the third chief executive of the Hong Kong Special Administrative Region (SAR), established in 1997 after sovereignty passed from the United Kingdom to the People's Republic of China (PRC). In this role, Leung Chun-ying would prove significant for three reasons: firstly, because his election as chief executive was regarded as unlikely and did not auger success; secondly, because of his close links to the PRC and claims that he was largely beholden to its interests, undermining his obligation to represent those of Hong Kong's; and thirdly, and perhaps most significantly, because of his role in the attempts to reform Hong Kong's constitution (the Basic Law) to allow for elections of the chief executive position in 2017. The proposals put forward by the SAR government over this issue in 2014 and into 2015 proved hugely controversial. Leung was to suffer public protests and low public approval ratings because of his part in this episode.

Early Career

Leung Chun-ying was born on 12 August 1954, and enjoyed an elite upbringing, attending the highly selective King's College in the city before studying at Bristol Polytechnic in the United Kingdom (now known as the University of the West of England). He returned to Hong Kong in the late 1970s to work in surveying, building up a successful practice. The property boom both in the city and on the mainland, which was experiencing the first flush of economic prosperity as a result of the reforms championed by the *Dèng Xiǎopíng 邓小平 leadership from 1978 onwards meant that by his mid-thirties, Leung was a wealthy and successful businessman. He was also able to build excellent relations with the mainland leadership during this period, advising different regional governments, and working as an informal consultant for figures as important as the fifth premier of the PRC, *Zhū Róngjī 朱荣基, who was allowing the property market, previously almost wholly under government control, to be liberalized.

Leung was politically active from early in his career. In 1985, he was appointed as one of 180 members of the Basic Law Consultative Committee. The Basic Law was meant to serve as a de facto constitution, and sort out the specific details of how the transition back to Chinese sovereignty would happen, while preserving Hong Kong's unique attributes as a trade, logistics, and finance center. The final law was passed in Beijing by the National People's Congress in 1990.

Leung was also a member of the Executive Council from the establishment of the SAR in 1997, serving through the 2000s as its Convenor. On this important advisory body, he continued to have

*People marked with an asterisk have entries in this dictionary.

a political role, even as he continued his surveying career, establishing a number of offices across China over the early 2000s, and eventually selling his company to the international property corporation DTZ. He sold all interests in DTZ when it was taken over by another company in 2011, before his run as chief executive.

An Unlikely Rise to Chief Executive

His opportunity to run as chief executive in 2012 was unforeseen. Until early 2012, the front runner had been Henry Tang 唐英年, former chief secretary of the SAR and with a high profile, experienced as a politician and well connected among business and establishment constituencies in the city. But Tang was dogged by claims he had built a huge illegal extension under his principle property in the city, along with other allegations about his private life. In the end, the March outcome was unequivocal. Of the twelve hundred members of the nominating council (expanded from four hundred in the first election in 2002, and eight hundred in 2007), Leung achieved 57 percent of the vote with 689 supporters, and Tang only 24 percent, with 285. A third candidate, Albert Ho 何俊仁, received only 76 votes. Leung was accordingly appointed as the third chief executive of the region.

Leung assumed power with a highly contentious mandate, however, and almost from the beginning hit a number of public, political, and private challenges. On the private front, it was claimed that he had also had an illegal extension added to his house in Hong Kong, exposing him to claims of hypocrisy because of the ways in which this line of attack had been used by his supporters against Tang in the election. On the public front, his many opponents in the city spread rumors that he had been a member of the Chinese Communist Party, something outlawed in the Basic Law. While no evidence has been produced to back up this claim, Leung had been a member of the Chinese government advisory body, the Chinese People's Political Consultative Conference (CPPCC), and the conviction remained among a large number of people that Leung's loyalties lay with Beijing.

Constitutional Challenges

Suspicions about Leung's loyalties seemed justified by two major proposals that Leung tried to implement once he came to power. The first concerned the education bureau of the city issuing proposals for "moral and national education" to be introduced into school curriculum. Along with an emphasis on deepening the civic and moral duties of citizens, this curriculum contained language concerning the development of a sense of the "China model" and of the Communist Party of China being "selfless." Such notions crossed a political line for many, who protested in

mid-2012, demanding that they be withdrawn. Activists proved victorious, with the proposals made voluntary, and subject to review at a later, unspecified date.

This defeat may have been the reason why the Beijing government was in no mood to see vacillation from the chief executive and SAR government over the second, much more important conflict—that of the appointment of chief executives after 2017, when the next election was due. From 1997, there had been a nominating committee, which had doubled in size each time elections were held, reaching twelve hundred people in 2012, appointed, elected, or chosen from different key constituencies in the city. Such a system was regarded as a long way from the universal suffrage that people had been led to expect, particularly as this seemed to have been proposed by the second chief executive, *Donald Tsang 曾蔭權, during remarks in 2007.

The Beijing government, under new, more authoritarian leadership since 2012 when *Xí Jìnpíng 习近平 had been appointed general secretary of the Communist Party, made its views clear in May 2014 when it issued a White Paper from the State Council on Hong Kong, stating clearly that while Hong Kong needed to be run by local people, these were in the end Chinese compatriots, and the final say on all constitutional matters still lay with the National People's Congress in Beijing. Hong Kong was part of China, and therefore any developments in the city detrimental to its remaining a stable part of the PRC were to be opposed.

The general suggestion contained in the August 31st Decision, as it was subsequently called, was a development of the existing system—a nominating committee to which candidates applied before they could go through to the five-million-strong electorate in Hong Kong. Candidates who did not get through the nominating committee would not be able to stand for election. And, crucially, the nominating committee would continue to be appointed, which meant a continuation of Beijing's close involvement in Hong Kong affairs.

Public response was furious, with people marching onto the streets in September during heavy downpours, inspiring the name "Umbrella Revolution." At a time when huge student protests in Taiwan had caused the government there to back down over attempts to pass a new trade deal with the mainland in May, the activists in Hong Kong felt even more emboldened. Many of them camped among the government buildings in the Central area, maintaining a vigil until they were finally cleared out in early December. The government was in no mood to compromise this time.

They were helped by the antics of the fragmented and often fractious opposition groups. For all the passion of the students, they lacked a coherent political message and a figurehead. And while there were perfectly powerful messages about searing inequality in the city,

declining living standards for many, and critical issues over housing costs and quality, on the whole those who spoke most vociferously during the Occupy Central campaign did so on the foundation of somewhat idealistic beliefs about how direct elections for a chief executive would be a panacea.

Leung Chun-ying himself proved a poor spokesperson for the merits of the constitutional change, with often ill-thought-out remarks about the city being immature and unprepared for full democracy. His enjoyment of extensive networks in the city's core constituencies did not compensate for his elitist background. He was not, like the first chief executive, *Tung Chee Hwa 董建華, a businessman with support from at least the tycoons. Nor was he, like Donald Tsang, a life-long civil servant with support from the bureaucracy. His one great source of support was in fact from Beijing, where the leadership maintained confidence in him and did all they could to ensure that he remained secure. The links he had assiduously cultivated over the 1980s and into the 1990s, at least in this area, paid off.

The details of the constitutional changes were formally announced by the SAR government in April 2015. As the August 31st Decision had stipulated, there was to be a nominating committee, with twenty-four hundred members, and those who wished to stand in public elections needed to get at least ten percent of the votes from this body.

The nominating committee would be appointed. When put before the Legislative Council, the body serving as Hong Kong's council, for ratification on 18 June, a walk-out by a large number of the legislators led to barely half the seventy-strong body casting their vote. The outcome was eight for the proposals, and twenty-eight against. They were therefore shelved, with continuing uncertainty. Symbolically, the large number of votes cast against the changes were embarrassing for Leung. As of the time of writing (October 2015) there have been no moves to reintroduce legislation on this issue, nor any sign that other proposals are being considered.

Assessment and Approval Ratings

From 2012 to 2015, Leung Chun-ying suffered some of the lowest ratings ever seen for a chief executive in Hong Kong. It was widely expected, though, that he would stand for election in 2017 for a second term. While the city maintained relatively good economic performance under his stewardship, it remained beset by issues over identity, its political future, and its role in the wider world. Leung evidently lacked the support, or the imagination, to find answers to these questions that were appealing to large sections of the Hong Kong public. But in view of the relatively poor performance of his two predecessors, the most charitable explanation was that his position in the end lacked the power and status to really address the huge issues that any chief executive would have faced.

Kerry BROWN
Lau China Institute, King's College

Further Reading

BBC. (2015). Profile: CY Leung, Hong Kong's third chief executive. Retrieved October 11, 2015, from http://www.bbc.com/news/world-asia-29426277

Cheung, Tony; Lam, Jeffie; & Ng, Joyce. (2015, 16 September). No one is above the law, says Hong Kong's top judge in surprise rebuke to leader CY Leung's defence of his 'transcendent' position. *South China Morning Post*. Retrieved October 11, 2015, from http://www.scmp.com/news/hong-kong/politics/article/1858653/hong-kong-leader-cy-leung-makes-fresh-defence-beijing?page=all

Lam Wai-man; Lui, Percy Luen-tim; & Wong, Wilson. (Eds.). (2012). *Contemporary Hong Kong government and politics* (2nd Ed.). Hong Kong: Hong Kong University Press.

☿ Lǐ Hóngzhì 李洪志

b. 1951—Founder of the Falun Gong religious movement, currently living in the United States

Summary

Li Hongzhi founded the Falun Gong religious movement in 1992, achieving public acclaim amid a national *qigong* revival. Combining elements of Buddhism, Daoism, and *qigong*, the movement quickly reached ten million practitioners in China by 1993. When thousands of practitioners surrounded the Zhongnanhai compound in Beijing in 1999, the government quickly suppressed the movement. Li has lived in the United States since 1995, but makes few public appearances.

T he biography of Li Hongzhi, founder of the Fǎlún Gōng 法轮功 movement, is the subject of some dispute. There are essentially two competing biographies. Li and Falun Gong members provide one account of his life, but it is substantially disputed in the biography published by the Chinese government. Critical scholars of Falun Gong generally agree that both these biographies are suspect and that there is little objective data on Li during the time that he lived in China.

Falun Gong Version of Li's Early Life

Both biographies agree that Li Hongzhi was born in Gongzhuling, Jilin Province, in northeast China. Li claims to have been born on 13 May 1951, whereas the Chinese government claims he was born on 27 July 1952. Li's claim is important because in China, 13 May 1951 corresponds to the eighth day of the fourth month in the Chinese lunar calendar, which is the traditional birthdate of Siddhartha Gautama, the Buddha. Sharing the same birthdate with the Buddha is one way that Li bolsters his claim to be a bodhisattva (an enlightened being) in his own right. Li admits to officially changing his birthday, but explains that it was incorrectly recorded during the Cultural Revolution (1966–1976). Having grown up during the tumultuous period of the Cultural Revolution, Li's early education was disrupted and curtailed by the extensive reeducation programs that took place during that time.

Li is the oldest of four children. According to the Falun Gong version of his biography, he was discovered to have extraordinary physical and spiritual capabilities early in life. At the age of four, the Buddhist master Quán Juě 全觉 sought him out and proceeded to teach him advanced Buddhist teachings for the next eight years. At the age of twelve, the Daoist (Taoist) master Bājí Zhēnrén 八极真人 recognized his spiritual potential and initiated him into advanced Daoist practices. In 1972, his Daoist training was completed under the supervision of master Zhēn Dàozǐ 真道子.

His spiritual training culminated with ten years of intensive study of *qìgōng* 气功 in the years 1982 through 1992. Qigong is a traditional Chinese practice combining physical and spiritual exercises that are thought to promote health, longevity, and spiritual abilities. China was in the midst of a qigong revival during the time that Li introduced his system and began teaching publically. It was during this period that Li claims to have developed the unique practices of Falun Gong. At the beginning of this period, Li married Lǐ Ruì

李瑞, and their daughter Lǐ Měigē 李美歌 was born sometime in the early 1980s.

Government Version of Li's Early Life

According to the official biography published by the Chinese government when the governmental suppression of Li and Falun Gong began (1999), Li was an ordinary and unexceptional child. His parents divorced and he moved, with his mother, to Changchun, Jilin Province, in 1955. His education was disrupted during the Cultural Revolution, and he was a mediocre student who received a limited education. After completing middle school, he worked at an army horse farm from 1970 through 1972. Following that, he worked as a trumpeter for the provisional forestry police, a position that was eliminated in 1978. Then he found work at the Grain and Oil Procurement Company in the city of Changchun, where he was employed through 1991. The government biography takes great pains to undermine Li's claim of extraordinary capabilities, instead portraying him as a mediocre, low-level worker who had no training or knowledge of qigong.

These two very different accounts of Li's early life clearly have competing objectives. Li's version is the earlier, first appearing in 1993, and seeks to lend credence to his assertion of extraordinary spiritual powers and his claim to be a spiritual master in his own right.

The governmental biography, on the other hand, seeks to justify the suppression of Falun Gong and paint a picture of Li as a spiritual imposter who, at best, led an ordinary, undistinguished early life. As noted above, most scholars observe that neither account can be verified and that the real truth about Li's early life likely lies somewhere between the two.

Li's Public Life

Li's public life, which began in 1992 with his first public teaching of Falun Gong in Changchun, is less contested since objective records are available. Following this teaching, Li traveled to Beijing, the geographic center of the burgeoning Chinese qigong movement. His first real success came in fall and winter of 1992–1993, when he taught at the Oriental Health Fair in Beijing. His teachings were the talk of the event. Accounts of his miraculous healings were broadly circulated. Equally important, he received wide support from the community of Chinese qigong teachers. News of his success traveled quickly, and he enjoyed a sudden popularity well beyond Beijing. Coming off this success, Li began a nationwide lecture tour and traveled extensively throughout China up to the end of 1994. His final lectures in China took place in Guangzhou in December 1994. In 1995, Li became concerned that he had attracted undue attention from the Chinese government officials.

He abruptly stopped teaching publically and began making arrangements to leave the country. In total, Li gave a little over fifty public teachings in China.

Li claims that Falun Gong is his unique invention that combines elements of Buddhism and qigong. Falun Gong (or Fǎlún Dàfǎ 法轮大法) means "Dharma Wheel Practice." Li moved quickly to build upon the success of his Beijing lectures in 1992–1993. His book *China Falun Gong* was first published in April 1993. About the same time, he founded the Falun Dafa Research Society that served as the seedbed of the Falun Gong organization. The organization was extremely successful and had an initial membership list numbering in the millions. The society was also financially successful through the distribution and sale of Falun Gong training materials. Li catapulted from obscurity to national popularity in a matter of mere months. In two years, he leveraged that popularity into a loosely organized national movement. In 1995, he published *Zhuǎn Fǎlún* 转法轮, and it quickly became one of the top ten best-selling books in China. *Zhuan Falun* is generally considered his masterwork. It eclipsed his first book, *China Falun Gong*, to become the central sacred text of the Falun Gong movement. *Zhuan Falun* posits that Li is an enlightened spiritual being with supernatural powers who plays an essential role in the history of the cosmos.

• Li Hóngzhì •

After Li discontinued teaching in public at the end of 1994, he traveled to the United States, first to Houston, Texas, and later to New York City, where he requested a permanent visa for himself, his wife, and daughter. Since 1995, he has made few public appearances and has kept a low profile while living in New York City.

Despite this seclusion, Li gained world attention on 25 April 1999, when ten thousand Falun Gong practitioners surrounded the Zhongnanhai compound in Beijing that houses the senior leaders of the Peoples' Republic of China. This protest was a reaction to a derogatory article about Falun Gong published in a Tianjin periodical earlier that month. The protestors sought governmental approval that would prohibit further derogatory publications. This was the largest public demonstration since the 1989 Tiananmen Square protests. The practitioners quietly stood or sat, and there was no confrontation with the police. Representatives of the demonstrators met with government officials and politely demanded that the Falun Gong organization be recognized officially and that demonstrators not be punished. None of the protestors' demands were met. At the end of the day, the crowd quietly disbanded. Li Hongzhi did not participate in the demonstration and denied any part in its planning or action. Chinese officials, however, pointed out that Li had visited Beijing from 22 April to 24 April, the day before the demonstration.

Government officials were clearly shocked by the unanticipated demonstration. They were particularly concerned that the government intelligence agencies had been caught completely unaware. Allowing Li to leave the country the day before the protest is an indication of the failure of governmental intelligence to uncover the protest in its planning stage. The Falun Gong movement's ability to rally ten thousand people without prior government knowledge was of grave concern. The Chinese government had to respond decisively, and less than three months later, it officially banned the Falun Gong organization and began systematic suppression of the organization, its practitioners, and Li Hongzhi.

In July 1999, the legal status of the Falun Gong movement was officially characterized as an "evil cult." At that time, the government estimated that the number of practitioners in 1999 was a little over two million, while unofficial estimates ranged from ten to seventy million. Over the following ten years, thousands of practitioners were sent to prison camps, where many eventually died. The suppression of Falun Gong led to international human rights complaints about the treatment of practitioners, which essentially politicized the movement. While the ongoing suppression has arguably been effective in limiting the public practice of Falun Gong within China, it catapulted Li Hongzhi and Falun Gong onto the world stage. Previously unknown outside China, the practice attracted significant international attention and consequently recruited practitioners around the world. Ironically, this international attention has continued to fuel resistance within China, while at the same time allowing Falun Gong to emerge as a truly international movement.

Craig BURGDOFF
Capital University

Further Reading

Chang, Maria Hsia. (2004). *Falun Gong: The end of days*. New Haven, CT: Yale University Press.

Falun Gong in China: Review and update: Hearing before the congressional-executive commission on China, One Hundred Twelfth Congress, second session, 18 December 2012. (2013). Washington: US Government Printing Office.

Li Hongzhi. (1998). *China Falun Gong* (Research society of Falun xiulian dafa, Trans.). Hong Kong: Falun Fo Fa Publishing.

Li Hongzhi. (1999). *Zhuan Falun* (Falun dafa disciples, Trans.). New York: Universe Publishing.

Li Hongzhi. (2000). *Falun Gong* (Rev. ed., 4th translation.). New York: Universe Publishing.

Ownby, David. (2008). *Falun Gong and the future of China*. Oxford, UK: Oxford University Press. doi:10.1093/acprof:oso/9780195329056.001.0001

Penny, Benjamin. (2003). The life and times of Li Hongzhi: Falun Gong and religious biography. *China Quarterly*, 175, 643–661.

Zhu Guobin. (2010). Prosecuting "evil cults": A critical examination of law regarding freedom of religious belief in mainland China. *Human Rights Quarterly*, 32(3), 471–501.

☿ Li Ka-shing

Lǐ Jiāchéng 李嘉誠

b. 1928—Business tycoon and billionaire

Alternate names: Lee Ka Shing; simpl. 李嘉诚

Summary

One of the most powerful and wealthiest tycoons in Asia, Li Ka-shing rose from an impoverished background to become known as a "superman" in the business world. His companies operate in fifty-five countries and span such interests as banking, construction, real estate, container ports, and health and beauty retail. A Chinese and Canadian citizen, Li has also donated generously to each country, and to the United States, through his Li Ka-shing Foundation.

Sir Li Ka-shing is among the richest people in Asia and in 2015 was the twentieth richest man in the world with a net worth of approximately US$33.5 billion. Described as a "superman" in business, and "Asia's most powerful man," Li is also an extremely generous philanthropist and is known for his unassuming lifestyle.

Early Life and Rise to Prominence

Born on 29 July 1928 to poor peasants in Chaozhou, Guangdong Province, Li Ka-shing had to flee with his parents to Hong Kong in 1940 to escape China's incessant political turmoil. Li and his family lived in the home of his very wealthy uncle, who became Li's inspiration to make a place for himself in the world. Li would ultimately marry the daughter of this uncle, Chong Yuet Ming (now deceased). At the age of fifteen, upon the sudden death of his father, Li was forced to quit school to work in a Hong Kong plastics factory for up to sixteen hours a day. A member of the Chaozhou (also rendered as Teochew) minority, Li displayed his entrepreneurial acumen early on by founding his own plastics company in 1950 with funds borrowed from family and friends. With Cheung Kong Industries, Li perfected the art of manufacturing plastic flowers that, with their unique color mixtures, resembled real flowers.

Within a few years, Li made a fortune by becoming the largest provider of plastic flowers in Asia, and diversified his business holdings by moving into the lucrative Hong Kong real estate market. As many of the colony's residents fled the riots and political turmoil that in 1967 had spilled over into Hong Kong from the ongoing Cultural Revolution in mainland China, Li quickly bought property at depressed prices and formally established his real estate company, Cheung Kong Holdings, which was listed on the Hong Kong Stock Exchange in 1972. Declaring his intention to become the largest developer of real estate in Hong Kong, surpassing even the Jardines-owned Hongkong Land Company, Li made a number of major real estate acquisitions, including prime locations just above the Central and Admiralty Mass Transit Railway (MTR) stations in the heart of the city. In 1979, Li further diversified his holdings by acquiring Hutchinson Whampoa Ltd., a massive conglomerate consisting of container terminals and ports, the world's largest, in Hong Kong, China, Canada, Rotterdam, the Bahamas, and the United Kingdom. The company also included A.S. Watson Group as a subsidiary, with 7,800 retail outlets worldwide specializing in health and beauty products. As chairman of the board of both Hutchinson Whampoa and Cheung Kong Holdings, Li's business interests span from banking, construction, real estate, hotels, retail outlets, and airports to plastics, cellular phones, satellite television, steel production, and shipping.

Operating in fifty-five countries, Li's companies have an estimated capitalization of US$647 billion which, until recently, included major real estate and retail holdings in the People's Republic of China. A major supporter of the economic reforms initiated by China's paramount leader *Dèng Xiǎopíng 邓小平 (1904–1997) in 1978–1979, including service at Deng's request on the board of China International Trust and Investment Corporation, Li invested in China from the 1990s onward. Citing China's enormous debt to gross domestic product (GDP) ratios that exceeded 200 percent, in 2014 Li sold off all his holdings including the prestigious Pacific Place Shopping Center in Beijing. A dual citizen of Hong Kong and Canada, Li also has had major economic interests in Canada, including serving as a major shareholder up to 2005 in Canadian Imperial Bank of Commerce, Canada's fifth largest, and also in such major Canadian energy companies as Husky Energy in Alberta. Throughout his business career, Li has proved his business prowess, earning the label of a "superman" in the business world, by structuring his companies in a way to retain disproportional control without incurring the cost of owning an equivalent economic interest. Li has also relied on his two sons: Victor, who works directly with his father as managing director and vice chairman of Cheung Kong Holdings, and Richard, who heads PCCW, the largest telecom company in Hong Kong. Both are Canadian citizens.

Philanthropy

Described in 2001 by *Asiaweek* as "Asia's most powerful man," Li Ka-shing has lent his considerable fortune to a host of charities and philanthropic activities, contributing over US$1.4 billion. Most notable is the Li Ka-shing Foundation established in 1980 with branches in both Hong Kong and Canada. Referred to affectionately as his "third son," the foundation has as its three main goals the nurturing of a culture of giving in Asia, fostering educational progress and reform, and supporting medical development and research. Included among the many programs and activities supported by the foundation was the substantial aid given to the victims of the disastrous 2008 earthquake in China's Sichuan Province; the establishment of Shantou University in Guangdong Province (near his native home of Chaozhou), and

Li Ka-shing (left, white shirt) at the construction site for Shantou University, Guangdong Province. Li's foundation contributed generously to the construction of the university's campus from the late 1980s onwards. Photo by Kelvin Tang.

the Cheung Kong School of Business, the only privately funded school of higher education in China; and support for cancer research at Cambridge University in the United Kingdom. Li has also made major donations to the bioscience and medical school programs at the University of California, Berkeley, and Stanford University, respectively.

While the Foundation has also invested in such high-technology companies as Facebook, future plans include a new technology institute to be built at Shantou University in conjunction with Technion, Israeli Institute of Technology. Emphasis at the institute will be on the life sciences and, in a few years' time, mechanical and aerospace engineering, with foundation money also going to Technion's main campus in Haifa, Israel. Li has also provided funding to Hong Kong Polytechnic University, where a building was named in his honor, and continues to invest in promising high-technology firms through his Horizon Ventures Inc.

Politics, Awards, and Lifestyle

As the most prominent Hong Kong tycoon, Li Ka-shing's politics are predictably conservative, as he supported the selection of Henry Tang as Hong Kong chief executive from 2007 to 2011 and opposed the demonstrations and protests of Occupy Central in 2014, asking Hong Kong students and protestors to return home. A target of protests from mainland China workers demanding payment of wages by companies under his control, Li is also under investigation for nonpayment of over US$700 million in back taxes in Australia. Li is recipient of several national awards, including the Grand Bauhinia Medal, the highest such award in Hong Kong since its transfer of sovereignty to the People's Republic of China in 1997, the Knight Commander of the Order of the British Empire, and the *Commandeur Légion d'honneur* of France. Li is known for his unassuming personal lifestyle, as he dresses simply and even sports a regular Seiko watch, though his home is in Deep Water Bay, one of Hong Kong's most expensive residential areas. An early riser, Li starts his day by playing golf with his friend and Hong Kong movie mogul Raymond Chow.

Lawrence R. SULLIVAN
Adelphi University

Further Reading

Chan, Anthony B. (1996). *Li Ka-Shing: Hong Kong's elusive billionaire.* Oxford, UK: Oxford University Press.

Singh, Sangeeta. (2009). Li Ka-shing. In Zhang Wenxian & Ilan Alon, (Eds.), *Biographical dictionary of new Chinese entrepreneurs and business leaders.* Northhampton, MA: Edward Elgar Publishing.

• Li Ka-shing •

♂ Lǐ Kèqiáng 李克强

b. 1955—Politician, premier of the PRC (2013–) and chair of the State Council

Alternate name: trad. 李克強

Summary

Li Keqiang rose from leadership positions in the Chinese Communist Youth League to ascend through the hierarchy of the Chinese Communist Party, serving as vice premier and then premier and chair of the State Council of the People's Republic of China. Promoting the idea of "overall reform" since coming into office, Li is known as a pragmatic reformer who aims to reduce corruption, pollution, and government waste, while building party discipline and instituting market reforms.

Li Keqiang is premier (2013–) and chair of the State Council (equivalent of the Cabinet) of the People's Republic of China (PRC). He was born in Dingyuan County, Anhui Province, in July 1955, the son of a midlevel provincial Chinese Communist Party (CCP) official, who joined the CCP in 1976. He was a "sent-down youth" during the latter part of the Cultural Revolution (1966–1976), when young people were removed from the cities and towns and sent to "learn" from peasants and workers, and spent four years (1974–1978) in the countryside of his native province. He used this experience to begin his career in the CCP and was chosen as party secretary of a production brigade.

Chinese Communist Youth League

Li reportedly rebuffed his father's efforts to groom him as a local party official. He was admitted to Peking University, China's most prestigious school, in 1978 and received a law degree four years later. He became a member of the Chinese Communist Youth League (CCYL), and most of his early jobs were connected with it. He was elected head of the student assembly in 1980 (he is, therefore, the only modern Chinese leader to win a competitive election), became secretary of the Peking University CCYL chapter in 1982, and worked his way up to first secretary of the CCYL by the early 1990s. In the CCYL he met *Hú Jǐntāo 胡锦涛 (b. 1942), who became his chief benefactor. While first secretary in the mid-1990s, Li served as president of the China Youth Political College and gained his doctorate in economics, studying under Li Yining, an early market reformer. He thus has benefited from membership in the CCYL throughout his career.

Government Career

Li began his government career as an official in Henan Province in central China. He served as deputy secretary and secretary of the provincial committee of the CCP and then as governor (1998–2004). As such, he was the youngest governor of the province and saw the provincial economy grow under his tenure, but he faced criticism for his slow response to the AIDS epidemic that swept the province. Many poor peasants had sold blood and had their plasma extracted and blood reinjected, and the resulting epidemic, caused by tainted blood and unhygienic practices, may have infected as many as a million people. Li cracked down on news media and AIDS activists that brought attention to the issue, yet he was accused of being indecisive by some of his CCP colleagues. He was then transferred to Liaoning Province in northeastern China, where

he served as secretary of the Liaoning CCP and chair of the Standing Committee of the Liaoning Provincial People's Congress (2003–2007). He was considered unlucky there due to a number of disasters, including major fires and coal mine explosions.

Li was selected as a member of the Standing Committee of the Politburo of the CCP Central Committee in 2007. The next year, he became a vice premier and was tasked with overseeing the Three Gorges Dam and South-to-North Water Diversion Construction Project. As vice chair of the Central Committee's "finance and economic leading small group," he is credited with helping Premier *Wēn Jiābǎo 温家宝 (b. 1942) guide the country through the 2008–2009 global financial crisis. Although President Hu promoted him as his successor for party secretary and president, these positions eventually went to *Xí Jìnpíng 习近平 (b. 1953), championed by *Jiāng Zémín 江泽民 (b. 1926) and the powerful Shanghai faction, instead. Li was again selected as a member of the Standing Committee of the Politburo in 2012 and was finally elevated to premier in March 2013.

Premiership, Governance, and Reform

Li is one of the leaders of the group on "Overall Reform" led by Xi Jinping and including Liú Yúnshān 刘云山 and Zhāng Gāolí 张高丽. Hong Kong reports indicated that he had appointed groups to

*People marked with an asterisk have entries in this dictionary.

Lǐ Kèqiáng

concentrate on six areas of reform: economy, environment, culture, democracy and law, party building, and party discipline.

Along with Xi, Li has staked out a clear reform agenda for his tenure. In his first annual policy speech in March 2014, he set the goals of greater market reforms, a 12.2 percent increase in military spending, reducing government waste, cutting urban smog by shuttering coal-fired industrial plants, cleaning up the nation's rivers, and advancing Xi's anti-corruption campaign. Li pledged that the economy would grow 7.5 percent in 2014, even though many forecasts expected a 7.3 percent rate. He departed from his script to promise a tough crackdown on terrorism after a horrific knife attack in Yunnan, apparently by Uygur separatists. In an obvious slap at Japan over historical issues and the recent Senkaku/Diaoyu Islands conflict (a territorial dispute over a group of islands between the two countries), Li said that China would "safeguard the victory of World War II and the postwar international order, and we will not allow anyone to reverse the course of history" (Xinhua 2014).

While not as ambitious as Wen Jiabao and his reform agenda, Li has apparently decided to focus on a few items, perhaps hoping that he will attain greater success than his predecessor. Wen was widely

Li Keqiang and his wife waving from their plane during a visit to Peru. Photo by Ministerio de Relaciones Exteriores.

viewed as pragmatic reformer, but he could not control the various CCP factions. Li had less experience than Wen as he came to power, and he is also struggling to gain control of the government. Reports in early 2014 suggested that Xi was consolidating his power at the expense of Li. Xi put together the CCP Third Plenum resolution in 2013, apparently by himself, and headed the Leading Group on deepening of reforms. Unlike Wen or *Zhū Róngjī 朱镕基 (b. 1928), the premier between 1998 and 2003, Li does not appear to be the leader on economic matters. Also, Li's welcoming dinner for the British prime minister, David Cameron, at the end of 2013 was canceled, partly due to tensions over visits by the Dalai Lama to the United Kingdom. (Li and Cameron did meet the next year in London.) Xi and Li nevertheless seem to be sharing diplomatic duties and visits abroad, like their predecessors.

Li is noted for his pointed intellect, mild temper, friendliness, and ability to convert enemies into friends. Many observers note that he displays a more cautious, less self-confident style than Xi, perhaps due to his more humble origins. In a US diplomatic cable released by WikiLeaks, he was called "engaging and well-informed on a wide range of issues," and had a "good sense of humor and appeared relaxed and confident." He also told US diplomats that he was very concerned about corruption and felt the best way to deal with it is to "create a transparent system of rules and adequate supervision that leaves corrupt officials no room to act" (Taylor 2012). He is reportedly the best English speaker among the top Chinese leaders and is said to be concerned about both the Chinese poverty and economic growth. Li's wife is a professor, and they have one daughter.

Joel R. CAMPBELL
Troy University

Further Reading

BBC News China. (2013, March 13). Profile: Li Keqiang . Retrieved October 25, 2014, from http://www.bbc.com/news/world-asia-china-19870221

Brookings Institution/John L. Thornton China Center. (2012). Li Keqiang: One of China's top future leaders to watch. Retrieved October 25, 2014, from http://www.brookings.edu/about/centers/china/top-future-leaders/li_keqiang

China Internet Information Center. (2012). Who's who in China's leadership. Retrieved October 25, 2014, from http://www.china.org.cn/english/MATERIAL/76257.htm

International Tibet Network. (2013). Chinese leaders. Retrieved October 25, 2014, from http://chinese-leaders.org/li-keqiang

Moore, Malcolm. (2013). Who is Li Keqiang? *Daily Telegraph*. Retrieved October 25, 2014, from http://blogs.telegraph.co.uk/news/malcolm-moore/100071283/who-is-li-keqiang/

Page, Jeremy; Davis, Bob; & Wei Lingling. (2013, December 20). Xi weakens role of Beijing's No. 2. *Wall Street Journal*. Retrieved October 26, 2014,

Lǐ Kèqiáng

from http://online.wsj.com/articles/SB10001424 0527023044777045792524938 57611618

Taylor, Adam. (2012, November 7). Here's what we know about the man everyone thinks will soon control China's economy. *Business Insider*. Retrieved October 26, 2014, from http://finance. yahoo.com/news/heres-know-man-everyone-thinks-224355227.html

Wong, Gillian. (2014, March 5). China vows tough reforms, stronger defense. *Washington Times*. Retrieved October 25, 2014, from http://www. washingtontimes.com/news/2014/mar/5/china-vows-tough-reforms-stronger-defense

Xi Jinping and Li Keqiang divide diplomacy like their predecessors. (2014, May 8). *China Times*. Retrieved December 30, 2014 from http://www. wantchinatimes.com/news-subclass-cnt. aspx?id=20140508000132&cid=1101

Xinhua. (2014, March 5). China vows to safeguard WWII victory. Retrieved May 2, 2015, from http:// www.chinadaily.com.cn/china/2014npcandcp pcc/2014-03/05/content_17323345.htm

Xinhua English News. (2013, March 15). Li Keqiang—premier of the State Council. Retrieved October 25, 2014, from http://news.xinhuanet.com/ english/china/2013-03-03/15/c_132236521.htm

李克强

♂ Lǐ Níng 李宁

b. 1963—Gymnast and founder of Li-Ning Company Ltd.

Alternate name: trad. 李寧

Summary

Known as the "Prince of Gymnastics," Li Ning is one of China's most well-known athletes. He won six of the seven gold medals at the Sixth Gymnastics World Cup in 1982, and then brought home six medals at the 1984 Olympic Games. After his retirement from professional gymnastics, he became a successful entrepreneur, founding his own sporting goods company called Li-Ning, and remains an active philanthropist in the sports arena.

Li Ning was a famous Olympic gymnast and is now a successful entrepreneur in China. He was born into a Zhuang minority family in Liuzhou, Guangxi Province, on 8 September 1963. His parents were teachers in Guilin, in southern China. Li Ning began practicing gymnastics at seven years old and joined the Guangxi provincial team at age ten. He was selected to be a member of the national gymnastics team in 1980 when he was seventeen. He won championships in floor exercise and pommel horse at the World University Games in 1981 and won six of the seven gold medals at the Sixth Gymnastics World Cup in 1982, becoming a gymnastics legend and earning the title of "Prince of Gymnastics" (Tǐcāo wángzǐ 体操王子).

Olympic Success

In 1984, at the Olympic Games in Los Angeles, Li Ning won gold medals in floor exercise, pommel horse, and rings; silver medals in the team all-around and the vault; and a bronze medal in the individual all-around. His success continued at the 1985, 1986, and 1987 World Championships and at the 1986 Seoul Asian Games. In 1987 he was selected as the only Asian member of the Athletes' Commission of the International Olympic Committee.

After the 1988 Olympic Games in Seoul, Li Ning retired from the national team because of an ankle injury, which caused his performance to suffer during the competition. In nineteen years as an athlete, he won a total of 106 gold medals at national and international competitions. He is an honorary member of the International Gymnastics Federation and was voted one of the "World's Most Excellent Athletes in the 20th Century" by the World Sports Correspondent Association (WSCA) in 1999. Li Ning was elected into the International Gymnastics Hall of Fame in 2000. A beloved and well-respected athlete in China, Li Ning was chosen to light the cauldron at the opening ceremony of the 2008 Summer Olympics in Beijing.

In it to Win it: Sports and the Olympic Games in China

The first modern Olympics in 1908 revived an ancient vigor for sporting competitions worldwide. Although China did not participate, for Zhāng Bólíng 張伯苓, who was visiting in London where the event was taking place, the Olympic Games sparked a deep respect for the principle upon which the competition rested—fair play. He taught the idea—and ideal—to his students back at Nankai University, which inspired China's journey to the Olympic Games. The nation's aspirations in future Olympic Games boiled down to three vital questions: When would China send its first athlete to the Olympics? When would one of their nation's athletes win the first gold medal? When would China host the Olympic Games?

The first two questions were answered within the century: in 1932, Liu Changchun went to the Olympics in Los Angeles; in 1984, sharpshooter Xu Haifeng won China's first gold medal. It wasn't until 2008 that China held the Olympics on its own soil. The lattermost achievement, which took place in Beijing, not only gave billions of Chinese citizens the chance to see their nation excel in sports, but also signified yet another landmark on China's road to modernization. As a result, the 2008 Beijing Olympics was one of the greatest national events of the twentieth and twenty-first centuries.

Especially in the Maoist era, between 1949 and 1976, China (like the rest of the world) believed sports played a critical role in politics and society. It was a method to show the superiority of socialism over capitalism. Since the 1980s, China's sporting success has evolved to incorporate its sense of ideological superiority and economic prosperity, as well as being an emblem of national resurgence. Every victory for a Chinese athlete is a victory for China as well.

Sources: Fan Hong. (2008). China's Olympic dream. In Fan Hong, Duncan Mackay, & Karen Christensen (Eds.), *China gold* (pp. ix–x). Great Barrington, MA: Berkshire Publishing Group.

Fan Hong. (2009). Olympic games—history. In Linsun Cheng (Ed.), *Berkshire encyclopedia of China* (pp. 1635–1641). Great Barrington, MA: Berkshire Publishing Group.

Business Career

Instead of becoming a coach after his retirement from gymnastics, Li Ning dedicated himself to business. At first, he worked as an assistant for the general manager at the Guangzhou-based soft drink producer Jianlibao Group Company Limited in 1989, which served as his introduction to the corporate world. Established in 1984, Jianlibao Group often sponsored sporting events during the 1990s, and the company supported Li as the main provider of his sportswear for the Eleventh Asian Games in 1990, a position that helped him found his own business, the Li-Ning Company Ltd., in Beijing later that year. The company mainly manufactures and sells sports and leisure footwear, apparel, accessories, and equipment in China. After two decades in operation, the company has become one of the leading sports brands in China: There are approximately eighty-five hundred exclusive shops, a retail network of more than six hundred thousand stores, and over two thousand outlets in 90 percent of mainland China. In addition, the company is continuously exploring overseas markets and developing its presence abroad.

Li Ning is dedicated to supporting sports-related and charitable causes at home and abroad. Since the 1992 Olympic Games in Barcelona, he has sponsored Chinese squads such as the table tennis, gymnastics, diving, and shooting teams so that they can attend major world tournaments. His company also provided footwear and apparel for professional athletes and teams abroad, both before and during the 2012 London Olympic Games, including the Argentina national basketball team, the US diving team, American high jumper Christian Taylor, Jamaican sprinter Asafa Powell, and Spanish basketball player Jose Calderon.

Li Ning featured on an Azerbaijani stamp (1996).

Li Ning established the Li Ning Foundation for the purpose of education, sport, and disaster relief, particularly aimed at providing sports facilities for schools in impoverished and remote areas and for people with disabilities. In addition, he supports retired Chinese athletes and coaches through the Chinese Athletes Education Foundation, which not only focuses on the educational needs of current athletes, but also on training retired athletes and coaches who are searching for new careers. In 2009 Li Ning was nominated by the United Nations World Food Programme (WFP) as China's first WFP Goodwill Ambassador against Hunger.

Just as Li Ning committed to developing himself as a gymnast, he committed to developing himself as a businessman. In 1998 he entered Peking University's law department and in 2004 he received his executive master of business administration from the Guanghua School of Management. Like the official slogans of his company, "Anything is Possible" and "Make the Change," Li Ning's life and career demonstrate the fundamental and lasting role sports played in changing his life and turning him from the "Prince of Gymnastics" into a successful business tycoon.

FAN Hong and LIU Li
The University of Western Australia

Further Reading

Le, Quinxi. (2013). Li Ning. In Song Yiwu (Ed.), *Biographical dictionary of the People's Republic of China* (pp. 178). Jefferson, NC: McFarland.

Li Ning—Prince of Gymnastics. (2009). Retrieved March 2, 2015, from http://www.china.org.cn/sports/characters/2009-09/11/content_18537780.htm

Li Yexin, & Zhou Junhong. (2010). *Li Ning: From Prince of Gymnastics to business tycoon.* Hangzhou: Zhejiang People's Press.

Official website of the Chinese Olympic Committee. (2003). Athlete Profile: Li Ning. Retrieved March 2, 2015, from http://en.olympic.cn/athletes/serch_L/2003-11-06/4683.html

Li-Ning Company Limited. (2014). Homepage. Retrieved March 2, 2015, from http://www.li-ning.com.cn/

Peking University Enrollment Information. (2014). Li Ning. Retrieved March 2, 2015, from http://www.gotopku.cn/index/detail/289.html

Sun, Sunny Li, & Quan, Martina Jing. (2009). Li Ning. In Zhang Wenxian, & Alon Ilan (Eds.), *Biographical dictionary of new Chinese entrepreneurs and business leaders* (pp. 84–85). Northampton, MA: Edward Elgar Publishing.

♂ Lǐ Péng 李鹏

b. 1928—Politician, premier of China (1987–1998)

Alternate name: trad. 李鵬

Summary

Li Peng was a protégé of Zhou Enlai, and a Party favorite who rose through the power sector to become premier of China (1987–1998) and chairman of the Standing Committee of the National People's Congress (1998–2003). Known as a conservative and a technocrat, Li took a hardline stance during the Tiananmen protests, following the bidding of more powerful elements in the Party.

Li Peng, the premier of China for over a decade, from 1987 to 1998, is likely to be remembered by history for his role in the Tiananmen Square Incident in June 1989. As head of the executive branch of the government at that time, Li had responsibility for day-to-day management of administration. It was in this role that he famously appeared at a meeting with leaders of the protesting students in the Great Hall of the People in Beijing in May. The image of him red-faced and angry, responding to some of the students' points with sour disdain has remained one of the strongest symbols of the mismatch between the two sides.

This view of him is almost certainly unrepresentative in as much as it imputes too much significance to his role. Li Peng was only the spokesperson and servant for far more powerful interests in the Party at this time, and ultimate responsibility for the tragedy of 1989 rests on the paramount leader, *Dèng Xiǎopíng 邓小平 (1904–1997). *The Tiananmen Papers* (2002), a compilation of "secret" official documents relating to the incident, which have dubious authenticity, are probably accurate when they portray a Li who was almost slavish in his solicitude to the senior leaders and who did what he could to keep them happy. While guilty of the crime of sycophancy, the

---

*People marked with an asterisk have entries in this dictionary.

Lǐ Péng

greater one of culpable slaughter has to be leveled elsewhere.

Early Life

Li was party aristocracy and fitted the model of technocrat down to the last detail. In that sense, he was more representative of the "third generation" leaders of China. Born on 20 October 1928 of Hakka ethnicity in Sichuan Province, southwest China, his father, the writer and Communist activist Lǐ Shuòxūn 李硕勋, was executed by the Nationalists when Li was three. A story grew up afterwards of Li being adopted by Zhōu Ēnlái 周恩来 (1898–1976), the first premier of the PRC, and his wife Dèng Yǐngchāo 邓颖超. Though it is hard to find evidence of an actual adoption, Li certainly enjoyed Zhou's patronage, and the link to one of the most admired and revered figures of revolutionary China served him well in his future career. Educated initially in natural sciences in the revolutionary base area of Yan'an, he joined the Party at age seventeen in 1945 and went to the Soviet Union to study engineering—something he has in common with many of the future political elite of his generation. He returned to China in 1955.

Career and Rise to Power

For the next three decades, Li was to work his way up the state enterprise leadership system in the power sector. He was an engineer and party administrator in the northeast of China from the 1950s up to the start of the Cultural Revolution when he moved to Beijing, where he was to spend the rest of his career. Li served in a number of positions in the power sector from 1966, seemingly unaffected by the purges and disruption visited on other figures around him. This culminated in him becoming the minister for the power industry in 1979 at the start of the Reform and Opening Up era (*gǎigé kāifàng* 改革开放). He moved to the State Education Commission as minister in 1983, and was appointed vice premier. Two years later, he joined the Politburo before being appointed premier in 1987 at the time of Party Secretary *Hú Yàobāng's 胡耀邦 (1915–1989) sidelining due to student protests that year and dissatisfaction with what were claimed to be his liberal leanings by the supposedly retired but still highly influential elder leaders around Deng.

Li Peng's role in the buildup to Tiananmen Square, and his part in the handling of the fall out, has been exhaustively studied. Although he has been categorized as a "hardliner," it is difficult to know what else might have been expected of a politician who had followed the most orthodox career path, and who had been a technocrat par excellence without any sign of real political imagination or flare. Declaring martial law in May 1989, Li put his name to the final orders to deal with the students by military intervention. To this day, the precise casualties are unknown. Li's close association with the event meant that he was never chosen to take up the top leadership position of party secretary.

That was given to *Jiāng Zémín 江泽民 (b. 1926), who had managed to handle matters as party head of Shanghai in such a way that there was no bloodshed in the city over this period, despite large demonstrations there.

Li was to prove to be deeply unpopular as a premier, someone largely avoided by foreign leaders and unwelcome abroad except under duress. There was also little real warmth towards him amongst people in China. The party secretary at the time, *Zhào Zíyáng 赵紫阳 (1919–2005), whom Li had worked with from 1987 to 1989, was put under house arrest for sixteen years but perhaps got the last word in, producing a highly unflattering portrait of Li in his memoirs smuggled out of China and published after his death in 2005. This may have prompted Li Peng himself to put pen to paper and produce memoirs that surfaced in Hong Kong in 2010–2011. The dry rendition of the correctness of the 1989 decision is unlikely to make these memoirs popular with historians, and they contain a largely defensive account, with few surprises and no revelations. Li's survival also means that a full reevaluation of the Tiananmen Square event by the modern leadership of the Party, most of whom have no link to it, has proved impossible.

From 1993 to 1998, Li served his second term as premier, though this time with the mandate to restart reforms after the Southern Tour of Deng Xiaoping in

Li Peng with Russian President Vladimir Putin in 2000. Photo by Russian Presidential Press and Information Office.

early 1992. Some commentators impute to him a supportive role in negotiations over China's entry into the World Trade Organization (WTO), though he probably did this through an awareness of how close the Party itself had come to collapsing in 1989 and how it needed to seek new forms of legitimacy and support through economic performance. This was pragmatism rather than penance. Li's public pronouncements were grimly formulistic, and the label "conservative" even in a very conservative system is probably deserved.

By 1998, with the need for a more imaginative and effective leadership, he was replaced by *Zhū Róngjī 朱镕基 (b. 1928), a far more palatable figure for the international community. From this period, Li stood as the second-ranking member of the Standing Committee of the Politburo, leading the National People's Congress. There was some irony in him being labeled China's chief lawmaker, when in fact he had been accused of riding roughshod over legality and due process only a decade before, during the student unrest. Li's tenure saw powerful opposition to the Three Gorges Plan, a project he personally supported, which managed to get record numbers of votes cast against it. The project went ahead, and will stand as perhaps his most significant physical contribution to China.

From his retirement in 2003, Li largely disappeared from public affairs, but managed to leave a continuing legacy in his children. With his wife Zhū Lín 朱琳, also a manager in the state energy sector in her early career, he has three children. *Lǐ Xiǎolín 李小琳 (b. 1961), his only daughter, is famous for being a major player to this day in the power sector, which has acquired enormous strategic and economic importance in China. His oldest son, Lǐ Xiǎopéng 李小鹏, was made vice governor of Shanxi Province in 2008 and governor in 2012.

Kerry BROWN
Lau China Institute, King's College

Further Reading

Li Peng. (2010). *Li Peng liusi riji zhenxiang* 李鹏六四记日真相 [Li Peng diary: The critical moments]. Macau: Au Ya Publishing.

Nathan, Adrew J.; Link, Perry E.; & Zhang Liang. (Eds.). (2002). *The Tiananmen Papers: The Chinese leadership's decision to use force against their own people—in their own words.* New York: PublicAffairs.

Mackerras, Colin; McMillen, Donald Hugh; & Watson, Donald Andrew. (1998). *Dictionary of the politics of the People's Republic of China* (p. 136). London: Routledge.

Sullivan, Lawrence R. (2007). Li Peng. In *Historical dictionary of the People's Republic of China* (pp. 316–317). Lanham, MD: Scarecrow Press.

Wang, James C. F. (1980). *Contemporary Chinese politics: An introduction.* Englewood Cliffs, NJ: Prentice Hall.

Wang, James C. F. (2002). Li Peng. In Pak-Wah Leung (Ed.), *Political leaders of modern China: A biographical dictionary* (pp. 86–88). Westport, CT: Greenwood Publishing Group.

♂ Lǐ Xiānniàn 李先念

1909–1992—Politician and central economic planner; president of the PRC (1983–1988)

Summary

Li Xiannian survived the most turbulent periods in the history of the Chinese Communist Party, and as president became a pillar of the Party establishment and a firm supporter of the state's central role in the economy. Opposed to many of the reforms that began during his term and lifetime, he is also known for his cautiousness and hardline stance against dissent.

Li Xiannian ranks as one of the great survivors of elite politics in the Chinese Communist Party (CCP) era. Someone who was able to survive the upheavals of the Cultural Revolution (1966–1976), the fall of the Gang of Four (who were ultimately blamed for the excesses of this period), and then the rise of *Dèng Xiǎopíng 邓小平 (1904–1997), he was to live on into the 1990s,

*People marked with an asterisk have entries in this dictionary.

associated with the "hardliners" who had authorized the military clampdown on the student demonstrators in Tiananmen Square in June 1989. Li was also one of the leaders with the longest membership in the Politburo, where he was continuously a member from the 1950s into the late 1980s.

Childhood and Early Years

Li, who had the most impeccable class background for a member of the CCP, was born on 23 June 1909 into a poor farming family in Hubei Province. A member of the Nationalist Party for only a year, in 1927 he was to join the rival Communists and become a military leader involved in the Long March over 1935–1936, when the Communists under Máo Zédōng 毛泽东 (1893–1976) fled from their southern base to the northern safe spot of Yan'an in Shanxi Province. Li had also been a guerilla leader back in his native Hubei, fighting against the Japanese in the Second Sino-Japanese

Li Xiannian in his Red Army uniform, 1937.

李先念

War (1937–1945), and was subsequently elected into the Central Committee of the Party.

A Career Through Tumultuous Times

With the 1949 Communist victory over the Nationalists after the three-year Chinese Civil War, Li was well placed to be appointed to a senior position and in 1952 became mayor of the major industrial center of Wuhan, Hubei's capital. Four years later, he was appointed to the Politburo, and in 1957 became minister

of finance, during the launch of the Great Leap Forward, with its ambitious plans to industrialize China to levels similar to the West in over a decade. The Great Leap Forward was to prove an immense failure and was followed by the famines of the early 1960s, which led to the premature deaths of up to forty million people. It was during this period that Li, already conversant in economic management from his work in the 1950s, worked with Liú Shàoqí 刘少奇 (1898–1969) and Deng Xiaoping, president and secretary general of the Communist Party then, to stabilize the economy and introduce reforms.

All of this was halted by the Cultural Revolution, beginning in 1966 with attacks on Liu and his allies, and their support for what were regarded as revisionist policies. Li was able to operate throughout this period, avoiding the brutal attacks launched against some of his colleagues, probably through his closeness to the veteran premier Zhōu Ēnlái 周恩来 (1898–1976). But he was sinuous enough to join in the attacks against Deng Xiaoping in 1976, just before Mao's death drew a line under the whole Cultural Revolution period and promoted Deng's own return to frontline politics.

Li's Later Years

Despite this attack on Deng only a few months earlier, Li was instrumental in approving and implementing the late

1976 removal of the Gang of Four, centered around Mao's wife, Jiāng Qīng 江青 (1914–1991). With their fall, Premier Huá Guófēng 华国锋 (1921–2008) and Deng were able to start initial reforms, which accelerated from 1978. Li was to serve as president from 1983 to 1987, but this was largely a ceremonial position that belied his influence behind the scenes.

His instincts as a hardline and orthodox supporter of the status quo came through in the manner in which he opposed reformists like *Hú Yàobāng 胡耀邦 (1915–1989), lobbying for his removal in 1987 as party leader. He then worked against *Zhào Zǐyáng 赵紫阳 (1919–2005), being part of the nominally retired leadership group around Deng who mandated the final clampdown of rebelling students in June 1989. Li was to subsequently strongly support the post-Tiananmen Square leader of the Party, *Jiāng Zémín 江泽民 (b. 1926), before his own death in 1992.

Influence and Legacy

Li was a pillar of the Party establishment throughout its history in rule, and a firm supporter of the state's role in the economy. He was far more wary of the sort of wholesale embrace of Western forms of economic management that were introduced after 1978, and in particular of the rise of a Chinese non-state sector and of deployment of foreign capital in the country's Special Economic Zones (SEZ, Jīngjì tèqū 经济特区). As president, while evidently dissatisfied with some of the reforms being implemented, he expressed only very moderate and careful reservations. It was cautiousness such as this that had managed to save him from the horrors reserved for many of the other leaders around him in the final Maoist decade.

Kerry BROWN
Lau China Institute, King's College

Further Reading

Brandt, Loren, & Rawski, Thomas G. (2008). *China's great economic transformation* (p. 102). Cambridge, UK: Cambridge University Press.

ChinaVitae. (2015). Li Xiannian. Retrieved April 8, 2015, from http://www.chinavitae.com/biography/Li_Xiannian|2534

Editorial Board. (2009). *Li Xiannian zhuan 1949–1992* 李先念传 1949–1992 [Biography of Li Xiannian, 1949–1992]. China: Central Documentary Press.

Law Yuk-fun. (2012). Li Xiannian. In Li Xiaobing (Ed.), *China at war: An encyclopedia* (pp. 226–227). Santa Barbara, CA: ABC-CLIO.

Li Xiannian 李先念. (1989). *Li Xiannian wenxuan* 李先念文选 [Collected works of Li Xiannian]. Beijing: People's Press.

♀ Lǐ Xiǎolín 李小琳

b. 1961—Business executive and daughter of former premier Li Peng

Summary

A major executive in the state power sector since the 1990s, Li Xiaolin has been criticized for profiting from her father's eminence as former premier of China. One of the Party "princelings" largely resented by the Chinese public, Li maintains a low profile within the country, working behind the scenes, and wielding much influence in the energy industry.

Typifying the phenomenon known as "princelings" in China, Li Xiaolin became a major player in the power sector from the 1990s as someone whose main prominence was due to being the daughter of former premier *Lǐ Péng 李鹏 (b. 1928), a man associated with the Tiananmen Square Incident of 1989, in which he had been a major influence.

*People marked with an asterisk have entries in this dictionary.

People like Li Xiaolin aroused as much resentment as awe at the ways in which they were able to leverage their family backgrounds not just for political and social capital, but for real financial returns. Li has maintained a low profile, however, and figured more in foreign press than in the domestic news, where her power remains discreet and behind-the-scenes.

Childhood and Early Education

Li enjoyed the full benefits of an elite background, born in 1961 in Beijing and subsequently educated in power engineering at Tsinghua University. She chose a timely subject to major in, given that as China's economy picked up in the 1980s and 1990s, its energy needs shot through the roof. Coal plants in particular were constructed across the country to power the new factories and the cities being built as China's economic model changed. Li's involvement in the state power sector culminated in her appointment as chief executive officer of China Power International Development Ltd. in 2004, and of its holding company. She is also the vice president for China Power Investment Corporation. In both of these positions, she was in charge of state companies running enormous state monopolies. Unsurprisingly, she soon became spoken of as one of the wealthiest individuals in the country.

In an interview in 2007, Li claimed that her successful career had nothing to do with her relationship with her father.

Anti-corruption Campaigns in Modern China

Anti-corruption campaigns against key players in the Chinese political system were put into effect under the *Xí Jìnpíng 习近平 (b. 1953) administration starting in 2012, a revitalization of past efforts to root out officials who took advantage of their positions in government. Already responsible for the capturing of several thousand officials in the People's Republic of China (PRC), the current campaign has taken its slogan—"killing tigers and swatting flies" 苍蝇和老虎一起打—very seriously, capturing small-scale officials (flies) as well as the more important lawmakers (tigers). One of the most notable officials ensnared by this crackdown is *Zhōu Yǒngkáng 周永康, who was a member of the Politburo Standing Committee, and the secretary of the Central Political and Legal Affairs Commission—in other words, a tiger. In December 2014, he was expelled from the Chinese Communist Party and arrested, making him the most senior official to be indicted since Liu Qingshan and Zhang Zishan, who were victims of the 1950s crackdowns.

The end of March 2015 saw further developments on the quest towards anti-corruption: the campaign began its search beyond the PRC borders, turning toward the United States, where it was rumored that 150 officials could be hiding. Though seemingly extensive compared to previous campaigns, president Xi Jinping believes this to be necessary in re-establishing authority. The CCP, with over 90 million members, lost much of its grip on local governments that struck deals with businesses to increase their profits—thus sacrificing the well-being of Chinese citizens, causing widespread unrest and protests. A decelerating economy has not helped matters, either.

• Lǐ Xiǎolín •

Underneath the vendetta against corruption, however, lies an important distinction in Xi's methods: instead of reforming the structure of the government itself, and exploring options beyond its one-party system, Xi is directing the reform towards the people who help run the country. Though originally modeled after Xunzi 荀子, a second-century BCE Confucian philosopher, the rigorous measures of the current campaign draws speculation from outside the country, leaving other governments wondering if it is the most efficient way to boost China's position in modern politics.

Eliza J. MITCHELL—*Berkshire Publishing Group*

Sources: Keliher, Macabe, & Wu, Hsinchao. (2015, April 7). How to discipline 90 million people. The Atlantic. Retrieved July 6, 2015, from http://www.theatlantic.com/international/archive/2015/04/xi-jinping-china-corruption-political-culture/389787/

Dillon, Michael. (2015). Zhou Yongkang. In Kerry Brown (Ed.), Dictionary of Chinese biography (vol. 4). Great Barrington, MA: Berkshire Publishing Group.

李小琳 •

Even so, netizens inside and outside China were keen to point out her expensive wardrobe and ostentatious displays of wealth, even mocking her when she appeared at a meeting of the Chinese People's Political Consultative Conference in a dress estimated to be worth over US$2,000. Her complaint in an interview that her greatest regret was not having more than one child also attracted ridicule. In light of China's One Child Policy, families are generally only allowed to have one child, but with enough financial means richer families easily manage to "buy" privileges for the second child that poorer families could never afford.

More seriously, she was connected to a deal in the mid 1990s that allowed Zurich Insurance to gain access into China for reportedly massive payments into offshore accounts. These came to light during US investigations, and were connected to a school-mate of Li's, who, it was claimed, had been persuaded by her to help the company in return for unspecified financial inducements.

More ominously, the power sector became a target of the sustained anti-corruption campaign beginning in 2013, after President *Xí Jìnpíng 习近平 (b. 1953) came to power. This, and her links to a father who was so contentious, stirred talk by some that she might be a potential target for the campaign, though it was unlikely this would happen while her father was still alive. Li remains representative of party aristocracy largely resented by the Chinese public, but feted

Li Xiaolin at the Fortune Global Forum in 2013. She was part of a discussion about Connecting with Women in an Emerging World. Photo by Fortune Live Media.

by some business people inside and outside China.

Kerry BROWN
Lau China Institute, King's College

Further Reading

Chen, Shu-Ching Jean. (2008). China's power queen. Retrieved April 8, 2015, from http://www.forbes.com/2008/01/03/li-xiaolin-china-face-markets-cx_jc_0103autofacescan01.html

Huang, Nellie. (2004). Li Xiaolin, star power. *Time* Asia edition.

Lam, Willy Wo-Lap. (2007). The traits and political orientation of China's fifth-generation leadership. In Joseph Y. S. Cheng (Ed.), *Challenges and policy programmes of China's new leadership* (pp. 35–62). Hong Kong: City University of HK Press.

Shankar, Sneha. (2015). Li Xiaolin, former Chinese Premier Li Peng's daughter, hid over $2M in HSBC Swiss account. Retrieved April 8, 2015, from http://www.ibtimes.com/li-xiaolin-former-chinese-premier-li-pengs-daughter-hid-over-2m-hsbc-swiss-account-1811000

Staff reporter. (2012). Chairwoman Li Xiaolin inherits power, creates her own. Retrieved April 8, 2015, fromhttp://www.wantchinatimes.com/news-subclass-cnt.aspx?id=20120409000045&cid=1601

♂ Lǐ Yànhóng 李彦宏

b. 1968—Chinese Internet entrepreneur, co-founder of Baidu

Alternate names: Robin Li; trad. 李彦宏

Summary

Li Yanhong is a Chinese Internet entrepreneur. He studied information management in China and the United States and co-founded the Chinese search engine Baidu in 2000. Li has been CEO of Baidu since January 2004.

Li (Robin) Yanhong was born on 17 November 1968 to an ordinary family in Yangquan, Shanxi Province. As a child he loved theater so much that he joined the local Jin Drama Troupe. By his high school days, however, he had decided to return to his normal schoolwork, at which he also excelled. In 1987 Li was admitted to Peking University to study information management after scoring first in his home district on the tough National College Entrance Examination (generally known as the *gāokǎo* 高考).

Education and Early Career

After Li graduated from Peking University, he continued his education in the Computer Science Department of the State University of New York at Buffalo. He had classes during the day and studied English or wrote computer programs at night. After just over a year at the school, Li got an internship at Panasonic. "It was a vital experience of the three-month internship to decide my later career," Li later said.

In the summer of 1994, Li received a job offer from the Wall Street firm Dow Jones. Li stated:

At the end of the internship, my achievement of studies had gained the appreciation from this area's most authoritative people, and the relevant papers had been published in the industry's most authoritative journals. These would be very helpful for my later Ph.D. dissertation...but at that time, there was a trend with Chinese students: a Ph.D. student would give up his studies once he found a job. At first, I didn't think

I would be like this. But my company boss, who was also a technical expert, influenced me. I decided to leave school and to accept the position of the company, as a senior consultant.

During his three and a half years on Wall Street, Li was responsible for designing the *Wall Street Journal*'s online real-time financial information system. He invented the so-called "Hyperlink Analysis" technology, which was awarded a patent. The full name of his invention is the Hyperlink Vector Voting method (HVV), a way to "rank" a website based on how often other sites link to it. This technology would become one of the foundational inventions for the development of the modern search engine. In 1997, Li left Wall Street and moved to Silicon Valley in California for a position with the famous search engine company Infoseek.

Silicon Valley and Baidu

During his time in the Silicon Valley, Li gained an appreciation for the business world. He often read the *Wall Street Journal* to learn how Microsoft competed against its rivals such as IBM, Sun Microsystems, and Netscape. He began to realize that "the technology itself is not the only decisive factor, but the business strategy is the real bread and butter."

During Li's eight years abroad, great changes were happening in China's Internet industry. Li was an avid observer of these changes and returned home every year to investigate business opportunities. Finally, in 1999 he decided that the timing was right. He returned to China, and he and his partner, Eric Xu, rented two rooms at the Resource Hotel near Peking University, along with five technicians and one accountant. The eight of them began to create Baidu Inc. Li quickly attracted the company's first venture investment of US$1.2 million. Nine months later, after the launch of Baidu, venture investment company Draper Fisher Jurvetson, along with the International Data Group, sent over US$10 million.

In the first couple of years after its founding, Baidu, like many Chinese Internet startups, struggled to find its

Lǐ Yànhóng

The Internet in China

In 2008, China had 253 million Internet users, surpassing the United States' total of 223 million users. Though Internet users made up only about 23 percent of China's population, compared to 73 percent in the United States, this marked China's ascent to the largest Internet country in the world. As a result of the rapid increase in Internet use, Chinese became the second Internet language after English.

Five years later, in 2013, not only were there about half a billion Internet users in China, but more than a billion mobile phone users as well. China has become one of the largest markets in the world for iOS and Android activations, and has been influential in manufacturing groundbreaking technologies for items such as the iPhone and the iPad. Lenovo, a Chinese technology company, became the world's third largest computer manufacturer almost as soon as it bought out IBM's personal computer division in 2005.

Even though Internet use has increased, it is still mainly accessed in urban areas. In general, citizens use it to read the news; download entertainment like music and movies; play games; and communicate with family members, friends, and colleagues. Blogging and social media have also grown in popularity. By 2012, the number of bloggers in China reached to about a third of a billion. Despite the large number of social and education outlets found on the Internet, however, a 2007 CNIP report revealed that 70 percent of those who took the survey in China believed that only a small portion of the information found online was reliable.

In light of the developments and setbacks that the Internet has seen in China, including Internet censorship and the infamous "Great Firewall", the country will still continue to have a massive influence when it comes to users worldwide. In fact, in the near future, Chinese characters will likely become a common sight in global URLs.

Eliza J. MITCHELL—*Berkshire Publishing Group*

Sources: Kluver, Randolph. (2014). Introduction. In Ashely Esarey & Randolph Kluver (Eds.), *The Internet in China: Cultural, political, and social dimensions (1980s–2000s)* (pp.1–3). Great Barrington, MA: Berkshire Publishing Group.

Christensen, Karen, & Guo Liang. (2009). Internet use. In Linsun Cheng (Ed.), *Berkshire encyclopedia of China* (vol. 3, pp.1179–1182). Great Barrington, MA: Berkshire Publishing Group.

identity and business model. In 2001 Li suggested to the board that Baidu should focus on creating an independent search engine and nothing else. This meant that the company would move away from its profitable business of providing technical service support for portal websites. The board resisted. Legend has it that it was Li's anger and attitude that finally got the board to agree with him. Since then, Baidu has been synonymous with the term "search engine" in China. A mere five years later, Baidu has become the world's second largest independent search engine and the largest Chinese-language search engine. Baidu's success also makes China one of only four countries in the world with search engine core technology, the other three being the United States, Russia, and South Korea. Successfully listed on NASDAQ in 2005, Baidu was the first Chinese company to trade its stocks on Wall Street. At present, Baidu is one of China's most valuable brand names.

Recognition and Significance

The success of Baidu not only has made Robin Li a wealthy man (he was ranked the second-richest man in mainland China with a net worth of US$12 billion as of December 2013), but also has brought him great honors and recognitions. In 2013, Li was appointed a member of the twelfth session of the Chinese People's Political Consultative Conference National Committee, vice chairman of the Eleventh National Federation of Industry and Commerce, and vice chairman of the Eighth Beijing Association for Science and Technology, as well as the global member of the United Nations Program on HIV/AIDS and the UN's public welfare ambassador of environmental protection.

In addition to these accolades, Robin Li has been actively involved in the future of Baidu. In 2015, Baidu made great strides in artificial intelligence and machine learning. On 13 May 2015, the company announced a new super computer whose software improved upon fields like speech, image, and language recognition. The company has also been working on driverless cars, with a release date sometime before the end of the same year. With innovations like these, Baidu has been pushing China to the forefront of scientific development, becoming a global influence in the future of technology.

QIN Ling
Sichuan University

Further Reading

Greenberg, Andy. (2009, October 5). The man who's beating Google. *Forbes Magazine*. Retrieved March 2, 2015, from http://www.forbes.com/forbes/2009/1005/technology-baidu-robin-li-man-whos-beating-google.html

Forbes.com (2010). #258 Robin Li. Retrieved May 3, 2014 from http://www.forbes.com/lists/2010/10/billionaires-2010_Robin-Li_XXXJ.html

MBAlib. (2012). Li Yanhong 李彦宏 [Li Yanhong]. Retrieved March 2, 2015 from http://wiki.mbalib.com/wiki/%E6%9D%8E%E5%BD%A6%E5%AE%8F

• Lǐ Yànhóng •

Taipei Times. (2006, September 17). Robin Li's vision powers Baidu's Internet search dominance. Retrieved March 2, 2015, from http://www.taipeitimes.com/News/bizfocus/archives/2006/09/17/2003328060

Li Yanhong. (1998). Toward a qualitative search engine. *IEEE Internet Computing*, 2(4), pp. 24–29. doi:10.1109/4236.707687

Watts, Jonathan. (2005). Interview: Robin Li, founder of Baidu.com. *The Guardian*. Retrieved March 2, 2015, from http://www.theguardian.com/technology/2005/dec/08/piracy.news

University of Buffalo Computer Science and Engineering. (2015). Alumni Profiles. Retrieved March 2, 2015, from http://www.cse.buffalo.edu/alumni/alumni_profiles.php

CCTV. (2006). Robin Li: Pioneer of China's information superhighway. Retrieved March 2, 2015, from http://english.cctv.com/program/upclose/20051226/100722.shtml

Shoham, Amir, & Zhang Wenxian. (2006). Li Yanhong. In Ilan Alon & Wenxian Zhang. *Entrepreneurial and business elites of China: The Chinese returnees who have shaped modern China* (pp. 85–87). Bingley, UK: Emerald Group Publishing.

♂ Li, Jet

Lǐ Liánjié 李连杰

b. 1963—Martial arts champion and actor

Alternate names: Cantonese: Li Nin Kit or Lee Nin Git; producer pseudonym: Li Yangzhong 李阳中; trad. 李連杰

Summary

As a global martial arts icon active in both Chinese-language and Hollywood films, Jet Li is one of the most recognizable Chinese celebrities in contemporary cinema. Li's long career is reflective of decades of cinematic change in the People's Republic of China, Hong Kong, and the United States. Li founded the One Foundation Project in 2007, and his philanthropic acts are inspired by his strong belief in Buddhism.

Jet Li's accomplished international career spans many fields, generations, and cultures. In the 1970s, Li was a highly acclaimed martial arts athlete in China and performed globally on diplomatic goodwill tours. By the early 1980s, Li became the first People's Republic of China–born transnational movie star after the post-Mao revival of martial arts films. While government control over job arrangements initially limited Li's career choices, Chinese economic reforms later allowed Li to immigrate to the United States and advance his career during the late 1980s. During the 1990s, Li's acting career flourished in Hong Kong, which helped him break onto the Hollywood scene. To this day he remains an international superstar active in both Chinese-language and Hollywood films.

Early Life and Education

Jet Li was born in Beijing on 26 April 1963 and was two years old when his father died, which left his mother, a bus-ticket collector, to single-handedly raise him and his older siblings, two brothers and two sisters, on a low income. At the age of eight, Li enrolled in the Beijing Amateur Sports School 北京业余体育运动学校, where he was chosen to practice *wǔshù* 武术, a form of traditional Chinese martial arts standardized for modern competitive sports under Wu Bin.

As a member of the Beijing Wushu Team, Li traveled internationally from 1974 to 1979, demonstrating wushu on goodwill tours. Some of these goodwill tours aimed to ease the tense international relations between the People's Republic of China (PRC) and Western countries, particularly between China and the United States.

By the end of the 1974 goodwill tour in the United States, Li's patriotic perspective, which reflected his absorption of Maoist ideologies, had changed drastically. Contrary to the PRC's negative representation of capitalism, which reinforced Li's expectations of a miserable and corrupt capitalist society, Li witnessed individuals acting with kindness and he also became aware of their material abundance. Li later described the tour as an eye-opening experience and a significant turning point in his life, which caused him to doubt his education and begin to think more independently (Voice of America 2012).

Shaolin Temple

Li's acting debut came in the 1982 PRC-Hong Kong co-production *Shaolin Temple* 少林寺. During this time many Hong Kong filmmakers were prohibited from filming in the mainland, but the PRC government viewed Cheung Yam-yim as a political leftist—that is, supportive of communism—and granted him exclusive filming rights.

Cheung shot *Shaolin Temple* in the Shaolin monastery in northern China, known as the cradle of Chinese martial arts, with Li as the film's protagonist. Cheung's use of long shots and long takes captured Li's exceptional wushu skills with a sense of realism and authenticity, which greatly contributed to the film's transnational success in East and Southeast Asia.

As a result of the Maoist era's ban on martial arts films (1949–1976), the domestic film audience had not seen a martial arts film in decades and found *Shaolin Temple* riveting. *Shaolin Temple* had a sensational box-office run, which resulted in a martial arts and Shaolin craze. The success of the film marked the beginning of a revival of the martial arts film genre and turned Li into the first PRC-born transnational movie star.

In Li's account of his experiences at the start of career, he recalls a great deal of physical pain and mental pressure instead of the glory of his accomplishments. Shortly after *Shaolin Temple* was released, Li broke his leg during training and Li's doctor warned him that continuing with his demanding wushu routines and rigorous practices could result in lifelong paralysis.

Aside from physical complications, Li was growing increasingly frustrated by the state-imposed restrictions on his career. Like the majority of urban citizens, Li was employed under the *dānwèi* 单位, or state-organized work unit system. His work unit, the Beijing Wushu Team, had nearly full control over every aspect of his career, from job arrangements to transfer possibilities. Initially, Li enjoyed significant privileges in the system. As an outstanding national

李连杰

athlete, his monthly salary of 88 yuan (about US$44) was at a state maximum usually reserved for professors and senior engineers. The sum, however, was nowhere near the exorbitant figure of six million yuan (about US$3 million) that a Hong Kong studio executive offered Li for starring in two films after his performance in *Shaolin Temple*. Li, however, was unable to accept the offer because of state restrictions and the regulations of his work unit.

Shaolin Sequels

After his injury, Li was no longer able to participate in competitive sports, and the Beijing Wushu Team loaned him on a five-year contract to a Hong Kong–based production company, the Sil-Metropole Organisation Ltd. 银都机构有限公司. Li had no choice but to accept the terms of the contract.

The Sil-Metropole featured Li in two sequels of *Shaolin Temple*: *Shaolin Kids* 少林小子 (1984) and *Martial Arts of Shaolin* 南北少林 (1986), both of which were filmed in mainland China. For these two films, Li was paid two and three yuan per day of filming (about US$1), respectively. Li knew that his earnings were a pittance by Hong Kong standards and a mere fraction of what the Beijing Wushu Team earned from his work: 50,000 yuan (about US$25,000) for each film. During the making of *Martial Arts of Shaolin*, Li experienced and witnessed infuriating disparities in income and treatment between Hong Kong and PRC cast and crew members.

As a result of his frustrations and hardships, Li nearly quit acting after *Martial Arts of Shaolin*. In an effort to persuade him to stay, however, the Sil-Metropole offered him the chance to direct a film. Li used this opportunity to produce a film that articulated his critique of the systematic and social discrimination against PRC citizens. Aware of the PRC's penchant for censorship, however, he avoided controversy by setting the film, called *Born to Defend* 中华英雄 (1986), in an earlier period during the Republic of China. The film starred Li as a Chinese veteran fighting against the occupation of Qingdao by the United States after the Second Sino-Japanese War (1937–1945). Li's character challenges the authority of the Chinese government, whose alliance with the United States results in the unjust treatment of Chinese citizens. Li later acknowledged that his resentment negatively affected his skills as a director and the quality of the storytelling. Moreover, Li's wushu performance, which used to captivate audiences, was no longer considered novel. The film was a box-office flop and considered a failure by both critics and Li himself, and he never directed again.

Hong Kong Films

In 1988, Li's five-year loan to the Sil-Metropole ended and economic reforms in the PRC loosened the state's control

Selected Filmography of Jet Li				
Year	**English Title**	**Chinese Title**	**Director**	**Notes**
1982	*Shaolin Temple*	少林寺 *Shàolín sì*	Cheung Yam-yim	Role: Chieh Yuan
1984	*Shaolin Temple: Shaolin Kids*	少林小子 *Shàolín xiǎozǐ*	Cheung Yam-yim	Role: San Lung
1986	*Martial Arts of Shaolin*	南北少林 *Nánběi Shàolín*	Lau Kar-Leung	Role: Zhi Ming
1986	*Born to Defend*	中华英雄 *Zhōnghuá yīngxióng*	Jet Li	Role: Jet
1989	*Dragon Fight*	龙在天涯 *Lóng zài tiānyá*	Lo Wei	Role: Jimmy Lee
1989	*The Master*	龙行天下 *Lóng háng tiān xià*	Tsui Hark	Role: Jet
1991	*Once Upon a Time in China*	黄飞鸿 *Huáng Fēihóng* (Cantonese: *Wong Fei-hung*)	Tsui Hark	Role: Wong Fei-Hung
1992	*Once Upon a Time in China II*	黄飞鸿之男儿当自强 *Huáng Fēihóng zhī nán'ér dāng zìqiáng* (Cantonese: *Wong Fei Hung II: Nam yee tung chi keung*)	Tsui Hark	Role: Wong Fei-Hung
1993	*The Legend*	方世玉 *Fāngshì yù* (Cantonese: *Fong sai yuk*)	Corey Yuen	Role: Fong Sai Yuk
1994	*Fist of Legend*	精武英雄 *Jīng wǔyīng xióng*	Gordon Chan	Role: Chen Zhen
1998	*Lethal Weapon 4*		Richard Donner	Role: Wah Sing Ku

Year	English Title	Chinese Title	Director	Notes
2000	*Romeo Must Die*		Andrzej Bartkowiak	Role: Han Sing
2001	*Kiss of the Dragon*		Chris Nahon	Role: Liu Jian
2001	*The One*		James Wong	Role: Gabe Law/Gabriel Yulaw/ Lawless
2002	*Hero*	英雄 *Yīngxióng*	Zhang Yimou	Role: Nameless
2007	*The Warlords*	投名状 *Tóumíng zhuàng* (Cantonese: *Tau ming chong*)	Peter Chan	Role: General Pang Qingyun
2010	*Ocean Heaven*	海洋天堂 *Hǎiyáng tiāntáng*	Xue Xiaolu	Role: Wang Xingchang
2010	*The Expendibles*		Sylvester Stallone	Role: Yin Yang

over his career. Li managed to leave his work unit for a private company, and soon after he immigrated to the United States as a wushu trainer. He was invited back to the Hong Kong film industry by director Lo Wei 罗维 and starred in *Dragon Fight* 龙在天涯 (1989), which told the story of a PRC wushu athlete turned American immigrant. *Dragon Fight* was not a commercial success, but it led to Li's employment by Golden Harvest 嘉禾, a major Hong Kong film studio. During his time at Golden Harvest, Li worked with Tsui Hark 徐克, an innovative and experimental director.

Li and Tsui first worked together on *The Master* 龙行天下, a low-budget film that was produced in 1989 but not released until after the positive reception of their second film, *Once Upon a Time in China* 黄飞鸿 (1991), which starred Li as the folk hero Wong Fei-hung (Huáng Fēihóng 黄飞鸿). In this film, Li abandoned his realistic wushu performance style for extravagant gravity-defying stunts and action sequences made possible by wire work. The film revived Li's celebrity status, and from 1992 to 1998 Li made seventeen films in Hong Kong. During this period of Li's prolific career, Li played various martial arts and action heroes in films set in ancient and modern times. To audiences of Chinese-language films, Li was indisputably one of the greatest icons of martial arts cinema.

The second wave of Li's high-profile celebrity career, however, was riddled with conflicts, just as the first wave had been. In 1992, Li had issues with the terms of his contract and fought with Golden Harvest and his manager, David Lo 罗大卫. In protest, he stopped acting during the production of *Once Upon a Time in China II* 黄飞鸿之男儿当自强 (1992) and changed his manager to Jim Choi 蔡子明. Under Choi's guidance, Li forced Golden Harvest to accept his conditions and agreed to return for his role in *Once Upon a Time in China II*. On 16 April 1992, Choi was mysteriously assassinated and Li felt threatened by these circumstances.

Global Icon

In desperate need of taking control over his own life and career, in 1992 Li launched his own production company, Eastern Production Ltd. 正东制作有限公司, with the support of Hong Kong producer Chui Bo-Chu 崔宝珠 and Taiwanese investor Yang Teng-Kuei 杨登魁. In 1993, Eastern released its first film, *The Legend* 方世玉, which starred Li as the main character and credited him as the producer under the pseudonym Li Yangzhong. *The Legend* was a box-office hit, and in 1993 and 1994

Li produced and acted in five more films under Eastern.

In one of the five films, *Fist of Legend* 精武英雄 (1994), Li cut back on his use of wire work, refocusing on realistic displays of diverse styles of martial arts and hoping the change could attract a wider audience. While the film was not as successful as expected in Asia, it became a cult favorite among many Western viewers, including American directors Quentin Tarantino and the Wachowski Brothers, who believed that it best captured Li's mastery of martial arts. With celebrity fans and endorsement, Li was able to begin a new stage of his career in Hollywood.

While Li was a highly acclaimed pan-Asian movie star, he was nearly unheard of in the West and began his Hollywood career as a relative unknown. Used to playing the heroic protagonist, Li found limited opportunities in Hollywood. He attended a competitive audition for a supporting role as a villain in *Lethal Weapon 4* (1998), and while he got the part he had to accept a final offer that was half of the promised payment. Li's Hollywood debut was well-received, and this marked a change in his Hollywood fortunes. In 2000 and 2001 he starred as the action hero in *Romeo Must Die* and *Kiss of the Dragon*. In the science fiction film *The One* (2001), Li played both the hero and the villain in the form of two variations of the same character in alternate universes.

Jet Li shows his talents on the set of the 2001 thriller *Kiss of the Dragon*. Photo by Maya Chow.

The martial arts epic *Hero* 英雄 (2002), directed by *Zhāng Yìmóu 张艺谋 (b. 1951), marked the start of Li's fourth and current career development. *Hero* was Li's first-ever collaboration with a PRC director. Since then, Li has been acting in both Hollywood films and Chinese-language cinema, which has seen the distinctions between PRC, Hong Kong, and Taiwanese films become increasingly blurred. Li has become a true global icon of martial arts and action. *Hero* was also Li's first experience working with a director recognized as an art-house auteur. Li's later films, *The Warlords* 投名状 (2007) and *Ocean Heaven* 海洋天堂 (2010), broadened his repertoire, proving Li capable of performing complex characters contrary to his usual action roles with little psychological depth. In *The Warlords*, Chan and Li endeavored to bridge high art with marketable filmmaking. Xue's *Ocean Heaven* was a noncommercial production made to raise awareness of autism. Li did not take any payment for making the film, and his role as a terminally ill father of an autistic child was his first that did not involve fighting. Li's most recent film was *The Expendables 3* (2014).

---

*People marked with an asterisk have entries in this dictionary.

Citizenship and Family

Li forfeited his PRC citizenship after immigrating to the United States. According to media reports, in 2009 he changed his citizenship to Singaporean. In 1987, Li married a fellow martial artist, Huáng Qiūyān 黄秋燕, with whom he has two daughters, Sī 思 and Tāimì 苔蜜. They divorced in 1990, and in 1999 Li married actress Nina Li 利智, with whom he also has two daughters, Jane and Jada. When Nina Li was pregnant, Li turned down the main role in the Oscar-winning *Crouching Tiger, Hidden Dragon* (2000), which went to *Chow Yun-fat 周潤發 (b. 1955).

Religion and Philanthropy

Li became a Buddhist in 1997 and has met with eminent Buddhist figures, such as master Sheng-Yen 圣严法师 and the fourteenth Dalai Lama. In 2004, Li and his family were vacationing in the Maldives when a devastating tsunami struck. They faced life-threatening danger but fortunately were not seriously injured. That same year Li had another near-death experience when he suffered from altitude sickness while vacationing in Tibet. From these experiences, he gained a profound understanding of the Buddhist concept of impermanence (*wúcháng* 无常), which inspired him to further explore the meaning of life through philanthropy.

In 2007, Li founded the One Foundation Project, which was formerly affiliated with the Chinese Red Cross but became an independent charity in 2010. Using the slogan "1 person + 1 dollar + 1 month = 1 big family," the One Foundation amasses small individual donations for large worldwide philanthropic projects. It is one of the most recognizable charities in China today.

Zhuoyi WANG
Hamilton College

Further Reading

Burr, Martha. (2001). The big Jet Li interview. *Kungfu qigong*. Retrieved July 5, 2015, from http://www.kungfumagazine.com/magazine/article.php?article=143

Farquhar, Mary. (2010). Jet Li: "Wushu master" in sport and film. In Elaine Jeffreys & Louise Edwards (Eds.), *Celebrity in China* (pp. 103–123). Hong Kong: Hong Kong University Press.

Hunt, Leon. (2003). *Kung fu cult masters: From Bruce Lee to Crouching Tiger*. London/New York: Wallflower.

Li, Jet. (n.d.). Jet Li's notes on *Shaolin Temple* and *Born to Defense* (Originally published but no longer available at the official Jet Li website: Jetli.com.). Retrieved November 7, 2014, from https://www.facebook.com/VerifiedJetLiFansite/notes

Li, Jet 李连杰. (2007). Luyu youyue 鲁豫有约 [A date with Luyu]. Phoenix Television.

Li, Jet 李连杰. (2009). Li Lianjie: Wode 2008 李连杰：我的 2008 [Jet Li: My 2008]. Phoenix Television.

Liao Xiaodong 廖小东. (2006). *Li Lianjie zhuan* 李连杰传 [Biography of Li Lianjie]. Wuhan, China: Hubei renmin chubanshe.

Major, Wade. (2000). The afterburner. In Stefan Hammond (Ed.), *Hollywood East: Hong Kong movies and the people who made them* (pp. 149–175). Chicago: Contemporary Books.

Marx, Christy. (2002). *Jet Li*. New York: Rosen Publishing Group.

Phoenix Television. (2009). Dujia zhuanfang Li Lianjie: Wo xue fo de zhenshi yuanyin 独家专访李连杰：我学佛的真实原因 [An exclusive interview with Jet Li: My true reason for studying Buddhism].

Stringer, Julian. (2003). Talking about Jet Li: Transnational Chinese movie stardom and Asian American Internet reception. In Gary D. Rawnsley & Ming-Yeh T. Rawnsley (Eds.), *Political communications in greater China: The construction and reflection of identity* (pp. 275–290). London/New York: RoutledgeCurzon.

Voice of America. (2012). Li Lianjie huigu meizhongwenhua jiaoliu 李连杰回顾美中文化交流 [Li Lianjie's recollections on the China-United States cross-cultural communications]. Retrieved April 8, 2015, from http://www.voachinese.com/content/article-20120302-nixon-40-years-141218483/943969.html

Wei Junzi. (2011). Cui Baozhu Li Lianjie zheng shuo "zhengdong" ershi nian 崔宝珠李连杰正说"正东"二十年 [An interview with Chui Bo-Chu and Li Lianjie on the 20 years of the Eastern Production Ltd.]. Retrieved November 4, 2014, from http://dailynews.sina.com/bg/ent/film/sinacn/m/c/2011-09-29/16283431341.html

Xinwenhui keting. (2005). Li Lianjie zuoke "Xinwenhui Keting": Cong Shaolinsi da haolaiwu 李连杰做客《新闻会客厅》：从少林寺到好莱坞 [Li Lianjie interviewed by *People in the News*: From Shaolin Temple to Hollywood]. Retrieved April 8, 2015, from http://ent.sina.com.cn/s/m/2005-12-06/2021919611.html

Yang Lan. (2008). Li Lianjie 李连杰 [An interview with Jet Li]. In Xiaoman Mao (Ed.), Yang Lan fangtanlu 2008 杨澜访谈录 2008 [*Interviews by Yang Lan in 2008*] (pp. 103–122). Shanghai: Shanghai jinxiu wenzhang chubanshe.

Yu, Sabrina Qiong. (2010). Jet Li: star construction and fan discourse on the internet. In Mary Farquhar & Yingjin Zhang (Eds.), *Chinese film stars* (pp. 225–236). London/New York: Routledge.

Yu, Sabrina Qiong. (2012). *Jet Li: Chinese masculinity and transnational film stardom*. Edinburgh, UK: Edinburgh University Press.

• Li, Jet •

♂ Lien Chan

Lián Zhàn 連戰

b. 1936—Taiwanese politician, former premier and vice president of Taiwan, and KMT chairman

Alternate name: simpl. 连战

Summary

Born into a rich Taiwanese family, Lien became the premier of Taiwan in 1993. He went on to be elected as Taiwan's vice president on Lee Teng-hui's ticket, but by the end of the 1990s, his relations with Lee had soured. After his defeat in the 2000 presidential elections, Lien took over the Nationalist Party and unsuccessfully ran again for Taiwan presidency in 2004. He then decided to focus on Taiwan's reconciliation with mainland China, actively contributing to President Ma Ying-jeou's rapprochement policy.

As with many successful politicians with long careers, Lien Chan has adopted contradictory positions and made conflicting alliances. He succeeded as a politician because he was perceived both by the Nationalists Party (Kuomintang 國民黨, KMT) and the Taiwan public as a clever person and an able administrator. His patrician background, however, has kept him removed from society. Considered by many as aloof and cold, he lacks charisma and as a result failed on two occasions to be elected president of the Republic of China (ROC, or Taiwan). After an election defeat in 2000, he moved so close to China in his ideology that he has alienated many Taiwanese and become even more isolated.

Lien Chan's Unusual Background

Lien Chan is different from other Taiwanese politicians in several respects. Firstly, he was born into a wealthy and well-known Tainan merchant family, originally from Longji, in southern Fujian. His paternal grandfather Lien Heng 連橫 (or Lien Ya-tang 連雅堂; 1878–1936), a historian, wrote the *General History of Taiwan* (*Táiwān tōngshǐ* 臺灣通史, 1921), a famous book that promoted the idea of a unified and strong Taiwanese identity. Secondly, Lien Chan was not born in Taiwan but on the mainland, in Xi'an, on 27 August 1936. The reason for this was that, after the 1931 Sino-Japanese Mukden incident, in which Japanese troops seized the city of Mukden (now Shenyang, Liaoning Province) as a prelude to invading the rest of Manchuria, and because of the growing tension between both countries, his grandfather, living on the mainland, asked his only son, Lien Chen-tung 連震東 (Lien Chan's father), to leave Japan where he was studying and come back to China. There he did some intelligence work for the KMT and met his future wife, Chao Lan-kun 趙蘭坤, a Yenching University student who came from a well-known Shenyang family. It is said that Lien Heng, just before his death, gave his grandchild the name "Chan" (zhàn 戰), meaning "war". Lien Chan is thus what is called in Taiwan a "half-mountain" person (bànshānrén 半山人), or a half-mainlander. After attending primary school in Xi'an, he moved with his family to Taiwan in 1945, when the island was handed over to ROC. His father accepted a position in the ROC provincial government and was later elected to various local public offices. He was the only Taiwanese on the powerful Central Reform Commission (1950–1952) and served as ROC minister of interior from 1960 to 1966. In the early 1960s, with the help of his wife, who managed the family's fortune, he became the seventh wealthiest man on the island, partly by speculating on land purchases and also benefitting from his connection to the KMT.

Thirdly, there are controversies about Lien Chan's grandfather's political inclinations: while most historians agree that Lien Heng was anti-Japanese and anti-Manchu, he is presented as a Taiwanese nationalist by some and a Chinese patriot by others, including Lien Chan himself. This ambiguity has served Lien Chan's political career, helping to reach out to larger segments of the local Taiwanese electorate. Fourthly, and contrary to most KMT officials, Lien Chan married a "beauty queen," former "Miss Republic of China" Fāng Yǔ 方瑀, who was born into a mainland family in Chongqing in 1943. They had two sons and two daughters, including Sean Lien (or Lien Sheng-wen 連勝文), a KMT politician and an unsuccessful candidate to Taipei mayorship in November 2014. This marriage boosted Lien Chan's profile, particularly in the 1980s and early 1990s, but it became less of an asset as Taiwan fully democratized.

Recognized by the KMT

As a good student who was interested in politics and diplomacy, Lien Chan was quickly identified by the KMT as a potential leader. In 1957, he graduated with a degree in political science from National Taiwan University (NTU) and went on to do his military service at the Political War College. He most likely

• Lien Chan •

joined the KMT at that time. In 1959, he went overseas to the University of Chicago in the United States, where in 1961 he obtained a master's degree in international law and diplomacy. In 1965, he earned a PhD in political science, with a thesis on the liberal Chinese thinker Hú Shì 胡适 (1891–1962), whose work was partly banned in Taiwan. After his marriage, Lien taught and did research for a while at the University of Wisconsin and the University of Connecticut. In 1968, he moved back to Taiwan and took up a visiting professorship in political science at NTU, later becoming chairman of the department and of the Graduate Institute of Political Science. Giving advice to and cultivating relations in the government, he became more active in the KMT and, in 1975, was appointed ambassador to the Republic of El Salvador. This was a stepping-stone in Lien's political career: in 1976, he was recalled and appointed as the director of the KMT Committee of Youth Affairs. Two years later, he became deputy secretary-general of the KMT Central Committee, and the commissioner of the National Youth Commission of the Executive Yuan, a ministerial post in charge of recruiting well-trained scholars and convincing those established abroad to come back to Taiwan.

Career in the Government

In 1981, Lien Chan was promoted to the post of minister of transportation and communications. Six years later and a few months before the January 1988 death of ROC President Chiang Ching-kuo 蔣經國, Chan rose to the position of vice premier (or number-two position) of the Executive Yuan in the Yu Kuo-hwa 俞國華 cabinet. But shortly after *Lee Teng-hui 李登輝, a local Taiwanese, succeeded Chiang as head of state and KMT chairman, he asked Lien Chan, whom he had befriended in the late 1960s, to become the minister of foreign affairs and to help him develop a more pragmatic diplomacy as Taipei's allies began to normalize ties with Beijing. Lien seems to have been only mildly successful as this post, since less than two years later he was replaced by Frederick Chien 錢復.

Lien's political career was hardly on the wane, however, especially since he decided to side with Lee Teng-hui in his battle against the conservatives in the KMT. As governor of Taiwan Province from 1990 to 1993, Lien was chosen by Lee, over Lin Yang-kang 林洋港, to become the premier of the first Executive Yuan confirmed by a fully democratically elected parliament, or Legislative Yuan. In this position he replaced General Hau Pei-tsun 郝柏村, a mainlander with whom Lee had a difficult relationship and whom could not have been reappointed by the new Legislative Yuan. Then emphasizing his Taiwanese

---

*People marked with an asterisk have entries in this dictionary.

identity, Lien was also clearly supportive of Lee's rapid democratization strategy.

During the rest of the 1990s, Lien worked closely with Lee Teng-hui, introducing additional constitutional reforms such as the direct election of the president of the ROC in 1994, and in developing a channel of communication with China while also intensifying Taiwan's pragmatic diplomacy. In 1996, he successfully ran as vice president on the same ticket as Lee and kept both his positions (premier and vice president), before being replaced in 1997 as premier by Vincent Siew (Hsiao Wan-chang 蕭萬長) after the Council of Grand Justices ruled that retaining these dual roles was "constitutional but inappropriate."

Lien then publicly backed Lee's mainland policy, in his willingness both to negotiate technical agreements with Beijing and, especially after the Third Taiwan Strait Crisis (during which China tested missiles in waters close to the island), to slow down factory transfers to and investment in the mainland. In 1999, he also approved Lee's qualification of the relations across the Strait as "quasi-state to state relations." Lien finally took an active role in Lee's attempt to enhance Taiwan's international status and return to the United Nations. For example, in 1995, Lien met with Václav Havel in Prague, underscoring on this occasion the similarities between Taiwan's democratization and Czechoslovakia's Velvet Revolution.

Lien Turns Conservative

Also assuming the post of vice chairman of the KMT (1993–2000), Lien quite logically became the KMT candidate in the 2000 presidential election. It has been argued that he was chosen by Lee in order to destroy the KMT. It has also been said that Lee publicized his "two state theory" to boost Lien's chances to win. In any event, Lee clearly initially supported Lien's campaign. Lee, however, was aware of Lien's deteriorating image after his disastrous management of the 21 September 1999 earthquake rescue operations, and eventually decided to secure independence-leaning Democratic Progressive Party (DPP) candidate *Chen Shui-bian's 陳水扁 (b. 1950) victory against James Soong Chu-yu 宋楚瑜, an ambitious KMT leader and mainlander who had run as an Independent against Lien Chan (and Chen) after falling out with Lee.

The year 2000 constituted a turning point in Lien Chan's career. After his defeat, he took the reins of a weakened KMT, where he started to develop a more conservative mainlander, or Chinese nationalist, orientation. For instance, he entertained the idea of setting up a confederation with the PRC, and opening party-to-party talks with the Chinese Communist Party (CCP). Later, in 2003, he was instrumental in forcing the Chen administration to open direct charter flights across the Taiwan Strait. He officially reconciled with James Soong

• Lien Chan •

and, to increase his chances of winning, put him on his ticket as a vice president candidate in the 2004 presidential election. After Chen Shui-bian managed to get reelected with a hair-thin majority, Lien and Soong decided to legally question the results, to no avail.

Lien's Rapprochement with China

Unable to accept his defeat, Lien Chan suddenly turned his attention to cross-Strait relations. Criticizing more and more forcefully Chen's mainland China policy, which he considered too confrontational, and supported by larger segments of the business community, he tried to regain some influence in restoring official relations between the KMT and the Chinese CCP. In April 2005, one month after Beijing enacted a new "anti-secession law," Lien travelled to the PRC and met *Hú Jǐntāo 胡錦濤 (b. 1942).

This "journey of peace," his timidity in promoting Taiwan's democracy on the mainland, and his silence on the "anti-secession law" precipitated his retirement from the KMT chairmanship, which was taken over in July 2005 by *Ma Ying-jeou 馬英九 (b. 1950). Since then and particularly since Ma's election as ROC president in 2008, Lien, who has kept the title of KMT honorary chairman, has travelled multiple times to China, giving the impression to many Taiwanese that he was drifting closer to Beijing than

Taipei. It is true that a kind of division of labor has taken shape between the Ma administration and Lien Chan, the latter (and other KMT patriarchs) being used to negotiating with the CCP authorities. Ma also used Lien's prestige on the mainland to appoint him Taiwan's (or "Chinese Taipei") representative at the Asia-Pacific Economic Cooperation (APEC) meetings between 2008 and 2012. Lien, however, has also tried to push Ma's rapprochement policy with China further than the majority of the KMT and Taiwanese society would have wished. For example, in February 2013 he took the occasion of his meeting with the CCP's new general secretary, *Xí Jìnpíng 習近平 (b. 1953), to pronounce a "16 character principle" for cross-Strait relations, which endorsed not only Beijing's "one China" and integration policies but also Xi's idea of "rejuvenation of the Chinese nation." The following year, he led eighty Taiwanese business leaders and civil group representatives to the mainland and publicly supported the PRC concept of a "one China framework" (*yīzhōng kuàngjià* 一中框架).

Today, Lien Chan seems a politician of the past. He accompanied Taiwan's democratization but did not make any major personal contribution to it. He only managed to get elected to a public office when running with Lee Teng-hui in 1996. And at the end of his career, he consoled himself by embarking into a rapprochement with the PRC that has been perceived by most Taiwanese, including many KMT voters, as exaggerated and putting him in a relationship with the CCP leaders that was too cozy for the representative of a democracy. In accord with the old Chinese proverb "old men go back to their roots" (*lǎorén guīgēn* 老人歸根), Lien, coming from a Taiwanese patrician family closely linked to the mainland and attached to its Fujian origins, is promoting in his old age a reunification of the Chinese nation and a dream that trumps political and ideological differences. As such, he represents a section of the Taiwanese political spectrum that is doomed to get smaller and smaller.

Jean-Pierre CABESTAN
Hong Kong Baptist University

Further Reading

Chao, Linda, & Myers, Raymond. (1992). *Democracy's new leader in the Republic of China on Taiwan*. Stanford, CA: Hoover Institution Press.

Conferment of the degree of Doctor of Laws, honoris causa. A citation: Dr Lien Chan. (2005, December 5) The Chinese University of Hong Kong: Press Release. Retrieved September 4, 2014, from http://www.cuhk.edu.hk/cpr/pressrelease/051208Lien_e.htm

Hu Chi-chiang (Ed.). (1995). *Premier Lien: A man of pragmatism*. Taipei: Government Information Office.

Jacobs, J. Bruce. (2012). *Democratizing Taiwan*. Leiden, The Netherlands: E. J. Brill.

Roy, Denny. (2003). *Taiwan: A political history*. Ithaca, NY: Cornell University Press.

Xu Han 许汉; Zhang Jueming 张觉明; & Zheng Meilun 郑美伦. (1995). *Lian Zhan qianzhuan. Taiwan zuiyou jinquan de nanren* 连战前传：台湾最有金权的男人 [Lien Chan prequel. The richest and most powerful Taiwanese man]. Taipei: Kaijin wenhua chubanshe.

♂ Liú Bīnyàn 刘宾雁

1925–2005—In-house investigative journalist and outspoken social critic

Alternate name: trad. 劉賓雁

Summary

As an outspoken investigative journalist during the 1950s and again in the 1980s, Liu Binyan became the Chinese Communist Party's most famous in-house critic during the first four decades of PRC history. His semi-fictionalized literary reportage won accolades from Chinese readers as incisive exposés of political corruption, bureaucratic autocracy, and censorship. For this Liu was ejected from the Party twice, imprisoned in labor camps for two decades, forced into permanent overseas exile in the late 1980s, and airbrushed out of official history by the government.

As in many other single-party authoritarian regimes throughout history, most citizens of the People's Republic of China (PRC) have been socialized to refrain from public expression of critical comments about regime misbehavior, daring to voice such comments only in private to relatives and trusted friends. Yet a tiny minority of courageous and well-educated spokespersons for the ordinary citizenry have repeatedly risked regime reprisals and stepped forward not only to voice trenchant dissent, but to do so in print. The investigative journalist and long-time Chinese Communist Party (CCP) member Liu Binyan exemplifies the admired traditional Chinese role of the loyal but conscientious Chinese official who would risk his personal freedom and even his life to upbraid an errant emperor or top official. In his semi-fictional literary reportage such as "People or Monsters?" ("Rén yāo zhījiān" 人妖之间), Liu openly sets out in writing a complaint about the CCP's unaccountable and autocratic mode of rule that many Chinese have uttered in private among trusted friends: "The Communist Party rides herd on everything—except on the Party itself" (Liu 1981, 180).

Witheringly detailed exposés of bureaucratic corruption, perfunctory work styles, and abuse of power within the CCP party-state won Liu prestige as the PRC's most outspoken and widely respected investigative journalist during much of the 1950s and 1980s. Unfortunately, it also led to his sacking at the *People's Daily* and ejection from the CCP in the late 1980s, along with his enforced exile from the PRC until his death in 2005. The authoritarian leaders who ruled the PRC since the sacking and house arrest of former reformist premier *Zhào Zǐyáng 趙紫阳 (1919–2005) repeatedly ignored Liu Binyan's requests to return to die in his native land. The authorities have also blacklisted all his writings and forbidden the mention of his name in the PRC media and publishing world. With signs of him only surviving in pre-1989 PRC editions of his books and on the Internet, Liu's fate of an Orwellian air-brushing from PRC history means that few PRC college students in the 2010s have even heard of him. Despite this, he remains a respected and renowned figure internationally and among millions of ethnic Chinese outside of the mainland.

Formative Years and Journalistic Career, 1925–1987

Born the son of a railway worker on 15 January 1925 in the northeastern city of Changchun and raised further north in Harbin, Liu Binyan received hardly any formal education beyond junior high school due to dislocations resulting from Japan's military invasion and annexation of northeastern China as its puppet state of Manchukuo 满洲国 (1931–1945). Liu nonetheless had an inquiring mind, gained a reading knowledge of Russian, Japanese, and English, and delved deeply into history, politics, and literature.

The first time Liu became closely involved with the CCP was in 1943 while participating in China's underground resistance to the Japanese military occupation, and he formally joined the CCP in 1944. After a stint as a middle-school teacher in the northern seaport Tianjin in 1945–1946, he worked in various youth organizations until 1950, when he began publishing what would become three decades' worth of translations of Soviet Russian writings into Chinese. His translations from Russian range from politics and aesthetics to literary works such as plays. Yet translation still paled beside Liu's keenest area of interest, namely investigative journalism, and he finally embarked upon his career as a reporter for *China Youth News* 中国青年报 in Beijing from 1951 to 1957. The year 1951 was also a turning point in his personal life, when he married an editor of children's books, Zhū Hóng 朱洪; the couple later had a son, Liú Dàhóng 刘大洪, and a daughter, Liú Xiǎoyàn 刘小雁.

What Liu learned on the job as a reporter in the 1950s provided the grist for two of his most renowned early

---

*People marked with an asterisk have entries in this dictionary.

• Liú Bīnyàn •

刘宾雁

pieces of literary reportage, "At the Bridge Construction Worksite" ("Zài qiáoliáng gōngdì shàng," 在桥梁工地上, 1956) and "Our Newsroom's Inside Story" ("Běnbào nèibù xiāoxì" 本报内部 消息, 1956). Both recount the struggle of youthful, thoughtful, and principled protagonists to raise the level of professionalism and efficiency at their workplace in the face of strong resistance from older, inefficient, and cynical party bosses and other bureaucrats with perfunctory work styles. The window of opportunity to critique shortcomings of Chinese society under single-party Leninist-Maoist authoritarian rule soon slammed shut as the CCP leadership shunted aside the Hundred Flowers Movement (1956–1957), in which the populace was encouraged to criticize the leadership, and cracked down hard on the intelligentsia in particular with the Anti-Rightist Campaign (1957–1958). Like hundreds of thousands of other intellectuals whose well-intentioned and mostly low-key social critiques were scathingly denounced as "rightist" or "anti-party," including Liu's fellow writers Bái Huà 白桦 (b. 1930) and Cóng Wéixī 从维熙 (b. 1933), Liu was ejected from the CCP, fired from his job, vilified as a "rightist" miscreant, and forced to remold (gǎizào 改造) his thinking in rural labor camps for most of the following two decades. In fact, Liu was permitted to spend only two weeks with his wife from the time he was taken away to Maoist prison camps and internal exile

in 1957 until his exoneration and restoration to CCP membership in 1978.

The peak of Liu Binyan's career as a journalist and writer dates from his exoneration in 1978 and return to work as a journalist, primarily at the *People's Daily* 人民日报, and concludes with his second punitive ejection from the CCP and blacklisting by the party-state as a writer and journalist in 1987, and subsequent permanent departure from China in 1988. His election by his fellow members of the Chinese Writers' Association to the post of vice-chairman in 1985 reveals the peer esteem he enjoyed at the time; it also marks the only time that the CCP has ever allowed PRC writers to elect their own leaders.

Yet more important still was Liu's role as an unflinching speaker of truth to power. Throughout the late 1970s and much of the 1980s, he commonly received enthusiastic readers' letters by the bagful about his literary exposés of official corruption and other wrongdoing on high—often with requests to visit a given reader's locale to investigate practically identical abuses of power by the local party bosses. The most famous example of such literary reportage is the aforementioned "People or Monsters?" (1979), which relates the province-wide network of rampant corruption and abuse of power in Heilongjiang Province by a CCP official named Wáng Shǒuxìn 王守 信 (?–1980), noting that it took the investigative effort of several low-ranking individuals and a more practical-minded national leadership mindset after Mao's Cultural Revolution to finally bring Wang to justice. Liu's second-most famous work of reportage is "A Second Type of Loyalty" ("Dì'èrzhǒng zhōngchéng" 第二种忠诚, 1985), which favorably compares the loyalty of two intellectuals, who criticized the party-state in hopes of reforming it, to the sort of slavishly uncritical loyalty to the CCP that the party-state has demanded and preached instead.

Liu's major literary satire of a top-level CCP official, in this case almost surely Mao Zedong's long-time spymaster and internal security czar Kāng Shēng 康生 (1898–1975), was the short story "Warning" ("Jǐnggào" 警告, 1980). This story features an old and terminally ill high official who is plagued by recurrent nightmares about the many innocent tortured victims of his grisly purges, and suggests that his spirit lives on in China and that such hair-raising injustices might well recur in the future.

A less well-known but more stylistically distinguished work by Liu Binyan is his short story "The Fifth Person to Wear the Overcoat" ("Dì wǔge chuān dàyī de rén" 第五个穿大衣的人, 1979), whose narrator is the overcoat-clad reporter and protagonist who has just been exonerated in 1978 after two decades in a prison camp on the political charge of "rightism." The reporter cannot forget the four other equally innocent former political prisoners who had in turn worn that same overcoat in their labor camp, before dying from the harsh conditions and unknowingly bequeathing the overcoat to a surviving inmate. Ironically, the very same party apparatchik who had persecuted all five of these political prisoners in the late 1950s with a "rightist" verdict, and thus sent four of them to an early grave in the labor camp, is still the top party boss of the newspaper bureau two decades later, and chillingly greets the reporter with a fake broad grin in 1978, obviously feeling neither remorse for his murderously criminal abuse of power nor qualms about his hypocrisy. This story is emblematic of how *Dèng Xiǎopíng's 邓小平 (1904–1997) wide-ranging economic reforms were not at all matched in the political realm, where most CCP officials remained unaccountable to the ordinary citizenry and unapologetically autocratic and opaque as leaders. Given the lack of meaningful political reform in post-Mao China, it was probably inevitable that a journalist and writer as outspoken as Liu Binyan would be ejected from the party and fired from his job as an in-house journalist for the second and final time in his career.

Life and Work in Overseas Exile, 1988–2005

Banned from working as a journalist or even publishing his writings in the PRC after his discharge from the Party in 1987, Liu had little choice but to try to keep writing and publishing outside of

刘宾雁

the PRC on a temporary basis, hoping in vain that future leaders of the party-state after Deng Xiaoping's exit from the scene might eventually reconsider their denunciation of him and allow him to return home to Beijing to resume his work. He thereby became a Nieman fellow at Harvard University in 1988–1989, along with teaching a course in Chinese about Chinese literature and politics at the University of California at Los Angeles in Spring 1988. He also assisted various translators who were rendering some of his writings into English and other languages, well beyond the reach of PRC government bans and censorship. From 1989 until his death in 2005, Liu held the formal position of writer in residence at Trinity College in Hartford, Connecticut. Yet during most of the final decade and half of his life in exile, Liu lived in a small suburban house near Princeton, New Jersey, where he continued to read, write essays and op-eds, and occasionally speak in public. He finally succumbed to a long bout with cancer on 5 December 2005.

While in exile, Liu Binyan publicly condemned the CCP party-state's June 1989 military crackdown on the people's protest movements in Beijing and nearly two hundred other PRC cities. Underestimating this single-party Leninist authoritarian regime's resilience and ability to bounce back from this nadir in its reputation at home and abroad, Liu opined on many occasions that the CCP party-state would not be able to survive for long unless it openly admitted the erroneousness of its June 1989 crackdown and set out on a new course of genuine political reform and democratization. Cut off from his native linguistic and cultural environment during the last seventeen years of his life in exile, Liu lacked the wherewithal to salvage an overseas professorship or equivalent post in the manner of his younger fellow exile and dissident, the astrophysicist *Fāng Lìzhī 方励之 (1936–2012). Liu's exile was thus a mostly frustrating dénouement to a career marked by many world-renowned achievements in the face of great adversity.

Legacy as the PRC's Preeminent Social Critic

Although repeatedly forced by higher-ranking CCP officials to write a formal *mea culpa* for this or that ideological "incorrectness" in one of his writings or speeches, Liu continued to speak out controversially as the CCP's most human face and the PRC's most famous in-house public intellectual—until CCP leaders permanently blacklisted him in 1987. Liu's trenchant and widely acclaimed socio-political critiques that he penned in 1956 and 1978–1986 made his name a household word for multiple generations of Chinese people. In spite of the attempts to airbrush Liu Binyan from PRC history and cast his life and work down an Orwellian memory hole, Liu's writings remain stubbornly persistent on myriad bookshelves and hundreds of websites, and together amount to an exemplary argument for a more just, transparent, and accountable socio-political order in China. As of the mid-2010s, no in-house Chinese intellectual in PRC history has yet achieved the public following and wide admiration for outspoken socio-political critique that Liu gained from his writings and speeches from 1978 to 1986.

Liu set a very high standard as an indefatigable, outspoken, and yet reasonable social critic who tried his best to work within the existing system, however autocratic and capricious it could be and often was in its dealings with him. Though no dissenting successor has yet arisen to equal the stature Liu attained in the PRC between 1978 and 1986, some in-house PRC intellectuals such as the CCP member and former Xinhua journalist Yáng Jìshéng 杨继绳 (b. 1940) have resembled Liu in conducting in-depth investigations and publishing detailed exposés such as that of the party-state's responsibility for the most deadly famine in world history, China's Great Famine of 1958–1962. The initial Chinese-language edition of Yang's book *Tombstone* (*Mùbēi* 墓碑) could only be published outside of mainland China, in Hong Kong (2008), and though later translated into other languages was immediately banned for importation into the PRC, where the CCP has always covered up the extent of its responsibility for the death of at least 30 million victims of the famine (Yang 2012). Although Yang Jisheng is much less famous than Liu Binyan was in his heyday, he has inherited the spirit of Liu to investigate and publicize problems that threaten human well-being or societal advancement in the PRC in spite of that regime's determination to cover these problems up—and has done so in the face of serious personal risk.

Philip F. WILLIAMS
Montana State University

Further Reading

Béjà, Jean-Philippe. (1989). *Liu Binyan: Le cauchemar des mandarins rouges* [Liu Binyan: nightmare of the red mandarins]. Paris: Gallimard.

Blank, Carolin, & Gescher, Christa. (1991). *Gesellschaftskritik in der Volksrepublik China: Der Journalist und Schriftsteller Liu Binyan* [A social critic in the PRC: The journalist and writer Liu Binyan]. Bochum, Germany: Universitätsverlag Dr. N. Brockmeyer.

Buruma, Ian. (2001). *Bad elements: Chinese rebels from Los Angeles to Beijing*. New York: Random House.

Duke, Michael S. (1985). Ironies of history in the reportage fiction of Liu Binyan. In *Blooming and contending: Chinese literature in the post-Mao era* (pp. 98–122). Bloomington: Indiana University Press.

Goldman, Merle. (1971). *Literary dissent in Communist China*. New York: Atheneum.

He Yuhuai. (1992). *Cycles of repression and relaxation: Politico-literary events in China 1976–1989*. Bochum, Germany: Universitätsverlag Dr. N. Brockmeyer.

• Liú Bīnyàn •

Lee, Gregory B. (2012). *China's lost decade: Cultural politics and poetics 1978–1990 in place of history.* Brookline, MA: Zephyr Press.

Link, Perry. (1992). *Evening chats in Beijing: Probing China's predicament.* New York: W.W. Norton.

Link, Perry. (2000). *The uses of literature: Life in the socialist Chinese literary system.* Princeton, NJ: Princeton University Press.

Liu Binyan. (1990). *China's crisis, China's hope: Essays from an intellectual in exile* (Howard Goldblatt, Trans.). Cambridge, MA: Harvard University Press.

Liu Binyan. (1990). *A higher kind of loyalty: A memoir by China's foremost journalist* (Zhu Hong, Trans.). New York: Pantheon.

Liu Binyan 刘宾雁. (1981). *Liu Binyan baogao wenxue xuan* 刘宾雁报告文学选 [An anthology of Liu Binyan's literary reportage]. Beijing: Beijing chubanshe.

Liu Binyan 刘宾雁. (1988). *Liu Binyan zixuan ji* 刘宾雁自选集 [An anthology of Liu Binyan's own favorite works]. Beijing: Zhongguo wenlian chuban gongsi.

Liu Binyan. (1983). *"People or Monsters?" and other stories and reportage from China after Mao.* (Perry Link, Ed.). Bloomington: Indiana University Press.

Martin, Helmut, & Kinkley, Jeffrey (Eds.). (1992). *Modern Chinese writers: Self-portrayals.* Armonk, NY: M.E. Sharpe.

Wagner, Rudolph G. (1986). Liu Binyan and the *texie. Modern Chinese Literature, 2*(1), 63–98.

Williams, Philip F., & Wu, Yenna. (2004). *The Great Wall of confinement: the Chinese prison camp through contemporary fiction and reportage.* Berkeley: University of California Press.

Yang Jisheng. (2012). *Tombstone: The great Chinese famine, 1958–1962* (Stacy Mosher & Guo Jian, Trans.; Edward Friedman et al., Eds.). New York: Farrar, Straus and Giroux.

刘宾雁

♂ Liǔ Chuánzhì 柳传志

b. 1944—Entrepreneur, founder of the computer company Lenovo

Alternate name: trad. 柳傳志

Summary

Liu Chuanzhi is the founder of Lenovo, one of the world's largest computer manufacturers, and chair of Legend Holdings. The most successful computer company in China, Lenovo gained international prominence when it purchased the PC division of IBM in 2004. Liu retired as Lenovo's board chairman in 2005 to focus on managing its parent company Legend Holdings, though he resumed his position to guide the company back to profitability after the global financial crisis of 2008. Recently, Liu has diversified Legend Holdings into a financial and commercial investment conglomerate.

A s chair of Legend Holdings and founder of Lenovo, Liu Chuanzhi was greatly assisted by his father's high rank and wide network of contacts in the Chinese and Hong Kong business communities. While these connections played a crucial role in the early success of Legend Holdings and Lenovo, Liu's own management talents, political skills, and personal integrity were equally important in building these companies into multinational conglomerates and cementing his reputation as one of China's most respected business leaders.

Childhood and Education

Before the Communist victory in 1949 in the Chinese Civil War, Liu's father Liǔ Gǔshū 柳谷书 (1921–2003), an executive at the Bank of China, had secretly worked with the Communist Party. After the Communists took power, Liu Gushu rose through a succession of senior positions in the finance bureaucracy; before and after the Cultural Revolution (1966–1976), he was a prominent official in the China Council for the Promotion of International Trade (CCPIT). In the 1980s, Liu Gushu set up a patent agency and legal consulting firm in Hong Kong to take advantage of the increasing trade between mainland China and Hong Kong (Cheng and Liu 2004, 226–227).

Due to his father's prominence, Liu Chuanzhi's upbringing in the 1950s was relatively privileged. Like millions of other children of Chinese cadres (*gànbù* 干部) and intellectuals, however, Liu had to survive the chaotic political turbulence of the Cultural Revolution. He was able to complete his education before the universities shut down, graduating from the Xi'an Military Communications Engineering Institute in 1966. In 1967, Liu was initially allocated a job in a scientific research institute in Chengdu attached to the Ministry of National Defense. In 1968, however, he was "sent down" to "learn from the peasants" by laboring on a rice farm in Zhuhai, Guangdong Province (China Vitae 2014).

A Legendary Career

This period of exile did not last long, and by 1970 Liu was transferred to the Chinese Academy of Sciences in Beijing where he worked as a researcher and later as a cadre until 1984. As part of the Chinese government's attempt to create a domestic computer industry, the Chinese Academy of Sciences provided the capital and office space for Liu and ten other researchers to found Legend (Liánxiǎng 联想) in 1984. The company initially distributed IBM, HP, and AST computers under license, but developed a Chinese character word processor in 1986 and started producing its own

computers in 1990 (Legend Holdings 2014a). Along with other pioneering Chinese computer companies, such as Stone and Founder, Legend was based in Zhongguancun, a district of Beijing with a high concentration of top universities and research institutes. The success of these companies partly resulted from their close proximity to the latest technological research, and the Chinese government later realized the importance of encouraging this kind of educational and technological hub, providing incentives for high-tech firms to set up research and development centers in Zhongguancun. The district soon became known as China's Silicon Valley, and has since expanded to encompass ten other high-tech hubs throughout Beijing under the umbrella of the Zhongguancun National Demonstration Zone (Z-Park 2014).

In 1994, Legend was one of the first Chinese companies to be listed on the Hong Kong Stock Exchange, and in 1997 it became the top-selling computer brand in China, a status it has maintained until today. In 2002, as part of the company's internationalization plan, Legend established a subsidiary with a more modern-sounding English name, Lenovo, and in 2004 Lenovo acquired IBM's personal computer division from the struggling American firm, including the famous Thinkpad brand of laptop computers. Lenovo soon became the world's third largest personal computer manufacturer (Legend Holdings 2014a).

Liu Chuanzhi has played a major role in the success of Legend and Lenovo. As chair of Legend Holdings, Liu was a pioneer in using incentives to promote innovation among employees, in particular by setting up one of the first employee-share systems in China. He has also become famous in China as an advocate of cultural management techniques, educating all employees in Legend's "core values" of defining clear goals, dividing goals into manageable phases, and "replaying the chess game" (in other words, constantly reviewing one's actions to see how they can be improved). Liu's cultural management approach has been imitated by many other private and state-controlled Chinese companies in recent years, and he has acted as a management mentor to numerous younger entrepreneurs, including the current chair and CEO of Lenovo, Yang Yuanqing (Legend Holdings 2014b; Hawes 2012).

Liu Chuanzhi is the founder of Lenovo. Photo by Cory M. Grenier.

• Liǔ Chuánzhì •

Liu's family connections also proved crucial to Legend during the firm's initial growth phase. One of the key investors in Legend's Hong Kong subsidiary was China Technology Transfer (Hong Kong) Corporation, whose CEO and deputy chair was Liu's father. Legend's ability to take out major loans with the Bank of China to overcome a cash flow crisis in the late 1990s was doubtless facilitated by Liu Gushu's longstanding connections with the Chinese financial bureaucracy (Cheng and Liu 2004, 226–227).

Liu Chuanzhi played a pivotal role in returning Lenovo to profitability after it became over-extended in the global financial crisis of 2008. By resuming his position as chair in 2009, restructuring the firm's management, and negotiating a capital injection by the large state conglomerate China Oceanwide Holdings Group, Liu ensured that Lenovo was soon back in the top ranks of highly profitable global computer manufacturers (Legend Holdings 2014c). Since 2011, Liu has once more resigned as chair of Lenovo to focus on the diversification of Legend Holdings into an investment conglomerate, adopting an approach similar in many ways to Warren Buffett's Berkshire Hathaway Inc.

Earlier in the 2000s, Legend had established a number of venture capital and real estate investment subsidiaries, including Legend Capital, Hony Capital, and Raycom Real Estate. The company particularly invested in start-up high-tech enterprises in need of capital to develop marketable products from new inventions. From 2010, Liu adopted a broader strategy, in which Legend Holdings began to acquire established companies in a range of industries, installing new managers or applying Legend's built-up institutional knowledge to restructure existing management systems and make the companies more efficient. Legend's subsidiaries now include various consumer goods and services businesses, such as China Auto Rental, Philion Battery, EnsenCare (an operator of senior homes), and Bybo Dental Group. They also include five companies engaged in production of new chemical materials, and the Joyvio Group, which controls several producers and importers of agricultural foodstuffs. Legend also owns a major insurance broker, a financing firm providing loans to small and medium-sized businesses, and an online payments business. Besides Legend's ownership, the only connecting feature of these diverse ventures is that they are all in industries with enormous long-term growth potential as China's middle-class consumer market expands (Legend Holdings 2014d; Flannery 2011).

Influence and Legacy

Liu Chuanzhi has become one of the most influential and respected business leaders in China, winning numerous national and international awards. Not only has he been instrumental in building Legend Holdings and Lenovo into outstanding business enterprises, but through these companies' investment arms, he has provided capital to hundreds of innovative private entrepreneurs who would otherwise find it almost impossible to finance their start-up businesses, due to the risk averse lending habits of Chinese banks. Liu has also acted as a management mentor both directly, through training younger entrepreneurs within the Legend group, and indirectly, through creating a cultural management model that succeeds in the Chinese business and political environment, and his approach has been regularly emulated by up-and-coming Chinese managers in their own companies.

Colin HAWES
University of Technology, Sydney

Further Reading

Cheng, Dongsheng, & Liu Lili. (2004). *Huawei zhenxiang* 化为真相 [The Truth about Huawei]. Beijing: Dangdai zhongguo chubanshe.

China Vitae. (2014). Liu Chuanzhi. Retrieved August 27, 2014, from http://www.chinavitae.com/biography/Liu_Chuanzhi/career

Flannery, Russel. (2011). Liu Chuanzhi has Legend Holdings in his sights. Retrieved September 16, 2014, from http://www.forbes.com/global/2011/1205/companies-people-liu-chuanzhi-lenovo-computer-ipo-flannery.html

Hawes, Colin. (2012). *The Chinese transformation of corporate culture.* London: Routledge.

Legend Holdings. (2014a). Our History. Retrieved December 7, 2014, from http://www.legendholdings.com.cn/en/About/FullHistory.aspx

Legend Holdings. (2014b). Corporate culture at Legend Holdings. Retrieved December 7, 2014, from http://www.legendholdings.com.cn/en/MgmtCulture/CorpCulture.aspx

Legend Holdings. (2014c). Management team. Retrieved December 7, 2014, from http://www.legendholdings.com.cn/en/Leadership/MgmtTeam.aspx

Legend Holdings. (2014d). Company overview. Retrieved December 7, 2014, from http://www.legendholdings.com.cn/en/About/Overview.aspx

Ling, Zhijun. (2006). *The Lenovo affair.* Singapore: John Wiley & Sons.

Sing, Sangeeta. (2009). Liu Chuanzhi. In Zhang Wenxian, & Ilan Alon, (Eds.), *Biographical dictionary of new Chinese entrepreneurs and business leaders* (pp. 98–100). Northampton, MA: Edward Elgar Publishing.

Z-Park. (2014). Zhongguancun Science Park profile. Retrieved December 7, 2014, from http://en.zgc.gov.cn/2013-12/04/content_17148863.htm

☿ Liú Xiáng 刘翔

b. 1983—Track and field athlete, winner of Olympic Gold Medal in 2004

Alternate name: trad. 劉翔

Summary

Liu Xiang, one of China's most successful athletes and a national icon, was simultaneously world record holder, world champion and Olympic champion in the 110-meter hurdles. He was the first Chinese athlete to win Olympic Gold in a men's track and field event. Injuries have put his career on hold, and he announced his retirement from the profession in 2015.

Liu Xiang, one of the most successful Chinese athletes in history and a national icon, was the first Chinese athlete to win Olympic Gold in a men's track and field event (110-meter hurdles). He was also the first athlete in China and Asia to hold three big titles at the same time: world record holder, world champion, and Olympic champion.

A Difficult Start

Liu was born in Shanghai on 13 July 1983. His career path is a classic tale of perseverance and overcoming hardships. At age twelve, Liu was placed in a special sports school, away from his family, so that he could study and train as a high jumper. When he was fifteen, however, Liu was asked to give up that event when a bone test showed that he would not grow tall enough to become a world-class jumper. Sūn Hǎipíng 孙海平, a prominent hurdles coach in China, eventually recognized Liu's potential in a different event. Sun persuaded Liu's family that Liu could excel at the hurdles and started training him. After making impressive progress, Liu joined the Shanghai Athletics Team in 1999. A year later, as a member of the Chinese Youth Team, Liu placed fourth in the men's 110-meter hurdles at the 2000 World Junior Championships.

Rise and Fall at the Olympic Games

In 2001 Liu launched his international career by impressively winning three major competitions: the East Asian

Games in Osaka, Japan; Universiade in Beijing; and the Ninth National Games of the People's Republic of China (PRC). The following year, Liu set an Asian record at the Athletissima meeting with a time of 13.12 seconds. This time broke the twenty-four-year-old world junior record held by Renaldo Nehemiah. In 2003 Liu secured bronze medals in the 60-meter hurdles at the International Association of Athletics Federations (IAAF) World Indoor Championships and in the 110-meter hurdles at the World Championships.

Liu did even better at the 2004 Olympic Games, winning the gold medal in the men's 110-meter hurdles. His time of 12.91 seconds matched the world record and set a new Olympic record. Liu became just the sixth man to run this event in under 13 seconds, improving on his own Asian record time from just two years earlier by more than 0.20 seconds. Two years later Liu reached another peak in his career when he set a new world record of 12.88 seconds at the Super Grand Prix in Lausanne on 11 July 2006. A year later Liu won gold in the World Championships in Osaka, Japan, and became world champion for the first time.

At the 2008 Olympic Games in Beijing, Liu was the favorite to win

Liu Xiang at the Doha 2010 World Indoor Championships. Photo by Erik van Leeuwen.

• Liú Xiáng •

and defend his Olympic title in front of a home crowd. Tragically, he had to pull out of the competition at the last moment due to the aggravation of a previously unrevealed, but serious Achilles tendon injury. Since Liu was considered a national hero, China relied upon his performance to bring success to the Beijing Olympic Games, and give "face" to the entire nation. As a result, his injury and subsequent decision to abstain from participation in the Games was a patriotic matter, and the entire nation was distraught (Qu 2015).

After thirteen months in recovery, Liu returned to the tracks in 2009. He was runner-up at the Shanghai Golden Grand Prix and then won gold medals at the Asian Athletics Championship, the East Asian Games, and the Eleventh Chinese National Games. Six months later he easily won his third consecutive title at the 2010 Asian Games in Guangdong, China.

In 2011 Liu marked his return to a world-class level by defeating David Oliver at the Shanghai Golden Grand Prix, receiving his first win on the 2011 IAAF Diamond League circuit. In August he won a silver medal at the World Championships. In June 2012 Liu was back atop the list of men's 110-meter hurdles, ranking first in the world again after a break of five years.

At the London Olympic Games in 2012, Liu again pulled his Achilles tendon while attempting to clear the first hurdle in the heats. He hopped the rest of the course and kissed the last hurdle before being put in a wheelchair and led away; a devastating event for Liu himself, the sport discipline in general, and viewers in China and across the world.

Future Plans

Since the 2012 Olympics, Liu has concentrated on recovering from his injury and has not competed. Hopes that he could return for the World Championships in Beijing in August 2015 were stifled in April of that year, when Liu announced his official retirement. "I'm afraid I have to leave behind the runway and hurdles. I am too 'old' and 'sick' to run freely. It's time to retire and begin a new journey," Liu wrote on his Sina Weibo account (Liu 2015). Just like any other retired athlete, Liu now needs to find a new career, but unlike many of his colleagues, Liu indicated not to be interested in coaching at this time, instead planning to continue his education and serve as a commentator at the upcoming World Championship in August 2015 (Qu 2015).

FAN Hong and MIN Ge
The University of Western Australia

Further Reading

BBC. (2012). China mourns hurdler Liu Xiang's Olympic exit. Retrieved March 2, 2015, from http://www.bbc.com/news/world-asia-china-19174696

China.org. (2010). Top 10 influential characters in China's sports history. Retrieved March 2, 2015, from http://www.china.org.cn/top10/2010-11/30/content_21452704_6.htm

Data Sports. (2010). Liu Xiang. Retrieved March 2, 2015, from http://data.sports.163.com/athlete/home/0005000E0IAe.html

International Association of Athletics Federations (IAAF). (2006). Athlete Profile: Liu Xiang. Retrieved March 2 , 2015, from http://www.iaaf.org/athletes/pr-of-china/xiang-liu-176546#biography

Liu Xiang. (2015, April 7). *Wode paodao! Wode lan!* 的跑道; 我的栏 [My track! My hurdles!]. Retrieved June 29, 2015, from http://www.weibo.com/liuxiang

Lu Zhouxiang & Hong Fan. (2014). *Sport and nationalism in China*. New York: Routledge.

Olympic.org. (2014). Liu Xiang—A true Chinese icon and Athlete Role Model. Retrieved March 2, 2015, from http://www.olympic.org/news/liu-xiang-a-true-chinese-icon-and-athlete-role-model/235545

Qu Chaonan. (2015). Liu Xiang says farewell to track. Retrieved June 29, 2015, from https://beijingtoday.com.cn/2015/04/liu-xiang-says-farewell-to-track

Wu Junkuan. (2011). Liu Xiang regains honor at Daegu worlds. Retrieved March 2, 2015, from http://english.cntv.cn/20110830/103287.shtml

• Liú Xiǎng •

☀ Liú Xiǎobō 刘晓波

b. 1955—Human rights defender and 2010 Nobel Peace Prize laureate

Alternate name: trad. 劉曉波

Summary

Liu Xiaobo is one of the most well-known human rights defenders in China. He first emerged in the mid-1980s as a literary critic and became a political activist during the Tiananmen Square protests of 1989. After several detentions for his activism and writings, he was sentenced to eleven years in prison in December 2009 for "inciting subversion of state power." When he was awarded the 2010 Nobel Peace Prize, his case became a *cause célèbre* for the defense of human rights and freedom of expression in China.

Liu Xiaobo is the first Chinese citizen residing in China to be awarded a Nobel Prize. While this makes him one of the most renowned Chinese dissident intellectuals abroad, he remains largely unknown within China because his name has been blacklisted by state censors since 1989. His first important contribution to the Chinese democracy movement took place during the 1989 protests, when he organized a hunger strike and negotiated with the students and the authorities a peaceful withdrawal of the students from Tiananmen Square, avoiding a possibly larger massacre. His second notable contribution was his role in the release of Charter 08, a manifesto calling for gradual political reforms and better protection of human rights in China. Between 1989 and 2008, Liu Xiaobo struggled to defend the human rights of his fellow citizens by mobilizing transnational civil society networks through the publication of open letters and as president of the Independent Chinese PEN Center, during which he monitored and documented various cases of human rights violations.

Early Life

Born on 28 December 1955 in the city of Changchun, Jilin Province, Liu Xiaobo was the third of five brothers. He grew up in China's northeast during an agitated period under the rule of

刘晓波

Máo Zédōng 毛泽东 (1893–1976). From the late 1960s until the end of the Cultural Revolution (1966–1976), urban people with education were sent to be "re-educated" in the countryside. Because his father was a university teacher, Liu Xiaobo spent three years in Inner Mongolia between 1969 and 1973, where he discovered his passion for learning outside the school system. In 1974, after finishing middle school, he spent two more years on a farm before returning to Changchun in 1977, when university entrance exams were re-established. Liu Xiaobo was admitted to the Chinese department of Jilin University, where he studied Western philosophy and with six other students formed a poetry group called the "Innocent Hearts" (Chìzǐ xīn 赤子心), at a time when writers and artists of the Democracy Wall Movement (1978–1979), who posted their dissent on a brick wall in Beijing, were being suppressed. After receiving his BA in 1982, he went to Beijing Normal University for graduate studies. In 1984, he married his classmate Tao Li and their son Liu Tao was born the following year.

From a Literary "Black Horse" to a "Black Hand"

In the second half of the 1980's, Liu joined the "cultural fever" (wénhuà rè 文化热) debates of intellectuals concerning Chinese and foreign literature by publishing critical articles. In 1986, he attracted attention in a symposium celebrating ten years of "New Era Literature" with an improvised speech entitled "The Crisis Facing New Era Literature" that denounced the traditionalism and lack of independence of Chinese writers and the "root-seeking literature" that was in vogue at that time and which put emphasis on Confucianism, Daoism, Buddhism, and regional culture. He argued that Chinese writers should focus on the development of their individual conscience and creativity by learning from authors like Lǔ Xūn 鲁迅 and *Gāo Xíngjiàn 高行健 (b. 1940) or T.S. Eliot and Joseph Conrad. His critiques were widely reprinted across China and quickly earned him the label of literary "black horse" for shocking old figures of the literary establishment.

In 1987, he published his first book to criticize the influential intellectual Lǐ Zéhòu 李泽厚 (b. 1930). Liu Xiaobo was influenced by Li's works on Kant but disliked his articulation of Western philosophy and Chinese traditional thought, arguing that Chinese people should break completely with Chinese tradition because of its incompatibility with democracy. As a result, Liu Xiaobo was seen as belonging to the school that advocates "radical Westernization" (quánpán xīhuà 全盤西化) of China as a precondition for democratization. In a few years, his critical interventions resulted in a "Liu Xiaobo Phenomenon" that sent shockwaves through China's

*People marked with an asterisk have entries in this dictionary.

literary circles. After obtaining a PhD in Chinese literature in 1988 with a dissertation entitled *Aesthetics and Human Freedom*, he became a lecturer whose growing reputation gave him the opportunity to travel for several months as a visiting scholar to the University of Oslo, the University of Hawaii, and Columbia University. On his way to Hawaii, he gave an interview in Hong Kong in which he said that mainland China would need "three centuries of colonialism" to become like Hong Kong, given that it took a century of British colonialism to make the city look like what it was in 1988. More than twenty years later, this quote would be used against him by his detractors in an attempt to discredit his struggle for human rights.

As the democracy movement of spring 1989 was unfolding after the death on 15 April of *Hú Yàobāng 胡耀邦 (1915–1989), ex-general secretary of the Communist Party, Liu refused to watch from a distance. He left Columbia University for Beijing to participate directly in the protests on Tiananmen Square by advising students and raising funds. Over several weeks, he gradually transformed from an observer to one of the leaders of the protests. He drafted speeches calling for institutional reforms and rejection of violence and class struggle ideology. He organized the 2 June hunger strike with three friends: Zhōu Duó 周舵, Gāo Xīn 高新, and Hóu Déjiàn 侯德健, who together later became known as the "Four Gentlemen" (Sì jūnzǐ 四君子). On the night of 3 June, Liu and his friends successfully negotiated with the leaders of the martial law troops a peaceful withdrawal of thousands of students from Tiananmen Square. Two days after the 4 June crackdown, he was arrested by the authorities who labeled him a "black hand" (*hēishǒu* 黑手) behind the "political turmoil" (*zhèngzhì fēngbō* 政治风波) and detained him for nineteen months in Qincheng prison. Meanwhile, he was expelled from Beijing Normal University and divorced from his first wife, who emigrated to the United States with their son. This historical movement would have a lasting effect upon his life trajectory and his position within China's democracy and human rights movement.

The Long Struggle of a "Doomsday Survivor"

After his release from prison, Liu Xiaobo painfully reflected upon the implications of the tragic events of 4 June and chose to continue campaigning for civil rights and constitutional government by co-signing open letters. In 1993, he was invited to Australia and the United States to give interviews for the documentary film *The Gate of Heavenly Peace*. Rejecting the advice of his friends to seek political asylum, he returned to China in May and published a confessional memoir entitled, *The Monologue of a Doomsday Survivor*, which stirred much controversy among domestic and overseas dissidents for its criticisms of the 1989 Democracy Movement. In 1995, he released with his friend Bāo Zūnxìn 包遵信 (1937–2007) and ten other intellectuals an "Anti-corruption Proposal" to the National People's Congress, calling for the implementation of short-term and long-term goals for political reform.

On the eve of the sixth anniversary of the 4 June Incident, he was detained yet again for six months after co-signing a joint statement asking the government to recognize the legitimacy of the 1989 movement. After his release in 1996, he signed a political declaration written by Wang Xizhe, a Democracy Wall activist, and was sent for three years to a "re-education through labor" camp (*láojiào*

劳教) in Dalian. From prison, he married Liú Xiá 刘霞 (b. 1961), an artist and poet he had met in literary gatherings in the 1980s. Through their monthly meetings and the poems they wrote to each other, their emotional bond deepened and transformed Liu Xiaobo's approach to his human rights defense.

After his third arrest ended in October 1999, he tried to avoid the risk of another imprisonment, hoping that Liu Xia would not have to again suffer the consequences. Although his writings became forbidden in China, foreign websites publishing articles on Chinese politics enabled him to earn a living as a freelance writer, together with his books printed in Taiwan and Hong Kong. During the 2000s, he invested most of his time

Liu Xiaobo's chair at the 2010 Nobel Prize Ceremony in Oslo remains empty since the imprisoned laureate was denied permission to attend. Photo by Kunshou.

and energy into publishing articles on current affairs and into monitoring human rights violations and Chinese civil society development, in which he saw the possibilities of a future free China. After helping establish the Independent Chinese PEN Center, he was elected its president from 2003 to 2007, during which time he focused on documenting and publicizing cases of writers in prison and on helping their relatives in need. Liu Xiaobo's activism was deeply inspired by and indebted to the Tiananmen Mothers (Tiān'ānmén mǔqīn 天安门母亲), especially Dīng Zǐlín 丁子霖, for their moral courage and perseverance in asking for justice for their children killed during the Tiananmen Incident. Each year on the anniversary of the crackdown, Liu Xiaobo writes an elegy to the "departed souls" (*wánglíng* 亡灵). Another key influence was the Czech writer and statesman Václav Havel, whose call to "live in truth" resonated with the importance Liu Xiaobo attached to ethics and the refusal to lie to one's conscience, which he considered essential for China's democratization. In October 2006, he took over the chief editor's position of the website Democratic China (Mínzhǔ Zhōngguó 民主中国) from Sū Xiǎokāng 苏晓康, until his fourth arrest.

Charter 08 and Conviction

After the 2008 Olympics, Liu Xiaobo worked together with Zhāng Zǔhuà 张祖桦 and Jiāng Qíshēng 江棋生 on Charter 08, which was planned to be released on 10 December for the sixtieth anniversary of the Universal Declaration of Human Rights. This political manifesto was inspired by Charter 77 written by Czechoslovakian dissidents including Václav Havel. As the twentieth anniversary of the 4 June crackdown was approaching and little progress had been made in redressing the injustice, Liu Xiaobo was willing to take risks once again. Two days before the launch of Charter 08, the police detained him in an undisclosed location until his formal arrest on 23 June 2009. On 23 December, he was put on trial and sentenced to eleven years imprisonment for "inciting subversion of state power" (*shāndòng diānfù guójiā zhèngquán zuì* 煽动颠覆国家政权罪) using six articles he wrote and Charter 08 as "evidence." While on trial, Liu Xiaobo said in his last statement: "I still want to tell the regime that deprives me of my freedom: I stand by the belief I expressed twenty years ago in my June 2nd hunger strike declaration: I have no enemies, I have no hatred." In May 2010, he was transferred to Jinzhou Prison in Liaoning Province in order to keep him away from public attention.

The World's Only Imprisoned Nobel Prize Laureate

Thanks to the solidarity of many individuals around the world, including

Nobel laureates and politicians, Liu Xiaobo received several international awards, notably the 2010 Nobel Peace Prize "for his long and non-violent struggle for fundamental human rights in China" which Liu dedicated to the "departed souls" of 4 June. Unable to attend the ceremony in Oslo in December, Liu was represented by an empty chair on the podium which became a symbol of an ongoing protest against his imprisonment. Since 2010, Liu Xia has been held illegally under house arrest but can visit her husband once a month. If not released earlier for medical reasons, Liu Xiaobo should get out of prison in June 2020, at the age of sixty-four.

Hermann AUBIÉ
University of Turku, Centre for East Asian Studies

Further Reading

Barmé, Geremie. (1991). Confession, redemption, and death: Liu Xiaobo and the protest movement of 1989. In George Hicks (Ed.), *The broken mirror: China after Tiananmen* (pp. 52–99). London: Longmans.

Béja, Jean-Philippe, Fu Hualing, & Pils, Eva. (Eds.). (2012). *Liu Xiaobo, Charter 08 and the challenges of political reform in China*. Hong Kong: Hong Kong University Press.

Chong Woei-Lien. (1993). The tragic duality of man: Liu Xiaobo on western philosophy from Kant to Sartre. In K. W. Radtke, & Tony Saich (Eds.), *China's modernisation: Westernisation and acculturation* (pp. 111–163). Stuttgart, Germany: F. Steiner.

Gu Xin. (1996). The irrationalistic view of aesthetic freedom and the philosophical sources of social discontent of Liu Xiaobo. *Issues & Studies*, 32(1), 89.

Liu Xiaobo. (2006). Reform in China: The role of the civil society. *Social Research*, 73(1), 121–138.

Liu Xiaobo. (2011). *La philosophie du porc et autres essais*. Paris: Gallimard.

Liu Xiaobo. (2012). *No enemies, no hatred: Selected essays and poems*. Cambridge, MA: Belknap Press of Harvard University Press.

Liu Xiaobo. (2012). *June Fourth Elegies*. Minneapolis: Graywolf Press.

Liu Xiaobo. (2015). Homepage. Retrieved July 6, 2015, from http://liuxiaobo.net

Liu Xiaobo et al. (2011). *"Watashi niwa teki wa inai" no shisō*私には敵はいない」の思想 [Philosophy of "I Have No Enemy"]. Tokyo: Fujiwara Shoten.

Leys, Simon. (2012). He told the truth about China's tyranny. *The New York Review of Books*. Retrieved December 1, 2014, from: http://www.nybooks.com/articles/archives/2012/feb/09/liu-xiaobo-he-told-truth-about-chinas-tyranny

Yu Jie 余杰. (2012). *Liu Xiaobo zhuan* 劉曉波傳 [Liu Xiaobo: A biography]. Hong Kong: Xinshiji chubanshe.

Zhang Yu 張裕. (2013). *Cong Wang Shiwei dao Liu Xiaobo: Zhongguo dangdai wenziyu qiutu bian nian lu* (1947–2010) 從王實味到劉曉波：中國當代文字獄囚徒編年錄 (1947–2010 年) [From Wang Shiwei to Liu Xiaobo: The prisoners of literary inquisition under Communist rule in Contemporary China (1947–2010)]. Hong Kong: Ziyou wenhua chubanshe.

♂ Mǎ Jūn 马军

b. 1968—Environmental journalist and activist

Alternate name: trad. 馬軍

Summary

Establishing the nonprofit Institute of Public and Environmental Affairs, Ma Jun has worked extensively on behalf of cleaner air and water across China by putting focus on the availability of pollution data rather than on direct confrontation with the government. With the publication of his book *China's Water Crisis,* **the release of the short video "The Other Side of Apple," and the use of social media, Ma has also put industry and foreign businesses on alert that pollution in China will no longer occur in secrecy.**

Ma Jun has become known across China and the world as one of the most prominent environmental journalists and activists in the country. Establishing the Institute of Public and Environmental Affairs (IPE) in 2006 as a major nongovernmental organization (NGO) in China, he has served as its director while publishing exposés on the extent of air and water pollution in China. Working to make data available to the public and using media outlets to involve the general public, Ma and his colleagues have been extremely effective in shedding light on China's environmental calamities.

Journalism and Activism

Born on 24 June 1968 in the city of Qingdao, Shandong Province, Ma majored in journalism and English at China's University of International Relations and also has studied law and forestry at Yale University. From 1993 to 2000, Ma was the Beijing reporter for Hong Kong's *South China Morning Post*, focusing on environmental issues that took him on visits to major sites around the country, including a trip to the construction site of the Three Gorges Dam in 1994. Throughout his travels, Ma has been shocked not just by the enormous damage being done to the country's environment—from the drought and drying up of rivers in

China's north, to devastating floods on the Yangzi (Chang) River, to the serious pollution of southern waterways—but even more so by the callous attitude of government officials, especially at the local level. Evidently oblivious to the impact on the environment of uncontrolled economic expansion, they have looked to large engineering projects, such as the Three Gorges Dam and the South-to-North Water Diversion project, as the flawed solution to every environmental problem. This was most evident in Ma's visit to the Yellow River Commission, whose chief engineer claimed victory over the river's periodic and hugely damaging flooding by noting that the various dams and diversion projects constructed on the waterway had led to its virtual dry-up several months out of the year.

Ma's response to this situation was to compose his book *China's Water Crisis* (*Zhōngguó shuǐ wēijī* 中国水危机), which was published in China in 1999 with an English translation produced in 2004 by the International Rivers Network. Relying on massive amounts of environmental data gathered from local Chinese government authorities, Ma provides an extensive documentary summary of the extent of China's severe water crisis, from the parched North China Plain to the Huang (Yellow) and Yangzi rivers, and virtually every major region of the country where water is quickly emerging as the country's number one environmental problem. According to this data, there is either too much, as in the increasingly devastating floods in central and southern China, or too little, as in northern and northeastern cities relying more and more on rapidly depleting underground aquifers for their water supplies. Frequently compared to *Silent Spring* (1962), a classic work by the US environmentalist Rachel Carson that documented the environmental impact of indiscriminate pesticide use, *China's Water Crisis* and Ma's subsequent work with IPE and Sinosphere, a major consultant group on environmental affairs for foreign companies operating in China, has made Ma Jun into an internationally renowned figure. In 2006, he was included in *Time* magazine's list of the "100 Most Influential People in the World," and in 2009, he was awarded the Ramon Magsaysay Award (so named for the former president of the Philippines in the 1950s), Asia's equivalent of the Nobel Prize. In 2012, he was awarded the prestigious Goldman Environmental Prize while also making the list of *Foreign Policy* magazine's 100 Leading Global Thinkers. A member of the Beijing Environmental Energy Roundtable (BEER) and named "China's Green Man of the Year" in 2006, Ma is currently a research fellow at the Woodrow Wilson Center, Princeton University.

Since its inception in 2006, IPE, under Ma's direction and with the assistance of a few staff members, has focused primarily on increasing transparency in China's environmental condition. Relying primarily on data gathered by local governments

• Mǎ Jūn •

and environmental protection bodies, critical information has been presented to the Chinese public in the form of pollution maps detailing water, air, and solid waste throughout the country and made available on the NGO's website. Reflecting Ma's view that water pollution is China's most serious environmental problem, IPE issued the China Water Pollution Map (Zhōngguó shuǐ wūrǎn dìtú 中国水污染地图) that brings together over ninety-five thousand environmental supervision records from various government departments, with data dating back to 2004. Monitoring the environmental performance of state-owned enterprises (SOEs) and companies that together account for 65 percent of China's industrial discharge, largely in traditional heavy industries, the map enables communities to understand the risks to their local water supplies from the surrounding environment. Also issued in conjunction with the Law School of the People's University in Beijing is the "Road Map to Blue Skies: China's Atmospheric Pollution," which assesses the quality of air pollution monitoring in twenty Chinese cities, with comparisons to ten international cities.

Unleashing the Facts

In a society increasingly composed of middle class citizens concerned with their environment, Ma and his allies, including the journalist *Dài Qíng 戴晴 (b. 1941),

---

*People marked with an asterisk have entries in this dictionary.

have taken a low-key approach that relies heavily on the passage of key environmental legislation in China, evidently spurred on by its election to the World Trade Organization in 2001. This includes the Environmental Impact Assessment Law, granting the Chinese public the right to participate in environmental policy decision making, and the Cleaner Production Promotion Law, both enacted in 2003. In addition, there is the 2004 Program for Implementation of Governance by Law and the 2007 Measures on Open Environmental Information, requiring local government bureaus, which constitute the bureaucratic heart of China's often highly insulated regional regulatory fiefdoms, to disclose key environmental information. Once considered a virtual state secret, air pollution data in major cities is now openly published, often in real time and especially in cities with concentrations of heavy industry, and includes measures of particulate matter less than 2.5 micrometers (for years totally unavailable in China despite its enormously deleterious effect on human health). China also produced its first National Water Report in 2011, while a new amendment to the Environmental Protection Law contains an entire chapter on increasing transparency. Aware that many of the thousands of annual social protests in China involve environmental issues, the government has also pressured Chinese and foreign multinationals to release social responsibility reports on their environmental impact, though many often refuse.

In conjunction with over forty NGOs, IPE expanded to create the Green Choice Alliance to promote global green supply chains by prodding foreign multinational corporations operating in China to concentrate on the environmental performance of their Chinese suppliers. With an emphasis on promoting transparency, the coalition, in conjunction with the United States National Resources Defense Council, issues an annual Pollution Information Transparency Index that allows international companies to track suppliers charged with violating China's environmental laws. With information on 113 cities across China, the index has become a productive channel for encouraging local government offices to strengthen the country's transparency on environmental issues. Overall, the Green Choice Alliance has exposed over nine thousand violations by local and multinational corporations operating in China, while five hundred of these companies have been convinced to disclose to the public their plans for cleaning up their facilities. This includes such prominent multinationals as Walmart, General Electric, and Panasonic, while companies making the environmental "blacklist" issued by the Ministry of Environmental Protection have been especially anxious to take creative action.

Ma Jun at the Annual Meeting of the New Champions in Tianjin, China (2012). Photo by World Economic Forum from Cologny, Switzerland.

• Mǎ Jūn •

Throughout his efforts to balance China's economic growth with environmental protection, Ma Jun has consistently emphasized the importance of involving the public, a process that the advent of social media in the country has made increasingly effective, especially since 2011 when large swaths of Chinese citizens learned to engage this medium. Employing China's increasingly popular microblogging website Sina Weibo 新浪微博, where he has over sixteen thousand followers, Ma Jun has called on citizens to identify offending production facilities with photos and videos, while IPE activists have also joined in a campaign to "take a picture to locate a polluter." A new smartphone app developed by IPE allows people to compare pollution readings for 190 cities in China and share emissions data from over fifteen thousand factories.

This use of social media was particularly evident in the case of Apple Inc., which for years resisted efforts to even reveal its major supply chains in China, let alone address possible environmental violations, including the use of heavy metals, amounting to 12 million tons of contamination into water supplies. As part of its "poison apple" campaign, IPE released a short video entitled "The Other Side of Apple," which contained interviews with present and former employees of Apple's suppliers in China, such as the Wintek Corporation and Dongguan Shengyi Electronics, as well as images in which the dangers of new toxic chemical compounds used in touch-screen production were shown juxtaposed to high-powered promotions by then-CEO Steve Jobs. With over 140,000 downloads of the video in China, Apple, under a new CEO, finally responded in 2011, and in 2012 issued a "supplier responsibility progress report" on the environmental and workplace improvements by 110 of its Chinese suppliers.

Similar tactics have been employed by IPE and the Green Alliance against well-known consumer and personal care companies in China by providing information to their customers, who then will bring pressure on transgressing firms that, at first, were unmoved by such appeals. The 2012 report "Cleaning Up the Fashion Industry" is part of this effort to shift the focus from heavy industrial to light industry polluters, which is part of a larger plan to encourage the central government to break the deadlock of weak enforcement, especially at the local level. Convinced that China has the technology and the capital to adequately address its pervasive environmental problems, Ma and his allied NGOs are convinced the problem lies with the need to impose checks on local governments that are all too willing to ignore environmental regulations in the name of attracting more industry, no matter how harmful this is to the local environment. Present plans call for establishing an environmental gold standard that will entail even greater transparency through online monitoring of data from top polluters, along with systematic and comprehensive public disclosure of government supervisory and enforcement information.

Lawrence R. SULLIVAN
Adelphi University

Further Reading

Foroohar, Rana. (2013, June 24). Cleaning up China. *Time*. Retrieved November 10, 2014, from http://content.time.com/time/magazine/article/0,9171,2145500,00.html

Green Earth Volunteers. (2015). China Green News. Homepage. Retrieved July 7, 2015, from http://eng.greensos.cn/default.aspx

Institute of Public & Environmental Affairs (IPE). (2015). Homepage. Retrieved July 7, 2015, from http://www.ipe.org.cn/en/default.aspx

Li, Naomi. (2006). Tackling China's water crisis online. Retrieved April 8, 2015, from https://www.chinadialogue.net/article/show/single/en/392-Tackling-China-s-water-crisis-online

Ma Jun. (2004). *China's water crisis* (Nancy Yang Liu & Lawrence R. Sullivan, Trans.). Norwalk, CT: EastBridge. (Original work published 1999)

Moustakerski, Laura. (2014). Publishing pollution data in China: Ma Jun and the Institute of Public and Environmental Affairs. Retrieved April 8, 2015, from https://casestudies.jrn.columbia.edu/casestudy/www/layout/standard.asp?case_id=135&id=978

• Mǎ Jūn •

♂ Ma Ying-jeou

Mǎ Yīngjiǔ 馬英九

b. 1950—Politician and third democratically elected president of the Republic of China (Taiwan)

Alternate name: simpl. 马英九

Summary

In 2008, Ma Ying-jeou became the third popularly elected president in the Republic of China (Taiwan), and won reelection in 2012. He is appreciated in the United States for his work in cross-Strait relations, and the Chinese have seen him as a relatively good cross-Strait partner. In the domestic arena, however, he is regarded as a poor leader, shown by his consistently low approval ratings.

Ma Ying-jeou was born in Hong Kong on 13 July 1950 though, as he emphasized in the 2008 presidential campaign, he was conceived in Taiwan. The son of a general, Ma led the life of a relatively privileged mainlander, going to school in Taipei where he graduated from the well-known Jianguo High School 建國高級中學. Ma then studied law at National Taiwan University (NTU), where he graduated in 1972. Later, Ma went to the United States where he received an LLM degree from New York University School of Law in 1976 and a SJD degree from Harvard Law School in 1981. His doctoral thesis from Harvard on the East China Sea was published as a monograph (Ma 1984).

Early Political Life

After working in the United States for a year, Ma returned to Taiwan in 1981 and became deputy director of the First Bureau in Chiang Ching-kuo's 蔣經國 presidential office as well as Chiang's English interpreter. From 1984 to 1988, he also served as deputy secretary-general of the Nationalist Party (Kuomintang 國民黨, KMT). Ma's appointment to these senior positions while still relatively young clearly indicated his high status among mainlander youth during Chiang Ching-kuo's rule.

In July 1988, after President *Lee Teng-hui 李登輝 (b. 1923) came to power,

---

*People marked with an asterisk have entries in this dictionary.

Ma Ying-jeou was appointed the youngest member of the cabinet as chairman of the Research, Development and Evaluation Commission, a position he held for about three years. In June 1991, he became deputy chairman of the Mainland Affairs Commission, then responsible for coordinating Taiwan's relations with China. On 27 February 1993, Ma again returned to the cabinet as minister of justice, though he was dismissed on 10 June 1996, reputedly for his zealous prosecution of political candidates who had bought votes. He then served as minister without portfolio for a year before moving to academia, where he taught as an associate professor at National Chengchi University.

In 1998, Ma campaigned to become mayor of Taipei. In 1994, against a divided KMT, *Chén Shuǐ-biǎn 陳水扁 (b. 1951) of the Democratic Progressive Party (DDP) won the first popular election of a mayor of Taipei since Taipei was elevated to provincial status in 1967. Taipei has a very large population of mainlanders, who vote ethnically (Cheng and Hsu 2002, 152; Jacobs 2012a, 134) and, despite Chen Shui-bian's very high approval rating, Ma Ying-jeou defeated Chen in 1998. Ma easily won reelection in 2002, and went on to serve the maximum two terms from 1998 to 2006. In 2005, Ma also became chairman of the KMT, a position he held until 2007, when he resigned after being indicted for corruption, though a court later found him not guilty.

Ma's Presidency

Ma Ying-jeou brought several positive features to his campaign for Taiwan's presidency. He was relatively young by KMT standards (fifty-seven in early 2008), handsome, and with a reputation as a reformer. Although a mainlander, he strongly asserted his Taiwan identity during the presidential campaign. On the other hand, many doubted his claim of Taiwan identity and Ma had a habit of saying one thing at one time and quite a different thing at another time. This inconsistency would cause him trouble. Critics also noted that he had in fact never implemented his party "reform" proposals.

Ma's presidential campaign against the DPP's nominee, Frank Chang-ting Hsieh (Xiè Chángtíng 謝長廷), demonstrated these inconsistencies. Ma moved closer to his opponent's policies, declaring late in the campaign that Taiwan is sovereign and that its future should only be decided by the people of Taiwan. Ma's campaign was also greatly helped when Hsieh suffered a minor stroke on 27 September 2007, which clearly inhibited Hsieh's campaign energy. Ma won the 22 March 2008 presidential election with a landslide victory, winning 58.45 percent of the vote (Jacobs 2012a, 234–236).

The strong sense of Taiwan identity that Ma tried to create in his campaign dissipated with his inauguration speech of 20 May 2008. The speech placed strong emphasis on how both sides of the

Ma Ying-jeou campaigning in 2008. Photo by Jimmy Yao.

Taiwan Straits were Chinese and Ma seemed to pull back on his commitment to Taiwan's sovereignty (Jacobs 2012a, 237–238).

Ma made clear to the United States that he was not a "troublemaker" and he made considerable efforts to deal with the Chinese, who, in order to give Ma credit, promulgated a number of agreements such as cross-Strait flights only after Ma's inauguration. On 29 June 2010, the Taiwan and Chinese sides signed an Economic Cooperation Framework Agreement (ECFA), which some Taiwan government officials saw as simply a framework for the future, while others called it a free trade agreement between China and Taiwan. Analyses four years

later suggest that ECFA has had little economic impact in Taiwan (Lee 2014, Fuller 2014). There was also considerable criticism of the Ma government's repression of the Republic of China flag and civil demonstrations during visits of senior Chinese envoys to Taiwan.

In the 2008 election campaign, Ma had promoted and capitalized on a perception that the previous Chen Shui-bian government was both corrupt and incompetent. Yet the Ma government too came to be seen as incompetent. In the words of a senior KMT official, President Ma liked to use people similar to himself. Thus, the disastrous appointment of Su Chi (Sū Qǐ 蘇起), whom Ma treated like a "brother," as secretary-general of the

National Security Council took almost two years to resolve (Jacobs 2010). Similarly, the appointment as premier of such people as Liu Chao-shiuan (Liú Zhàoxuán 劉兆玄) (2008–2009), Sean Chen (Chén Chōng 陳冲) (2012–2013), and Jiang Yi-huah (Jiāng Yíhuà 江宜樺) (2013–2014) has also proven disastrous. None of these premiers had been elected to public office or served the Taiwan government outside of Taipei. None could speak Taiwanese or Hokkien (the mother language of over 75 percent of Taiwan's population). Only Premier Wu Den-yih (Wú Dūnyì 吳敦義) (2010–2012) had won several electoral offices and served outside Taipei in his native Nantou and in Kaohsiung, but he was removed as premier when he became vice-president in the 2012 presidential election.

President Ma won a lackluster campaign for reelection on 14 January 2012 against the DPP nominee, Tsai Ing-wen (Cài Yīngwén 蔡英文), winning 51.6 percent of the vote, a significant decline from 2008, but still a majority of votes cast. Ma benefited because Tsai failed to make clear her policy towards China (she urged a meaningless "Taiwan consensus") and because she relied upon a very small and incompetent group of advisors to run her campaign (Jacobs 2012b).

Ma's leadership ineptness continued in his second term. On 7 September 2013 he accused long-term Speaker of the Legislature Wang Jin-pyng (Wáng Jīnpíng 王金平) of influence peddling. Ma attacked Wang, a Taiwanese and

leading member of the Kuomintang, while he was in Malaysia attending his daughter's wedding. Wang immediately fought back and the court decisions have unanimously backed Wang. Ma's attack on Wang proved counterproductive when the student-led Sunflower Movement (Tàiyánghuā xuéyùn 太陽花學運) occupied the Legislative Yuan to protest the Cross-Strait Service Trade Agreement (CSSTA) in March and April 2014 and Wang, as speaker, became critical to the solution of the occupation. Ma also proved incompetent when he called a major international press conference during the Sunflower Movement and only answered three questions from friendly sources, relenting only after the press protested vociferously.

In the November 2014 local elections, the KMT suffered a devastating defeat at the polls. The cabinet of Jiang Yi-huah resigned to take responsibility and a few days later Ma Ying-jeou resigned as chairman of the KMT. Eric Chu (Zhū Lìlún 朱立倫), mayor of New Taipei City became the party's new chairman. The KMT under Eric Chu also dropped its appeals against Speaker Wang Jin-pyng.

Evaluating Ma Ying-jeou

For a president who was elected by a landslide and reelected comfortably, Ma's approval ratings have been very low. During his first term, ratings were generally in the low 30 percent range and even dropped to 16 percent on one occasion, much below Chen Shui-bian's approval ratings (Jacobs 2012a, 254–261). Ma's second-term approval ratings have been even lower, falling to less than 20 percent in May 2014 (Hsu and Chang 2014).

A Bifurcated Image as President

For many Americans, especially conservatives, Ma Ying-jeou has been seen to reduce tensions across the Taiwan Strait and has not become a "troublemaker" for the United States. After initial difficulties with Japan and the Philippines, Ma managed to resolve those relations, which became much smoother. Relations with China, however, appear to have deteriorated and Ma did not get to meet *Xí Jìnpíng 习近平 (b. 1953) at the Asia-Pacific Economic Cooperation (APEC) meeting in Beijing, though much of the responsibility for the deterioration also rests with China. Domestically, however, he has proven an incompetent leader who has possibly damaged Taiwan's international standing by negotiating poor economic agreements with China and being unwilling to speak clearly about Taiwan's sovereignty.

J. Bruce JACOBS
Monash University

Further Reading

Cheng, Tun-jen & Hsu, Yung-ming. (2002). The March 2000 election in historical and comparative perspectives: Strategic voting, the Third Party, and the non-Duvergerian outcome. In Bruce J. Dickson & Chen-min Chao (Eds.), *Assessing the Lee Teng-hui legacy in Taiwan's politics: Democratic consolidation and external relations* (pp. 148–174). Armonk, NY: M.E. Sharpe.

Fuller, Douglas. (2014). ECFA's empty promise and hollow threat. In Jean-Pierre Cabestan & Jacques deLisle (Eds.), *Political Changes in Taiwan under Ma Ying-jeou: Partisan conflict, policy choices, external constraints and security challenges* (pp. 85–99). London and New York: Routledge.

Hsu, Stacy & Chang, Richard. (2014, May 14). Separate polls put Ma's approval rate under 18 percent. *Taipei Times*, p. 1. Retrieved April 17, 2015, from http://www.taipeitimes.com/News/front/archives/2014/05/14/2003590295

Jacobs, J. Bruce. (2010, February 24). Su Chi's resignation long overdue. *Taipei Times*, p. 8. Retrieved April 17, 2015, from http://www.taipeitimes.com/News/editorials/archives/2010/02/24/2003466473

Jacobs, J. Bruce. (2012a). *Democratizing Taiwan.* Leiden, The Netherlands: E.J. Brill.

Jacobs, J. Bruce. (2012b, January 16). DPP faces hard truths after defeat. *Taipei Times*, 2012, p. 8. http://www.taipeitimes.com/News/editorials/archives/2012/01/16/2003523315

Lee Hsin-fang. (2014, August 17). ECFA benefited trade little: ministries. *Taipei Times*. p. 3. Retrieved April 17, 2015, from http://www.taipeitimes.com/News/taiwan/archives/2014/08/17/2003597611

Ma Ying-jeou. (1984). *Legal problems of seabed boundary delimitation in the East China Sea.* Baltimore: Occasional Papers/Reprints Series in Contemporary Asian Studies, School of Law, University of Maryland.

馬英九

☿ Ma, Jack

Mǎ Yún 马云

b. 1964—Internet entrepreneur, founder and executive chairman of Alibaba

Alternate name: trad. 馬雲

Summary

Known as one of China's first and most successful Internet entrepreneurs, Jack Ma is the founder and executive chairman of Alibaba, an e-commerce site that went public in 2014; Taobao, China's largest online shopping platform; and Alipay, China's first third-party online payment system. Since 2013, Ma has also founded new Internet companies and worked on behalf of environmental causes in China.

Born in the south-central city of Hangzhou, Zhejiang Province in September 1964 with the Chinese name Ma Yun (lit. "Horse Cloud"), Jack Ma is founder and executive chairman of Alibaba Group Holding Limited, China's largest e-commerce Internet company. Currently the third richest man in China and eighteenth in the world with an approximate net worth of over US$30 billion, Ma and friends, including Péng Lěi 彭蕾, established Alibaba in 1999 as a consumer-to-consumer, business-to-consumer, and business-to-business company. The first entrepreneur from the People's Republic of China (PRC) to appear on the cover of *Forbes Magazine*, Jack Ma is the recipient of many international awards including an honorary doctorate from Hong Kong University of Science and Technology. Ma, who is fluent in English, often appears in Western media, and has become the "face" of Alibaba, much as Steve Jobs was the face of Apple.

From English to Computers

As a young man in Hangzhou, Ma exhibited an early desire to learn English by biking to local foreign tourist hotels where in return for leading city tours of Hangzhou, considered one of China's most beautiful urban areas, he would engage English-speaking foreigners in conversation. Having failed the National College Entrance Examination (generally known as the *gāokǎo* 高考) twice, he enrolled in the Hangzhou Teachers

Institute and graduated in 1988 with a degree in English. This was followed by a stint at Hangzhou Dianzi University where he taught courses in both English and international trade. Ma also attended the Cheung Kong Graduate School of Business in Beijing founded by Hong Kong's *Li Ka-shing 李嘉誠 (b. 1928), one of the richest men in Asia. At age thirty-three Ma first encountered computers, then a rarity in China, and became aware of the Internet in 1994–1995 during a visit to the United States. Relying on a small loan, he established his first company named "China Yellow Pages" in 1995, to assist Chinese companies in creating their own websites, which within three years earned 5 million yuan (around US$800,000).

Founding Alibaba

Following work at an electronics company established by the Ministry of Foreign Trade and Economic Cooperation, he left his job in 1999 and returned to Hangzhou where he and a few friends set up Alibaba. Taking the name from the legendary wise-man character from medieval Arabic literature, Alibaba quickly took advantage of the rapid growth of the computer industry in China, creating the web domain alibaba.com. In short order, Ma took his concept global by hiring American executives and engineers to build the technology

platform and advertising in numerous foreign markets, especially in the United States as a portal to connect Chinese manufacturers with domestic and overseas buyers. This was greatly facilitated by US$25 million in venture capital investments from numerous sources including China Development Bank, Goldman Sachs, Japan's Softbank and, most importantly, by Jerry Yang of Yahoo! who bought a significant stake in the company. In 2003–2004, additional companies were created including Táobǎo 淘宝 (lit. "searching for treasure"), which quickly emerged as China's largest online shopping platform, providing a wide variety of product offerings; and Alipay which, modeled on Pay-Pal, was China's first third-party online payment solution.

According to its official website, Alibaba has 300 million registered users, 60 million regular visitors, and currently executes about 80 percent of China's e-commerce transactions. In 2009, Ma announced that Alibaba would become heavily involved in cloud computing, an aim to build an advanced, data-centered service platform, including e-commerce data mining, high-speed massive e-commerce data processing, and data customization, this from a man who admitted he had never written a single line of computer code and who famously once said "I know nothing about technology." The same year saw Ma's invention of what became the widely popular "singles day" (11 November) when young Chinese are encouraged to celebrate their

---

*People marked with an asterisk have entries in this dictionary.

unmarried status by employing Alibaba to purchase discounted consumer products. As online transactions in 2012 exceeded one trillion yuan (US$170 million), Ma was dubbed by his employees as "trillion *hou*" 万亿侯 ("trillion yuan marquis"). Known for his hard-driving administrative style, Ma announced in 2013 a significant restructuring of the company, dividing its original six major subsidiaries into twenty-five separate units as a way to ensure that the company would keep pace with the rapidly growing e-commerce industry in China and internationally. At the same time, in an open letter to his employees, he announced plans to retire as CEO as he claimed he was too "old" for the Internet business and has even commented that he often finds being rich "tiring." Yet Ma has a lighter side, often entertaining his employees by cross-dressing and regaling them with songs that reflected his parents' career as traditional musicians.

Post-Alibaba

Despite Ma's retirement as CEO of Alibaba in 2013, he remains on as executive chairman and is still actively involved in the company's management. He led the effort to take the company public with an initial public offering (IPO) that was introduced on the New York Stock Exchange in 2014. While US$25 billion was successfully raised, the fact that the offering bypassed the Hong Kong Hang Seng provoked the chagrin of many Chinese who were effectively prevented from buying stock in the company. Ma is currently taking on China's state-dominated finance industry with his newly named business, Zhejiang Ant Small and Micro Financial Services Group, which processes payments, sells insurance, and runs one of the world's largest money market funds. The company is going head-to-head with China's highly profitable banks, operating in a highly regulated market, and standing against competitors largely owned and subsidized by the Chinese government. In the future, according to Ma, the company will focus on three pillars of future business: e-commerce, finance (providing loans to small and medium enterprises in China), and data mining, since it has just begun to scratch the surface of analyzing the reams of user data generated through its business-to-business e-commerce site and consumer-to-consumer platform, Taobao.

Since 2013, Ma has also devoted himself to many interests including serving on the board of Japan's Softbank and acting as the trustee for the Nature Conservancy China Program, reflecting his growing interest in environmentalism. In 2015, Ma bought a 28,100-acre property in upstate New York, planning to turn it into a conservation area. In China, Ma has already been involved in setting up a nature reserve in Sichuan Province, and he is a founding member of the Sichuan Nature Conservation Foundation, the nongovernmental organization that runs the reserve (Tilton 2015). Ma has also joined such prominent Chinese as basketball star *Yáo Míng 姚明 (b. 1980) in proposing a ban on Chinese consumption of shark-fin soup because of its highly destructive effects on the world's shark population. Ma also sits on the board of the Breakthrough Prize in Life Sciences, which includes other well-known international billionaires such as Facebook's Mark Zuckerberg. Reflecting his international reputation, Ma is frequently invited to lecture at some of the world's most popular and prominent universities, such as the University of Pennsylvania's Wharton School, Massachusetts Institute of Technology, and Harvard University, from which Ma claimed he had been rejected for admission on ten separate occasions. Ma is married to Zhāng Yīng 张瑛 and they have one son and one daughter.

Lawrence R. SULLIVAN
Adelphi University

Further Reading

D'Onfro, Jillian. (2014). How Jack Ma went from being a poor school teacher to turning Alibaba into a $160 billion behemoth. Retrieved March 4, 2015, from http://www.businessinsider.com/the-story-of-jack-ma-founder-of-alibaba-2014-9#ixzz3TPYvDUht

Erisman, Porter. (2015). *Alibaba's world: How a remarkable Chinese company is changing the face of global business.* New York: Palgrave MacMillan.

Erisman, Porter. (Producer & Director). (2012). *Crocodile on the Yangtze.* United States: Taluswood Films.

Liu Shiying, & Avery, Marthy. (2009). *Alibaba: The inside story behind Jack Ma and the creation of the world's biggest online marketplace.* New York: Harper Collins.

Stone, Madeline, & D'onfro, Jillian. (2014). The inspiring life story of Alibaba founder Jack Ma, now the richest man in China. *Business Insider.* Retrieved June 9, 2015, from http://www.businessinsider.com/the-inspiring-life-story-of-alibaba-founder-jack-ma-2014-10?op=1&IR=T

Sun Jianmin, & Cui Huijian. (2009). Ma Yun. In Zhang Wenxian & Ilan Alon (Eds.), *Biographical dictionary of new Chinese entrepreneurs and business leaders.* Northampton, MA: Edward Elgar Publishing.

Tilton, Sarah. (2015, June 24). Alibaba's Jack Ma buys $23 million property in New York's Adirondacks. *The Wall Street Journal.* Retrieved July 27, 2015, from http://www.wsj.com/articles/alibabas-jack-ma-buys-23-million-property-in-new-yorks-adirondacks-1435155612

Greeven, Mark J. (2014). *The Alibaba group and Jack Ma.* In Tony Fu-Lai Yu & Yan Ho-Don. (2014). *Handbook of East Asian entrepreneurship.* London: Routledge.

☩ Mò Yán 莫言

b. 1955—Chinese author, winner of the 2012 Nobel Prize in Literature

Alternate name: b. Guǎn Móyè 管谟业

Summary

Mo Yan, winner of the 2012 Nobel Prize in Literature, burst onto the Chinese literary scene in the 1980s and quickly established himself as one of the most popular and influential contemporary Chinese writers. Working with the themes of hunger, loneliness, and violence, Mo Yan writes about Chinese people's will for survival in times of pain and suffering.

Mo Yan, winner of the 2012 Nobel Prize in Literature and one of China's most celebrated novelists, was born into a peasant family in Northeast Gaomi Township, Shandong Province. His birth name was Guan Moye. Mo Yan is his pen name, which literally means "don't speak," an ironic twist for a writer known for his metaphors and loquaciousness.

Mo Yan had a difficult childhood. Hunger is the central theme of his memories about growing up in the rural village where his family has been for generations. To make matters worse, he was expelled from primary school for some mischief during the height of the Cultural Revolution (1966–1976), so the future literary giant of China officially received only a fifth-grade education. Lonely and hopeless, Mo Yan escaped into the world of books when he was not helping with the family's farm work. His elder brother, who was studying Chinese language and literature at a college in Shanghai, was an inspiration and a great help for Mo Yan's early literary aspirations. Mo Yan read all his brother's secondary school textbooks and many other books, improving his literacy skills. At that time in rural China, however, the only way out for young men was to join the People's Liberation Army. Joining the army was not only an honorable profession, but also a chance for a better life. Mo Yan did so in 1976, but he would turn out to be a soldier with pens, not guns.

Mo Yan burst on the literary scene in 1981 after he published his first short story, titled "Falling Rain on a Spring

Night" ("Chūnyǔ yèfēi fēi" 春雨夜霏霏), while in the army. In 1985, Mo Yan gained recognition for his short story titled "The Transparent Carrot" ("Tòumíng de hóngluóbo" 透明的红萝卜). A year later his novel *Red Sorghum* (*Hóng gāoliáng* 红高粱) firmly established him as one of the most important writers of his generation. Mo Yan subsequently wrote another four novels, together named *The Family Saga of Red Sorghum* (*Hóng gāoliáng jiāzú* 红高粱家族) which was quickly made into a film by director *Zhāng Yìmóu 张艺谋 (b. 1951) and won the Golden Bear prize at the 38th Berlin International Film Festival. In 1997 Mo Yan left the army. Many works of fiction followed, each pushing him closer to the highest honor for contemporary Chinese literature. In 2012, Mo Yan won the Nobel Prize for Literature. Although the Chinese-French writer *Gāo Xíngjiàn 高行健 (b. 1940) won the same prize in 2000, Mo Yan is officially recognized as the first Chinese citizen to win the prize while living in China, thus fulfilling the country's long-standing "Nobel Prize dream."

Inspiration and Style

The 1980s were a "golden era" for arts and literature in China. The economic reforms brought about an unprecedented openness that encouraged creativity and learning from the West. Mo Yan has repeatedly acknowledged his

indebtedness to foreign writers during his formative years, including William Faulkner, Gabriel García Márquez, Gustave Flaubert, and James Joyce. At the same time Mo Yan has found even greater inspiration from Chinese masters of the past, particularly the great short story writer Pú Sōnglíng 蒲松龄 (1640–1715), who lived not too far from Mo Yan's hometown. Although Chinese critics tend to group Mo Yan with "root-seeking" and "avant-garde" writers, he truly found his own voice for telling his stories.

Mo Yan so far has published more than eighty short stories, thirty novellas and eleven novels, plus a dozen plays and many essays. His works have been translated into many foreign languages, including English, Swedish, Russian, Japanese, and Korean. The fictional world that he creates is colorful and various, filled with fascinating people from China's past and present who live and die in spectacular fashion. There are references to historical events in modern China that reveal Mo Yan's cultural sensitivity and social criticism, but more often he relishes in presenting stories of the supernatural, the grotesque, and the bizarre that illuminate his power of imagination.

Mo Yan has captured the attention of millions of readers and has won all of the major literary awards in China, but he is not without critics. In fact, debates about his works have been occurring since the beginning of his literary career. When "The Transparent Carrot" came out,

---

*People marked with an asterisk have entries in this dictionary.

Gaomi Township in Mo Yan's Imagination

The following passage from Mo Yan's famous novel Red Sorghum *describes Gaomi, the hometown of the protagonist, which also happens to be Mo Yan's own real-life hometown.*

[...] I had learned to love Northeast Gaomi Township with all my heart, and to hate it with unbridled fury. I didn't realise until I'd grown up that Northeast Gaomi Township is easily the most beautiful and most repulsive, most unusual and most common, most sacred and most corrupt, most heroic and most bastardly, hardest-drinking and hardest-loving place in the world. The people of my father's generation who lived there ate sorghum out of preference, planting as much of it as they could. In late autumn, during the eighth lunar month, vast stretches of red sorghum shimmered like a sea of blood. Tall and dense, it reeked of glory; cold and graceful, it promised enchantment; passionate and loving, it was tumultuous.

The autumn winds are cold and bleak, the sun's rays intense. White clouds, full and round, float in the tile-blue sky, casting full round purple shadows onto the sorghum fields below. Over decades that seem but a moment in time, lines of scarlet figures shuttled among the sorghum stalks to weave a vast human tapestry. They killed, they looted, and they defended their country in a valiant, stirring ballet that makes us unfilial descendants who now occupy the land pale by comparison. Surrounded by progress, I feel a nagging sense of our species' regression.

Source: Mo Yan. (1992). *Red Sorghum* (Howard Goldblatt, Trans.), p. 4. London: Arrow Books.

• Mo Yan •

some critics were taken aback by its pseudo-fairytale narrative and its dark view on life and humanity, yet years later the short story became required reading for high school students. Concerns also linger about the substantial contents of sex and violence in Mo Yan's novels, such as the titillating sex scenes in his novel *Big Breast and Wide Hips* (*Fēng rǔ féi tún* 丰乳肥臀) and the excruciating details of torture in *Sandalwood Death* (*Tán xiāng xíng* 檀香刑). Even his characteristic language of narration has been criticized as verbose, with overblown images and metaphors that convey nothing but eloquent nonsense on occasion. His noted silence on China's current social and political issues is also a point for criticism and discussion. In China's rapidly changing social environment where competing values (including literary values) have become a normal way of life, such controversies about Mo Yan and his works are not surprising and they certainly have not diminished his reputation as one of the most important Chinese writers living today.

Setting and Themes

The setting for all of Mo Yan's novels has the same name as his hometown, Northeast Gaomi Township; the people who live there and the legends kept alive by oral storytelling are the fabrics of his narratives. He records what happens at this place, but he also creates it. For example, in the novel *Red Sorghum* Mo Yan uses a dislocated narrator who returns home to search for lost stories about his ancestors, yet the stories he finds are half historical and half imaginative, all reconstructed to highlight his ancestors' lives of passion and abandonment in times of great social turmoil and national crisis.

Hunger, loneliness, and violence are prominent themes in Mo Yan's fiction. On many occasions, Mo Yan recalls his experiences with them during his childhood in the extremely impoverished countryside. In some way, writing for him is an escape from these memories because of the distance it creates between the past and the present. It is for the same reason that Mo Yan often uses a child's perspective and highly sensual language to tell his stories. For example, "The Transparent Carrot" centers on a "black child," a thin and reticent boy who uses his senses of smell, sight, and taste to experience the world. This boy has an obsession with the taste of burned skin and loves the image of the carrot glowing in the sunlight, which becomes a thing of magic through Mo Yan's stylistic language. The deprived life of a twelve-year-old is somewhat enriched by this surreal image of the radish.

Creative narration is Mo Yan's signature. Every novel is a new stage for his language experiment and narrative innovation, a testimony to his talent and unlimited resources. He has used more elements from Chinese dialects and folk traditions than any other modern writer; his extensive use of absurdity and irony helps to expose the fallacy of history and reality; and his creation of endless fresh metaphors and similes fully explores the symbolic power of the Chinese language to reveal the light and the dark sides of the human existence. Nobody has done more in the last four decades than Mo Yan to expand the narrative possibilities for the contemporary Chinese novel.

In his essay "Writing as the People," Mo Yan says that there are two kinds of writers: one who writes for the people, and the other who writes *as* people (Mo Yan 2012). He belongs to the latter group. This is a novel way for a Chinese writer to locate himself within Chinese society. It is Mo Yan's way of saying that his writings are as much about himself as they are about others. In every story of hunger, loneliness, and violence, there is the shadow of Mo Yan's own impoverished childhood and tortured family history. At the same time Mo Yan can describe universal experiences such as pain and suffering with such compassion and can imagine life with such passion. This is also why he is recognized as one of the best storytellers of our time by readers in China and elsewhere.

YU Minhua
Zhejiang Normal University

Further Reading

Cai, Rong. (2003). Problematizing the foreign other: Mother, father, and the bastard in Mo Yan's *Large Breasts and Full Hips. Modern China, 29*(1), 108–137.

Chan, Shelley W. (2011). *A subversive voice in China: The fictional world of Mo Yan.* Amherst, NY: Cambria Press.

Davis-Undiano, Robert Con. (2013). A Westerner's reflection on Mo Yan. *Chinese Literature Today, 3*(1/2), 21–25.

Mo Yan. (1991). White dog and the swings. (Michael S. Duke, Trans.). In Michael S. Duke (Ed.), *Worlds of modern Chinese fiction: Short stories & novellas from the People's Republic, Taiwan & Hong Kong*. Armonk, NY: Sharpe. (Original work published 1985)

Mo Yan. (1993). *Red sorghum: A novel of China* (Howard Goldblatt, Trans.). New York: Viking Penguin. (Original work published 1987)

Mo Yan. (1995). *The garlic ballads* (Howard Goldblatt, Trans.). New York: Viking Penguin. (Original work published 1988)

Mo Yan. (2000). *The republic of* wine (Howard Goldblatt, Trans.). New York: Arcade. (Original work published 1993)

Mo Yan. (2001). *Shifu, you'll do anything for a laugh* (Howard Goldblatt, Trans.). Hodder Paperback. (Original work published 1999).

Mo Yan. (2004). *Big breasts and wide hips* (Howard Goldblatt, Trans.). New York: Arcade. (Original work published 1995)

Mo Yan. (2008). *Life and death are wearing me out* (Howard Goldblatt, Trans.). New York: Arcade. (Original work published 2006)

Mo Yan. (2012). *Zuowei laobaixing de xiezuo* 作为老百姓的写作 [Writing as the people]. In *Yong erduo yuedu* 用耳朵阅读 [Reading with ears] (pp. 65–72). Beijing: Zuojia chubanshe.

Riemenschnitter, Andrea. (2013). A gun is not a woman: Local subjectivity in Mo Yan's novel Tanxiangxing. *Frontiers of literary studies in China, 7*(4), 590–616.

Yang Xiaobin. (1998). The republic of wine: An extravaganza of decline. *Positions, 6*(1), 7–25.

Zhu Ling. (1993). A brave new world? On the construction of 'masculinity' and 'femininity' in The Red Sorghum Family. In Lu Tonglin (Ed.), *Gender and sexuality in twentieth-century Chinese literature and society* (pp. 121–134). Albany, NY: SUNY Press.

• Mò Yán •

♂ Péng Zhēn 彭真

1902–1997—Political leader and influential legal advisor

•彭真•

Summary

Peng Zhen was one of the most influential political leaders of Maoist and early post-Mao China. After being purged from Chinese Communist Party leadership at the outset of the Cultural Revolution in 1966, Peng resumed responsibility for the legal system in 1978 and oversaw the emergence of the National People's Congress as a key political and policy actor. Peng's discourse of socialist legalism remains a key feature of China's legal system today.

Peng Zhen had a lasting impact on the socialist legal system of the People's Republic of China (PRC). His leadership in the Chinese Communist Party's (CCP) political-legal (*zhèngfǎ* 政法) system during the 1950s and again in the early 1980s shaped the ideological and institutional foundations for legal reform in the post-Mao period. As chair of the National People's Congress Standing Committee beginning in 1983, Peng exercised unparalleled authority over content and process of legislation. Peng's slogan, "the party leads the people in enacting the law and leads the people in observing the law" (Peng 1991a, 389), remains a dominant theme of party orthodoxy on ruling the country by law (*yīfǎ zhìguó* 依法治国) (Wu 2000; Zhang 2000; Tian 2000, 412). Peng's views on law and political authority reflected the political conditions of his time. Early on, he was associated with some of the most repressive aspects of communist rule, but after the Cultural Revolution (1966–1976), Peng called for increased reliance on more-formal rules and procedures. Nonetheless, the theme of CCP control remained constant and continues to characterize China's legal policies.

Rise and Fall

Born in remote Shanxi Province on 12 October 1902, Peng lived through periods of warlord strife, Japanese invasion, and civil war. While most authorities agree that Peng came from a poor peasant family, during the Cultural Revolution, Red Guard criticisms of Peng claimed that his was a rich peasant background (Mao 1967; Klein and Clark 1970). He joined the Chinese Communist Party in 1923 and became active in labor-organizing work among factory and railway workers in Shijiazhuang (Hebei CPC 1998). He was also active in underground labor-organizing in Tianjin and Tangshan. For these actions, he spent time in Nationalist Party prisons in Tianjin and Beiping (later renamed Beijing). Following his release from prison in 1935, Peng began a long standing relationship with Liú Shàoqí 刘少奇 (1898–1969) when Liu took over the CCP's North China Bureau in Tianjin, where Peng was director of the Organization Department (Huang 1998). In 1938, Peng was appointed party secretary and later chairman of the Government Council of the Jinchaji Border Region (covering areas of Shanxi, Chahar, and Hebei). Peng went to Yan'an in 1941 to become vice-president of the Central Party School. In this capacity, Peng played a key role in the Party's Rectification Campaign (1942–1944), aimed at enforcing Maoist orthodoxy on CCP cadres, particularly those newly admitted to the Party.

With responsibilities for urban work and party organization, Peng was appointed to the Politburo at the Seventh National CCP Congress in 1945 and served as an alternate member of the Secretariat. After the Japanese surrender in the Second Sino-Japanese War (1937–1945), Peng was appointed secretary of the Northeast Bureau in Manchuria and political commissar for the army commanded by Lín Biāo 林彪 (1907–1971). Peng was removed from these posts in 1946 due to policy conflicts with Lin and Mao over political and military strategy—primarily the question of whether to emphasize urban (Peng) or rural (Lin and Mao Zedong) areas in resisting the Nationalist Party's expansion into Manchuria after the defeat of Japan (Ebon 1970, 260). This effectively ended Peng's involvement in military matters, although his antagonistic relationship with Lin continued in subsequent years and no doubt played a role in ideological attacks on Peng during the Cultural Revolution by staunch Mao supporters.

From 1947 to 1949, Peng focused on land reform issues in Jinchaji and other liberated areas of North China. He also began to take on greater responsibilities in preparation for the capture and ultimately the administration of Beijing (Peng 1991b). After the establishment of the PRC in 1949, Peng was made secretary of the Beijing Party Committee and held concurrent positions in the Chinese People's Political Consultative Conference and the Central People's Government Council. Peng was also appointed vice-chairman and party secretary of the government's Political-Legal Affairs Commission.

Péng Zhēn

Mao Zedong, Peng Zhen, Norodom Sihanouk, and Liu Shaoqi in 1956. Official US Army Photograph.

In the early 1960s, Peng was given responsibility for the Party's culture policies, possibly due to his role in the Yan'an Rectification Campaign, which saw Mao's famous 1942 speech to the Yan'an Forum on Literature and Art extol the need for party control over culture. As a result of the political infighting that had intensified following the Great Leap Forward (1958–1960) and the Socialist Education Campaign (1963–1966), indirect criticism of Mao soon became prominent in the literary circles for which Peng had responsibility. As head of a five man Cultural Revolution Group charged by Mao to direct the criticism of the writer Wu Han and his play "Hai Rui Dismissed from Office" 海瑞罢官, Peng attempted to confine criticism of Wu to academic rather than political issues. This led to a final break with Mao, and Peng was dismissed from his posts in May 1966; this event is often taken as the opening salvo of the Cultural Revolution. Peng was initially confined at one of the Central Case Examination Group prisons on the outskirts of Beijing (Schoenhals 1996). After 1975, however, he appears to have been exiled to Shaanxi Province (Seymour 1980, 194).

Political Rehabilitation

Following the landmark Third Plenum of the Eleventh Central Committee in late 1978, Peng was rehabilitated along with many other Cultural Revolution victims. Peng was appointed chairman of the NPC Committee for Legislative Affairs and vice-chairman of the NPC Standing Committee (World Broadcasts 1979). He also soon regained his former position on the Politburo (Bartke 1981). As vice-chairman of the Committee for Revising the Constitution, Peng played a key role in designing the document that remains the foundation for CCP rule in China. In December 1982 Peng became first secretary of the Party's Central Political-Legal Committee, although he was passed over for appointment to the Politburo Standing Committee. Instead, he was appointed chairman of the Sixth NPC Standing Committee in June 1983. In this position he played an active role in drafting a wide range of legislation, including the General Principles of Civil Law (1986) and the Bankruptcy Law (1986). Peng resigned from the Central Political-Legal Committee and Politburo in October 1987 and was replaced by *Wàn Lǐ 万里 (b. 1916) as chair of the NPC Standing Committee the following spring.

Following his formal retirement, Peng remained active politically, participating on the informal council of elders that advised *Dèng Xiǎopíng 邓小平 (1904–1997) on key issues, including the handling of the Tiananmen crisis in 1989. Empowered by his status as an elder statesman, Peng continued to make periodic pronouncements on legal reform throughout the late 1980s and early

1990s. Gradually, however, his advanced age and associated health problems confined him to a wheelchair and, despite occasional televised inspection tours of Beijing in 1995 and 1996, Peng limited his public appearances. He died 26 April 1997 at age ninety-five.

Legacy: From Leninist Discipline to Socialist Legalism

As leader of the CCP's *zhengfa* system and chair of the NPC Standing Committee, Peng exercised unparalleled leadership over post-Mao legal reform efforts. Despite the obvious parallels to his legal responsibilities for CCP political-legal work in the 1950s, Peng's career during the post-Mao era reflected changing priorities—both his own and those of the party-state. In the 1950s, for example, questions of revolutionary consolidation and class struggle dominated political and policy discourse, while in the 1980s economic development became a key priority. Peng's positions on law and governance during the post-Mao period reflected these changed conditions, revealing a transition from relying on the Party's policy discretion toward emphasis on formal rules and processes interpreted and enforced by the party-state. This transition from Leninist discipline to socialist legalism stands as Peng's legacy to the PRC legal system. Whereas the 1950s typology of Leninist discipline

---

*People marked with an asterisk have entries in this dictionary.

• Péng Zhēn •

placed a premium on strict compliance by subordinates, with party policies decided at higher levels, the socialist legalism that emerged in the 1980s combined policy goals of collective and state ownership in the economy with autocratic norms of the Qín 秦 dynasty (221–206 BCE) legalist school of governance. The typology of socialist legalism was a dominant theme in PRC legal reform efforts in the post-Mao period, and has been reiterated under the leadership of *Xí Jìnpíng 习近平 (b. 1953).

Through a combination of personal circumstances, ambition, and contemplation, Peng came to articulate a vision for the role of law in socialist China. Associated with the legislative system as chair of the NPC Standing Committee, Peng worked to expand the influence of the NPC in the policy processes that inform lawmaking in China. Peng supported socialist policy priorities of public property and state economic planning, while his views on the content and application of law echoed traditional legalist notions about formalism, generality, and punishment. While the punitive elements were consistent with a public law discourse that had become well-entrenched throughout the PRC's history, Peng's views on the centrality of general principles as the basis for legislation and on the formal application of law to party members, and ultimately to the CCP itself, represented important developments in official conceptions of law in the PRC. What emerged was a doctrine of socialist legalism—a view that combined, on the one hand, adherence to socialist ideologies of state control of the economy and narrowly limited parameters for social and cultural discourse with, on the other hand, a system reminiscent of pre-Han legalism that embodied formal laws and institutions characterized by coercive norms of general application. By combining tenets of socialism and legalism, Peng modeled a discourse that, although diminished by the short-term political ambitions of recent leaders, stands as a powerful paradigm for legal reform in China and remains an important component of the discourse of law in the PRC.

Pitman B. POTTER
University of British Columbia

Further Reading

Bartke, Wolfgang. (1981). Peng Zhen. In *Who's who in the People's Republic of China* (pp. 287–289). Armonk, NY: M.E. Sharpe.

Bodde, Derk, & Morris, Clarence. (1967). *Law in Imperial China* (pp. 25–26). Philadelphia: University of Pennsylvania.

Ebon, Martin (Ed.). (1970). Lin Piao's most significant speech (Informal address of Politburo meeting, 1966). In *Lin Piao: The life and writings of China's new ruler* (pp. 252–269). New York: Stein and Day.

Friedman, Edward. (1989). Theorizing the democratization of China's Leninist state. In Arif Dirlik & Maurice Meisner (Eds.), *Marxism and the Chinese experience* (pp. 171–189). Armonk, NY: M.E. Sharpe.

Hebei CPC Committee Party History Research Office and Hebei Academy of Social Sciences. (1998). Peng Zhen tongzhi zai Hebei de geming huodong 彭真同志在河北的革命活动 [Comrade Peng Zhen's revolutionary activities in Hebei]. In Huang Huoqing, et al (Eds.), *Mianhuai Peng Zhen* 缅怀彭真 [Remembering Peng Zhen] (pp. 500–520). Beijing: Central Literature Press.

Huang Huoqing, et al. (Eds.). (1998). Zhuinian jing'ai de lao lingdao Peng Zhen tongzhi 追念敬爱的老领导彭真同志 [Recalling esteemed old leader comrade Peng Zhen]. In *Mianhuai Peng Zhen* 缅怀彭真 (pp. 13–15). Beijing: Central Literature Press.

Hulsewe, A.F.P. (1985). *Remnants of Ch'in law: An annotated translation of the Ch'in legal and administrative rules of the 3rd century B.C. discovered in Yun-meng Prefecture, Hu-pei Province, in 1975*. Leiden, The Netherlands: E.J. Brill.

Mao Zedong. (1969). Counter-revolutionary revisionist Peng Zhen's towering crimes of opposition of the party, socialism and the thought of Mao Tse tung (June 10, 1967). In *Selections from China mainland magazines* 639 (January 6, 1969).

Klein, Donald W., & Clark, Anne B. (1970). Peng Zhen. In *Biographical dictionary of Chinese communism 1921–1965* (pp. 713). Cambridge MA: Harvard University Press.

Peng Zhen. (1991a). Guanyu difang ren da changweihui de gongzuo 关于地方人大常委会的工作 [On the work of local people's congress standing committees] (April 18, 1980). In *Peng Zhen wenxuan* 彭真文选 [Collected works of Peng Zhen]. Beijing: People's Press.

Peng Zhen. (1991b). Zuohao tongyi zhanxian gongzuo 做好统一战线工作 [Do a good job in united front work)] (January 6, 1949). In *Peng Zhen wenxuan* 彭真文选 [Collected works of Peng Zhen] (pp. 170–192). Beijing: People's Press.

Potter, Pitman B. (1986). Peng Zhen: Evolving views on party organization and law. In Carol Lee Hamrin & Timothy Cheek (Eds.), *China's establishment intellectuals* (pp. 21–25). Armonk, NY: M.E. Sharpe.

Potter, Pitman B. (2003). *From Leninist discipline to socialist legalism: Peng Zhen on law and political authority in the PRC*. Stanford, CA: Stanford University Press.

Schoenhals, Michael. (1996). The central case examination group, 1966–1979. *China Quarterly*, 145, 87–111.

Seymour, James. (1980). Document No. 49, Peng Zhen (from *Beijing Spring*). In *The fifth modernization: China's human rights movement 1978–1979*. Stanfordville, NY: Human Rights Publishing Group.

Tian Jiyun. (Ed.). (2000). *Zhongguo gaige kaifang yu minzhu fazhi jianshe* 中国改革开放与民主法制建设 [China's reform and opening up and construction of democracy and the legal system]. Beijing: China Democracy and Legal System Press.

World Broadcasts (Far East). (1979, February 27), p. BII/2.

Wu Fumin. (2000, April 19). Zou yifa zhiguo lu 走依法治国路 [Walking the road of ruling the country by law]. *Fazhi ribao* [Legal System Daily], 1–2.

Zhang Zhiming. (2000). *Cong minzhu xin lu dao yifa zhiguo* 从民主新路到依法治国 [From the new road of democracy to ruling the country according to law]. Nanchang: Jiangxi Higher Education Press.

Péng Zhēn

♂ Qián Xuésēn 钱学森

1911–2009—Rocket scientist who contributed to China's missile, nuclear weapon, and space program

Alternate names: Hsue-Shen Tsien; H. S. Tsien; trad. 錢學森

Summary

As the pioneer of China's rocket science, Qian Xuesen made important contributions to the missile program, nuclear weapon development, and space technology. As a general and politician, he also served as one of the national leaders of China's strategic weapon programs, defense industry, and international military technology. The founder and first director of the Fifth Academy (China's space agency), Qian became known as the "Father of Chinese Missiles" and the "King of Rocketry."

Qian Xuesen was born on 11 December 1911 in Hangzhou, the capital of southeastern Zhejiang Province. He received his college degree in mechanical engineering from National Jiaotong University in Shanghai in 1934. In 1935, he left China for the United States on a Boxer Indemnity Scholarship Program (Gēngzǐ péikuǎn jiǎngxuéjīn 庚子赔款奖学金), allocated by the US government for the education of Chinese students at US institutions (from war reparations of US$333 million paid by the Chinese government to foreign powers, according to the Boxer Protocol of 1901). Qian began graduate study at Massachusetts Institute of Technology (MIT) in August of 1935. He used the name Hsue-Shen Tsien or H. S. Tsien while he was in the United States (the spaceship *Tsien* in Arthur C. Clarke's 1982 science fiction novel *2010: Odyssey Two* is named after him.) After he received his master's degree from MIT in 1936, he went on to the California Institute of Technology (Caltech) on referral from the aerodynamic engineer and physicist Theodore von Kármán (1881–1963) to study applied mechanics, including jet propulsion and engineering control theories.

He obtained his PhD from Caltech in 1939 with a thesis on slender body theory at high speeds. He then worked with the US military ballistic missile (ICBM) program (which developed the Titan rockets) as a designer and later as a director of the Jet Propulsion Laboratory in Pasadena, California. In 1945, Qian became an associate professor at Caltech. After World War II ended in 1945, he served in the US Army as a lieutenant colonel and was sent to Germany as part of the team examining captured German V-2 rockets. In 1947, he married Jiang Ying, the daughter of General Jiang Baili, one of the leading military strategists of Chiang Kai-shek (1887–1975), leader of the Republic of China (ROC) in the mainland (1927–1949) and on Taiwan (1949–1975). In 1947, Qian worked as a professor at MIT while designing an intercontinental space plane. His work would inspire the X-20 Dyna-Soar, which would later influence the development of the American space shuttle. In 1949, Qian became the first director of the Daniel and Florence Guggenheim Jet Propulsion Center at Caltech. He became a US citizen in 1950.

During the Cold War (1946–1991), the post-WWII world was divided between the US-led "free-world" and the Soviet Union–controlled Communist bloc. In the early 1950s, an anti-Communist sentiment, also known as McCarthyism,

Qian Xuesen served as a consultant to the United States Army Air Forces. Here he is pictured together with Ludwig Prandt (left, German scientist) and Theodore von Kármán (right, Hungarian-American scientist), who was his doctoral advisor (1944). Photo by US Army.

• Qián Xuésēn •

swept America. While the detrimental impact of this "Red Scare" persisted, the Federal Bureau of Investigation (FBI) made allegations that Qian was a Communist, revoking his security clearance in 1950. This became a turning point in his life, since he found himself unable to pursue his career. Within two weeks, he announced plans to return to mainland China, or the People's Republic of China (PRC). Due to his background and knowledge, the US government wavered between deporting him and refusing to allow his departure. Before he could leave for China, the FBI detained him and his wife at Terminal Island, a federal prison near Los Angeles, in 1950. For five years, he was subjected to constant surveillance and house arrest. Qian then became the subject of negotiations between the United States and the PRC.

From April to July 1954, during the Geneva Conference to discuss Indochina settlement after the French-Indochina War (1946–1954), the PRC delegation, headed by Zhōu Ēnlái 周恩来 (1898–1976), China's premier from 1949 to 1976, held five meetings with the US delegation and raised the question of Chinese people being prohibited from leaving the United States. To pressure the US government, between 1950 and 1953, Beijing released four American pilots captured during the Korean War (during which China sent 3.1 million troops to Korea to fight against the United Nations forces). The US and PRC ambassadors continued to meet fourteen times after the Geneva

Conference and eventually reached an agreement on 18 October 1954. In exchange for Dr. Qian and other Chinese citizens who studied in America, the PRC government would release eleven more American pilots. On 17 September 1955, Qian, his wife, and their two American-born children left the United States on a passenger liner for China via Hong Kong. Premier Zhou later said that China had gotten Qian back from America at Geneva. Had it been the only Chinese achievement at Geneva, the Sino-American ambassadorial talks could not have been more valuable. Qian became a prominent scientist and soon founded modern science and technology for the strategic force of the People's Liberation Army (PLA), which includes China's army, navy, and air force.

After his return, Qian began leading Chinese nuclear and rocket programs by working at the Institute of Chinese Academy of Sciences (CAS) and China Science and Technology University. On 17 February 1956, he submitted a proposal to the Central Committee of the CCP, which controlled national budget and defense programs, with the request to establish a ballistic missile program. On 14 March, Premier Zhou, who also served as vice chairman of both the Central Committee and the Central Military Commission (CMC), chaired a CMC meeting and established the State Commission of Aviation Industry in April, which included Zhou himself; Marshal Niè Róngzhēn 聂荣臻 (1899–1992), vice chairman of the CMC, chief of the PLA General Staff, and vice premier; and Qian as its leading members. Thereafter, Qian became one of the three top leaders in charge of China's aviation and space programs.

On 18 February 1957, Qian founded the Fifth Academy (China's space agency) under the Ministry of Defense, and he served as its first director until 1970. The Fifth Academy was in charge of missile and space technology; in the 1960s it became the Seventh Industrial Ministry, and in the 1980s, the Space and Navigation Ministry. The missile program's first priority was to develop medium-range surface-to-surface missiles within three years and long-range ones in five years. Qian helped to reverse-engineer the Soviet P-2 missile, an improved version of the German V-2 rocket. During the Anti-Rightist Movement in 1957, when intellectuals and scientists, as well as those critical of the Chinese Communist Party (CCP) were persecuted, Marshal Nie quietly transferred most of the civilian employees at the nuclear and missile research institutes into military service. He successfully built up a "fire wall" in October 1958 by founding the Commission on Science, Technology, and Industry for National Defense (COSTIND) of the CMC and served as its chairman. As vice chairman of the COSTIND, Qian became a lieutenant general of the PLA in 1957 and a CCP member in 1958. Thereafter, Qian survived the ensuing political movements and campaigns during the era of Máo Zédōng 毛泽东(1893–1976).

On 9 September 1960, Qian launched the first Chinese-made short-range missile, the Dongfeng-01, modeled on the Soviet P-2, at the northwestern desert testing ground (the ballistic surface-to-surface missile system went under the name of Dongfeng, meaning "east wind"). On 15 November, he launched the first Chinese-designed short-range surface-to-surface missile. On 6 and 16 December, he tested three more missiles of his own design. In June and July 1964, three China-designed medium- and long-range missiles, Dongfeng-02, were successfully tested. In December, China began manufacturing surface-to-air missiles, Hongqi-01 (the surface-to-air missile system went under the name Hongqi, meaning the "red flag"). In 1965, Qian became vice minister of the Seventh Industrial Ministry (or the Missile Industrial Ministry). After China's first nuclear bomb test on 16 October 1964, Qian and Nie successfully launched a medium-range missile to carry a nuclear warhead, on 27 October 1966. The PRC government named 1966 the "missile year" (dǎodàn nián 导弹年).

In 1966, China established its strategic missile force, the PLA Second Artillery Corps. From the beginning, the corps maintained the arsenal for both conventional and nuclear-armed missiles. Qian also designed and developed the widespread Silkworm missiles. In 1980, China tested its first intercontinental ballistic

Qián Xuésēn

missile; two years later, it tested its first submarine-launched ballistic missile. As chief designer and one of the major leaders, Qian played a key role in the research, testing, and manufacture of carrier rockets, guided missiles, satellites, and aerospace programs. Due to his extraordinary contribution to China's nuclear and missile program, Mao Zedong met Qian on several occasions.

In the 1980s, Qian led the designs, tests, production, and launching of China's space rocket system under the name of the Changzheng (meaning the "Long March"). Although Chinese leaders admitted the shortcomings of their missile system, they expressed little doubt that missile technology was one area in which China would make great strides in the late 1970s and 1980s. As one of the pioneers of China's missile and space science, Qian became the "Father of Chinese Missiles" and "King of Rocketry." In 1992, China used Qian's research as the basis for its manned space program and successfully launched the Shenzhou V mission in October 2003. Asteroid (3763) Qianxuesen is named after him, which is a main belt minor planet discovered at the Purple Mountain Observatory in Nanjing in 1980.

Career in Education and Politics

Qian also made important contributions to China's higher education. He established the Institute of Mechanics

Engineering and trained Chinese scientists and engineers in the techniques he had learned in the United States. He founded a library and taught methodology of research aeronautics. He was the first chairman of the Department of Mechanics at the University of Science and Technology of China (USTC). In 1980, he was elected vice chairman of the China Association for Science and Technology, and was elected chairman in 1984.

Qian rose in politics after being elected national congressman at the Second National People's Congress (NPC) in 1959. He was reelected as national congressional representative at the Third, Fourth, and Fifth NPCs in 1964, 1975, and 1978, respectively. He was also elected party representative of the CCP Ninth National Congress and an alternative member of the Ninth Central Committee in 1969, and then reelected representative of the CCP Tenth, Eleventh, Twelfth, Thirteenth, Fourteenth, and Fifteenth National Congresses from 1973 to 1997, and an alternative member of the CCP Tenth, Eleventh, and Twelfth Central Committees from 1973 to 1982. Qian was elected vice chairman of the National Committee of the Chinese People's Political Consultation Conference (CPPCC) at the Sixth CPPCC National Congress in 1982. He continued to serve as the vice chairman for the CPPCC Seventh and Eighth National Committees. He supported many CCP policies in the 1960s and associated with Maoist leaders in the Cultural Revolution (1966–1976), including Jiāng Qīng 江青 (1914–1991), the wife of Mao and a member of the Gang of Four, who was sentenced to life in prison in 1980.

After the United States and China normalized diplomatic relations on 1 January 1979, Caltech awarded Qian the "Distinguished Alumni Award" of that year, but he did not make the trip to California for his award ceremony. Only in 2001 did Caltech President David Baltimore (1997–2006) ask Frank E. Marble, one of Qian's friends, to bring the award to him in Beijing. In the early 1980s, the American Institute of Aeronautics and Astronautics (AIAA) invited him again to visit the United States, but he declined the invitation, asking for a formal apology for his detainment in the early 1950s.

Qian retired in 1991 and maintained a low public profile in Beijing. In 1995, *Jiāng Zémín 江泽民 (b. 1926), China's president from 1990 to 2002, inscribed Qian Xuesen's name for the library of Xi'an Jiaotong University. In 2008, Qian was named *Aviation Week and Space Technology* "Person of the Year." In the same year, China Central Television (CCTV) named Qian as one of the eleven most inspiring people in China. He died on 31 October 2009 in Beijing.

Xiaobing LI
University of Central Oklahoma

Further Reading

Chang, Iris. (1996). *Thread of the silkworm*. New York: Basic Books.

Harvey, Brian. (2004). *China's space program: From conception to manned spaceflight*. New York: Springer.

Jencks, Harlan W. (1982). *From muskets to missiles: Politics and professionalism in the Chinese army, 1945–1981*. Boulder, CO: Westview.

Lewis, John Wilson, & Xue Litai. (1988). *China builds the bomb*. Stanford, CA: Stanford University Press.

Li Hongshan. (2008). *U.S.-China educational exchange: State, society, and intercultural relations, 1905–1950*. New Brunswick, NJ: Rutgers University Press.

Li Xiaobing. (2007). *A history of the modern Chinese army*. Lexington: University Press of Kentucky.

MacDonald, Bruce W. (2008). *China, space weapons, and US security*. New York: Council on Foreign Relations.

*People marked with an asterisk have entries in this dictionary.

• Qián Xuésēn •

♂ Qiáo Shí 乔石

1924–2015—Chinese Communist revolutionary and high-ranking politician

Alternate names: b. Jiǎng Zhìtóng 蒋志彤; trad. 喬石

Summary

Qiao Shi was a leader of the Chinese Communist Party and Chinese state government. At the peak of his career, he ranked as the third highest in China's leadership structure. Although he never rose to the top position as had been speculated, his dedication to the ideas and practice of socialist democracy and legality helped charter the course of China's "opening and reform" and continues to resonate in the country's political landscape.

Qiao Shi was born in December 1924 in Shanghai. His political career started at his high school, where he was a student leader in protests against the ruling Nationalist Party (Guómíndāng 国民党, GMD). In 1940, at the tender age of sixteen, he joined the Chinese Communist Party (CCP). Then he spent the following years going to high schools and colleges in Shanghai, identifying potential CCP members and mobilizing students to cause troubles for the Nationalist government. It was dangerous work because the government often resorted to ruthless measures to deal with "red communists" who tried to sabotage the Nationalists' war effort against the CCP. As a precaution, he changed his name from Jiang Zhitong to Jiang Qiaoshi. While occupying himself in this underground work, he also managed to earn a science degree from Tongji University in Shanghai.

When the CCP took over Shanghai in 1949, he was sent to Hangzhou, Zhejiang Province, to do youth work within local party organizations. From 1954 to 1962, possibly because of his college training, he was reassigned to the iron and steel industry and moved around state-owned companies in the northeast and northwest. He gained valuable experience from middle- to high-level management positions and rose steadily in China's cadre system, but he remained one of thousands of undistinguished officials throughout the 1950s.

Qiao Shi's breakthrough came in 1962 when he was selected to spend a year at the CCP's Central Party School in Beijing for theory training, a first step for important new assignments for Chinese cadres. Although his first job after the Central Party School was as a mere researcher with the CCP's Ministry of International Liaisons, he was visible and near the center of power. His promising political career took a step back during the Cultural Revolution (1966–1976), and he suffered serious criticism and suspension, even arrest and brief imprisonment. Not much public information is available concerning the reasons for Qiao Shi's hardships, but his fate was hardly unique in that time of mass persecution. There is speculation that Qiao Shi was a remote relative of Chiang Kai-shek, the leader of the Nationalist Party and government. They share the same family name, and their ancestral homes in Zhejiang Province are close to each other. To prevent suspicion of association, one of Qiao Shi's sons suggested that the family drop the surname Jiang (which uses the same character as Chiang) and go by their middle name, Qiao. The suggestion was accepted, and Jiang Qiaoshi has since been known as Qiao Shi.

Rise to Power

In 1977, Qiao Shi was restored to his former rank and position. Soon afterward, he began a rapid ascent in power: in 1982 he was appointed as the minister of international liaisons and elected as an alternate member of the Central Secretariat. A mere year later he became the chief of staff and the minister of organization of the CCP, a vital position in charge of vetting cadres before important appointments within the party as well as the state government.

In 1985, succeeding Chén Pīxiǎn 陈丕显 (1916–1995), Qiao Shi was appointed to the position of head of the Bureau of National Security and Intelligence after Yú Qiángshēng 俞强声, a high-ranking official of the bureau, defected to the United States, resulting in the exposure of Larry Wu-Tai Chin, a Chinese agent inside the Central Intelligence Agency (CIA). Qiao Shi also took charge of the CCP's Central Security Committee from 1985 to 1998. In addition, in 1986 he began to serve as a vice premier of the State Council, responsible for maintaining law and order in China. During this time, he was highly visible in his efforts to advocate the creation of laws that would respond to the needs of the country. This was seen as a progressive pursuit within the CCP, which, after years of power abuse and personal worship during the Mao-era, strived to establish the principle of "rule by law" (*fǎzhì* 法治) in contrast to the conventional practice of "rule by person"(*rénzhì* 人治).

Between 1987 and 1997, Qiao Shi stood as a member of the Politburo Standing Committee of the CCP, the real seat of power in China. In the first five

• Qiáo Shí •

years, Qiao Shi also simultaneously held the position of secretary of the Central Commission for Disciplinary Inspection, a feared organization that investigates and punishes corrupted party members. In the second five years, he served as the chairman of the Standing Committee of the National People's Congress, theoretically the highest office in the Chinese state government. By this time, in public appearances with other Chinese leaders, Qiao Shi would be ranked third highest in the country leadership structure. Using his positions as head of the state legislature and the CCP's chief disciplinary officer, Qiao Shi continued to push his agenda of rule by law and election reform in local governments.

In the early 1990s Qiao Shi started to attract the attention of political observers outside China. Some speculated that Qiao Shi would rise to further prominence. They held this idea mainly for two reasons: first, although Qiao Shi clearly demonstrated pro-democracy sympathies, he escaped unscathed in the fallout of the Tiananmen Square student protests in 1989; second, he responded actively to the call by *Dèng Xiǎopíng 邓小平 (1904–1997) to continue to push for the course of Reform and Opening Up, yet his political rival *Jiāng Zémín 江泽民 (b. 1926) did not. Others pointed out, however, that his assignment as the chairman of the Standing Committee of

the National People's Congress was virtually a demotion, for this post ranked equally with his previous posts, and in essence was a mostly ceremonial position. Still others held out hope for Qiao Shi to be a power player in China. They argued that, because of "Jiang," the surname Qiao Shi was born with, he might be a person of choice to solve the issue of Taiwan. In addition, the CCP had shown much interest in pursuing further reforms toward a more legalist and democratic system of government. Qiao Shi becoming its top leader would certainly help achieve this goal.

Power Struggles and Retirement

All the conjectures turned false when Qiao Shi retired from all his positions in 1998. Officially Qiao Shi's retirement was due to his age (he was seventy-four at the time), but there were widespread reports in media outside China suggesting that it was a failed power struggle with CCP's top leader Jiang Zemin that sent Qiao Shi home. The fact that unlike many other political leaders of his generation, Qiao Shi retired not just from his official positions but from political life altogether seems to confirm this theory.

In the eyes of most Chinese people, Qiao Shi was a leader of unquestionable moral rectitude, with an earnest tendency toward pro-democracy reform and rule by law. He held a pragmatic attitude about the issues of government

---

*People marked with an asterisk have entries in this dictionary.

and development in China, emphasizing that the construction of socialist democratic politics should be based upon real situations and carried out in a proper order, so that it could better serve the interests of the party and the Chinese people. His dedication to the ideas and practice of socialist democracy and legality has helped chart the proper course of China's openness and reform and continues to resonate in the country's political landscape today.

Qiao Shi's wife, Yù Wén 郁文, died of illness in 2013 at the age of eighty-seven. Qiao passed away in Beijing two years later, on 14 June 2015. Together they had two sons and two daughters.

Quan LI
Sichuan University, China

Further Reading

Gao Xin 高新. (1996). *Zhong gong ju tou Qiao Shi* 中共巨头乔石 [Qiao Shi: A magnate of the CCP]. Shanghai: Shijie shuju.

Qiao Shi 乔石. (2012). *Qiao Shi tan min zhu yu fa zhi* 乔石谈民主与法制 [Qiao Shi's opinions on democracy and rule by law]. Beijing: Renmin Chubanshe.

Qiao Shi. (1998). In Mackerras, Colin; McMillen, Donald H.; & Watson Andrew (Eds.), *Dictionary of the politics of the People's Republic of China* (pp. 185–186). London: Routledge.

Song, Yuwu. (2013). Qiao Shi. In Yuwu Song (Ed.), *Biographical dictionary of the People's Republic of China* (pp. 258). Jefferson, NC: McFarland.

Tian Ji Yun 田纪云. (2012). Yi Qiao Shi zhu chi ba jie ren da chang wei hui gong zuo 忆乔石主持八届人大常委会工作 [A recollection of Qiao Shi during Eighth People's Congress when he presided the work of the Standing Committee]. *Party & Government Forum, 25*(2), 42–43.

Zou Aiguo 邹爱国. (1992). *Di san dai ling dao ren de zu ji* 第三代领导人的足迹 [Footprints of the third-generation leaders of PRC]. Beijing: Zhongongzhongyangdangxiao Chubanshe.

• Qiáo Shí •

☿ Rèn Zhèngfēi 任正非

b. 1944—Entrepreneur and founder of Huawei Technologies

Summary

Ren Zhengfei is the founder and CEO of Huawei Investment Holding Corporation, a highly successful but controversial communications technology firm, with a core business focused on Internet and telephone network hardware. Ren was born in a poor and remote area in western China, and started his career in the army. He founded Huawei in 1987 and built it into a company with global impact that he is still leading as CEO, well into his seventies.

Ren Zhengfei founded Huawei (Huáwèi tóuzī kònggǔ yǒuxiàn gōngsī 华为投资控股有限公司) in 1987 to sell simple telephone exchange switches imported from Hong Kong, and the firm grew rapidly along with the massive increase in telephone and Internet usage in China. Huawei's rapid growth and success are closely tied up with Ren Zhengfei's character and personal values, which were formed during the period of the Great Chinese Famine (1959–1962) and the Cultural Revolution (1966–1976).

Childhood and Early Education

Ren Zhengfei was born on 25 October 1944 and grew up in a remote town in the mountains of an autonomous region in Guizhou, one of China's poorest provinces. His father, Rèn Móxùn 任摩逊, had been the only member of his family to attend university, but was unlucky enough to come of age in the chaotic period of the late 1930s. The Nationalists and Communists had created a so-called Second United Front in 1936 to cooperate in fighting the Japanese invaders, and during this period of uneasy alliance, Ren Moxun worked as an accounting clerk in a Nationalist army factory in Guizhou. At the same time, he set up an independent bookstore to sell socialist literature and maintained contacts with Chinese Communist Party (CCP) sympathizers, yet without actually joining the Party himself. This ambivalent stance, coupled with his class status as an "intellectual," would cause Ren Moxun to suffer great persecution during the extremist days of the Cultural Revolution, even though he had dedicated his life to educating poor peasants as a poorly paid Guizhou high school principal for two decades. Ren Zhengfei's mother, Cheng Yuanzhao, was less educated than her husband, but through self-study she managed to become qualified as a high school teacher. She also raised seven children, of whom Ren Zhengfei was the eldest (Ren 2001).

Even before the Cultural Revolution, Ren's parents struggled to cover the costs of raising such a large family, especially during the Great Chinese Famine, following the Great Leap Forward. This was when Ren Zhengfei first learned that survival depended on being selfless, and he later recalled that if any of his family had acted selfishly during this time, it would have been impossible for all of them to avoid starvation (Ren 2001). Despite these privations, Ren Zhengfei was able to study well enough to gain a place at Chongqing Construction and Engineering College in 1964 (Wang 2013). He was therefore absent from Guizhou in 1966 when his father was imprisoned in a small cell and forced by Red Guards to undergo numerous violent "struggle sessions." His parents refused to let Ren return home, saying it would only cause their family to suffer more persecution. Instead, Ren's father

told him: "Remember that knowledge is strength, so even if no-one else is studying, you should go against the main current and keep on studying" (Ren 2001). So during the chaos of the late 1960s, when universities throughout China became class battlegrounds, Ren spent his days in Chongqing tagging along on the peripheries of various "revolutionary gangs," while in his spare time teaching himself electronics, math, and foreign languages from old textbooks (Ren 2001).

These traumatic youthful experiences molded Ren's character in several ways and strongly influenced his management style at Huawei. In particular, he has been motivated by a kind of crisis consciousness—a painful awareness that everything can be taken away in a moment—which has led him to drive himself and his employees to constantly innovate in order to stay ahead of the competition. He has also consistently emphasized the need for self-sacrifice and sharing Huawei's success with all of its stakeholders, as this has allowed the firm to survive and prosper in a business environment that has been very challenging for private entrepreneurs.

Career in Telecommunications

Due to the social chaos of the Cultural Revolution and his father's suspect class background, Ren's career options were limited. In the early 1970s, he managed to get a job in the engineering corps of

• Rèn Zhēngfēi •

the People's Liberation Army (PLA), where he spent several years leading a team working on the construction of a major chemical plant in Liaoyang. Ren's team was responsible for creating automated processes for refining oil, and in 1978 his innovative work was recognized when he was chosen as one of several PLA delegates to attend the Chinese Science Congress (Wang 2013; Rogers and Ruppersberger 2012; CNPC 2014). Another source claims that Ren also worked in a military aircraft factory in Guizhou designing communications systems, but Ren himself has never confirmed this, and it may be incorrect (Cheng and Liu 2004, 202). Around this time, Ren's father was cleared of all wrongdoing as part of the post-Cultural Revolution rehabilitation of intellectuals, and this paved the way for Ren to join the CCP. He attended the Twelfth National Party Congress in 1982 as an army delegate. Soon afterwards, the Chinese government began downsizing the PLA and disbanding many of its noncombat divisions, including the engineering corps. Ren was discharged in 1983 and after losing a couple of jobs in quick succession at a Shenzhen government construction firm and an electronics company, he decided to become a private entrepreneur by setting up Huawei in 1987 (Ren 2001; Wang 2013).

Huawei's first few years were extremely difficult, with Ren and his first few employees working and living together in a small warehouse in Shenzhen. As a private company, it was hard for Huawei to convince their customers, which were mainly the local branches of China Telecom, to buy their products rather than those of state-owned competitors. Ren hit on the idea of creating a "community of shared interests" (*lìyì gòngtóngtǐ* 利益共同体) with these customers by setting up joint ventures between Huawei and local telecom branches. When the telecom branches purchased Huawei's products, they would share in the profits, and as the Chinese telecom industry expanded rapidly and was constantly upgrading its technology, it was in the telecom officials' interests to continue ordering products from Huawei rather than from their less generous competitors (Cheng and Liu 2004, 76–78, 104–109; Wang 2007, 283–286).

To avoid direct competition with powerful state-owned competitors, Ren also told his sales staff to focus on smaller towns and cities that had been neglected by the bigger equipment manufacturers. This was a strategy called "first take the countryside, then encircle the cities" which Ren adapted from the early Communist military leaders like Máo Zédōng 毛泽东 (Cheng and Liu 2004, 223–224). Ren also paid his employees mainly with Huawei shares, while requiring any employees who left the firm to give up their shares. This not only motivated employees to maximize the firm's profits—and during the 1990s, Huawei's share returns regularly reached 70 percent—but also reduced the risk that employees would jump ship to work for a competitor. With this remuneration system, Huawei's employees soon became the highest paid in the industry, and the firm was able to attract some of the top technology graduates from Chinese universities (Zhang 2007, 17–19).

Finally, Ren realized early on that only constant innovation would keep Huawei's products from becoming obsolete, so he ploughed at least 10 percent of the firm's annual revenues into researching and developing new communications technologies. The real breakthrough came with the invention of a fully digital telephone exchange in 1993, a technology that only one other company in China, the Sino-American joint venture Shanghai Bell, was able to manufacture (Cheng and Liu 2004, 28–30).

Influence and Legacy

Under Ren's forceful leadership, Huawei has continued to follow these strategies while internationalizing its business. In 2013, Huawei's revenues reached US$39.6 billion, placing it 285th on the Global Fortune 500 list, and it currently employs around 150,000 staff with sales in around 170 countries (Huawei 2014a). Rather than directly competing with multinational competitors like Cisco Systems, Huawei focused first on selling its cheaper products in poorer developing nations that could not afford the most advanced equipment. It used the profits to finance further innovations to the point where currently Huawei's technology is able to satisfy the world's top telecom providers such as BT and Vodaphone in Europe, and Telus and Bell in Canada (Zhang 2007; Huawei 2014c). Ren's early decisions to plough a large proportion of Huawei's annual sales revenues back into research and development and to generously share the firm's profits with its employees created a highly innovative and committed workforce. The firm now has over 36,000 patents, many of which were invented by its own employees (Huawei 2014b). And the firm continues to be an employee-owned company, with approximately half of its staff owning units in Huawei's employee share fund, which in turn owns almost 99 percent of Huawei's shares. Ren Zhengfei himself only owns around 1.4 percent of Huawei's shares (Huawei 2013, 108).

To build up a huge multinational firm from nothing obviously requires a strong character, and Ren has often been criticized for his short temper and his tendency to insult and publicly humiliate his senior managers with obscene language when they have made mistakes. But as Huawei's longstanding chair, Sūn Yàfāng 孙亚芳, explained to one offended Huawei executive, "The more he trusts you, the more he will curse you!" (Zhang 2007, 244). Ren has also consistently expected his senior employees to follow his lead in sacrificing their personal interests for Huawei. Ren admitted that his health was ruined during the 1990s due to overwork and he rarely had time to visit his parents before they died in the late 1990s (Ren 2001). He has also publicly stated that he suffered from depression for many years, including occasional suicidal thoughts, until he realized that he needed medical treatment (Ren 2008). Many other Huawei employees have also suffered serious health problems and long separation from their families while posted to poor developing countries or remote parts of China. And the pressure to constantly innovate and compete has allegedly led some employees to commit suicide. This kind of pressure, however, is apparently quite common among Chinese companies, and unlike many manufacturing firms, Huawei rewards its employees very generously for their sacrifices (Zhang 2007, 235–242; Yang 2008).

Another major controversy that has caused problems for Huawei is its supposed "close ties" to the Chinese military and government. A report by the RAND Corporation in 2005 suggested that Huawei and other Chinese high-tech firms were part of a digital triangle formed between Chinese industry, military intelligence, and the government seeking to develop Chinese high-tech military capabilities and use cyber-warfare to undermine the national and economic security of the United States and its allies (Medeiros et al 2005, 218–221). This report was the main source used by the US Permanent Select Committee on Intelligence in its 2012 investigation of

Huawei. The evidence, however, was remarkably thin: Ren Zhengfei had served in the PLA for several years in the 1970s, and Huawei had sold some standardized telephone exchange and network equipment to the Chinese military (Rogers and Ruppersberger 2012). Huawei's history as a private enterprise and its current governance structure do not suggest any government or state control over the firm or its management, and there is no evidence that Ren Zhengfei maintained any relationship with the Chinese military after he was demobilized in 1983. Certainly after Huawei became successful in the late 1990s, the Chinese government encouraged the big four Chinese banks to extend loans to the company on regular commercial terms, and invited Ren Zhengfei along with several other successful Chinese private entrepreneurs to accompany trade missions to Africa and the Middle East. But these kinds of efforts to promote the growth of private enterprise and overseas investment are common among governments throughout the world (Cheng and Liu 2004, 284–288; Anderson 2013; Hawes 2015).

Unfortunately for Huawei, US government suspicions about the firm have prevented it from bidding on major government broadband contracts in the United States and in countries like Australia, India, and Canada (Hawes 2015). This has not stopped the firm from selling its products and services in over 170 countries, but it has meant that

Huawei must spend a lot of resources dealing with the damage to its reputation, caused by what it sees as unfounded allegations. For Ren, this is a classic example of how a Chinese private entrepreneur can become swept up by larger geopolitical forces.

Ren Zhengfei is now in his seventies and still CEO of Huawei, but he recently selected three "rotating co-CEOs" to take turns sharing the top job with him (Huawei 2013, 115). He may retire soon, but it does not appear that retirement would suit his hard-driving character. He is married and has three children, but he has always kept his family out of the limelight. He once stated that his wife never had a career but instead focused on raising and educating their children (Wang 2013). His daughter Meng Wanzhou (also known as Cathy Meng) worked her way up Huawei's ranks to become the firm's CFO in 2011. One of his sons and some of Ren's brothers and sisters also work at Huawei, but Ren has publicly stated that none of his family members will become the next CEO of the company, and none of the current rotating co-CEOs is related to Ren (Fierce Wireless 2013; Chon 2013).

Colin HAWES
University of Technology, Sydney

Further Reading

Anderson, Eric. (2013). *Sinophobia: The Huawei story*. Kindle Books.

Cheng Dongsheng, & Liu Lili. (2004). *Huawei zhenxiang* 化为真相 [The truth about Huawei]. Beijing: Dangdai zhongguo chubanshe.

Chon, Gina. (2013). Huawei CEO says his son and daughter don't have what it takes to succeed him. *Quartz, 29*. Retrieved December 6, 2014, from http://qz.com/79280/huawei-ceo-ren-zhengfei-says-his-son-and-daughter-dont-have-what-it-takes-to-succeed-him

CNPC. (2014). Zhongguo shiyou Liaoyang shihua gongsi 中国石油辽阳石化公司 [CNPC's Liaoyang Petrochemical Corporation]. Retrieved December 6, 2014 from http://www.cnpc.com.cn/cnpc/lhqy/201404/836ac6d706684274b72077d9cfc7514b.shtml

Fierce Wireless. (2013). Cathy Meng, CFO, Huawei: 2013 Women in Wireless. Retrieved December 6, 2014 from http://www.fiercewireless.com/special-reports/cathy-meng-cfo-huawei-2013-women-wireless

Hawes, Colin. (2015). "Framing" Chinese hi-tech firms: A political and legal critique. *Australian Journal of Corporate Law, 30*(1), 1–24.

Huawei Technologies. (2013). Annual Report. Retrieved December 6, 2014, from http://www.huawei.com/en/about-huawei/corporate-info/annual-report/2013/index.htm

Huawei Technologies. (2014a). Corporate Information. Retrieved December 6, 2014, from http://www.huawei.com/en/about-huawei/corporate-info/index.htm

Huawei Technologies. (2014b). Gongsi jieshao 公司介绍 [Corporate profile]. Retrieved December 6, 2014, from http://www.huawei.com/cn/about-huawei/corporate-info/index.htm

Huawei Technologies. (2014c). Milestones. Retrieved December 6, 2014, from http://www.huawei.com/

• Rèn Zhèngfēi •

en/about-huawei/corporate-info/milestone/index.htm

Medeiros, Evan S.; Roger. Cliff; Crane, Keith; & Mulvenon, James C. (2005). *A new direction for China's defense industry*. Arlington, VA: RAND Corporation.

Ren Zhengfei. (2001). Wo de fuqin muqin 我的父亲母亲 [My father and mother]. In Cheng Dongsheng & Liu Lili, *Huawei zhenxiang* 化为真相 [The truth about Huawei] (pp. 242–250). Beijing: Dangdai zhongguo chubanshe.

Rogers, Mike, & Ruppersberger, Dutch. (2012). Investigative report on the U.S. National Security issues posed by Chinese telecommunications companies Huawei and ZTE. Retrieved December 6, 2014, from http://intelligence.house.gov/legislation/committee-reports

Wang Peng. (2013). Ren Zhengfei: Huawei ming yuanzi zhonghua youwei; women yao jiao waiguoren zenme nian 任正非：华为名源自中华有为 我们要教外国人怎么念 [Ren Zhengfei: Huawei's name comes from "Zhonghua youwei" (China's potential); we need to teach foreigners how to pronounce it properly]. Retrieved December 6, 2014, from http://tech.ifeng.com/telecom/detail_2013_12/01/31700411_0.shtml

Wang Yongde. (2007). *Langxing guanli zai Huawei* 浪形管理在华为 [Wolf-style management at Huawei]. Hubei: Wuhan University Press.

Yang Jiang. (2008, April 7–13). Miwu zhong de Huawei zishamen 迷雾中的华为自杀们 [Suicides at Huawei shrouded in mist]. *Xinmin zhoukan*, 17–27.

Zhang Guanjing. (2007). *Huawei si zhang lian* 化为四张脸 [The four faces of Huawei]. Guangdong: Jingji chubanshe.

♂ Róng Yìrén 荣毅仁

1916–2005—Economic advisor, vice president of the PRC (1993–1998)

Alternate name: trad. 榮毅仁

Summary

Rong Yiren, who served as vice president of the People's Republic of China from 1993 to 1998, is most widely known for his advisory role in the opening up of the Chinese economy. Setting up the China International Trust and Investment Corporation (CITIC) in 1978, Rong leveraged foreign investment and the expertise of returning Chinese nationals to rebuild the Chinese economy. For his loyalty to the Communist Party and his efforts on behalf of Deng Xiaoping's policies, Rong was called the "red capitalist."

On 16 January 1979, five former industrialists and businessmen who had not met for over a decade (Rong Yiren, Hú Juéwén 胡厥文, Hú Zǐ'áng 胡子昂, Gǔ Gēngyú 古耕虞, and Zhōu Shūtāo 周叔韬) all received a message that *Dèng Xiǎopíng 邓小平 (1904–1997),

*People marked with an asterisk have entries in this dictionary.

then vice premier of the People's Republic of China (PRC), wanted to see them. They gathered at Rong's house that evening to consider what he wanted to discuss and what proposals they might put forward for the reconstruction of the Chinese economy. At ten o'clock on the morning of 17 January, Deng met the five men in the Great Hall of the People and spoke frankly to them about the political situation. The Third Plenum of the Eleventh Central Committee, meeting in December 1978, had decided to shift the entire focus of the party's work to constructing "socialist modernization" and they could not afford to lose any more time. China now had access to foreign capital and technology, and Chinese experts, many living overseas, who might be willing to return to rebuild the economy. Of these "five elders" whom Deng had taken into his confidence, it was Rong Yiren who was of most importance, and Deng charged him with the responsibility of attracting and managing foreign capital.

Early Life and Career

Rong had a background in business and in the 1940s, after graduating from the elite St. John's University in Shanghai, an Anglican foundation, he ran his family's flour and cotton mills in the city of Wuxi in Jiangsu Province. Rong's father, Róng Déshēng 荣德生, had been one of the wealthiest industrialists in China before World War II (by 2000, Rong Yiren would be named as China's richest individual). Rong Yiren had chosen to stay on the mainland after the Chinese Communists Party's (CCP) victory in 1949, unlike many business owners who moved, along with their assets, to Hong Kong or Taiwan. This decision was judged to have been patriotic and he was one of the few pre-1949 industrialists who worked closely with the government of the PRC. During the 1950s, Rong was closer to Máo Zédōng 毛泽东 (1893–1976) and Zhōu Ēnlái 周恩来(1898–1976) than to Deng Xiaoping, but he came to Deng's attention when he contributed to the cost of aircraft during the Korean War (1950–1953) and cooperated with the CCP when large private businesses were brought under state control. He became deputy mayor of Shanghai in 1957, and in 1959 Deng even recommended him for the post of deputy minister with responsibility for the textile industry. Rong was criticized severely during the Cultural Revolution (1966–1976) but may have been protected from the worst excesses of Red Guards by the intervention of Zhou Enlai.

A New Kind of Trust

Deng Xiaoping initially brought Rong into the Beijing political elite by inviting him to take on the role of deputy chairman of the Chinese People's Political Consultative Conference (CPPCC), the national forum for people and groups outside the Communist Party. Deng was beginning to assemble the personnel he needed and asked Rong to set aside all other business interests and to concentrate his efforts on rebuilding China's national economy. Deng emphasized that whatever methods and instruments were used internationally in capitalist countries should be brought to China. On Deng's instructions, Rong began work to create a new inward investment organization operating on the basis of modern international financial principles rather than political doctrine. This would eventually become the China International Investment Trust Corporation (Zhōngguó zhōngxìn jítuán gōngsī 中国中信集团公司, CITIC). It would be Rong's job to find the right people, manage the business, and take responsibility for the whole enterprise. No such body existed in China, and Deng wanted a report to the Central Committee as soon as possible. Rong had no assistants and spent many late nights in the study of his traditional Beijing courtyard house, working to create the concept and determine how it would operate, with his wife, Yang Jianqing, acting as his unofficial secretary.

The Central Committee received the report and rapidly approved it. Deng Xiaoping, economic strategist *Chén Yún 陈云 (1905–1995), and *Lǐ Xiānniàn 李先念 (1909–1992), vice chairman of the CCP, were unequivocally enthusiastic, but there was still doubt and even outright opposition to the Reform and Opening Up (gǎigé kāifàng 改革开放) policy. Deng tried to smooth Rong's path and remove predictable obstacles: he warned Rong against allowing other bodies to try to take over his responsibilities, but insisted that he and CITIC should not become bureaucratized. Deng kept a watching brief on Rong and his organization, conscious of the fact that a non-party person must have real power in order to be effective—he must be seen to be the bearer of the emperor's sword (shàngfāng bǎojiàn 尚方宝剑). Only with the public support of Deng would Rong be able to complete his task.

The preparatory group of what would eventually become CITIC was established on 8 July 1978, the same day that a law on Chinese-foreign joint ventures was promulgated, and CITIC came into being formally on 4 October of the same year. It developed into a powerful financial and industrial conglomerate with extensive international connections and functioned as the government's investment banking arm and as China's key link to the international capital market.

Extended Family

One of Rong Yiren's major assets was that he had over four-hundred relatives scattered about the world in various locations where the Chinese diaspora had settled. Many were well known in the commercial, technical, or scientific fields. In June 1986, over half of this extremely extended family—two-hundred overseas members of five generations of the Rong clan and twenty who still lived in China—travelled to Beijing for what turned out to be a cross between a family reunion and a political rally. Members of the clan had travelled from many countries, including the United States, Canada, Australia, Brazil, West Germany, and Switzerland. This reunion was unprecedented in the history of the Rong clan and it brought together many whose business and professional interests had already brought them to China, or back to China, since President Nixon's visit of 1972. On 18 June 1986, Deng met representatives of Rong's huge family at a reception in the Great Hall of the People in Beijing. The overseas Rongs stayed in Beijing for three days before embarking on a tourist itinerary that took in Xi'an, the family ancestral home of Wuxi, and Shanghai. The reunion was a personal triumph for Rong Yiren, whose authority was strengthened by the direct involvement of Deng, and for the worldwide Rong family. As so often happened in the Beijing political elite, the political relationship also led to more personal links, and the Deng and Rong families became very close.

Red Capitalist

Although Rong worked closely with the government and the CCP—Deng was reputed to have called him his "red capitalist"—it was assumed that he had remained outside the Communist Party. Rumors persist that he did eventually join (some say in 1985) but that there was an agreement that this would not be revealed during his lifetime. An obituary in a news release in Chinese from the New China News Agency (Xinhua) on 27 October 2005 referred to him as a "fighter for communism" (*gòngchǎn zhǔyì zhànshì* 共产主义战士) but did not claim that he was a member of the CCP (Xinhua Net 2005). Rong served as deputy chairman of the National People's Congress between 1988 and 1993 and as vice president of China from 1993 to 1998, but he had been so closely identified with the

investment body which he had created that, right up to his death, he was often referred to as Mr. CITIC.

Michael DILLON
Independent Scholar

Further Reading

Dillon, Michael. (2014). *Deng Xiaoping: The man who made modern China*. London: I.B. Tauris.

Liu Jianhua 刘建华, & Liu Li 刘丽. (2011). *Deng Xiaoping jishi* 邓小平纪事 [Chronicle of the life of Deng Xiaoping]. Beijing: Zhongyang wenxian chubanshe.

McNeill, David. (2005, October 29). Rong Yiren: China's billionaire "red capitalist." *The Independent*. Retrieved January 23, 2015, from http://www.independent.co.uk/news/obituaries/rong-yiren-6143281.html

Xinhua Net. (2005, October 27). Yuan guojia fuzhuxi Rong Yiren Tongzhi zai jing shishi xiang nian 89 sui 原国家副主席荣毅仁同志在京逝世享年 89 岁 [Comrade Rong Yiren, vice president of China, dies in Beijing at age 89]. Retrieved January 23, 2015, from http://news.xinhuanet.com/politics/2005-10/27/content_3690438.htm

荣毅仁

♂ Shih, Stan

Shī Zhènróng 施振榮

b. 1944—Entrepreneur, co-founder, chairman, and CEO of the Acer Group (1987–2004)

Alternate name: simpl. 施振荣

Summary

Crowned the "Godfather" of Taiwan's PC industry, Stan Shih founded Acer, Taiwan's famous computer brand. Extolled as an entrepreneur and a trailblazer, Shih led two major reorganizations at Acer, in 1992 and 2000, both of which set strong examples in corporate governance and branding management. His exit-planning for retirement, which took place when he turned sixty in 2004, resulted in an exemplar of business succession. Shih to this day remains active in promoting public interests.

Stan Shih was the key founder of Multitech International, incorporated in 1976, which in 1987 was renamed Acer, the first Taiwan-made globally known computer brand. Shih not only led Acer to prominence, but also set examples in a wide array of issues in strategic management, corporate governance, and leadership. Due to his extensive influence, Shih has been praised as the "Godfather" of Taiwan's personal computer (PC) industry.

Life and Career

Stan Shih was born on 8 December 1944 in the countryside village of Lu-Kang, located on the western coast of central Taiwan. Raised in a poor family, Shih helped his young widowed mother to sell duck eggs. A natural entrepreneurial instinct began to take shape while he learned business acumen, mathematics, utilizing resources, and the importance of credibility (*Reader's Digest* 2002) from these simple tasks. After graduating from high school, Shih entered National Chiao Tung University in Taiwan, where he received his bachelor's and master's degrees in electrical engineering. Unlike many of his classmates, who sought out higher education in the United States, Shih started his career in Taiwan, which would change the course of his entire life (Lin 2011).

After graduation, Stan Shih's first job was at Unitron Industrial Corporation, where he successfully designed, developed, and commercialized Taiwan's first desktop calculator in 1971. He then moved on to work at Qualitron Industrial Corporation, a sister company of Unitron, in 1973 and led a team to design the world's first pen watch. Disappointed at how his profitable innovations were unable to prevent Qualitron from being pulled down by the poor performances of other family businesses, in 1976, Shih, together with his wife Carolyn Yeh and four partners, established Acer with US$25,000 in capital. In its early years, Acer produced computer peripherals, traded electronic components, and ran a computer training center (Shih et al. 2006). In the mid-1990s, Shih successfully transformed it into one of the top international PC brands and began to compete with the global giants, such as Japan's NEC and Toshiba, and America's Dell and Hewlett-Packard. Shih not only established the Acer Group as a truly global company, but also was instrumental in helping to launch Taiwan's IT industry and reshape the island's national image (Lin and Hou 2010, 6). In 2006, *Time* magazine featured him as one of its "60 Years of Asian Heroes" for helping Taiwan to become a PC-manufacturing powerhouse.

Throughout his career, Stan Shih has received a plethora of awards (Acer Group 2014). For his innovative capabilities, in 1976 Shih was honored with his first prominent award by The Outstanding Young Persons Foundation as one of the Ten Most Outstanding Young Persons 台灣十大傑出青年 in Taiwan. In 1981, the Youth Career Development Association Headquarters awarded Shih Young Model for the Founding of a Business 青年創業楷模 in Taiwan. Junior Chamber International in 1983 selected Shih as one of the Ten Most Outstanding Young Persons in the World 世界十大傑出青年. The success of Acer's endeavor in going global won him another award in 1989, as one of "25 People You Ought to Know for Doing Business in Asia," by *Fortune* magazine. In 1995, at the International Monetary Fund (IMF) and the World Bank's annual meeting, Shih received the Emerging Markets CEO of the Year Award. In the year that Stan Shih retired from Acer, *Business Week* selected him as one of the 25 Stars of Asia.

Cherishing an admonition of his mother's, "Be a useful person," after retirement from Acer, Stan Shih turned another page in his career. He took seats on various boards of directors in the IT industry, including that of honorary chairman of Acer Incorporated Group, chairman of iD Soft Capital, and a member of the boards of directors at Ben Q, Wistron, and TSMC. It bears noting that iD Soft Capital Group, which aims to speed up the development of the knowledge-based economy, was founded by Shih with the other founders of Acer and

施振榮

former senior managers in order to contribute their management expertise to the benefit of society. Shih has also extended his influence in public and social services. He is the chairman of the National Culture and Arts Foundation and a member of the boards of directors of the National Chiang Kai-Shek Cultural Center and Taiwan Public Television Service Foundation.

Recognition and Influence

Stan Shih keenly observed that the rise of globalization, enhanced by information and communication technology (ICT), has revolutionized the structure of the electronics industry, along with the prevalence of the global supply chain and vertical disintegration in the computer industry (Shih 2002, 3). He aptly demonstrated that the growth strategy of a firm can be effectively positioned by applying his widely cited concept of the "smiling curve," which was first proposed around 1992 in order to convince Acer's employees to embrace the firm's first organizational re-engineering. The smiling curve illustrates value-adding potentials of different components of the value chain in the personal computer industry. Shih asserted that both ends of the value chain, research and development and brand marketing, command higher value added to a product than the middle part, assembly.

Many entrepreneurs in Taiwan have focused on practicing original equipment manufacturing (OEM), or assembling, for multinational corporations (MNCs) and believe that investing in brands does not work. Shih delved quixotically into creating a global brand by focusing on original brand manufacturing (OBM). He particularly emphasized brand creation, the right end of the smiling curve, and was able to extend the concept of smiling curve to different industries, such as service, agriculture, restaurant, medical, etc. (Shih 2012, 12). As a company, Acer has exemplified the example of a small firm transformed into a global corporation in terms of growth strategy, organization governance, and leadership.

While the smiling curve provides a useful concept for a corporate strategy to win a war, Stan Shih favored Go, a game invented in the ninth century by the Chinese but which flourished in Japan, and which offers tactics to score in a battle. The tactics of Go are useful in the initial stage of entrepreneurship, when resources are limited. For instance, to avoid head-on-head competition with powerful MNCs, Acer first entered markets in Southeast Asia, then Latin America, followed by the European Union, and finally the United States. This tactic of "village embracing a city" is an application of the game of Go (Shih 1996).

In regards to organization governance, Stan Shih believes that to maintain a sustained competitive advantage in an ever-changing business environment, a company should undertake re-engineering every five years (Shih 2002, 219). After two organizational re-engineering transformations, Stan Shih shared the experiences of Acer in his books, *Me Too is Not My Style* (Shih 1996) and *Millennium Transformation* (Shih 2004). After witnessing plummeting prices of personal computers in the early 1990s, Shih sensed that change was imperative and used the first re-engineering to convert Acer into a disintegration and delegation business model. The strategy of "global brand, local touch" under the first re-engineering has been deemed as a useful mode to implement an international partnership (Shih 1996). The second re-engineering aimed to clear up the division of responsibility between production and marketing, and the ensuing dilemma of straddling both OEM and OBM businesses (Shih 2004). Acer Group thereafter was divided into three separate corporations: Acer, BenQ, and Wistron.

Unlike conventional Taiwanese entrepreneurs and executives, Shih openly eschewed family parochialism in favor of meritocracy and proclaimed that his three children will not take over his business. Stan Shih has also tried to set an example in exit planning. When he passed the Acer baton to his successor, all the other founders retired as well and were invited to co-found iD SoftCapital Group in order that Acer's new executive team have free rein. Stan Shih thus ensured a smooth transition, when many other Taiwanese corporations have been troubled by various leadership transition problems (Chen and Wang 2009).

Acer continued its growth trend under Shih's successor, Jen-tang Wang, and became the number one brand globally for PCs and number two for notebooks. Failing to sense the turning trend of the IT industry toward mobile devices, however, Acer's growth started to decline. In 2012, Acer was dealt a heavy blow with the announcement of the ouster of Gianfranco Lanci, an Italian national who joined Acer in 1997 and was promoted to CEO in 2005. With the objective of leading the company through a third corporate transformation, Stan Shih was summoned to return for a six-month stint as chairman in November 2013 to complete the transition. In this and his other endeavors, Shih has been recognized around the globe for his achievements in brand-business building and for his management models (Chen and Miller 2010).

YAN Ho-Don
Feng Chia University, Taiwan

Further Reading

Acer Group. (2014). Stan Shih. Retrieved November 30, 2014, from http://www.acer-group.com/public/The_Group/management.htm

Chen, Ming-Jer, & Miller, Danny. (2010). West meets East: Toward an ambicultural approach to management. *Academy of Management Perspective*, 24(4), 17–24.

Chen Yi-Shan, & Wang Hsiao-Wen. (2009). Taiwan's corporate succession crisis. *CommonWealth Magazine*, 23, 431.

Lin Ling-Fei. (2011). *Taiwanese IT pioneers: Stan (Chen-Jung) Shih*. Computer History Museum. Retrieved March 10, 2015, from http://archive.computerhistory.org/resources/access/text/2012/02/102746001-05-01-acc.pdf

Lin Hao-Chieh, & Hou Sheng-Tsung. (2010). Managerial lessons from the East: An interview with Acer's Stan Shih. *Academy of Management Perspective*, 24(4), 6–16.

Reader's Digest. (2002). *Face to face with Stan Shih*. Retrieved March 10, 2015, from https://laofutze.files.wordpress.com/2010/07/ow-ying-chuan-stan-shih-2009.pdf

Shih, Stan. (1996). *Me-too is not my style: Corporate visions, strategies and business philosophies of the Acer Group*. Acer Foundation.

Shih, Stan. (2002). *Growing global: A corporate vision masterclass* (Fu-Yuan Xiao, Ed.; Minn Song, Trans.). Singapore: John Wiley & Sons.

Shih, Stan. (2004). *Millennium transformation—Change management for New Acer*. Aspire Academy.

Shih, Stan. (2012). *Weixiao zouchu ziji de lu* 微笑走出自己的路 [Smile and beat your own path]. Taiwan: Commonwealth Publishing Group.

Shih, Stan; Wang, Jen-Tang; & Young, Arthur. (2006). Building global competitiveness in a turbulent environment: Acer's journey of transformation. *Advances in Global Leadership*, 4, 201–217.

• Shih, Stan •

♂ Sū Tóng 苏童

b. 1963—Avant-garde novelist, short-story writer, and essayist

Alternate names: b. Tóng Zhōngguì 童忠贵; trad. 蘇童

Summary

Though rising to international fame with the adaptation of his novel into the movie *Raise the Red Lantern*, Su Tong had long established himself as an important Chinese writer and a master of the avant-garde novelistic style. His consistent dedication to "serious" literature does not reduce his popularity among Chinese readers and has also won him acclaim on the world literary stage.

Su Tong, whose real name is Tong Zhonggui, is among the few pioneers of Chinese avant-garde literature, a style popular since the early 1980s, who remain active and productive today. His Toon Street Series (Xiāngchūnshù jiē 香椿树街) and Maple-Poplar Village Series (Fēngyángshù xiāng 枫杨树乡) of novels and novelettes have left a deep imprint on Chinese literary history and on the literary memories of contemporary Chinese people. At least four of his novels have been adapted into movies, including the award-winning *Wives and Concubines*, which was made into the movie *Raise the Red Lantern* (*Dàhóng dēnglóng gāogāo guà* 大红灯笼高高挂) directed by *Zhāng Yìmóu 张艺谋 (b. 1951). Because of Su Tong's achievements and influence in Chinese literary circles, David Der-wei Wang, professor of Chinese literature at Harvard University, described him as "one of the most important novelists of contemporary mainland China" (Wang 2010, 50).

Early Works

Su Tong was born to a typical working-class family in Suzhou, Jiangsu Province on 23 January 1963. With an elder brother and two elder sisters, his childhood was by no means free from want, and this was made worse by nationwide poverty and deprivation during the Cultural Revolution (1966–1976). When he was

---

*People marked with an asterisk have entries in this dictionary.

nine, he was stricken by severe nephritis and sepsis and was hospitalized for over half a year. As he later recalled, that illness had a direct bearing on his approach to death in his novels (Wang and Lin 2003, 197). The years of schooling following his illness were smooth and of no special note except that he was always good at writing. In 1980, he was admitted to the department of Chinese language and literature of Beijing Normal University. This life-changing opportunity gave him the chance to become one of China's few academically trained professional writers after the Cultural Revolution.

Su Tong published his first short story in 1983. When he graduated from Beijing Normal University the following year, he was assigned to work at Nanjing Arts University as a student counselor. As he was more interested in literature, he continued to write and publish short stories, and managed to transfer to work as an editor for the literary magazine *Zhongshan*. Su Tong's period at *Zhongshan* was said to be important for his career because he was able to contact famous authors such as Jiǎ Píngwā 贾平凹, Tiě Níng 铁凝, and Lù Yáo 路遥, and to work on their manuscripts (Zhang 2012, 73).

In 1987, Su Tong published his first novella *On the Run in 1934* (*1934 nián de táowáng* 一九三四年的逃亡), which attracted critical attention as an avant-garde rewriting of history. In 1988, he published another pioneering novelette *Opium Family* (*Yīngsù zhījiā* 罂粟之家). In 1989, he published his third novelette in a row, *Wives and Concubines* (*Qīqiè chéngqún* 妻妾成群), which was well received by Chinese readers largely owing to its depictions of sexuality and the fantasy of polygyny. In 1991, *Raise the Red Lantern*, an adapted movie from *Wives and Concubines* directed by Zhang Yimou became a cinematographic success, winning the Silver Lion for Best Director at the Venice International Film Festival, and a nomination for Best Foreign Language Film at the Oscars. As a result, Su Tong's name as a novelist became much better known in China and internationally. In 1990, Su Tong joined the Chinese Writers Association, an authoritative organization that receives authors who are not only famous and influential but are also capable of maintaining a tactful harmony with the dominant ideology of the Communist Party.

An Avant-garde Approach to History

It is generally believed that Su Tong's avant-garde approach to "historical situations saturated with illicit sexuality, bold female characters and unrelieved depravity" (Gunn 2005, 790) found the best expression in his first novel *Rice* (*Mǐ* 米), which delved deeply into the intricacies of hunger, sexuality, and brutality, and in his novel *Hóngfěn* 红粉, in which he depicted the love affairs of two Shanghai prostitutes at the end of the Chinese Civil War, around 1949. Both novels were

• Sū Tóng •

Su Tong's *The Boat to Redemption*

In 2009, the novel The Boat to Redemption *won Su Tong the Man Asian Literary Prize. The story, set during the Cultural Revolution, is told from the perspective of the boy Dongliang who grows up among the boat people together with his father. Below are the opening paragraphs of the novel.*

Son

Most people live on dry land, in houses. By my father and I live on a barge. Nothing surprising about that, since we are boat people; the terra firma does not belong to us. Everyone knows that the Sunny-side Fleet plies the waters of the Golden Sparrow River all year round, so life for Father and me hardly differs from that of fish: Whether heading upriver or down, most of our time is spent on the water. It's been eleven years. I'm still young and strong, but my father, a rash and carless man, is sinking inexorably into the realm of the aged.

Ever since the autumn he has been exhibiting strange symptoms, some age-related, some not. The pupils of his eyes are shrinking and becoming increasingly cloudy- sort of fish-like. He hardly ever sleeps any more; from morning to night he observes life on the shore through fish eyes filled with dejection [...] I've noticed spots on the backs of his hands and along his spine; a few are brown or dark red, but most glisten like silver, and it's these that are beginning to worry me. I can't help thinking that my father will soon grow scales on his body. He has lived an extraordinary life, and I'm afraid he's on the verge of turning into a fish.

Source: Su Tong. (2010). *The Boat to Redemption* [*Hé'àng* 河岸] (Howard Goldblatt, Trans.) (pp. 7–8). New York: Doubleday.

published in 1991 and were soon adapted into controversial films, with *Rice* adapted into *Dàhóng mǐdiàn* 大鸿米店 by Huang Jianzhong in 1995, and *Hongfen* into *Blush* by Li Shaohong in 1994 and *Rouged Beauties* by Huang Shuqin in 1995.

The 1990s witnessed a resurgence in people's interest in history. In response to this trend, Su Tong further developed his neo-historicist approach and created a number of works in this category, most notably *My Life as Emperor* (*Wǒde dìwíng shēngyá* 我的帝王生涯) in 1992 and *Empress Dowager Wu Zetian* (*Wǔ Zétiān* 武则天) in 1994.

As one of the few avant-garde novelists still productive in the twenty-first century, Su Tong seems to be giving more importance to the literary quality and literary-historical significance of his new works. His major novels over the past fifteen years include *Binu and the Great Wall of China* (*Bìnú* 碧奴) published in 2006, *The Boat to Redemption* (*Hé'àn* 河岸) in 2009, and *Tales of the Siskin* (*Huángquè jì* 黄雀记) in 2013. *The Boat to Redemption* especially has proved a great critical success, with David Der-Wei Wang calling it an important transition in Su Tong's novel writing and his best work in years (Wang 2010, 50). In 2009, it won Su Tong the Man Asian Literary Prize. Two years later, he became one of the first Chinese writers to be nominated for the Man Booker International Prize, along with the realist writer Wāng Ānyì 王安忆. In 2012, Su Tong became a writer-in-residence of the Hong Kong University at the age of fifty.

As a Chinese writer whose career has synchronized with the most rapid social transformations in China, Su Tong and his works have reflected some important features, both old and new, of contemporary Chinese literature. On the one hand, he shared a strong fascination in his works with the native soil, or the so-called cultural "root." His preference for the Toon Street or the Maple-Poplar Village as the setting of his stories is strongly reminiscent of the Shen Congwen's "border town" in Western Hunan or of *Mò Yán's 莫言 "Northeast Township" of Gaomi County. On the other hand, like his contemporary *Yú Huá 余华 (b. 1960), who is often mentioned alongside him and thought to be his major competitor, Su Tong has shown a liking for the literary representations of violence, sexuality, and the dark side of human nature amidst absurd social realities. They both also have the readiness and capability to explore and communicate with the international literary community. Their distinct approaches to novel creation, one neo-historicist and the other realist, may provide a full and thought-provoking picture of the contemporary Chinese novel and avant-garde literature.

Huaiyu LUO
Beijing University of Chemical Technology

Further Reading

Gunn, Edward. (2005). Su Tong. In Edward L. David (Ed.), *Encyclopedia of contemporary Chinese culture*. New York: Routledge.

Li Jie 李劼. (1998). Lun zhongguo dangdai xinchao xiaoshuo 论中国当代新潮小说 [On China's contemporary avant-garde novels]. *Zhongshan Literary Bimonthly*, 5.

Su Tong. (1995). *Rice* [*Mǐ* 米]. (Howard Goldblatt, Trans.). New York: W. Morrow and Co. (Original work published 1991)

Su Tong. (2005). *My Life as Emperor* [*Wǒde dìwíng shēngyá* 我的帝王生涯] (Howard Goldblatt, Trans.). New York: Hyperion East. (Original work published 1992)

Su Tong. (2008). *Binu and the Great Wall of China* [*Bìnú* 碧奴] (Howard Goldblatt, Trans.). Melbourne: Text Publishing Company. (Original work published in 2006)

Su Tong. (2010). *The Boat to Redemption* [*Hé'àng* 河岸] (Howard Goldblatt, Trans.). New York: Doubleday. (Original work published in 2009)

Wang, David Der-Wei. (2010a). "Brothers" offers a sweeping satire of modern China. Retrieved August 20, 2014, from http://www.npr.org/templates/story/story.php?storyId=100423108

Wang, David Der-Wei. (2010b). He yu an: Su Tong de he'an 河与岸：苏童的《河岸》 [The river and the bank: Su Tong's *The Boat to Redemption*]. *Contemporary Writers Review*, 1.

Wang Yao 王尧, & Lin Jianfa 林建法. (2003). *Su Tong Wang Hongtu duihua lu* 苏童王宏图对话录. [Dialogues between Su Tong and Wang Hongtu]. Suzhou : Suzhou Unversity Press.

Zhang Xuexin 张学昕. (2012). Su Tong wenxue nianpu 苏童文学年谱 [A literary cronicle of Su Tong]. *Soochow Academic*, 6.

• 苏童 •

♂ Tán Dùn 谭盾

b. 1957—Musician, composer, and conductor

Alternate name: trad. 譚盾

Summary

The musician, conductor, and contemporary composer Tan Dun absorbed the sights, sounds, and stories of China's countryside, first from his home village, and later from the farming commune where he served during the Cultural Revolution, and channeled them into music. Now based in New York, Tan combines "organic" sounds of water, paper, and ceramics while blending elements of East and West in historical or literary themes and orchestration. He has transformed contemporary composition into a popular, edgy art form, and remains critically and commercially successful.

As classical music struggles to retain audiences, impresarios, program directors, and conductors look to contemporary music to keep orchestras alive. Tan Dun is a China-born, New York-based contemporary composer who fuses East and West, shamanism and realism, the organic and the inorganic. He also favors leather pants and black T-shirts, and emphasizes the visual as much as the aural. Tan has brought hipness to a misunderstood, even feared, musical genre, and while some accuse him of cultural superficiality, he is loved, respected and admired on both sides of the International Date Line.

Childhood and Early Education

Born on 18 August 1957, Tan grew up in Simao, Hunan Province, in south-central China. His medical doctor mother and food researcher father were transferred to the provincial capital of Changsha, so Tan stayed with his grandmother in a village teeming with Taoists, shamans, ghost stories, and rituals—later forbidden in the changing political climate.

Chinese leader Máo Zédōng's 毛泽东 (1893–1976) Cultural Revolution lasted for ten years (1966–1976), but the effects still reverberate. During that time, a recognizable legal system ceased to exist. Schools were closed while teachers and other intellectuals were publicly harassed and sometimes imprisoned and, in the most extreme cases, killed. Red Guards, teenaged paramilitary organizations, roamed the streets and tore through private houses searching for forbidden bourgeois or traditional objects. Those with international experience, ancestry on the wrong side of the Chinese Civil War (1946–1949), or "bad backgrounds" were subjected to job discrimination, forced relocation or even incarceration and death.

Officials transferred millions of urban teenagers to the countryside to experience firsthand how the peasants lived. Considering China's top-heavy agricultural society, this idea had some merit; however, terms of service could last over a decade. There were no visits home, food was scarce, and housing often woefully inadequate. "Imagine," Tan said. "You were told to report to an office and made to swear to leave your family, to feed pigs, to plant rice, for your entire life. I cried. How could I do this my entire life?" (Buruma 2008).

Tan was fortunate: Mao's death in 1976 cut short his stay in the farming commune and rendered his service comparatively painless. He spent his time charming the farmers by setting Maoist texts to their now-forbidden ghost operas, and making music by playing cooking implements, farming tools, and even a three-stringed violin. Then a freak accident catalyzed his career. A Peking opera troupe's boat capsized near the commune, killing several musicians, and the self-taught Tan filled an empty slot. A few years of on-the-job training and touring accelerated his music skills, and when the politics changed, he was ready for a career in music.

Cultural Revolution policies proscribed playing or listening to any traditional or Western music; arts lovers were limited to the so-called "Eight Model Operas" which included one cantata, two ballets, and five revolutionary operas. Western instruments not confiscated or destroyed were for playing odes to Mao. But when the revolution collapsed, Tan was finally exposed to composers such as Beethoven and Bach. Soon after, he applied to Beijing's now-reopened Central Conservatory of Music, and secured one of thirty slots among thousands of applicants. This graduating class is now legendary, spawning compositional luminaries such as Zhōu Lóng 周龙 (b. 1953) and his wife Chén Yí 陈怡 (b. 1953). Tan, along with Yè Xiǎogāng 叶小纲 (b. 1955), Guō Wénjǐng 郭文景 (b. 1956), and Qú Xiǎosōng 瞿小松 (b. 1952), was known as one of the "Four Talents." And even among this elite group of Third Generation composers of New Wave music (*xīncháo yīnyuè* 新潮音乐), Tan has achieved worldwide recognition.

Musical Career

Tan moved to New York City in 1986, but upon meeting fellow composer John

Cage, his ideas about contemporary composition underwent a permanent shift. "What he really pushed me to do was to listen to the sounds of nature and listen to myself," Tan says. "If I didn't meet with John Cage, I'm thinking my life is different" (Chute 2012). Listening has made Tan a master of blending disparate sounds, and for some, bringing Chinese sensibilities to life. His "organic music" series, which includes his *Water Concerto* (1998), *Paper Concerto* (2003), *Earth Concerto* (2009), and *Water Music* (2004), as well as more traditional works such as his opera *Tea: A Mirror of the Soul* (2002) use natural elements such as paper, stones, ceramics, and splashing water. "It's a huge statement from me that organic sounds are the most important musical instrument," says Tan. For him, organic sounds literally hit close to home. "Life is music, and music is my life; if not, I don't think I can master the sounds," he continued. "When I was growing up in Hunan countryside, all those people doing laundry, washing their rice and their bodies in the river, created beautiful sounds" (N. Pellegrini, personal communication with Tan Dun, 2008).

Tan is equally captivated by ancient Chinese culture. His first opera, *Nine Songs* (1989), draws on the poetry of Qu Yuan, an imperial official from almost 2,500 years ago and called the father of Chinese poetry, who drowned himself after falling victim to palace intrigue (this tragedy supposedly inspired the Chinese Dragon Boat Festival holiday).

Tan's operas *Peony Pavilion* (1998) and *Marco Polo* (1996) both melded East and West; *Peony* included Kun opera staging and *Marco* used instruments from Medieval Europe and the Silk Road. For *The First Emperor* (2006), which addressed China's national unification under the Qin, he collaborated with Chinese-American novelist Ha Jin on the English-language libretto. Tan is also known for his film soundtracks, most notably director *Ang Lee's 李安 (b. 1954) *Crouching Tiger, Hidden Dragon* (2000), which earned him Grammy and Academy Awards.

Influence and Legacy

Many Chinese composers combine East and West by playing pentatonic (five-tone, traditionally Asian) scales on orchestral instruments, but Tan draws on academic, historical, sentimental, and sensual influences. Some critics accuse him of surface-level interpretations, but his work introduces Western audiences to a different side of China, and reminds Chinese listeners of sights, sounds, and subjects they have forgotten, or maybe never learned. A prolific composer of operas, concertos, film scores and symphonic, chamber and solo works, not to mention a Bach-inspired oratorio, Tan also experiments with technology. His 2002 piece *The Map: Concerto for Cello, Video and Orchestra* combined video projections with orchestral music, while his *Internet Symphony*

---

*People marked with an asterisk have entries in this dictionary.

Album cover for a CD with three of Tan Dun's compositions. Photo by iClassical Com.

No. 1 "Eroica," for the YouTube Orchestra (2009) blended cyber-auditions with a concert date at Carnegie Hall, and included disc brakes and automobile rims in the percussion section. Perhaps his greatest legacy, however, is making contemporary music popular. "Composing contemporary music is a niche market… so you can enjoy your freedom," says Chinese composer and former classmate Guo Wenjing (b. 1956). "Some are dissatisfied with the status quo and get media attention; Tan Dun is a typical example. But this is understandable, and very good for contemporary music," he continues. "If no one cares about it, the genre is going to die" (N. Pellegrini, personal communication with Guo Wenjing, 2008).

Nancy PELLEGRINI
Stage Editor/Writer for Time Out Beijing/
Time Out Shanghai

Further Reading

Buruma, Ian. (2008). Of musical import: East Meets West in the art of Tan Dun. *The Asia-Pacific Journal: Japan Focus.* Retrieved February 7, 2015, from http://www.japanfocus.org/-Ian-Buruma/2753

Chute, James. (2012, July 28). There's no composer in the world like Tan Dun. *San Diego Union Tribune.* Retrieved February 7, 2015, from http://www.utsandiego.com/news/2012/jul/28/La-Jolla-Music-Society-Summerfest-Tan-Dun/all/?print

Dun, Tan. (2005). In *Encyclopedia of world biography.* Retrieved February 7, 2015, from http://www.encyclopedia.com/doc/1G2-3435000066.html

Kouwenhoven, Frank. (1991/1992). Composer Tan Dun: The ritual fire dancer of China's new music. *China Information*, 7(1), 17–39.

Harris, Craig. (no date). Tan Dun. *Billboard biography.* Retrieved February 7, 2015, from http://www.billboard.com/artist/1496600/tan-dun/biography

Home page. Tan Dun. Retrieved January 14, 2015, from http://tandun.com/about

Hughes, Mary Joe. (2013). Musical interplay: Tan Dun's *The Map* and other examples. In *The move beyond form: Creative undoing in literature and the arts since 1960* (pp. 49–66). London: Palgrave Macmillan.

Liu Jingzhi. (2010). *A critical history of new music in China* (Caroline Mason, Trans.). Hong Kong: The Chinese University of Hong Kong.

Melvin, Sheila, & Cai Jindong. (2004). *Rhapsody in red: How Western classical music became Chinese.* New York: Algora Publishing.

Music Sales Classical. (2013). Tan Dun. Retrieved January 14, 2015, from http://www.musicsales-classical.com/composer/long-bio/Tan-Dun

Schulman, David, & Freymann-Weyr, Jeffrey. (2006). Tan Dun's cultural evolution. *NPR Morning Edition.* Retrieved February 7, 2015, from http://www.npr.org/templates/story/story.php?storyId=5148259

Revolutionary New Music. (no date). *Other minds.* Retrieved February 7, 2015, from http://www.otherminds.org/shtml/Tan.shtml

Swed, Mark. (2013, January 7). Classical music review: Tan Dun offers fresh sounds for a new year. *Los Angeles Times.* Retrieved February 7, 2015, from http://articles.latimes.com/2013/jan/07/entertainment/la-et-cm-la-phil-review-tears-of-nature-20130107

Utz, Christian. (2002). *Neue Musik und Interkulturalitaet: von John Cage bis Tan Dun.* Stuttgart, Germany: Steiner.

Utz, Christian. (1998). Extreme cross-over, extremely personal music—Interview with Tan Dun. *Chime*, 12/13, 142–150.

Van Putten, Bas. (1996). Tan Dun's Marco Polo: A multi-cultural journey. *Chime*, 9, 57–62.

• Tan Dun •

♀ Teng, Teresa

Dèng Lìjūn 鄧麗君

1953–1995—Taiwanese pop star, famous for her romantic ballads

Alternate names: b. Teng Li-yun 鄧麗筠; nickname: Little Deng; simpl. 邓丽君

・鄧麗君・

Summary

As a superstar throughout East and Southeast Asia, Teresa Teng was one of the most revered singers of Chinese ethnicity. A multilingual singer famous for her romantic ballads and folk-style songs, she enjoyed world-wide success, including in mainland China, before semi-retiring in the late 1980s. Her songs have influenced and inspired a younger generation of singers across China, Taiwan, Hong Kong, and even Japan.

Teresa Teng is one of the most influential and memorable singers in the Chinese-speaking world in modern times. She made a decisive career decision to be a full-time singer at the age of fourteen and rose to stardom beyond political boundaries. She died in 1995, but her sweet voice and delicate appearance remain vivid for millions of Chinese around the world, so much so that it is claimed that wherever there are Chinese people, the songs of Teresa Teng can be heard.

Childhood and Early Education

Born in Yunlin County, Taiwan on 29 January 1953, Teresa Teng was the only daughter in a family of five children. Her father, an officer of the Republic of China Armed Forces, moved from the mainland to Taiwan with the military in 1949. The Teng family finally settled down in Taipei County (now New Taipei City) in 1959 when the father retired from the military. She attended Luzhou Elementary School and then Ginling Girls High School.

Teng developed her passion for singing at elementary school by participating in various talent performances, military entertainment events, and singing competitions. She won her first major award in 1963 by singing "Visiting

Yingtai" 訪英台 from the 1962 Shaw Brothers' film *The Love Eterne* (*Liáng shānbó yǔ zhù yīngtái* 梁山伯與祝英台) in a competition hosted by Chinese Radio Station (Zhōnghuá guǎngbō diàntái 中華廣播電台), and was on track to build a stellar career in music. She attended singing lessons offered by Chengsheng Broadcasting Corp. (Zhèngshēng guǎngbō gōngsī 正聲廣播公司) and completed the training program as the highest-ranking student in 1966.

Music Career

Having won awards in various competitions, she quit high school with her father's approval in 1967 in order to pursue a professional singing career. She was signed to Yeu Jow Records 宇宙唱片 and released her first record in the same year. She also started to perform on *All Stars Event* (*Qúnxīng hùi* 群星會), the first-ever TV singing program in Taiwan, for Taiwan Television and on live radio shows for the Broadcasting Corporation of China, as well as in night clubs such as Paris Night 夜巴黎 and Seventh Heaven 七重天.

The year 1969 saw more "firsts" in Teng's early career. She made her film debut in *Thanks to the General Manager* (*Xièxiè zǒng jīnglǐ* 謝謝總經理), recorded the theme song for the first TV drama *Crystal Girl* (*Jīngjīng* 晶晶) in Taiwan, hosted a singing program for China Television, and delivered her first overseas performance in Singapore. In 1971 she began a tour in Hong Kong and some Southeast Asian countries for more than two years, which made her a well-known star in overseas Chinese communities and laid a solid foundation for her future development.

In order to set her sights further afield, Teng signed with Polydor (Japan) and started to record Japanese songs to foray into the Japanese market in 1973. After winning the Best New Artist of Japan Record Awards in the next year, her popularity boomed in East and Southeast Asia. In 1979 she was deported from Japan for having an Indonesian passport which she obtained illegally. She was therefore banned from entering the country for one year, which led to unprecedented frustration in her career. Despite this incident, she signed a contract with Taurus Records in 1983, making a successful comeback in Japan. Her career reached its pinnacle in the 1980s. She also performed frequently in Hong Kong, Taiwan, Japan, and North America until the late 1980s when she became semi-retired.

Teng took up residence in Paris in 1989, where she performed in a concert to express her support during the 1989 Tiananmen student protests, and met her boyfriend, the French photographer Quilery Paul Puel Stephane. Unmarried and with no children, she lived there on her record royalties until she died from a severe asthma attack while on holiday in Thailand on 8 May 1995.

Style and Success

Enchanting the audience with sincerity, sweetness, and skills, Teng had a perfect voice for romantic ballads and folk-style songs. Mandarin pieces such as "The Moon Represents My Heart" 月亮代表我的心 and "Small Town Story" 小城故事 were standards in her lifetime. She also reinterpreted works from 1930s and 1940s Shanghai, such as Zhou Xuan's "When Will You Come Back Again" 何日君再來 and Li Xianglan's "Fragrance of the Night" 夜來香, so impressively that she was closely identified with these tunes.

The Chinese popular music industry started in Shanghai in the late 1920s. After 1949, Hong Kong served as a major production center for Mandarin pop for two decades, with Taiwan replacing Hong Kong by the time Cantopop took shape in the 1970s. Teng was not only a successor to old Shanghai, but also a post-war Taiwanese singer who opened up new horizons in her own right. Well-received in many Asian countries, she recorded songs not only in her native Mandarin but also in Taiwanese, Cantonese, Japanese, English, and Indonesian. Some of her works were published in more than one language and became transnational hits. For example, her original Japanese hit "Give Yourself to the Flow of Time" 時の流れに身をまかせ, which won the Gold Award of Japan Record Awards in 1986, was later covered in Mandarin as the famous "I Only Care About You" 我只在乎你.

Teng set several records in her music career. For example, from 1976 to 1981 (except for 1979, when she took an English-language program at the University of Southern California), she performed sold-out concerts at the prominent Lee Theatre in Hong Kong every year. She was the first singer of Chinese ethnicity to perform at the Lincoln Center in New York City, in 1980. From 1984 onwards, she was the Grand Prix winner both of All Japan Cable Broadcasting Awards, Osaka 全日本有線放送大賞 and of Japan Cable Awards, Tokyo 日本有線大賞 at the same time for three consecutive years.

Influence and Legacy

Born to parents from mainland China, brought up and beginning a career in an era when military hostilities across the Straits were extremely high, Teng's voice not only appealed to the general public but also comforted many soldiers through frequent volunteer performances for servicemen. She was thus dubbed the "eternal sweetheart of the military" in Taiwan. But apart from her homeland, given the continuing political tension between China and Taiwan, her songs also broke through the "bamboo curtain."

After Chinese economic reform, with the ban on popular music from Taiwan and Hong Kong relaxed, Teng's

• 鄧麗君 •

popularity began to take China by storm in the 1980s. Her songs were played everywhere and pirated recordings could be found even in remote villages. Instead of patriotic love and praise for the party, the Chinese audience could now hear about romantic love, a theme absent from popular culture since the founding of the People's Republic. People said humorously, "While old Deng [Deng Xiaoping] rules China by day, little Deng [Teresa Teng] rules by night" and "Listen to old Deng during the day, little Deng at night." She never performed in China, however, though she was repeatedly invited. She stated firmly that she would never set foot on the mainland until democracy was realized there.

Many musicians in China, Taiwan, and Hong Kong mention Teng as one of the most important influences on their early musical development. Her songs have been covered by many singers, including the celebrated singer Faye Wong 王菲, who released a tribute album *Decadent Sound of Faye* (*Fēi mǐmǐ zhī yīn* 菲靡靡之音) of Teng's popular hits in 1995. The multi-award-winning pop singer Fish Leong (Liáng Jìngrú 梁靜茹), who used to sing Teng's songs in competitions, affirms that her professional career might not have been possible if she had never heard Teng's work in her childhood.

Teng's songs have been used in many films, for example, the Hong Kong film *Prison on Fire* (*Jiānyù fēngyún* 監獄風雲, 1987), Hollywood-produced *The Game* (1997), *Rush Hour 2* (2001), and even Italian *Gomorrah* (2008). Her life has also been commemorated in various forms. In 1996, *Comrades: Almost a Love Story* (*Tián mìmì* 甜蜜蜜) was produced in memory of Teresa Teng. Not only does the Chinese title of the film come from the title of her song "Sweet as Honey" 甜蜜蜜, but her music is featured throughout the film and her untimely death is an important subplot to the main story. In 2007, to mark the thirteenth anniversary of her death, Japanese TV Asahi also produced a biographical drama, *The Story of Teresa Teng* (*Teresa Teng monogatari* テレサ・テン物語). Teng's wax figures are exhibited in Madame Tussauds branches in Hong Kong, Beijing, Shanghai, and Wuhan.

Funded by Chinese Television System (Taiwan), Polygram Records (Hong Kong), and Taurus Records (Japan), her family set up the Teresa Teng Culture and Education Foundation to promote her legacy and music education.

Szu-wei CHEN
National Taiwan University

Further Reading

Baranovitch, Nimrod. (2003). *China's new voices: Popular music, ethnicity, gender, and politics, 1978–1997.* Oakland: University of California Press.

Broughton, S., & Ellingham, M. (2000). *World Music: Latin and North America, Caribbean, India, Asia and Pacific* (Vol. 2). Rough Guides.

Davis, E. L. (2009). Deng Lijun. In *Encyclopedia of contemporary Chinese culture*. Taylor & Francis. Retrieved February 16, 2015, from http://contemporary_chinese_culture.academic.ru/183/Deng_Lijun

Gold, Thomas B. (1993). "Go with your feelings": Hong Kong and Taiwan popular culture in greater China. *China Quarterly, 136*.

Jones, Andrew. F. (1992). *Like a knife: Ideology and genre in contemporary Chinese popular music*. Ithaca, NY: Cornell University, East Asia Program.

Latham, Kevin. (2007). *Pop culture China!: Media, arts, and lifestyle*. Santa Barbara, CA: ABC-CLIO.

Moskowitz, Marc L. (2010). *Cries of joy, songs of sorrow: Chinese pop music and its cultural connotations*. Honolulu: University of Hawai'i Press.

Shambaugh, David. (Ed.). (1995). *Greater China: The new superpower?* (pp. 255–273). Oxford, UK: Oxford University Press.

☿ Tsang, Donald

Zēng Yīnquán 曾蔭權

b. 1944—Politician, second chief executive of Hong Kong (2005–2012)

Alternate names: Yam-kuen Tsang; simpl. 曾蔭权

Summary

Serving from 2005 to 2012 as the second chief executive of Hong Kong after China reassumed sovereignty in 1997, Donald Tsang oversaw a period of financial growth and successful infrastructure development. Critics, however, have claimed that he did little to address the political and social issues that beleaguer the city to this day.

Donald Tsang was the second chief executive of the Hong Kong Special Administrative Region (SAR) after its reversion from British to Chinese sovereignty in 1997, and served from 2005 to 2012. Under this arrangement, Hong Kong was granted a "high degree of autonomy" over its domestic and fiscal policy, allowed to have its own flag, currency, and run a capitalist system with a free market.

Political Career

Tsang, born on 7 October 1944 when Hong Kong was under Japanese occupation during World War II, came to the position of chief office holder in the city more by accident than design. His predecessor, the first chief executive *Tung Chee-hwa 董建華, had resigned in March 2005, two years before his second (and final) term had been meant to end. Tung had cited health reasons, though it was widely accepted inside and outside Hong Kong that the real reasons was the precipitous drop in his credibility and approval ratings since trying to secure passage of an anti-subversion bill (Article 23) through the local parliament, the Legislative Council, in 2003. Huge protests had brought more than half a million onto the streets in August and September 2003, almost a tenth of Hong Kong's population, and by March 2005 Tung had exhausted the patience even of his stalwart political overlords in Beijing.

Tsang was an ambiguous choice to succeed Tung. He had been a civil servant since 1967, and had a huge knowledge of

---

*People marked with an asterisk have entries in this dictionary.

the highest level of local bureaucracy. Since the resignation of the highly regarded chief secretary of administration (in effect, the number two power-holder in the city, in charge of the entire civil service) *Anson Chan 陳方安生 in 2001, again for personal reasons, Tsang had been Tung's deputy, working closely with him. But he was not particularly favored by Beijing, not least because of his close working relationship with the last British governor of the city, Christopher (subsequently Lord) Patten. Patten, since his appointment in 1992 and after losing his own parliamentary seat in the United Kingdom, had pushed through a number of democratic reforms in Hong Kong, infuriating the Chinese government. Tsang's good service to the British was symbolized by the granting of a knighthood to him by Prince Charles just hours before the formal handover in July 1997.

Such an award would, in the normal order of things, have been toxic for any successful political career in Hong Kong after 1997, but Tsang reaped good fortune, at least initially, from Tung's own woes. He did bring a good understanding of the economic and trade dynamics of the city, too, from his jobs in the civil service in the 1980s and into the 1990s dealing with finance and business. A trade officer earlier in his career (he had even, in the 1960s after leaving university worked very briefly as a salesman for an American company), Tsang was financial secretary from 1995 to 2001, during the handover period, and had been instrumental in helping weather the worst impacts of the Asian Financial Crisis in 1997–1998 when unemployment soared, growth collapsed, and the city entered a serious recession.

These experiences weighed against his more negative aspects for Beijing, and his election in March 2005 was uncontested. Out of the nomination committee of eight hundred, he reportedly secured over seven hundred votes. His immediate challenge, however, was to restore at least some of the influence and authority of the chief executive position.

Chief Executive and Legacy

Tsang can best be described as the luckiest of the three chief executives the territory has had up to 2015. Unlike his predecessor Tung Chee-hwa, he did not have to make his job up from scratch and have the burden of first incumbency with all the expectations that carried. Nor did he, initially, have to deal with a major economic crisis. And he did not have to figure out answers to constitutional change and the huge public protests these inspired from the public that his successor, *Leung Chun-ying 梁振英, wrestled with. Hong Kong, under Tsang's leadership until 2012, was blessed with largely positive gross domestic product (GDP) growth, even managing to weather the 2008

曾蔭權

global financial crisis by a largely effective fiscal stimulus package and reliance on the energy of the expanding mainland economy.

Even so, Tsang's legacy will largely be seen as an underwhelming one. He left major political, financial, and social issues for the city unanswered. That he was formally charged with two counts of misconduct in October 2015 only adds to the ambiguity about his legacy. The only area where his leadership from 2005 to 2012 might have had a lasting impact is in the huge infrastructure projects commenced over this period.

Political Legacy

In terms of political legacy, Tsang did little to push through substantive constitutional change for the chief executive elections, either in 2007 or 2012. The 2007 election maintained the eight hundred-strong nominating committee. The 2012 one extended it only by another four hundred, to a total of twelve hundred members. Tsang had been closely associated with Lord Patten's fierce criticisms of Beijing and its refusal to countenance democratic reforms in the city during the 1990s. Even so, he enjoyed a frosty relationship with the pan-democrats in the city, and while he never had to deal with huge protests as both Tung Chee-hwa and Leung Chun-ying did, neither did he leave a coherent approach to constitutional reform for after he left office. The issue was simply shelved.

Financial Legacy

The same could be said of fiscal issues. Hong Kong often seems to operate more like a company than a government. Its public spending as proportion of gross domestic product (GDP) rarely rises above 20 percent, one of the lowest in the world. The government also has sufficient reserves to cover its expenditure for several months even were it to take in no revenue. Despite this, it has one of the lowest tax rates for individuals and corporations in the world (currently 17 percent). Once more, despite raising government expenditure during the financial crisis modestly, and allowed small grants to be made to the public to buy energy-saving light bulbs, Tsang did little to reform the welfare, health, and education systems dramatically, nor to address the huge issue of inequality in the city, rising poverty levels, and soaring housing costs. He did introduce proposals for a consumption tax, but after two years of consultations, these were also put on hold and have not been resurrected since.

Social Legacy

In environment, too, Tsang did little, despite the city suffering rising levels of pollution largely due to its proximity to the huge manufacturing base of Guangzhou Province. Public health scares continued to plague the city, with the most noticeable being around avian bird flu. None got out of hand, but they were reminders of how vulnerable the

A mocking poster of Donald Tsang at the 2009 Hong Kong democracy protests. The sign reads "I'll make a good dog", referring to Tsang's "obedience" to the Chinese government. Photo by David Yan.

city was to health and environment issues from the mainland, neither of which it could do much about.

Infrastructure Development

In one area, that of infrastructure development, Tsang had a major impact. From 2007, talk started of the "ten major projects," which were aimed at making the city more integrated into the mainland, where a major fast rail and motorway construction boom was taking place. In order to maintain its place as an international logistics hub, Hong Kong put into place a twenty-year development plan running from 2009, part of which was to build a major motorway link-up between Guangzhou, Shenzhen, and Hong Kong, population centers that came to a total of 50 million people. The other component was to construct a bridge, scheduled to be one of the world's longest, with part of it under water, between Hong Kong, Macau, and

Zhuhai in Guangdong. A third was to redevelop the former airport of Kai Tak in the city. While Hong Kong had opened a new airport on reclaimed land on Lantau Island in the late 1990s just after the handover, the old airport with its famously dramatic close proximity to the city, occupied prime real estate to the east of Kowloon. The issue was that the land was heavily contaminated and needed major investment before it could be reused. Years of consultation finally resulted in agreement to build a major cultural and public center there, something that was ultimately achieved. Even so, by 2015 large parts of Kai Tak were still under construction and reclamation. And ironically, the airport built to replace this one was already almost at capacity, with a new plan to reclaim more land to its north and construct another runway.

The infrastructure master plan also involved building a new mass rail transport system, and an extension to the subway on the island area. These at least took the pressure off the city's already crowded roads. But through challenges over planning, finance, and political objections, the most ambitious of them ended up having completion times extended far into the future. No one disputed, however, that the city needed this investment. In that sense, this was Tsang's biggest legacy.

Tsang himself was the son of a member of the Royal Hong Kong Police force. He was a devout Roman Catholic, attending mass every morning. Despite this, his policies received trenchant criticism from the local Roman Catholic representatives who felt they fueled social injustice and inequality. Tsang's most distinctive habit was to wear bow ties, a sartorial habit he had picked up reportedly from a British official resident in the city in the 1990s, Stephen Bradley. On leaving office in 2012, he spent part of his time in a house he had designed and built for him in Shenzhen, across the border in the mainland. It was this luxury house that was to figure in claims made against him when charged for misconduct in October 2015.

Kerry BROWN
Lau China Institute, King's College

Further Reading

BBC News. (2007). Profile: Donald Tsang. Retrieved May 13, 2015, from http://news.bbc.co.uk/2/hi/asia-pacific/4335331.stm

Chan, Ming K., & Lo, Shiu Hing. (Eds.). (2010). Tsang, Donald. In *The A to Z of the Hong Kong SAR and the Macao SAR* (pp. 197–198). Lanham, MD: Rowman & Littlefield.

Cheng, Joseph Y. S. (Ed.). (2013). *The second chief executive of Hong Kong SAR: Evaluating the Tsang years, 2005–2012.* Hong Kong: City University of Hong Kong Press.

The Economist. (2005, June 16). A knight of the people's paradise. Retrieved October 11, 2015, from http://www.economist.com/node/4091570?zid=309&ah=80dcf288b8561b012f603b9fd9577f0e

Fong, Brian C. H. (2014). *Hong Kong's governance under Chinese sovereignty: The failure of the state-business alliance after 1997*. New York: Routledge.

Loh, Christine, & Lai, Carine. (2007). *Reflections of leadership: Tung Chee Hwa and Donald Tsang (1997–2007)*. Hong Kong: Civic Exchange.

♂ Tung Chee-hwa

Dǒng Jiànhuá 董建華

b. 1937—Businessman and politician, first chief executive of Hong Kong (1997–2005)

Alternate names: C. H. Tung; simpl. 董建华

Summary

Tung Chee-hwa served as Hong Kong's first chief executive after the 1997 handover to China. With little political experience, Tung was an unlikely candidate who faced three major hurdles during his time in office: the Asian Financial Crisis, the SARS epidemic, and wide-spread protests against the anti-secession legislation, known as Article 23. He resigned in 2005, just two years into his second term.

Tung Chee-hwa will go down in history if for no other reason than that he was the first leader of Hong Kong after it reverted from British to Chinese sovereignty as a Special Administrative Region (SAR) in July 1997. Appointed as chief executive under the transitional system agreed upon by the British and Chinese governments, Tung was in effect the main spokesperson for Hong Kong's interests internationally, and to the new political overlords in Beijing. But his fate was to prove how hard of a job this new position was, and he was unable to see out the second full term granted him under the Basic Law, Hong Kong's de facto constitution, resigning early in 2005.

Family Business in a Changing City

Tung had been a controversial choice for the position of chief executive. Born in Shanghai on 7 July 1937, his family subsequently moved to the British colony of Hong Kong because of the turbulence suffered on the mainland as a result of the devastating Sino-Japanese War between 1937 and 1945. Hong Kong itself, however, was controlled by the Japanese until their defeat, when it reverted once more to British control. Tung's father, Tung Chao Ying, established a shipping company, the Oriental Overseas Containment Line (OOCL), at a time when the small city was lifting itself from poverty and backwardness to become one of the great logistic and merchant hubs of the post-War world. With spectacular growth over the 1960s and into the 1970s, Hong Kong acquired its position as a major finance and services center, a manufacturing base, and the interface between a People's Republic of China (PRC) still largely closed off from the rest of the world.

This function was to be energized by the *Dèng Xiǎopíng 邓小平 leadership reforms from 1978, with the mainland opening up Special Economic Zones (SEZ, jīngjì tèqū 经济特区). One of those SEZs, Shenzhen, was directly adjacent to Hong Kong, and became a place where Hong Kong business people were able to establish manufacturing centers taking advantage of cheap labor, land, and amenity costs. Ironically, the start of this new phase in the city's history had an ultimately deleterious effect on OOCL. With the death of Tung's father in 1981, the business went into gradual decline, nearly going bankrupt in 1985 as a result of spiraling costs, fierce competition from other shipping lines, and poor management.

Tung Chee-hwa himself, while he had been involved in the business since graduating in the late 1950s from the University of Liverpool in the United Kingdom with a degree in marine engineering, was immediately pushed into the position of having to devise a strategy to save the company. He did so through

pursuing two paths. The first, which was to have great significance later in his career, was to secure support from the Beijing government for a major bailout. Through an intermediary, Hong Kong and Macau businessman and property magnate *Henry Fok 霍英東, he was able to secure US$110 million of funding to keep the company going. His second approach was to ruthlessly cut costs, lay off workers, and reduce OOCL's huge expenses. His strategy worked: OOCL survived, and in the ensuing years prospered, still ranking as one of the world's major shipping lines.

Political Career

That Tung figured at all in the considerations over who should be Hong Kong's first chief executive after the handover in 1997 surprised many, even though he had been a member of the China Consultative Committee for the Basic Law since 1985 (until 1990, when a Basic Law was agreed upon), and held other positions in the Honk Kong colonial government, most notably as a member of the Executive Council (1992–1996). Described as a "little known businessman" by veteran Hong Kong-based journalist Philip Bowring at the time of Tung's appointment in July 1997, it was soon clear that his greatest attribute had been his palatability to a wide group of stakeholders, rather than any necessary experience for the position he had been granted (Bowring 1997). For the British, at least he had

---

*People marked with an asterisk have entries in this dictionary.

good links and an understanding of the United Kingdom through his time as a student there and his years as a businessman. For China, he had grown familiar to them through the OOCL events in the 1980s. He was not Cantonese, the primary linguistic and cultural group in Hong Kong, and so was immune to accusations of being overly pliant to them. In the end, he had the somewhat unexciting advantage of having the least amount of antagonism towards his appointment.

Asian Financial Crisis and Political Challenges

Despite this, his lack of any relevant political background was soon to show. Elected by a majority in the Nominating Council, made up of four hundred appointed and community individuals, his first major challenge was to handle the impact of the Asian Financial Crisis which devastated Hong Kong's growth figures and, in an unprecedented way, raised its unemployment levels over 1998. Hong Kong's lauded finance center was engulfed by accusations of crony capitalism, something that was hard to combat by Tung largely because of his own origins as a business rather than a political leader. And while Hong Kong was eventually able to stabilize its markets by a huge state purchase of stocks, which were eventually sold on the open market again for a profit,

it was a torrid baptism into his new role.

Tung was in charge of a city that had been granted special status for fifty years from 1997 by the Chinese government. Except in international affairs and defense, it had been given a "high degree of autonomy" over its domestic matters—setting interest rates, levying taxes (none of which it had to give to the Beijing government), maintaining a capitalist system, and setting local social welfare policies. It was in this area that the public had the most concerns, because Hong Kong relied on its economic prowess and its ability to produce growth. In addition to the impact of the Asian Financial Crisis, Tung had to face down three other challenges. The first was the parlous state of housing in the city, with prices rising, pressure on land growing, and increasing challenges over how the young and less well-off actually housed themselves. The second was how to find new sources of growth at a time when the mainland economy was increasingly open to the outside world, without relying on Hong Kong's mediatory role, and Hong Kong businesses in turn getting less of a benefit from manufacturing on the mainland, through increases in costs and greater regulation. The third challenge was purely political, but impacted on the other areas, namely how to maintain good relations with Beijing, while ensuring that the city did enjoy autonomy and the Basic Law promises and provisions were kept.

• Tung Chee-hwa •

SARS

The severe acute respiratory syndrome (SARS) crisis in 2003 highlighted just how unexpected events could put all Hong Kong under intense scrutiny. Probably originating in Guangdong Province in late 2002, the disease, which involved flu and fever symptoms and could prove fatal, spread to Hong Kong, which suffered the largest impact. The appearance of SARS created a major panic because of the initial failure to control its spread. The World Health Organization (WHO) was highly critical of both Hong Kong and Beijing's handling of the spread of the virus, which was believed to come from civets and to have crossed across species. Mainland China imposed strict quarantine conditions, and restrictions on movement, with Hong Kong becoming a ghost town as people became fearful of moving in public spaces. The disease was successfully combated in the summer of 2003, but it had been a nasty scare.

Article 23 and Tung's Second Term

On top of the SARS crisis was the more political issue of Article 23. This regulation was part of the Basic Law, approved by the Beijing government at its National People's Congress in 1990, in which "anti-secession" activities were to be outlawed. Pro-democracy and rights activists, along with a sizeable part of the public, felt that over-strict interpretation

of this, and attempts to implement it by taking action against those exercising their rights to free speech and peaceful demonstration, was a violation of the Basic Law promise to preserve Hong Kong's autonomy.

Tung himself was unable to communicate to the public the need to have a security law based on the Article 23 stipulation. When the draft Security Bill was presented in late 2002, there were immediate demonstrations, with over half a million initially protesting, and 170,000 signing a petition opposed to the bill. The Legislative Council, in effect Hong Kong's parliament, was unable to pass the proposed bill, with heated arguments over its provisions and implications. For many in Hong Kong it was read as a clear sign that they were being amalgamated into the PRC and their promised rights were being eroded. In mid-2003, just after the SARS crisis, over 600,000, almost 10 percent of the city's population, marched in protest against the bill, with a crowd of fifty-thousand surrounding the Legislative Council building on the day on which the bill was to be discussed.

Tung himself had been re-elected for a second term as chief executive in July 2003, with 714 out of the expanded electoral committee of eight hundred members supporting him. But he was the sole candidate. Even so, his withdrawal of the Security Bill legislation in September the same year was a huge loss of face. For his final two years in position, he faced pressure on two fronts, the first being dwindling public confidence in his ability to defend Hong Kong's interests in the city. The second was lack of support for him in Beijing, with the PRC president *Hu Jintao in effect criticizing his performance in early 2005. The political reality was that while Tung could deal with the loss of one of these pillars of support, to have neither was politically devastating. He resigned on 12 March 2005, to be replaced by his chief secretary, *Donald Tsang 曾蔭權. Since his retirement, Tung has continued to serve on the mainland Chinese People's Political Consultative Conference (CPPCC), and established a group working on China-Unites States relations. He was part of the delegation led by Hu Jintao's successor, *Xí Jìnpíng 习近平, to the United States in September 2015.

Legacy and Evaluation

Historians will likely be kinder to Tung than many of his contemporaries were. With very little preparation, he took up a new and challenging position in 1997, having to face hugely different stakeholders with no real road map of what he was meant to achieve, and how he could best be judged. The subsequent record of his successors has shown that the position of chief executive is a hugely difficult one to truly do well. Like Tung, both his successor Donald Tsang and the third chief executive *Leung Chun-ying 梁振英 were to be torn between keeping Beijing happy and making sure that they were seen to preserve the autonomy of the city. None were entirely successful, and there must be a question mark about whether it is in fact possible to fulfill these two obligations.

Tung did make a lasting impact on the city, if only through support of huge infrastructure projects, and through allowing Disneyland to establish a theme part there in the early 2000s. Neither of these were free of controversy, with claims of over-expenditure and inefficient planning. Even so, Hong Kong under Tung maintained its premier position as a finance center, and, after the Asian Financial Crisis, maintained solid growth even though it continued to be blighted by soaring housing costs, rising inequality, poor provision of social welfare, and environmental challenges.

Kerry BROWN
Lau China Institute, King's College

Further Reading

Bowring, Philip. (1997). Tung Chee Hwa. *Prospect Magazine*. Retrieved October 11, 2015, from http://www.prospectmagazine.co.uk/features/tungcheehwa

Chan, Ming K. (Ed.). (2008). *China's Hong Kong transformed: Retrospect and prospects beyond the first decade*. Hong Kong: City University of Hong Kong Press.

ChinaVitae. (2015). Tung Chee Hwa. Retrieved January 30, 2015, from http://www.chinavitae.com/biography/Tung_Chee%20Hwa|535

Goodstadt, Leo. (2014). *Poverty in the midst of affluence: How Hong Kong mismanaged its prosperity* (2nd rev. ed.). Hong Kong: Hong Kong University Press.

Horlemann, Ralf. (2002). *Hong Kong's transition to Chinese rule*. New York: Routledge.

Lau Siu-kai. (Ed.). (2002). *The first Tung Chee-Hwa administration: The first five years of the Hong Kong Special Administration Region*. Hong Kong: Chinese University Press.

Loh, Christine, & Lai, Carine. (2007). *Reflections of leadership: Tung Chee Hwa and Donald Tsang (1997–2007)*. Hong Kong: Civic Exchange.

Sing, Ming. (2008). *Politics and government in Hong Kong: Crisis under Chinese sovereignty*. New York: Routledge.

• 董建華 •

♂ Wàn Lǐ 万里

1916–2015—Politician, economist and party elder

Alternate name: trad. 萬里

Summary

With one of the longest careers in the history of the Communist Party, Wan Li served as chair of the National People's Congress, and as an influential member of the Politburo since 1987. He played key roles in the remodeling of Beijing under Mao, in the economic reforms that began with farmers in Anhui Province, and in the promotion of the Three Gorges Dam project.

Wan Li, as part of one of the earliest generations of Communist Party leaders, had a career that ranged from local government positions in his native Shandong Province in the 1930s to leadership of the National People's Congress (NPC) in Beijing, China's de facto parliament, from 1988 to 1993. Close enough to *Dèng Xiǎopíng 邓小平 (1904–1997) to be his bridge partner, Wan Li was also a more elusive political force than many of his colleagues, associated with the critical agricultural reforms of the late 1970s that led to the break-up of the communes, and then critical of the military clampdown on the Tiananmen Square student demonstrators of 1989, he was also blamed in the 1990s for blocking opposition in the NPC to the environmentally problematic Three Gorges Dam project. Into his ninth decade, he expressed support for deeper democratization of China.

Childhood and Early Career

Wan Li was born on 1 December 1916, in Dongping Country, in the northern province of Shandong, and spent most of his formative years there, joining the Communist Party after the Long March in 1936 and occupying a number of administrative positions through the Sino-Japanese War, into the foundation of the People's Republic in 1949. He was brought to Beijing to take up a position in

---

*People marked with an asterisk have entries in this dictionary.

the central government as a vice minister of architectural engineering in 1953, and minister of urban construction two years later. In these roles, he played a key part in the remodeling of Beijing, approving the removal, at Máo Zédōng's 毛泽东 behest, of the ancient city walls in order to run vast, wide Soviet-style boulevards through the city center, and then remaking Tiananmen Square with a vast open space (to this day, the largest central city square in the world) where a consular area had once stood, with the monumental National People's Congress and Museum of Revolutionary History standing on either side. This evidently received Mao Zedong's recognition, as he reportedly joked about Wan Li's name being a homophone for the term "ten thousand li" (*li* is a Chinese unit of measure, coming to just under a kilometer) and said that with Li in charge of projects they would go a long distance.

Occupying positions in the Beijing municipal government from 1958, Wan served under the mayor of the city, *Péng Zhēn 彭真 (1902–1997), reaching the position of deputy mayor. Affected by Peng's dramatic fall from grace at the start of the Cultural Revolution in 1966, Wan was removed from office, and only made a return in the 1970s when he was supportive of Deng Xiaoping during his rehabilitation, serving as minister of railways from 1975 to 1976. Like Deng, his return was short-lived and he was sidelined after the Tiananmen Square protests after the death of Premier Zhōu Ēnlái 周恩来 in April 1976, up until the death of Mao a few months later.

Career in the Upper Ranks

It was while an official in Anhui Province in the late 1970s that Wan started to support reforms being tried by farmers in places like Zongyang County, one of the areas worst affected by the famines of almost two decades before. Yields from crops in these areas had risen remarkably due to a new system devised by local farmers, where they were allowed to sell any of their crops leftover once they had given a certain agreed-upon proportion to the local government. This incentivized farmers to be more efficient, and became known as the Household Responsibility System, adopted by the rest of the country in the early 1980s. Grassroots experimentation by farmers like this leading to something resembling a free market would have been anathema during the Maoist period, but became one of the key lynchpins of reform in the Deng era from 1978, and revolutionized productivity in the rural areas.

Despite initial controversy, and opposition in Beijing from Mao Zedong's successor Huá Guófēng 华国锋 (1921–2008), Wan Li was to prevail, and with Deng's ascendancy from 1978 his closeness to the new dominant leader was rewarded with promotion. In 1982, he became party secretary of Anhui, before being promoted to the Politburo in Beijing after the fall of *Hú Yàobāng

胡耀邦 (1915–1989) as party secretary in 1987. He achieved this elevation despite opposition from hardliners in the party elite who were mistrustful of his more economically liberal tendencies. But Deng's support meant that, while he was not appointed country president, he at least became chair of the National People's Congress in 1988.

Tiananmen and Later Career

Wan was on a visit overseas to North America when the Tiananmen Square protests of 1989 exploded, and he reportedly expressed support for the student demands for more openness and democracy from the party. There were rumors that he intended to return to Beijing and stand by his colleague, the then-party secretary, *Zhào Zǐyáng 赵紫阳 (1919–2005). But he went instead to Shanghai, and it was there that the leader of the city, *Jiāng Zémín 江泽民 (b. 1926), was said to have talked him into supporting the hardening government line. Jiang himself was summoned to Beijing after 4 June and the removal of Zhao.

While Wan was able to continue in his position at the NPC until he retired in 1993, the Tiananmen Square issue did not disappear, and he was associated a decade after the event with calls, on the fifteenth anniversary of the crackdown, to rehabilitate Zhao Ziyang (then still under house arrest) and to re-evaluate the whole event by not labeling it a counter-revolutionary movement. He also spoke about the need to modernize democracy in China and to implement political reforms within the party. Despite this, he was firm against opposition to one of Premier *Lǐ Péng's 李鹏 (1909–1992) main projects, the vast Three Gorges Dam, which was planned in southwest China at great environmental cost, closing down debate of the issue despite significant numbers of opponents in the NPC when a vote was taken in 1992. As the last of the "Eight Immortals" (or "Eight Elders"), Wan Li died on 15 July 2015 in Beijing at age ninety-eight.

Kerry BROWN
Lau China Institute, King's College

Further Reading

Becker, Jasper. (1996). *Hungry ghosts: China's secret famine*. London: John Murray.

Editorial Board. (1989). Wan Li. In *Who's who in China: Current leaders* (pp. 662). Beijing: Foreign Language Press.

Lamb, Malcolm. (1984). *Directory of officials and organizations in China, 1968–1983*. New York: M.E. Sharpe.

Le, Quinxi. (2013). Wan Li. In Song Yuwu (Ed.), *Biographical dictionary of the People's Republic of China* (pp. 295–296). Jefferson, NC: McFarland.

Lee, Khoon Choy. (2005). *Pioneers of modern China: Understanding the inscrutable Chinese*. Singapore: World Scientific.

Leung, Pak-Wah. (2002). Wan Li. In *Political leaders of modern China: A biographical dictionary* (pp. 163–165). Westport, CT: Greenwood Press.

☿ **Wāng Huī** 汪晖

b. 1959—Academic, historian, and social critic

Alternate name: trad. 汪暉

Summary

Wang Hui is a renowned scholar in China. Considered by many to be the leading voice of China's New Left, he is known for his original studies of the issue of modernization in China. From his early study of the author Lu Xun to his later research on intellectual history and modernity, Wang Hui has covered a broad academic spectrum and has become a leading social theorist in the Chinese-speaking world, with an international reputation.

Wang Hui is a renowned scholar in China and is considered by many to be the leading voice of China's New Left, a school of intellectual thought that is critical of capitalism and in favor of socialism.

Early Scholarship

Wang Hui was born in October 1959 in Yangzhou, Jiangsu Province. After high school he worked at a factory as an apprentice for a year and a half before becoming a college student in 1977, the year when Chinese colleges and universities resumed admitting students by exams after suspending operations during the Cultural Revolution, which began in 1966. In 1985, he went to the Chinese Academy of Social Sciences in Beijing to pursue a PhD in modern Chinese literature and then stayed on to work at the Institute of Literature after earning his degree. In 1991, he co-founded a journal called *The Scholar* (*Xuérén* 学人). From 1996 to 2007, he was the editor of *Reading* (*Dúshū* 读书) and helped make the magazine an influential forum for cultural and social discussions in China. Since 2002, he has been on the faculty of the College of Humanities at Tsinghua University.

Wang Hui's major works include 1991's *Against Despair: Lu Xun and His Literary World* (*Fǎnkàng juéwàng: Lǔ Xùn jíqí wénxué shìjiè* 反抗绝望： 鲁迅及其文学世界), 2000's *Rekindling a Dead Fire*

(*Sǐhuǒ chóngwēn* 死火重溫), and 2004's four-volume *The Rise of Modern Chinese Thought* (*Xiàndài Zhōngguó sīxiǎng de xīngqǐ* 现代中国思想的兴起). His works have been translated into several languages, including the following three English versions: 2006's *China's New Order: Society, Politics, and Economy in Transition*; 2011's *The End of the Revolution: China and the Limits of Modernity*; and 2011's *The Politics of Imagining Asia*. Wang Hui's scholarship has received considerable attention outside China. In 2008, the American journal *Foreign Policy* named him one of the world's Top 100 Public Intellectuals. In October 2013, he was awarded the prestigious Luca Pacioli Award in Venice, an award given to scholars with an outstanding record in the area of creative interdisciplinary research. The prominent German philosopher Jürgen Habermas was the other recipient of the award in the same year.

Wang Hui has emerged as one of China's most original and controversial intellectuals during the past decades. He is known for his original studies of the issue of modernization in China. From his early study of Lu Xun, a leading figure in modern Chinese literature, to his later research on intellectual history and modernity, Wang Hui has covered a broad academic spectrum to become a leading social theorist in the Chinese-speaking world with an international reputation. In 2010, Wang Hui was involved in a plagiarism scandal. The plagiarism accusations concerned the improper citations in some of his work, especially *Against Despair*, the book based on his doctoral dissertation. This event rapidly stirred a controversial argument over his scholarly integrity. Nonetheless, there are many scholars at home and abroad who ardently defend his academic reputation.

Eschewing the Western Model

The 1980s saw the launch of China's market-oriented economic reforms and the influx of various Western thoughts and theories, which stimulated scholars and intellectuals, especially those in Beijing, the political and cultural center of China. They embraced a progressive narrative of tradition and modernity, in which the West was viewed as the model of the modern world with which China was forever forced to catch up. Intellectuals saw themselves as agents of a new enlightenment movement and facilitators of China's forward march toward modernization. Many of these people identified with liberalism and neo-liberalism and provided the intellectual arguments for more openness and reform.

But Wang Hui was not one of them. He often found himself "mentally distant from the surrounding environment." In 1988, when he finished his dissertation (later published as *Against Despair*), he immediately went to work on his second book project on May Fourth intellectuals—those involved in the movement to cast off traditional Confucian values and embrace a modern, Western-inspired worldview for China. This book focused on the possible potential internal crisis hidden in the so-called "enlightenment movements." Spending nearly one year working and living in a remote and poor county in Shaanxi Province in 1990 gave Wang Hui a new perspective on China's problem. Having witnessed the disorders resulting from the dissolution of rural communes in the countryside, he became dissatisfied with the elitism of his generation. After returning to Beijing, he founded *The Scholar* with a group of friends. It was the first magazine established by intellectuals in 1990s China. Focused on academic history, it aimed at transferring excessive political passions of the last decade to serious academic endeavors, thus encouraging scholars to engage in history and society with academic means.

In the 1990s, market economy started to shape China on a massive scale. This period also brought a rapidly growing wealth gap between segments of society. Official corruption and materialistic fever ran rampant. Wang Hui wrote a series of papers in response to what he saw as a societal crisis, criticizing the contemporary trend of neo-liberalism. He redefined the problems through elaborate and sensitive historical analysis, believing that it was impossible for China to borrow its development model from the West. China must find its own unique way of transformation, he

maintained. Wang Hui believed that only by abandoning the idea of total marketization driven by neo-liberalism would China's intellectuals be able to regain the possibility to understand and criticize contemporary issues.

When he became executive editor of *Reading* in 1996, Wang Hui created a new forum to mobilize scholars and intellectuals to think about and to intervene in China's new realities. Previously limited to literary reviews and humanistic critiques, the journal under Wang's editorship was expanded to include contents about politics and economics, eventually becoming an all-encompassing public space for the discussion of contemporary issues in China. It was perhaps due to the journal's bold and sometimes critical commentary on current affairs that Wang Hui was forced to leave his editor position in 2007.

The Rise of Modern Chinese Thought

An interdisciplinary approach and a social-political objective as reflected in the contents of *Reading* are also the features of *The Rise of Modern Chinese Thought*, Wang Hui's four-volume tour de force. In this ambitious work that was ten years in the writing, Wang Hui rejects the teleological and progressive narrative of modernization and the dichotomies brought about, like China/West, state/society, and empire/nation. Instead, he offers an alternative version of "modernity." Traversing across Chinese history from the Sòng 宋 dynasty (960–1279) to the twentieth century, he suggests that China has its own modernity within Chinese traditions that could be garnered to construct a society different from that of the capitalist West. He insists that the dominance of Western modernity in twentieth-century China was merely the result of a set of very contingent causes. In tracing the "anti-modern modernity" in Chinese history, his work is not only an immense contribution to historical and historiographical scholarships but also a self-conscious political intervention. Specifically, he highlights the role of intellectual history to recover repressed elements of the past in order to question the structures that govern the present.

The idea of modernity that we know today, Wang Hui writes, has its origin in the official discourse of the collective awakening of the 1980s, which gave rise to market economy and globalization. It also connects with China's revolutionary past. In view of the trend of "de-politicization" and emerging problems caused by marketization and globalization since the 1990s, he argues that China's revolutionary history and its current liberalization are part of the same discourse of modernity. He therefore calls for alternatives to both its capitalist trajectory and its authoritarian past, in the hope of forging a new path for China's future. The developmental crisis in China that Wang Hui so eloquently describes, however, may not be limited to the country alone. As Theodore Huters writes in the introduction to his new English translation of Wang Hui's *The Politics of Imagining Asia*, "Wang Hui's concerns extend beyond China and Asia to an ambition to rethink world history as a whole" (Wang 2003, 4). Indeed, as we reflect on the many economic issues and developmental problems facing the world today, Wang Hui's work could inspire other non-Western intellectuals to look at their own history and traditions on their terms and beyond a Western-oriented modernity model.

He LIN
University of Electronic Science and Technology of China

Further Reading

Brown, Kerry. (2011). China and the battle with modernity. *Journal of Contemporary Asia, 41*(2), 324–330.

Day, Alexander. (2011). Depoliticization and the Chinese intellectual scene. *Criticism, 53*(1), 141–151.

Huang, Philip C. C. (2008). In search of a Chinese modernity: Wang Hui's *The rise of modern Chinese thought. Modern China, 34*(3), 396–404.

Murthy, Viren. (2006). Modernity against modernity: Wang Hui's critical history of Chinese thought. *Modern Intellectual History, 3*(1), 137–165.

Wang Hui. (1998). Contemporary Chinese thought and the question of modernity (Rebecca E. Karl, Trans.). *Social Text, 55*, 9–44.

• Wáng Huī •

Wang Hui. (2000). *Fankang juewang: Lu Xun jiqi wenxue shijie* 反抗绝望: 鲁迅及其文学世界 [Against despair: Lu Xun and the literary world.]. Shijiazhuang: Hebei Jiaoyu Press.

Wang Hui. (2003). *China's new order: Society, politics and economy in transition* (Theodore Huters, Trans.). Cambridge, MA: Harvard University Press.

Wang Hui. (2004). *Xiandai Zhongguo sixiang de xingqi* 现代中国思想的兴起 [The rise of modern Chinese thought] (4 vols.). Beijing: Sanlian Bookstore.

Wang Hui. (2009). *The end of the revolution: China and the limits of modernity*. London: Verso Books.

Wang Hui. (2011). *The politics of imagining Asia* (Theodore Huters, Trans.). Cambridge, MA: Harvard University Press.

江晖

♂ **Wáng Shuò** 王朔

b. 1958—Author and scriptwriter, known for his so-called "hooligan literature"

Summary

Wang Shuo is a contemporary Chinese writer and cultural icon, known as one of the most provocative and controversial figures on the Chinese literary scene in the 1980s and 1990s. Creating a new type of writing, called "hooligan literature," Wang has written novels, screenplays, and television series that mostly deal with the fall-out of the Cultural Revolution and the later Reform Era.

Wang Shuo is an influential contemporary Chinese writer and was one of the most provocative and controversial figures on the Chinese literary scene in the 1980s and 1990s. He single-handedly created a new type of writing, called "hooligan literature" (*pīzi wénxué* 痞子文学), which has drawn the attention of literary critics both in China and in the West. Wang Shuo's popularity was such that one of his characters jokes boastfully: "You must have read his stuff. The only book with a larger print run is *Selected Works of Chairman Mao*" (Wang 1997, 44–45). While challenging and subverting the line between "low-brow" literature and "high-brow" or serious literature, Wang Shuo also has served as a public apologist for his hooligan protagonists by claiming them to be the true vanguards of the era of reform: "All the motivating forces of reform and openness come from hooligans…Take a look, all those who have really succeeded, who have already become rich, are all hooligans" (Gao 1993, 217).

Early Life and Education

Wang Shuo was born in 1958 in Nanjing and grew up in a military compound in Beijing during the Cultural Revolution. He joined the People's Liberation Army (PLA) Navy in 1976 and worked in a state-owned pharmaceutical company in Beijing in the early 1980s. In 1983, he quit his job and was engaged in various

• Wáng Shuò •

enterprises with his friends and went broke. Only then did he determine to sit down to write fiction as a freelance writer, and started with what was then viewed as pulp fiction, including urban romances and crime stories. Wang Shuo's own life experiences in particular provided unique material for his early hooligan sagas, including the novellas *Flight Attendant* (*Kōngzhōng xiǎojiě* 空中小姐, 1984), *Emerging from the Sea* (*Fú chū hǎimiàn* 浮出海面, 1985), *Half Is Flame, Half Is Sea* (*Yībàn shì huǒyàn, yībàn shì hǎishuǐ* 一半是火焰，一半是海水, 1986), and *The Rubber Man* (*Xiàngpí rén* 橡皮人, 1986). By creating a gallery of hooligans born at the dawn of the reform era and making them his morally ambivalent, first-person protagonists, Wang Shuo also teased his readers with the first taste of a dizzying, almost sinful new world of post-socialist "reform."

The Playing Masters

Wang's trilogy, The Playing Masters, is comprised of three novellas: *The Playing Masters* (*Wán zhǔ* 顽主, 1987), *Nothing Real or Serious* (*Yīdiǎn zhèngjīng méiyǒu* 一点正经没有, 1989), *You Are Not a Vulgar Person* (*Nǐ bùshì yīgè súrén* 你不是一个俗人, 1992). Under the cover of extremely simple or almost non-existent plots, the first-person sentimental hooligans of his early hooligan sagas are now expanded into a collective gang of "frivolous hooligans" or "playing masters": with their characters and identities

deliberately flat and interchangeable, they keep themselves entertained by inventing seemingly endless new schemes and farces against a comic and almost-virtual reality, which turns out to be a quite accurate representation of reality in China's era of reform. That is to say, unlike many of his contemporary writers in the mid-1980s who attempt either cultural "roots-seeking literature" (*xúngēn wénxué* 寻根文学) or metaphorical exploration of modern Chinese history (experimental fiction, *shíyàn xiǎoshuō* 实验小说), Wang boldly reveals that the urban Chinese reality has already evolved into such a fluid and hybridized state that it presents itself as a hollow void where not only the official ideology of socialism is increasingly petrified and useless but also various newly imported Western intellectual jargons and discourses are equally superficial and "pseudosizing." By deciding parody and pastiche to be the only originality allowed in this new social reality, indeed Wang Shuo can be called the first true postmodernist writer in contemporary China.

In 1988, Wang Shuo published his first full-length, and arguably most acclaimed novel, *Playing for Thrills* (*Wán de jiùshì xīntiào* 玩的就是心跳). The narrative of *Playing for Thrills* is a highly engaging and innovative one that combines farce and suspense, two modes that Wang Shuo has deftly deployed in his previous works. The story starts in 1988, when Fang Yan, the first-person narrator and protagonist, as well as the alter ego of Wang himself, indulges in his usual activities of gambling and womanizing. But all of a sudden, in a Kafkaesque scene, he is suspected by the police of having committed a murder ten years previously. In order to prove his innocence, he has to recount what he has done during a certain seven-day period ten years ago. The search for his lost past and identity soon gains a historical or metaphysical dimension as a journey of self-discovery.

The novel ends in 1978, the year when the post–Cultural Revolution open-door policy was officially adopted and the economic reforms had just started. Far beyond most people's scope of understanding back then, however, Wang Shuo was providing an alarming, alternative vision of the ten years of "reform" from 1978 to 1988, in the fashion of a recharged Cultural Revolution, or, a new capitalist revolution, along with all its vehemence and violence.

In a surreal way, the apocalyptic scene of a fire on a large square towards the end of the novel can also be understood as foreseeing the upcoming apocalyptic scene of fire and smoke in Tiananmen Square barely one year later in 1989. In retrospect, *Playing for Thrills* actually stands as the only literary work produced in the 1980s that correctly predicted—albeit through the crystal ball of a so-called hooligan writer—the true colors of the misnamed "decade of reform" and its catastrophic exit in 1989.

Rewriting the Cultural Revolution

Yearnings (*Kěwàng* 渴望, 1990), a television drama series that Wang co-scripted, is his attempt after the events of 1989 to refresh or refashion the collective cultural memory of the Cultural Revolution. It became an instant national hit by representing in a melodramatic mode ordinary people's lives throughout the Cultural Revolution.

In the meantime, Wang also wrote the novella *Vicious Animals* (*Dòngwù xiōngměng* 动物凶猛, 1991), which could be loosely seen as a sequel to *Playing for Thrills*, a semiautobiographical story about a group of Beijing adolescents coming of age during the later period of the Cultural Revolution. In particular, the story focuses upon the young protagonist's sexual awakening and initiation, which was eventually effected through both psychological and physical violence.

Under Wang Shuo's pen, the Cultural Revolution evolved into a new cultural signifier in the 1990s, to be appropriated according to various cultural and ideological, as well as public and personal, agendas.

Pre- and Post-1989

There is a decisive divide between the pre-1989 Wang Shuo and the post-1989 Wang Shuo. In the former, we see a more blasphemous author who embodies play with a residual ideology of

• Wáng Shuò •

revolution. For the latter, however, this revolution has gradually been refashioned into the object of a conservative nostalgia in the mass imagination and collective memory. Having admitted the failure of his fantasy of invoking a new Cultural Revolution in *Playing for Thrills,* Wang Shuo has finally succeeded in remodeling himself in *Vicious Animals*—through re-packaging and consuming a past revolutionary age. Via such play, Wang Shuo has, in the end, regained his status as a playing master: he is now the star author of bestsellers, the darling of the media, and the cultural idol and "godfather" for an entire new generation of ambitious "Rastignacs" (so named for the social climber in Honoré de Balzac's *Old Goriot*).

Within a few years, the once-provocative and subversive Wang Shuonian popular literature of the 1980s assumed a new role and became much more conservative or conformist in the 1990s. Since the mid-1990s, Wang Shuo has mostly stopped fiction writing altogether and has turned instead to work in other cultural arenas, such as working with film directors like Jiang Wen (b. 1963), who adapted his *Vicious Animals* into a critically acclaimed film *In the Heat of the Sun* (*Yángguāng cànlàn de rìzi* 阳光灿烂的日子, 1995), and *Féng Xiǎogāng 冯小刚

(b. 1958) as a scriptwriter on demand. Sporadically, Wang Shuo tried make a comeback as a fiction writer, such as with the novel *It Looks Beautiful* (*Kàn shàngqù hěn měi* 看上去很美, 1999), which was yet another sequel to both *Playing for Thrills* and *Vicious Animals*, tracing the genealogy of his "hooligans" even further back to their kindergarten and elementary school days in Beijing, from 1961 to the very eve of the Cultural Revolution in 1966. His more recent literary efforts include a hybrid compilation of fiction and non-fiction entitled *My Thousand Years of Coldness* (*Wǒ de qiānsuì hán* 我的千岁寒, 2007). But none of these attempts has fared well with either critics or common readers. It seems that while still active as a high-profile cultural celebrity, Wang Shuo has already largely left his prolific, peak years as a literary author behind.

In all of his works, careful readers can discern a deep-seated pessimistic attitude toward the world in which he lives. For example, his often neglected novel, *Please Don't Call Me Human* (*Qiān wàn bié bǎ wǒ dāng rén* 千万别把我当人, 1989), an ambitious, somewhat uneven, but utterly "anti-humanist" novel, presents another apocalyptic scene at the end of the story: "The city fell dark, as the enormous shadow of the mushroom cloud spread across high-rise buildings, streets and boulevards, parks and grassy lawns, rivers and lakes" (Wang Shuo 2003, 288–289).

---

*People marked with an asterisk have entries in this dictionary.

Wang Shuo's Influence

Wang Shuo's admirers and followers are many, and he has influenced at least several generations of readers since the 1980s. Director Feng Xiaogang publically acknowledged Wang Shuo's influence in his own script writing. Another popular fiction writer, Shí Kāng 石康 (b. 1968), who is also based in Beijing and has often been compared to Wang Shuo, equally gave Wang Shuo high praise and stated: "When it comes to contemporary Chinese writers, one simply can't avoid Wang Shuo's existence, at least that's how I would think" (Shi 2002, 240).

In the end, Wang Shuo should be viewed as one of the very few contemporary Chinese writers who has most pointedly represented the locality and hybridity of contemporary China. He has deftly shown the crisis-charged, sometimes dystopian nature and the complexities of the transformation from socialism to capitalism. As a bastard child of both the Cultural Revolution and postmodernism, his contribution and impact as a provocative yet conformist, high-spirited yet disillusioned "hooligan"—not to mention his linguistic ingenuity in terms of creating and introducing lively, poignant slang and expressions into contemporary Chinese lexicon—is very real, and deserves to be reassessed by future cultural and literary historians.

Yibing HUANG
Connecticut College

Further Reading

Barme, Geremie. (1992). Wang Shuo and *liumang* ('hooligan') culture. *The Australian Journal of Chinese Affairs, 28,* 23–66.

Gao Bo. (Ed.). (1993). *Wang Shuo: dashi haishi pizi* 王朔：大师还是痞子 [Wang Shuo: Master or hooligan]. Beijing: Beijing Yanshan chubanshe.

Huang Yibing. (2007). Wang Shuo: Playing for thrills in the era of reform, or, a genealogy of the present. In *Contemporary Chinese literature: From the Cultural Revolution to the future.* New York: Palgrave Macmillan.

Huang Yibing. (2002). Vicious animals: Wang Shuo and negotiated nostalgia for history. *Journal of Modern Literature in Chinese,* 5(2), 81–102.

Lombardi, Rosa. (2013). Wang Shuo. In Thomas Moran & Ye (Dianna) Xu (Eds.), *Chinese fiction writers, 1950–2000. Dictionary of literature biography* (vol. 370, pp. 228–234). Detroit: Thomson Gale.

Shi Kang 石康. (2002). Wang Shuo. In *Ji yizui Ya yizui* 鸡一嘴 鸭一嘴. Nanning: Guangxi chubanshe.

James, Jamie. (1997, April 21). Bad boy: Why China's most popular novelist won't go away. *New Yorker,* 50–53.

Noble, Jonathan. (2003). Wang Shuo and the commercialization of literature. In Joshua Mostow & Kirk A. Denton (Eds.), *Columbia companion to modern East Asian literatures* (pp. 598–603). New York: Columbia University Press.

Rojas, Carlos. (2008). Wang Shuo and historical portraiture. In *The naked gaze: Reflections on Chinese modernity* (pp. 244–273). Cambridge, MA: Harvard University Asia Center.

• Wǎng Shuò •

Shu, Yunzhong. (1999). Different strategies of self-confirmation: Wang Shuo's appeal to his readers. *Tamkang Review, 29*(3), 111–126.

Wang Jing. (1997). Wang Shuo: Pop goes the culture. In *High culture fever: Politics, aesthetics, and ideology in Deng's China* (pp. 261–286). Berkeley: University of California Press.

Wang Shuo. (1997). *Playing for thrills* (Howard Goldblatt, Trans.). New York: Penguin Books. (Original work published 1988)

Wang Shuo. (2003). *Please don't call me human* [*Qiān wàn bié bǎ wǒ dāng rén* 千万别把我当人] (Howard Goldblatt, Trans.) Boston: Cheng & Tsui Company. (Original work published 1989)

Yao Yusheng. (2004). The elite class background of Wang Shuo and his hooligan characters. *Modern China, 30*(4), 431–469.

♂ Wāng Yáng 汪洋

b. 1955—Politician, "fifth generation" liberal leader

Summary

As a vice premier since 2013 focusing on the economy, Wang Yang is poised to ascend to the highest levels of leadership in China. He is considered one of the most competent and liberal members of the so-called "fifth generation" leadership.

Wang Yang is a core member of what has come to be called, at least outside the People's Republic of China, the "fifth generation" of leadership. This group follows former leaders Máo Zédōng 毛泽东 (1893–1976), *Dèng Xiǎopíng 邓小平 (1904–1997), *Jiāng Zémín 江泽民 (b. 1926), and *Hú Jǐntāo 胡锦涛 (b. 1942). Widely expected to join the Standing Committee of the Politburo during the leadership transition of 2012, Wang had to settle for a position on the full Politburo. But he remains highly regarded as one of the most competent

*People marked with an asterisk have entries in this dictionary.

and most liberal current Chinese leaders, serving as a vice premier dealing with microeconomic issues.

Childhood and Early Education

Wang was born in Anhui Province on 12 March 1955 into a family of modest means. Unable to attend university due to the suspension of tertiary education during the Cultural Revolution that began in 1966, Wang worked in a food-processing factory from 1972 to 1976 before being chosen to study political economy at the Central Party School in Beijing, the key political training ground. Like other elite figures, from Hu Jintao to his colleague *Lǐ Kèqiáng 李克强 (b. 1963), Wang was involved in the China Youth League in the early 1980s, the body in charge of recruiting and training Chinese Communist Party (CCP) members under twenty-six years of age. This experience provided Wang with a powerful network, which was useful for his future political career. From 1986 to 1998 he worked in a number of party and government roles in his native Anhui Province, rising to vice governor beginning in 1993. When *Zhū Róngjī 朱镕基 (b. 1928) was appointed premier in 1998 and began undertaking difficult reforms of the state-owned sector, Wang was brought to Beijing to become deputy director of the State Development Planning Commission, in charge of implementing the national Five-Year Plans (this body is now named the National Development and Reform Commission). He became deputy secretary general of the State Council from 2003 to 2005, at the start of the Hu Jintao and *Wēn Jiābǎo 温家宝 (b. 1942) era.

Provincial Leadership

In 2005, Wang was appointed party secretary of Chongqing, a vast province-sized municipality, under the direct control of the central government, that had been carved off from Sichuan Province five years earlier. With its population of over 30 million, Chongqing had been called the most populous city on earth. But it was also one of China's most impoverished places, with major developmental challenges. Wang's most notable achievement in his two years there was to promote campaigns to place Chongqing on the global map. For example, he started a campaign encouraging "the world to come to Chongqing" and even compared its panorama at night

full of brightly lit skyscrapers and neon advertisements to that of Hong Kong. More surprising, and novel, was his liberalization of news coverage in the city; he allowed the media to cover stories they felt should take priority rather than automatically giving top news slots to political stories.

After Wang moved to the important southern province of Guangdong, however, his replacement in Chongqing, *Bó Xīlái 薄熙来 (b. 1949), attracted attention by supporting popular housing projects and undertaking an extensive, brutal crackdown on mafia groups in the city. These actions were interpreted as criticisms of Wang, implying that he had presided over the city at a time when problems had grown and he had done nothing significant about them. The two also engaged in a debate about what to do with "the cake" (relating to economic development)—with Bo insisting it needed to be grown bigger before being divided and Wang arguing that it needed to be divided now, regardless of its future growth. Such arcane language concealed a debate about what the party's priorities should be—either to try to build equity now or to tolerate rising social inequality until a future time when China would be wealthy enough to deal with its challenges. These arguments, however, proved academic when Bo was felled in 2012 after his wife was accused of murder and he was tried a year later for corruption following his removal from office.

Wang Yang (middle right) meets with German officials in Beijing (2014). Photo by Dragan Tactic.

In Guangdong, Wang had attracted attention as one of the most conciliatory leaders, someone who was able to deal with unrest and dissension through negotiation rather than deployment of violence and state security. The Wukan uprising in 2011 was the most celebrated example. The incident involved a town of about twenty thousand people who had rebelled against the requisition of their land, at very low levels of compensation by local officials, and launched a mass campaign of civil disobedience. Wang allowed for compromise, letting the villages elect new leaders and defusing what could have been a long-term revolt. For this, he received plaudits from Beijing.

Wang was also associated with a campaign called "Happy Guangdong," in which he made the focus of government policy more than just an obsession with pumping out raw gross domestic product (GDP) growth. Instead, he encouraged local officials to look at living conditions and well-being indices in order to improve the overall standard of living.

In 2013, Wang was appointed one of four vice premiers, with a particular focus on the economy. His relative youth means that he is poised to be elevated to the Standing Committee of the Politburo during what is expected to be the next leadership change in 2017.

Kerry BROWN
Lau China Institute, King's College

Further Reading

Brown, Kerry. (2014). *The new emperors: Power and the princelings in China.* London & New York: I. B. Tauris.

• Wāng Yáng •

ChinaVitae. (2015). Wang Yang. Retrieved April 29, 2015, from http://www.chinavitae.com/biography/Wang_Yang/career

Du Zijia 窦梓稼. (2009). *Wang Yang zhuan: Zhongguo zhengtan na pi "lang"* 汪洋传: 中国政坛那匹 "狼" [Biography of Wang Yang: That "wolf" in China's political arena]. New York: Mirror Books.

Wang Yaohua 王耀华. (2009). *Zhu hou zheng feng* 诸侯争锋 [Competition among provincial chiefs] (pp. 13–58). New York: Mirror Books.

Cheng Li. (2008). Hu's southern expedition: Changing leadership in Guangdong. *China Leadership Monitor, 24*, 1–13.

☝ Wáng Zhèn 王震

1908–1993—General and hardline politician

Summary

Wang Zhen was instrumental to the development of the Chinese Communist Party. A distinguished military commander, he became a party leader known for his hardline and often brutal approach to dealing with intellectuals and liberals.

Wang Zhen was one of what came to be called the "Eight Immortals" who were central to the development of the Chinese Communist Party (CCP) from its foundation period after 1921 to its period in power from 1949 onward. A distinguished military commander in the Second Sino-Japanese War and later the Chinese Civil War, he became a trenchant hardliner once the CCP came to power, supporting Maoist-style policies even after the Reform and Opening Up (*gǎigé kāifàng* 改革开放) era began in 1978. Loathed by intellectuals and liberals, Wang supported the military clampdown on the Tiananmen student protesters in 1989.

Childhood and Early Career

Wang was born in 1908, during the twilight of the Qīng 清 dynasty (1644–1911/12), in Liuyang, Hunan Province, the same province as fellow future Communist leaders Máo Zédōng 毛泽东 (1893–1976) and Liú Shàoqí 刘少奇 (1898–1969). In 1927, after working briefly as an assistant in a railways master's office, Wang joined the Communist Youth League and the CCP during the violent attacks against them by the Nationalists. He joined the newly established Red Army (which later became the People's Liberation Army), serving as a political commissar and surviving the Long March in 1935. During the Second Sino-Japanese War (1937–1945), Wang was once more a political commissar and field commander, working under Marshal Péng Déhuái 彭德怀 (1898–1974). It was during this time that Wang reportedly was put in charge of one of the first rectification campaigns against intellectuals, in an effort to assert Communist culture; Mao believed that because Wang had no formal education, he would know how to deal with them best. Wang undertook a vicious purge against figures like the scholar and writer Wáng Shíwèi 王实味, incarcerating him for five years before his execution. Wang Zhen would repeat this uncompromising approach throughout the rest of his life.

Political Life

Because of his military skills, Wang was made responsible for the conquest of the Xinjiang area in 1949, after four years of independence for some parts of the region as an independent republic. Soviet leader Joseph Stalin had accepted Mao's demand that the area would be retaken, and Wang headed the army forces sent to achieve this. The effectiveness and brutality with which he carried out this assignment created resentment that lingered for decades. Unlike Tibet, Xinjiang was made an autonomous region within the People's Republic of China almost immediately after its foundation.

Wang Zhen's statue outside of the Army Reclamation Museum in Shihezi, Xinjiang Province. Photo by Mypowercell.

Wang had planned to pursue a military career throughout the 1950s, before becoming the minister for agriculture in 1958. He was largely unaffected by the political turmoil of the Cultural Revolution (1966–1976) due to his closeness to Mao. Wang was famously reputed to be one of the few people who was able to carry a gun in Mao's presence, though as the story goes he did this only once. Wang became a vice premier in the final year of the Cultural Revolution. After the end of the revolution, he was appointed first as a vice chairman of the newly created Central Advisory Commission (which was headed by its president, *Lǐ Xiānniàn 李先念 [b. 1961]) and then as vice president of the country from 1988 to 1993, serving under *Yáng Shàngkūn 杨尚昆 (1907–1998), another former military leader.

While this position was largely meant to be a ceremonial one, it gave Wang a platform from which to fully support the hardline approach against the protesting students in Tiananmen in June 1989. According to the "Tiananmen Papers," a contested collection of so-called internal reports that detailed the meetings between leaders up to and during the protests and their clampdown, Wang took a consistently tough stance. For him, the final decision of *Dèng Xiǎopíng 邓小平 (1904–1997) to send in the military to quash the students with tanks and live ammunition was a wholly correct one,

and Wang was shown on television soon after the clampdown congratulating soldiers for their actions. His more extreme suggestion of setting up internal prison camps for those associated with the protests, however, was not carried out.

Wang continued as vice president until 1993. Despite being close to Deng personally, he was largely opposed to many of the economic liberalizations connected to his period as paramount leader. Wang remained faithful to the memory of Mao until his death and was, according to one obituary, "a scourge of writers and free-thinkers for the last 50 years. . . . Chinese intellectuals detested few people among the Communist leadership as Mr. Wang."

Kerry BROWN
Lau China Institute, King's College

Further Reading

Kristoff, Nicholas D. (1993). Wang Zhen, Chinese hardliner decried by intellectuals, dies aged 85. *The New York Times*. Retrieved March 11, 2015, from http://www.nytimes.com/1993/03/13/obituaries/wang-zhen-chinese-hard-liner-decried-by-intellectuals-dies-at-85.html

Luard, Tim. (1993). Wang Zhen: Obituary. *The Independent*. Retrieved March 11, 2015, from http://www.independent.co.uk/news/people/obituary-wang-zhen-1497308.html

Nathan, Adrew J.; Link, Perry E.; & Zhang Liang. (Eds.). (2002). *The Tiananmen Papers: The Chinese leadership's decision to use force against their own people—in their own words*. New York: PublicAffairs.

*People marked with an asterisk have entries in this dictionary.

• Wáng Zhèn •

♂ Wèi Jīngshēng 魏京生

b. 1950—Democracy activist affiliated with the Democracy Wall Movement (1978–1979)

Summary

As one of the most prominent democratic activists in the early post-Mao years, Wei Jingsheng was a leading participant in Beijing's 1978–1979 Democracy Wall Movement, an editor of the short-lived publication *Exploration*, and author of the movement's most famous essay, "The Fifth Modernization." He spent over eighteen years in prison and since 1997 has lived in exile in the United States.

Wei Jingsheng's given name, meaning "born in the capital" is apt since he was born in Beijing on 22 May 1950, into a family that was privileged within the Communist system. His father was an air force officer, and most of his adult relatives were (and would remain) party members. Wei's secondary education was acquired at a top high school connected with Beijing's People's University. From his mid-teens on, he was caught up in the Cultural Revolution (1966–1976), during which time he traveled around the country briefly as an eager Red Guard and also as leader of a musical troupe. But he saw much injustice and everywhere witnessed abject poverty, and this experience eventually caused him to turn against the regime. In the meantime, he served a stint in the army. As the Cultural Revolution wound down, Wei gained employment as an electrician in the Beijing zoo.

In the wake of the Cultural Revolution, there were sporadic efforts from the public to promote liberalization. The first of these occurred in Beijing's Tiananmen Square in 1976, during the 5 April Tiananmen Incident 五四天安门事件, when citizens gathered in the square first to commemorate former premier Zhōu Ēnlái 周恩来 (1898–1976), who had died earlier that year, and then to protest the removal of their mourning objects. The protests were crushed by the military. Only five months later, however, Máo Zédōng 毛泽东 died, and

*Dèng Xiǎopíng 邓小平 (1904–1997) eventually made a return to power. Deng promoted liberalization in industry and agriculture, and the modernization of the armed services and of science/technology (altogether comprising the "Four Modernizations"). At this point, the question for many was: Would all of this be accompanied by any *political* liberalization, or was the crushing of the earlier Tiananmen incident the final word on the matter? Among the most strident of those promoting a second pro-democracy wave would be Wei Jingsheng.

The Advent of the Democracy Wall

In March 1978, a new constitution was promulgated which promised (though hardly for the first time) that civil liberties would be respected and that popular participation in public affairs would be allowed. Accordingly, in November 1978 some people began advocating democracy, human rights, and rule of law, as well as venting a wide assortment of more specific grievances. In the early autumn, Chén Ěrjìn 陈尔晋 from Guizhou mounted some posters near Tiananmen Square. Soon such actions were replicated by similar activists in cities around the county, including Shanghai, Guangzhou, Hangzhou, Guiyang, and even Lhasa. Essays, variously the works of individuals

acting on their own, or associated with different new organizations, were widely circulated. Civil society seemed to be in the making.

For a while, the movement was allowed to proceed. After all, it was not directed against Deng Xiaoping, in whom many had placed their trust. Rather, Deng and the protesters shared a common ground in their battle against remnant hardline leftists, who had been silenced but not eliminated from the political scene.

How could the activists get the word out in this pre-Internet age, since no publishers dared to cooperate with them? Faced with this dilemma, the amorphous group took a page from Deng's own book and resorted to the mimeograph machine. (As a student-worker in France in the early 1920s, Deng had been known as Mr. Mimeograph.) These printed materials were distributed by hand, but to attract other readers they were often posted on a wall outside of a bus depot in Beijing's Xidan 西单 area, which came to be known as the "Democracy Wall."

The most daring essay which appeared on the wall under Wei's name was an exposé of China's most notorious prison, Qincheng (Qínchéng jiānyù 秦城 监狱). Although the inhumanity of the place was described, Wei's larger message was the role of political imprisonment in the oppression of the proletariat:

The tool has been used so effectively that all of the dictator's opponents have been eliminated,

---

*People marked with an asterisk have entries in this dictionary.

魏京生

even "comrades-in-arms" from the era of the Long March. . . . If the majority would benefit from democracy and freedom, why do we go to such extremes to maintain dictatorship? . . . Qincheng proves that our government is not a people's government, because it has deprived the people of free speech. . . . Only those who lack the support of the people have to resort to making false charges and torturing their opponents in order to perpetuate their dictatorship. (Seymour 1980, 220–221)

Arrest and Life in Prison

Wei was arrested in March 1979, charged with counterrevolutionary incitement and also revealing secrets in connection with the ongoing war between China and Vietnam. (After the cessation of hostilities, he had told foreign journalists that China suffered nine-thousand deaths—only a slight exaggeration.) A trial was held at which Wei defended himself without a lawyer. He was found guilty, and remained in prison most of the time until 1997.

While in prison, Wei did much writing. Whereas his pre-arrest writings were aimed at the public, his serious prison writings were addressed to officials. These sometimes seemed to be a genuine reaching out to China's leaders, but more were often acerbic attacks on them and probably intended ultimately

for a wider audience. A selection translated into English was published in the anthology *The Courage to Stand Alone* (Wei 1997).

Much of the time he was kept in solitary confinement and was seriously abused, his medical conditions receiving little attention. By the mid-1980s, human rights organizations abroad were beginning to take up such cases; Deng professed lack of concern. But Wei was released in the spring of 1993, apparently as part of China's ill-fated bid to attract the 2000 Olympics. His period of freedom turned out to be only six months. On 16 November 1993, he was re-arrested on grounds of plotting against the state and sentenced to fourteen years, of which he served four. Finally, in late 1997, he was sent into permanent exile, ostensibly to receive medical treatment in the United States, but more likely

Wei Jingsheng (second from the left) in front of the White House, together with President George W. Bush and other Chinese activists, including Ciping Huang, Sasha Gong, Rebiya Kadeer, Harry Wu, and Bob Fu. Photo by the White House/Eric Draper.

because of the growing international campaign for his freedom.

Life in Exile

In a post-release American television interview (PBS, 21 November 1997) Wei declared his patriotism, and expressed optimism for the democracy movement. Wei believed he would to be the leader of the exile democracy movement. It did not work out that way, and he had to struggle to try to remain relevant. By now there was a large younger generation of exiles, including "graduates" of the Tiananmen incident of 1989, who were better attuned than Wei to developments in China, were fluent in English, and often had degrees from Western universities. In contrast to the more "sensible" exiled dissidents, Wei often came across as somewhat paranoid. Although there would always be some who supported him, his advocacy increasingly fell on deaf ears. As Columbia University's Andrew Nathan observed, "Wei is pretty much discounted because his views are not relevant to policy" (Chang 2000). His call for America to use trade as a weapon to force China's political modernization was supported internationally neither by many liberals (who often saw trade as a way of opening China up to Western ways) nor conservatives (who often wanted a strong business presence in China). He shocked many when, in 2010, he seemed to oppose the awarding of the Nobel Peace Prize that year to jailed dissident *Liú Xiǎobō 刘晓波 (b. 1955), who in Wei's view was unduly moderate.

Wei Jingsheng's Philosophy

In his writings, Wei concedes that humans are social beings, but he insists that "people's individuality enjoys priority over their sociality" (Seymour 1980, 57). A system based on the individual, however, requires rule of law, the absence of which had been as much a problem throughout Chinese history as the absence of democracy. "Law has been in the hands of a small group which has been defying all law, while the citizenry has been ruled, enslaved, and deprived of all rights" (Seymour 1980, 59). Law has always been a tool in the hands of China's autocrats; "it was neither beneficial to the people nor conducive to democracy" (Seymour 1980, 67).

As for China's current plight, Wei's central message is that, while Deng Xiaoping's Four Modernizations were a good start, they would be of little value to the Chinese people if not accompanied by the modernization of the political system. Thus, Wei published his three-installment essay "The Fifth Modernization," which instantly caught people's attention. "To accomplish modernization, the Chinese people should first practice democracy, and modernize China's social system...Without this condition, society will become stagnant" (Seymour 1980, 53f.).

Wei Jingsheng

Human Rights and Democracy

For Wei, central to the concept of democracy are the issues of human rights and equality, which he conflates in the term "the equal human rights issue" (*píngděng rénquàn de wèntǐ* 平等人权的问题). As Wei points out, human rights means little even in those "democracies" where there is great inequality. Originally, in Wei's view, this pair of principles had been part of socialism, but over time they came to be separated, with civil liberties being completely neglected. As a result, "Marxist economics—'scientific socialism'—has led to nothing!" (Seymour 1980, 141).

Rights, for Wei, are inherent, not bestowed. They are conditioned by the social environment and by the times, and must be achieved gradually. Human rights are not above or independent of politics. "Politics is the activity of obtaining or suppressing human rights" (Seymour 1980, 142). Specifically, Wei cites freedom of speech, assembly, association, the press, religion, movement, and the right to strike as essential to the achievement of equality. "These freedoms must be unrestricted in theory and unregulated in reality" (Seymour 1980, 143).

The link between rights and equality may be obvious to Westerners, but in China at the time, where total emphasis had previously been on equality at the expense of other values, the point was an important contribution to the discourse. Equality for Wei does not mean sameness or averaging, but rather giving people choices. People's achievements will vary, but "the important thing is that these different results be obtained by everyone under the same conditions, enjoying the same opportunities. Thus the outcome will be uniquely satisfying for the people taken as a whole; it is the result from which the people can enjoy the most satisfaction" (Seymour 1980, 143).

In the late 1970s Wei was filled with optimism that the Chinese public shared his vision: "We need neither gods nor emperors. We do not believe in the existence of any savior. We want to be masters of the world and not instruments used by autocrats to carry out their wild ambitions" (Seymour 1980, 53). The "new leader" is not a person, but the banner of democracy

The Tibetan Cause

Wei (who in the late 1970s had a Tibetan girlfriend) has always been a strong supporter of the Tibetan cause. While in prison he wrote a letter intended for Deng Xiaoping in which he charged the party with incompetence, ignorance, and distorting and lying about the situation on the plateau. While he does not suggest Tibet's separation from China, he argues that Chinese policies toward Tibet would drive the Tibetans, including those in areas attached to Chinese provinces, to seek independence. While, according to Wei, China's claim to sovereignty over the area is "vague," his

魏京生

solution was to bring the situation in line with historic realities, and perhaps move in the direction that Europe was going—that is, unity would be voluntary and the jurisdictions would have the right to break away. But China has been moving in "the wrong" direction with regard to Tibetan policy, resulting in "mutual discrimination and distrust." For this, he declared Deng himself responsible. During his period of exile he continuously stood in solidarity with the Tibetans.

Legacy of a Lone Dissident

What sustained Wei in China, namely the "courage to stand alone," became something of a liability in the West, where those who had any chance of advancing the movement were more apt to be those who could work together with individuals holding non-identical views. "The biggest criticism of me is that I don't listen to anyone else's opinion. But why should I when my opinion is right? All people with great achievements share this trait." Such a go-it-alone approach precluded his being an effective participant in the exile democracy movement.

Nonetheless, Wei Jingsheng's role in China's democracy movement should be assessed primarily on the basis of the positions he took in China. His contribution was phenomenal, and earned him a distinguished place in Chinese history.

James D. SEYMOUR
Chinese University of Hong Kong

Further Reading

Chang, Leslie. (2000, November 16). Chinese dissident turns U.S. life into a jail of sorts—After years in solitary, Mr. Wei pursues his ideals. *Wall Street Journal*.

Seymour, James D. (Ed.). (1980). *The fifth modernization: China's human rights movement, 1978–1979*. Stanfordville, NY: Earl M. Coleman Enterprises.

Wei Jingsheng. (1992). Letters from prison: To Deng Xiaoping on the Tibetan question. *Wei Jingsheng Foundation*. Retrieved December 17, 2010, from http://www.weijingsheng.org/tibet/tibet%20letter%20to%20deng.html

Wei Jingsheng. (1997). *The courage to stand alone: Letters from prison and other writings*. New York: Viking Press.

Wei Jingsheng Foundation. (2010). Homepage. Retrieved December 17, 2010, from http://www.weijingsheng.org

☿ Wēn Jiābǎo 温家宝

b.1942—Politician, premier of China (2003–2013)

Alternate name: trad. 溫家寶

Summary

Wen Jiabao was premier of China from 2003 to 2013, and while in office, he was known as a competent administrator. His tenure as premier was noted for a number of crises and natural disasters that the government had to handle, from SARS to the 2008 Wenchuan earthquake, but it was crowned by the successful staging of the Beijing Olympics, the handling of the impact of the global financial crisis, and an era when China almost quadrupled its economy. Wen left office calling for the kind of major political reforms that he was unable to implement as government leader.

Premier of China from 2003 to 2013, Wen Jiabao was known as a competent administrator and was respected for his empathy to ordinary people. Commonly called "the People's Premier," he possessed a strong work ethic but also was considered reserved and unassuming. He nonetheless traveled throughout the country to reach out to those who did not benefit from China's economic growth in the reform era. He frequently spoke about the need for political and social reform, and warned about weaknesses in China's political economy. Even so, he was part of a leadership that presided over widespread government suppression of political expression, along with a tightening of state controls on the Internet (the "Great Firewall of China") and other news and information media.

Early Life and Career

Wen was born on 15 September 1942 in Beichen, Tianjin City. He attended Nankai High School, from which Zhōu Ēnlái 周恩来 (1898–1976), former premier of China, also graduated. He joined the Chinese Communist Party (CCP) in 1965. At the Beijing Institute of Geology, he majored in geological structure and graduated in 1968. He took some postgraduate courses but, later that year, moved to Gansu Province, where he held increasingly important positions over the next thirteen years. He was a member of a geo-mechanics survey team and worked his way up to deputy director of the Gansu Provincial Geological Bureau. In 1982, under the tutelage of Party Secretary *Hú Yàobāng 胡耀邦 (1915–1989), Wen was transferred to Beijing, where he joined the CCP Secretariat of the Central Committee.

His first job in Beijing was as head of the Policy and Regulations Research Section of the Ministry of Geology. Later, he moved up to vice minister, while serving as deputy secretary of the Leading Party Members' Group and director of the CCP Political Department. In 1985, he was appointed deputy director of the party's General Affairs Office, which oversees daily activities of party leaders, and then promoted to director the next year. He worked under Party Secretary *Zhào Zǐyáng 赵紫阳 (1919–2005), who had replaced Hu after student protests in several cities, from December 1986 to January 1987, and accompanied Zhao when he visited the Tiananmen Square protesters in May 1989 (he can be seen standing with a pained expression beside Zhao in photographs of that evening). When Zhao was thereafter relieved of his posts and put under house arrest, Wen was not punished for his association with the former party leader, as his

administrative abilities were valued by colleagues.

Wen continued to hold key positions in the 1990s. In 1992, he became an alternate Politburo member and member of the CCP Central Committee Secretariat. Returning to his science roots, he served as vice chair of the National Committee on Minerals Resources and was deputy head of the State Leading Group for Science and Technology by 1996. He then rejoined the Central Committee. In the most significant posting yet, he was appointed vice premier of the State Council in 1998 (under Premier *Zhū Róngjī 朱镕基 [b. 1928]) and was made a member of the Standing Committee of the Politburo the same year. As vice premier, Wen directed work in agriculture, rural areas, development planning, and finance. He drafted the reforms carried out in the wake of the Asian Financial Crisis (1997–1998). He also directed the government's response to serious flooding along the Yangzi (Chang) River in 1998. He was finally elevated to premier in 2003.

Premier During Rapid Growth and Turmoil

Wen and president and CCP secretary *Hú Jǐntāo 胡锦涛 (b. 1942) were the core of the "fourth generation" of Chinese leadership. The two men are the same age, had worked around the same time in Gansu Province in the 1960s and 1970s, were close to Hu Yaobang, and reportedly got on well together. Both

---

*People marked with an asterisk have entries in this dictionary.

agreed on Hu's "harmonious society" program to promote greater opportunities for those left behind by the reforms (farmers, day laborers, minorities, and others). Due to his experience in Gansu and as vice premier, Wen has always had a strong interest in agriculture and rural issues. He introduced a fee-to-tax plan that he hoped would lessen tax burdens on farmers.

In his first term, Wen confronted two serious health issues. In spring 2003, the severe acute respiratory syndrome (SARS) crisis was made worse by official denial and secrecy. Once the magnitude of the crisis became apparent, Wen worked to improve Chinese cooperation with the World Health Organization (WHO) and control the disease. In 2004, he became the first Chinese leader to acknowledge the AIDS devastation in southwestern China.

While SARS was successfully contained finally, the year 2008 proved to be a hugely challenging one for the government. During the Chinese New Year, severe weather stranded many tens of millions of Chinese trying to return home for the festival. Wen famously went to one of the worst affected places to console those affected and handle the crisis. He formally began his second term in office after reappointment at the National People's Congress in 2008, facing a major uprising in Tibet in April that year by Tibetans who were demanding reform in the province and a return of the Fourteenth Dalai Lama (b. 1935). The demonstrations were designed to draw attention to the province's status in the run-up to the 2008 Beijing Olympics. The Olympics, however, were generally regarded as successful.

In May of the same year, Wen visited the site of the Wenchuan earthquake that struck Sichuan Province on 12 May, to assuage anger at local officials who were blamed for lax building codes and inaction that exacerbated the disaster. As the year wore on, Wen's government was forced to focus primarily on economic problems. At the beginning of 2008, the concern was inflation, but the global financial crisis swiftly shifted focus to economic stabilization and stimulus. The government undertook one of the world's largest economic stimuli, concentrating on infrastructure projects as a means of pumping money back into the economy.

Wen had frequently made statements on the need for democracy and economic restructuring while in office, and this gave him the reputation as one of the leadership's most liberal members over this period. An article he wrote about Hu Yaobang, admiring the former leader's reformist instincts in the *People's Daily* in 2010, was the first in a series of public statements where he showed more political reformist leanings. In an interview with CNN's Fareed Zakaria the same year, he spoke about the need for more democracy but then backtracked on those comments when he returned to China. At the National Party Congress in March 2012, he gave perhaps his fullest support for democratic reform: "Without successful political reform, it is impossible for us to fully institute economic system reform. The gains in this area may all be lost" (Radio Free Asia 2012). He also raised the specter of a return to the Cultural Revolution (1966–1976) if reforms were not implemented. Various observers felt that Wen was attempting to use such statements in his last year in office to cement his legacy as a reformer, but that any movement toward genuine democracy was likely to be slow. When Chongqing party leader *Bó Xīlái 薄熙来 (b. 1949) was implicated in a major scandal at about the same time, Wen's government hesitated at first, then swiftly arrested the former CCP rising star and convicted his wife, Gǔ Kāilái 谷开来 (b. 1958), for the murder of a British businessman. Bo was convicted of corruption and attempting cover up of his wife's guilt in 2013 and sentenced to fifteen years in prison.

As premier, Wen was noted for his strong preparation, hard work, and casual demeanor (often wearing casual clothes and shoes while on countryside tours). He traveled to most Chinese provinces and a majority of counties, and made a point of visiting areas hit by natural disasters. Early in his tenure, he even descended into a coal mine to talk with miners.

Eventually, Wen left office with a mixed record in 2013. While pushing anti-corruption campaigns and talking up the need for political reform, he undertook no major groundbreaking initiatives and was hesitant in dealing with major issues engendered by rapid economic development, such as environmental pollution, declining public service, endemic poverty, and economic inequality. At the end of his tenure, the *New York Times* alleged that members of his family had hidden billions of dollars gained through corrupt practices. Wen's supporters strongly denied this account, but it cast a pall over Wen's legacy as a corruption fighter. Willy Lam, a China politics expert at Chinese University of Hong Kong, notes that, although he tried to promote political reform and further economic liberalization, Wen could not take much action in these areas and did not present a strong personal example of personal integrity (Lam 2006).

Wen is married to Zhāng Péilì 张培莉, who has a jewelry investment business. Their son, Wen Yunsong, is CEO of a networking firm. A daughter, Wen Ruchan, is a bank employee and, by one report, managing director of Great Wall Computer Company. She is married to Liu Chunhang, director of the statistics department and research bureau of the China Banking Regulatory Commission.

Joel R. CAMPBELL
Troy University

Further Reading

Anderlini, Jamil. (2013, March 6). Wen takes final bow leaving divided legacy. *Financial Times.* Retrieved December 3, 2014, from http:www.ft.com/cms/s/0/6f32731e-8595-11e2-9ee3-06144feabdc0.html#axzz3KolCZQM3

• Wēn Jiābǎo •

Barboza. David. (2012, October 25). Billions in hidden riches for family of Chinese leader. *New York Times*. Retrieved December 3, 2014, from http://www.nytimes.com/2012/10/26/business/global/family-of-wen-jiabao-holds-a-hidden-fortune-in-china.html?pagewanted=all

Brown, Kerry. (2013, March 14). What did Hu Jintao and Wen Jiabao do for China? *BBC News*. Retrieved December 3, 2014, from http://www.bbc.com/news/world-asia-china-21669780

4to40: Kids Portal for Parents. (n.d.). Wen Jiabao: The people's premier. Retrieved March 5, 2015, from http://www.4to40.com//wordpress/biographies-for-kids/wen-jiabao/

Hutzler, Charles. (2012). Chinese premier warns of specter of turmoil. *Washington Times*. Retrieved May 9, 2012, from http://www.washingtontimes.com/news/2012/mar/14/premier-warns-of-specter-of-turmoil/

Lam, Willy. (2006). *Chinese politics in the Hu Jintao era: New leaders, new challenges*. New York: M. E. Sharpe.

Lampton, David. (2008). *The three faces of Chinese power: Might, money, and minds*. Berkeley: University of California Press.

Nathan, Andrew, & Gilley, Bruce. (2003). *China's new rulers: The secret files*. London: Granta Books.

Nguyen, Hai Hong. (2012, November 24). Wen Jiabao's legacy and Chinese politics today. *East Asia Forum*. Retrieved December 3, 2014, from http://www.eastasiaforum.org/2012/11/24/wen-jiabao-legacy-and-chinese-politics-today/

Radio Free Asia. (2012, March 14). Wen warns China over reform. Retrieved May 2, 2015, from http://www.rfa.org/english/news/china/warns-03142012154212.html

Shambaugh, David. (2009). *China's communist party: Atrophy and adaptation*. Berkeley: University of California Press.

Want China Times. (2012). Wen Ruchuan, Wen Jiabao's mysterious daughter. Retrieved March 5, 2015, from http://www.wantchinatimes.com/news-subclass-cnt.aspx?id=20120513000052&cid=1601

Xinhua News Agency. (2003). Wen Jiabao, premier of State Council. Retrieved May 9, 2012, from http://news.xinhuanet.com/english/2003-03/16/content_780876.htm

溫家宝

♂ Wong Kar-wai

Wáng Jiāwèi 王家衛

b. 1958—Film director, screenwriter, and producer

Alternate name: simpl. 王家卫

Summary

Hong Kong filmmaker Wong Kar-wai is one of the most artistically renowned Chinese directors working today. His films consistently press the medium's formal limits, displaying a level of experimentation rare in Hong Kong cinema. His aesthetic style not only sets him apart from local contemporaries but also has influenced international filmmakers. Several of his films, including *In the Mood for Love*, are considered by critics worldwide as among the greatest films ever made.

The most world-renowned of Hong Kong's contemporary filmmakers, Wong Kar-wai is also among the most controversial. He is alleged to be profligate, reckless with investors' money, and indifferent to production deadlines. Of his actors and crew he demands endless takes, stretching over several years of production. He shoots copious amounts of footage, and even major stars find their roles reduced to mere cameos. He dispenses with screenplays, discovering the story as he goes; often the plot coalesces as late as the editing phase. Detractors castigate him as irresponsibly tardy; at the Cannes Film Festival he notoriously delivered his competing entry twelve hours late and unfinished. Yet Wong is revered as one of the greatest filmmakers in world cinema. His films—fastidiously designed, achingly romantic, and rich in emotional depth—have won prestigious prizes at Cannes and other major festivals, increasing the global visibility of Hong Kong's art cinema. Wong's stylistic influence spreads far beyond Asia, and his Western supporters include Hollywood directors Martin Scorsese and Quentin Tarantino.

Childhood and Filmography

Born on 17 July 1958 in Shanghai, Wong immigrated to Hong Kong with his parents when he was five years old. As a child he was a voracious consumer of movies, from Hollywood westerns and British horror films to French *policiers* and Cantonese musicals. In his teens he studied graphic design at Hong Kong Polytechnic, and in the early 1980s he enrolled in a local television station's training program. From there he secured employment at Cinema City, a local mainstream studio, where he worked as a staff writer of formulaic comedies and supernatural thrillers.

Selected Filmography of Wong Kar-wai			
Year	English Title	Chinese Title	Notes
1988	*As Tears Go By*	旺角卡門 *Wàngjiǎo kǎmén*	Director, screenwriter
1990	*Days of Being Wild*	阿飛正傳 *Ā fēi zhèngzhuàn*	Director, screenwriter
1994	*Chungking Express*	重慶森林 *Chóngqìng sēnlín*	Director, producer, screenwriter
1994	*Ashes of Time*	東邪西毒 *Dōngxié xidú*	Director, producer, screenwriter
1995	*Fallen Angels*	墮落天使 *Duòluò tiānshǐ* (Cantonese: *Do lok tin si*)	Director, producer, screenwriter
1997	*Happy Together*	春光乍洩 *Chūn guāng zhà xiè*	Director, producer, screenwriter
2000	*In the Mood for Love*	花樣年華 *Huā yàng nián huá* (Cantonese: *Fa yeung nin wa*)	Director, producer, screenwriter
2004	*2046*	2046	Director, producer, screenwriter
2007	*My Blueberry Nights*		Director, producer, screenwriter.
2013	*The Grandmaster*	一代宗師 *Yī dài zōngshī*	Director, producer, screenwriter
2015	*Blossoms*		Director, screenwriter

Disenchanted, Wong co-founded his own firm, In-Gear, and launched his directorial career. His first film, *As Tears Go By* 旺角卡門 (1988), belonged to the popular formulaic triad-gangster genre, but its recasting of MTV-style imagery and its use of a step-printing technique (whereby some frames are deleted and others multiply printed) infused the genre's gunplay scenes with a fresh staccato energy. It was his next film, however, that introduced Wong as a major new cinematic stylist. *Days of Being Wild* 阿飛正傳 (1990), unlike *As Tears Go By*, seemed indifferent to popular trends. The story of a dissolute *ah fei* (delinquent), it defied genre conventions, embraced aleatory plotting, and demoted scenes of physical action (de rigueur in Hong Kong films, regardless of genre). A star-packed and costly venture, this film was a conspicuous commercial failure, but Wong was feted as a cinematic stylist of the first order.

An extravagant venture into *wǔxiá* 武俠 (swordplay) cinema—*Ashes of Time* 東邪西毒 (1994)—earned Wong a reputation for self-indulgence and profligacy, but *Chungking Express* 重慶森林 (1994) won almost universal adulation. An uplifting romantic comedy, it became Wong's international breakthrough film. *Fallen Angels* 墮落天使 (1995) and especially *Happy Together* 春光乍洩 (1997) solidified his presence in the global film scene; the latter, a haunting gay love story, earned Wong recognition at Cannes. Through these films Wong became associated with a set of signature techniques: step-printing, smudge motion (whereby the image dissolves into iridescent streaks of light), handheld camerawork, elliptical editing, and an audio-visual style adapted from MTV.

His next film, *In the Mood for Love* 花樣年華 (2000), marked a stylistic departure and is perhaps the film for which Wong is best known internationally. An unofficial sequel, *2046* (2004), emerged after years of delays. Another hiatus was broken by the release of *My Blueberry Nights* (2007), a flop financed by French capital and shot in the United States with Hollywood stars. Wong reworked *Ashes of Time* for Western theatrical distribution (*Ashes of Time Redux* [2008]) and scored a major success with *The Grandmaster* 一代宗師 (2013), a long-gestating foray into the kung fu genre.

An Aesthetic of Disturbance

In the 1980s and 1990s, Hong Kong filmmakers embraced a principle of expressive clarity. Plotlines built out of discrete episodes displayed a structural transparency. Composition, camera movement, and editing combined to render the onscreen action perspicuous, amplifying the visceral qualities of a swordfight or a shootout. Local filmmakers carried this legibility principle into all genres—not only the martial arts and action films, but also supernatural fantasies, romantic melodramas, urban comedies, and historical dramas. The result was a local cinema bursting with expressive force, visceral sensation, and piercing emotion. Hong Kong films depicted and elicited the "basic" emotions of sadness, happiness, anger, disgust, fear, and surprise in palpable ways. Within and against this milieu, Wong cultivated an innovative aesthetic, neither wholly embracing nor wholly rejecting the legibility schema. Instead, he opted to "disturb" and qualify this schema, complicating the expressive clarity favored by his peers.

Visual Style

His visual style combines sensuousness with obfuscation, aesthetic engrossment with cognitive detachment. On the one hand, he presents a pictorially lush stylistic program, enriched by colleague William Chang's sumptuous costume design and set decoration (and betraying Wong's own background in graphic design). On the other hand, he thwarts the image's seductiveness by placing perceptual obstacles within the frame, blocking or obscuring the shot's apparent object of attention. In Wong's aesthetic of "disturbance," the faces of characters are often perversely blocked from view. Step-printing may preclude the viewer from comprehending the image. Elliptical editing may create spatial ambiguities, sending the viewer's grasp of scenic geography into disarray. In numerous ways, Wong distresses the local norm of legibility. Critics claim that his ravishing imagery induces a

dreamlike passivity, but his films actually demand an active viewer: Only by processing a host of perceptual and cognitive obstacles can the viewer properly comprehend the action. Wong's visual style, then, is simultaneously sensuous and difficult, at once pleasing and perplexing to the eye.

This aesthetic allowed Wong to subject genre conventions to fresh variation. In *Ashes of Time*, the obligatory swordfight becomes a study in ellipticality and obliqueness. Images of swordsmen in combat—which in other Hong Kong *wuxia* films would be presented through legible shot design—are obscured by smudge motion, discontinuous editing, canted angles, rapid camera movement, fast editing, and abrupt figure movement within the frame. Yet intermittent close-up shots of the swordsmen's faces, decelerated images of a clash of weapons, and communicative sound effects help to orient the viewer. Consequently, the viewer's uptake of the action proceeds haltingly: Only in spasmodic bursts does the swordfight become intelligible. For much of the combat, the oblique presentation of bodies in extremis obscures the specifics of the duel, making it impossible to determine which swordsman has the upper hand. In such sequences Wong's visual style becomes highly palpable, but this is not, as his detractors allege, a case of mere ornamentation. Rather, his tactics of obfuscation ratchet up suspense (which duelist will triumph?), while the sheer

王家衛

kineticism of the action conveys the fighters' otherworldly athleticism. *Ashes of Time*'s swordfights resembled no other action scene in 1990s Hong Kong cinema, and they not only rejuvenated *wuxia* genre conventions but further distinguished Wong from his contemporaries.

Narrative Style

At the narrative level, too, Wong defied local convention. He adopted the local custom of building plots out of discrete episodes, but he introduced ellipses and digressions that seemed to throw the plotline off track. Tacit ellipses (i.e., jumping ahead in story time without overtly signaling as such) misdirect the viewer's inferences about how and when the action unfolds, as when *In the Mood for Love*'s unmarked ellipses encourage erroneous inferences about the protagonists' illicit relationship. On other occasions plot episodes bear no apparent relation to the principal narrative. In *Fallen Angels* a contract killing is sidetracked when the assassin randomly encounters his former classmate, a digression ostensibly disrupting the film's genre plot. If such scenes seem incidental, they in fact communicate both character psychology and thematic concerns. Overall, ellipticality and digression obscure the episodic clarity of the plot's architecture, without abandoning episodic plotting altogether. Here again Wong's cinema reworks but does not reject Hong Kong storytelling norms.

Emotional Response

Then there is the local cinema's moral perspicuity. Hong Kong movies, like those of other popular cinemas, stage Manichean conflicts that pit morally virtuous characters against morally depraved ones. Yet Wong at times flouts this tradition, emphasizing malevolent or apathetic protagonists and soliciting sympathy for them. For example, Killer in *Fallen Angels* is an emotionally opaque assassin, while Yuddy in *Days of Being Wild* displays the traits of a sociopath.

Moreover, if Hong Kong films teem with emotional displays and arouse strong emotions in the viewer, Wong's cinema ushers in relatively diffuse and complex emotional states. Because his characters are often either taciturn or emotionally repressed (or both), they are disinclined to express their feelings—hence Wong hints at their private passions by evocative shots of the surrounding milieu: a turbulent sea (*Ashes of Time*), curlicues of cigarette smoke (*In the Mood for Love*), a cascading waterfall (*Happy Together*). This tactic averts the melodramatic excess characterizing most Hong Kong cinema and creates instead a pervasive sense of mood. Evoking complex rather than basic emotions, Wong's films avoid both the emotional salience of popular cinema and the affective detachment found in art films. In sum, his films disturb both the moral and emotional clarity of popular Hong Kong cinema.

Wong Kar-wai amidst a crowd of press photographers at the Berlin Film Festival (2013). Photo by Siebbi.

王家衛

Influences

There are several reasons Wong cultivates this aesthetic of disturbance. From the start he sought distinctiveness. A self-conscious auteur, he pursued aesthetic options that would separate his work from a plethora of local films (he began directing during the industry's late-1980s production boom). He also coveted the international film festival market, and, knowing that festival programmers favor directors with "personal visions," he challenged local cinema norms and genre conventions. These festivals also tend to prize cerebral filmmaking, hence Wong's penchant for cognitively complex "mood pieces." Moreover, the directors he cites as influences specialize in stylistic experimentation: Alain Resnais retards the viewer's story comprehension (*Last Year at Marienbad*, 1961), Jean-Luc Godard employs ludic audio-visual style (*Pierre le Fou*, 1965), François Truffaut playfully reworks genre (*Shoot the Piano Player*, 1960), and Michelangelo Antonioni flaunts visual sensuousness (*Red Desert*, 1964).

Wong's influences from Hong Kong cinema—chiefly the Shaw Brothers studio films on which he was weaned—demonstrate a rich visual sensuousness through bold schematic color palettes, widescreen compositions, and intricate costume and set design. If Wong's authorial sensibility mostly aligns with that of European art filmmakers, it should be remembered that his career began in the mainstream popular industry as a screenwriter. The tension his films exhibit—between clarity and opacity, immersion and detachment—may stem from a synthesis of aesthetic taste and this background in mainstream production.

Trendsetter

One measure of Wong's global importance is the breadth of influence exerted by his authorial style. His international breakthrough, *Chungking Express*, inspired a flurry of Asian films embellished by step-printing, smudge motion, ticking clocks, and other derivative traits. Films from South Korea (*All About My Wife* 내 아내의 모든 것, dir. Min Kyu-dong, 2012) and mainland China (*Keep Cool* 有话好好说, dir. *Zhāng Yìmóu 张艺谋, 1997; and *Suzhou River* 苏州河, dir. Lóu Yè 娄烨, 2000) also owed stylistic debts to Wong, while the Hong Kong cinema mercilessly parodied his trademark visual aesthetic and character types in films such as *Days of Being Dumb* (*Yǎfēi yú yǎjī* 亞飛與亞基, dir. Blackie Ko, 1993).

Averse to being pigeonholed, Wong sought new stylistic territory. He settled on a sedate, almost classical style, substituting languorous camera movement for the erratic handheld cinematography of *Chungking Express. In the Mood for Love* also exemplified this aesthetic, and it too spawned imitators. Now Wong's influence reached Hollywood. Sofia Coppola's *Lost in Translation* (2003), Spike Jonze's *Adaptation* (2002), and David O. Russell's *Silver Linings Playbook* (2012) allude to *In the Mood for Love*, while European art films such as Abbas Kiarostami's *Certified Copy* (2010) and Xavier Dolan's *Heartbeats* (2010) and *Tom at the Farm* (2013) also pay homage.

Again and again, Wong strives to differentiate himself from his imitators. If his efforts to do so qualify him as a polystylist, he nonetheless remains committed to the aesthetic of disturbance, balancing sensuous absorption and cognitive challenge. He endeavored to stay one step ahead of his rivals with another stylistic departure in *The Grandmaster*, which blended *In the Mood for Love*'s stately rhythms with the kinetic energy of *Ashes of Time*. Just months after *The Grandmaster*'s theatrical release, its striking visual narration was lampooned in a new Hong Kong comedy (*Golden Chickensss* 金雞SSS, dir. Matt Chow, 2013). Though it may irk him, Wong Kar-wai remains an irrepressible trendsetter.

Gary BETTINSON
Lancaster University

---

*People marked with an asterisk have entries in this dictionary.

Further Reading

Abbas, Ackbar. (1997). *Hong Kong: Culture and the politics of disappearance*. Minneapolis & London: University of Minnesota Press.

Bettinson, Gary. (2015). *The sensuous cinema of Wong Kar-wai: Film poetics and the aesthetic of disturbance*. Hong Kong: Hong Kong University Press.

Bettinson, Gary. (Ed.). (2012). *Directory of world cinema: China*. Bristol & Chicago: Intellect Press.

Bordwell, David. (2000). *Planet Hong Kong: Popular cinema and the art of entertainment*. Cambridge, MA: Harvard University Press.

Brunette, Peter. (2005). *Wong Kar-wai*. Champaign: University of Illinois Press.

Dissanayake, Wimal. (2003). *Wong Kar-wai's* Ashes of Time. Hong Kong: Hong Kong University Press.

Ma, Jean. (2010). *Melancholy drift: Marking time in Chinese cinema*. Hong Kong: Hong Kong University Press.

Riviere, Daniele. (Ed.). (1997). *Wong Kar-wai*. Paris: Editions Dis Voir.

Tambling, Jeremy. (2003). *Wong Kar-wai's* Happy Together. Hong Kong: Hong Kong University Press.

Teo, Stephen. (2005). *Wong Kar-wai*. London: BFI.

Teo, Stephen. (1997). *Hong Kong cinema: The extra dimensions*. London: BFI.

Yau, Esther C. M. (2001). *At full speed: Hong Kong cinema in a borderless world*. Minneapolis: University of Minnesota Press.

王家衛

☦ Woo, John

Wú Yǔsēn 吳宇森

b. 1946—Hong Kong film director and producer

Alternate names: Ng Yu-Sum; simpl. 吴宇森

Summary

One of the most globally acclaimed Chinese film directors, John Woo exerted a heavy influence on action cinema both in Hong Kong and in Hollywood. His transnational career made him a pioneer in Hollywood's assimilation of Hong Kong cinema and in Hong Kong and Chinese-language cinema's globalization in the 1990s. Woo's distinct brand of kinetic yet graceful presentation of action scenes has had a profound impact on filmmakers working both inside and outside of Hong Kong.

John Woo was born on 1 May 1946 in Guangzhou (Canton), Guangdong Province. In 1951, his family immigrated to British-colonized Hong Kong to flee the Communist takeover of China. Living an impoverished life, Woo was only enrolled in school with the aid of an American Lutheran family. This Christian education played a part in Woo's conversion to Christianity and his naming himself in English after John the Baptist; Christian iconography would also become a recurring feature in his films. During his teenage years, Woo was surrounded by gangsters, and these experiences found their way into his later films. He immersed himself in cinema from an early age and acquainted himself with a diverse range of film schools, movements, and genres—from the French New Wave to New Hollywood films, and from musicals to westerns. With no formal training in film, he joined a student film group in 1967 and made five short films over the course of the following two years. His cinematic inspirations include Chang Cheh (Zhāng Chè 张彻), King Hu (Hú Jīnquán 胡金铨), Akira Kurosawa, Stanley Kubrick, Martin Scorsese, Sam Peckinpah, Sergio Leone, and, especially, French crime-film specialist Jean-Pierre Melville.

Woo started his professional career at Hong Kong's major studios when the local industry was in transition from studio production to independent production. He joined the Cathay Organization 国泰 as a script supervisor in 1969 and moved on to Shaw Brothers 邵氏 Studio the following year. There he became assistant director to martial arts director Chang Cheh, whose thematic preference for male-bonding, an aesthetic inclination toward violence, and stylistic devices of slow-motion cinematography and freeze-frame editing, among other things, left an indelible imprint on Woo's work. Woo's directorial debut, *The Young Dragons* 鐵漢柔情 (1973), a kung fu film, was released by independent studio Golden Harvest 嘉禾 in 1974. Woo simultaneously left Shaw Brothers and signed a contract with Golden Harvest. In 1981, he also started to make films for Cinema City 新艺城 before making a permanent move and ending his time at Golden Harvest two years later.

During his tenures with these large companies, Woo made fourteen films covering a range of genres, including martial arts, comedies, melodramas, fantasies, and musicals. Most of these early works fall into either the martial arts or comedy category, which constituted the two major genres in local cinema from the mid-1970s to the mid-1980s. Notwithstanding the ups and downs at the box office, these films helped Woo hone his skills as a versatile director, with his first local hit being the comedy *Money Crazy* 發錢寒 (1977). During the same period, he extended his role to become a producer. Two films that he oversaw were released during his sojourn to Taiwan, after he was sent there by Cinema City. Two years later, Woo returned to Hong Kong, calling a close to both a frustrating exile experience and a not-so-glamorous early career.

Hong Kong Heroic Bloodshed

Upon returning to Hong Kong in 1985, Woo collaborated with local producer-cum-director Tsui Hark 徐克, who provided funds for *A Better Tomorrow* 英雄本色 (1986). The film became an immediate box-office sensation and a monumental achievement in Hong Kong film history. Although the stylized violence and altruistic themes that characterize the "heroic bloodshed" genre had previously appeared in Chang Cheh's films, with *A Better Tomorrow*, Woo carved out a name for the genre on the world stage. Heroic bloodshed became a staple sub-genre of Hong Kong action cinema. It differs from previous local kung fu action films in its heavy presentation of gunplay, which is choreographed in a stylized, romantic, even surrealistic manner. Thematically, Woo's heroic bloodshed films usually feature gangsters and highlight friendship, loyalty, and sacrifice among his heroes.

A Better Tomorrow was a turning point in Woo's career. It established his cinematic style, transformed him into an action-film director, and launched him on his road to auteur status. In the wake of

吳宇森

Selected Filmography of John Woo			
Year	English Title	Chinese Title	Notes
1973	*The Young Dragons*	鐵漢柔情 *Tiě hàn róuqíng*	Director, writer
1977	*Money Crazy*	發錢寒 *Fā qián hán*	Director, writer
1986	*A Better Tomorrow*	英雄本色 *Yīngxióng běn sè*	Director, writer, producer, actor
1986	*Heroes Shed No Tears*	英雄无泪 *Yīng xióng wú lèi*	Director, writer, producer
1987	*A Better Tomorrow II*	英雄本色2 *Yīngxióng běn sè 2*	Director, writer, producer
1989	*The Killer*	喋血雙雄 *Dié xuè shuāng xióng*	Director, writer
1989	*Just Heroes*	義膽羣英 *Yì dǎn qún yīng*	Director
1990	*Bullet in the Head*	喋血街頭 *Dié xuè jiē tóu*	Director, producer, writer
1990	*Once a Thief*	縱橫四海 *Zòng héng sì hǎi*	Director, writer
1992	*Hard Boiled*	辣手神探 *Là shǒu shéntàn*	Director, writer
1993	*Hard Target*		Director
1996	*Broken Arrow*		Director
1997	*Face/Off*		Director
2002	*Windtalkers*		Director, producer
2003	*Paycheck*		Director
2008–2009	*Red Cliff*	赤壁 *Chì bì*	Director, producer, writer
2014–2015	*The Crossing*	太平輪 *Tài píng lún*	Director, producer

Doves are one of John Woo's signature images. Another example of his use of Christian iconography is the church as an often-used setting. Photo by Darius Family.

吳宇森

the film's commercial and critical success, Woo directed another six features in Hong Kong: five in the same vein as *A Better Tomorrow*—*A Better Tomorrow II* 英雄本色2 (1988), *The Killer* 喋血雙雄 (1989), *Just Heroes* 義膽羣英 (1989), *Bullet in the Head* 喋血街頭 (1990), and *Hard Boiled* 辣手神探 (1992)—and one crime romance, *Once a Thief* 縱橫四海 (1990). Among these titles, *The Killer* earned him best director at the Hong Kong Film Awards and received wide critical acclaim in the West, especially for its action sequences. The film toured at film festivals from Europe to the United States and gave Woo a cult reputation among audiences. Meanwhile, Hollywood's major studios started to show interest in the director, enticing him to make films for Hollywood.

Hollywood Career

Escaping the Hong Kong film industry's decline in the mid-1990s and the anxious political climate caused by China's 1997 takeover of Hong Kong, Woo moved to the United States in 1992 to make his first Hollywood film, *Hard Target* (1993), which made him the first Asian filmmaker to direct a major Hollywood studio feature. Having enjoyed much of the creative control since his Golden Harvest career in Hong Kong, he experienced difficulty with both his limited directorial authority in the Hollywood system and the relatively strict censorship of violence in American cinema. As a result, *Hard Target* did not allow Woo full self-expression. Yet its financial success earned him contracts to stay in Hollywood to direct *Broken Arrow* (1996) and *Face/Off* (1997). These two action thrillers became enormous hits and made Woo a bankable name. From *Hard Target* to *Broken Arrow* to *Face/Off*, the gradual yet large increase in production costs attested to Woo's rising profile, with the films exhibiting the director's constant fight for artistic freedom. In 1999, Woo became a US citizen, and he directed *Mission: Impossible II* (2000) with a blockbuster budget, which announced his status as an A-list director in Hollywood. The following two commercial disappointments, however, the World War II film *Windtalkers* (2002) and science-fiction thriller *Paycheck* (2003), led to the end of his Hollywood tenure.

A theme throughout Woo's career is his struggle against studio interference. Such struggles back in Hong Kong in 1990 resulted in his first effort to establish his own production house. During his Hollywood stint, with accumulated experience and networks, he founded WCG Entertainment with his long-time business partner Terence Chang (Zhāng Jiāzhèn 张家振) and American producer Christopher Godsick in 1994. After that, he assumed the roles of producer and supervisor on a number of films. In 1999, Lion Rock Productions, which he formed with Chang, replaced WCG to continue his transnational production agenda. In 2007, Lion Rock started to support and cultivate Asian filmmakers, anticipating Woo's return to Asia.

Return to Chinese-Language Cinema

In the context of the prosperity of the Chinese film market in the 2000s, while Lion Rock devoted most of its focus to Chinese-language films, Woo himself returned to the Chinese cinematic landscape in 2008 with a two-part period war epic *Red Cliff* 赤壁 (2008–2009). Produced on a record-breaking budget and becoming a box-office sensation in Asia, *Red Cliff* demonstrated Woo's absolute influence in the Chinese-language and Asian film industries. His blockbuster-scale epics then extended to the two-part *The Crossing* 太平輪 (2014–2015), which also mainly targeted the Asian market, especially mainland China.

In the midst of a career still going strong, Woo received a Golden Lion for Lifetime Achievement, for his contribution to action films worldwide, from the Venice Film Festival in 2010. Yet his return to China has witnessed two new tendencies: as a director, he is moving beyond the action genre, for which he is renowned, toward a more transnational, transcultural production direction; and as a producer and supervisor, he is reassuming responsibility for the development of Chinese-language cinema.

Legacy and Contribution

Woo is seen as one of the world's most successful and influential action-film masters. A groundbreaker in the development of the action genre in Hong Kong, he played a principal role in the transition from martial arts films to heroic bloodshed films in local cinema in the late 1980s. His soulful, sensitive heroes and their balletic, poetic gunfights revived local action films in terms of both narrative and style. His work further affected the characterization in Hollywood action films by introducing an alternative to macho masculinity. His visual devices, such as characters holding guns in both hands and characters pointing guns at each other, have become staples in action films worldwide. Woo's films are a cross-national, cross-cultural phenomenon due to the wide range of works from which they derive inspiration. In turn, his work influences filmmakers across the globe. In Hong Kong, this is particularly clear in the films of Johnnie To (Dù Qífēng 杜琪峰). In Hollywood, his successors include Quentin Tarantino, Robert Rodriguez, and the Wachowski brothers.

In addition to the interest in Hong Kong cinema by Western film industries, critics, and audiences as result of his 1980s heroic bloodshed movies, Woo was also a major player in Hong Kong cinema's globalization and in the shaping of its image in the West in the 1990s. By bringing Hong Kong cinema's influence to Hollywood during his overseas adventure, he also made a contribution to Hollywood's assimilation of foreign film cultures. He is among a small number of Asian filmmakers whose contributions to film art and transnational cultural exchange are internationally recognized.

Sun YI
University of Nottingham

Further Reading

Ciecko, Anne T. (1997). Transnational action: John Woo, Hong Kong, Hollywood. In Sheldon Hsiao-peng Lu (Ed), *Transnational Chinese cinemas: Identity, nationhood, gender* (pp. 221–237). Honolulu: University of Hawai'i Press.

Fang, Karen. (2004). *John Woo's* A Better Tomorrow. Hong Kong: Hong Kong University Press.

Hall, Kenneth E. (2009). *John Woo's* The Killer. Hong Kong: Hong Kong University Press.

Hall, Kenneth E. (2011). *John Woo: The films* (2nd ed.). Jefferson, NC: McFarland.

McDonagh, Maitland. (1993). Action painter: John Woo. *Film Comment, 29*(5), 46–49.

Sandell, Jillian. (1996). Reinventing masculinity: The spectacle of male intimacy in the films of John Woo. *Film Quarterly, 49*(4), 23–34.

Stringer, Julian. (1997). "Your tender smiles give me strength": Paradigms of masculinity in John Woo's *A Better Tomorrow* and *The Killer. Screen, 38*(1), 25–41.

Szeto, Kin-Yan. (2011). Facing off East and West in the cinema of John Woo. In *Martial Arts Cinema of Chinese Diaspora: Ang Lee, John Woo, and Jackie Chan in Hollywood* (pp. 71–112). Carbondale: Southern Illinois University Press.

Williams, Tony. (2009). *John Woo's Bullet in the Head.* Hong Kong: Hong Kong University Press.

Williams, Tony. (1997). Space, place, and spectacle: The crisis cinema of John Woo. *Cinema Journal, 36*(2), 67–84.

Woo, John. (2005). *John Woo: Interviews.* Oxford: University Press of Mississippi.

吳宇森

♀ Wú Yí 吴仪

b. 1938—Politician, vice premier of the PRC (2003–2008)

Alternate name: trad. 吳儀

Summary

Named by *Forbes* magazine in 2007 as the second most powerful woman in the world, Wu Yi has held several political positions in the Chinese Communist Party and Chinese government, including vice premier. She has been called the "dragon lady" for her tough approach to international negotiations, tackling trade and intellectual property rights issues as well as public health initiatives in China.

Born on 17 November 1938 in the central Chinese city of Wuhan in Hubei Province to a modest family of intellectuals, Wu Yi went on to become one of the highest-ranking women in the Chinese government since the establishment of the People's Republic of China (PRC) in 1949.

As a young girl Wu aspired to become an entrepreneur but instead trained as a chemical engineer in the male-dominated field of the petroleum industry. She began her studies at the National Defense Department of the Northwest Polytechnic Institute and then attended the Oil Refinery Department of the Beijing Petroleum Institute, where she received a degree in petroleum engineering in 1962. That same year, at the height of the famine brought on by the Great Leap Forward (1958–1960), she joined the Chinese Communist Party (CCP).

Wu worked at the Lanzhou Oil Refinery in China's far northwest Gansu Province from 1962 to 1965 and then as a technician in the Production and Technology Department of the Ministry of Petroleum Industry from 1965 to 1967. This was followed by her work as a technician at Beijing Dongfanghong ("East is Red") Refinery, where over the next fifteen years she advanced within the company from technician to technology section chief to deputy chief engineer and finally to deputy director of the refinery. From 1983 to 1988, she was deputy manager and Communist Party secretary at the Beijing Yanshan Petroleum Corporation.

Early Political Career

After spending twenty years in what she later described as the country's "backwater," where she was consumed by her work and never married, Wu began her political career in 1988, serving as deputy mayor of the municipality of Beijing. Charged with overseeing the city's industrial development and foreign trade endeavors, Wu played a crucial role after the June 1989 military crackdown on demonstrators in Tiananmen Square when she worked to prevent workers at the city's electrical power generation plants from striking in protest over the killings of defenseless students.

In 1990 she made her first trip to the United States as a member of a delegation of the China Council for Promotion of International Trade; this signaled a move toward renewal of normal US-China relations following the Tiananmen crackdown and provided an opportunity to address concerns over the prevalence of pirated music and software from America in China. Subsequently, Wu was appointed minister of foreign trade and economic cooperation, serving in that role from 1993 to 1998, and a member of the all-important Leading Party Group in the State Council. A protégé of then premier *Zhū Róngjī 朱镕基 (b. 1928), Wu was just one of five state councilors in China in 1998, and then from 2003 to

2008 served as a vice premier—the first woman to hold this position since 1998 and only the third in the history of the PRC. Wu also served on the Fifteenth Central Committee of the CCP and as an alternate member of the ruling Politburo (1997–2002), and later on the Sixteenth Central Committee and as a full member of the Politburo (2002–2007).

As minister of foreign trade and economic cooperation and a vice premier, Wu was intimately involved in various aspects of China's trade and economic relations with foreign nations, especially the United States, Japan, the European Union, and Russia. In the run-up to the PRC's successful entry into the World Trade Organization (WTO) in 2001, Wu became internationally known when, while hammering out the trade deal with the United States and other relevant parties, she also dealt with continued complaints from the United States about widespread violation of intellectual property rights, which led her to order a major reorganization of the country's customs service. Her responsibilities also included overseeing China's industry and state-owned enterprises, including the government's efforts to promote economic development in China's poor interior, a policy pushed by Premier Zhu. Wu also played a major role in working to increase foreign direct investment in China, promoting the growth of the country's own high-technology exports while also encouraging Chinese firms to invest in assembly plants overseas. In

---

*People marked with an asterisk have entries in this dictionary.

1999 Wu was credited with completing five trade agreements with Russia.

Public Health Advocate

In the midst of the devastating severe acute respiratory syndrome (SARS) epidemic in China in the early 2000s, Wu was appointed minister of health, a position she held from 2003 to 2005. True to her reputation as an "enforcer of last resort," Wu quickly reversed the widespread cover-up of the epidemic by her predecessor, Zhāng Wénkāng 张文康, by imposing quarantines on thousands of suspected SARS carriers and heading a committee that instituted a system of monitoring the outbreak. Under her leadership, the epidemic was finally brought under control. As head of a "patriotic public health campaign," Wu also pushed for improved organizational and educational measures along with improved indoor and outdoor sanitation to control the disease.

When China confronted an outbreak of AIDS in 2005, Wu personally visited villages and other areas where the outbreak was especially severe, meeting face-to-face with people infected by the disease while stressing the importance of programs designed to educate a fearful population about AIDS.

With an allocation of 3.5 billion yuan (US$585 million), Wu authorized the establishment of a nationwide public health network along with the creation of the Center for Disease Prevention and Control, modeled after similar organizations in the United States and the rest of the developed world. A major proponent of improving food and drug safety in China, she banned the use of lead in children's toys, closed over nine hundred unlicensed food processing plants along with two thousand factories making fake goods, and suspended the licenses of 1,200 drug and medical equipment manufacturers.

Elected president of the China Association of Foreign Funded Enterprises, Wu played a central role in the second round of the China-US Strategic Economic Dialogue initiated by the George W. Bush administration. Her negotiating style was described by then Secretary of the Treasury Henry Paulson as a "force of nature." Also known as the "iron lady" and "dragon lady" for her tough approach to international negotiations, Wu was praised for being sincere and candid and for "telling it like it is" with great attention to detail. While she vehemently opposed those in the United States Congress who wanted to impose sanctions and penalties on China for currency manipulation and other supposed misdeeds, she believed trade between the two countries was a win-win situation and so was equally hard on local officials in China for tolerating widespread violation of intellectual property rights for foreign-made goods. In meetings held between the United States and China in April 2004, Wu and her team made numerous promises and concessions,

Wú Yí

signaling Beijing's desire to soften its position on global commerce matters. In addition to better enforcement of intellectual property rights, Wu helped broker deals in wireless communication standards.

Labeled the "goddess of transparency" by *Time* magazine in 2004 and ranked by *Forbes* magazine as the second most powerful woman in the world in 2007, Wu also devoted her considerable political energies to promoting the development of China's poverty-stricken interior, where she had worked as a young chemical engineer, and to improving the circumstances of women and children. Yet Wu could also be hard-nosed, such as when she dismissed appeals by authorities in Taiwan for China's assistance during the SARS crisis and when she openly opposed Chongqing mayor *Bó Xīlái 薄熙来 (b. 1949) as her successor to vice premier, citing his apparent unwillingness to consider the opinions of others. A lover of Western music and literature, Wu continued to work on intellectual property rights and toy safety issues with the United States right up until her formal retirement in 2008. At that point, she declared that she was cutting all ties with work and "leaving with nothing," including the usual honorary posts and positions.

Lawrence R. SULLIVAN
Adelphi University

Further Reading

China Vitae. (n.d.). Wu Yi. Retrieved November 10, 2014, from http://www.chinavitae.com/biography/33

Edwards, Louise. (2006). Sport, fashion, and beauty. New incarnations of the female politician in contemporary China. In Fran Martin & Larissa Heinrich (Eds.), *Embodied modernities: Corporeality, representation, and Chinese cultures* (pp. 146–161). Honolulu: University of Hawai'i Press.

Hermann, Eve M. B. (2005). Wu Yi. In *Encyclopedia of world biography*. Retrieved March 11, 2015, from http://www.notablebiographies.com/newsmakers2/2005-Pu-Z/Wu-Yi.html

Sullivan, Lawrence R. (2007). Wu Yi. In *Historical dictionary of the People's Republic of China* (pp. 574). Lanham, MD: Scarecrow Press.

Wu Yi. (2009). In Zhang Weidong, & Ilan Alon (Eds.), *Biographical dictionary of new Chinese entrepreneurs and business leaders* (pp. 198–200). Northampton, MA: Edward Elgar Publishing.

• 吴仪 •

☌ Xí Jìnpíng 习近平

b. 1953—Top leader of the "fifth generation" leadership, president of the People's Republic of China (2013–)

Alternate name: trad. 習近平

Summary

A top leader of the "fifth generation" leadership and son of a veteran revolutionary, Xi Jinping became general secretary of the Chinese Communist Party and chairman of the Central Military Commission in November 2012, and president of the People's Republic of China in March 2013. Since then he has called for an anti-corruption campaign and further reforms. He has also coined the phrase "China Dream" to describe his overarching plans for China.

As son of a veteran revolutionary, Xi Jinping enjoyed a huge advantage as a young politician. He was appointed a deputy party secretary of a county only three years after his graduation from university and experienced rapid promotions in subsequent years. He worked in Hebei Province for three years, in Fujian Province for seventeen years, in Zhejiang Province for five years, and in Shanghai for seven months. Without particularly impressive performances, he was promoted to higher positions once every two to three years.

The least popular alternative member of the Fifteenth Central Committee of the Chinese Communist Party (CCP) in 1997, Xi became a member of the Politburo Standing Committee ten years later. Xi then became the top leader of China as general secretary of the CCP, chairman of the Central Military Commission, and president of the People's Republic of China (PRC) in another five years. He managed to consolidate his power over the party, the state, and the military within two years and introduced the "China Dream" (*Zhōngguó mèng* 中国梦) as his vision for China.

Early Life

A native of Shaanxi Province, Xi Jinping was born on 15 June 1953 in Beijing. His father, Xí Zhòngxūn 习仲勋 (1913–2002), joined the Communist Youth League at the age of twelve and the Chinese

Communist Party at the age of fourteen. At the time of Xi Jinping's birth, Xi Zhongxun was one of the high officials of the CCP. He was in charge of the party's propaganda work as director of the Central Propaganda Department under CCP Chairman Mao Zedong (1893–1976). Three months later, he also became concurrently secretary general of the State Council under Premier Zhōu Ēnlái 周恩来 (1898–1976). Xi Jinping's mother, Qí Xīn 齐心 (b. 1926), the second wife of Xi Zhongxun, was also a veteran Communist who joined the CCP at the age of seventeen in 1943 and worked at the Central Party School.

Xi Jinping's privileged life as son of a high-ranking official was shattered in 1962 when his father was dismissed from all of his posts for his "anti-party" activities. Xi Zhongxun was accused of instigating anti-party activities because of his involvement in the writing of a novel. The novel, named after the revolutionary martyr Liú Zhìdàn 刘志丹 (1903–1936), was considered an attempt to reverse the verdict on a former Politburo member, Gāo Gǎng 高岗 (1905–1954), who had committed suicide for his "anti-party factionalist activities." Xi Zhongxun had been consulted on the writing of the novel because he had been a comrade-in-arms of both Liu Zhidan and Gao Gang, and the trio were from the same province of Shaanxi.

In the beginning of the Cultural Revolution (1966–1976), Xi Jinping was not even allowed to join the Red Guards because he was considered a child of "bad elements" (hēi bāng 黑帮). In January 1969, at the age of fifteen, Xi left Beijing for Shaanxi (his home province) for physical labor. In contrast to many youngsters who were bidding a tearful farewell, Xi seemed thrilled about the departure. "I would have to cry if I could not leave," Xi recalled. "Because I would have lost my life had I stayed" (Wu 2010, 64).

In the subsequent seven years, Xi made great efforts to get used to rural life in Shaanxi and to accumulate political credentials. Because of his father's problems, he had to make extra effort to be admitted to the Chinese Communist Youth League and the Chinese Communist Party. He was recruited to the Youth League after his eighth application and was made a member of the CCP after ten applications (Wu 2010, 588, 589). He was admitted to the CCP in January 1974 at the age of twenty and was soon appointed as party secretary of his village. In October 1975, with the recommendation of his county, he was enrolled in the Department of Chemical Engineering at Tsinghua University as a "worker-peasant-soldier" student.

Political Career

During his years at Tsinghua, his father was rehabilitated politically. After a hiatus of sixteen years, Xi Zhongxun was brought back to politics in 1978. He was appointed the second party secretary of Guangdong in April 1978 and was promoted to the first party secretary of the province in December of that year. He was at the forefront of policies to open up to the outside world and was responsible for setting up special economic zones in Guangdong.

Through his father's connections, upon his graduation from Tsinghua University in April 1979, Xi Jinping got a job as personal secretary to Gěng Biāo 耿飚 (1909–2000), then Politburo member, vice premier of the State Council, and secretary general of the Central Military Commission (CMC). After *Dèng Xiǎopíng 邓小平 (1904–1997) took over as chairman of the CMC in June 1981, however, Geng Biao was gradually sidelined. He was replaced by *Yáng Shàngkūn 杨尚昆 (1907–1998) as secretary general of the CMC and was demoted from a vice premier of the State Council to a state councilor.

While Geng Biao was in political decline, Xi Jinping decided to embark on a political career in the provinces. With a father who was a rising political star in China as a member of the Secretariat of the Central Committee of the CCP, twenty-eight-year-old Xi was appointed deputy party secretary of Zhengding County in March 1982, barely three years after his graduation from Tsinghua University. But he quickly gained the confidence of local people for his down-to-earth work style and was promoted to party secretary of the county in a year and a half.

*People marked with an asterisk have entries in this dictionary.

Rapid Promotions

In June 1985, Xi Jinping was promoted to vice mayor of Xiamen through his father's connections. The first party secretary of Fujian at the time was Xiàng Nán 项南 (1918–1997), son of Xiàng Yúnián 项与年 (1894–1978), a colleague of Xi Zhongxun in the 1930s and 1940s in Shaanxi. Xi Zhongxun also worked very closely with Xiang Nan in the 1980s.

Although Xiang Nan was removed from his position within nine months of Xi's arrival, Xi Jinping experienced rapid promotions in Fujian. He was promoted to party secretary of Ningde Prefecture in May 1988 and to party secretary of Fuzhou City, the capital of Fujian, in May 1990. He was further inducted in the Standing Committee of the Fujian Provincial Party Committee in September 1993 and was made deputy party secretary of Fujian in October 1995.

Xi's rapid promotions were not without merit. He was responsible for drafting a well-received fifteen-year strategic plan for economic and social development in Xiamen, took tough measures against corruption in Ningde, and promoted government efficiency and cross-Strait economic cooperation in Fuzhou.

But his promotions have been attributed more to his family connections than to his personal achievements. At the Fifteenth National Party Congress of the CCP in September 1997, Xi barely made it to the CCP Central Committee as an alternate member: out of 151 alternate members, he was ranked last. It is reported that Xi, in fact, had failed to be elected to the Central Committee, but his name was added to the list of alternate members because he was to be groomed for future leadership positions.

Although Xi was not directly implicated in various corruption scandals in Fujian, some of his successors in Ningde, such as Jing Fusheng (b. 1952); his partners in Fuzhou such as Hong Yongshi (b. 1942) and Jin Nengchou (b. 1941); and his superiors in Fujian, such as Jia Qinglin (b. 1940), were either implicated in major corruption scandals or faced disciplinary actions because of corruption.

Xi's career, however, was not adversely affected. He was appointed as acting governor of Fujian in August 1999 and became governor in January 2000. In the meantime, he also managed to beef up his academic credentials by acquiring a doctor of law degree from Tsinghua University without a requisite master's degree and with a dissertation of suspicious originality. He was transferred to Zhejiang in October 2002 as acting governor and was promoted to party secretary of Zhejiang in November 2002, a few days after he had become a full member of the Sixteenth Central Committee.

Racing to the Top

During his tenure in Zhejiang, Xi became one of rising political stars in China. Along with Henan party secretary *Lǐ Kèqiáng 李克强 (b. 1955), Jiangsu party secretary Lǐ Yuáncháo 李源潮 (b. 1950), and commerce minister *Bó Xīlái 薄熙来 (b. 1949), Xi was in a race to the top. He articulated a new development strategy based on *Hú Jǐntāo's 胡锦涛 scientific outlook on development and promoted the "Zhejiang experience" as a role model for other provinces.

After Chén Liángyǔ 陈良宇 (b. 1946) was dismissed as party secretary of Shanghai for a social security fund scandal in September 2006, Xi was transferred to Shanghai in March 2007 as the party chief of this metropolis. Seven months later, he was made a Politburo Standing Committee member at the Seventeenth Party Congress. Most significantly, his name was listed ahead of Li Keqiang's in the ranking of the Politburo Standing Committee members.

In subsequent years, Xi took over as president of the Central Party School in December 2007, was elected vice president of the PRC in March 2008, and was installed into the Central Military Commission in October 2010.

In a year of leadership transition with dramatic twists and turns, and when another rising political star, Bo Xilai, was dismissed from his position as party chief in Chongqing and then from the Politburo, Xi's succession was not affected. He moved on to succeed Hu Jintao as general secretary of the CCP and chairman of the Central Military Commission both on the same day, 15 November 2012.

A Game Changer

A politician with no particularly impressive track record as an effective leader in his career of thirty years, Xi has surprised many observers as a leader of strong personality and great power. Within two years, he accumulated more titles than all of his predecessors except for Huá Guófēng 华国锋 (1921–2008), Mao Zedong's designated successor who was both party chairman and premier from 1976 to 1980.

In addition to general secretary of the party, chairman of the Central Military Commission, and president of the People's Republic of China, Xi also became chairman of the National Security Commission, head of the Leading Small Group for Comprehensive Deepening Reform, head of the Leading Small Group on Internet Security and Informatization, and head of the Leading Small Group for Deepening Reform on National Defense and the Military.

Xi also promoted his personality cult in the military and at large. His instructions to the military were ordered to be hung on the wall of the meeting rooms of the People's Liberation Army units, along with those of other great leaders of the Central Military Commission such as Mao Zedong, Deng Xiaoping, *Jiāng Zémín 江泽民 (b. 1926), and Hu Jintao. Military officers were organized to study Xi's speeches and to pledge loyalty to Chairman Xi as the commander-in-chief. The party propaganda machine was employed to project another new great leader, following Mao Zedong and Deng Xiaoping. The number of times Xi's name was mentioned in the *People's Daily*, the mouthpiece of the CCP, is more than that of another other leader during the same time period, except for Mao Zedong.

He has articulated a slogan of the China Dream as his signature ideology in order to turn China into a strong and prosperous country. He has also introduced a series of reform measures in all aspects of China's economic and social life.

With a sweeping anti-corruption campaign, Xi is creating fear among party officials and military officers. By October 2014, fifty officials with a vice-ministerial rank and above had been placed under investigation. In particular, Xi broke the rule of not taking down any member of the Politburo Standing Committee for corruption and investigated the case of *Zhōu Yǒngkāng 周永康 (b. 1942), a former Politburo Standing Committee member in charge of the public security apparatus. He also had General Xu Caihou, former vice chairman of the Central Military Commission and Politburo member, expelled from the party.

In his foreign policy, Xi ignored Deng Xiaoping's advice on keeping a low profile and began to assert China's interests in international affairs. He surprised the United States, Japan, and South Korea with the introduction of an air defense identification zone over the East China Sea, which has areas overlapping with similar zones of Japan and

Besides the many national issues that Xi Jinping is dealing with, maintaining international relations is still an important responsibility. Here, Xi welcomes the president of Mexico, Enrique Peña Nieto, during his visit to Sanya, Hainan Island (2013). Photo by Enrique Peña Nieto.

习近平

South Korea. He played tough over territorial issues with the Philippines and Vietnam, frightening Southeast Asian countries. He also introduced a Monroe Doctrine in Asia by claiming that Asians could deal with their own security issues without interference from others (in particular, the United States).

In the meantime, he has also tried to soothe China's neighbors by offering economic incentives through an economic outreach program known as the "Silk Road Economic Belt" or "Maritime Silk Road of the Twenty-first Century" (Yīdài yīlù 一带一路, lit. "one belt, one road").

With China's rise, Xi's international stature is also increasing. Hopefully, during his tenure of ten years, he will make some difference in creating not only a clean government but also a clean environment, with China becoming a responsible stakeholder in world affairs.

Xi had a short marriage to Kē Línglíng 柯玲玲, daughter of Kē Huā 柯华 (b. 1915), China's ambassador to Britain from 1978 to 1983. He is currently married to Péng Lìyuán 彭丽媛 (b. 1962), a famous singer in the People's Liberation Army. They have a daughter, Xí Míngzé 习明泽 (b. 1992), who studies at Harvard University under a different name.

Xi has been listed as one of the "100 Most Influential People in the World" by *Time* Magazine since 2011.

Zhiyue BO
New Zealand Contemporary China Research Centre

Further Reading

Albert, Melissa. (2013). Xi Jinping. In *Encyclopaedia Britannica*. Retrieved March 11, 2015, from http://www.britannica.com/EBchecked/topic/1490336/Xi-Jinping

Bo Zhiyue. (2014). *China's elite politics: Governance and democratization* (vol. 19). Singapore: World Scientific.

Brown, Kerry. (2014). *The new emperors: Power and the princelings in China*. London: I. B.Tauris.

Callahan, William A. (2013). *China dreams: 20 visions of the future*. Oxford, UK: Oxford University Press.

ChinaVitae. (n.d.). Xi Jinping. Retrieved March 11, 2015, from http://www.chinavitae.com/biography/Xi_Jinping|303

Kuhn, Robert Lawrence. (2011). *How China's leaders think: The inside story of China's past, current and future leaders*. Singapore: John Wiley & Sons.

Li Taohua 李涛华, & Hu Lili 胡丽丽. (2013). *Xi Jinping dazhuan* 习近平大传 [A biography of Xi Jinping]. Deer Park, NY: Mirror Books.

Song Yuwu. (2013). Xi Jinping. In Song Yuwu (Ed.), *Biographical dictionary of the People's Republic of China* (pp. 334–335). Jefferson, NC: McFarland.

Wu Ming 吴鸣. (2010). *Zhongguo xinlingxiu Xi Jinping zhuan* 中国新领袖习近平传 [A biography of China's new leader Xi Jinping]. Hong Kong: Xianggang Wenhua Yishu Chubanshe.

Zheng Yongnian, & Gore, Lance L. P. (Eds.). (2014). *China entering the Xi Jinping Era*. London: Routledge.

♂ Xú Bīng 徐冰

b. 1955—Internationally acclaimed visual artist

Summary

Xu Bing is a visual artist whose work combines techniques and ideas characteristic of Westernized modernist and postmodernist art with aspects of traditional Chinese cultural practice. His work is widely regarded as a modernizing innovation within China and has been celebrated internationally as exemplary of globalized contemporary art. As an artist and teacher, he has also made significant contributions to the development of art in the People's Republic of China during the post-Mao period.

Xu Bing was born in Chongqing in 1955. Though his family has historical associations with the city Wenling, in Zhejiang Province, Xu spent much of his childhood in Beijing. Like many of his generation within the People's Republic of China (PRC), during the Cultural Revolution (1966–1976) Xu was "sent down" to the countryside to experience materially impoverished peasant life, spending more than two years in northern China as a farm laborer between 1974 and 1977. While in the countryside he made drawings, established amateur art groups, and organized cultural events.

Training and Early Career in China

Following the end of the Cultural Revolution, Xu was among the first generation of students selected to enroll at the recently reopened Central Academy of Fine Arts (CAFA) in Beijing, entering the department of printmaking there in 1977. While a student at the academy, Xu trained initially in the socialist-realist style of the Maoist period, though later he developed a more expressive and individualistic approach to image making. Xu received his bachelor's degree in printmaking from CAFA in 1981 and then joined the academy as an instructor. At this time, Xu's early work as a printmaker was shown in Europe, North

America, and Asia. His work also entered the collection of the British Library in London. Xu enrolled as a graduate student at CAFA in 1984, receiving his master's degree in fine art in 1987 after producing a 100,000-word dissertation on the teaching of drawing.

Shortly after graduating in 1987, Xu began his first major internationally recognized work, *Book from the Sky* (*Tiān shū* 天书). For this work he would eventually produce a series of four thousand hand-carved wood blocks, each inscribed with an invented and unintelligible "Mandarin Chinese" character. These woodblocks were used to print numerous volumes and scrolls that were displayed as a large-scale museum/gallery installation placed on the floor and suspended from the ceiling. The idiomatic meaning of the title *Book from the Sky* in traditional Chinese—天書—is suggestive of an alien and incomprehensible system of writing, one that has "fallen from the sky." The first completed section of *Book from the Sky* was shown at an exhibition of his work staged at the China National Museum of Fine Arts in Beijing (now the National Art Museum of China) in 1988. This exhibition attracted significant attention both in China and internationally. In 1988 Xu took up a position as a visiting artist at the Academy of Fine Arts in Paris.

Book from the Sky and other similar text-based works by Xu can be interpreted (like many other contemporary art works) as suspending the notion of authoritative meaning by demonstrating the constant openness of language to shifts in cultural and historical context and new meanings arising in relation to those shifts. Xu's "deconstructivist" approach to linguistic meaning can be further understood within the specific context of the PRC as a resistance to governmental authoritarianism (Erickson 2001; Silbergeld 2006), including the nationwide imposition of simplified Chinese (*pǔtōnghuà* 普通话) by the Chinese Communist Party (CCP) during the 1950s and the ideological entanglement of imagery and text throughout the Maoist period—in particular during the early years of the Cultural Revolution—as part of the dissemination of state propaganda.

In 1989 Xu participated in China/Avant-Garde, a major retrospective of contemporary art produced in China during the 1980s, staged at the China National Museum of Fine Arts shortly before the Tiananmen protests of the same year. The exhibition, which included a highly diverse array of works from across China associated with the avant-garde artistic movement known as the 1985 New Wave (Bāwǔ xīncháo měishù yùndòng 八五新潮美术运动), became a focus for controversy after an unscheduled performance involved the firing of a gunshot within the museum and then anonymous bomb threats, which led to its permanent closure by city authorities.

During the following year, Xu began work on another major project,

Ghosts Pounding the Wall (*Guǐ dǎ qiáng* 鬼打墙). This site-related installation, whose initial making took place from 18 May to 10 June 1990, involved collaboration between art students and local farmers on the production of an immense 32- by-15-meter, twenty-nine-part ink-on-rice-paper frottage (i.e., rubbing) of the Jinshanling section of the Great Wall in Hebei Province, north of Beijing. It is possible to interpret *Ghost Pounding the Wall* as a monumental satire on the CCP's use of iconic symbols of Chinese tradition to gloss over the increasingly unsettling effects of *Dèng Xiǎopíng's 邓小平 (1904–1997) modernizing policy of Opening and Reform. This reading is encapsulated by the art historian and curator Wu Hung's description of the work as a "counter-monument" (Wu 2008, 18). The subject matter and immense scale of *Ghosts Pounding the Wall* also resonates critically with the political isolationism in China before and during the Maoist period, as well as invoking the Confucian aesthetic *dà* 大 (literally, big or vast) as part of the moral supplication to power seen throughout China's imperial and post-imperial histories. With respect to the latter, it is possible to view the monumentality of Xu's work as a continuation of as well as a critical breaking with China's authoritarian aesthetic traditions.

---

*People marked with an asterisk have entries in this dictionary.

International Career

As part of the conservative crackdown on culture that took place in the wake of the Tiananmen protests, Xu's work was subject to strong criticism within the PRC as a perceived focus for anti-CCP and even anti-patriotic sentiment. In the face of this criticism and renewed governmental restrictions on freedom of self-expression, in 1990 Xu, like many other artists in mainland China, decided to leave for the United States, taking up an invitation to be an honorary fellow at the University of Wisconsin–Madison. From 1990 to 1991, Xu held his first exhibition in the United States at the university's Elvehjem Museum of Art (now the Chazen Museum of Art). This exhibition included versions of the installations *Book from the Sky* and *Ghosts Pounding the Wall*.

In 1992 Xu moved briefly to Vermillion, South Dakota, where he studied Western bookbinding and papermaking techniques. The following year he relocated to the East Village in New York City, exhibiting work at the 45th Venice Biennale before returning temporarily to Beijing. There Xu worked on *Case Study of Transference* (*Yīge zhuǎnhuàn ànlì de yánjiū*一个转换案例的研究), a performance work recorded on video involving two pigs, a sow and a boar—the former inscribed with Chinese characters and the latter, romanized letters—whose indifference to their audience and violent mating stirred a highly emotional

Xu Bing's artwork named *Phoenix* is made completely of scraps from urban construction sites in China. The male phoenix is 27 meters long, and the female 100 meters. In 2014–2015, the installation was on display in the Cathedral Church of St. John the Divine (New York). Photo by Bosc d'Anjou.

response among viewers. This work can be interpreted as an extension of Xu's apparently deconstructivist approach to the relationship between words and meaning in the context of cultural identity and issues of post-colonialism. In particular, he examines this issue as it relates to the dominance of Western discourses and cultural models over Eastern ones in the twentieth century.

As such, Xu's work has been readily assimilated by post-colonialist discourses prevalent within the Westernized art world since the 1990s. The strong identification of Xu's work throughout the 1980s and 1990s with an often exceptionalist Chinese cultural tradition, however, suggests a problematic divergence from the residual universalism of such internationalist thinking in a way that prefigures similarly resistant discourses and art works presently associated with scholarly uses of the term *contemporaneity* (e.g., Smith, Enwezor, and Condee 2008).

In 1994 Xu exhibited a major new work, *Square Word Calligraphy* (*Yīngwén fāngkuàizì shūfǎ rùmén* 英文方块字书法入

门), at the Reina Sofia Museum of Art in Spain. *Square Word Calligraphy* incorporates romanized letters written in a characteristically Chinese calligraphic manner that are meaningless to Mandarin Chinese speakers. Xu titled this approach "New English Calligraphy," conducting a series of public classes on how to write the characters.

Since the late 1990s Xu has participated in a series of high-profile international exhibitions, including shows at the Ludwig and Bonn Museums of Art in Germany and at the Museum of Modern Art (MoMA), New York, in 1999; at the then newly established Chinese Arts Centre in Manchester, United Kingdom, in 2003; at the National Museum for East-Asian Art in Berlin in 2004; and at the Metropolitan Museum of Art, New York, in 2007. Xu has also received numerous honors and prizes, including a MacArthur Foundation Genius Grant, the 14th Fukuoka Asian Culture Prize, an honorary professorship by the Central Academy of Fine Arts in Beijing, and an honorary doctor of humane letters from Columbia University, New York.

Xu was awarded the Artes Mundi Prize for his work *Where Does the Dust Collect Itself?* (*Hé chù ruò chén'āi?* 何处若尘埃?), an installation using dust collected by the artist in New York City the day after the 11 September 2001 attack on the World Trade Center. Inscribed in a layer of dust spread on the gallery floor were words taken from a Chan Buddhist poem written by the Sixth Patriarch of Chan Buddhism in China, Huìnéng 惠能 (638–713 CE): "As there is nothing from the first, where does the dust itself collect?" Like many of Xu's other works, *Where Does the Dust Collect Itself?* can be understood to invite differing cultural perspectives, giving rise to what might be seen in this instance as an unresolved shuttling between materialist and spiritual responses to transnational conflict and its resulting trauma.

In 2007, Xu was named vice president of CAFA by the PRC's Ministry of Education. Since his appointment, Xu has set aside any conspicuous critique of governmental authority in the PRC to make works that engage with larger international issues such as global warming and urbanization. These works include *Forest Project* (*Mù, lín, sēn jìhuà* 木, 林, 森计划), which supported transfers of funding from developed countries to Kenya to use for the reversal of deforestation. They also include *The Phoenix* (*Fènghuáng* 凤凰), an assemblage of construction-site debris initially commissioned for the World Financial Center in Beijing, although *The Phoenix* was eventually rejected by the World Financial Center. It was exhibited, instead, outside the Today Art Museum in Beijing before being shown at the Shanghai Expo in 2010, and then at the Cathedral of Saint John the Divine in New York City in 2014.

Paul GLADSTON
University of Nottingham

Further Reading

Borysevicz, Mathieu. (Ed.). (2014). *The book about Xu Bing's* Book from the Ground. Cambridge, MA: MIT Press.

Erickson, Britta. (2001). *The art of Xu Bing: Words without meaning, meaning without words.* Washington DC: Freer Gallery of Art and Arthur M. Sackler Gallery.

Silbergeld, Jerome. (Ed.). (2006). *Persistence-transformation: Text as image in the art of Xu Bing.* Princeton, NJ: Princeton University Press.

Smith, Terry; Enwezor, Okwui; & Condee, Nancy. (Eds.). (2008). *Antinomies of art and culture: Modernity, postmodernity, contemporaneity.* Durham, NC: Duke University Press.

Spears, Katherine. (Ed.). (2009). *Tianshu: Passages in the making of a book.* London: Bernard Quaritch.

Wu Hung. (2008). *Making history: Wu Hung on contemporary art* (pp. 11–28). Hong Kong: Timezone 8.

Xu Bing. (2014). *Book from the ground: From point to point.* Cambridge, MA: MIT Press.

• Xú Bīng •

♀ Yáng Jiàng 杨绛

b. 1911—Playwright, translator, essayist, intellectual, and wife of Qian Zhongshu

Alternate names: b. Yáng Jìkāng 杨季康; trad. 楊絳

Summary

Best known for her translation of Cervantes's *Don Quixote* and for her memoirs detailing the hardships she and her husband, the famed writer Qian Zhongshu, suffered during the Cultural Revolution, Yang Jiang is one of China's most important literary figures from the twentieth century. Long-lived and the author of comedic plays, a novel, and many essays, Yang wrote her latest collection well into her nineties.

Yang Jiang is one of the most important Chinese female writers of the twentieth century, a figure whose life typifies the journey that intellectuals had to travel over this period. Her one novel and her memoirs are powerful but subtle works, and while her reputation is overshadowed by that of the great work of her husband Qián Zhōngshū 钱锺书 (1910–1998), in her own right as translator, playwright, and author her achievements are significant ones.

Education and Early Career

Born in the final months of the Qīng 清 dynasty (1644–1911/12) in Wuxi, Jiangsu Province, Yang graduated from Soochow University in 1932. It was while at Tsinghua University in Beijing that she met her future husband, the writer and intellectual Qian Zhongshu, also a student there. Married in 1935, they traveled to Europe where they both studied in the United Kingdom, she in London and Qian at Oxford. It was also in Europe that their daughter Qián Yuàn 钱瑗 was born. After their return to China in 1938, Yang Jiang lived in Shanghai while her husband taught at Southwestern University, which moved around the interior of the country due to the war. During this time, she served as a headmistress of the girls' high school she herself had attended, and earned extra money as a playwright, producing comedies that consciously ignored the war and focused instead on "homely" issues such as marriage (Lioi 2014, 107). After the founding of the People's Republic of China, both Yang and Qian taught English literature back at Tsinghua University in Beijing.

With the intensification of the Maoist-inspired campaigns against intellectuals from the late 1950s, Yang and her husband experienced increasing hardship. Their background was one that drew immediate suspicion, both because of their strong intellectual identity and also because of their years spent abroad. This period is alluded to in *Baptism* (*Xǐzǎo* 洗澡), a novel published in 1988 and only translated into English twenty years later. As with the protagonists of the novel, Qian and Yang taught at the newly established Chinese Academy of Social Sciences in Beijing, beginning in 1953. Exposed to a number of rectification campaigns, they were able to survive into the 1960s. But with the onset of the Cultural Revolution, the toughest period of their lives began.

Yang herself produced an account of this era in her brief, but deeply moving *A Cadre Life in Six Chapters* (*Gànxiào liù jì* 幹校六記; also translated as *Six Chapters from My Life "Downunder"*). Issued in 1981 in Hong Kong, it was translated not once but twice soon after publication, by China scholars and celebrated translators Geremie Barmé and Howard Goldblatt. Yang and her family were sent to one of the "May 7 Cadre Schools" in the central province of Henan. These institutions, named after the date on which they had been set up by a central directive from the Cultural Revolution Leading Group,

were places of hard labor and detention, the regime of which is described with sparse prose in Yang's account. One of the most moving passages of the book is when the man evidently based on her husband is inspected by a doctor who declares that the patient has the same name as the great author. The doctor is evidently unable to reconcile the illustrious writer of *Cities Besieged* (*Wéichéng* 围城), Qian's popular classic from 1946, with the pathetic, malnourished figure before him. In her later memoir, *We Three* (*Wǒmen sā* 我們仨), Yang describes the deep suffering that her beloved daughter also endured in this period, reduced to cleaning out latrines and working in the fields. *Six Chapters* arguably remains one of the few enduring literary works to come out of the ten years of the Cultural Revolution. In an essay on the piece from 1983, the sinologist Simon Leys stated that "Paradoxically, [Six Chapters] is also heavy with all that it does not say" (Yang 1989, 3). The meaning lies between the lines.

Life after the Cultural Revolution

Returning to Beijing in 1972, the family settled at the Chinese Academy of Social Sciences. Yang herself worked on the first translation of Miguel de Cervantes's *Don Quixote* from Spanish to Chinese, which was issued in eight volumes over the ensuing decade. In the 1980s she produced her sole novel, *Baptism*.

The death of her daughter in 1997 and her husband in 1998 were immense blows to her in her eighties. The memoir *We Three*, issued in 2002 in Chinese, testifies in its title to how close she was to "Ah Yuan" (her affectionate nickname for her daughter). A popular book among the Chinese reading public, it went through several reprints in the first year of print. The first five chapters were in fact written by Yang's daughter. Five years later, at the age of ninety-six, Yang produced her latest work, *Reaching the Brink of Life* (*Zǒu dào rénshēng biān shàng* 走到人生邊上). This too had shades of the influence of her husband, being a disparate memoir similar in style and tone to a work he had produced in the 1970s and into the 1980s, the epic five-volume *Limited Views* (lit. *Pipe-Awl Collection, Guǎn zhuī biān* 管锥编).

Yang Jiang continues to live, well into her eleventh decade, in the same Beijing house she has occupied since 1976.

Kerry BROWN
Lau China Institute, King's College

Further Reading

Armory, Judith, & Shihua Yao. (2007). Yang Jiang and *Baptism*. In Yang Jiang, *Baptism* (pp. vi–xii). Hong Kong: Hong Kong University Press.

Goldblatt, Howard. (1980). The Cultural Revolution and beyond: Yang Jiang's *Six Chapters from My Life "Down Under."* Modern Chinese Literature Newsletter. 6(2), 1–11.

Gewurtz, Margo. (2008). The afterlife of memory in China: Yang Jiang's Cultural Revolution memoir. *ARIEL, Life Writing in International Contexts Issue*, 39(1–2), 29–45.

Lioi, Tiziana. (2014). 100 years of Qian Zhongshu and Yang Jiang: A centennial perspective. In Ikuko Sagiyama & Valentina Pedone (Eds.), *Perspectives on East Asia* (pp. 103–116). Florence, Italy: Firenze University Press.

Rea, Christopher G. (2011a). Yang Jiang's 楊絳 Conspicuous inconspicuousness. A centenary writer in China's "Prosperous Age." *China Heritage Quarterly*. Retrieved March 17, 2015, from http://www.chinaheritagequarterly.org/features.php?searchterm=026_yangjiang.inc&issue=026

Rea, Christopher G. (2011b). "To thine own self be true": One hundred years of Yang Jiang. *Renditions*, 76, 7–14.

Renditions. (2011). Special edition on Yang Jiang. *Renditions, 76.* Research Centre for Translation: The Chinese University of Hong Kong.

Swislocki, Mark. (2002). Yang Jiang. In Lily Xiaohong Lee (Ed.), *Biographical dictionary of Chinese women: The twentieth century* (pp. 618–622). Armonk, NY: M. E. Sharpe.

Yang Jiang. (1989). *Lost in the crowd: A Cultural Revolution memoir* (Geremie Barmé, Trans.). Melbourne: McPhee Gribble.

Yang Jiang. (2007). *Baptism* (Judith Armory & Shihua Yao, Trans.). Hong Kong: Hong Kong University Press. (Original work published 1988)

☿ Yáng Shàngkūn 杨尚昆

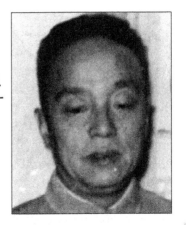

1907–1998—Politician and military general

Alternate name: trad. 楊尚昆

Summary

Though his position in the Chinese Communist Party was often tenuous due to factions within the Party jockeying for power, Yang Shangkun enjoyed considerable power and influence. Yang was one of the most important veteran leaders and military generals during the 1980s and early 1990s, and one of the key supporters of Deng Xiaoping and his policies. Yang also played a leading role in the crackdown on pro-democracy demonstrators in Tiananmen Square in 1989.

Yang Shangkun, former chairman of the People's Republic of China (PRC) and vice chairman and secretary general of the Central Military Commission (CMC), was a powerful military leader during the 1980s who played a crucial role in the crackdown on pro-democracy demonstrators in Tiananmen Square in 1989. Though he held many leadership positions in the Chinese Communist Party (CCP), he frequently found himself in jeopardy due to factions within the Party jockeying for power. Yang retired from the position of chairman in March 1993 after he was forced to hand over his leading military position as the vice chairman of the CMC in October 1992 amid fears that he had too much power and influence in the People's Liberation Army (PLA).

Early Years

Born on 5 July 1907 to a land-owning family in Sichuan, Yang was influenced politically by his father, Yáng Huáiqīng 杨淮清, a local gentry and a Communist sympathizer, and his older brother, Yang Shangshu (style name Yáng Yàngōng 杨闇公), one of the founders of the Chinese Communist movement in Sichuan. Yang Shangkun joined the Communist Youth League in 1925 and became a Communist member one year later. In November 1927, after six months of study at Shanghai University, he was sent to Moscow, where he enrolled in Sun Yat-sen University, a training ground for Communist cadres founded and controlled by the CCP.

During his study in Moscow, Yang emerged as a member of the 28 Bolsheviks, a group of bright leftist Chinese students who took an anti-Trotsky stance and who supported Pavel Mif, rector of Sun Yat-sen University (Terrill 1999, 138–139). The 28 Bolsheviks later became an influential pro-Stalin political faction within the CCP, which controlled party leadership during the early 1930s. After returning to China, Yang worked underground in Shanghai for the CCP from 1931 to 1932 and was appointed by the CCP leadership to lead the Propaganda Department in the All-China General Labor Union and later the CCP Jiangsu Party Committee.

Following a series of successful but bloody campaigns of suppression launched by the Nationalist Party against the CCP in Nationalist-controlled areas during the early 1930s, the CCP leadership was forced to move from Nationalist-controlled Shanghai to the Jiangxi base areas. Yang was also transferred to there, and he was appointed a key associate of Zhāng Wéntiān 张闻天, a leading figure of the 28 Bolsheviks who led the CCP Propaganda Department and was a member of the Politburo Standing Committee.

Yang played an essential role as vanguard against the so-called Luo Ming line, a campaign that attacked Máo

Yang Shangkun as a young man in 1940.

Zédōng 毛泽东 (1893–1976) and Mao's supporters for their views. Yang's experience in Moscow and his early career ties with the Comintern and the returned students, however, played a role in Yang's failure to win Mao's trust throughout Yang's career—especially when the CCP leadership jockeyed for power. This was the case, for example, during the Cultural Revolution (1966–1976) in which Mao launched a crusade of mass violence against the CCP bureaucracy led by Liú Shàoqí 刘少奇 (1898–1969) and *Dèng Xiǎopíng 邓小平 (1904–1997). On the eve of the Cultural Revolution, Yang Shangkun was the first high-ranking leader to be purged by Mao, due not only to his ties to Liu and Deng but also to his proximity to core CCP secrets and his leadership role over

*People marked with an asterisk have entries in this dictionary.

the elite security forces, including the Central Guard Bureau and the Central Guard Regiment (Unit 8341).

Military Credentials and Rise in Party Central Bureau

Yang's career benefited from the backing he received from politician and diplomat Zhōu Ēnlái 周恩来 (1898–1976). Although Zhou and Yang got to know each other in 1928 when Zhou visited Moscow, their close ties were not formally established until February 1931 when Yang returned to China from the Soviet Union. After Zhou was appointed party secretary of the CCP Jiangxi Central Bureau to lead the Jiangxi base areas, he asked for Yang's transfer in early 1933 from Shanghai to Jiangxi and appointed Yang deputy director of the General Political Department under the CMC and director of the Political Department under the First Front Army in June 1933. Perhaps the most significant military position that Yang held under Zhou's leadership was that of political commissar of the Third Army Group, led by Commander Péng Déhuái 彭德怀 (1898–1974) in the winter of 1933 (Yang 2001c, 35). Like the First Army Group led by Lín Biāo 林彪 (1907–1971) and Niè Róngzhēn 聂荣臻, the Third Army Group headed by Peng and Yang played an indispensable role in safeguarding the CCP and its Red Army from being destroyed by the Nationalist armies during the Long March (1934–1935) when Chinese Communists marched from Jiangxi Province in southeast China to Shaanxi Province in northwest China.

At the famous Zunyi Conference, an enlarged meeting of the Politburo of the CCP during the Long March held in January 1935, the party leadership resolved to establish Zhou Enlai's authority in leading the Red Army and giving him the final say in any military decisions after abolishing the so-called Three Corps—Bo Gu (a leading figure of the party's pro-Russian faction), Otto Braun (the Comintern-appointed German advisor), and Zhou Enlai—as commanders of the Red Army. Mao was accepted into the Politburo and appointed Zhou's "helper" in executing military decisions. Yang supported these resolutions (Yang 2001a, 120). It was the Zunyi Conference that became the crucial first step in establishing Mao's leadership as he slowly moved to take over military leadership from Zhou Enlai in its aftermath.

With the outbreak of the Second Sino-Japanese War (1937–1945), Yang was appointed deputy secretary of the CCP Northern Bureau and became a key associate of Liu Shaoqi, party secretary of the CCP Northern Bureau. From November 1938 to February 1942, Yang replaced Liu as party secretary of the CCP Northern Bureau, which commanded the party organizations in northern China and supported and cooperated with the CCP-controlled Eighth Route Army against the Japanese

Army. Yang co-led the well-known Hundred Regiments Campaign, one of the largest offensive campaigns conducted by the CCP against Japanese forces.

Career in the Central Party Organization

Yang was a target in the 1942–1943 Yan'an rectification campaign, in which Mao supporters attacked the so-called dogmatism led by Wáng Míng 王明 (1904–1974) and empiricism headed by Zhou Enlai (Teiwes 1990, 205). As a member of the 28 Bolsheviks, Yang was accused of being a key member of the "dogmatism faction" and was forced to make "self-criticisms" at numerous party meetings (Gao 2000, 617; Yang 2001a, 211–213). Benefiting from his intimate associations with the party central organization and army, as well as the profound personal ties he had with high-ranking leaders including Liu Shaoqi, Zhou Enlai, Zhū Dé 朱德 (1886–1976), *Chén Yún 陈云 (1905–1995), Liú Bóchéng 刘伯承 (1892–1986), and Deng Xiaoping, Yang survived the Yan'an rectification campaign and his political status was reaffirmed. Yang particularly benefited from Zhou Enlai retaining his leadership positions and influence after Mao was compelled to give up his attacks against him, partially due to the strong disapproval from the Comintern and many high-ranking party and army leaders (and partially due to Zhou's willingness to

comply with Mao's leadership), a sign indicating that Zhou was no longer a political rival and competitor of Mao (Gao Wenqian 2003, 75–84). Mao's distrust of Yang remained, however, and Yang's promotion in the CCP slowed significantly in later years.

In 1944, Yang was appointed secretary general of the party's military commission, which assisted Zhou Enlai in conducting the daily administrative work of the CCP and the People's Liberation Army (PLA). A year later Yang became director of the CCP Central Committee's General Office, a post he maintained for twenty-one years (official appointment took place in 1948) and one that cemented his ties to Liu Shaoqi, Zhou Enlai, and Deng Xiaoping (who became the party's secretary general in 1956). Owing to Yang's excellent skills in coordinating the relationships among the CCP central organizations, the government departments, the PLA, and high-ranking leaders, he quickly became highly regarded by the top leadership including Mao.

Yang remained in charge of the CCP Central Committee's General Office following the defeat of Nationalist forces and the founding of the PRC in 1949, giving him a degree of direct control over deciding CCP affairs. Mao's attempt to gain personal control over the General Office began at the end of 1964 when Yang was sent to Shaanxi for the Socialist Education Movement. Yang's authority and influence were further undermined

杨尚昆

Yang Shangkun (far right) and Mao Zedong during a visit from the prominent Soviet politician Nikolai Bulganin (third from right) in 1957. On the far left is Soong Ching-ling, the second wife of Sun Yat-sen.

after the Party Committee of the General Office, headed by Wang Dongxing, Mao's longtime bodyguard, was established in September 1965 (Yang 2001b, 668). The dismissal of Yang in November 1965 and his later imprisonment in December 1966 was undoubtedly part of Mao's strategy to secure control over the party's high-ranking leaders through control over the General Office as well as the use of the elite security forces. Once Yang was no longer a threat, Wang Dongxing moved quickly to monopolize the authority of the General Office for Mao. In May 1966, Yang was transferred from Guangdong to Shanxi, where he was demoted to take a position as a prefecture-level deputy party secretary in Linfen. In December 1966, at the onset of the Cultural Revolution (1966–1976), Yang was jailed and transferred to Beijing where he was imprisoned for nine years until June 1975, when he was sent back to Linfen.

Reform Era: A Key Figure Among Veteran Leaders

Yang was reintegrated into the CCP after Mao died and Deng Xiaoping rose to power in 1978 following a successful effort to seize control of the party leadership from the neo-Maoists headed by Hua Guofeng. As an influential party veteran before the Cultural Revolution and as a close associate and a longtime personal friend of Deng Xiaoping, Yang was recalled to Beijing from Shanxi and was appointed the second CCP secretary and vice-chairman of the Guangdong Provincial Revolutionary Committee from January 1979 to October 1980. Yang was then promoted to secretary general of the CMC in July 1981, and a year later was appointed a member of the Polit-buro and vice chairman of the CMC. Deng Xiaoping gradually focused more attention on party leadership, effectively allowing room for Yang to consolidate military power and authority. In 1988, Yang was elected president of the PRC.

In 1989, Yang played a crucial role in implementing the CCP's decision to use military force to harshly suppress pro-democracy student demonstrations in Beijing's Tiananmen Square. At first Yang agreed with the sympathetic approach promoted by *Zhào Zǐyáng 赵紫阳 (1919–2005) in handling the crisis, but he quickly changed his position to ally himself with the hard-liners after Deng decided to crack down on the student demonstrations by using force (Xu 1993, 373–374, 377).

After 1989, Yang's influence in the PLA was bolstered due to the army's successful role in cracking down on the student demonstrations. Additionally, Yang's power in controlling the military was greatly expanded after the PLA stood firmly behind Deng Xiaoping by announcing that it would "escort and protect" (*bǎojià hùháng* 保驾护航) economic reforms during Deng's "Southern Tour" 南巡 in 1992 to reassert his economic agenda. By this time Deng had officially retired but was still regarded as the most prominent leader in the CCP and in China. He had openly expressed his disappointment with *Jiāng Zémín 江泽民 (b. 1926), general secretary of the CCP and chairman of the CMC, and Jiang's slow pace in reforming the economy.

Yang and his younger half-brother, Yang Baibing, secretary general of the CMC and director of the PLA General Political Department, arranged a large number of their followers and supporters to take senior military positions and began purging generals from other military factions. This generated resentment among military elders, who accused Yang of attempting to dominate the army and possibly challenge Deng's authority by developing a "Yang family clique."

The measures taken by the Yang brothers to challenge Jiang raised Deng's vigilance about the powerful influence they were acquiring in both the CCP and the PLA. Deng's concern deepened after senior party leaders and senior PLA officers expressed concerns about the Yang brothers' power-building efforts and petitioned Deng to remove Yang Baibing from his military post. While dissatisfied with Jiang, Deng was more concerned that the party leadership would be seized by powerful military generals who might end economic reforms or return purged members like Zhao

Ziyang to redress issues with the 1989 Tiananmen student demonstration. In October 1992, the Fourteenth Party Congress was held in Beijing and the Yang brothers were ordered to hand over their military power to the new CMC headed by Jiang Zemin. Six months later, Yang Shangkun retired from the position of PRC chairman.

Yang's influential role was derived from his extensive experience in very powerful central party organs, long-term service within the leading administrative body of the CCP central organizations, his leading role in the PLA, and his dominance in the central committee's General Office. Yang was one of the most important and influential leaders in China during the 1980s and one of the key supporters of Deng Xiaoping and his reform policies. As one of the "Eight Elders" or (Eight Immortals), a group of elderly members of the CCP who held substantial power during the 1980s and 1990s, Yang was a well-known "open-minded" (*kāimíng* 开明) veteran leader who shared Deng Xiaoping's "cat theory" —"it doesn't matter if a cat is white or black, as long as it catches mice." This modern version of pragmatic rationalism supported freeing China's economic reform from ideological constraints, but maintaining communist rule by adopting a two-pronged capitalism-communism development approach.

Xuezhi GUO
Guilford College

Further Reading

Center for Chinese Research Materials. (1992). *Hongweibing ziliao, xubian* II 红卫兵资料，续编II [Red Guard publications, supplement II] (vol. 8). Oakton, VA: Center for Chinese Research Materials.

Gao Hua. (2000). *Hong taiyang shi zenyang shengqi de—Yan'an zhengfeng de lailong qumo* 红太阳是怎样升起的—延安整风的来龙去脉 [How did the sun rise over Yan'an? A history of the rectification movement]. Hong Kong: The Chinese University of Hong Kong.

Gao Wenqian. (2003). *Wannian Zhou Enlai* 晚年周恩来 [Zhou Enlai's later years]. Hong Kong: Mirror Books.

Terrill, Ross. (1999). *Mao: A biography*. Redwood City, CA: Stanford University Press.

Teiwes, Frederick C. (1990). *Politics at Mao's court: Gao Gang and party factionalism in the early 1950s*. Armonk, NY: M.E. Sharpe Inc.

Xu Jiatun. (1993). *Xu Jiatun xianggang huiyilu* 许家屯香港回忆录 [Xu Jiatun's Hong Kong memoirs] (vol. 2.). Hong Kong: Xianggang lianhe bao youxian gongsi.

Yang Shangkun. (2001a). *Yang Shangkun huiyilu* 杨尚昆回忆录 [Memoirs of Yang Shangkun]. Beijing: Zhongyang wenxian chubanshe.

Yang Shangkun. (2001b). *Yang Shangkun riji* 杨尚昆日记 [Diary of Yang Shangkun] (vol. 2.). Beijing: Zhongyang wenxian chubanshe.

Yang Shangkun. (2001c). *Zhuiyi lingxiu zhangyou tongzhi* 追忆领袖战友同志 [Recollecting leaders, comrade-in-arms, and comrades]. Beijing: Zhongyang wenxian chubanshe.

• Yáng Shàngkūn •

♂ Yáo Míng 姚明

b. 1980—Basketball player who played in the NBA

Summary

The tallest player in the National Basketball Association during his last season, Yao Ming is arguable China's most famous face abroad and is known for playing eight seasons for the Houston Rockets as well as in the Olympics and World Championships. Yao has also acted as an "ambassador" for China and has been featured in many advertising campaigns in China and the United States.

Asked to name a famous current Chinese figure, many people—at least in the United States—would probably name the basketball star Yao Ming. His face is certainly one of the most recognized throughout the world, from advertisements to newspapers to television. For visitors to his native city of Shanghai, he looks out from advertising billboards; he must rank as one of the great modern ambassadors for his home city. He is one of the very few Chinese sports stars who are featured in advertising campaigns outside the country, but he is also someone whose sportsmanship, sense of fair play, and general patriotism have become powerful assets for Chinese "soft power" as it becomes a more global and higher profile country.

Basketball in China

Basketball was introduced to China at the Tianjin Young Men's Christian Association (YMCA) in 1895 and then spread to other cities such as Beijing and Shanghai. China's inaugural "international" game occurred during the 1913 Far East Championship Games in Manila, the Philippines. But it took another twenty years before China competed for the first time in the sport, during the 1936 Olympic Games in Berlin.

Another half century was to pass before basketball began to gain real popularity. It was one of the team sports in which China was to enjoy some of its earliest and best successes, with the Chinese men's basketball team, in particular, dominating. From 1975 to 1983, they won five consecutive Asian Basketball Confederation Championship (renamed as FIBA Asia Championship in 2005) titles. The Chinese women's basketball team, while not as successful, finished third at the 1983 (FIBA) World Championship for women. Despite these successes, it was only in 1995 that the Chinese Basketball Association (CBA) was established.

Early Career

Born in Shanghai on 12 September 1980, Yao Ming came from a family who could be said to have basketball prowess in their genes, literally. His granfather Yáo Xuémíng 姚学明 was exceptionally tall but, unfortunately, not discovered early enough to become a professional basketball player. Yao's mother, Fāng Fèngdì 方凤娣, and father, Yáo Zhìyuán 姚志源, however, were both basketball players, and when they married in 1979, they were recognized as the tallest couple of China, being 1.9 meters and 2 meters tall respectively. Yao's mother captained the national woman's team in the 1970s. Yao himself weighed twice as much as the average Chinese baby when born. Brook Larmer, in his book *Operation Yao Ming: The Chinese Sports Empire, American Big Business, and the Making of an NBA Superstar*, even goes as far as claiming that

Chinese officials had "planned" Yao for the purpose of creating a basketball star, based on the combination genetics of his parents, and they tracked his development from a very early stage. Whether accurate or not, this shows some of the importance China placed, even at this early stage in its opening up to the outside world, in becoming competitive in international sport.

Yao's career certainly started very early; at thirteen he practiced basketball for some ten hours a day. He played for the Shanghai Sharks' first junior team, then its senior team, reaching the Chinese Basketball Association's finals two times (both times, his team was defeated by the Bayi Rockets, from Ningbo, Zhejiang Province). A rivalry over this period developed between Yao and Wáng Zhìzhì 王治郅, a Beijinger who played for the Bayi Rockets and became the first Chinese basketball player to be drafted into the US National Basketball Association (NBA). Later in his career, Yao was to buy the Shanghai Sharks team in 2009, when it was experiencing financial difficulties.

Standing 2.29 meters tall, Yao entered the NBA draft in 2002. He joined the Houston Rockets in 2002 and managed to score his first basket against the Denver Nuggets that same year. During his career, he played in the Olympics three times—in 2000, 2004 and 2008—and also in the FIBA Asian Championships and the 2006 FIBA World Championships.

Yáo Míng •

姚明 •

Yao Ming, standing 2.29 meters tall, makes a slam dunk (2008). Photo by Keith Allison.

In 2007, Yao married Yè Lì 叶莉, a fellow basketball player. Together they have one daughter, Yáo Qìnlěi 姚沁蕾, who was born in 2010 in the United States.

While in Shanghai in 2011, Yao announced his retirement. In the final few years of his professional career, he had suffered from a number of ankle and foot injuries that kept him out of the game. Yao is famous as a Chinese national who has succeeded at one of the most competitive sports in the United States and also as the face of a number of brands, including Nike, Reebok, Visa, McDonalds, and Apple, with which he signed sponsorship deals. He has also supported charity events, in particular during the tragic Sichuan earthquake in 2008, when he gave generously to the relief work. According to former NBA commissioner David Stern,

Yao Ming has been a transformational player and a testament to globalization of our game. His dominant play and endearing demeanor along with his extensive humanitarian efforts have made him an international fan favorite and provided an extraordinary bridge between basketball fans in the United States and China. (Associated Press 2011)

Kerry BROWN
Lau China Institute, King's College

Further Reading

Associated Press. (2011). Chinese great Yao Ming retires from NBA. Retrieved February 18, 2015, from http://www.cbc.ca/sports/basketball/chinese-great-yao-ming-retires-from-nba-1.1029363

Larmer, Brook. (2005). *Operation Yao Ming: The Chinese sports empire, American big business, and the making of an NBA superstar.* New York: Penguin.

Yao Ming, & Bucher, R. (2005). *Yao: A life in two worlds.* Santa Monica, CA: Miamax.

Xiao Chunfei. (2000). *Yao Ming: The road to the NBA.* San Francisco: Long River Press.

Zhang Ling. (2008). Basketball. In Fan Hong, Duncan Mackay & Karen Christensen (Eds.), *China Gold: China's quest for global power and Olympic glory* (pp. 37–40). Great Barrington, MA: Berkshire Publishing Group.

• Yao Ming •

♂ Yè Jiànyīng 叶剑英

1897–1986—Politician and military official

Alternate names: b. Yè Yíwěi 叶宜伟; courtesy name: Cāng bái 沧白; trad. 葉劍英

Summary

One of the ten marshals of the People's Liberation Army, Ye Jianying ultimately served as vice chairman of the Chinese Communist Party. Lacking interest in personal power, his influence lay in his role as an advisor at key junctures in party history, such as when he saved Mao Zedong during the Long March and when he helped Hua Guofeng arrest the Gang of Four and set China on its modernizing course. Towards the end of his life, he served a key role as patriarch during the early post-Mao years.

When Ye Jianying passed away in late October 1986 at the age of eighty-nine, general secretary *Hú Yàobāng 胡耀邦 (1915–1989), delivered the official eulogy, hailing Ye's brilliant career as a founding father of the People's Republic of China (PRC) who had dedicated half a century to the party cause. In less than two months, Hu, formally the number-one official of the Chinese Communist Party (CCP), was ousted by the paramount leader, *Dèng Xiǎopíng 邓小平 (1904–1997). Two years after this dismissal, Hu's own passing triggered the massive student demonstration at Tiananmen Square that ended with the crackdown of 4 June 1989, a defining historical moment that still haunts the Communist regime today. People close to Hu, reflecting on these tragic events, have commented that had Ye Jianying lived just a bit longer, Hu's political skin could have been saved, and the history of this period would have been very different. While the comment justifiably reflects Ye's pivotal role as patriarch during the early post-Mao years, it drastically overstates his influence once Deng emerged as the fiercest "mother-in-law" (*pópo* 婆婆, matriarch ruler) in China's "old man politics" (*lǎorén zhèngzhì* 老人政治) of the 1980s that extended into the 1990s (Gao 2010).

Ye was indeed the king-maker in the months after Mao's death in 1976. Huá

---

*People marked with an asterisk have entries in this dictionary.

Guófēng 华国锋 (1921–2008), though Mao's anointed successor, was faced with insurmountable obstructions from radical leaders, including Mao's wife and others known as the Gang of Four, who were entrusted by Mao to carry on the Cultural Revolution. When Hua decided to deal with the Gang of Four, he needed and secured the full support of the military, with Ye's blessing. Ye was not only a vice chairman of the Party, but also the only marshal, among the surviving four, still in a position to control the gun. In the immediate aftermath of the arrest of the Gang of Four, notwithstanding his absolute seniority, Ye declined Hua's offer to take up the chairmanship, saying modestly that he was merely a soldier and not suited to handling civilian affairs. This gracious gesture reflected Ye's total loyalty to Mao's perceived wish that "I'm entrusting Hua Guofeng to you," as well as his fear that, being the defense minister, his taking the number-one spot could be construed as staging a rightist military coup. Instead, he threw all his weight behind Hua. Ironically, in the political culture of the CCP tradition, wherein the pecking order was decided by seniority and revolutionary status, Ye's proactive promotion of Hua's personal cult raised the ire of many of the other 18,000-plus veterans more senior to Hua, especially Deng and *Chén Yún 陈云 (1905–1995), that, despite little policy difference, led to Hua's eventual demise.

While duly exercising his role as the grand counselor to bolster Hua's leadership, Ye also brought back Deng in 1977, in the hope that the capable statesman, although twice banished from politics by Mao, would show the same loyalty and help Hua to run the ailing country and "bring back order out of chaos." Quickly, by a joint effort in what was called "the New Long March," Hua and Deng began to shake off Mao's shadow and ushered in the new era of reform and opening. By June 1980, however, when Deng activated his long-held plan to topple Chairman Hua, Ye not only could not save his young master, he himself was also kicked upstairs, however ceremoniously. The new party center, now with Deng and Chen Yun being the twin towers of Chinese power politics, rejected his repeated request for resignation. But Ye had to make a tearful self-criticism for his "feudalistic" mentality of emulating the legendary Kong Ming (Zhūgě Liàng 諸葛亮) of the Three Kingdoms period, who went on to serve the young king loyally and selflessly after his lord passed away.

With little lust for power, playing the role of the consigliere, so to speak, was Ye's natural role, and he did it well. Throughout his long career he had been happy to play the second or third fiddle. When Mao conferred ten marshal titles in 1955 to acknowledge the most outstanding lieutenants in a revolutionary struggle that was won in battle, there was speculation that the inclusion of Ye, listed last, was merely to make up the numbers (apparently because of Ye's lack of a track

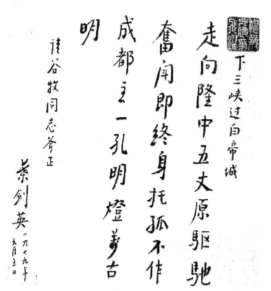

Ye Jianying's poem, written on 5 September 1979, in which he implicitly portrays himself as the modern version of Kong Ming (Zhuge Liang), loyally serving Chairman Hua Guofeng.

record as a brilliant commander on the battlefield). Yet back in September 1935, during the Long March, it was in his position as "principal advisor" (*cānmóuzhǎng* 参谋长) of the Fourth Front Army that Ye was able to intercept a "secret telegram" allegedly containing a mortal threat by Mao's rival Zhāng Guótāo 张国焘 and he warned Mao in time for him to escape. Even twenty years later, Mao remembered Ye's loyalty at that critical juncture and rewarded him with the status of marshal for "saving the Party as well as for saving the Red Army" (Yan 1997–2008). The intended recipient of the telegram, Chén Chānghào 陈昌浩, however, never confirmed its existence, and after Mao's death, the content of this

"confidential telegram" resurfaced as a point of fierce dispute. Marshal Xú Xiàngqián 徐向前, the other alleged recipient of the telegram, declared in 1982 and 1988 (when Ye's political clout had dwindled dramatically and after Ye's passing) that he never saw such a telegram. This episode and Ye's self-assured claim that Mao had entrusted Hua to him, instead of, one may wonder, entrusting his loyal and dear wife Jiang Qing to Ye, the two major turning points in Ye's distinguished long career, may both remain intriguing mysteries.

With this long-standing loyalty to Mao, Ye became one of the very few favorite lieutenants in Mao's court. But unlike the other two favorites, Lín Biāo 林彪 (1907–1971) and Deng Xiaoping, who both displeased Mao and lost power at one point or the other, Ye went largely unscathed. He repeatedly demonstrated his loyalty, as in his active role in the purge of Luó Ruìqīng 罗瑞卿 (chief of staff of the PLA) on the eve of the Cultural Revolution, with one exception being a famous incident in February 1967. With the intention of protecting the military from the interference of radicals, Ye, with Lin Biao's support, fractured his wrist after smashing the table and played the leading role in fiercely confronting the Central Cultural Revolution Small Group led by Mao's wife—an event Mao furiously described as the "February Adverse Current" (against the Cultural Revolution) (Liu 2007, vol. 2, 956, 961). Ye was consequently sidelined for four years. But soon after Lin Biao's downfall, Mao turned to Ye, the sole-remaining trustworthy marshal who did not have his own "mountaintop" (faction) precisely because he was never a field army or army corps commander.

From late 1971, Mao relied heavily on Ye to shake up and rectify a fractured and fragmented military force after the predominance of Lin Biao's Fourth Field Army during the Cultural Revolution period. By the time of Mao's death, Ye had truly become the mainstay of the PLA and reached the pinnacle of his own power and prestige. With Mao's passing, China was a nation at the crossroads, waiting for new leadership. Despite being in his twilight years, Ye, in assisting Hua, left his enduring stamp at this stage of historical transition. His influential role was only cut short by the arrival of the Deng era, as indicated, inter alia, by his inability to veto Deng's determination to "teach Vietnam a lesson," hence the costly border war with Vietnam in February and March 1979. He formally and completely retired in 1985.

In his personal life, Ye was apparently the most cultured among the ten marshals. He composed many classical verses, a rare gift for a career soldier, and was thus sometimes dubbed a "literary general." Even Mao, a poet himself, was impressed and had advised Chén Yí 陈怡, the other poetry-loving marshal, to learn from Ye. On the other hand, he was notoriously dubbed a "flirting marshal." It's not clear whether there is any basis for the rumors about his womanizing, but it does indicate a stark contrast to the puritanical lifestyle of his peers, such as Péng Déhuái 彭德怀 (1898–1974) and Lin Biao. Ye, a handsome man, was surrounded by women throughout his life and reportedly had six marriages and four partners. At the time of his death, seven of them still survived. To avoid public embarrassment, and an unpleasant confrontation between the women, the authorities had to intervene to ensure that none of the widows appeared at Ye's state funeral.

Influence and Legacy

Unlike Deng Xiaoping, who never revisited his birthplace in Sichuan, Ye was perceived to have a strong bond with his native province of Guangdong. As early as 1952, he was accused of committing the mistake of localism and of being too lenient on local gentry and landlords. Mao ordered his removal and brought in the outsiders Táo Zhù 陶铸 and *Zhào Zǐyáng 赵紫阳 (1919–2005) to run the region. After Mao's death in 1979, and still at the height of his political power, Ye reiterated the critical importance of nurturing local cadres in Guangdong. Despite the official narrative that glorifies Deng as the "grand architect" of China's economic reform, Ye's quiet role in establishing the Special Economic Zones (SEZ, Jīngjì tèqū 经济特区) in Guangdong is perhaps more instrumental to their success. He supported the then-first secretary of Guangdong Xí Zhòngxūn's 习仲勋 call for allowing Guangdong to take one step ahead in opening China, as well as the timely National People's Congress legislation on the SEZs and Chinese-foreign equity joint ventures during his chairmanship of the NPC (March 1978–June 1983).

Due to his acute sense of the treacherous and precarious nature of politics at the center of power, Ye reportedly advised his children not to pursue high positions in Beijing, but to stay put and consolidate their power base in Guangdong. There is little doubt that they remain the most powerful family in Guangdong, and their influence goes far beyond the province nowadays, through princelings' connections, and of course Ye's iconic status in the history of the PRC. What is more difficult to pin down is Ye's real legacy. At least for the intellectuals in China, Marshal Ye may be remembered most for his tolerance of dissenting voices, as implied in the proposal to hold the "Theory Work Forum" in early 1979 for an open debate on Mao and the party's past (which was quickly thwarted by Deng and his declaration of the "four cardinal principles" 四项基本原则—upholding the socialist path, the people's democratic dictatorship, the leadership of the CCP, and Mao Zedong Thought and Marxism-Leninism—to perpetuate the CCP's monopoly of power), as well as in his often suppressed remark in late 1978: "The Third Plenum [referring to the "Party Center Work Conference" presided over by Hua Guofeng] is the role model of our Party's inner democracy; the Democracy Wall at Xidan is the role model of our people's democracy" (Zhu 2010).

Warren SUN
Monash University

Further Reading

Deng Xiaoping. (1983). *Selected works of Deng Xiaoping* (pp. 158–184). Beijing: Remin chubanshe.

Gao Yu. (2010). Liusi 21 zhounian de sikao 六四21周年的思考 [My reflections on the 21th anniversary of the June fourth tragedy). Retrieved May 20, 2015, from http://tw.aboluowang.com/2010/0601/167954.html#sthash.5YvW4b8Y.dpbs

Fan Shuo. (2002). *Ye Jianying zai feichang shiqi 1966–1976* 叶剑英在非常时期 1966–1976 [Ye Jianying in an Extraordinary Period, 1966–1976] (2 vols.). Beijing: Huawen chubanshe.

Liu Jixian 刘继贤. (2007). *Ye Jianying nianpu* 叶剑英年谱 [Chronological account of Ye Jianying] (2 vols.). Beijing: Zhongyang Wenxian chubanshe.

Song Kanfu 宋侃夫, & Qi Te 齐特. (1982/2000). Hong sifangmian jun diantai shimo 红四方面军电台始末 [The whole story about the telegram issue of the Fourth Frontal Army]. Retrieved June 4, 2015, from http://blog.sina.com.cn/s/blog_9aaa13ff0100xgci.html#comment2

Teiwes, Frederick & Sun, Warren. (2007). *The end of the Maoist Era: Chinese politics during the twilight of the Cultural Revolution, 1972–1976* (pp. 550–608). New York and London: M. E. Sharpe.

Xinhua Net. (n.d.). Mianhuai kaiguo yuanxun Ye jianying—Dashi nianbiao 念坏开国元勋叶剑英—大事年表 [A chronological list of major events—In memory of the founding father Ye Jianying]. Retrieved April 29, 2015, from http://news.xinhuanet.com/politics/2008-04/28/content_8065590_1.htm

Xiong Lei. (2008). Yijiuqiliu nian, Hua Guofeng he Ye Jianying shi zenyang lianshou de 1976 年, 华国锋和叶剑英是怎样联手的 [How Hua Guofeng and Ye Jianying formed an alliance in 1976]. *Yanhuang Chunqiu, 10.*

Yan Baohuang. (1997–2008). Ye Jianying yu Zhongguo minzhu geming de liangci lishixing zhuanzhe 叶剑英与中国民主革命的两次历史性转折 [Ye Jianying and the two historical turning points during the Chinese democratic revolution period] Retrieved June 4, 2015, from http://cpc.people.com.cn/GB/69112/118416/118423/7036520.html

Ye Jianying biography editorial board. (1995). *Ye Jianying zhuan* 叶剑英传 [Biography of Ye Jianying]. Beijing: Dangdai Zhongguo chubanshe.

Ye Xuanji. (2008, October 30). Ye shuai zai shiyijie sanzhong quanhui qianhou 叶帅在十一届三中全会前后 [Marshal Ye around the time of the Third Plenum]. *Nafang Zhoumo* [South China Weekend]. Retrieved June 4, 2015, from http://www.infzm.com/content/19143/0

Zhang Jiangming. (1997). *Lishi zhuanzhe guantou de Ye Jianying* 历史转折关头的叶剑英 [Ye Jianying at the historical turning point]. Beijing: Zhonggong dangshi chubanshe.

Zhu Huaxin. (2010). Renmin ribao: jiaoyisheng tongzhi taichenzhong 人民日报：叫一声同志太沉重 [Remembering my days at People's Daily with a heavy heart]. Retrieved May 20, 2015, from http://www.zmw.cn/bbs/thread-113763-1-1.html

• Ye Jianying •

♂ Yú Huá 余华

b. 1960—Avant-garde novelist, short-story writer, and essayist

Alternate name: trad. 余華

Summary

In his stories and novels, the avant-garde writer Yu Hua transcends style and experimentation to reveal the struggles of the individual during tumultuous and often brutal periods in China's recent history. Although his novels such as *To Live* and *Brothers* have received much acclaim, Yu remains ardent about breaking new ground, leaving readers much to look forward to from a writer many consider a contender for a future Nobel Prize.

One of the most translated writers of contemporary China, Yu Hua has enjoyed great success and favor by readers of Chinese novels since the early 1990s. His novels *To Live* (*Huózhe* 活着), *Chronicles of a Blood Merchant* (*Xǔ sānguān mài xuè jì* 许三观卖血记), and *Brothers* (*Xiōngdì* 兄弟) have not only been bestsellers, but have also won awards and critical acclaim both in China and abroad. His writing style, commonly known as

avant-gardism, represents an important literary trend in China that began in the 1980s and continues to the present day. Rather than mere stylistic experimentation, however, Yu Hua has had the intent to reveal the pain of the individual as situated against the collective pains of the times and of the nation (Wang and Yu 2010). Because of this combination of style and approach, some critics have called him "a most prominent successor to the cultural legacies of Lu Xun" (Li 1998) or a writer with a "mysterious Dickensian gift" (Corrigan 2009).

Early Life and Career

Yu Hua was born on 3 April 1960 in Hangzhou, Zhejiang Province. His father worked as a surgeon after being released from military service and his mother was a nurse. The hospital thus became the place where Yu Hua spent most of his childhood apart from home and school (Yu 1995, 381–386). It is thought that the descriptions of blood, death, and the mortuary in some of his novels may have originated with these early experiences. When Yu Hua was in primary and middle school, the Cultural Revolution (1966–1976) was reaching every corner of Chinese society. As Yu Hua later recalled, the big-character posters that he frequently saw, with their violent language, fictive content, and exaggerated rhetoric became his initial acquaintance with "literature" (Wang 2012, 109). After failing the first college entrance examination given after the Cultural Revolution, Yu worked as a dentist with the help of his parents. But the tedium of examining mouths and extracting teeth was disillusioning for a young man who dreamed of writing. Five years later, he managed to get transferred to the Cultural Center of Haiyan County, and gradually started a career as a professional writer.

Success as a Writer

Yu Hua started to publish short novels in the early 1980s, a period full of literary ideals and enthusiasm during which many of today's best-known Chinese writers began to emerge. With the success of "Leaving Home at Eighteen" ("Shíbā suì chūmén yuǎnxíng" 十八岁出门远行) in 1987 (which was also used as the name of his first short story collection) and the publication of other stories, Yu Hua soon established himself as one of China's rising avant-garde writers. He then began to try his hand at novellas

and full-length novels. In 1991, he published his first novel, *Cries in the Drizzle* (*Zàixìyǔzhōng hūhǎn* 在细雨中呼喊), which was hailed by critics as a remarkable autobiographical and psychological novel. Over the ensuing decade, Yu went on to develop his distinctive writing style, which became clear years later when he acknowledged a few important intellectual precursors, among them Lǔ Xùn 鲁迅 (1881–1936), China's greatest writer for much of the 20th century, for his critical sharpness (Zhao 1991, 33–38); Japanese writer Yasunari Kawabata for his handling of narrative details (Yu 2007, 10); and Franz Kafka for his allegorical surrealism (Yu 2004, 112–113).

International Acclaim

The year 1992 was significant for Yu Hua, as he not only married poet Chén Hóng 陈虹 (the next year they moved to Beijing), but also published his most influential novel, *To Live*. By far the most popular of his novels, *To Live* deals diachronically with the pain and suffering of an ordinary man faced with the stark and absurd realities of life caused by drastic socio-political transformations. A movie of the same name was directed by *Zhāng Yìmóu 张艺谋 in 1994, and while garnering a number of awards from Cannes and elsewhere, the movie was banned in China due to its political

---

*People marked with an asterisk have entries in this dictionary.

The Walking Dead in a Chinese Ghost Town

Yu Hua's 2013 novel The Seventh Day *is a surreal story about the "living" dead who roam in a foggy city, unable to find an appropriate final resting place. Below are the opening paragraphs of the story, introducing the recently deceased main character Yang Fei.*

The First Day

The fog was thick when I left my bedsit and ventured out alone into the barren and murky city. I was heading for what used to be called a crematorium and these days is known as the funeral parlor. I had received a notice instructing me to arrive by 9:00 a.m., because my cremation was scheduled for 9:30.

The night before had resounded with the sounds of collapsing masonry—one huge crash after another, as though a whole line of buildings was too tired to stay standing and had to lie down. In this continual bedlam I drifted fitfully between sleep and wakefulness. At daybreak, when I opened the door, the din suddenly halted, as though just by opening the door I had turned off the switch that controlled the noise. On the door a slip had been posted next to the notices that had been taped there ten days earlier, asking me to pay the electricity and water bills. in characters damp and blurry in the fog, the new notice instructed me to proceed to the funeral parlor for cremation.

Source: Yu Hua. (2015). *The Seventh Day* (Alan H. Barr, Trans.). New York: Random House. (Original work published 2013)

sensitivity. This in turn contributed substantially to Yu Hua's literary fame, as well as the novel's circulation, and it has since been published in many languages, including English, French, German, Italian, Swedish, Japanese, and Korean. The novel also received the Grinzane Cavour Prize in Italy in 1998.

In 1995, Yu Hua impressed China's literary circles again with his *Chronicle of a Blood Merchant*. He then became involved in various literary and cultural activities both inside and outside of China, his work during this period consisting mainly of essays and casual writings. In 2002, the English-version collection of short stories, *The Past and the Punishments*, made him the first Chinese writer to receive the prestigious James Joyce Award given by the Literary and Historical Society of University College Dublin. In 2004, Yu received a Barnes & Noble Discover Great New Writers Award in the United States, as well as France's Chevalier de l'Ordre des Arts et des Lettres. In 2005, he received the China Books Special Contribution Award, given by the Chinese government. Yu Hua published his other influential novel, *Brothers* in 2005 (the first part) and in 2006 (the second part). This coming-of-age novel, the longest of all Yu Hua's books, tells the story of the destinies and pains of two stepbrothers through the changing realities of love, family, and society. Perhaps owing to some degree to readers' anticipation following the success of *To Live*, *Brothers* turned out a great success in China in terms of circulation, reaching about 800,000 in the first year. Critics, however, have become divided as to the literary merits of the novel, especially in regards to its language and structure. For example, some have criticized its verbosity or the misplaced social context of many of its expressions, or the apparent absurdity of several points in its plot. Despite this, the novel received the Prix Courrier International in France and was shortlisted for the Man Asia Literary Prize in 2008.

Yu Hua's most recent publications include a collection of essays entitled *China in Ten Words* (*Shíge cíhuì lǐ de Zhōngguó* 十个词汇里的中国, 2011), not available on the mainland, most likely due to the sensitivity of certain aspects of its content, and the experimental novel, *The Seventh Day* (*Dì qī tiān* 第七天, 2013).

As a contemporary Chinese writer, Yu Hua differs from most of his peers not only because he has been so influenced by Western literature and literary ideas, but also because he is actively engaged in international communication, especially with academic institutions and the media. The Nobel laureate *Mò Yán 莫言 (b. 1955), for example, was much more reserved in his interaction with the media and non-literary circles before he was awarded the prize in 2012. In August 2003 alone, Yu Hua visited some thirty American universities on a public speaking tour (Wang 2012, 117). Since 2013, he has also served as a contributing opinion writer for the *International New York Times*.

Huaiyu LUO
Beijing University of Chemical Technology

Further Reading

Corrigan, Maureen. (2009). 'Brothers' offers a sweeping satire of modern China. Retrieved August 20, 2014, from http://www.npr.org/templates/story/story.php?storyId=100423108

Li Jie 李劼. (1998). Lun zhongguo dangdai xinchao xiaoshuo 论中国当代新潮小说 [On China's contemporary avant-garde novels]. *Zhongshan Literary Bimonthly*, 5.

• Yú Huá •

Shank, Megan. (2013). The challenges of conveying absurd reality: An interview with Chinese writer Yu Hua. Retrieved August 20, 2014, from http://lareviewofbooks.org/interview/conveying-absurd-reality-yu-hua

Wang Kan 王侃, & Yu Hua 余华. (2010). Wo xiang xiechu yige guojia de tengtong 我想写出一个国家的疼痛. [I want to write about the pains of a nation]. *Soochow Academic*, 1.

Wang Kan 王侃. (2012). Yu Hua wenxue nianpu 余华文学年谱. [A literary chronicle of Yu Hua]. *Soochow Academic*, 4.

Yu Hua 余华. (1995). *Yu Hua zuopin ji 余华作品集*. [Collection of works by Yu Hua]. Beijing: China Social Sciences Publishing Press.

Yu Hua. (2003). *Chronicle of a blood merchant* (Andrew F. Jones, Trans.). New York: Anchor Books. (Original work published in 1995)

Yu Hua. (2003). *To Live*. (Michael Berry, Trans.). New York: Anchor Books. (Original work published in 1992)

Yu Hua 余华. (2004). *Meiyou yitiao daolu shi keyi chongfu de* 没有一条道路是可以重复的. [There is no road that can be repeated]. Shanghai: Shanghai Literature and Art Publishing House.

Yu Hua 余华. (2007). *Wo nengfou xiangxin ziji: Yu Hua suibi ji* 我能否相信自己：余华随笔集. [Can I believe in myself: Collection of casual essays by Yu Hua]. Jinan: Tomorrow Publishing House.

Yu Hua. (2008). *Cries in the Drizzle*. (Allan H. Barr, Trans.). New York: Anchor Books. (Original work published in 1993)

Yu Hua. (2009). *Brothers* (Eileen Cheng-yin Chow & Carlos Rojas, Trans.). New York: Pantheon Books. (Original work published 2005–2006)

Yu Hua. Opinion page on the website of *The New York Times*. Retrieved August 20, 2014, from http://topics.nytimes.com/top/reference/timestopics/people/y/yu_hua/index.html

Zhao Yiheng 赵毅衡. (1991). Fei yuyihua de kaixuan: xidu Yu Hua 非语义化的凯旋：细读余华. [The triumph of desemantization: Close reading of Yu Hua]. *Contemporary Writers Review*, 2.

余华

♂ Yuán Lóngpíng 袁隆平

b. 1930—Agricultural scientist, developer of hybrid rice

Summary

Yuan Longping is a Nobel Peace Prize nominee, and best known for developing hybrid rice in the 1970s. Due to his continued research and innovations, rice yields increased significantly, allowing China to produce the nutrition it needs for its growing population. Well past the official retirement age, Yuan remains committed to advancing agricultural research.

Born on 7 September 1930 to a father who worked on the Beijing-Wuhan railway and a mother who taught him English, Yuan Longping is known as the "father of hybrid rice" for his successful development of the first such varieties during the 1970s.

After moving around China with his family as a child during the Second Sino-Japanese War (1937–1945), Yuan enrolled in Southwest Agricultural College in 1949 as an agronomy major, which marked the beginning of his lifelong work in agriculture. Upon his graduation in 1953, he took a teaching job at the Anjiang Agricultural School in Hunan Province, where he taught Russian, botany, crop cultivation, breeding, and genetics. While teaching, he also conducted scientific experiments involving asexual crossings between crops, employing the then dominant theories of I.V. Michurin and T.D. Lysenko imported from the Soviet Union. After realizing that Lysenkoist methods had fatal flaws, Yuan fundamentally altered his research methods based on his reading of Western magazines such as *Crop Science*, where he learned the hereditary principles of G. Mendel and T.H. Morgan.

Hybrid Rice Research

The widespread famine that hit China from 1960 to 1963 following the disastrous policies of the Great Leap Forward (1958–1960) led Yuan to begin his research on hybrid rice, backed by a research program sponsored by the

Chinese government at the Academy of Agriculture in Changsha, Hunan Province. Observing the results of hybridization in corn, he developed the idea of using hybrids to increase rice yield, despite the widespread belief among agronomists worldwide that hybrid vigor—or heterosis—could not be bred in a self-pollinating crop like rice. Even as virtually no solutions for high-yielding hybrid seed production were on the horizon, Yuan believed that heterosis was a universal phenomenon and that rice was no exception. His earliest research efforts, however, met with little success.

With the beginning of the Cultural Revolution in 1966, Yuan, like many scientists in China, saw his research disrupted. Because of his perceived affront to the views of Chinese Communist Party Chairman Máo Zédōng 毛泽东 (1893–1976) on agriculture, Yuan's experimental seedlings were seized. He moved his research operations from Hunan to Yunnan Province in China's southwest and to Hainan Island off the coast of southeast China. It was on Hainan in 1970 that he and his research team discovered a natural male-sterile wild rice plant (wild rice with flowers containing no pollen). This led to rapid progress in the development of hybrid rice, which was aided by a decision by China's State Science and Technology Commission in 1972 to list hybrid rice as a key national research project.

Yuan and his team succeeded in breeding unique genetic tools, which consisted of a three-line system essential for developing high-yielding hybrid rice: male-sterile line, maintaining line, and restore line (or A, B, R line). By 1974 they successfully developed the technology to produce Indica, a long-grained glutinous rice, with a yield 20 percent higher than that of common species. With experimental planting carried out in 1975, the species was made available for widespread use by Chinese farmers in 1976.

When news of Yuan's work on hybrid rice reached Western scientific circles, many were skeptical. Among the skeptics were scientists at the International Rice Research Institute (IRRI) in the Philippines, which had attempted to develop hybrid rice research before 1962 but eventually gave up. In 1979, Yuan introduced Chinese hybrid rice at an international conference sponsored by the research institute, and IRRI restored its own hybrid rice research the following year. In 1995, Yuan and his team made further advances by developing a two-line system of hybrid rice that promised even higher yields.

The impact on production in China and other parts of the world has been dramatic. The number of acres planted in hybrid rice in China increased from zero in 1974 to 17 million in 1983, accounting for 20 percent of the country's total rice acreage; in recent years that figure has risen to 50 percent and accounts for 60 percent of the country's total rice crop. With average increases

20 percent higher than conventional rice, total rice output in China, which in 1950 was 5.7 billion tons, rose to 19.5 billion tons in 2012 with annual increases large enough to feed 60 million people. Much of this is due to Yuan's innovations. Whereas in the late 1960s rice production in China averaged 300 kilograms per hectare (or 2.47 acres), at present the average is 700 kilograms per hectare, with experimental fields in Hunan reaching 870 kilograms per hectare.

Internationally, Yuan's hybrid rice has been adopted in over twenty other countries. In addition, the United Nations' Food and Agricultural Organization (FAO) chose hybrid rice as its first program to increase world grain production and appointed Yuan the chief consultant. He and his research associates have traveled to India, Vietnam, Myanmar, Bangladesh, Sri Lanka, and the United States to provide advice and consultation to rice research personnel, while Yuan's research institute has trained over 3,000 scientists from more than fifty countries. Additionally, the Yuan Longping Foundation in China grants awards to promising agricultural researchers.

Accolades and Continuing Research

Yuan has published more than sixty articles and six monographs, including "Hybrid Rice Breeding and Cultivation and Technology of Hybrid Rice Production" (published by FAO). His work has also greatly influenced other research fields, such as plant sciences, agriculture, and applied biotechnology. He has won numerous awards and honors for his work, including the 1981 first Special-Class National Invention Prize, 1987 UNESCO Science Prize, 2000 National [China] Preeminent Science and Technology Award, 2004 World Food Prize and 2004 Wolf Prize in Agriculture, and 2011 Mahathir Science Award. Additionally, he was named a foreign associate of the National Academy of Sciences in the United States in 1997. Yuan is currently director-general of the China National Hybrid Rice Research and Development Center located in Hunan, as well as a professor at Hunan Agricultural University and a member of the Chinese Academy of Engineering. An associate of former Chinese Communist Party Chairman Huá Guófēng 华国锋 (1921–2008), Yuan has also served on the Chinese People's Political Consultative Congress of Hunan Province. In 1999, the Longping High-Technology Agricultural Company was formed; Yuan owns 2.5 million shares in it. In 2014, Yuan was nominated for the Nobel Peace Prize.

Despite his advancing age, Yuan continues to develop new approaches to enhance the heterosis level and to simplify the methodology for hybrid rice breeding. This includes conducting ongoing analysis of available yield-limiting factors and breeding technologies, with the goal of developing a variety of "super hybrid rice" with potential yield increases of 20–30 percent. Current projects also include preparing to plant hybrid rice in the far western and arid regions of Xinjiang Province using a water-saving drip irrigation system.

While Yuan believes that the future will inevitably involve genetically modified crops, he has so far successfully expressed opposition to the commercial introduction of genetically modified rice in China, at least for the near future. Yuan has also called for imposing fines on consumers in China who waste food, especially at the innumerable and extravagant official banquets, where the wasted and uneaten food could, he estimates, potentially feed upwards of 200 million people annually.

A lover of the Chinese game of mahjong, Yuan also plays the violin and stays in shape by swimming. Four asteroids and a college in China have been named after Yuan.

Lawrence R. SULLIVAN
Adelphi University

Further Reading

Chen Zhiyuan. (2013). Yuan Longping. In Song Yuwu (Ed.), *Biographical dictionary of the People's Republic of China* (pp. 381–382). Jefferson, NC: McFarland.

Deng Xiangzi, & Deng Yinru. (2007). *The man who puts an end to hunger: Yuan Longping, "Father of Hybrid Rice"*. Beijing: Foreign Languages Press.

Yuan Longping, & Peng Jimin (Ed.). (2004). *Hybrid rice and world food security*. Beijing: China Science and Technology Press.

Ma Guohui, & Yuan Longping. (2003). Hybrid rice achievements and development in China. In S. S. Virmani, C. X. Mao, & B. Hardy (Eds.), *Hybrid rice for food security, poverty alleviation, and environmental protection* (pp. 247–256). Manila, Philippines: International Rice Research Institute.

袁隆平

☿ Zen, Joseph

Chén Rìjūn 陳日君

b. 1932—Spiritual leader, bishop of the Catholic Diocese of Hong Kong (2002–2009)

Alternate names: Zen Ze-kiun; simpl. 陈日君

Summary

Cardinal Joseph (Ze-kiun) Zen was the sixth bishop of the Catholic Diocese of Hong Kong. He often criticized the Chinese and the Hong Kong SAR governments for violating human rights and, as an advisor to the Vatican for Sino-Vatican negotiations, expressed his critical views on the Chinese government's control over the Catholic Church. He has received a number of humanitarian awards from local and international organizations.

Cardinal Joseph (Ze-kiun) Zen served as an educator, a religious leader, and an advisor to the Vatican for Sino-Vatican negotiations. He was born into a Catholic family in Shanghai on 13 January 1932. Zen's father worked for an electric light company and later a tea company, and Zen's mother worked for a telephone company. Zen's mother gave birth to ten children.

In 1937 the Japanese army occupied Shanghai, and the house of Zen's family was bombed by Japanese soldiers. The family found itself in difficult times, and in 1944 Zen's mother took him to the Salesian Minor Seminary in Shanghai (part of the Society of St. Francis de Sales, commonly known as the Salesians of Don Bosco) to receive his education. It was during this period that Zen responded to the calling of the vocation of priesthood. As Zen recalled, "My faith was born in Shanghai" (Malovic 2007b, 9).

In 1948 Zen entered the novitiate in the Salesian House of Studies in Hong Kong, where he spent the next four years. In 1949 the Communists became the ruling party in China, and the new regime held that the Catholic Church was a manifestation of Western imperialism. The Catholic Church was soon severely oppressed. Catholic missionaries were expelled from the country from 1949 to 1952, including Antonio Riberi, the Vatican representative to China. Later, the Chinese Communist Party established the Chinese Catholic

Patriotic Association to exercise state supervision over China's Catholics.

Zen was accused of being an agent who received training from foreign powers; as such, he was not able to return to Shanghai, so he stayed in Hong Kong. He received training in Salesian pedagogy from Salesian institutions in Hong Kong and Macau from 1952 to 1955.

From 1955 to 1964, Zen continued his studies at the Salesian Pontifical University in Rome and was ordained to the priesthood in Turin, Italy, on 11 February 1961. He earned a Licentiate in Theology in 1961 and a Doctorate in Philosophy in 1964.

The period from 1962 to 1965 marked the time of the Second Vatican Council. The renewal of Catholic doctrines, particularly Catholic social teachings, deeply influenced Zen's understanding of faith and society.

Sociopolitical Context

Zen's life coincided with three closely related sociopolitical environments: Chinese society ruled by the Communist regime; Hong Kong society changing from a British colony to a Special Administrative Region (SAR) under a Communist state; and the Sino-Vatican relationship, which was full of tension. Zen was engaged in the issues of all three environments.

On the one hand, because he taught at a number of seminaries in mainland China, Zen embraced China as his motherland; on the other hand, he experienced a political reality in which the Communist regime severely controlled Chinese society and oppressed the Catholic Church. Important events during Zen's life included the establishment of the People's Republic of China (1949), the Cultural Revolution (1966–1976), and the Tiananmen pro-democracy movement in Beijing (1989).

Zen also witnessed the changes that took place in Hong Kong society in 1997, when Hong Kong went from being a comparatively stable British colony to a SAR under the sovereignty of a Communist country. The Hong Kong SAR government (or, more precisely, the Chinese government behind it) has since refused to introduce constitutional reforms and implement universal suffrage, and many of its social policies have breached human rights (Hong Kong Human Rights Monitor 2006, 2013). Important events during Zen's life included the signing of the Sino-British Joint Declaration in 1984, declaring Hong Kong's return to China in 1997, and 1.5 million Hong Kong people taking part in a march to protest the Chinese government's suppression of the Tiananmen Democratic Movement in 1989.

Zen also was involved in the Sino-Vatican relationship. He often criticized the Chinese government's control over the Catholic Church and its clergy, particularly the state's Chinese Catholic Patriotic Association, which advocated independence from the Roman Catholic

Church and the consecration of its own bishops. He urged the Vatican to take a strong stance against the Chinese government and the Chinese Catholic Patriotic Association in defense of religious freedom. Important events during Zen's life included Pope Pius XII appointing Bishop Antonio Riberi as apostolic nuncio to China in 1946 (he was later expelled by the Communist regime in 1951); the establishment of the Chinese Catholic Patriotic Association in 1957; and Pope John Paul II's canonization of 120 martyrs in China on 1 October 2000, which angered the Chinese government because that date is the National Day of the People's Republic of China.

Zen as an Educator

After completing his postgraduate studies, Zen returned to the Salesian House of Studies Hong Kong, where he taught philosophy and theology from 1964 to 1970. He began teaching at the Holy Spirit Seminary College in 1971. He was the provincial superior of Salesians (Hong Kong, Macau, Taiwan, and China) from 1978 to 1983 and the dean of the Philosophy Division at the Holy Spirit Seminary College from 1984 to 1991. He was also the rector of the Salesian Community of Aberdeen Technical School from 1986 to 1989.

Zen taught at a number of seminaries in mainland China for six months each year from 1989 to 1996, including in Shanghai, Wuhan, Xi'an, Shi Jiazhuang, Shenyang, and Beijing. He provided students with training in modern theological education, particularly the new ideas of the Second Vatican Council, during a time when the Catholic community in China had long been separated from the outside world.

Zen as a Bishop

Zen was appointed as the coadjutor bishop of Hong Kong in 1996 and was installed as the sixth bishop of Hong Kong on 23 September 2002. In this role, Zen focused on the deteriorating condition of human rights in Hong Kong. In 1999, the Hong Kong SAR government denied mainland-born children the right of abode in Hong Kong by overturning the ruling of the Court of Final Appeal and asking the National People's Congress to reinterpret the Hong Kong Basic Law. Later, the government refused to allow mainland-born children to attend school because of their illegal status. Zen held that these children had the right to an education, and he invited them to attend the schools run by the Catholic Church. Thereafter, Zen often openly criticized the government's social policies, and the Catholic Church became a powerful social organization that defied the government.

In 2001, the Hong Kong SAR government proposed the "Education (Amendment) Ordinance," requiring all primary and secondary schools to set up incorporated management committees by 2010.

Joseph Zen's coat of arms. His motto *Ipsi cura est* means "for he cares about you" and is taken from a line in Peter 5:7. Photo by SajoR.

The ordinance was passed by the Legislative Council in July 2004. Under this law, the incorporated management committees could easily be infiltrated and controlled by political organizations. Zen strongly opposed this law, stating that it would weaken the autonomy of the schools run by the Catholic Church. In 2002, the Hong Kong SAR government attempted to enact laws to protect national security according to Article 23 of the Hong Kong Basic Law. Zen openly opposed the legislation and called on Catholics to take part in a march, at which he prayed for them at the opening rally. Zen thought that the religious policies of China would be easily implemented in Hong Kong after the legislation, which meant that the Catholic Church would be under absolute state control (Zen 2009, 109). In 2005, Zen and a group of Protestant church leaders criticized "The Fifth Report of the Constitutional Development Task Force" for not providing a direction, a timetable, and steps for achieving universal suffrage in Hong Kong by 2017 and 2020. Later, the report was rejected by the pan-democrats in the Legislative Council.

During this period Zen became an influential opinion leader in Hong Kong and was frequently invited by journalists to comment on social policies. As a powerful social organization defending human rights, the Catholic Church built a strong civil society in Hong Kong.

Zen as Advisor to the Vatican

On 22 February 2006 Zen was named by Pope Benedict XVI as a member of the Sacred College of Cardinals and was formally elevated to the Cardinalate on 24 March 2006. As a member of the Vatican Commission for the Catholic Church in China, Zen was able to express his critical views on Chinese manipulation of the Catholic Church.

After 1949, the Chinese Communist Party held that the Catholic Church represented the power of Western imperialism, therefore the Catholic Church in China had to cut ties with the Vatican. The Vatican had begun its negotiations with the Chinese government after Pope John Paul II assumed his position in 1978. Thereafter, the Vatican and the Chinese government intermittently negotiated on the normalization of relations. As a Chinese bishop in Hong Kong, Zen had both insider and outsider perspectives on the social and political situation in mainland China. He regularly sent his reports to the rector major of the Salesians of Don Bosco, explicating observations on Chinese society gleaned through his teaching in China. These reports were forwarded to the Vatican.

At that time there were divergent positions on how to negotiate with the Chinese government. Father Jeroom Heyndrickx of the Ferdinand Verbiest Foundation at the Catholic University of Leuven, Belgium, believed that the Vatican should continuously engage in dialogue with the Chinese government. Zen disagreed: He maintained that the bishops and clergy in China found it difficult to engage in such dialogue with the Chinese government because they were not equal in power. Zen recommended that the Vatican stop negotiating with the Chinese government in matters violating the principles of the church. The two priests often debated with each other in publications and on the Internet.

Public Reaction and Recognition

Zen has received a number of honors and awards regarding human rights and humanitarianism from local and international organizations. These awards include the Reporter's Courage Prize, granted in 2001 by the Hong Kong Journalist Association, Foreign Correspondents' Club, Hong Kong, and Amnesty International Hong Kong for defending human rights in media in recognition of his article "We Thought That This Kind of 'Campaign' Was History," which was published in *Ming Bao* in 2000; Hong Kong "Person of the Year" in 2002, as named by *South China Morning Post*; Defender of the Faith Award in 2006, granted by the Italian review *Il Timone* (*The Helm*) for his commitment to religious freedom in Hong Kong and China; the Sienna Liberty Award in 2006, granted by the Fondazione Liberal of Italy for defending human rights and freedom of beliefs and for pushing Chinese democracy; an honorary Doctor of Humane Letters from Amherst College in the United States in 2007 for his courage in and contributions to defending religious freedom; the Lifetime Companionship Award from the Chung Chi Divinity School in 2013 in recognition of his decades of pastoral care for prisoners in Hong Kong; and the John Diefenbaker Defender of Human Rights and Freedom Award in 2013, granted by the Canadian government for his commitment to human rights, democracy, and religious freedom. John Baird, Minister of Foreign Affairs of Canada, remarked that Zen had rightly earned a reputation as "the new conscience of Hong Kong" and said

Zen represented the best traits of humanity (*Sunday Examiner* 2013).

Influence after Retirement

In 2007, at age seventy-five, Zen submitted his application for retirement to Pope Benedict XVI, and he officially retired on 15 April 2009. He continues to express his views on social and political issues and to participate in social movements. He has urged the Chinese and the Hong Kong SAR governments to allow Hong Kong to elect their chief executive and legislators. In 2014 he and two other priests, Father Louis Ha and Father Chan Moon-hung, formed a "Three-people Concern Group for Constitutional System," publishing articles in *Gōngjiāo bào* 公教報 (a Chinese Catholic weekly in Hong Kong) and encouraging Hong Kong people to call for universal suffrage. He took part in the "Umbrella Movement" (also known as the Occupy Movement) from September through December 2014, which was pressing for universal suffrage. Zen is an example showing how Christianity can act as a strong social force in Hong Kong. Generally, Christians support universal values such as democracy, freedom, and human rights, and they act upon social and political issues. They provide moral and spiritual energy to social activism and they themselves are an integral part of civil society in Hong Kong.

Shun-hing CHAN
Hong Kong Baptist University

陳日君

Further Reading

Hong Kong Human Rights Monitor. (2006). Joint NGO submission to the United Nations Committee on International Covenant on Civil and Political Rights regarding the report of the Hong Kong Special Administrative Region of the People's Republic of China, March 2006. Retrieved May 3, 2015, from http://www.hkhrm.org.hk

Hong Kong Human Rights Monitor. (2013). Joint shadow report by Hong Kong NGOs coordinated by the Hong Kong Human Rights Monitor to the UN Human Rights Committee for its hearing of the HKSAR report under the ICCPR, 12 March 2013. Retrieved from http://www.hkhrm.org.hk

Lam, Annie. (2012). Cardinal Joseph Zen: "I am just a conscientious teacher." *Tripod*, *32*(166), 64–72.

Ma, Ngok. (2005). Civil society in self-defense: The struggle against national security legislation in Hong Kong. *Journal of Contemporary China*, *14*(44), 465–482.

Malovic, Dorian. (2007a). Mgr Zen, un home encolére. Entretiens avec le cardinal de Hong Kong [Bishop Joseph Zen, an angry man: Interviews with the Cardinal of Hong Kong]. Paris: Bayard. (French language source.)

Malovic, Dorian. (2007b). *Chen Rijun: Zhaolianggongyi de shuji (Chen Rijun shuji qinzi xiuding ban)* 陳日君: 照亮公義的樞機 (陳日君樞機親自修定版) [Zen Ze-kiun: A Cardinal fighting for justice (Revised by Cardinal Joseph Zen Ze-kiun)] (Ng Wing Yan, Liu Oi Ping, and Pun Hoi Ying, Trans.). Hong Kong: Next Publications Ltd.

Sunday Examiner. (2013, November 16). Cardinal Zen accepts Canadian human rights award on behalf of the voiceless. *Sunday Examiner*. Retrieved October 18, 2014, from http://sundayex.catholic.org.hk/node/1661

Zen, Ze-kiun 陳日君. (2009). *Ping'an di anquan kao ta: Chen Rijun shuji gongjiao bao wenji (1996–2009)* 平安抵岸全靠祂: 陳日君樞機公教報文集 [Arriving safely on the shore by trusting him: Collected essays of Cardinal Joseph Zen Ze-kiun, 1996–2009]. Hong Kong: Gongjiaobao.

Zen, Ze-kiun 陳日君. (2004–2006). *Zhaoxi xiangsui: Zhurijiangdao (1998–2001)* 朝夕相隨: 主日講道 (1998–2001) [Following him day and night: Sunday homilies, 1998–2001] (3 vols.). Hong Kong: Gongjiaobao.

• Zen, Joseph •

♀ Zhāng Àilíng 张爱玲

1920–1995—Author of short stories, novels, essays, and screenplays

Alternate names: b. Zhāng Yīng 张煐; Eileen Chang Reyher; penname: Liáng Jīng 梁京; trad. 張愛玲

Summary

Zhang Ailing is an iconic figure in modern Chinese literature and culture. Her evocative portrayals of urbanites were an immediate success in 1940s Shanghai, but were later seen as contaminated by bourgeois ideology and decadent values. Forced into exile, she spent the latter half of her life in obscurity in the United States. Chinese readers flocked to her again at the end of the twentieth century, when a potent mix of economic resurgence and cultural nostalgia swept through urban centers.

Zhang Ailing, or Eileen Chang in English, was a tall, slender woman whose virtuoso commitment to style is evident throughout her oeuvre, which includes stories, essays, novels, screenplays, letters, and translations, as well as line drawings and a carefully curated set of personal photographs. She first became famous in her early twenties, as a writer of psychologically incisive stories and essays that carefully ignored the Japanese occupation/collaborationist regime within which she worked, often by invoking a wider frame of consciousness, a mythical-historical or existential level of experience. This perspective shaped much of her later writing as well.

Zhang's multi-tiered perspective is perhaps a result of her own elite, storied ancestry: she was the great-granddaughter (though not a direct patrilineal descendant) of Lǐ Hóngzhāng 李鸿章, one of the late Qing empire's most eminent and effective officials. This, together with her devotion to Qing classics like *Dream of the Red Chamber* (*Hónglóu mèng* 红楼梦) and championing of the lesser-known *Flowers of Shanghai* (*Hǎishàng huā* 海上花) would go far towards explaining why the past is always present, and sometimes subsumes the present, in her fictional worlds.

Equally important must be the traumatic conflict she experienced in her immediate family and the cool gaze learned from those experiences—a

张爱玲

coolness that could still readily give way to delight in simple, sensory pleasures, or quiet sympathy for her characters' toilsome difficulties. In any event, this nuanced, balanced perspective, which served her so well in the 1940s publication market, became the basis for a lifelong commitment to literary writing, even when political and cultural winds blew against her. That is why, for many readers and critics, she is, as the scholarly critic C.T. Hsia has said, "the best and most important writer" in mid-twentieth-century China (Hsia 1961/1999, 389).

Childhood and Early Education

Zhang Ailing was born into once-prosperous gentry in Shanghai in 1920, one year after the May Fourth Movement, during which calls were made to cast off traditional Confucian values for cultural rejuvenation and a more modern (Western-inspired) worldview, and a decade after the fall of the Qing regime. According to the writer's memoir-essays, for example "Whispered Words" ("Sīyǔ" 私语) and "Dream of Genius" ("Tiāncái mèng" 天才梦), her father, Zhāng Tíngzhòng 张廷重 (1896–1953), indulged in opiates and women, and quarreled with both his sister and his wife, Huang Yifan (1896–1957). When Zhang was about three years old, her mother, having by then given birth to a son, went to Europe with her sister-in-law to study art. Some

years later, the couple reunited and moved into a Western-style villa in Shanghai, but the addiction and quarrels resumed and Huang Yifan obtained a divorce. Zhang Tingzhong remarried, but Zhang, now in her teens, boarded at her school, St. Mary's Hall. While on a visit home, she angered her father, who battered her, then kept her imprisoned in a room for half a year, refusing to call a doctor even though she had fallen ill. Eventually she escaped and moved into her mother's apartment. But money was tight, and mother-daughter relations were often strained.

Zhang Ailing qualified for university study in England, but wartime travel restrictions meant she went to Hong Kong instead. Her academic studies were cut short by the Japanese invasion of the British colony in 1941. After making her way back to Shanghai, she launched her career as a self-supporting writer, publishing first in an English-language nonfiction magazine aimed at expatriate readers, then more widely in Chinese magazines that, prior to the Japanese invasion, had been part of a lively literary scene in Republican China. Her pungent portrayals of moral mishap in culturally mixed milieus and her personal reflections on a wide range of topics, from the artsy to the mundane, were quickly collected in two bestselling volumes, *Romances* (*Chuánqí* 传奇, 1944) and *Written on Water* (*Liúyán* 流言, 1945), that eventually became foundational texts in her oeuvre.

At the time, however, because Shanghai was held by Japanese or Japanese-friendly forces, a public profile carried significant risks. Those risks were exacerbated when she responded to the romantic overtures of Hú Lánchéng 胡兰成, a literary adventurer who became a cultural affairs official in the collaborationist regime. The couple made a private marriage agreement in 1943, but Zhang ended the relationship after three years, due to Hu's liaisons with other women. Hu Lancheng was by then persona non grata in China; he eventually moved to Japan, then Taiwan.

Middle and Later Years

The association with Hu Lancheng, in combination with her elite family background and dogma-averse temperament, dimmed Zhang's chances for success when the Communists rose to power. Nonetheless, for several years, while using the penname Liáng Jīng 梁京, she made observable efforts to adapt her writing to changing conditions, most notably in the 1950–1951 novel *Eighteen Springs* (*Shíbāchūn* 十八春), which ends in a determinedly upbeat manner. By 1952, however, she had decided to flee to Hong Kong. There she wrote two novels— *The Rice-sprout Song* 秧歌 and *Naked Earth* 赤地之恋—that offer a nuanced, often heart-breaking portrayal of misguided efforts to carry out agricultural reforms and recruit young people for patriotic causes. She wrote each of these novels in English, then re-wrote them in Chinese. She also translated stories and essays by American writers—Washington Irving, Ralph Waldo Emerson, and Ernest Hemingway—into Chinese. These efforts were supported by the United States Information Agency and, in 1955, helped her gain immigrant refugee status in the US. She was, conversely, banned in the PRC.

In 1956, Zhang Ailing met and married Ferdinand Reyher, a divorced American novelist, screenwriter, and playwright. Reyher was almost thirty years older than Zhang (there had been fourteen years between her and Hu Lancheng); he had been active in promoting left-wing European intellectuals like Berthold Brecht; and, as it turned out, he was near the end of his productive writing career. Despite these seemingly great differences, the two writers had a meaningful companionship until Reyher's health declined and he died in 1967.

These were also the years when Zhang Ailing tried to publish several novels about China in English, but except for *The Rouge of the North*, published in London in 1967, the results were disappointing. She was able, however, to sell screenplays in Hong Kong, and hold posts as a visiting writer or researcher at Miami University, Radcliffe College, and the University of California at Berkeley.

By 1968, the Taipei-based publisher Crown 皇冠 had offered her a contract for the re-publication of her early work, and a new generation of younger readers in Taiwan and Hong Kong was reading and admiring her stories. One of her first new projects was the re-working of *Eighteen Springs* into *Half a Lifelong Romance* (*Bànshēng yuán* 半生缘), by changing the ending and strengthening the overall development of this story about a promising young couple's painful derailment. The plot was originally, and largely, inspired by *H.M. Pulham, Esq.*, a 1940 novel by the American writer John P. Marquand, but Zhang's novel greatly expands the narrative around the female protagonist and makes artful use of Chinese narrative traditions and locations, cinematic Gothicism, and her own experience of family repression.

This novel, along with a steady stream of essays and canon-building projects like her extended commentary on *Dream of the Red Chamber* and Mandarin translation of *Flowers of Shanghai* kept Zhang Ailing in the public eye in Taiwan, Hong Kong, and among the overseas Chinese from the 1970s onward. Even so, she preferred a reclusive lifestyle in California; for many readers, this only made her more fascinating. By the 1980s, the ban on her writing had been lifted in China, and the news of her death in 1995 became a media sensation throughout the Chinese-speaking world. The sense of loss was compounded by an affecting image of loneliness—she died unattended, in a scantly furnished rental apartment in Los Angeles. Her ashes, in accordance with her wishes, were scattered at sea.

Posthumous Career and Legacy

The groundswell of commemorative appreciation after Zhang's death has inspired more than a dozen biographies (including a television serial), as well as multiple academic conferences and publications, translations and re-issues of her work, and multi-media and stage performances. The 2007 release of director *Ang Lee's 李安 (b. 1954) *Lust, Caution* (*Sè, jiè* 色戒), a gripping version of a complex, cautionary tale that Zhang set in 1940s Shanghai but did not finish writing till three decades later, stirred considerable interest and controversy. Then, in 2009, following the release of various posthumous collections of minor work, Crown and the University of Hong Kong Press began publishing a set of autobiographical novels, one written in Chinese (*A Small Reunion* [*Xiǎo tuányuán* 小团圆]), and two in English (*Fall of the Pagoda*, *The Book of Changes*), all dealing with the formative first decades of the author's life and written between the late 1950s and mid-1970s but never previously published. These novels generated another round of discussion and debate, partly because the style is so

*People marked with an asterisk have entries in this dictionary.

• Zhāng Àilíng •

spare it is almost affectless. But the last title in this posthumous series probably will be the 2014 Chinese translation of an unfinished, unpublished English novel, *The Young Marshall*, which focuses on a fictional romance involving Zhāng Xuéliáng 张学良, a 1930s Nationalist general.

Although the most avid phase of attention seems to have passed, scholarly and popular interest in Zhang Ailing remains strong. After a long and tumultuous historical process, her high ranking among modern Chinese writers is assured, and is widely agreed to rest on creative integration of Qing, Anglophone, and cinematic influences; penetrating studies of gendered, quotidian experience in both Republican and Communist China; and a distinctive personal style. The particular social conditions that she analyzed so sympathetically and provocatively are to some extent passing away, due to middle-class Chinese women's greater access to positive forms of agency. Future readers nevertheless will still find in her work vivid portrayals of a former age, and a sensibility that is by turns sensuous, laconic, and severe.

Karen S. KINGSBURY
Chatham University

Further Reading

Chang, Eileen. (1995). *The rice-sprout song*. Berkeley: University of California Press. (Original work published 1955)

Chang, Eileen. (1998). *The rouge of the north*. Berkeley: University of California Press. (Original work published 1967)

Chang, Eileen. (2000). *Traces of love and other stories*. (Eva Hung et al., Trans.). Hong Kong: Renditions.

Chang, Eileen. (2005). *Written on water*. [*Liuyan* 流言] (Andrew F. Jones, Trans.). New York: Columbia University Press.

Chang, Eileen. (2007). *Love in a fallen city* [*Qingcheng zhi lian* 倾城之恋]. (Karen S. Kingsbury, Trans.). New York: New York Review Books. London: Penguin. (Original work published 1943)

Chang, Eileen. (2007). *Lust, caution and other stories*. (Julia Lovell et al., Trans.) London: Penguin.

Chang, Eileen. (2010a). *The fall of the pagoda*. Hong Kong: Hong Kong University Press.

Chang, Eileen. (2010b). *The book of change*. Hong Kong: Hong Kong University Press.

Chang, Eileen. (2014). *Half a lifelong romance*. (Karen S. Kingsbury, Trans.). London: Penguin. (Original work published 1950)

Chang, Eileen. (2015). *Naked earth*. New York: New York Review Books. (Original work published 1956)

Ding Yamin 丁亚民, & Sun Zhuo 孙卓. (Dir.). (2005). *Ta cong Shanghai lai – Zhang Ailing chuanqi* 她从海上来 – 张爱玲传奇 [The Legend of Eileen Chang] (24 episodes). Dongsen Meizhou. DVD.

Gao Quanzhi 高全之. (2008). *Zhang Ailing xue* 张爱玲学 [Eileen Chang reconsidered]. Taipei: Maitian.

Hsia, C.T. (1999). *A history of modern Chinese fiction*. (3rd Ed.). Bloomington: Indiana University Press. (Original work published 1961)

Lee, Ang. (Dir.). (2007). *Lust, Caution* (Se, jie 色, 戒). Focus Features.

Li Oufan 李欧梵. (2006). *Cangliang yu shigu: Zhang Ailing de qishi* 苍凉与世故：张爱玲的启示 [Desolation and Sophistication: Eileen Chang's Revelation]. Hong Kong: Oxford University Press.

Lin Xingqian 林幸谦. (Ed.). (2007). *Zhang Ailing: wenxue, dianying, wutai.* 张爱玲：文学. 电影. 舞台 [Zhang Ailing: literature, cinema, stage]. Hong Kong: Oxford University Press.

Lin Xingqian 林幸谦. (Ed.). (2012). *Zhang Ailing: chuanqi, xingbie, xipu.* 张爱玲：傳奇. 性別. 系谱 [Zhang Ailing: legend, gender, genealogy]. Taipei: Lianjing.

Louie, Kam. (Ed.). (2012). *Eileen Chang: Romancing languages, cultures and genres.* Hong Kong: Hong Kong University Press.

Sima Xin 司马新. (1996). *Zhang Ailing yu Laiya* 张爱玲与赖雅 [Eileen Chang and Ferdinand Reyher]. (Xu Si 徐斯 and Sima Xin, Trans.) Taipei: Dadi.

Yang Ze 杨泽. (1999). *Yuedu Zhang Ailing: Guoji yantaohui lunwenji* [Reading Eileen Chang: International conference proceedings]. Taipei: Maitian.

Zhang Ailing 张爱玲. (2009–2012). *Zhang Ailing diancang xinban* 张爱玲典藏新版 [Zhang Ailing new archival edition] 18 vols. Reissued edition. Taipei: Huangguan.

Zhang Ailing 张爱玲. (2014). *Xiao shuai* 小帅 [The Young Marshall]. (Zheng Yuantao 郑远涛, Trans.) Taipei: Huangguan.

• Zhāng Àilíng •

♂ Zhāng Cháoyáng
张朝阳

b. 1964—Businessman, founder and CEO of Sohu Company

Alternate names: Charles Zhang; trad. 張朝陽

Summary

Zhang Chaoyang, CEO and chairman of the board of directors of Sohu Company, helped China leap into the Internet age. Sohu, a household name in China, has won numerous awards for innovation and performance, and it was the only company to have Internet broadcast rights for the 2008 Beijing Olympic Games. Zhang is widely admired for his vision and entrepreneurial spirit.

Zhang Chaoyang, known for his key role as a pioneer in the field of information technology and the Internet industry, was born into a working-class family in Xi'an, Shanxi Province, on 31 October 1964. His parents were both doctors who created a rather free environment for him during his childhood. He led a mostly carefree life and was able to pursue his own interests, which included painting, music, and other cultural activities.

Because he performed very well in his school studies, he was admitted to Xi'an High School of Shanxi Province, a renowned school with a history spanning more than one hundred years. He graduated from the school and entered Tsinghua University in 1981, after scoring very highly on the difficult national college entrance exam. Five years later, he graduated from the university with a degree in physics and was selected by the China-United States Physics Examination Application (CUSPEA) scholarship program to study in the United States. The program was a joint effort between the Chinese government and the renowned Chinese American scientist and physics Nobel laureate Tsung-Dao Lee. Zhang ended up at the Massachusetts Institute of Technology (MIT), where he earned his doctoral degree in 1993. He would stay on there for three more years conducting postdoctoral research before he returned to China to embark on his Internet business adventures.

Building a Company

"Opportunities will only befall those who are well-prepared" is Zhang's motto. Before he achieved success, Zhang endured many challenges and setbacks. For instance, in order to raise the money needed for his Internet project in China, he spent countless hours in public phone booths on Boston's streets. He also was kicked out of a potential investor's office more than once. But he was not one to give up. Finally, his efforts paid off. With help from professor Nicholas Negroponte, head of the MIT Media Lab, and professor Edward Robert from MIT's Sloan School, Zhang was able to start his Internet company in China with the funding provided by the two professors.

Zhang not only brought new Internet technologies to China but also introduced "venture capital" into the Chinese business language. In 1998 the company that he founded, Internet Technologies China, officially launched "Sohu," a new product that combined the functions of search, information, and communication. Sohu was so popular that Zhang renamed his company after it.

Zhang became an instant sensation because of his ground-breaking role in China's nascent Internet industry. Later that year, Zhang debuted in *Time* magazine, on their list for the world's top fifty digital elite; he would be featured again in the same magazine, on the 15 Global Tech Gurus list in 2003. On 7 July 2000, Sohu began to trade its stock on the NASDAQ; it was one of the first initial public offerings in the United States for a Chinese company. In 2003, Zhang ranked second on a list of wealthy Chinese people in science and technology, a list based on statistics from the Shanghai Stock Exchange, US Securities and Exchange Commission (SEC), HKSE, and Yahoo! Finance in the fields of IT and ICT industry for listed companies. The same year also witnessed his rise to the top three on a list of China's fifty wealthiest figures in the Internet industry in the Hunrun China Rich List 2013.

Zhang is recognized for more than his rapidly accumulating wealth, however, and his influence on China's business world as well as on Chinese society is shown by a long list of honors and awards. In 2000, for example, he was selected by *China Youth Daily* as one of the "Ten Most Influential IT Figures of the Year"; and in 2004 he was given the "Annual Outstanding Manager Award" by the Chinese Academy of Management.

A New Type of Businessman

Apart from his professional achievements, Zhang leads a very active and culturally diverse personal life. Painting and music are among his many interests. He has said he would have become a rock and roll singer if his Internet business did not work out. He is also very fond of mountain climbing and has organized several expeditions under the banner of his company. In 2003, to commemorate

Zhāng Cháoyáng •

the fiftieth anniversary of the first successful ascent of Mount Everest, he led the China Sohu Climbing Team and reached the high point of 6,666 meters.

Zhang thrives under the spotlight of the media and frequently appears in reality and talk shows on television. Fully aware of his influence among China's youth, he connects with them through online writings and guest appearances at college campuses around the country. These speeches have been collected in *Overcoming 300 Years of Inferiority: Zhang Chaoyang's View on the Internet, Cyber Culture, and Life*, a popular book among young readers.

China's economic reform and openness have brought business opportunities to millions. Many who have seized the opportunities have become successful, wealthy, or famous. Zhang has become all these and more, but he stands apart from the stereotype of the ruthless and self-indulgent businessmen in many ways. He wants profit, but he also cares about public interest; he lives a corporate life, but he fully engages with Chinese society and culture. He is the new face of the Chinese businessman: passionate, intelligent, and fluent in the languages of the East and the West. He is a leader not only in business but also in cultural life. In an article titled "The Basic Contradictions of Life," Zhang held that human culture tells you that as long as you are engaged in something,

you will feel fulfilled and happy, but he chose to live life differently: though he is engaged in his work, he finds happiness and fulfillment beyond it as well, in China's society and culture, in the world around him. It is not just his absorbing career that sustains him. His pursuit of success in the first half of life aims to help him have more room and freedom in seeking fulfillment and longevity later in life.

Peina ZHUANG
Sichuan University, China

Further Reading

Jiang Di 江堤. (Ed.). (2011). *Kuayue sanbainian de zibei: Zhang Chaoyang tan wangluo, wangluowenhua yu shenghuo* 跨越三百年的自卑：张朝阳谈网络·网络文化与生活 [Overcoming 300 Years of Inferioirty: Zhang Chaoyang's view on the internet, cyber culture, and life]. Changsha: Hunan University Press.

Tian Yu 天宇. (2006). *Sousuo Zhang Chaoyang— Zhang Chaoyang yu SohuSougou de Gushi* 搜索张朝阳—张朝阳与搜狐搜狗的故事 [Searching for Zhang Chaoyang—Zhang Chaoyang's story with Sohu and Sougou]. Beijing: World Knowledge Press.

Dong Guoyong 董国用. (2011). *Meiyou bu keneng— bing bu mosheng de Zhang Chaoyang* 没有不可能—并不陌生的张朝阳 [Beyond impossibilities—the familiar Zhang Chaoyang]. Beijing: CITIC Press Group.

• 张朝阳 •

☿ Zhāng Yìmóu 张艺谋

b. 1951—Contemporary film director, key figure of the Fifth Generation

Alternate names: b. Zhāng Yímóu 张诒谋；trad. 張藝謀

• Zhāng Yìmóu •

Summary

Arguably one of the most talented and versatile filmmakers in contemporary China, Zhang Yimou has been a prolific and influential director for nearly three decades. As one of the so-called Fifth Generation directors, Zhang has played a key role in defining the landscape of Chinese cinema after the Cultural Revolution and introducing Chinese films to a Western audience. His filmmaking not only helped shape the post-socialist "national cinema," but also permanently changed the ways in which Chinese films are produced, financed, distributed, and consumed.

As arguably the most admired and criticized Chinese director following the Cultural Revolution, Zhang Yimou has attracted world attention for his tapestries of color, bold depictions of desire, timely engagement with politics, and continuous quest for cinematic freedom from genres and conventions. Both his art-house productions and market-oriented blockbusters reflect his complex relationships with Chinese authority, international film festivals, and domestic and foreign markets. Although often a target of criticism, and known for dancing a fine line between domestic censorship and international appeal, Zhang has succeeded in terms of artistic recognition and box office proceeds, resulting in his status as a leader in new Chinese cinema.

Early Life

Born on 14 November 1951 as Zhāng Yímóu 张诒谋 to a mother who was a dermatologist and a father who served in the defeated Nationalist army and thus belonged to a suspect social class, Zhang Yimou spent his childhood feeling isolated and restricted. Sensitive and quiet, he found consolation in drawing and asserted himself at school by taking charge of blackboard propaganda. His artistic talent was a source of pride until he was challenged by a girl who had transferred from Beijing. This girl, named Xiāo Huá 肖华, later became Zhang Yimou's wife after a persistent courtship.

In 1968, Zhang was "sent down" to the countryside (*shàng shān xià xiāng* 上山下乡) as part of the relocation of urban youth during the Cultural Revolution (1966–1976). He convinced Xiao Hua to go with him to a remote village in Shaanxi Province, where they stayed for three years doing manual labor, until both got a chance to return to the city to work in factories. These harsh years spent working in the village and a cotton mill would later become sources of inspiration for his filmmaking.

Selected Filmography of Zhang Yimou			
Year	**English Title**	**Chinese Title**	**Notes**
1987	*Red Sorghum*	红高粱 *Hóng gāoliáng*	Director
1988	*Codename Cougar*	代号美洲豹 *Dàihào měi zhōubào*	Co-director
1990	*Ju Dou*	菊豆 *Jú Dòu*	Director
1991	*Raise the Red Lantern*	大红灯笼高高挂 *Dà hóng dēnglóng gāogāo guà*	Director
1992	*The Story of Qiu Ju*	秋菊打官司 *Qiūjú dǎ guānsī*	Director
1994	*To Live*	活着 *Huózhe*	Director
1995	*Shanghai Triad*	摇啊摇，摇到外婆桥 *Yáo a yáo, yáo dào wàipó qiáo*	Director
1997	*Keep Cool*	有話好好說 *Yǒuhuà hǎohǎo shuō*	Director
1999	*Not One Less*	一个都不能少 *Yīgè dōu bùnéng shǎo*	Director
1999	*The Road Home*	我的父亲母亲 *Wǒ de fùqīn mǔqīn*	Director

Year	English Title	Chinese Title	Notes
2000	*Happy Times*	幸福時光 *Xìngfú shíguāng*	Director
2002	*Hero*	英雄 *Yīngxióng*	Director
2004	*House of Flying Daggers*	十面埋伏 *Shímiàn máifu*	Director
2005	*Riding Alone for Thousands of Miles*	千里走单骑 *Qiānlǐ zǒu dānqì*	Director, writer
2006	*Curse of the Golden Flower*	满城尽带黄金甲 *Mǎnchéng jìn dài huángjīn jiǎ*	Director, writer
2008	Beijing 2008: Games of the XXIX Olympiad		Director (opening and closing ceremony)
2009	*A Woman, a Gun and a Noodle Shop*	三枪拍案惊奇 *Sānqiāng pāi àn jīngqí*	Director
2010	*Under the Hawthorn Tree*	山楂树之恋 *Shānzhāshù zhī liàn*	Director
2012	*The Flowers of War*	金陵十三钗 *Jīnlíng shísān chāi*	Director
2013	*Coming Home*	归来 *Guī lái*	Director
2016	*The Great Wall*	长城 *Chángchéng*	Director

During his time at the cotton mill, he developed an interest in photography and allegedly sold his blood to buy a camera. It was also during this time that he changed his name to Yìmóu 艺谋 (*yì* 艺 meaning art) to avoid the embarrassment of people mispronouncing the character *yí* 诒 (bequeath, gift). His works soon appeared in art journals such as *Chinese Photography*. In 1978, his portfolio of photographs impressed those in authority enough to admit him to the cinematography department at the Beijing Film Academy, although at age twenty-seven, he had officially passed the age limit for admission. This became a turning point in Zhang Yimou's life.

• Zhāng Yìmóu •

Turning Point

Zhang's eligibility to attend the Academy was attacked, and this experience reinforced his reticence, motivating him to devote all his time and energy to his studies. After graduating in 1982, he accepted an assignment to Guangxi Film Studio, a remote regional studio generally not favored by students. This, however, gave Zhang Yimou the opportunity to work independently, with other young college graduates, instead of assisting senior filmmakers for years. Zhang served as the cinematographer for Zhāng Jūnzhāo's 张军钊 *One and Eight* (*Yīgè hé bāgè* 一个和八个, 1983), and *Chén Kǎigē's 陈凯歌 *Yellow Earth* (*Huáng tǔdì* 黄土地, 1984) and *The Big Parade* (*Dà yuèbīng* 大阅兵, 1986). Steering away from the socialist realist mode of filmmaking that had dominated Chinese cinema since the 1950s, these films corresponded with the socioeconomic reform in the 1980s and adopted more of a humanistic perspective to portray revolutionary history and the present. Zhang's bold, powerful images immediately seized people's attention and, as critics have noted, helped forge a new cinematic language utterly unlike previous Chinese filmmaking conventions. Zhang and his contemporaries became known as the "Fifth Generation" that brought about a revolutionary breakthrough in Chinese cinema, refreshing

————
*People marked with an asterisk have entries in this dictionary.

the image of China for Western audiences. For Zhang Yimou, this was a period when he found an outlet to express himself, and his creative energy was finally unleashed. The loosening up in ideological control and the thriving market allowed for more freedom in cinematic expression and international collaboration, paving the way for Zhang's stylistic innovation as well as the way of production.

A Controversial Director

Encouraged by the public recognition of his cinematography, Zhang made his debut as a director in 1987 with the feature film *Red Sorghum* 红高粱, which was an instant hit in China and subsequently won the Golden Bear award at the Berlin Film Festival, the first Chinese film ever to win. Adapted from *Mò Yán's 莫言 (b. 1955) 1986 serialized novel *The Family Saga of Red Sorghum* (*Hóng gāoliáng jiāzú* 红高粱家族), the film quickly established Zhang Yimou as a director whose groundbreaking mode of storytelling, marked by sensuous, sumptuous visual display, delivered not only a powerful visual impact, but also examined compelling cultural forces. The film also introduced *Gǒng Lì 巩俐 (b. 1965), the leading actress, to the international red carpet. She went on to become a cultural icon and together with Zhang, as with many other directors and their muses, began eight years of collaboration in films and romance off-screen.

Zhang's marriage with Xiao Hua soon came to an end.

Set in the 1920s and 1930s in rural China, *Red Sorghum* portrays an unconventional fairytale about an assertive girl, Jiu'er (Gong Li), her rescuer-rapist, and a legendary battle led by peasants against the invasion of the Japanese. Fraught with bold symbolism and visceral brutality, and marked by the use of a powerful red color, the film offers a fresh glimpse into the social ethos of the mid-1980s as well as an alternative history that is exotic, colorful, and passionate.

Following the success of *Red Sorghum*, which highlighted the liberating energy hidden in Chinese culture, Zhang made two films that mainly focused on the theme of oppression, particularly that of women, in Republican China. Both *Ju Dou* 菊豆 (1990) and *Raise the Red Lantern* 大红灯笼高高挂 (1991) tell the stories of young women being treated as commodities, sold to older husbands and confined in hopeless situations. As with *Red Sorghum*, Zhang continued to employ sensuous, even voluptuous, colors to accentuate the stunning image of Gong Li, whose characters, although striving to exercise some agency to assert their position and sexuality, end as victims silenced by an ironclad patriarchal system. What were usually considered "corrupt" and "obscene" cultural flaws, such as concubinage and taboos like incest, were packaged in stunning images and brilliantly displayed on screen, astonishing Western audiences.

Although garnering multiple awards, these films also invited tremendous controversy and criticism. Some critics believed that Zhang intentionally exhibited an exotic, feminine, and impotent image of China to satisfy the voyeuristic, fetishistic, Orientalist Western gaze, to reinforce their conception of China as an eternally backward nation.

Zhang's signature style of colorful and dramatic storytelling was restrained with his surprising turn to another method of filmmaking: documentary-style realism. *The Story of Qiuju* 秋菊打官司 (1992) traces a peasant woman's untiring search for justice and dignity for her husband after an unapologetic local official kicks him in the groin. This time, Zhang, while again featuring Gong Li, avoided his extravagant style and employed local amateurs to play characters like themselves, often using hidden cameras amid the crowd to capture spontaneity. A unique exploration of the decency and persistence of peasants as a valuable characteristic of Chinese culture, the film prompted critics to comment on Zhang's changing relationship with the Chinese government, believing he made this film to cater to the national project of legal reform at that time.

The 1990s saw Zhang become an influential director who drew criticism that swayed between whether his films bowed to the ideological mainstream promoted by Chinese government or appealed to the Western fantasy of an exotic or inhumane China. The fate of

• Zhāng Yìmóu •

the films often reflected his complex relations with Chinese authorities and foreign markets. For example, the 1994 historical epic *To Live* 活着 (based on the novel by *Yú Huá 余华 [b. 1960]), a sensitive and rousing look at the life of an ordinary man and his family from the 1940s to 1970s as they struggle to survive in the ever-changing sociopolitical milieu of China, was banned in China yet won the Grand Prix du Jury at the Cannes Film Festival. Banned from accepting international investment, Zhang shot *Shanghai Triad* 摇啊摇, 摇到外婆桥 (1995), a moderately funded gangster movie, which marked the end of Zhang's professional collaboration and romantic relationship with Gong Li. The two would not work together until 2006 in *Curse of the Golden Flower* 满城尽带黄金甲.

With Gong Li's departure, Zhang made a lighthearted black comedy, *Keep Cool* 有话好好说 (1997) and in 1999, two films set in the countryside though radically different in terms of style. *Not One Less* 一个都不能少 is a documentary-style film that offers a moving account of a substitute teacher's effort to keep children from dropping out of school in contemporary rural China. *The Road Home* 我的父亲母亲 presents a nostalgic look at an innocent yet profound love relationship during the Maoist period, which launched the career of Zhāng Zǐyí 章子怡 (b. 1979), the second international superstar that Zhang discovered.

By the 2000s, Zhang had firmly established himself as one of the most successful art-house directors in China, capable of attracting significant financial resources to make big-budget blockbusters. This period also witnessed Zhang's increasing compromise with the government and conscious appeal to the mass market. Apart from a couple of comedies, *Happy Times* 幸福时光 (2000), and *A Woman, a Gun, and a Noodle Shop* 三枪拍案惊奇 (2009) and a light drama, *Riding Alone for Thousands of Miles* 千里走单骑 (2005), Zhang's most notable achievement was his revitalization of the martial arts genre. His 2002 hit, *Hero* 英雄, remains the highest-grossing motion picture in the Chinese film industry. Instilling the Chinese political ideal of *tiānxià* 天下 (all under heaven) into the *wǔxiá* 武侠 (knight errands) genre, showcasing traditional Chinese arts of music, calligraphy, and swordplay in extravagant visual images, the film also generated criticism for its promotion of authoritarianism at the same time as it mesmerized global audiences for its breathtaking splendor.

Despite these criticisms, the box office success of this film encouraged Zhang to make two more martial arts films set in imperial times: *House of Flying Daggers* 十面埋伏 (2004) and *Curse of the Golden Flower* (2006). Packed with international superstars from the mainland, Hong Kong, and Taiwan, these films repeat Zhang's lavish use of color, music, and movement in *Hero*, but with neither its level of heroics or artistic originality.

To date, Zhang has made nineteen feature films and continues to reinvent

张艺谋

Zhang Yimou was commissioned to direct the opening ceremony for the 2008 Beijing Olympics. Photo by Tim Hipps/U.S. Army.

himself in various genres and styles. His last two films were both adapted from the novels of female writer Yán Gēlíng 严歌苓 (b. 1958). *Flowers of War* 金陵十三钗 (2012) features Hollywood superstar Christian Bale, retelling the atrocities and sacrifices which took place during the Nanjing Massacre of 1937. *Coming Home* 归来 (2013) narrates a family tragedy rooted in the Cultural Revolution. Both are weighty topics in modern Chinese history and sensitive to censorship, yet Zhang chose to approach the topics by dramatizing sentimental themes of love, sacrifice, and redemption.

Acting and Producing

Zhang's talent has not been limited to filmmaking. Without professional training in acting, he played the male lead in Wú Tiānmíng's 吴天明 (1939–2014) film *Old Well* (*Lǎo jǐng* 老井, 1986) and won multiple best-actor awards for it. He also co-starred with Gong Li in a Hong Kong production, *Fight and Love with a Terracotta Warrior* (*Gǔjīn dà zhàn qínyǒng qíng* 古今大战秦俑情, 1989). Since the 1990s, he has delved into a variety of other artistic ventures, including opera, ballet, and outdoor multimedia productions, most famously the opening and closing ceremonies of the 2008 Beijing Olympics. In 2010, Yale University recognized his genius with both camera and choreography by awarding him an Honorary Doctorate of Fine Arts.

Kun QIAN
University of Pittsburgh

Further Reading

Berry, Michael. (2005). Zhang Yimou: Flying colors. In Michael Berry, *Speaking in images: Interviews with contemporary Chinese filmmakers*. New York: Columbia University Press.

Chow, Rey. (1998). The force of surfaces: Defiance in Zhang Yimou's films. In Rey Chow, *Primitive passions: Visuality, sexuality, ethnography, and contemporary Chinese cinema*. New York: Columbia University Press.

Cui, Shuqin. (1997). Gendered perspective: The construction and representation of subjectivity and sexuality in *Ju Dou*. In Sheldon Lu (Ed.), *Transnational Chinese cinema: Identity, nationhood, gender*. Honolulu: University of Hawaii Press.

Gateward, Frances. (Ed). (2001). *Zhang Yimou: Interviews*. Jackson: University Press of Mississippi.

Gong Haomin. (2011). Zhang Yimou. In Yvonne Tasker (Ed.), *Fifty contemporary film directors*. London and New York: Routledge.

Huang Xiaoyang 黄晓阳. (2008). *Yinxiang Zhongguo: Zhang Yimou Zhuan* 印象中国：张艺谋传 [The impression of China: a biography of Zhang Yimou]. Beijing: Huaxia chuban she.

Kong, Haili. (1996). Symbolism through Zhang Yimou's subversive lens in his early films. *Asian Cinema*, 8(2): 98–115.

Lan, Feng. (2008). Zhang Yimou's Hero: Reclaiming the martial arts film for 'All Under Heaven.' *Modern Chinese Literature and Culture*, 20(1), 1–43.

Li Erwei. (2002). *Zhimian Zhang Yimou* 直面张艺谋 [Face to face with Zhang Yimou]. Beijing: Jingji ribao chubanshe.

Lu, Sheldon H. (1997). National cinema, cultural critique, transnational capital: The films of Zhang Yimou. In Sheldon H. Lu (Ed.), *Transnational Chinese cinema: Identity, nationhood, gender*. Honolulu: University of Hawai'i Press.

Lu, Tonglin. (2002). The Zhang Yimou model. In Tonglin Lu, *Confronting modernity in the cinema of Taiwan and mainland China*. Cambridge, UK: Cambridge University Press.

Zhang, Yingjin. (2002). Seductions of the body: Fashioning ethnographic cinema in contemporary China. In Yingjin Zhang, *Screening China: Critical interventions, cinematic reconfigurations and the transnational imaginary in contemporary Chinese cinema*. Ann Arbor: Center for Chinese Studies, University of Michigan Press.

张艺谋

♂ Zhào Zǐyáng 赵紫阳

1919–2005—Party leader, political and economic reformer

Alternate names: b. Zhào Xiūyè 赵修业; trad. 趙紫陽

Summary

Zhao Ziyang was an innovative party leader who was instrumental in the late twentieth century's political and economic reforms in China. Among other issues, he advocated secret-ballot elections in villages, local markets and greater flexibility for farmers, and a loosening of the commune system. He is best remembered as China's leader during the tumultuous student demonstrations of 1989 during which he lost his position, spending the next sixteen years under house arrest.

If there was an abiding image of the 1989 disturbances that rocked Beijing and the People's Republic of China (PRC)—beyond that of the lone man standing defiantly before the tank coming down the Avenue of Heavenly Peace—it was of Zhao Ziyang, then head of the Chinese Communist Party (CCP), holding a megaphone to his mouth and trying to address students on 19 May 1989, as the revolt was growing. Zhao was to be effectively felled from power on this date.

The journey from one of the most innovative and effective provincial party secretaries in the Maoist period to one of the key economic decision makers in the early Reform and Opening Up period, peaking as leader of the party from 1987 to 1989 and ending with sixteen years under house arrest and a death in 2005 that was barely noted in China, must rank as one of the most remarkable in modern Chinese politics. Zhao Ziyang was to prove himself the ultimate "almost" man in the story of modern China.

Early Years

Zhao was born in central China's Henan Province in 1919. He joined the Communist Youth League during the early 1930s and was an underground worker for the Communist Party itself during the Second Sino-Japanese War (1937–1945). His impeccable revolutionary credentials were only reinforced when his father was killed in the late 1940s during the

Chinese Civil War (1946–1949) with the Nationalists. By 1951, he had become a key official in Guangdong, where he piloted numerous economic programs, many of them in partial defiance of central diktats that stressed increasing levels of centralized economic planning and worked to impose a heavy-handed commune system upon the whole country. The tragic effects of this were felt in the early 1960s in the aftermath of the Great Leap Forward 大跃进, when a famine swept China, leading to the deaths of over thirty million people. By then, Zhao started simply to disband the commune system, marking a temporary return to rational economic policy making. A simple household responsibility system was introduced, and marketization tolerated. By 1965, Zhao was party secretary of Guangdong, despite not being on the Central Committee of the party.

The Cultural Revolution (1966–1976) abruptly ended this period. Like many leaders at provincial and national levels who were perceived as being "revisionist," Zhao was an immediate target for hardline Red Guard (Hóngwèibīng 红卫兵) rebellion groups in Guangdong in 1967. Zhao survived this violent and dangerous period, serving in a rural factory. Like *Dèng Xiǎopíng 邓小平 (1904–1997), who was to be his greatest and most important political patron in the future, Zhao was eventually summoned from this form of

internal exile once some form of stability had returned. It wasn't until 1973, however, that Zhao was partially rehabilitated, invited to join the Central Committee of the Communist Party's elite leaders, and sent first back to Guangdong to continue his work there, and then, in 1975, to Chengdu in Sichuan Province.

Sichuan Years

Sichuan was to be Zhao's final launchpad for central leadership. An immense, populous province with rich agricultural and natural reserves, it had been economically decimated by the Cultural Revolution. In the final year of Mao's life (he died in 1976), Zhao started to implement the economic system that was to be introduced nationwide from 1978. Tearing up the rule book of commune-based, revolutionary productivity methods that had been state orthodoxy until then, Zhao allowed the creation of local markets and greater flexibility for farmers to sell their surpluses to the state cooperatives. Introduced to the Politburo first as an alternate member, and then in 1979 as a full member, Zhao was now finally part of the new inner circle of decision makers around Deng Xiaoping, looking to rebuild China's economy, repair some of the damage done to its international image, and create, finally, a fully modernized and efficient system.

Return to Beijing

Along with *Hú Yàobāng 胡耀邦 (1915–1989), appointed the party's general

赵紫阳

—————
*People marked with an asterisk have entries in this dictionary.

secretary in 1980, Zhao was to be closely associated with the initial years of reform, creating the town and village enterprise network—a diverse group of local government-supported enterprises that covered sectors from industry to hotels and service providers—which was to eventually employ more than 70 percent of Chinese workers, delivering efficiency in the state and agricultural sector, liberalizing laws that allowed foreign investment into China, and rebuilding the key relationship with the United States. In a series of bold moves beginning in 1981, many of them instigated by Zhao (who had become premier in 1980, in effect in charge of China's administration after the peaceful removal of then party chairman Hua Guofeng), four Special Economic Zones (Jīngjì tèqū 经济特区, SEZs) opened up to allow foreign investment. Through these SEZs, China started an epic investigation of financial models available abroad, looking at almost every area of economic policy and governance. Zhao himself was recorded as saying that Deng simply told his two protégés, Hu Yaobang and Zhao, to "sort the economy, leave the politics to me."

Zhao records in his memoirs that the key challenge was productivity. Years of ideological battles had made China's fragile industrial sector and its all-important agricultural sector inefficient. China had next to no reserves of foreign currency. It had to import almost all machine technology, and was even forced to import food staples. Zhao

suffered none of the ideological hang-ups of previous leaders, however, and he had proved in Sichuan that he was willing to experiment. The SEZs, launched between 1981 and 1983, were perhaps the most symbolic change because they shattered the resistance to foreign investment and brought both capital and know-how into China. The second greatest change was the final introduction of the household responsibility system that allowed farmers to dismantle centrally imposed communes and sell surpluses of crops back to the state. Both delivered huge benefits.

Agricultural sector reform was more complex and much more profound in its impact on society generally in China. Allowing greater freedom to farmers, to incentivize them and improve efficiency, was critical even though it cut across much of Maoist orthodoxy that had reigned till then. Now, banks could start lending to a wider group of people. Town and village enterprises became genuinely entrepreneurial. Efficiency in the agricultural sector shot up, releasing many people to pursue other areas of economic activity. The impact of this is best seen on China's gross domestic product (GDP) growth rate, which in 1981 started to climb steadily up into double digits.

Political Costs

As premier and finally as a full member of the Politburo Standing Committee in 1983, Zhao soon found that such changes

• Zhào Zǐyáng •

created plenty of opposition. Through-out the 1980s the remaining hardline leftists mounted various attacks on what they saw as the anti-Maoist, overly lib-eral policies of Zhao and Hu Yaobang. Frequent "spiritual pollution" cam-paigns were held from 1982 onward, slapping down those who tried to link economic reform with political reform in particular, eventually leading to Hu Yaobang's removal from his position as party secretary in 1987. Zhao took over this position, and held on to the pro-found conviction that China had no choice but to continue its Reform and Opening Up policy, and that returning to a more leftist model would be a huge

impediment and lead to even greater political consequences.

Party Secretary (1987–1989)

Zhao was to be head of the Party for only two years. The three great issues for Zhao and which led up to the events of June 1989 were dealing with increasing inflation in China, continuing reform of the party so that the growing issue of corruption could be managed, and con-tinuing opening up to former strategic enemies, in particular the USSR, which was itself undergoing dramatic reform under its then general secretary, Mikhail Gorbachev.

Ronald Reagan (right) and Zhao Ziyang (left) at the White House, 1984. Photo by Doug Kanter/ U.S. Department of State.

One policy instigated by Zhao during this period would have a lasting positive effect: the National Organic Law of Village Committees of 1988, allowing secret ballot elections to be held at the village level throughout China. Delivering a popular mandate to village committees meant that they were able to undertake the responsibilities of gathering taxes and implementing the one-child policy, which was introduced in 1981, more robustly. Village elections continue to this day, a testament to their success.

During the 1987 Party Congress, Zhao promoted two major policy developments. The first was to record that the Party was now building "the primary stage of socialism." This legitimized the utilization of a more market-based, entrepreneurial economic model. It meant that "socialism with Chinese characteristics" could be hybrid, able to encompass different forms of ownership and embrace a wider role of the non-state sector, which was increasingly producing growth, innovation, and employing people in rural and city areas. In addition to this, Zhao also sanctioned support for wider forms of non-state enterprises, something typified by companies associated with the Wenzhou area of Zhejiang Province, which were largely free of government involvement, highly entrepreneurial in their activity, and working increasingly in small manufacturing and industry. These companies would become increasingly important as they occupied areas of the Chinese economy the state was keen to relinquish.

But neither these economic and ideological changes, nor village elections were sufficient to deal with the dislocations and complex forces in Chinese society that resulted from a few years of very rapid and unequal economic reform. By the start of 1989, inflation in particular had pushed staple-food prices up dramatically, meaning that harsher rationing had to be introduced. This only accentuated the problem of party corruption. Finally, in April 1989, Hu Yaobang died, precipitating the events of the next three months that led ultimately to Zhao's fall and house arrest.

June 1989

The two most authoritative firsthand accounts of 1989 are, first, the widely accepted as authentic documents that appeared in *The Tiananmen Papers* (Zhang et al. 2001), which consist of the minutes of top-level meetings and accounts of discussions on how to handle the student demonstrations; and, secondly, Zhao's own account in his memoirs. Both show that there was a clear division in the leadership over how to deal with the threat posed by students to party authority. Their demands for democracy and for fundamental party reform were hard to take even for so-called liberals like Zhao. For the hard-liners they were confirmation of many of the negative and risky effects that China had brought

• Zhào Zǐyáng •

on itself after undertaking such rapid, wholesale reform since 1980. With China's universities not functioning and riots already taking place in over 250 other Chinese cities, fear of instability and a return to the chaos of the Cultural Revolution ran high. When this happened, Deng crucially withdrew his all-important support for Zhao.

Zhao himself states in his memoirs that by mid-May 1989, just before the visit of Gorbachev to China, demonstrators had cooled off, and had he been able to deal unfettered with their demands, he could have avoided what happened a month later. Hard-liners in the party elite were toughening their stance, however, and when an editorial in the *People's Daily* in mid-May labeled the student demonstrators as "anti-party, counter-revolutionary" elements, the situation became enflamed. The continuation and—even worse—escalation of demonstrations after mid-May only proved to his many opponents within the elite that he was part of the cause, and Zhao's position was increasingly precarious.

From late May, Zhao was effectively politically marginalized to such an extent that he had already been removed from power, even though he still held the position of party secretary until 24 June. The most famous final public moment of his career came on the night of 19 May, when he appeared—to the astonishment of demonstrators—in the square itself with his political private secretary, *Wēn Jiābǎo 温家宝 (b. 1942), standing grim

faced at his side. He apologized to the students and, overcome by emotion, told them that they had achieved what they needed, been listened to, and now needed to return to their universities and homes. It was a piece of advice that went unheeded. On 4 June, in the early hours, Tiananmen Square was filled with troops, and live ammunition was turned on those who had been brave enough to remain. China deals with the legacy of this moment to this day.

House Arrest

Zhao was never to speak to or meet with Deng again after May 1989, despite writing to him. He was never formally charged with any crime, but his own successor, *Jiāng Zémín 江泽民 (b. 1926), ensured that he enjoyed no freedoms or a public profile. His official residence in Beijing became a prison. While not treated as brutally as former key leaders who fell from power, he was to become China's forgotten leader. This was symbolized by the news of his death in January 2005, when only the briefest notice appeared in the official state media. There were no events or obituaries.

But in 2009, Zhao's voice finally returned in the form of twenty cassette tapes that he had secretly recorded and then hidden in his own home; they were discovered by his son and carefully transcribed and published in Hong Kong. The evenhanded, sometimes dry descriptions of the tumultuous events in 1989

赵紫阳

only added to their credibility. More remarkably, it is in the description of his involvement with the early period of the Reform and Opening Up era that Zhao offers the most insight—as well as in his final admission that in order to move forward, China has to look at greater political reforms.

Zhao's relaxed, open manner had always impressed those who had met him when he traveled abroad. He made a major contribution to the positive development of China in a very short space of time, and he will be remembered for the impact of this and for being a decent, pragmatic, and courageous leader.

Kerry BROWN
Lau China Institute, King's College

Further Reading

Brook, Timothy. (1992). *Quelling the people: The military suppression of the Beijing democracy movement.* New York: Oxford University Press.

Wu, Guoguang, & Lansdowne, Helen. (Eds.). (2013). *Zhao Ziyang and China's political future.* London: Routledge.

Zhang Liang; Nathan, Andrew J.; Link, Perry; & Schell, Orville. (Eds. & Trans.). (2001). *The Tiananmen papers.* New York: PublicAffairs.

Zhao Ziyang. (2009). *Prisoner of the state: The secret journal of Chinese premier Zhao Ziyang* (Bao Pu, Renee Chiang & Adi Ingantius, Eds. & Trans.). New York: Simon & Schuster.

• Zhào Zǐyáng •

⚥ Zhōu Yǒngkāng 周永康

b. 1942—Politician and party member charged with corruption in 2015

Summary

As a leader in the oil and gas industry, a member of the Politburo Standing Committee, and the secretary of the Central Political and Legal Affairs Commission, Zhou Yongkang wielded great influence over China's industries and security apparatus. His arrest and expulsion from the Chinese Communist Party was seen as a major victory for the anticorruption campaign pursued by the Xi Jinping administration.

The arrest and expulsion from the Chinese Communist Party (CCP) of Zhou Yongkang, former member of the Politburo Standing Committee and secretary of the Central Committee's Political and Legal Committee, was announced after a meeting of the Politburo on 5 December 2014. It was seen by many commentators as a major victory for the anticorruption campaign pursued by the *Xí Jìnpíng 习近平 (b. 1953) administration.

*People marked with an asterisk have entries in this dictionary.

The decision to proceed against Zhou put an end to a tacit understanding that the most senior members of the party would not be prosecuted: "tigers" such as Zhou were no longer any more immune from prosecution for corruption than the lower level "flies." Zhou was the most senior member of the CCP to be prosecuted for many years, and his case has been compared to the trial of Liu Qingshan and Zhang Zishan, two "great tigers" who were executed during the Three-Anti Campaign of the early 1950s.

Early Life and Career

Zhou Yongkang was born into a poor family in 1942, in the countryside near the city of Wuxi in Jiangsu Province. He did well at school and enrolled in the survey and exploration department of the Beijing Petroleum Institute (now named the China Petroleum University). He graduated in 1966, having joined the CCP two years previously, and worked in the oil industry in Liaoning Province in the northeast of China.

He also began his political career in Liaoning as mayor of the oil town of Panjin, while gaining increasing managerial responsibilities in the industry.

His first central government position was as deputy minister of the petroleum industry in 1985. After reorganization and the creation of what would become the China National Petroleum Organization (CNPC), Zhou was named deputy general manager. He became general manager in 1996, after CNPC bid successfully for pipeline construction and other petroleum-related projects in Sudan, Venezuela, and Kazakhstan, and he was also responsible for the stock exchange listing of PetroChina, a CNPC subsidiary. He served as an alternate member of the Central Committee from 1992.

Political Rise and Fall

Zhou's political career took off rapidly when he became a full member of the Central Committee in October 1997, and the following March he was appointed minister of land resources by premier *Zhū Róngjī 朱镕基 (b. 1928). In 1999, he took over as party secretary of Sichuan, running the province until 2002 and acquiring a reputation as an efficient modernizer. His involvement in high-value international oil contracts and land deals, and the complex and wide-ranging network of contacts he had cultivated, gave him access to immense financial resources, and CCP investigators allege that he profited personally from these in a corrupt manner.

After the Sixteenth CCP Congress, held in Beijing in November 2002, a new administration under general secretary *Hú Jǐntāo 胡锦涛 (b. 1942) took over, and Zhou was appointed as minister of public security and as deputy secretary (under Luó Gàn 罗干) of the Central Committees Political Legal Committee, which oversees the courts, the police, and the entire security apparatus. He also became a member of the Politburo and the State Council. In 2007 he succeeded his boss, Luo Gan, as secretary of the Political Legal Committee and was promoted to the Standing Committee of the Politburo, becoming one of the most powerful men in China.

Zhou's time in charge of security is regarded by many as a period when tough policing led to repression and abuse by the police and other official and unofficial security organizations. In 2007, Zhou publicly supported the policies of his protégé *Bó Xīlái 薄熙来 (b. 1949), the party secretary of Chongqing. Bo had combined a drive to promote quasi-Maoist "red culture" with a ruthless crackdown on organized crime that also affected many innocent citizens. Bo was removed from his party and government positions in March 2012, following the death of the British businessman Neil Heywood (Bo's wife, Gu Kailai, was later convicted of his murder). It became clear that Zhou had been protecting Bo and had even resisted the Politburo's decision to dismiss him. Reports of an attempted coup by Zhou, or that he threatened to use the People's Armed Police to get his way, cannot be substantiated, but in the political infighting that ensued, Zhou was forced to hand over control of the Political and Legal Committee to Mèng Jiànzhù 孟建柱, the minister for public security, in advance of his own retirement from the Politburo, which was due to take place at the Eighteenth CCP Congress in the autumn of 2012. Following this meeting, at which the new administration of Xi Jinping took power, the role of the Political and Legal Committee was downgraded and the new party secretary, Meng, was not given a seat on the Politburo Standing Committee.

The decision to investigate and charge Zhou with corruption involved a long and tortuous process, and was resisted because of his status and the political support he had gained within the leadership. A formal investigation into Zhou's activities was launched in December 2013 by the Central Commission for Discipline Inspection and the results were reported to the Politburo on 29 July 2014. Several key associates of his were arrested and some tried for corruption, but there was a delay in bringing a prosecution against Zhou. This was due in part to his seniority and to difficulties experienced in obtaining evidence, but it also reflected the support he enjoyed among senior CCP figures and the degree of factional wrangling over his future. The decision to expel Zhou from the CCP (thus leaving the way clear for a trial) was taken during the fourth plenary session of the Central Committee that opened on 17 October 2014 but, contrary to expectations, he was not expelled during the plenum.

After further delay, the announcement that he had been expelled came during a meeting of the Politburo on 5 December 2014. According to the official Chinese news agency, Xinhua:

The investigation found that Zhou seriously violated the Party's political, organizational and confidentiality discipline. He took advantage of his posts to seek profits for others and accepted huge bribes personally and through his family, the statement said.

He abused his power to help relatives, mistresses and friends make huge profits from operating businesses, resulting in serious losses of [state-owned] assets.

Zhou leaked the Party's and country's secrets. He seriously violated self-disciplinary regulations and accepted a large amount of money and properties personally and through his family.

Zhou committed adultery with a number of women and traded his power for sex and money.

Added were other clues of suspected crimes by Zhou, also found during the investigation.

On 2 April 2015 Zhou Yongkang was formally charged with taking bribes, abusing his power and deliberately leaking state secrets. It was announced that the trial would take place in Tianjin but the precise date was not specified. As he is being tried, inter alia, for violations of "party and organizational discipline and secrecy," leaking state secrets, the hearings will not be mainly held in public. Insiders expect him to be treated more harshly than Bo Xilai, who was sentenced to life imprisonment, and commentators have predicted a sentence of death suspended for two years.

Michael DILLON
Independent Scholar

Further Reading

Chan, Minnie. (2014, December 7). Zhou Yongkang can expect tougher treatment than Bo Xilai: Analysts. *South China Morning Post*. Retrieved April 29, 2015, from http://www.scmp.com/news/china/article/1657113/zhou-yongkang-can-expect-tougher-treatment-bo-xilai-analysts-say

China's top judge says Zhou Yongkang probe proves nobody is above "cage" of the law (2014, August 27). *South China Morning Post*.

China Vitae. (2015). Zhou Yongkang. Retrieved April 29, 2015, from http://www.chinavitae.com/biography/Zhou_Yongkang

Cui Min. (2014). Zhou Yongkang an de fansi yu jianyan 周永康案的反思与检验 [Reflections and opinions on the Zhou Yongkang case]. *Yanhuang chunqiu, 11*, 18–21.

Du Daozheng. (2014). Ye yi Zhou Yongkang an de genben qishi 也易周永康案的根本其实 [More fundamental disclosures on the Zhou Yongkang case]. *Yanhuang chunqiu, 11*, 9–12.

Mu Xuequan (Ed.). (2014, December 6). Zhou Yongkang arrested, expelled from CPC. *Xinhua News Agency*. Retrieved April 29, 2015, from http://news.xinhuanet.com/english/china/2014-12/06/c_127281433.htm

⚥ Zhōu Yǒuguāng 周有光

b. 1906—Linguist and co-inventor of the romanization system pinyin

Alternate name: b. Zhōu Yàopíng 周耀平

Summary

Originally a banker both in China and in the United States, Zhou Youguang will go down in history as the creator of pinyin, perhaps the world's most successful transliteration system, which romanizes Chinese characters and is the main system by which Chinese and foreigners learn Mandarin to this day.

Interviewed soon after his 109th birthday in 2015, Zhou Youguang dryly joked that he had been "forgotten by God." A man whose life ran from the dying years of the Qīng 清 dynasty (1644–1911/12), through the Republican Era (1911–1949), and deep into the first decades of the twenty-first century and the entirety of Communist China rule, Zhou impressed those meeting him with his liveliness, wit, and free-spirited nature. A fierce critic of the Chinese Communist Party in his later years, he commented, when asked whether this made him afraid, that the government had little option but to let him be, as the likelihood of detaining such a venerated and immensely long-lived figure was non-existent. In that sense not only was he one of modern China's longest-lived people, but also perhaps its most free.

Early Life and Career

Zhou was born Zhou Yaoping in Changzhou, Jiangsu Province in January 1906, six years before the collapse of the Qing dynasty, into a relatively wealthy family of officials. Educated at the US-supported St John's University in Shanghai in the 1920s, he married Zhāng Yǔnhé 张允和 in 1933. Over the period of the start of the Second Sino-Japanese War, he moved to the Nationalist wartime capital of Chongqing, working for the Xinhua Trust and Savings Bank. During this period he had one piece of very bad luck—the death of his five-year-old daughter from appendicitis—and one piece of good luck—meeting

周有光

with the future Chinese premier, Zhōu Ēnlái 周恩来 (1898–1976). This link was to see him appointed to the Language Commission, established in 1955 after the People's Republic had been in power for six years.

In 1946, Zhou moved to the United States with his wife and son, working at One Wall Street for Xinhua Bank. Years later he was to recall meeting Albert Einstein during this time, but said the subject of their conversations had grown hazy in the intervening years. After the Communists won the Chinese Civil War in 1949, Zhou heeded the great patriotic plea to return to the motherland to assist in China's reconstruction. It was as part of this movement that Máo Zédōng 毛泽东 (1893–1976) and his colleagues decided something needed to be done about the pitifully low literacy levels of 15 percent among Chinese people.

Inventing Pinyin

Set up in 1955, the Language Commission first had to address how to create a better phonetic system to learn the sounds of Chinese characters. Previous systems had proved inaccurate or too cumbersome. At the time, Zhou was working as a teacher in Shanghai, but was summoned to Beijing to lead the commission, largely at Zhou Enlai's request (despite their shared family names, the two were unrelated). Zhou Youguang had developed an interest in linguistics in the early 1950s, and he put these skills to use to help to create a flexible but accurate new system. The result, three years later, was *pīnyīn* 拼音, a relatively straightforward transliteration using the Roman alphabet, with diacritical marks to indicate tones, and one which proved easy for both native and non-native Chinese speakers to master.

Later, it was his involvement with this project and the link with the premier that probably saved him from the worse excesses of the Anti-Rightist Campaigns, waged from 1957 onwards, and then the Cultural Revolution (1966–1976). On paper, at least, he had all the attributes of a class enemy as it was defined in the new era of Maoist purism. As someone who had worked for many years in finance, and who had worked abroad in the United States, Zhou could have been labelled as politically suspect and compromised. He was attacked at struggle meetings a number of times in the late 1960s, but then was shipped off to the relative peace and quiet of the western Ningxia region for a period of rustication and reeducation. There he stayed until the early 1970s, when he was allowed back to be with his family in Beijing

Becoming a Critic

After the 1978 reforms, Zhou was once more able to offer his linguistic skills to his country, and was appointed as one of the main editors and translators of the first complete Chinese edition of the *Encyclopaedia Britannica* in 1985. Ostensibly retiring in 1991, he proceeded to produce in the next two and a half decades over ten books on aspects of Chinese language, culture, and history. He also started to opine more freely on the need for political reform in China, arguing that Chinese were no different than anyone else and therefore were perfectly capable of adopting democratic systems. Such frankness saw him rewarded with the label "sensitive person," and his name was removed from the invite list for a party attended by top-level Chinese leaders to celebrate the twentieth anniversary of the *Encyclopaedia Britannica* publication in Beijing.

Zhou's insatiable curiosity about the world extended well into his eleventh decade of life, as he ran a successful blog, under the catching title "Centennial Scholar," on which he posted about issues from Confucianism in modern China to social problems he had noticed.

Zhou Youguang is still an active writer and blogger well into his nineties (2012). Photo by Fong Carlie.

Alert and sprightly, he looked ready to continue for another decade or more, one of the most remarkable and significant figures of modern Chinese history, but among its quietest, most self-effacing, and for this reason, most impressive. His contribution was a large part of the reason why China now has some of the best literacy rates in the world, rising above 95 percent. Few people have contributed so much to human development and improvement, and yet sought so little in return.

Kerry BROWN
Lau China Institute, King's College

Further Reading

Chen Ping. (1999). *Modern Chinese: History and sociolinguistics.* Cambridge, UK: Cambridge University Press.

Goodman, Kenneth S.; Wang Shaowei; Iventosch, Miko; & Goodman, Yetta M. (2012). *Reading in Asian languages: Making sense of written texts in Chinese, Japanese, and Korean.* London: Routledge.

Hancock, Tom. (2015). China's 109-year-old dissenter is still fighting for democracy. Retrieved March 17, 2015, from http://uk.businessinsider.com/afp-china-linguists-109th-birthday-wish-democracy-2015-1?r=US#ixzz3Uf6x964x

LaFraniere, Sharon. (2012). A Chinese voice of dissent that took its time. *The New York Times.* Retrieved March 17, 2015, from http://www.nytimes.com/2012/03/03/world/asia/a-voice-of-dissent-in-china-that-took-its-time.html?pagewanted=all&_r=0

Lim, Louisa. (2011). At 105, Chinese linguist now a government critic. Retrieved March 17, 2015, from: http://www.npr.org/2011/10/19/141503738/at-105-celebrated-chinese-linguist-now-a-dissident

Rogers, Brown. (2012). Zhou Youguang: The father of Pinyin. Retrieved March 17, 2015, from http://www.theworldofchinese.com/2012/03/zhou-youguang-the-father-of-pinyin

Taylor, Insup, & Taylor, Martin M. (1995). *Writing and literacy in Chinese, Korean and Japanese.* Amsterdam: John Benjamins Publishing.

Zhou Youguang 周有光. (2003). *The historical evolution of Chinese languages and scripts* 中國語文的時代演進 (Zhang Liqing 張立青, Trans.). Ohio State University National East Asian Language Resource Center.

Zhou Youguang. (2011). Zhou Youguang de boke 周有光的博客 [Zhou Youguang's blog]. Retrieved March 17, 2015, from http://blog.sina.com.cn/zhouyouguang

• Zhōu Yǒuguāng •

♂ Zhū Róngjī 朱镕基

b. 1928—Politician, liberal and economic reformer, premier of the PRC (1998–2003)

Alternate name: trad. 朱鎔基

Summary

Known as China's "economics tsar" during the first decade of the twenty-first century, Zhu Rongji served as vice premier and premier during a period in which China joined the WTO, inflation was brought under control, and foreign investment flourished. While critics cite growing inequality during this time, as well as increasing unemployment and the decline of services for the most needy, Zhu Rongji is remembered as a liberal reformer who managed to dismantle the old system and integrate China more firmly into the global capitalist economy.

After two decades in the political wilderness during the Mao era, Zhu Rongji is best known for his return to the center of Chinese politics in the early 1990s and for serving a decade as China's "economics tsar." He oversaw a number of economic and administrative reforms that altered the very foundations of China's political economy: national finances became more stable, inflation was brought under control, the financial burdens of unprofitable state enterprises were reduced, government administration was streamlined, and market-based mechanisms of macroeconomic control were strengthened. In 2001, China finally joined the World Trade Organization (WTO), after fifteen years of on-and-off negotiations.

Despite outspoken criticism against Zhu's objectives and reforms, as time passes, Zhu's reputation has been enhanced—particularly among the general population. He is remembered as a "man of the people" who liked Chinese opera and playing the *húqín* 胡琴 (spike fiddle). Compared to other Chinese leaders Zhu was also considered to be approachable and candid by Chinese and foreign journalists. A more than competent English speaker, he was renowned for his sense of humor and disarming way of dealing with those critical of China's political system.

Early Career: Planning and Purges

Zhu was born in Changsha, Hunan Province, on 1 October 1928. His early life was one of deprivation, poverty, and illness; his father reportedly died before he was born, he was orphaned by the age of nine (some sources say ten), and he only just survived a life-threatening illness. Although he managed to get an education through support from his wider family and scholarships, the idea of Zhu as "one of the people" is well founded.

Like many of his generation, his formal educational training was technical, as an electrical engineering student at Tsinghua University. Zhu joined the Communist Party in October 1949, and also served as president of the Tsinghua Students' Union. This mix of political affiliation and academic expertise made him an ideal candidate for a career in the political system. When he graduated in 1951, Zhu was initially assigned to the industries ministry for northeast China before transferring to the State Planning Commission in Beijing in 1952.

His progress through the ranks, however, came to an abrupt halt in 1958, when Mao's preference for continued radical reform of the countryside replaced the policies of *Chén Yún 陈云 (1905–1995) that promoted industrial development through centralized control, leading ulti-

mately to the Great Leap Forward 大跃进 (1958–1960). Those like Zhu who criticized the change in policy were labeled as "rightists"—just as those who were deemed to have opposed Mao in the Hundred Flowers Campaign 百花运动 (1956–1957) had been. Zhu survived, but still lost his party membership and was sent to work in a cadre training school. As the economic and social costs of the Great Leap began to become clear in the early 1960s, policy tipped back to the more cautious planning agenda of Chen Yun, and those who had been criticized just a few years earlier began to take the steps back towards rehabilitation. In 1962, Zhu became an engineer in the National Economy Bureau of the State Planning Commission in Beijing.

But the political wind was to change yet again with the onset of the Cultural Revolution (1966–1976), and those who had previously been branded as rightists were obvious targets for criticism, forced re-education, and (physical) abuse. From 1970 to 1975, Zhu was "transferred" to work in a "May 7 Cadre School" 五七干部学校 where errant officials and intellectuals were supposed to be re-educated by learning from the experience of the masses through manual labor. This time Zhu's rehabilitation was rather slow and undramatic, working from 1975 as an engineer in the petroleum industry, though also holding an academic appointment. Mixing academic and state appointments was something he would continue until his

---

*People marked with an asterisk have entries in this dictionary.

retirement in 2001, including the position of (founding) dean of the Tsinghua University School of Economics and Management since 1984. It was not until 1978, however, that Zhu was effectively rehabilitated and his party membership was renewed. Like many of his generation, not just his political career but his person life had been subject to the vagaries of Chinese politics. But at least he had survived and was in a position to resume a long uninterrupted career—a career that was to take a new turn in 1987 with his appointment as vice mayor of Shanghai, under the city's party secretary *Jiāng Zémín 江泽民 (b. 1926).

Reviving Shanghai

Shanghai is an important city and financial center for China, so while other local governments were allowed to increase amounts of locally generated income to spend on local projects in the 1980s, Shanghai was simply too important to be given the same freedom. Not surprisingly, there was a feeling in Shanghai that local development was being impeded and sacrificed to support the growth of other parts of the country.

After considerable lobbying, a new system was introduced in which Shanghai was effectively allowed to keep any surplus income it generated for local projects until 1991—after that, any surplus was to be split fifty-fifty between the local and central government. And it was in this new economic environment

that Zhu made his mark in Shanghai. Elevated to mayor in the spring of 1988, and concurrently local party leader the following summer, for two years Zhu set in motion a number of local reforms that laid the foundations of what would become the transformation of Shanghai into a global city. Most notably was the expansion of what had been farmland on the eastern side of the Huangpu River 黄浦江, across from the historical and famous Bund, into a Special Economic Zone that has become almost the symbol of China's emergence as a modern global economy: Pǔdōng 浦东.

Zhu's time in Shanghai, however, was not all about his economic record. When the initial small group of mourners commemorating the life of former party secretary *Hú Yàobāng 胡耀邦 (1915–1989) began to swell and morph into protests in Tiananmen Square, Beijing in the spring of 1989, a smaller but similar movement also occurred in Shanghai. In the end, the Shanghai protests dissipated and ultimately ended without the recourse to military force, as had occurred in Beijing on 4 June, and Zhu came through the events looking to China's leaders like a man who could cope with a crisis.

Back to the Center

The next transition from a period of post-Tiananmen economic retrenchment and little political change to a new period of reform is usually said to start with *Dèng Xiǎopíng's 邓小平 (1904–1997) visit of

朱镕基

sourthern China during his "Southern Tour" *nánxún* 南巡 in the spring of 1992. In some ways, however, perhaps the real start date should be April 1991, when Zhu took the same path as Jiang Zemin from Shanghai to the central leadership in Beijing. Initially as vice premier in charge of the State Council Production Office, Zhu was elevated to become the first ranking of China's vice premiers in 1993 and was concurrently governor of the People's Bank of China (China's Central Bank) from 1993–1995. These positions effectively left Zhu as the key leader in charge of economic affairs until his retirement in 2003.

Zhu's first tasks as "economics tsar" were not to push forward with liberalization, but rather to fight fires and to prevent economic problems leading to social discontent. Faced with growing inflation in part fuelled by bank lending to support the initiatives of local governments, Zhu attempted to build a new financial system that tipped the balance of authority back from the provinces to the center, including fiscal and banking reforms.

As important as these reforms were, they did not deal with the basic problem that many state-owned enterprises (SOEs) simply could not survive without sustained injections of capital from the banks. In September 1995, the Central Committee announced a new national strategy of "grasping the big and letting go of the small" (*zhuādà fàngxiǎo* 抓大放小). Larger SOEs were to remain within the state sector while small enterprises left the state

sector by undergoing "shareholding transformation" (*gǔfenhuà* 股份化, calling it "privatization" 私有化 was still a step too far). These reforms did not resolve all of China's financial problems, but a large financial crisis was avoided and China achieved what was typically called a "soft landing" from the investment-fueled inflation of the early 1990s. The basic nature of the Chinese economy had also been changed to a hybrid economic system where the state tries to "regulate" economic activity rather than "plan" and "control" it. Given that virtually all of the changes that Zhu oversaw were intended to change the status quo, it is not surprising that these changes upset a wide range of people, from unemployed workers to top officials who found their formal agencies and channels of influence were disappearing. Zhu's leadership style also caused resentment at times. By his own admission, he had a very direct way of dealing with officials, demanding immediate answers and wanting to know who was responsible when things went wrong.

Verdicts on Zhu's record as an economic manager were divided. On the one hand, critics pointed to growing inequality; increasing unemployment; the decline in the provision of health, education, and welfare for the most needy; the growing influence of foreign economic interests; and a rising individualist/materialist obsession at the heart of Chinese society—as perhaps shown by the search for profits from schools-cum-firework factories. Supporters conversely focused on

Zhū Róngjī

the enormous structural problems that Zhu had to take on to turn China around, the relatively low rates of unemployment given the extent of state-owned enterprise reform, the soft landing from inflation, increasing amounts of foreign investment, and the fact that near 10 percent growth had still been achieved despite the outbreak of economic crisis in much of the rest of Asia in 1997.

Joining the WTO

Negotiations over China's WTO entry with what was then still the GATT had been ongoing since 1986 but entered a new phase in April 1999, when Zhu offered a range of compromises to the US during a visit to Washington intended to finally settle the issue. Many within the Chinese policy elites thought that these concessions went too far; to make matters worse for Zhu, even these concessions failed to gain an affirmative response from the United States.

Then, on 7 May, US forces as part of NATO operations in Yugoslavia bombed the Chinese embassy in Belgrade, killing three and injuring more. The Chinese people were outraged, and protestors flocked to the US embassy and consulates across the country, and while the United States was the primary target of hostility, Zhu also came under criticism for not defending China's interests and being too soft on the United States.

In some respects, this "crisis" helped turn things around for Zhu. The US administration was already under domestic pressure from economic groups that wanted to engage China further. After the events of April and May, the need to mend relations with Beijing and concerns about a potential retreat from Zhu and liberalization in China, the Clinton administration changed tack and signed a bilateral deal extending the Permanent Normal Trade Relations (PNTR) to China that Zhu wanted. While this was a key step on the road to WTO entry, negotiations with various WTO members continued for the better part of two years before China eventually joined in December 2001. The more apocalyptic warnings of a collapse of rural incomes and mass urban unemployment as a result of WTO entry proved wide of the mark. Entry into the WTO also helped ensure that foreign investment continued to flood into China, helping maintain economic growth in the first decade of the new millennium. Attaining the objective of joining the WTO in the face of considerable domestic opposition was a major political achievement for Zhu, and one for which he will be long remembered.

Evaluating Zhu Rongji: Liberal, Pragmatist, or Party Loyalist

In retiring from the premiership in 2003, Zhu more or less disappeared from public life altogether. He remains highly popular among China's (online) community, however, and praise for his honesty, devotion, and common touch (and origins) abound.

Zhu has often been referred to as a "liberal" reformer, and with good reason. His reforms went a long way towards dismantling the old state-planning system, introducing a greater role for markets, and integrating China more firmly into the global capitalist economy. Zhu's aim, however, does not appear to have been to destroy the state's economic role, but to change it, partly to make it more responsive to market pressures but also to make it more efficient and more able to regulate economic activity across the country.

Politically, Zhu also seemed to be more prepared to listen and solve problems peacefully rather than through force. In April 1999, for example, when ten thousand Falun Gong 法轮功 (also known as Fǎlún Dàfǎ 法轮大法) members assembled in Beijing to call for an end to repression, Zhu is reported to have come out of Zhongnanhai, the well-protected party-state headquarters, to encourage the demonstrators to choose representatives who could talk to him and air their grievances. That the Falun Gong was subsequently outlawed and suppressed is usually attributed to Jiang Zemin's intervention.

Like Deng Xiaoping, the man who helped bring him back from obscurity to the center of politics, Zhu was a party man. His goal was never to weaken party rule, even when he was trying to pull apart the status quo. On the contrary, the aim was to strengthen party rule by finding new ways to legitimate it because the old style of economic control was no longer sustainable, and corruption was undermining popular faith in the system. That his predecessors have continued to struggle to control corruption suggests how deeply seated the problem had become—and perhaps also explains why, in the popular mind at least, it is this side of Zhu's leadership that seems to be remembered rather than the at times rather bitter disputes over his management of the economy.

Shaun BRESLIN
University of Warwick

Further Reading

Brahms, Laurence J. (2002). *Zhu Rongji and the transformation of modern China*. Hoboken, NJ: John Wiley & Sons.

Breslin, Shaun. (2003). Reforming China's embedded socialist compromise: China and the WTO. *Global Change, Peace and Security*, 15 (3), 213–230.

Fewsmith, J. (2001). The political and social implications of China's accession to the WTO. *The China Quarterly*, 167, 573–591.

Giles, John; Park, Albert; & Cai, Fang. (2006). How has economic restructuring affected China's urban workers? *The China Quarterly*, 185, 61–95. Retrieved October 22, 2010, from www.msu.edu/~gilesj/gilesparkcaiCQ.pdf

Zhū Róngjī

Guo Sujian. (2003). The ownership reform in China: What direction and how far? *Journal of Contemporary China*, 12(36), 553–573.

Lau, Lawrence J; Qian Yinyi; & Roland, Gerard. (2000). Interpretation of China's dual track approach to transition. *Journal of Political Economy*, 108(1), 120–163.

Nathan, Andrew J. (2003). Authoritarian resilience. *Journal of Democracy*, 14(1), 6–17. doi: 10.1353/jod.2003.0019

Naughton, Barry. (2001). Zhu Rongji: The twilight of a brilliant career. *China Leadership Monitor*, 1, 1–10.

Naughton, Barry. (2005). SASAC rising. *China Leadership Monitor*, 14, 1–11.

Yang Guohua, & Cheng Jin. (2001). The process of China's accession to the WTO. *Journal of International Economic Law*, 4(2), 297–328.

Yang Yao. (2004). Government commitment and the outcome of privatization. In Takatoshi Ito & Anne O. Krueger (Eds.), *Governance, regulation, and privatization in the Asia-Pacific region* (pp. 251–278). Chicago: University of Chicago Press.

Zweig, David. (2001). China's stalled "fifth wave": Zhu Rongji's reform package of 1998–2000. *Asian Survey*, 41(2), 231–247.

朱镕基

Acknowledgements

We have many people to thank for ideas, advice, and conversations about the value of a biographical project such as this. We benefited from the expertise of many individuals who responded to our requests, both online and in person, for guidance. These individuals—amongst them, many of the leading China experts of our particular period of history—greatly contributed to the work you hold in your hands or see on your screen.

In particular, we thank the scholars and experts who reviewed and commented on the initial headword list and helped us prioritize and select the final hundred individuals who are profiled in this volume. A few chose to remain anonymous, and we thank them along with Jan Berris, Bill Bishop, Michael Chang, Anne Chao, Timothy Cheek, Ja Ian Chong, Maghiel van Crevel, Carine Defoort, Susan Finder, Edmund Fung, Qian Gao, Liangyan Ge, Sam Geall, Natascha Gentz, Phillip Grimberg, Tom A. Grunfeld, John Holden, Sylvia Hui, Bruce Jacobs, Jeremiah Jenne, Yu Jiang, Thomas Kampen, David Kelly, André Laliberté, Cheuk-Yi Lee, Huaiyu Luo, Catherine Lynch, Sheng-mei Ma, Colin Mackerras, Jonathan Markley, Alexus McLeod, Jimmy Mitchell, Sherry Mou, Jonathan Noble, Steven Phillips, Yuri Pines, John Rapp, Shelley Rigger, Stanley Rosen, Patrick Fuliang Shan, Mei Ah Tan, Harold Tanner, Lik Hang Tsui, Winnie Wai Tsui, Stephen Wadley, Jeff Wasserstrom, Philip Wen, Jeffrey R. Williams, Wai-ying Wong, Sophia Woodman, Shelton Woods, Zhiyi Yang, Maochun Yu, Hanmo Zhang, Yunshuang Zhang; and the many anonymous reviewers. A special thanks goes to the many peer reviewers, whose comments and suggestions greatly improved the content; to Dian Li for helping locate several Chinese contributors; to Kerry Brown, Joel R. Campbell, Colin Hawes, and Lawrence R. Sullivan for writing multiple entries; and to the National Committee on U.S.-China Relations for providing images. The positive reviews and feedback on the first three volumes from Benjamin A. Elman, Philip J. Ivanhoe, Jeffrey L. Richey, Alice Miller, Rana Mitter, Stephen A. Orlins, Alexander Pantsov, and Wm. Theodore de Bary are much appreciated, as are the encouragement and helpful suggestions from Lucien Ellington and Frank Shulman.

We at Berkshire Publishing Group also appreciate the enthusiasm of a much older and much, much larger academic publisher, Oxford University Press, for recognizing the quality and importance of this project and proposing that they host and distribute the online version of the DCB.

The editor in chief and publisher especially want to thank Marjolijn Kaiser, Berkshire's China projects editor, who ably managed this complex project and conceived and compiled the appendices on individuals, geographical locations, pinyin terms, historical events, and general resources, that users find a valuable addition to the biographies themselves.

Contributors

COHEN, Jerome A. New York University School of Law

Chen Guangcheng

DILLON, Michael Independent Scholar

Rong Yiren
Zhou Yongkang

FAN Hong The University of Western Australia

Li Ning (co-author: Liu Li)
Liu Xiang (co-author: Min Ge)

FENG Chongyi University of Technology, Sydney

Bao Tong

FENG Lin University of Hull

Chow Yun-fat

FRISCH, Nicholas Independent Journalist

Cha, Louis

GARNAUT, John The Sydney Morning Herald

Bo Xilai

GLADSTON, Paul University of Nottingham

Xu Bing

GONG Haomin Case Western Reserve University

Chen Kaige

GREEN-WEISKEL, Lucia Queen's College, CUNY

Chen Xitong

GUO Xuezhi Guilford College

Yang Shangkun

HARGITTAI, Balazs Saint Francis University

Lee, Yuan Tseh (co-author: Istvan Hargittai)

HARGITTAI, Istvan Budapest University of Technology and Economics

Lee, Yuan Tseh (co-author: Balazs Hargittai)

HAWES, Colin University of Technology, Sydney

Huang Guangyu
Liu Chuanzhi
Ren Zhengfei

HOCKX, Michel SOAS, University of London

Han Han

HUANG Yibing Connecticut College

Wang Shuo

HUI, Dennis Lai Hang The Hong Kong Institute of Education

Gou, Terry
Ho, Stanley

HUNG, Chung Fun Steven The Hong Kong Institute of Education

Chan, Anson

JACOBS, J. Bruce Monash University

Lee Teng-hui
Ma Ying-jeou

KALDIS, Nicholas A. Binghamton University (SUNY)

Ba Jin

KINGSBURY, Karen S. Chatham University

Zhang Ailing

KIRCHBERGER, Sarah Katharina University of Hamburg

Hu Yaobang

LEE, Mabel The University of Sydney

Gao Xingjian

LI Dian Sichuan University

Bei Dao

LI Quan Sichuan University

Qiao Shi

LI Xiaobing University of Central Oklahoma

Qian Xuesen

LIN He University of Electronic Science and Technology of China

Wang Hui

LIU Li The University of Western Australia

Li Ning (co-author: Fan Hong)

LUO Huaiyu Beijing University of Chemical Technology

Su Tong
Yu Hua

MACKERRAS, Colin Griffith University

Lang Lang

MAK, Grace Yan-yan Hong Kong Baptist University

Lee, Ang

MIN Ge The University of Western Australia

Liu Xiang (co-author: Fan Hong)

PELLEGRINI, Nancy Time Out Beijing/Time Out Shanghai

Tan Dun

POTTER, Pitman B. University of British Columbia

Peng Zhen

POUJOL, Patrice Independent Researcher

Chan, Jackie

QIAN Kun University of Pittsburgh

Zhang Yimou

QIN Ling Sichuan University

Li Yanhong

SEYMOUR, James D. Chinese University of Hong Kong

Wei Jingsheng

SO, Clement Y. K. Chinese University of Hong Kong

Lai, Jimmy

STEEN, Andreas Aarhus University

Cui Jian

SULLIVAN, Lawrence R. Adelphi University

Dai Qing
Li Ka-shing
Ma Jun
Ma, Jack
Wu Yi
Yuan Longping

SUN, Warren Monash University

Ye Jianying

TAVARES DA SILVA, Jorge Institute of Information and Administration Science (ISCIA), University of Minho

Chen Shui-bian

VOGEL, Ezra F. Harvard University

Deng Xiaoping

WANG Zhengxu University of Nottingham

Jiang Zemin (co-author: Marcel Austin-Martin)

WANG Zhuoyi Hamilton College

Li, Jet

WILLIAMS, Philip F. Montana State University

Liu Binyan

YAN Ho-Don Feng Chia University, Taiwan

Shih, Stan

YEUNG, Chee Kong Chinese University of Hong Kong

Fok, Henry

YI Sun University of Nottingham

Woo, John

YU Minhua Zhejiang Normal University

Mo Yan

ZHANG Jie Trinity University

Chen, Joan

ZHANG Rui Tsinghua University

Feng Xiaogang

ZHANG Weidong Winona State University

Lai Changxing

ZHUANG Peina Sichuan University

Zhang Chaoyang

Editors and Staff

Editor in Chief

Kerry BROWN Professor of Chinese Studies and Director of the Lau China Institute, King's College, London

Associate Editors

Patrick BOEHLER University of Hong Kong

Wai (Winnie) TSUI Chinese University of Hong Kong

Sylvia HUI Independent Scholar, London

Publisher

Karen CHRISTENSEN

Editorial Staff

Marjolijn KAISER Project Editor

Amanda PRIGGE Indexing

Cindy LI, Eliza J. MITCHELL, Evelyn WANG, Zoe Yizhou ZHANG Editorial and Photo Research Assistants

Erin BINNEY, Kathy BROCK, Olette TROUVE Copyeditors

Design and Production

Aptara, Inc Pagination

Trevor YOUNG, Rachel CHRISTENSEN Information and Database Management

Image Credits

Page 1: Ba Jin (1958).

Page 9: Chinese ex-official Bao Tong at home (2008). Photo by Renee Chiang.

Page 13: Contemporary poet Bei Dao in Freedom Square, Tallin, Estonia (2010). Photo by Avjoska. CC by 3.0.

Page 20: Government official Bo Xilai (2011). Photo by Voice of America.

Page 26: Bo Yibo in Peking (1946).

Page 30: Louis Cha during a keynote speech at the Chinese University of Hong Kong (2007). Photo courtesy of The Chinese University of Hong Kong.

Page 36: Anson Chan addressing the media (2005). Photo by Fuzheado. Flickr, CC by-SA 2.0.

Page 41: Jackie Chan at the Cannes Film Festival (2012). Photo by Georges Biard. CC by-SA 3.0.

Page 48: Chen Guangcheng in New York. Photo by Karen Christensen.

Page 55: Chen Kaige at the 26th Tokyo International Film Festival (2013). Photo by Dick Thomas Johnson. Flickr, CC by 2.0.

Page 62: Chen Shui-bian speaking (2009). Photo Jamali Jack. CC by-SA 3.0.

Page 68: Portrait of Chen Xitong, from the cover of his book *Conversations with Chen Xitong* (2012).

Page 74: Chen Yun in Zhongnanhai (1959). Author unknown.

Page 78: Joan Chen at the 30th San Francisco International Asian American Film Festival (2012). Photo by jchan7388. CC by-SA 2.0.

Page 86: Maggie Cheung (2007). Photo by Roger Wo. CC by 2.0.

Page 93: Chow Yun-fat signing his name in support of preserving the Queen's Pier at Edinburgh Place in Hong Kong (2007) (cropped). Photo by Sliceof. CC by-SA 3.0.

Page 101: Cui Jian with his guitar in front of Tiananmen Square (cropped) (1990). Photo courtesy of Cui Jian and Beijing East West Music & Art Production Co., Ltd.

Page 107: Dai Qing with the Ourobouros Environmental Award (1993). Photo courtesy of the Goldman Environmental Prize.

Page 113: Deng Xiaoping in Washington D.C. listening to Jimmy Carter (cropped) (1979). Photo by Library of Congress.

Page 123: Fang Lizhi with his wife and Chen Kuide (cropped). Photo by Voice of America.

Page 128: Fei Xiaotong at Yangqing University (c. 1920–1930).

Page 135: Feng Xiaogang (middle with cap) surrounded by the cast from *Aftershock* (cropped) (2010). Photo by Walter Lim. Flickr, CC by 2.0.

Page 143: Papercut artwork of Henry Fok. Photo by Ben Dalton. Flickr, CC SA 2.0 Generic.

Page 147: Portrait of Gao Xingjian in Luxembourg (2012). Photo by Jwh. CC by-SA 3.0.

Page 156: Gong Li at Cannes Film Festival (2011). Photo by Georges Biard. CC by-SA 3.0.

Page 162: Terry Gou and Dilma Rouseff shaking hands (cropped) (2011). Photo by Roberto Stuckert Filho. Flickr, CC by-SA 2.0.

Page 166: Han Han at the Hong Kong Book Fair (2010). Photo by laihiuyeung ryanne. CC by 2.0.

Page 170: Stanely Ho holding a moon cake (cropped) (2006). Photo by 太皮. Flickr, CC by-SA 2.0

Page 174: Hou Hsiao-Hsien. NO IMAGE

Page 180: Portrait of Hu Jia (2014). Photo by Voice of America.

Page 184: Hu Jintao in Cannes (2011). Photo by Dilma Rouseff. CC by-SA 2.0.

Page 191: Hu Yaobang, on cover of a brochure for his Former Residence (2014). Photo by Huangdan2060.

Page 199: Huang Guangyu. NO IMAGE

Page 204: Jia Zhangke (2008). Photo by RanZag. CC by-SA 2.0.

Page 209: Jiang Zemin visiting Hickam Air Force Base, Hawai'i. Photo by Tina M. Ackerman, U.S. Navy.

Page 217: Rebiya Kadeer at the Forum on Minority Issues (2012). Photo by United States Mission Geneva. CC by 2.0.

Page 224: Lai Changxing. NO IMAGE

Page 229: Jimmy Lai walking in Hong Kong (2013). Photo by Voice of America.

Page 235: Pianist Lang Lang at the Opening of Chopin Year, Warsaw (2010). Photo by Chancellery of the President of the Republic of Poland. GNU Free Documentation License (Version 1.2).

Page 240: Lee Teng-hui at an election rally (2004). Author unknown. CC by-SA 3.0.

Page 248: Ang Lee at the 66th Venice Film Festival (2009). Photo by nicolas genin. CC by-SA 2.0.

Page 255: Bruce Lee as Kato from *The Green Hornet* (1967). Photo by ABC Television.

Page 262: Martin Lee at the twentieth anniversary of the Tiananmen Square Incident (2009). Photo by laihiu. CC by 2.0.

Page 268: Lee Yuan Tseh in Lindau, Germany, during an annual meeting of Nobel laureates (2005). Photo courtesy by Istvan Hargittai.

Page 274: Leung Chun-Ying at the 2013 Policy Address (2013). Photo by Voice of America.

Page 279: Li Hongzhi being recognized for his teachings in Houston, TX (cropped) (1999). Cropped photo by Kaiger. CC by-SA 3.0. Original photo by ClearWisdom.net, CC by-SA 3.0.

Page 284: Li Ka-shing at EdTech Stanford University School of Medicine (2010). Photo by EdTech Stanford University School of Medicine. CC by 2.0.

Page 288: Li Keqiang visiting the Minister of Foreign Affairs in Peru (2015). Photo by Ministerio de Relaciones Exteriores. Flickr, CC by 2.0.

Page 293: Li Ning at the 2008 Beijing Olympics opening ceremony (cropped) (2008). Photo by Tim Hipps/U.S. Army.

Page 297: Li Peng (2003). Photo by World Economic Forum. CC by-SA 2.0.

Page 301: Li Xiannian taking part in the celebration of the thirtieth anniversary of Romania's liberation from Nazi occupation. Photo by FOCR. Wikimedia, from the Romanian National Archives. Digital ID: 37860X14X66.

Page 304: Li Xiaolin (2012). Photo by Pacific Aviation Museum. Flickr, CC by 2.0.

Page 306: Li Yanhong at Web 2.0 Summit (2010). Photo by Kevin Krejci. Flickr, CC by 2.0.

Page 313: Jet Li at the opening of *Fearless* (2006). Photo by Gavatron.

Page 322: Lien Chan (2013). Photo by Voice of America.

Page 328: Liu Binyan as a young man. Cropped from a picture together with his wife.

Page 335: Liu Chuanzhi at the 2005 National Committee on U.S.-China Relations. Photo courtesy by NCUSCR and Elsa M. Ruiz.

Page 340: Liu Xiang at Shanghai University of Sport (2014). Photo by Shanghai University of Sport. CC by-SA 4.0.

Page 344: Liu Xiaobo, Nobel Peace Prize laureate (2010). Photo by Blatant World. Flickr, CC by 2.0.

Page 350: Ma Jun with the Ourobouros Environmental Award (2012). Photo courtesy of the Goldman Environmental Prize.

Page 356: Ma Ying-jeou (2011). Photo by jamiweb. CC by 2.0.

Page 361: Ma Yun (Jack Ma) speaking at The World Economic Forum Annual Meeting of the New Champions (2008). Photo by Natalie Behring, World Economic Forum. CC by-SA 2.0.

Page 365: Mo Yan at a reading in Hamburg (2008). Photo by Johannes Kolfhaus, Gymn. Marienthal. CC by-SA 3.0.

Page 370: Peng Zhen (1949).

Page 376: Qian Xuesen (1938).

Page 382: Qiao Shi. NO IMAGE

Page 386: Reng Zhengfei (2014). Photo by Rory Cellan. Flickr, CC by-SA 2.0.

Page 393: Rong Yiren. NO IMAGE

Page 397: Stan Shih in his early years. Photo by oneVillage Initiative. Flickr, CC by-SA 2.0.

Page 402: Su Tong. NO IMAGE

Page 407: Tan Dun (2011). Photo by Iluv2write. CC by-SA 3.0.

Page 412: Teresa Teng. Photo by jdxyw. Flickr, CC by-SA 2.0.

Page 417: Donald Tsang at the 2012 World Economic Forum. Photo by World Economic Forum. CC 2.0.

Page 423: Tung Chee Hwa visiting Alar Streimann (cropped) (2011). Photo by Estonian Foreign Ministry. CC by 2.0.

Page 429: Wan Li. NO IMAGE

Page 432: Wang Hui at Holberg Prisen Symposium (2008). Photo by Holberg Prisen. CC by 2.0.

Page 437: Wang Shuo. NO IMAGE

Page 443: Wang Yang at US-China Dialogue (2013). Photo by U.S. Department of State.

Page 447: Wang Zhen in military uniform (1955).

Page 450: Wei Jingsheng at the European Parliament of Strasbourg (2013). Photo by Claude Truong-Ngoc. CC by-SA 3.0.

Page 456: Wen Jiabao with the president of Korea (2009) (cropped). Photo by Republic of Korea. Flickr, CC by-SA 2.0.

Page 461: Wong Kar-wai at the premier for *Ashes of Time* (2008). Photo by Karen Seto/司徒嘉蘭. Flickr, CC by 2.0.

Page 469: John Woo at the Cannes Film Festival (2005). Photo by Jakob Montrasio. CC by 2.0.

Page 475: Wu Yi with Colin Powell (cropped) (2004). Photo by Michael Gross.

Page 479: Xi Jinping in Russia (2013). Photo by Antilong. CC by-SA 3.0.

Page 486: Xu Bing at Asian Contemporary Art Fair, New York City (cropped) (2007). Photo by watashiwani. CC by-SA 2.0.

Page 492: Yang Jiang (1941).

Page 495: Yang Shangkun (1958). Photo by 哈军工纪念馆.

Page 502: Yao Ming during a game (2006). Photo by Keith Allison. Flickr, CC by 2.0.

Page 506: Ye Jianying in uniform (1955). Photo by Liu Feng.

Page 512: Yu Hua at Singapore Writers' Festival (2005). Photo by Chouca. CC by 3.0.

Page 517: Yuan Longping reading (1962).

Page 521: Portrait of Joseph Zen (2013). Photo by Iris Tong, Voice of America.

Page 528: Zhang Ailing in Hong Kong (1954).

Page 534: Zhang Chaoyang. NO IMAGE

Page 537: Zhang Yimou at the opening of *Under the Hawthorn Tree*, Busan International Film Festival (2010). Photo by Injeonwon. CC by-SA 3.0.

Page 545: Zhao Ziyang (1985). Photo by Rob Bogaerts/Anefo. CC by-SA 3.0.

Page 552: Zhou Yongkang (2006). Photo by Barry Bahler.

Page 556: Zhou Youguang as a young student (c.1920).

Page 560: Zhu Rongji leading the Chinese delegation at the European Management Symposium in Switzerland (1986). Photo by World Economic Forum. CC by-SA 2.0.

Appendix 1: Pronunciation and Conversion Table

Pinyin is the system used to transcribe Chinese characters into the Latin alphabet; it was developed in China in the 1950s, and is currently the most commonly used transcription system. Other systems, however, have been used in the past, most notably the Wade-Giles system, named after the two scholars Thomas Wade and Herbert Giles. The pinyin system uses the Latin alphabet, but the pronunciation differs somewhat from other languages. Below is a short pronunciation guide to Mandarin Chinese, followed by a conversion table between pinyin and Wade-Giles.

Vowels and Syllables

a	as in Ba**ha**mas
(w)o	long o as in "bore"
e	"er" as in "hers"
(y)e	as in "nest"
ai	as in "eye"
ei	as in "a" in "way"
ao	as in "aue" in "sauerkraut"
ou	similar to "o" in "go"
en	as in "un" in "under"
er	"e" with the tongue curled back (retroflex)
(y)i	"e" as in "be"
(w)u	"oo" as in "boom"
yu	purse your lips and position the tongue high and to the front

Consonants

b	"b" as in "bowl"—softened to approach a "p" sound
p	as "p" as in "top"—same shape as "b," but with aspiration (air)
m	"m" as in "may"
f	"f" as in "far"
d	"d" as in "down"—softened to approach a "t" sound
t	"t" as "top"—same shape as "d," but with aspiration (air)
n	"n" as in "nail"
l	"l" as in "look"
g	"g" as in "go"—softened to approach a "k" sound
k	"k" as in "kiss"—same shape as "g," but with aspiration (air)
h	"h" as in "hope"—with a slight rasp as in "loch"
j	"j" as in "jeep"—tongue positioned below lower teeth

Consonants (*continued*)

q	"ch" as in "cheap"—tongue is positioned below lower teeth
x	"sh" as in "sheep"—tongue is positioned below lower teeth
zh	"j" as in "jam"—tip of the tongue rolled back into mouth (retroflex)
ch	"ch" as in "cheap"—tip of the tongue rolled back into mouth (retroflex)
sh	"sh" as in "ship"—tip of the tongue rolled back into mouth (retroflex)
r	"z" as in "azure"
z	"ds" as in "woods"
c	"ts" as in "bits"
s	"s" as in "see"

Pinyin / Wade-Giles Conversion Table

The conversion table below shows both pinyin and Wade-Giles syllables, arranged in alphabetical order of the pinyin.

Pinyin	Wade-Giles	Pinyin	Wade-Giles	Pinyin	Wade-Giles
A		biao	piao	chan	ch`an
a	a	bie	pieh	chang	ch`ang
ai	ai	bin	pin	chao	ch`ao
an	an	bing	ping	che	ch`e
ang	ang	bo	po	chen	ch`en
ao	ao	bu	pu	cheng	ch`eng
B		**C**		chi	ch`ih
ba	pa	ca	ts`a	chong	ch`ung
bai	pai	cai	ts`ai	chou	ch`ou
ban	pan	can	ts`an	chu	ch`u
bang	pang	cang	ts`ang	chuai	ch`uai
bao	pao	cao	ts`ao	chuan	ch`uan
bei	pei	ce	ts`e	chuang	ch`uang
ben	pen	cen	ts`en	chui	ch`ui
beng	peng	ceng	ts`eng	chun	ch`un
bi	pi	cha	ch`a	chuo	ch`o
bian	pien	chai	ch`ai	ci	tz`u

Pinyin	Wade-Giles
cong	ts`ung
cou	ts`ou
cu	ts`u
cuan	ts`uan
cui	ts`ui
cun	ts`un
cuo	ts`o
D	
da	ta
dai	tai
dan	tan
dang	tang
dao	tao
de	te
deng	teng
di	ti
dian	tien
diao	tiao
die	tieh
ding	ting
diu	tiu
dong	tung
dou	tou
du	tu
duan	tuan
dui	tui
dun	tun
duo	to
E	
e	o
en	en
er	erh

Pinyin	Wade-Giles
F	
fa	fa
fan	fan
fang	fang
fei	fei
fen	fen
feng	feng
fo	fo
fou	fou
fu	fu
G	
ga	ka
gai	kai
gan	kan
gang	kang
gao	kao
ge	ko
gen	ken
geng	keng
gong	kung
gou	kou
gu	ku
gua	kua
guai	kuai
guan	kuan
guang	kuang
gui	kuei
gun	kun
guo	kuo
H	
ha	ha
hai	hai

Pinyin	Wade-Giles
han	han
hang	hang
hao	hao
he	ho
hei	hei
hen	hen
heng	heng
hong	hung
hou	hou
hu	hu
hua	hua
huai	huai
huan	huan
huang	huang
hui	hui
hun	hun
huo	huo
J	
ji	chi
jia	chia
jian	chien
jiang	chiang
jiao	chiao
jie	chieh
jin	chin
jing	ching
jiong	chiung
jiu	chiu
ju	chü
juan	chüan
jue	chüeh
jun	chün

Pinyin	Wade-Giles	Pinyin	Wade-Giles	Pinyin	Wade-Giles
K		liao	liao	**N**	
ka	k`a	lie	lieh	na	na
kai	k`ai	lin	lin	nai	nai
kan	k`an	ling	ling	nan	nan
kang	k`ang	liu	liu	nang	nang
kao	k`ao	long	lung	nao	nao
ke	k`o	lou	lou	nei	nei
ken	k`en	lu	lu	nen	nen
keng	k`eng	lü	lü	neng	neng
kong	k`ung	luan	luan	ni	ni
kou	k`ou	lüe	lüeh	niang	niang
ku	k`u	lun	lun	nian	nien
kua	k`ua	luo	lo	niao	niao
kuai	k`uai	**M**		nie	nie
kuan	k`uan	ma	ma	nin	nin
kuang	k`uang	mai	mai	ning	ning
kui	k`uei	man	man	niu	niu
kun	k`un	mang	mang	nong	nung
kuo	k`uo	mao	mao	nou	nou
L		mei	mei	nu	nu
la	la	men	men	nü	nü
lai	lai	meng	meng	nuan	nuan
lan	lan	mi	mi	nüe	nüeh
lang	lang	miao	miao	nuo	no
lao	lao	mie	mieh	**O**	
le	le	min	min	ou	ou
lei	lei	ming	ming	**P**	
leng	leng	miu	miu	pa	p`a
li	li	mo	mo	pai	p`ai
lian	lien	mou	mou	pan	p`an
liang	liang	mu	mu	pang	p`ang

Pinyin	Wade-Giles
pao	p`ao
pei	p`ei
pen	p`en
peng	p`eng
pi	p`i
pian	p`ien
piao	p`iao
pie	p`ieh
pin	p`in
ping	p`ing
po	p`o
pou	p`ou
pu	p`u
Q	
qi	ch`i
qia	ch`ia
qian	ch`ien
qiang	ch`iang
qiao	ch`iao
qie	ch`ieh
qin	ch`in
qing	ch`ing
qiong	ch`iung
qiu	ch`iu
qu	ch`ü
quan	ch`üan
que	ch`üeh
qun	ch`ün
R	
ran	jan
rang	jang

Pinyin	Wade-Gile
rao	jao
re	je
ren	jen
reng	jeng
ri	jih
rong	jung
rou	jou
ru	ju
ruan	juan
rui	jui
run	jun
ruo	jo
S	
sa	sa
sai	sai
san	san
sang	sang
sao	sao
se	se
sen	sen
seng	seng
sha	sha
shai	shai
shan	shan
shang	shang
shao	shao
she	she
shen	shen
sheng	sheng
shi	shih
shou	shou

Pinyin	Wade-Gile
shu	shu
shua	shua
shuai	shuai
shuan	shuan
shuang	shuang
shui	shui
shun	shun
shuo	shuo
si	ssu
song	sung
sou	sou
su	su
suan	suan
sui	sui
sun	sun
suo	so
T	
ta	t`a
tai	t`ai
tan	t`an
tang	t`ang
tao	t`ao
te	t`e
teng	t`eng
ti	t`i
tian	t`ien
tiao	t`iao
tie	t`ieh
ting	t`ing
tong	t`ung
tou	t`ou

Pinyin	Wade-Gile	Pinyin	Wade-Gile	Pinyin	Wade-Gile
tu	t`u	xue	hsüeh	zeng	tseng
tuan	t`uan	xun	hsün	zha	cha
tui	t`ui	**Y**		zhai	chai
tun	t`un	ya	ya	zhan	chan
tuo	t`o	yai	yai	zhang	chang
W		yan	yen	zhao	chao
wa	wa	yang	yang	zhe	che
wai	wai	yao	yao	zhen	chen
wan	wan	ye	yeh	zheng	cheng
wang	wang	yi	i	zhi	chih
wei	wei	yin	yin	zhong	chung
wen	wen	ying	ying	zhou	chou
weng	weng	yo	yo	zhu	chu
wo	wo	yong	yung	zhua	chua
wu	wu	you	yu	zhuai	chuai
X		yu	yü	zhuan	chuan
xi	hsi	yuan	yüan	zhuang	chuang
xia	hsia	yue	yüeh	zhui	chui
xian	hsien	yun	yün	zhun	chun
xiang	hsiang	**Z**		zhuo	cho
xiao	hsiao	za	tsa	zi	tzu
xie	hsieh	zai	tsai	zong	tsung
xin	hsin	zan	tsan	zou	tsou
xing	hsing	zang	tsang	zu	tsu
xiong	hsiung	zao	tsao	zuan	tsuan
xiu	hsiu	ze	tse	zui	tsui
xu	hsü	zei	tsei	zun	tsun
xuan	hsüan	zen	tsen	zuo	tso

Source: *People's Republic of China: Administrative Atlas.* Washington, DC: Central Intelligence Agency, 1975, pp. 46–47.

Appendix 2: Biographical Directory

The following is a list of prominent people mentioned in the Berkshire Dictionary of Chinese Biography *(volume 4), in alphabetical order. Those people who have an article devoted to them in the DCB are marked in* **bold**.

A

Āh Chéng 阿城 (b. 1949)—Writer, also known as Zhōng Āchéng 钟阿城

Ān Mín 安民 (b. 1945)—Politician; vice minister of commerce (2003–2005)

Ān Zǐwén 安子文 (1909–1980)—Director of the CCP Central Organization Department; his secretary was **Bao Tong**

B

Bā Jīn 巴金 (1904–2005)—Writer, editor; b. Lǐ Yáotáng 李尧棠, style name: Lǐ Fèigān 李芾甘

Bái Huà 白桦／白樺 (b. 1930)—Writer, poet, playright; b. Chén Yòuhuā 陈佑华

Bājí Zhēnrén 八极真人／八極真人—Daoist master

Bào Tóng 鲍彤／鮑彤 (b. 1932)—Government official, activist, writer

Bāo Zūnxìn 包遵信 (1937–2007)—Intellectual; friend of **Liu Xiaobo**

Běi Dǎo 北岛／北島 (b. 1949)—Contemporary poet, member of Misty Poetry movement; b. Zhào Zhènkāi 赵振开

Bó Xīlái 薄熙来 (b. 1949)—Politician, arrested for corruption; son of **Bo Yibo**

Bó Yībō 薄一波 (1908–2007)—Party elder, political and military leader; father of **Bo Xilai**

C

Cha, Louis (Zhā Liángyōng 查良镛／查良鏞) (b. 1924)—Author, media tycoon; also known by his pen name Jīn Yōng 金庸

Chan, Anson (Chén Fāng Ānshēng 陈方安生／陈方安生) (b. 1940)—Politician; chief secretary of Hong Kong (1993–1997)

Chan, Charles 陈志平／陳志平 (1914–2008)—Father of **Jackie Chan**

Chan, Jackie (Chén Gǎngshēng 陈港生／陳港生) (b. 1954)—Hong Kong actor, stuntman, and director

Chan, Lee-Lee 陈莉莉／陳莉莉 (1916–2002)—Mother of **Jackie Chan**

Chan, Willie Chi-Keung (b.1941)—Manager and friend of **Jackie Chan**

Chang Chen 张震／張震 (b. 1976)—Taiwanese actor

Chang, Eileen—*See* **Zhang Ailing**

Chao Lan-kun 赵丽坤／趙蘭坤 (1910–2011)—Mother of Taiwanese politician **Lien Chan**

Chén Ěrjìn 陈尔晋／陳爾晉—Activist

Chén Guāngchéng 陈光诚／陳光誠—Civil rights activist and lawyer

Chén Huái'ǎi 陈怀皑/陳懷皑 (1920–1994)—Film director, father of **Chen Kaige**

Chén Kǎigē 陈凯歌/陳凱歌 (b. 1952)—Fifth Generation film director

Chen Kun-hou 陈坤厚/陳坤厚 (b. 1939)—Cinematographer

Chén Liángyǔ 陈良宇/陳良宇 (b. 1946)—Politician, party secretary of Shanghai

Chén Pīxiǎn 陈丕显/陳丕顯 (1916–1995)—Revolutionary and politician

Chén Shuǐ-biǎn 陈水扁/陳水扁—Taiwanese politician, president of the ROC (2000–2008)

Chén Xītóng 陈希同/陳希同—Politician, mayor of Beijing (1983–1993)

Chén Yí 陈怡/陳怡 (b. 1953)—Musician

Chén Yún 陈云/陳雲 (1905–1995)—PRC politician, one of the "Eight Immortals"

Chen, Joan (Chén Chōng 陈冲/陳沖) (b. 1961)—Actress, director, and producer

Chen, Sean (b. 1949)—Taiwanese politician

Cheng, Adam 郑少秋/鄭少秋 (b. 1947)—Actor

Cheung, Leslie (Zhāng Guóróng 张国荣/張國榮) (1956–2003)—Actor and musician

Cheung, Mabel 张婉婷/張婉婷 (b. 1950)—Film director

Cheung, Maggie (Manyuk) (Zhāng Mànyù 张曼玉/張曼玉) (b. 1964)—Transnational Hong Kong actress

Cheung, Terence 张家振/張家振 (b. 1949)—American film producer

Chiang Ching-kuo 蒋经国/蔣經國 (1910–1988)—Son of Chiang Kai-shek; stepson of Soong Mei-ling; leader of Taiwan after his father's death

Chiang Kai-shek 蒋介石/蔣介石 (1887–1975)—Leader of the Nationalists after Sun Yat-sen; father of Chiang Ching-kuo

Chien, Frederick 钱复/錢復 (b. 1935)—Taiwanese politician; replaced **Lien Chan** as minister of foreign affairs

Choi, Jim 蔡子明—Manager of **Jet Li**

Chow Keung (Zhōu qiáng 周强)—Producer, editor

Chow Yun-fat (Zhōu Rùnfā 周润发/週潤發) (b. 1955)—Hong Kong action film star

Chu Tien-wen 朱天文 (b. 1956)—Author, screen-writer

Chu, Eric (Zhū Lìlún 朱立伦/朱立倫) (b. 1961)—Taiwanese politician

Chui Bo-Chu 崔宝珠/崔寶珠—Hong Kong film producer

Cóng Wéixī 从维熙/從維熙 (b. 1933)—Writer

Cuī Jiàn 崔健 (b. 1961)—Musician, composer, author, film director

D

Dài Kèjǐng 戴克景—Chinese translator

Dài Qíng 戴晴 (b. 1941)—Environmental journalist, writer, and human rights activist

Dèng Xiǎopíng 邓小平/鄧小平 (1940–1997)—Politician, paramount leader of China

Diāo Yìnán 刁亦男 (b. 1969)—Film director

Dīng Zǐlín 丁子霖 (b. 1936)—Leader of the Tiananmen Mothers

Duō Duō 多多 (b. 1951)—Poet, member of the Misty Poets movement, b. Li Shizheng 栗世征

F

Fàn Bīngbīng 范冰冰 (b. 1981)—Actress

Fāng Lìzhī 方励之/方勵之 (1936–2012)—Physicist, dissident

Fāng Yǔ 方瑀 (b. 1943)—Former "Miss Republic of China"; wife of **Lien Chan**

Fèi Dáshēng 费达生/費達生 (c. 1905)—Pioneer of rural industry; sister of **Fei Xiaotong**

Fèi Pǔān 费朴安/費樸安—Father of **Fei Xiaotong**

Fèi Xiàotōng 费孝通/費孝通 (1910–2005)—Founder of sociology in China; professor of sociology and anthropology

Fèi Zōnghuì 费宗惠/費宗惠—Daughter of **Fei Xiaotong**

Féng Xiǎogāng 冯小刚/馮小剛 (b. 1958)—Film director, known for his New Years Films

Fěng Yóulán 冯友兰/馮友蘭 (1895–1990)—Western-educated Chinese scholar

Fok, Henry (Huò Yīngdōng 霍英东/霍英東) (1923–2006)—Hong Kong businessman, politician, and sportsman

Fù Dàqìng 傅大庆/傅大慶 (1900–1944)—Father of **Dai Qing**

Fung, Elmer Hu-hsiang (Féng Hùxiáng 冯沪祥/馮滬祥) (b. 1948)—Taiwan politician, pro-KMT philosopher

G

Gāo Gǎng 高岗/高崗 (1905–1954)—Member of the Politburo

Gāo Xíngjiàn 高行健 (b. 1965)—Author and artist; won the 2000 Nobel Prize for Literature

Gāo Yuányuán 高圆圆/高圓圓 (b. 1979)—Actress

Gě Yōu 葛优/葛優 (b. 1957)—Actor

Gěng Biāo 耿飚/耿飈 (1909–2000)—Politburo member

Gǒng Lì 巩俐/鞏俐 (b. 1965)—Actress

Gou, Terry (Guō Táimíng 郭台铭/郭台銘) (b. 1950)—Entrepreneur; founder and chairman of Foxconn

Gǔ Kāilái 谷开来/谷開來 (b. 1958)—Second wife of **Bo Xilai**, convicted of murdering British businessman Neil Heywood

Gǔ Lóng 古龙/古龍 (1938–1985)—Taiwanese martial arts novelist; b. Xiong Yaohua

Guō Wénjǐng 郭文景 (b. 1956)—Musician; one of the "Four Talents"

H

Hán Hán 韩寒 (b. 1982)—Blogger, writer, racecar driver

Hán Jié 韩杰/韓傑 (b. 1977)—Film director

Hán Rénjūn 韩仁均/韓仁均—Father of **Hán Hán**

Hán Sānpíng 韩三平/韓三平 (b. 1953)—Film producer

Ho, Stanley (Hé Hóngshēn 何鸿燊/何鴻燊) (b. 1921)—Entrepreneur

Hou Hsiao-hsien (Hóu Xiàoxián 侯孝贤/侯孝賢) (b. 1947)—Taiwanese director, producer, and screenwriter

Hóu Jì-rán 侯季然 (b. 1973?)—Actor

Hsieh Tung-min (Xiè Dōngmǐn 谢东闵/謝東閔) (1908–2001)—Taiwanese politician

Hsieh, Frank Chang-ting (Xiè Chángtíng 谢长廷/謝長廷) (b. 1946)—Taiwanese politician

Hú Déhuá 胡德华/胡德華 (b. 1949)—Scientist; son of **Hu Yaobang**

Hú Dépíng 胡德平 (b. 1942)—Politician; son of **Hu Yaobang**

Hú Gē 胡戈 (b. 1974)—Amateur director; made a spoof of **Chen Kaige's** The Promise

Hú Jiā 胡佳 (b. 1973)—Environmental, HIV/AIDS, democracy, and human rights activist

Hú Jǐntāo 胡锦涛/胡錦濤 (b. 1942)—Politician, president of the PRC (2003–2013)

Hú Qiáomù 胡乔木/胡喬木 (1912–1992)—Politician

Hú Qǐlì 胡启立/胡啟立 (b. 1929)—Politician, minister of Electronics Industry (1993–1998)

Hú Yàobāng 胡耀邦/胡耀邦 (1915–1989)— High-ranking official of the PRC; economic and political reformer

Huá Guófēng 华国锋/華國鋒 (1921–2008)— Handpicked successor of **Mao Zedong**; Chairman of the PRC (1976–1981)

Huáng Guāngyù 黄光裕/黃光裕 (b. 1969)— Entrepreneur; founder of Gome

Huáng Qiūyān 黄秋燕/黃秋燕 (b. 1961)—Martial artist; wife of **Jet Li** (m. 1987–1990)

Hui, Ann 许鞍华/許鞍華 (b. 1947)—Director

J

Jì Jūnxiáng 纪君祥/紀君祥—Thirteenth century dramatist, wrote *The Orphan of Zhao*

Jiǎ Píngwā 贾平凹/賈平凹 (b. 1952)—Writer

Jiǎ Zhāngkē 贾樟柯/賈樟柯 (b. 1970)—Sixth Generation director, screenwriter, and producer

Jiǎng Bǎilǐ 蒋百里/蔣百里 (1882–1938)—Military advisor under Chiang Kai-shek, **Qian Xuesen**'s father-in-law

Jiang He (b. 1941)—Poet, member of the Misty Poets movement

Jiāng Qīng 江青 (c. 1914–1991)—Last wife of **Mao Zedong**; leader of the "Gang of Four"; known in the West as "Madame Mao"; led purges during Cultural Revolution (1966–1976)

Jiāng Qíshēng 江棋生—Intellectual, dissident

Jiāng Wén 姜文 (b. 1963)—Director and author

Jiang Yi-huah (Jiāng Yíhuà 江宜桦/江宜樺) (b. 1960)—Taiwanese politician

Jiāng Zémín 江泽民/江澤民 (b. 1926)—Politician, president of the PRC (1993–2003)

K

Kadeer, Rebiya (Rèbǐyǎ Kǎdé'ěr 热比娅·卡德尔) (b. 1946)—Businesswoman and political activist

Kāng Shēng 康生 (1898–1975)—Internal security czar

Kao, Jack 高捷 (b.1958)—Actor

Kē Línglíng 柯玲玲—First wife of **Xi Jinping**

Kwan, Stanley 关锦鹏/關錦鵬 (b. 1957)—Director

L

Lài Chāngxīng 赖昌星/賴昌星 (b. 1958)— Entrepreneur (Yuanhua Group) and criminal

Lai, Jimmy (Lí Zhìyīng 黎智英) (b.1948)— Founder of *Apple Daily* and Next Media Group

Lam, Ringo 林嶺東 (b. 1955)—Director, producer, writer

Láng Guórèn 郎国任/郎國任—Father of **Lang Lang**

Láng Lǎng 郎朗 (b. 1982)—Pianist, composer

Lau, Andy 刘德华/劉德華 (b. 1961)—Actor

Lau, Damian 刘松仁/劉松仁 (b. 1949)—Actor

Lau, Emily 刘慧卿/劉慧卿 (b. 1952)—Hong Kong politician, chair of Democratic Party

Law, Clara 罗卓瑶/羅卓瑤 (b. 1957)—Director

Lee Hsing 李行 (b. 1930)—Director

Lee Teng-hui (Lǐ Dēnghuī 李登辉/李登輝) (b. 1923)—First democratically-elected president of the Republic of China (Taiwan)

Lee Tian-lu 李天禄/李天祿 (1910–1998)—Actor

Lee, Ang (Lǐ Ān 李安) (b. 1954)—Taiwanese American director

Lee, Bruce (Lǐ Xiǎolóng 李小龙/李小龍) (1940–1973)—Martial artist and kung fu film star

Lee, Lillian (Lǐ Bìhuá 李碧华/李碧華) (b. 1959)—Writer; known for *Farewell, My Concubine*, later adapted by **Chen Kaige**

Lee, Mark Ping-bing 李屏宾/李屏賓 (b. 1954)—Cinematographer

Lee, Martin (Lǐ Zhùmíng李柱銘/李柱铭) (b. 1938)—Lawyer, legislator, and political activist in Hong Kong

Lee, Yuan Tseh (Lǐ Yuǎnzhé 李远哲/李遠哲) (b. 1936)—Scientist; Nobel Prize in Chemistry laureate (1986)

Leung Chun-ying 梁振英 (b. 1954)—Politician; chief executive of Hong Kong since 2012

Lǐ Bīngbīng 李冰冰 (b. 1973)—Actress

Lǐ Gōngpǔ李公朴/李公樸 (1902–1946)—Democratic intellectual; assassinated by the Nationalists

Lǐ Héng 李恒/李恆 (b. 1952)—Daughter of **Hu Yaobang**

Lǐ Hóngzhāng李鸿章/李鴻章 (1823–1901)—Qing empire official; great grandfather of **Zhang Ailing**

Lǐ Hóngzhì 李洪志 (b. 1952)—Spiritual leader, founder of Falun Gong

Li Ka-shing (Lǐ Jiāchéng 李嘉誠/李嘉诚) (b. 1928)—Entrepreneur; billionaire

Lǐ Kèqiáng 李克强/李克強 (b. 1955)—Politician, premier of the PRC (2013–)

Lí Lìlì 黎莉莉 (1915–2005)—Actress

Lǐ Měigē 李美歌 (c. 1980s)—Daughter of **Li Hongzhi**

Lǐ Níng 李宁 (b. 1963)—Olympic gymnast; founder of Li-Ning Company Ltd.

Lǐ Péng 李鹏 (1909–1992)—Politician, premier of PRC (1987–1998)

Lǐ Ruì 李瑞—Wife of **Li Hongzhi**

Lǐ Shūxián 李淑娴/李淑嫻—Wife of **Fang Lizhi**

Lǐ Xiānniàn 李先念 (1909–1992)—Politician; president of the PRC (1983–1988)

Lǐ Xiǎolín 李小琳 (b. 1961)—Business executive; daughter of **Li Peng**

Lǐ Xīmíng 李锡铭/李錫銘 (1926–2008)—Politician; Communist Party leader

Li Yang-kang 林洋港 (1927–2013)—Taiwanese politician

Lǐ Yànhóng 李彦宏 (b. 1968)—Internet entrepreneur; co-founder of Baidu

Li Yin-wo 李彦和/李彦和—Father of **Martin Lee**; general

Lǐ Yuáncháo 李源潮 (b. 1950)—Politician

Lǐ Zhāo 李昭—Wife of **Hú Yàobāng**

Lǐ Zéhòu 李泽厚/李澤厚 (b. 1930)—Intellectual

Li, Jet (Lǐ Liánjié 李连杰/李連杰) (b. 1963)—Martial artist and film star

Li, Nina 利智 (b. 1961)—Actress; married **Jet Li** in 1999

Liáng Shíqiū 梁实秋/梁實秋 (1902–1987)—Human rights campaigner, with **Hu Shi**

Liáng Yǔshēng 梁羽生 (1926–2009)—Martial arts novelist; b. Chen Wentong

Liáng Zhènyīng 梁振英 (b. 1954)—Politician, Hong Kong

Liao Ching-sung 廖庆松/廖慶鬆 (b. 1950)—Editor and producer

Lien Chan (Lián Zhàn 连战/連戰) (b. 1936)—Taiwanese politician

Lien Chen-tung 连震东/連震東—Father of **Lien Chan**

Lien Heng 连横/連橫 (Lien Ya-tang 连雅堂/連雅堂) (1878–1936)—Writer, wrote the *General History of Taiwan*; grandfather of **Lien Chan**

Lien, Sean (Lien Sheng-wen 連勝文/连胜文) (b. 1970)—Politician; son of **Lien Chan**

Lim Giong 林强/林強 (b. 1964)—Composer

Lín Biāo 林彪 (1907–1971)—Politician; replaced Peng Dehuai

Liú Bīnyàn 刘宾雁/劉賓雁 (1925–2005)—Journalist and activist

Liú Bóchéng 刘伯承/劉伯承 (1892–1986)—High-ranking political official

Liu Chao-shiuan (Liú Zhàoxuán 刘兆玄/劉兆玄) (b. 1943)—Taiwanese politician and educator

Liǔ Chuánzhì 柳传志/柳傳志 (b. 1944)—Founder of Lenovo

Liú Dàhóng 刘大洪/劉大洪—Son of **Liu Binyan**

Liú Dí 刘荻/劉荻 (b. 1981)—Blogger

Liǔ Gǔshū 柳谷书/柳谷書 (1921–2003)—Bank executive, father of **Liu Chuanzhi**

Liú Hú 刘湖/劉湖 (b. 1945)—Son of **Hu Yaobang**

Liú Shàoqí 刘少奇/劉少奇 (1898–1969)—Revolutionary, chairman of the PRC (1959–1968)

Lǐ Shuòxūn 李硕勋/李碩勳 (1903–1931)—Writer and Communist activist, father of **Li Peng**

Liú Xiá 刘霞/劉霞 (b. 1961)—Artist and poet; wife of **Liu Xiaobo**

Liú Xiáng 刘翔/劉翔 (b. 1983)—Olympic athlete in track and field

Liú Xiǎobō 刘晓波/劉曉波 (b. 1955)—Activist, 2010 Nobel Peace Prize laureate

Liú Xiǎodōng 刘小东/劉小東 (b. 1963)—Artist

Liú Xiǎomíng 刘晓明/劉曉明 (b. 1956)—China's ambassador to Great Britain

Liú Xiǎoyàn 刘小雁/劉小雁—Daughter of **Liu Binyan**

Liú Yànchí 刘燕驰/劉燕馳—Script editor, and film consultant; mother of **Chen Kaige**

Liú Yǒngqīng 刘永清/劉永清 (b. 1940)—Wife of **Hu Jintao**

Liú Yúnshān 刘云山/劉雲山 (b. 1947)—Politician, member of the "Overall Reform" group, led by **Li Keqiang** and **Xi Jinping**

Liú Zhìdān 刘志丹/劉志丹 (1903–1936)—Revolutionary martyr

Lo Wei 罗维/羅維 (1918–1996)—Hong Kong film director

Lo, David 罗大卫/羅大衛—Film manager of **Jet Li**

Lǔ Xūn 鲁迅/魯迅 (1881–1936)—Writer, "father" of modern Chinese literature

Lù Yáo 路遥/路遙 (1949–1992)—Writer

Lung, Sihung (Láng Xíong 郎雄) (1930–2002)—Taiwanese actor

M

Mǎ Jūn 马军/馬軍 (b. 1968)—Environmentalist and journalist

Ma Ying-jeou (Mǎ Yīngjiǔ 马英九/馬英九) (b. 1950)—Politician; president of the ROC (2008–)

Ma, Jack (Mǎ Yún 马云/馬雲) (b. 1964)—Internet entrepreneur; founder and executive chairman of Alibaba

Máo Zédōng 毛泽东/毛澤東 (1893–1976)—
Founding father of the PRC

Master Sheng-Yen 圣严法师/聖嚴法師 (1930–
2009)—Buddhist monk, religious scholar

Máng Kè 芒克 (b. 1951)—Poet, co-founder of the
literary journal *Today* together with **Bei Dao**

Méi Lángfāng 梅兰芳/梅蘭芳 (1894–1961)—
Peking Opera master, topic of Chen Kaige's
semi-biopic *Forever Enthralled*

Mèng Yín 孟吟—Second wife of **Fei Xiaotong**

Mò Yán 莫言 (b. 1955)—Writer, Nobel Prize in
Literature laureate (2012)

N

Ng, Lawrence 伍卫国/伍衛國 (b. 1964)—Actor

Ní Kuāng 倪匡 (b. 1935)—Martial arts novelist

Niè Róngzhēn 聂荣臻/聶榮臻 (1899–1992)—
Military leader, one of the ten Marshals

P

Péng Déhuái 彭德怀/彭德懷 (1898–1974)—Former
minister of defense, dismissed by Mao Zedong

Péng Léi 彭蕾—Co-founder of Alibaba, together
with **Jack Ma**

Péng Lìyuán 彭丽媛/彭麗媛 (b. 1962)—Wife of
Xi Jinping

Péng Zhēn 彭真 (1902–1997)—Politician,
National People's Congress chairman

Pú Sōnglíng 蒲松龄/蒲松齡 (1640–1750)—Writer,
inspiration of **Mo Yan**

Q

Qí Xīn 齐心/齊心 (b. 1926)—Mother of
Xi Jinping

Qián Xuésēn 钱学森/錢學森 (1911–2009)—
Rocket scientist

Qián Yuàn 钱瑗/錢瑗—Daughter of **Yang Jiang**
and Qian Zhongshu

Qián Zhōngshū 钱锺书/錢鍾書 (1910–1998)—
Influential scholar, writer, literary critic,
husband of **Yang Jiang**

Qiáo Shí 乔石/喬石 (1924–2015)—Politician; b.
Jiǎng Zhìtóng 蒋志彤

Qú Xiǎosōng 瞿小松/瞿小鬆 (b. 1952)—
Musician; one of the so-called Four Talents

Quán Juě 全觉/全覺—Buddhist master

R

Rèn Zhèngfēi 任正非 (b. 1944)—Entrepreneur;
founder of Huawei Technologies

Róng Yìrén 荣毅仁 (1916–2005)—Politician;
economic advisor

Ruǎn Língyù 阮玲玉 (1910–1935)—Actress

S

Shěn Cóngwén 沈从文 (1902–1988)—Writer

Shih, Stan (Shī Zhènróng 施振榮/施振荣,
b. 1944)—Entrepreneur; co-founder of
Acer Group

Shū Qí 舒淇 (b. 1976)—Actress

Siew, Vincent (Hsiao Wan-chang 蕭萬長/萧万长)
(b. 1939)—Taiwanese politician; vice president
of the ROC (2008–2012)

Soong, James (Sòng Chǔyú 宋楚瑜) (b. 1942)—
Taiwanese Independent politician

Su Chi (Sū Qǐ 苏起/蘇起) (b. 1949)—Taiwanese
politician

Sū Tóng 苏童/蘇童 (b. 1963)—Writer, b. Tóng
Zhōngguì 童忠贵

Sū Xiǎokāng 苏晓康/蘇曉康 (b. 1949)—Writer, intellectual

Sūn Hǎipíng 孙海平/孫海平 (b. 1955)—Hurdles coach of **Liu Xiang**

Sūn Yàfāng 孙亚芳/孫亞芳 (b. 1955 or 1956)—Chairman of Huawei

Sun Yat-sen 孙中山/孫中山 (1866–1925)—Politician; first president of the ROC

Szeto Wah 司徒华/司徒華 (1931–2011)—Hong Kong politician, co-founder of the Hong Kong Alliance in Support of Patriotic Democratic Movements in China together with **Martin Lee**

T

Tam, Patrick 谭嘉明/譚嘉明 (b. 1969)—Hong Kong director

Tán Dùn 谭盾/譚盾 (b. 1957)—Composer, musician; one of the so-called Four Talents

Tang, Harry 唐英年 (b.1952)—Hong Kong politician

Téng Biāo 滕彪 (b. 1973)—Human rights lawyer

Teng, Teresa (Dèng Lìjūn 邓丽君/鄧麗君) (1953–1995)—Musician; pop singer

Tián Zhuàngzhuàng 田壮壮/田壯壯 (b. 1952)—Fifth Generation director, worked with **Chen Kaige** and **Zhang Yimou**

Tiě Níng 铁凝/鐵凝 (b. 1957)—Writer

Tiong Hiew King 張曉卿 (b. 1935)—Malaysian-Chinese tycoon, owner of Ming Pao Holdings

Tsai Ing-wen (Cài Yīngwén 蔡英文) (b. 1956)—Taiwanese politician

Tsang, Donald (Zēng Yìnquán 曾荫权/曾蔭權) (b. 1944)—Politician; chief executive of Hong Kong (2005–2012)

Tseng Wen-hui (Zēng Wénhuì 曾文惠) (b. 1926)—Wife of **Lee Teng-hui**

Tsui Hark 徐克 (b. 1950)—Director

Tu Tu-chi 杜笃之/杜篤之 (b. 1955)—Sound designer

Tung Chee-hwa (Dǒng Jiànhuá 董建华/董建華) (b. 1937)—Businessman; first chief executive of Hong Kong (1997–2005)

W

Wàn Lǐ 万里/萬里 (b. 1916)—Economist and politician; vice premier of the PRC (1983–1988)

Wàn Yánhǎi 万延海/萬延海 (b. 1963)—AIDS activist

Wāng Ānyì 王安忆/王安憶 (b. 1954)—Writer

Wáng Bǎosēn 王宝森/王寶森 (1935–1994)—Vice mayor of Beijing, protégé of **Chen Xitong**

Wāng Dàohán 汪道涵 (1915–2005)—Party cadre, mentor and supporter of **Jiang Zemin**

Wáng Déjiā 王德嘉—Husband of **Dai Qing**

Wáng Dùlú 王度庐/王度廬 (1909–1977)—Writer; author of the martial arts-romance series Crane-Iron Pentalogy 鹤鐵系列

Wāng Huī 汪晖/汪暉 (b. 1959)—Academic and social critic

Wang Jin-pyng (Wáng Jīnpíng 王金平) (b. 1941)—Taiwanese politician

Wáng Lìjūn 王立军 (b. 1959)—Former police chief of Chongqing, associated with and later testifying against **Bo Xilai**

Wáng Míng 王明 (1904–1974)—CCP leader; one of the "28 Bolsheviks"

Wáng Ruòwàng 王若望 (1918–2001)—Intellectual, author, dissident

Wáng Shíwèi 王实味/王實味 (1906–1947)—Writer and scholar; imprisoned and executed

Wáng Shǒuxìn 王守信 (?–1980)—CCP official, corruption exposed by **Liu Binyan**

Wáng Shuò 王朔 (b. 1958)—Writer, actor, filmmaker, worked together with **Feng Xiaogang**

Wáng Tónghuì 王同惠—Wife of **Fei Xiaotong**

Wáng Xiǎojiā 王小嘉—Daughter of **Dai Qing**

Wāng Yáng 汪洋 (b. 1955)—Politician; candidate for future leader of China

Wáng Zhèn 王震 (1908–1993)—Central Advisory Committee vice chairman

Wáng Zhèng 王政—Translator

Wèi Jīngshēng 魏京生 (b. 1950)—Activist during the Democracy Wall Movement of 1979

Wēn Jiābǎo 温家宝/溫家寶 (b. 1942)—Politician; premier of the PRC (2003–2013)

Wén Yīduō 闻一多/聞一多 (1899–1946)—Democratic intellectual, poet; assassinated by the Nationalists

Wong Kar-wai (Wáng Jiāwèi 王家卫/王家衛) (b. 1958)—Director, screenwriter, and producer

Woo, John (Wú Yǔsēn 吴宇森/吳宇森) (b. 1946)—Director, producer, screenwriter

Wu Den-yih (Wú Dūnyì 吴敦义/吳敦義) (b. 1948)—Taiwanese politician

Wú Shìcháng 吴世昌 (1904–1974)—Political commentator (1930s/1940s); uncle of **Bao Tong**

Wu Shu-shen 吴淑珍 (1904–1974)—Wife of **Chen Shui-bian**

Wú Tiānmíng 吴天明 (1939–2014)—Director

Wú Wénzǎo 吴文藻/吳文藻 (1901–1985)—Anthropologist, sociologist, ethnologist

Wú Yí 吴仪/吳儀 (b. 1938)—Politician; vice premier of the PRC (2003–2008)

X

Xí Jìnpíng 习近平/習近平 (b. 1953)—Chinese Communist Party leader

Xí Míngzé 习明泽/習明澤 (b. 1992)—Daughter of **Xi Jinping**

Xí Zhòngxūn 习仲勋/習仲勛 (1913–2002)—Politician; father of **Xi Jinping**

Xiàng Nán 项南/項南 (1918–1997)—Politician; son of Xiàng Yúnián

Xiàng Yúnián 项与年/項與年 (1894–1978)—Politician

Xiāo Huá 肖华/肖華—Wife of **Zhang Yimou**

Xiè Jìn 谢晋 (1923–2008)—Director

Xú Bīng 徐冰 (b. 1955)—Visual artist

Xú Fān 徐帆 (b. 1967)—Actress; wife of **Feng Xiaogang**

Xú Zhìmó 徐志摩 (1897–1931)—Shanghai poet; distant relative of **Louis Cha**

Y

Yán Xíshān 阎锡山 (1883–1960)—Shanxi Province warlord

Yán Yúnxiáng 严云翔/嚴雲翔 (b. 1954)—Writer, anthropologist

Yáng Àngōng 杨暗公/楊闇公 (Yang Shangshu)—One of the founders of the Chinese Communist Movement in Sichuan; brother of **Yang Shangkun**

Yáng Huáiqīng 杨淮清/楊淮清—Father of **Yang Shangkun**

Yáng Jiàng 杨绛/楊絳 (b. 1911)—Author and intellectual, wife of Qian Zhongshu

Yáng Jié 杨洁/楊潔 (d. 1944)—Mother of **Dai Qing**; executed during the War of Resistance against Japan

Yáng Jìshéng 杨继绳/楊繼繩 (b. 1940)—Intellectual, former Xinhua journalist, author of the book *Tombstone*, covering the period of China's Great Famine

Yáng Rènlán 杨纫兰/楊紉蘭—Mother of **Fei Xiaotong**

Yáng Shàngkūn 杨尚昆/楊尚昆 (1907–1998)—Politician; president of PRC (1988–1993)

Yang Teng-Kuei 杨登魁/楊登魁 (1938–2012)—Taiwanese investor and film producer

Yáng Zhōngměi 杨中美/楊中美 (b. 1945)—Biographer of **Hu Yaobang**

Yang, Edward 杨德昌/楊德昌 (1947–2007)—Taiwanese director

Yao Hung-I 姚宏易—Director

Yáo Míng 姚明 (b. 1980)—Basketball player; played in the NBA for the Houston Rockets

Yáo Wényuán 姚文元 (1931–2005)—Member of "Gang of Four"

Yáo Yīlín 姚依林 (1917–1994)—Politician; vice premier of the PRC (1988–1993)

Yáo Zhìyuán 姚志源 —**Yao Ming's** father, basketball player

Yè Lì 叶莉/葉莉—Basketball player, **Yao Ming's** wife

Yè Jiànyīng 叶剑英/葉劍英 (1897–1986)—High-ranking marshal in the People's Liberation Army (PLA); stepfather of **Dai Qing**

Yè Xiǎogāng 叶小纲/葉小綱 (b. 1955)—Musician; one of the so-called Four Talents

Yeoh, Michelle 杨紫琼/楊紫瓊 (b. 1962)—Actress

Yeung Sum 杨森/楊森 (b. 1947)—Succeeded **Martin Lee** in the United Democrats of Hong Kong

Yú Huá 余华/余華 (b. 1960)—Writer, essayist

Yu Jim-yuen (Yú Zhānyuán 于占元) (1905–1997)—Martial arts and drama master; taught **Jackie Chan**

Yu Pun Hoi 于品海—Hong Kong media entrepreneur

Yú Zhōng 俞钟/俞鍾—Director and actor

Yuán Lóngpíng 袁隆平 (b. 1930)—Scientist; developed hybrid rice

Z

Zen, Joseph Ze-Kiun (Chén Rìjūn 陈日君/陳日君) (b. 1932)—Spiritual leader, cardinal in Hong Kong

Zēng Jīnyàn 曾金燕 (b. 1983)—Director, blogger, and activist

Zéng Míngnà 曾明娜—Ex-wife of **Lai Changxing**

Zhāng Àilíng (Eileen Chang) 张爱玲/張愛玲 (1920–1995)—Influential novelist; wrote *Lust, Caution*, later adapted into a film by **Ang Lee**

Zhāng Cháoyáng 张朝阳/張朝陽 (b. 1964)—Businessman; CEO and a chairman of Sohu Company

Zhāng Gāolí 张高丽/張高麗 (b. 1946)—Politician, member of the "Overall Reform" group, led by **Li Keqiang** and **Xi Jinping**

Zhāng Wénkāng 张文康/張文康 (b. 1940)—Minister of health; covered up the SARS epidemic

Zhāng Wéntiān 张闻天/張聞天 (1900–1976)—Politician

Zhāng Yìmóu 张艺谋/張藝謀 (b. 1951)—Prominent Fifth Generation film director

Zhāng Yuán 张元/張元 (b. 1963)—Sixth Generation director; director of *Beijing Bastars*, featuring **Cui Jian**

Zhāng Yǔnhé 张允和/張允和—Wife of **Zhou Youguang**

Zhāng Zǔhuà 张祖桦/張祖樺—Intellectual

Zhào Tāo 赵涛/趙濤 (b. 1977)—Actress

Zhào Zǐyáng 赵紫阳/趙紫陽 (1919–2005)— Former premier of PRC who sympathized with Tiananmen Square protesters; friend of **Bao Tong**

Zhèng Xiǎolóng 郑晓龙/鄭曉龍 (b. 1952)— Director, worked together with **Feng Xiaogang**

Zhōu Ēnlái 周恩来/周恩來 (1898–1976)— Politician; first premier of the PRC (1949–1976)

Zhōu Guópíng 周国平/周國平 (b. 1945)— Essayist and philosopher

Zhōu Lóng 周龙/周龍 (b. 1953)—Musician

Zhōu Xùn 周迅 (b. 1974)—Actress

Zhōu Yǒngkāng 周永康 (b. 1942)—Politician; charged with corruption in 2015

Zhōu Yǒuguāng 周有光 (b. 1906)—Intellectual; co- inventor of the pinyin romanization system

Zhū Dé 朱德 (1886–1976)—High-ranking political leader

Zhū Hóng 朱洪—Wife of **Liu Binyan**

Zhū Róngjī 朱镕基/朱鎔基 (b. 1928)—Politician; premier of the PRC (1998–2003)

Appendix 3: Geographical Directory

This list of geographical locations includes names of cities, towns, villages, regions, rivers, and mountains, in both simplified and traditional characters (if only one set of characters is provided, there is no difference between the two). A list of all contemporary provinces, municipalities, autonomous regions, and special administrative regions is included at the top. Alternative spellings are mentioned in parentheses when appropriate.

Provinces, Autonomous Regions, Special Administrative Regions, and Municipalities of the People's Republic of China		
TOTAL ESTIMATED POPULATION MAINLAND CHINA (2013)		1.36 BILLION (1,360,720,000)
Provinces	Abbr.	Population
Ānhuī Province 安徽省	AH	60.3 million (2013)
Fújiàn Province 福建省	FJ	37.74 million (2013)
Gānsù Province 甘肃省	GS	25.82 million (2013)
Guǎngdōng Province 广东省	GD	106.44 million (2013)
Guìzhōu Province 贵州省	GZ	35.02 million (2013)
Hǎinán Province 海南省	HI	8.95 million (2013)
Héběi Province 河北省	HE	73.33 million (2013)
Hēilóngjiāng Province 黑龙江省	HL	38.35 million (2013)
Hénán Province 河南省	HA	94.13 million (2013)
Húběi Province 湖北省	HB	57.99 million (2013)
Húnán Province 湖南省	HN	66.91 million (2013)
Jiāngsū Province 江苏省	JS	79.39 million (2013)
Jiāngxī Province 江西省	JX	45.22 million (2013)
Jílín Province 吉林省	JL	27.51 million (2013)
Liáoníng Province 辽宁省	LN	43.9 million (2013)
Qīnghǎi Province 青海省	QH	5.78 million (2013)

Provinces	Abbr.	Population
Shǎnxī (Shaanxi) Province* 陕西省	SN	37.64 million (2013)
Shāndōng Province 山东省	SD	97.33 million (2013)
Shānxī Province* 山西省	SX	36.3 million (2013)
Sìchuān Province 四川省	SC	81.07 million (2013)
Yúnnán Province 云南省	YN	46.87 million (2013)
Zhèjiāng Province 浙江省	ZJ	54.98 million (2013)

*Shǎnxī 陕西 (Shaanxi) and Shānxī 山西 provinces should not be confused; Shaanxi with two As is the home of the ancient capital of Xi'an, site of the famous terracotta armies; Shanxi is the eastern neighbor of Shaanxi.

Autonomous Regions	Abbr.	Population
Guǎngxī Zhuàng Autonomous Region 广西壮族自治区	GX	47.19 million (2013)
Inner Mongolia (Nèiměnggǔ) Autonomous Region 内蒙古自治区蒙	NM	24.98 million (2013)
Níngxià (Huí) Autonomous Region 宁夏回族自治区	NX	6.54 million (2013)
Tibet (Xīzàng) Autonomous Region 西藏自治区	XZ	3.12 million (2013)
Xīnjiāng (Uygur) Autonomous Region 新疆维吾尔自治区	XJ	22.64 million (2013)

Municipalities	Abbr.	Population
Běijīng Municipality 北京市	BJ	21.15 million (2013)
Chóngqìng Municipality 重庆市	CQ	29.7 million (2013)
Shànghǎi Municipality 上海市	SH	24.15 million (2013)
Tiānjīn Municipality 天津市	TJ	14.72 million (2013)

Special Administrative Regions	Abbr.	Population
Macau (Àomén) Special Administrative Region 澳门特别行政区	MC	592,000 (2013)
Hong Kong (Xiānggāng) Special Administrative Region 香港特别行政区	HK	7.188 million (2013)

Population statistics: National Bureau of Statistics of China.

Population and Special Municipalities of the Republic of China (Taiwan)		
TOTAL ESTIMATED POPULATION REPUBLIC OF CHINA (TAIWAN) (2014)		**23.3 MILLION (23,374,000)**
Special Municipalities	**Abbr.**	**Population**
Kaohsiung (Gāoxióng Shì) 高雄市	KHH	2.78 million (2014)
New Taipei (Xīnběi Shì) 新北市	TPE	3.97 million (2014)
Taichung (Táizhōng Shì) 臺中市		2.72 million (2014)
Tainan (Táinán Shì) 臺南市		1.88 million (2014)
Taipei (Táiběi Shì) 臺北市		2.67 million (2014)
Taoyuan (Táoyuán Shì) 桃園市		2.07 million (2015)

Population statistics: Official Websites of Municipalities.

A

Altay (XJ)

Ānyuè County 安岳 (SC)

B

Bǎnqiáo 板桥/板橋 (TW)

Běichén 北辰 (TJ)

Běijīng 北京 (Peking) (BJ)

C

Chángchūn 长春 (JL)

Chángzhōu 常州 (JS)

Cháozhōu 潮州 (GD)

Chéngdū 成都 (SC)

Chóngqìng 重庆/重慶 (CQ)

D

Dàlián 大连/大連 (LN)

Dìngyuǎn 定远 (AH)

Dōngchéng District 东城/東城 (BJ)

Dōngpíng 东平/東平 (SD)

F

Fēnyáng 汾阳/汾陽 (SN)

G

Gànzhōu 赣州/贛州 (JX)

Gāomì 高密 (SD)

Gōngzhǔlǐng 公主岭/公主嶺 (JL)

Guǎngyuán 广元/廣元 (SC)

H

Hǎiníng 海宁 (ZJ)

Hángzhōu 杭州 (ZJ)

Harbin (Hā'ěrbīn) 哈尔滨 (JL)

Héféi 合肥 (AH)

Hsi-chuang 西莊 (TW) (Guantian Township of Tainan County)

Hsinchu (Xīnzhú) 新竹 (TW)

Huālián County 花蓮縣 (TW)

I

Inner Mongolia (Nèiménggǔ 内蒙古)

J

Jǐnán 济南/濟南 (SD)

Jìnchájì 晋察冀/晉察冀 (historical border region, covering areas in current-day Shanxi, Inner Mongolia, and Hebei)

Jìnjiāng 晋江/晉江 (FJ)

Jìxī County 绩溪/績溪 (AH)

K

Kaohsiung (Gāoxióng) 高雄 (TW)

Kowloon 九龙/九龍 (HK)

Kūnmíng 昆明 (YN)

L

Liúyáng 浏阳/瀏陽 (HN)

Lùgǎng 鹿港 (TW)

M

Mei County 眉县/眉縣 (GD)

N

Nánjīng 南京 (JS)

Nántóu 南投 (TW)

Nánxiāng 南乡 (HN)

P

Píngdōng 屏东/屏東 (TW)

Q

Qīngdǎo 青岛/青島 (SD)

Quánzhōu 泉州 (FJ)

Qǔwó Country 曲沃 (SN)

S

Shànghǎi 上海 (ZJ)

Shàntóu 汕头 (GD)

Shěnyáng 沈阳/沈陽 (LN)

Shēnzhèn 深圳 (GD)

Shíjiāzhuāng 石家庄/石家莊 (HE)

Shíshī 石狮 (FJ)

Sīmáo 丝茅 (HN)

Sūzhōu 苏州/蘇州 (JS)

T

Táiběi 台北/臺北 (TW)

Táidōng 台东/臺東 (TW)

Tàinán 太南 (TW)

Tàiyuán 太原 (SX)

Tamshui (Dànshuǐ) 淡水 (TW)

Táng County 唐县 (HE)

Tángshān 唐山 (HE)

Tiānjīn 天津 (TJ)

Tóngnán 漳南 (SC)

U

Urumchi 乌鲁木齐/烏魯木齊 (XJ)

W

Wènchuān 汶川 (SC)

Wújiāng 吴江 (JS)

Wǔhàn 武汉/武漢 (HB)

Wūkǎn 乌坎/烏坎 (GD)

Wūxī 巫溪 (JS)

X

Xī'ān 西安 (SN)

Xiàmén 厦门/廈門 (FJ)

Xīdān 西单/西單 (BJ)

Y

Yán'ān 延安 (SN)

Yúnlín 云林/雲林 (TW)

Z

Zhèngdìng 正定 (HE)

Zhènjiāng 镇江/鎮江 (JS)

Zhènníng 镇宁/鎮寧 (GZ)

Zhōngguāncūn District
中关村/中關村 (BJ)

Zhōnghé 中和 (TW)

Appendix 4: Pinyin Glossary

This list contains terms and concepts discussed in the Berkshire Dictionary of Chinese Biography, *arranged alphabetically by pinyin pronunciation, and including traditional and simplified characters.*

Terms and Concepts

A

ah fei 阿飞/阿飛—juvenile delinquent

B

bàofāhù 暴发户/暴發戶—"get rich quick" entrepreneur

bǎojià hùháng 保驾护航/保駕護航—escort and protect

bàolì de měixué 暴力的美学/暴力的美學— aesthetics of violence, film technique associated with **Hou Hsiao-hsien**

bànshān rén 半山人—half-mainlander

bǐzhàn 笔战/筆戰—pen wars

C

chā 差—a horizontal dimension of relational distance and differentiation

chāxùgéjú 差序格局—differential mode of association (concept developed by **Fei Xiaotong**)

D

dà 大—big, vast

dānwèi 单位/單位—state-organized work unit system

dǎodàn nián 导弹年/導彈年—missile year (1966)

dàyuàn 大院—grand courtyard (a compound with apartments, offices, and other public facilities)

dì liù dài 第六代—Sixth Generation (referring to film directors)

dízi 笛子—bamboo flute

E

è'gǎo 恶搞—spoof, parody

Èrshíyī tiáo 二十一条—Twenty-One Demands (made by Japan after World War II)

F

Fǎnfēnliè Guójiā Fǎ 反分裂國家法—Anti-Secession Law, which allowed "non-peaceful means" to be used if the mainland's territorial integrity was threatened

fǎzhì 法治—rule of law

fèi 废/廢—waste

fēngbǐ 封笔/封筆—completing ones work/canon

G

gǎizào 改造—remold

gànbù 干部/幹部—cadres

gāojí gànbù 高级干部/高級幹部—high-level cadre position

gètǐhù 个体户/個體戶—individual entrepreneurs

Gòngchǎndǎng 共产党/共產黨—Chinese Communist Party (CCP)

Guānchá 观察—*The Observer*, a key journal of Chinese liberal intellectuals in the 1940s

guójiā ānquánfǎ 国家安全法/國家安全法—martial law

Guólì Táiwān Dàxué 國立台灣大學—National Taiwan University

Guómín gémìng jūn 国民革命军/國民革命軍—National Revolutionary Army (NRA)

Guómíndǎng 国民党/國民黨—Nationalist Party, also called Kuomintang (KMT), particularly in Taiwan

gǔzhēng 古筝—zither

H

hēi bāng 黑帮/黑幫—bad elements

hēishǒu 黑手—black hand (referring to people who are accused of inciting others)

hèsuìpiàn 贺岁片/賀歲片—New Year film/ comedy (film genre)

héxié shèhuì 和谐社会/和諧生活—harmonious society (concept presented by **Hu Jintao**)

hóngbāo 红包/紅包—red envelopes with money in them

Hóngwèibīng 红卫兵/紅衛兵—Red Guard (during the Cultural Revolution)

hóu 侯—marquis

Huángpǔ jūnxiào 黄埔军校/黃埔軍校—Whampoa Military Academy

J

Jeet Kune Do 截拳道—"The Way of the Intercepting Fist"; **Bruce Lee's** martial art form

jīngjì tèqū 经济特区 經濟特區—Special Economic Zones (SEZ)

jīngjù 京剧/京劇—Peking Opera

Jīntiān 今天—*Today*; name of a 1978 "underground" poetry journal

K

kāimíng 开明/開明—open-minded

Kèjiā 客家—Hakka (people)

L

láojiào 劳教/勞教—re-education through labor

lǎorén guīgēn 老人归根/老人歸根—old men go back to their roots (proverb)

liǎng guó lùn 两国论/兩國論—two state theory (**Lee Teng-Hui**)

Lìfǎ Yuàn 立法院—Legislative Yuan (Taiwan's de facto parliament)

lìyì gòngtóngtǐ 利益共同体/利益共同體—community of shared interests

lǐ zhì shèhuì 礼治社会/禮治社會—ritual-based society

lǐzhì 礼治/禮治—rule of ritual

M

Máo Zédōng sīxiǎng 毛泽东思想/毛澤東思想—Mao Zedong Thought (collected wisdom of Mao Zedong)

mínbīng zǔzhī 民兵组织/民兵組織—guerilla units

Mǐnnánrén 闽南人/閩南人—Hokkiens (people)

mínshēng 民生—socialism

mínzú yīngxióng 民族英雄—national hero

N

Nánxún 南巡—southern inspections tours (taken by emperors, as well as **Deng Xiaoping**)

P

pīdòuhuì 批斗会/批鬥會—struggle sessions

píngděng rénquàn de wèntí 平等人权的问题/平等人權的問題—the equal human rights issue

pǐnyǐn 拼音—pinyin (the romanization system of the Chinese language)

pǐzi wénxué 痞子文学/痞子文學—hooligan literature

pópo 婆婆—matriarch ruler; also "mother-in-law"

pǔluó wénxué 普罗文学/普羅文學—proletarian literature

pǔtōnghuà 普通话/普通話—standard (simplified) Chinese

Q

qìgōng 气功/氣功—practice to cultivate and balance vital energy (*qi*)

quánpán xīhuà 全盘西化/全盤西化—radical westernization (seen by some as a precondition for China's democratization)

R

rénròu sōusuǒ 人肉搜索—human flesh search engine; a phenomenon where netizens use the Internet to publically punish (perceived) wrongdoers

rénzhì 人治—rule of man

S

sān kǔ nián 三苦年—three bitter years (referring to 1960–1962, aftermath of the Great Leap Forward)

sān bù zhèngcè 三不政策—Three No's policy: no contact, no compromise, no negotiation 不接触, 不谈判, 不妥协 (Chiang Ching-Kuo, referring to dealings with the mainland in the 1980s)

sānmín zhǔyì 三民主义/三民主義—Sun Yat-sen's Three Principles of the People: nationalism (*mínzú* 民族), democracy (*mínquán* 民權), and welfare (*mínshēng* 民生)

shāndòng diānfù guójiā zhèngquán zuì 煽动颠覆国家政权罪/煽動顛覆國家政權罪—inciting subversion of state power

shēngyuán 生员/生員—civil service degree

shīfu 师傅/師傅—martial-arts teacher

shí 实/實—true; immediate and tangible (subject matter of poetry)

shíyàn xiǎoshuō 实验小说/實驗小說—experimental fiction

shíshì qiúshì 实事求是/實事求是—Seek the truth (correct path) from facts (Mao Zedong)

Sì jūnzǐ 四君子—the "Four Gentlemen" of Tiananmen (**Liu Xiaobo**, Zhou Duo, Gao Xin, Hou Dejian)

Sìgè xiàndàihuà 四个现代化/四個現代化—Four modernizations: science and technology, industry, agriculture, and national defense (**Deng Xiaoping**, 1980s)

Sìrén bāng 四人帮/四人幫—Gang of Four, originally called the Cultural Revolution Small Group (Jiāng Qīng 江青, Wáng Hóngwén 王洪文, Zhāng Chūnqiáo 张春桥, and Yáo Wényuán 姚文元)

suǒnà 唢呐—(Chinese) oboe

T

tiānxià 天下—all under Heaven

Tóngménghuì 同盟会/同盟會—Revolutionary Alliance

tuántǐgéjú 团体格局/團體格局—organizational mode of association (concept developed by **Fei Xiaotong**)

W

wánglíng 亡灵/亡靈—departed souls

wěidà dǎoshī 伟大导师/偉大導師—great teacher (referring to Mao Zedong)

wén yì fù xīng 文艺复兴/文藝複興—cultural revival

wǔshù 武術—a traditional martial arts form

wǔxiá 武侠/武俠—martial hero; knight errand

wǔxiá piān 武侠片—swordplay films

wǔxiá xiǎoshuō 武侠小说/武俠小說—martial arts novel

wúyòng 无用/無用—(social) uselessness

X

xiào 孝—filial piety

Xǐtóng dǐng 希同顶—Xitong hats (after **Chen Xitong**); small pagodas and traditional-looking pavilions on modern buildings

xù 序—a vertical dimension of moral hierarchy and order (**Fei Xiaotong**)

xúngēn wénxué 寻根文学/尋根文學—roots-seeking literature

Y

yáogǔn jīngshén 摇滚精神/搖滾精神—rock spirit

yì 义/義—righteousness, rightness, propriety, justice (Confucian concept)

yì 艺—art

yí 诒—bequeath, gift

yīfǎ zhìguó 依法治国/依法治國—ruling the country by law

yī zhōng kuàngjià 一中框架—one China framework (concept in which there is one state called China, not two separate states (i.e., mainland China and Taiwan) with the same claim)

yuān jiǎ cuò àn 冤假错案/冤假錯案—unjust verdicts

Z

záwén 杂文/雜文—polemical essays

zhàn 战/戰—war

zhānghuí xiǎoshuō 章回小说/章回小說—late imperial vernacular chapter-style fiction

zhèngfǎ 政法—political-legal

zhèngzhì fēngbō 政治风波/政治風波—political turmoil

zhīshi qīngnián 知识青年—sent-down youth

zhōng 忠—loyalty

zhuādà fàngxiǎo 抓大放小—grasping the big and letting go of the small

Events and Movements

Bǎi huā yùndòng 百花运动/百花運動—Hundred Flowers Campaign (1956)

Báisè kǒngbù 白色恐怖—White Terror, purge of Communists

Bāwǔ xīncháo měishù yùndòng 八五新潮美术运动/八五新潮美術運動—1985 New Wave (artistic) movement

Dǎngwài 黨外—lit. outside the party; Tangwai movement (mid-1970s, early 1980s, Taiwan)

Dàyuèjìn 大跃进/大躍進—Great Leap Forward (1958)

Fǎlún Dàfǎ 法轮大法/法輪大法— also called Falun Gong, lit. Dharma Wheel Practice; a combination of Buddhism and *qigong*, founded by **Li Hongzhi**

Fǎnfēnliè Guójiā Fǎ 反分裂國家法—Anti-Secession Law (China imposes on Taiwan, 2005)

Gǎigé kāifàng 改革开放—Reform and Opening Up era (starting 1978)

Gāoxióng Shìjiàn 高雄事件—Kaohsiung (Gaoxiong) Incident, pro-democracy demonstrators suppressed and jailed (1979, Taiwan)

Liǎng gè fán shì 两个凡是/兩個凡是—Two Whatevers; policy initiated by **Hua Guofeng** in 1977

Mínjìndǎng 民进党/民進黨 or *Mínzhǔ jìnbù dǎng* 民主进步党/民主進步黨—Democratic Progressive Party (DPP), Taiwan

Pī Lín pī Kǒng 批林批孔—"Criticize Lin [Biao], criticize Confucius [Zhou Enlai]" Campaign (1974)

Sān fǎn-Wǔ fǎn 三反五反—Three and Five Antis Campaigns (1951–1952)

Shínián hàojié 十年浩劫—Ten-Year Disaster, Cultural Revolution

Táiwān xīn diànyǐng 台湾新电影/臺灣新電影—New Taiwan Cinema (movement)

Táiwān xīn làngcháo 台湾新浪潮/臺灣新浪潮—Taiwan New Wave (alternate name for New Taiwan Cinema)

Tàiyánghuā xuéyùn 太阳花学运/太陽花學運—Sunflower Movement (Taiwan)

Wénhuà dàgémìng 文化大革命—Cultural Revolution (1966–1976)

Xīdān mínzhǔ qiáng 西单民主墙/西單民主牆—Democracy Wall Movement (1978)

Xīncháo yīnyuè 新潮音乐/新潮音樂—New Wave music

Yěbǎihé 野百合—Wild Lily (student demonstrations for political reform in Taiwan, 1990)

Yīdài yīlù 一带一路 一帶一路—One belt, one road; outreach program called "Silk Road Economic Belt" ("Maritime Silk Road of the 21st Century") (2013–present)

Appendix 5:
General Bibliography

The amount of (re)sources on modern China is enormous and continues to grow both in number and scope. It is impossible to present a "complete" bibliography, but in this appendix you will find a small collection of resources focused on biographical information, as well as some general reference works, both online and in print.

Art and Literature

Davis, E. L. (2009). *Encyclopedia of contemporary Chinese culture.* Abingdon, UK: Taylor & Francis.

Latham, Kevin. (2007). *Pop culture China!: Media, arts, and lifestyle.* Santa Barbara, CA: ABC-CLIO.

Martin, Helmut, & Kinkley, Jeffrey. (Eds.). (1992). *Modern Chinese writers: Self-portrayals.* Armonk, NY: M.E. Sharpe.

Sullivan, Michael. (2006). *Modern Chinese artists: A biographical dictionary.* Berkeley: University of California Press.

Zhang, Yingjin, & Xiao, Zhiwei. (Eds.). (2002). *Encyclopedia of Chinese film.* London: Routledge.

Business and Economy

Lamb, Malcolm. (1994). *Directory of officials and organizations in China: A Quarter Century Guide.* Armonk, NY: M. E. Sharp.

Poza, Ernesto J., & Daugherty, Mary S. (2014). *Family business.* Mason, OH: Cengage Learning.

Wang, Huiyao. (2012). *Globalizing China: The influence, strategies and successes of Chinese returnee entrepreneurs.* Bingley, UK: Emerald Group Publishing.

Zhang, Wenxian, & Alon, Ilon. (Eds.). (2009). *Biographical dictionary of new Chinese entrepreneurs and business leaders.* Northhampton, MA: Edward Elgar Publishing.

Government and Politics

Brown, Kerry. (2014). *The new emperors: Power and the Princelings in China.* London: I. B. Tauris.

Dietrich, Craig. (1994). *People's China: A brief history.* New York: Oxford University Press.

Klein, Donald W., & Clark, Anne B. (Eds.). (1971). *Biographic dictionary of Chinese Communism, 1921–1965* (2 vols.). Cambridge, MA: Harvard University Press.

Lee Hong Yung. (1991). *From revolutionary cadres to party technocrats in Socialist China.* Berkeley: University of California Press.

Leung, Edwin Pak-wah. (Ed.) (2002). *Political leaders of modern China: A biographical dictionary.* Westport, CT: Greenwood Publishing Group.

Li, Cheng. (2001). *China's leaders: The new generation.* Lanham, MD: Rowman & Littlefield.

Li, Xiaobing. (Ed.) (2012). *China at war: An encyclopedia.* Santa Barbara, CA: ABC-CLIO.

Link, Perry. (1992). *Evening chats in Beijing: Probing China's predicament.* New York: Norton.

Mackerras, C., McMillen, D. H., & Watson, A. (2003). *Dictionary of the politics of the People's Republic of China.* Routledge.

Sullivan, Lawrence R. (2007). *Historical dictionary of the People's Republic of China.* Lanham, MD: Scarecrow Press.

Wortzel, Larry M., & Higham, Robin D. S. (1999). *Dictionary of contemporary Chinese military history.* Westport, CT: Greenwood Press.

General Biographical Resources

Lee, Khoon Choy. (2005). *Pioneers of modern China: Understanding the inscrutable Chinese.* Singapore: World Scientific.

Lee, Lily Xiao Hong, & Stefanowska, A. D. (Eds.). (2003). *Biographical dictionary of Chinese women: The twentieth century (1912–2000).* Armonk, NY: M.E. Sharpe.

Song, Yuwu. (Ed.). (2013). *Biographical dictionary of the People's Republic of China.* Jefferson, NC: McFarland.

Online Resources

China Vitae http://www.chinavitae.com/

An online resource that contains biographies of more than 4000 modern Chinese leaders in government, politics, the military, education, business, and the media.

Chinese Biographical Database (CBD)

http://www.berkshirepublishing.com/chinesebiodb/

This project was designed and created by Marilyn A. Levine and has been archived online by Berkshire Publishing Group.

Appendix 6:
Timeline (from 1949)

The following is a selection of major historical events, including events from mainland China, Hong Kong, and Taiwan. As with any timeline, countless events have been omitted here; this timeline serves to give the reader a general sense of the recent history and development of Greater China.

1949, 1 October: Chinese Revolution: **Mao Zedong** proclaims new People's Republic of China in Beijing; the Nationalists under Chiang Kai-shek flee to Taiwan and establish the Republic of China on Taiwan

1950: North Korea under Communist leader Kim Il Sung bids to reunite the two halves of Korea by force; Mao Zedong sends the People's Liberation Army to support Pyongyang; Communist China becomes major Cold War player

1950: Deng Xiaoping dispatches troops to take over **Tibet**

1951–1952: CCP launches the **Three Antis Campaign** against waste, corruption, and bureaucratism; and the **Five Antis Campaign** against bribing, evading taxes, stealing state assets, cheating on government contracts, and stealing capital

1953: armistice is signed keeping North and South Korea separate

1953: death of Joseph Stalin

1954: first high-level purge of the PRC (by Mao Zedong, of Gao Gang, ally of Stalin)

1954: British sinologist and chemist Joseph Needham publishes the first volume of his massive *Science and Civilisation of China*

1956: PRC attempts to promote literacy by simplifying Chinese characters, now the standard on the mainland; Taiwan, Hong Kong, and Macao still use traditional (or complex) characters

1956: Hundred Flowers Campaign: Mao Zedong announces that the government will relax its strict control over thought and expression; an estimated 500,000–750,000 intellectuals who accepted this offer denounced or blacklisted

1957–1958: Anti-Rightist Campaign is primarily aimed against intellectuals that have spoken out against Mao and the Party during the Hundred Flowers Campaign

1957: Bo Yibo launches first Five Year Plan to encourage the growth of industry and technology over agriculture

1958: launch of the Great Leap Forward: campaign to advance China's agricultural and industrial development to the level of the West; leads to widespread famine killing an estimated 30 million people

1959: the 14th Dalia Lama flees to India, and Tibet becomes a special administrative region under the central government

1959: Lushan Conference to review the results of Mao's Great Leap Forward program; it was not received well by many leaders, including defense minister Peng Dehuai, who Mao later replaced.

1964: French President Charles de Gaulle announces France's recognition of the PRC as the sole representative of China at the United Nations

1964: China tests first nuclear weapon

1966: **Qian Xuesen** and Nie Rongzhen launch China's first medium-range missile to carry a nuclear warhead, hence the year is dubbed the "missile year"

1966–1976: Cultural Revolution; violent period of social disruption; Jiang Qing officially commissioned "advisor on questions in literature and art of the People's Liberation Army; removal of president Liu Shaoqi from all party posts for being a revisionist with the Soviet Union in 1966; he dies in 1969

1967: China tests first hydrogen bomb

1968: Mao dismisses the Red Guards

1969: military clash between Soviet and Chinese forces on northern border of China

1971: military leader Lin Biao dies under suspicious circumstances in a plane crash over Inner Mongolia, supposedly fleeing after a failed coup to oust Mao

1972: United States President Richard M. Nixon visits the PRC

1973: end of Vietnam War

1974: "Criticize Lin [Biao], criticize Confucius [Zhou Enlai]" Campaign

1975: death of Nationalist leader Chiang Kai-shek

1975: Deng Xiaoping sends troops to Jiangsu Province, where badly needed coal and other supplies have piled up because rebels have blocked the smooth flow of freight; it is a quick success that instantly increases industrial production

1976: Tomb No. 5, excavated northwest of Xiaotun Village in Anyang, Henan Province, confirmed to be that of late thirteenth century BCE warrior and queen Fu Hao of the Shang dynasty

1976: death of Communist leaders Mao Zedong, Zhou Enlai, and Zhu De; protestors gather in Tiananmen Square, upset over removal of mourning displays for the recently deceased Zhou Enlai; square cleared by orders of the Gang of Four.

1976: Deng Xiaoping declares that Mao Zedong was 70 percent correct and 30 percent mistaken

1976: Tangshan earthquake kills an estimated 250,000 people

1976: Gang of Four arrested a few weeks after Mao's death; the official end of the Cultural Revolution

1977: Zhongli Incident in Taiwan: streets protests after accusations of vote rigging in favor of the ruling Nationalist Party

1977: Deng Xiaoping criticizes **Hua Guofeng's** "Two Whatevers," a doctrine that spoke of total loyalty to Mao

1978–1979: launch of economic reform under Deng Xiaoping at the Third Plenum of the Eleventh Congress of the Communist Party in Beijing in December

1978–1979: Democracy Wall Movement; calling for more political liberalization occurs in Beijing, spreading across the country; it is closed down in the spring of 1979 with one of its chief advocates, **Wei Jingsheng**, jailed for 15 years

1978: Chiang Kai-shek's son, Chiang Ching-kuo, becomes president of the Republic of China (Taiwan); reelected in 1984

1978: United States President Jimmy Carter "de-recognizes" the Republic of China

1978: Reform and Opening Up era begins

1978: The Great Truth Criterion Debate to support Deng's reform agenda

1979: Kaohsiung Incident on Taiwan: pro-democracy demonstrators suppressed and jailed

1979: one-child policy introduced in PRC as population control measure; some estimates put prevented births at 400 million

1980s: Taiwan New Wave movement (cinema)

1980s: Smuggling is rampant in China's southern coastal region

1980s: regeneration of Hong Kong cinema

1980s: Chiang Ching-kuo implements "Three Nos" policy: "no contact, no compromise, and no negotiation" with the PRC; the ROC is forced to breach this policy on 3 May 1986, following the hijacking of a China Airlines cargo plane, which is forced to land in Guangzhou; the ROC sends a delegation to negotiate for the return of the crew and plane

1980: creation of the first Special Economic Zone in Shenzhen, opposite Hong Kong; these become the main economic interfaces between China and world economy

1982: China's **population reaches 1 billion**

1982: Twelfth National Party Congress

1983: The Anti-Spiritual Pollution Campaign (October–December) aims to reign in liberal attitudes among the people, often claimed to be inspired by Western influences

1984: China is considered one of the most equal countries in the world (in terms of income distribution)

1985: Mikhail S. Gorbachev becomes general secretary of the Communist Party in the Soviet Union

1986: Democratic Progressive Party (DPP) forms in Taiwan; first opponent to ruling Nationalist Party

1986: **Lee Yuan Tseh** is co-recipient of the Nobel Prize in Chemistry

1987, 15 July: martial law officially ends in the ROC after nearly four decades

1987, April: Fall of CCP general secretary, Hu Yaobang

1989: Berlin Wall torn down

1989, 4 June: Tiananmen Square Incident; student protestors gathered on Beijing's central Tiananmen Square to call for political reforms. Talks with the Party leadership lead nowhere, and on the night of 4 June, the square is violently cleared out by the military. Many protesters are killed, jailed, or exiled.

1989: Pro-independence riots and protests in Lhasa reach peak, after the beginnings of unrest in 1987

1990: the United Democrats of Hong Kong (UDHK) is formed in Hong Kong

1991: Cold War ends with collapse of the Soviet Union; China now the largest remaining Communist power

1991: suicide of Jiang Qing, wife of Mao Zedong and leader of the Gang of Four, main purgers during the Cultural Revolution

1994: the Chinese Film Import and Export Corporation signs a contract with major Hollywood studios to import ten Hollywood films each year; upon China's entry into the WTO, the limit would become non-existent for large periods of time

1994: Legend (founded by **Liu Chuanzhi**) becomes one of the first Chinese companies to be listed on the Hong Kong Stock Exchange

1997: Asian Financial Crisis

1997: Hong Kong handover back to China from Britain; becomes special administrative region (SAR) of China

1997: **Deng Xiaoping** passes away

1997: **Jiang Zemin** makes a landmark visit to the United States

1998: the China Internet Network Information Center (CNNIC) issues first Statistical Report on Internet Development in China; issued twice yearly

1999: Macao becomes a special administrative region (SAR) of China; was colony of Portugal starting in 1887

1999, May 7: United States bombs, as part of a NATO operation, hit the Chinese embassy in Yugoslavia

1999, April 25: ten thousand Falun Gong practitioners protest outside the Zhongnanhai compound in Beijing

2000: Nationalists on Taiwan lose election for the first time, to the Democratic Progressive Party

2000: **Gao Xingjian** wins the Nobel Prize for Literature

2000: Jiang Zemin presents his influential **Three Represents** theory for the first time

2001, 11 September: terrorist attacks on the United States

2001: China enters the World Trade Organization

2002: Basketball player Yao Ming joins the National Basketball Association (NBA)'s Houston Rockets

2002/2003: Hu Jintao and Wen Jiabao, representatives of the "fourth generation" leadership, become party secretary and premier, respectively

2002/2003: SARS epidemic spreads in China and Hong Kong

2003: Soong Mei-ling, commonly known as Madame Chiang Kai-shek, dies in New York at age 106

2003: First Chinese crewed space program launched: the Shenzhou 5; third country in the world after the Soviet Union and the United States

2003, July 1: Protests in Hong Kong against Basic Law Article 23, which many feared would affect rights like freedom of speech and universal suffrage

2003: implementation of the Environmental Impact Assessment Law and the Cleaner Production Promotion Law; both put environmental knowledge into the hands of Chinese citizens, including the right to participate in policy decision making.

2004: The Program for Implementation for Governance by Law (and eventually the 2007 Measures on Open Environmental Information) require local government bureaus to share important environmental information with the public.

2005: **Han Han** posts his first blog; becomes China's (and the world's) most-read blogger

2005: mainland China approves the Anti-Secession Law, which allows "non-peaceful means" to be used against actions that endanger territorial integrity.

2007: China becomes as unequal in its income distribution as Brazil

2008: relocation complete of over 1 million residents for construction of controversial Three Gorges Dam

2008: Sichuan (Wenchuan) earthquake kills an estimated 68,000 people

2008: Tibetan uprising (also called 3.14 Riots)

2008: Summer Olympic Games held in Beijing

2009: Tibetan monks begin campaign of self-immolation in protest of rule by the PRC

2009: **Chen Shui-bian** receives a life sentence for embezzlement, bribery, and money laundering

2009: China overtakes the United States as the world's biggest market for cars

2010: Liu Xiaobo becomes the first Chinese citizen living in China to receive the Nobel Peace Prize

2011: Unrest in Inner Mongolia over treatment of indigenous culture and mining developments

2011, September: Wukan protests (Siege of Wukan), sparked when government officials sold land in Wukan to developers without consulting the villagers. A peaceful resolution is eventually reached, with much of the credit going to **Wang Yang**.

2011: China's first National Water Report is released

2012/2013: The Senkaku (Diaoyu) Islands Dispute. Japan and China fight over rights to the islands after Japan buys three of them from a private owner.

2012: The Writers Legal Protection Union wins a copyright law battle against Internet service company Baidu

2012: Three Gorges Dam (on the Yangzi River) is finished

2012: Chinese Communist Party leader Xi Jinping's "Chinese Dream" speech

2012: by December, China has 564 million Internet users, and an Internet penetration rate of 42.1 percent

2012: writer **Mo Yan** wins the Nobel Prize for Literature

2013: trial of Bo Xilai, former rising star in Communist Party; sentenced to life in prison

2014: Sunflower Movement, Taiwan. Students protest the Cross-Strait Trade Service Agreement (CSSTA), and eventually occupy the Legislative Yuan in March and April.

2014/2015: Occupy Central, Hong Kong. Thousands gather in Hong Kong's financial district for a mass civil disobedience movement, protesting the direction of the government's proposed electoral reform, which was threatening to become more restrictive. Here, the Umbrella Movement (a pro-democracy political group) is born. The last tents from Occupy Central's spillover group were removed on 25 June, 2015.

2014, June: 25th Anniversary of the Tiananmen Square Incident

2015, August: a fire and consequent explosions, caused by dangerous chemicals stored in the harbor of Tianjin, kills nearly 200 people

2020: Xi Jinping's first "Chinese Dream" goal: China will be a "moderately well-off society" by now, the 100th anniversary of the Chinese Communist Party

2022: Beijing hosts the 2022 Winter Olympic Games

2049: Xi Jinping's second "Chinese Dream" goal: China will be a fully developed nation by now, the 100th anniversary of the People's Republic of China

Dictionary of Chinese Biography **Index**

Bold entries and page numbers denote people with an article about them in the *DCB*.

Bold entries and page numbers denote people with an article about them in the *DCB*.

CPSIA information can be obtained
at www.ICGtesting.com
Printed in the USA
BVOW09*2229270217

477036BV00011B/70/P